MEASUREMENT AND ADJUSTMENT
SERIES
Edited by Lewis M. Terman

DESCRIPTION AND MEASUREMENT OF PERSONALITY

by

Raymond B. Cattell

Research Professor of Psychology
University of Illinois

Yonkers-on-Hudson, New York
WORLD BOOK COMPANY

Reprinted with the permission of R. B. Cattell

Johnson Reprint Corporation   Johnson Reprint Company, Ltd.
111 Fifth Ave., N.Y., N.Y. 10003   Berkeley Square House, London, W. 1

First reprinting, 1969, Johnson Reprint Corporation

Printed in the United States of America

Preface

BECAUSE of the great importance of an understanding of personality to so many human interests — medical, religious, political, educational — some personal, some practical, some purely scientific — one would imagine that research on this subject, despite its difficulties, would be pursued with great intellectual vigor and substantial popular support. Because of its intrinsic scientific fascination one would imagine that the best minds of our generation would be found at work on it and that elementary blunders would rarely have any role in the theoretical formulations. Neither of these suppositions is confirmed by the present state of the subject.

The present work is the first of two volumes — one cross-sectional, the other developmental in approach — attempting to bring into perspective the knowledge we have as yet obtained regarding personality, and aiming to suggest problems and methods for further organized research. The work is on the absurdly inadequate scale which is alone possible for the unaided investigator, and it has many gaps which are inevitable when research in the field is left to a collection of isolated pioneer investigators distracted by many duties inimical to seeing the field well and to seeing it whole.

That the reader may correct, according to his own standards, whatever bias or astigmatisms may unwittingly have entered into the author's approach to a subject in which comprehensiveness and nice judgment are of paramount importance, it is necessary to digress briefly into the personal origins of this undertaking.

Fifteen years ago, the writer, deeply interested in the purely scientific understanding of personality, left an academic laboratory (where there seemed many capable psychologists incapable of finding any worth-while research problems), to take charge of a psychological clinic where there was an embarrassing abundance of intriguing and suggestive research material mainly handled by overworked medical men untrained in research methods. In this environment, congenial in all respects save for its lack of sufficient leisure for research thought, the writer initiated a number of systematic inquiries. It was proposed to gather these together, along with a growing crop of similarly oriented researches in many parts of the world, in a book to be entitled *The Empirical Study of Personality*. This title was intended to express, quite militantly, a truly scientific approach and a definite break with the majority of writings having intuitive, "individual," pedagogical, religious, and literary foundations which then commanded the field in the clinical and general study of personality.

Fortunately, as this research work accumulated, the swift evolution of psychological opinion made the challenging epithet "empirical" no longer necessary in the title. Indeed, in the last five years the sheer volume of experimental and statistical data has grown with the rapidity of a careering snowball and, alas, with the same flimsiness of integration. So that we are now faced with two new problems. First, that research has lost deliberation and planning, principally in that no one has stopped to deal thoroughly with the task of describing and *measuring* personality variables. For it is on measurement that all further scientific advance depends. Too many psychologists are trying to run ahead of this disciplined advance, intent on looting the fascinating novelties and discoveries in the realm of personality development, without first having consolidated the "supply lines" of measuring technique through which alone an effective attack can be supported.

Secondly, the time and energy available for research in personality are frittered away in many overlapping, inconsecutive, and frequently trivial researches, uninformed by any wide vision of what is happening in the field as a whole. Under the present conditions of academic life, things could not be otherwise; no individual has time or a sufficient research staff to become thoroughly immersed in the wide range of research in personality, extending from the experimental studies on learning to educational measurement, social psychology, physiological psychology, psychiatry, and the most advanced statistical researches. Research has not developed specialization too far; it has only developed specialization without the necessary complementary machinery of integration. The blind socio-financial growth of learned institutions on traditional lines has failed to make any provision for the training, selection, and support of those who could act as bridge builders and integrators. A psychologist is a specialist or a dilettante; no other category seems to be admitted. The results of this outlook, defective in foresight and creativeness, are sadly prevalent throughout the attempts of the past fifty years to describe and measure personality. In some fields there is constant repetition and overlap; in others, equally important, there is a complete dearth of data; throughout there is an almost complete absence of cross reference or of the collection of data which would permit ready integration.

To remedy this situation, the present writer has proposed and organized a central Institute for Research in Personality, with an advisory board composed of leading research workers in the chief branches of psychology, education, psychiatry, and sociology. Granted adequate support, this can be staffed with a small group of research leaders of wide interests and proved power who can be given the leisure and equipment to overstep the partitions dividing specialized fields and hold the whole realm in focus in a creative synthesis. For the mere publication of "symposia" by collections of specialists is no answer to the real needs of research advance; the data must be known, integrated, and constructively applied within single minds, grasping the whole and perceiving interconnections.

Further argument for this reform is outside the purpose of the present book, except in so far as it may persuade research foundations to deflect some support from mere orgies of accumulation of "data" to repeat the integrative task attempted here (in, say, five or six years' time) on a scale and by an organization commensurate with the importance of the undertaking to pure and applied psychology.

For the present, this study has to make the best of the unorganized research available. If lack of resources prevents key questions being put directly to the touchstone of planned experiment on an adequate scale, it may yet be possible to find some existing studies which permit being used, more or less satisfactorily, to render answers. We have set out to rescue from this incontinent flux that which can be utilized as secondhand building material. This is not easy, because, owing to changing fashions of nomenclature, material is frequently misclassified in abstracts. (More than once a study on, for example, the special senses has proved to have its chief importance in personality.) In any case, valuable material is often hidden under an avalanche of debris. The specialist with duties other than research generally throws up his hands in despair at the very idea of reading all that comes in the present rather turbid torrent of psychological publications. But in this case the task has had to be faced, and the writer has spent much time in the years since this book was first envisaged in the work of reviewing abstracts, turning up original studies, and adapting and evaluating researches which might bear in any way on crucial issues of personality description and measurement.

The bulk of this kind of work has been demanded by the

second volume, on personality development. The present volume deals with only some 286 studies, most of which were in any case designed by their authors to bear aptly and directly on the description and measurement of personality; for this field has not lacked a core of excellent methodology and a disciplined viewpoint among researchers.

Since the completion of the second volume has had to be postponed, owing to interruption by war work, it has seemed best to publish this volume on its own. The straight description and measurement of personality — the cross-sectional, instantaneous depiction of personality in being — forms an entirely natural unit of study in itself. The longitudinal, developmental study, dealing with hereditary, environmental, and somatic factors determining personality formation and change, begins with equal naturalness, but complete sequential dependence, upon the foundation established by the present descriptive study. The publication of this first volume without further delay was also dictated by the fact that many problems in the rehabilitation program and in the rapidly expanding postwar personnel and guidance schemes will depend intimately on such a complete appraisal of personality factors as is presented, for the first time, in these pages. Finally, since the findings gathered together here are structured by a large-scale original research on personality factors, which has not yet been made available elsewhere and which provides a new framework for practical personality measurement, it seemed best to make the volume available at the earliest opportunity.[1]

Being an attempt to contribute toward a more complete scientific understanding of personality, this book is primarily of interest to serious students — especially those in advanced courses dealing with personality, clinical and abnormal psychology, and psychometry. Since this is at present the

---

[1] Not only the data and final interpretation, but also many of the theoretical formulations and suggestions for revised terminology, have not yet been published elsewhere. Some three brief articles, thrown off like fragments from the parent body as it spun itself out of the initial stages of chaos, have appeared in journals.

only book offering a complete or ordered catalogue of correlation cluster and factor researches, it is also practically a necessity for those planning research or reinterpretation of data in this field. Finally, it is hoped that it will be of value to practicing psychologists in guidance, education, and industrial and other personnel work; for it offers, in place of the unfounded and speculative factors on which "personality measurement" is now based, a set of factors well attested by research, thoroughly discussed and described, and incorporated in a sound theory of measurement.

As it is my intention to bring this text and reference book, integrating data on the measurement of personality, periodically up to date, I should very much appreciate receiving from readers notice of any unpublished theses or researches contributing in any way to the systematic description of personality.

Acknowledgments

Through the kindness of the Ella Lyman Cabot Foundation trustees I was enabled to have a year free from academic duties, which made possible the completion of the main research (involving, in its separate aspects, the calculation of over 20,000 correlation coefficients, apart from other statistical work) and the writing up of the completed survey of other researches in the field. Without this aid the work could not have been completed for several years.

I wish to express my great indebtedness to Dr. Gordon Allport, for his constant friendship and ever ready help in overcoming difficulties which presented themselves in the course of this research. This helping hand was offered despite sharp differences of theoretical viewpoint and regardless of the brusque way in which I have sometimes hammered on the anvil of his systematic psychology! Among my colleagues I am also indebted to Dr. E. G. Boring, for his active sympathy in reconstruction when work involving several months of arduous computations was ruined by a laboratory accident.

In an enterprise requiring so many diversely qualified helpers it is difficult, in a few words, to express even the outstanding sentiments of gratitude. But I think the primary acknowledgment should go to the voluntary assistants who carried out those services which are only well done by those who work from interest in the scientific project itself. Notably I would mention Dorothy Benner, who patiently and skillfully labored over the trait foundation; Karen Schuettler, who faced with me the task of working out the first 15,000 correlations; and Guinevere Cordingley, who enriched the population of subjects with Boston Brahmins, Bohemians, and other rarer types not usually given due representation in academic personality studies!

I am most grateful to Dr. Cyril Burt, Dr. Karl Holzinger, Dr. Truman Kelley, and Dr. Phillip Rulon for the benefit of individual discussion on various aspects of statistical procedures; to Dr. Louis Thurstone for his generosity in supplying me with manuscript copies of the forthcoming revised *Vectors of Mind*, the improved statistical methods in which substantially shortened our labors; to Dr. Harry Murray and Dr. Robert White for the freedom and resources of the Harvard Psychological Clinic; to Dr. Carroll Pratt and Major Merriam for augmenting and normalizing my population with two platoons of soldiers; to Dr. Reyburn, Dr. Taylor, and Dr. Karlin, of Cape Town University, for painstaking criticism, through correspondence, of my original trait list. Finally, for some of the more intangible yet most valuable help I have great pleasure in expressing my gratitude to Dr. P. S. de Q. Cabot.

RAYMOND B. CATTELL

Contents

Editor's Introduction

THE number of research publications in the field of personality during the last quarter century runs well into the thousands. In a recent ten-year period there appeared more than 130 articles dealing with a single personality test. Testing devices on the market are numbered in the hundreds. Unfortunately, the scientific outcome of this tremendous activity is not in proportion to the labor expended. The explanation, according to Dr. Raymond Cattell, is that so much of the work has been done haphazardly, by piecemeal attacks, and without adequate integration of findings. The purpose of this book is to take stock of all that has been accomplished and by the exposition of improved techniques to prepare the way for more systematic and searching explorations.

The book begins with an incisive discussion of the nature of traits. The greater part of the first half is devoted to the principles and methods of personality trait measurement, and the last half to a detailed account of the resulting harvest of established traits, syndromes, and factors. Although emphasis is placed on the necessity of defining trait terminology as a preliminary to experimentation, the author makes it clear that the definition of personality variables can proceed only by successive approximations and that many of the concepts involved must remain flexible.

The author's approach to the problems of personality research is by way of psychometrics, and particularly through the techniques of factor analysis. This does not betoken a lack of interest in or acquaintance with the applications of psychology in life situations. As a matter of fact the author is an experienced clinical psychologist, and it was his interest in this field that decided him to take time out from his work as a practitioner to lay a more scientific foundation for the analysis of personality structure.   Nor does the author's constant resort to psychometrics imply that he regards the statistical as the only profitable approach to the study of personality. On the contrary, he specifically points out that psychological progress requires, not that we choose between statistical and clinical procedures, but that we bring them together.   What he does inveigh against is the blind application of clinical methods that have not been scientifically validated.   He is, if possible, even more critical of the so-called "objective" tests of personality than he is of clinical procedures, for the objective test can be worthless or misleading despite all the statistical labor that has gone into its manufacture and standardization.

Many of the issues discussed are admittedly controversial, and the critical reader may occasionally find himself in disagreement with opinions and conclusions expressed by the author.   One example is the assertedly greater importance of internal (statistical) validation of personality traits as contrasted with validation against life situations.   Another example is the alleged superiority of trait ratings over testing devices.   Some will think that the author is putting his case a bit strongly when he says that the self-inventory "represents the nadir of scientific inventiveness and subtlety," and when he dismisses the Rorschach test as something analogous to a patent medicine.   Whether the reader always agrees does not matter.   What does matter is that he should be compelled to think, as he certainly will be by this book.

The climax of the treatise is appropriately reserved for the final chapter, in which the author makes a list of the dozen traits the existence of which he considers most convincingly established by the use of ratings, questionnaires, tests, and clinical practice.   He not only names the twelve traits but also lists them in a rank order of certainty, and essays, one by one, their interpretation. This is one of the many bold and challenging features of the book. Readers will await with interest the publication of the author's tests for measuring these twelve primary personality traits.

Because a given trait as measured and identified by different methods of trait assessment are not exactly the same, cross matching of the results of different investigations is regarded as very important. The author does not accept a trait as even tentatively identified until its existence has been confirmed by at least three satisfactory studies. As he rigidly adheres to this criterion, the list of traits at which he finally arrives must be taken seriously.

Especially worth noting is the author's distinction between "source" traits and "surface" traits. The latter, because they are more open to observation, can be rated with greater reliability and thus seem to be more convincing, whereas the source traits have to be assessed indirectly. It is understandable that personality research has hitherto concerned itself very largely with the traits that are most accessible, but the need now is for more systematic and determined attack upon source traits.

No less important than the identification and measurement of primary personality traits is the little-understood problem of trait interaction. As the author points out, the presence of a given factor may act as a catalyst, multiplying the effect of other existing factors. It is probably just as true that in certain cases the presence of a given factor suppresses the effect of other factors. A particular trait possessed in equal degrees by two persons may therefore have a dynamic quality in one that it almost entirely lacks in the other.

The author has prepared the way for future confirmation or modification of his trait list. The ultimate value of his work is to be judged, not by the degree to which his exact conclusions are confirmed, but by the amount and quality of the research it provokes. This book will be indispensable to advanced students of personality, clinical or abnormal psychology, and psychometrics. Ultimately its influence will extend to practitioners in the fields of educational guidance, personnel research, and industrial psychology.

LEWIS M. TERMAN

Chapter One

THE ENTERPRISE OF DESCRIBING, DIAGNOSING, AND MEASURING PERSONALITY

1. THE PRIORITY OF DESCRIPTIVE RESEARCH AMONG PERSONALITY RESEARCH PROBLEMS

The ignoring of a problem. Although the endless variety and colorfulness of human personality intrigue the artist and challenge the ingenuity of the scientist who function together harmoniously in the mind of any good psychologist, many psychometrists have nevertheless fled from this richness of human nature as from some fearsome incubus. They have left reality to the novelist, and escaped into the cloistered order of the laboratory, where the husk of measurement may be exhibited even when the kernel is lost. Some experimentalists have thus gained what is really a barren scientific victory either by maneuvering themselves into false assumptions about human nature, or at the price of relinquishing three fourths of the wide domain of human behavior.

The high psychological enterprise of faithfully exploring human nature and grappling with its precise description and measurement has been neglected equally by applied psychologists of a less sensitive stamp — those misendowed with callous confidence and eager for "results." These "practical" psychologists rush in where angels fear to tread, being impatient to predict and control, without having first observed, described, and measured. A third group which essentially ignores the problem is composed of psychologists religiously

1

anxious to prove all sorts of fond theories about the working of personality, but indisposed to experiment. They invent personality traits, syndromes, types, and mechanisms with easy, magic words, scattering them like thistledown in the harvest fields of precise research and realistic discussion. This censure of a generation of personality study may seem to overstate the neglect; yet how else can one account for the failure to attempt advances where realistic thinking would indicate that they are most urgently needed? True, the advancing front of psychological research suffers partly from being underorganized, so that whenever some different point has to be attacked the ranks of psychologists are apt to resemble a mob rather than a disciplined army, preferring the looting of more or less immediately useful data to the overcoming of central issues of principle or method. But a newcomer, seeing the neglect of cross-sectional studies in current literature, might be forgiven for supposing that there is indeed some positive repression of attention to this foundation on which all developmental studies must ultimately be built.[1]

[1] That scientific psychology has "repressed" these issues is itself worthy of some investigation. Anyone familiar with the history of psychology will recognize that it has been a problem child among the sciences, attempting from an early age to gain the privileges of adult stature without first submitting to the discipline of an exact descriptive stage. This evasion of a laborious apprenticeship arises, first, from psychology's unfortunate and traumatic experience of essaying to become a descriptive science in the wrong medium. For it spent much time, with Titchener and James (in America) attempting to classify the elements of the stream of consciousness. When it turned from this cul-de-sac into a study of behavior, it fell foul of old semantic pitfalls and traded in such artifacts as "faculties" or, more commonly, became imprisoned in a mechanically rigid doctrinaire system which considered all personality traits as "reflexes" and so never came to grips with real personality problems.

The evasion and methodological backwardness of personality study, visible in present research approaches, arose, secondly, from the quite disproportionate difficulties in the descriptive phase of psychology when compared with that of many other sciences. A third factor determining the lack of methodological development has been the quite plausible exactness which can be reached by systems — e.g., clinical, dynamic systems — which do not trouble to describe personality any more precisely than by terms of popular speech, and which avoid exposure of their superficiality by avoiding the challenge of measurement.

The growth of applied, personnel psychology no indicator of real advance. Applied psychologists, it may be objected, have necessarily given a great deal of attention to personality description. Hosts of psychologists, professional and amateur, are busily engaged in measuring or predicting with respect to individual differences, and not merely in the field of abilities alone. Rating scales, "tests," and questionnaires on personality swell the files of business and social agencies. Psychotherapy and education are increasingly based on comprehensive reports attempting to depict the total personality. These meticulous procedures may impress the general public indefinitely; yet for the most part they are not science. The thought which goes into them lacks not only the methodological standards but, indeed, the very subtlety, vigor, and honesty of science. Essential investigation of the foundations on which these pseudomeasurements are supposed to depend for their scientific validity, and even for their practical commercial efficiency in terms of time and money, appears to be nobody's responsibility. Applied psychology has in some respects grown like a monstrous cancer on the body of pure science. It has diverted attention from essential theoretical issues and has supplied no sustenance for the laborious basic research that needs to be done.

This historical outcome is explicable but not excusable. For when the applied psychologist is hounded for immediate results, the teeming variety of actual personalities naturally holds no scientific fascination for him. He must force those realities into arbitrary stereotypes (usually in questionnaire data) no matter how ill-founded, which will permit him to make attractive statistical tables, rating scales, profiles, and index systems, giving his work the semblance of a scientific rigor which it fundamentally lacks.

The challenge of real measurement. The aim of this book is to examine in a radical fashion the whole question of personality description and measurement. Only by so doing can developmental, clinical, social, hereditary, and physiological studies be put on a sound footing or applied psychology be rescued from the public judgment of inefficiency, or even quackery, to which, in some quarters, it is constantly liable.

The psychologist who undertakes to take personality measurement seriously has to be prepared to cope with a great number of viewpoints and criticisms — from those of philosophy to those of the physical scientist. He has to find an answer on the one hand to those mystics, especially in art and literature, who smile at the very idea of applying measurement to personality. He has to reply, on the other, to those applied psychologists who ask, a little indignantly, what is amiss with their present "successful" personality testing, using categories and methods slavishly and unimaginatively copied from aptitude testing, or possibly from bookkeeping or plumbing.

The descriptive phase in the development of a science. Measurement, of course, is only a final specialization of description. It can come into its own only when qualitative description has truly ripened. For this reason the study of measurement must begin with discussion and analysis of such matters as the nature of traits and the mode of representation of the total personality. In the first part of this book it is necessary to study the intriguing and beautiful techniques by which so subtle a phenomenon as human personality can be represented symbolically. Only when this is accomplished is it fitting or profitable to take up practical problems of psychometry and personnel prediction.

If, as the bulk of contemporary writing suggests, there remains an appreciable body of psychologists still unaware of the primary importance of this theoretical study of descriptive technique, it may help them if one points out that no science has reached adult stature without passing through a well-developed descriptive stage. The chemist began his science with some mystical quest after the elixir of life and a recipe for gold, but also, and primarily, with a sense of wonder which led him accurately and graphically to describe a great variety of minerals and fluids. The botanist built his science on a classification of plants and trees. Love for the material has to be prior to love of theories. No psychologist worthy of the name can be content with a hasty and slipshod treatment of this morphological phase in the development of his science.

2. RELATION OF CROSS-SECTIONAL TO LONGITUDINAL STUDIES

The present position of descriptive devices. The basic contention of the above opening paragraphs has been that a fruitful exploration of the origins and transformations of personality structure can proceed only on a foundation of correct description, classification, and measurement of personality manifestations existing at any given moment. It is further argued that psychology has tried, to its cost, to abort this phase of descriptive, cross-sectional development.

What is the general position today regarding progress made in description and measurement? From the standpoint of sheer quantity of data it is true that there is not much evidence of neglect. Measures and statistical observations come in richly from many kinds of research interest and from all angles of approach — except, unfortunately, that kind of research directed to the methodological heart of the problem. Extremely little research has been directed, in fact, to obtaining meaningful, defined measurements of personality variables or toward systematizing the task of describing personality. Psychologists have met their difficulties with a vigorous smothering attack, but the apparently endless booty of this onslaught, sometimes of dazzling novelty, must not be allowed to blind us to the fact that exactness of prediction and depth of theoretical understanding have made practically no advance at all.

It is as if the forces of research, advancing by sheer pressure of numbers on the flanks, have been held up by an impassable resistance before their main objective. This resistance prevents the transition from description of personality by age-old popular concepts, by ratings and measures of a rough nature and uncertain foundation, or by fanciful but unestablished syndromes, to a new era of description by truly conceived measurements based on explicit premises and fundamental exploration.

One cannot reiterate too frequently that it is unsafe and wasteful to attempt to advance in other fields of research until this resistance has been overcome. It is of no use, for example, to multiply publications on the origins of the inferiority sense, or the relative frustration tolerance of differently educated individuals, or the inheritance of emotional instability, unless and until these variables have been defined and measured in such a way that the data are meaningful and fit to be combined with those of other researches presumably on the same variables.[1]

The meaning of cross-sectional research. Personality research, like any other research, deals with changes, under certain influences, of known entities. Longitudinal, developmental studies, as well as simultaneous comparisons of groups or individuals under different conditions, can go forward only when cross-sectional studies have first established the *boundaries* of the traits or forms of behavior to be compared. This becomes most readily evident in longitudinal studies, where one sees at once that the history of a personality trait or neurotic syndrome, and observations on the manner in which

---

[1] A recent comment by Harrison (*109*), typical of the findings of conscientious researchers in a host of similar studies, deserves quotation here. Surveying twenty or thirty years of research on the "personal tempo," its inheritance, significance for personality, etc., he stops amidst the confusion of conflicting findings, obviously due to different workers having measured different variables under the impression that they were dealing with a single tendency, and remarks dryly, "Logically the specificity-generality (of the trait) should have been one of the first, not one of the last, issues to be investigated." Always this realization seems to come too late to save decades of research.

it is affected by various factors, cannot be undertaken until one can infallibly recognize the trait and estimate it well enough to establish changes in its magnitude. Variously expressed, this axiom reads: the cross-sectional study must precede longitudinal study; definition of phenotypes must precede attempts to understand genotypes; the study of anatomy and morphology must precede the study of function. Ultimately this amounts to saying that the distance between two points cannot be measured until one can recognize the points — a fact which is overlooked in some otherwise very impressive psychological writings.

The research sequence must not be rigid. Needless perhaps to add, the foregoing does not mean that developmental hypotheses cannot be entertained until the description and measurement of personality at every age, and through cross sections at every stage of life, are complete, or that the longitudinal study may not be used in turn as a means of aiding the isolation and definition of traits. The functional unity of a trait, indeed, needs frequently to be established, or at least confirmed, by developmental studies of its growth and fate, made simultaneously with the cross-sectional studies.[1]

However, facile hypotheses concerning dynamic developmental mechanisms and learning are all too plentiful and cheap, whereas successful attempts to measure and define personality at any given moment are woefully few. Consequently our first need today, in reforming the methodology of personality research, is an explicit statement of the theory and practice of founding the study of personality on a thorough treatment of the problems of personality description. Though the actual course of research has to be responsive to tactical considerations and to hunches which would suffer grievously from any attempt to impose a rigid ''cross-sectional

---

[1] As will be seen from Section 2 of Chapter 5, the recognition and definition of a functional unity can, theoretically, be just as well established by longitudinal as by cross-sectional studies. The present criticism is of those numerous longitudinal studies which *assume* the existence of a unity and proceed to other issues.

to longitudinal'' sequence, the general line of advance from descriptive to developmental studies will always remain the most promising; moreover, the accuracy of prediction of developmental changes will always be limited by and proportional to the degree of precision attained in describing and measuring the personality characteristics which change.

3. AIMS AND METHODS OF THE PRESENT INQUIRY

Plan. The book falls essentially into two parts: the first, comprising Chapters 1 through 6, dealing with principles and methods of personality measurement; and the second, extending through the remaining five chapters, dealing with the research harvest of actual syndromes or factors and the means for their measurement. However, the first part does not plunge instantly into the most strenuous problems of methodology, nor does the theoretical discussion ascend too abruptly to the tenuous atmosphere of advanced abstractions. It begins by presenting naïvely the accepted syndromes resulting from the direct and common-sense observations of clinical psychology and psychiatry. It departs from the simplicity of these concepts only when investigation and certain doubts raised by reasoned analysis force further refinement. The theoretical discussions of the first part are thus a preparatory schooling between an initial conventional presentation of personality syndromes and a more sophisticated technical treatment, developed as it becomes necessary.

Presentation of theoretical advances. Apart from the initial glance at clinical syndromes, the major concern of the first part is, as stated, to bring into the open the technical problems and to develop the theoretical analysis. This is a closely reasoned discussion and, because of its condensation, makes relatively abstract and difficult reading. The understanding of Chapters 3 through 6 will be helped by familiarity with the important viewpoints and discussions already published in regard to personality structure; e.g., Allport's

Personality, Murray's *Explorations in Personality*, McDougall's *Energies of Men*, and Freud's later writings. It positively *demands*, however, familiarity with correlation procedures, general statistics, and the basic devices of factor analysis.

Practitioners in clinical, guidance, educational, and personnel work, whose immediate interest is in devising and standardizing tests for the traits and primary factors systematically reviewed in the second half of the book, may prefer to go directly to the chapters concerned. This may be convenient, but it is recommended only if the reader returns as soon as possible to studying the underlying theoretical concepts. There is no mistake more costly than the assumption that vocational-guidance experts, educators, industrial psychologists, personnel workers, and psychiatrists can intelligently utilize the results of psychological tests without fully understanding the theory on which they are based. One of the comic spectacles of our generation is the rise of a body of practicing psychologists who are prepared to give momentous advice on personality, and who claim and believe that theirs is a new, superior, and entirely scientific profession, but who insist at the same time that they shall not be asked to learn anything more complicated than simple addition and the drawing of test profiles and who lose patience at once with any text which attempts to disentangle the complex interaction of factors in the organic unity and developmental history of personality. They wish to direct the lives of others with almost godlike insight, but without the effort of reasoning necessary even for adjusting the mechanism of a wheelbarrow. Parenthetically, one, may add that the practicing psychologist needs to be of a mental caliber and a profundity of training which exceed those of the medical practitioner as much as the adjustments of the total organism to a living society exceed in complexity the merely physiological adjustments of the organism.

The theoretical framework which can deal with all individual differences of personality, and the prediction of their consequences in relation to occupations, educational systems, clinical therapeutic influences, and social life generally, cannot be simple. Moreover, since a substantial number of entirely new [1] concepts are put forward here with some of the tentativeness and perhaps lack of clarity with which a writer deals with new concepts, the first part of this book inevitably presents difficult chapters requiring more than one reading.

The catalogue of traits and syndromes. As indicated, the second part of the book is essentially a survey or catalogue of syndromes, factors, traits, etc., discovered to date and the measurement of which is now tolerably well understood. In the first evaluation and integration of research findings the results are kept in four separate divisions, according to the nature of the source data — i.e., the way in which the original "measurements" are gathered. (1) Syndromes based on clinical observation; (2) Syndromes clusters and factors based on behavior ratings; (3) Factors based on self-inventory data; and (4) Factors and clusters based on objective test measurements.

The final chapter attempts cross identifications, matching factors from the four different sources in a complete list of factors for describing and measuring personality.

Within each chapter the plan has been followed of first literally cataloguing the individual researches on which the later conclusions rest, numbering the discovered syndromes and factors of individual researches serially as they occur, for reference. This is called the "catalogue of available research data." The preliminary catalogue numbering has no particular significance; it merely follows a rough chronological order. The magnitude of the populations and number of trait elements, etc., in the various researches are set out, so

---

[1] They have been foreshadowed, however, in two recent articles by the present writer (52) (54).

of each common trait, or a certain possession of unique traits, one describes him.

The concept of traits involves far greater difficulties than that of types. We can proceed to a reasonably satisfactory definition of a type immediately and employ it in the cataloguing of actual types and syndromes in the next chapter, long before we approach the complex theory of traits. In so doing we are following the historical development of personality psychology. This order is dictated also by the fact that we regard the clinical approach — in which the use of type and syndrome is embedded — as a desirable, naturalistic, perspective-giving preliminary to the more intensive, technical methodology of traits; for the latter demands at once certain experimental and statistical refinements.

Terms for the major divisions, aspects, or "modalities" of personality. Whether the psychologist is dealing with types or traits, he has to employ terms to denote certain broad aspects of personality and their subdivisions. Contingently we shall use the following labels, with the relationships as shown, and in the senses used in common by such recent standard works as those of Allport (6), Murray (190), or McDougall (173)(174).

1. Abilities.   (a) More constitutional abilities and aptitudes; e.g., intelligence, musical aptitude, spatial reasoning.
     (b) Attainments. Acquired information, verbal and other skills.
2. Interests.   (a) Considered quantitatively as interests, object cathexes of love or aversion.
     (b) Considered qualitatively as sentiments, attitudes, tastes, infatuations, and phobias.
3. Manner of character integration. Stability, moral orientation, and other general characters of the dynamic structure.
4. Temperament, including temper and emotionality. Constitutional reactivity.
5. Disposition. The predominant dynamic drives and purposes coloring personality.

that the reader may judge for himself the confidence to be assigned to various findings.

Following this mere exhaustive cataloguing, an evaluation, synthesis, and final classification is made into the syndromes that can be considered established by these researches. These new syndromes formed by the overlapping, confirmatory syndromes of the actual researches are arranged roughly in order of importance and of soundness of foundation. They are numbered by Roman numerals, as well as tentatively named. These numbers are intended to form a relatively "permanent" index system to facilitate later discussion and research reference, and it is possible that the reference system will prove convenient to psychologists beyond the confines of the discussion in this book. The index number is prefixed by C, BR, Q, or T to indicate that the source or foundation is, respectively, Clinical Observation, Behavior Rating, Questionnaire, or Objective Test Measurement.

Scientific standards and flexibility of method. The reasons for the above dual listing — in terms of original data and of finished conclusions — spring not only from a need for convenient arrangement but also from the spirit and canons of method embraced in this whole study.[1] In a first survey of personality description of this kind one has to build on the uneven ground provided by a few sound researches intermixed with many others that are fragmentary in scope and sometimes approximate in method. If the latter are summarily

[1] This permits temporary "working" syntheses and a free development of hypotheses which can be readily restructured. It is an adaptation to gain two distinct objectives with respect to the usefulness of this book in advancing research. By clearly separating data from conclusions, in two distinct presentations, we are at greater liberty to use the hunches which come from experience and individual insight in this field. We can proceed with less paralyzing caution in foreshadowing the factors which will be of greatest use in practical measurement, and we can venture more original propositions to guide the next phase of research, without damaging our foundation or preventing the reader from using them for his independent conclusions.

Moreover, it permits the book to be used when necessary simply as an exhaustive reference work, offering a succinct and ordered catalogue of all available research — a catalogue which can be kept up to date in later editions.

rejected, through the mechanical application of some rigid, and often arbitrary, rule or standard of statistical and experimental validity, without regard to the total situation and the cumulative suggestiveness of several perhaps individually defective researches, valuable findings may be lost.   From incomplete researches, nuances of distinction capable of guiding the search in further and final experiment have been gleaned.

Consequently, our first catalogue list has not presumed to rule out, for example, any syndrome which has the pragmatic sanction of sound clinical experience, merely because it lacks further investigation by correlation methods;   nor does it leave unrecorded a factor at which some statistician might demur because it rests on only twenty or thirty cases.

Instead, all researches meeting all-round scientific criteria have been included in the first cataloguing, but with precise records of their foundations, so that they may be employed in arriving at the second listing but with a clear view of their limitations as evidence.   The labeling of trait patterns in the catalogue by C, BR, Q, or T is part of this methodological plan of indicating categories of certainty, for these clinical, testing, and other sources have different validities and often lead to different evaluations.

4. ASSUMPTIONS REGARDING THE STARTING POINT OF THE PRESENT PERSONALITY INVESTIGATION

Existing terms and concepts.   Although an inquiry of radical scope has to question much that is regarded as solid ground, it must nevertheless take its start from some definitive point of firmness and consent explicitly to use some existing equipment of concepts until its own are developed.

The platform from which we start will be little more than the relatively permanent core of common-sense notions about personality existing in intelligent discussion and the elements of which have been traditionally defined in the dictionary.
Beyond that we accept the refinements and stabilizations of

meaning which the majority of psychologists ha use in the first part of this century — refinements v to description, not to interpretation or formalized

Personality measurement deals essentially with tions: (1) What are the things to be measured? an can the measurement be made and expressed?   Out ters are concerned to explore the nature of the en measured.

Psychology down the ages has used many conc scribe personality and to which quantitative adject attached, but in essence they reduce to only t
(*a*) Types (with which we may include syndr
(*b*) Traits (symptoms, measured attributes, etc. pursue our examination we shall see that the between these two systems ultimately dissolves in prehensive mathematical formulations.   But s and for certain restricted purposes they are very Following the first method, one picks out an (a real individual or an ideational composite of vations) — e.g., an extravert, a rogue, a schizo musical genius, or a Mongolian imbecile — and u a reference picture, median sample, standard ca pigeonhole for the classification of others.   The type picture may occur to the scientist through h observed a whole group of individuals manifesting characters in common, or, less inductively and mo tively, as a logically elaborated creation from son principle in the psychologist's mind.

By the second or trait method of describing perso picks out a certain mode or modes of behavior a this behavior as the expression of a trait.   It may be trait — i.e., something which all people possess extent — or it may be entirely peculiar to the indi i.e., a unique trait.   By invoking a comprehensiv such traits and assigning to the individual a definit

Naturally, our later investigation may not support these divisions in this form or admit that they are ultimately independent; but they seem the most tested and proved equipment with which to begin.

Irrelevance of "normal" and "abnormal." Throughout this inquiry normal and abnormal patterns and behavior manifestations are considered in a common field of reference and under the illumination of single comprehensive concepts. As indicated in the Preface, we feel that the dichotomy, though legally necessary and therapeutically convenient, is scientifically pointless and stultifying. Normal and abnormal behavior manifestations differ in frequency and quality and may not be part of a single continuum; they are equally manifestations of what we call personality, just as psychiatry, as a body of knowledge, is a part of psychology.

What is personality? In Allport's scholarly survey (*8*) of personality theory, some fifty-three definitions of personality are cited as existing in the literature. Murphy and Jensen, after an almost equally exhaustive acquaintance with the discussions, say, with seemingly genuine surprise and disappointment, "We do not believe that anyone today can seriously undertake to say that he knows what personality is."

The ritual of beginning a dissertation with a precise definition of what is being studied seems to be beloved almost as much by students as by professors. Yet it frequently implies a serious misunderstanding of scientific method. If anything can be fully defined, it is pointless to investigate it. In the present instance we have only to describe the *fields of phenomena* which we set out to understand. While doing so, if we use the term "personality" at all, it is to be understood in a common dictionary sense. At the end of this book we shall be in a position to make a better approximation — still, of course, not final — to a true definition of personality.

The reactions which constitute the data of personality study are all the reactions of the organism: its reactions to people, things, and ideas; its partial reaction, as in reflexes, and its total reaction; its conscious reactions and its unconscious reactions.

Utility of results to the practicing psychometrist. Although practical measurement is implicit in every theme and section of this work, it is only in the last chapter that direct consideration is given to testing as a routine procedure and with respect to the practical situations in which prediction is required.

This betokens no neglect of the needs of the practicing psychologist; indeed, the emphasis on first understanding the nature of measurement and sharpening its concepts can alone give an efficient foundation for these practical ends. Today the urgent need of psychometry is not any addition to the already prolific "measurement scales," questionnaires, and tests, but a clearer evaluation of what really needs to be measured and of the terms in which such measurement can be understood. Above all, psychometry needs guidance as to the nature of the primary factors of personality, both in orectic and in ability fields, if practicing psychometrists are ever to use their available testing time less wastefully than at present. As soon as these basic traits are made clear, the production of actual rating scales and standardized tests can be depended upon to ensue quickly.[1]

In any case, the final step of producing actual scales, norms, item validities, consistency coefficients, and comparatively foolproof instructions for administration is now — fortunately for future progress — within the competence of a considerable army of practicing psychometrists who will consequently have no difficulty in adapting the present findings to their needs.

---

[1] A description of tests and norms for most of the personality factors and special abilities discussed here is already available in the present writer's *Guide to Mental Testing*, Revised Edition, University of London Press; 1946.

Chapter Two

THE NATURE AND VARIETIES OF CLINICALLY DISTINGUISHABLE PERSONALITY FORMS

1. THE DISTINCTION BETWEEN CONTINUOUS TYPES AND SPECIES TYPES

Origin of the type concept and its duality. The description of personality through typologies has grown up primarily in the clinical realm. For that reason it has been far more concerned with the phenomena of psychopathology than of normal personality, so that the examples used in this chapter to illustrate the theory of types are more likely to come from abnormal than normal psychology and to be syndromes which in the first place were the discoveries of the medical practitioner.

However, the theoretical clarifications of type concepts with which we must first concern ourselves apply equally to normal and abnormal behavior. As we have seen, a type was customarily defined initially by pointing to some total, unanalyzed individual, real or imaginary, as the representative of it; but ever since Plato and the application of type concepts to personality by Hippocrates and Galen, there has been a double meaning in notion of types. Regarding stature, for example, we could speak of two types — a tall and a short type. By a tall type we mean a person of long over-all dimension and with other dimensions to match. In any actual population, however, except one of mixed and unmiscegenated tall and short people — e.g., a settlement of Swedes and Japanese — there is

17

a continuous grading of statures from tall to short, and the "intermediate type" is in fact the most numerous.   This is an instance of a continuous typology, in which a series of characteristics — height, leg length, weight, arm length, shoulder breadth — vary, in company and congruently, from one extreme pole, "shortness," to the opposite pole, "tallness."

What are called "types," in a continuous typology, are thus nothing more than the descriptions of the bounding extremes of a continuous distribution.   The great majority of continuous typologies therefore have only two polar types, but it is possible to have type labels in such a situation for more than two types.   Thus it has been said that human beings can be divided into two types, those who play golf and those who do not; but the good player is forced to recognize the existence of a third type, those intermediates who believe they play golf!

Species types.   Contrasted with continuous types are species types, which can best be illustrated first by a physical example, in fact by the lowly example of breeds of dogs or cattle.   In well-regulated kennels of dog breeders one finds a population divisible into a number of well-marked groups, each substantially homogeneous within itself.   There are, apart from hybridization, no continuities between — and certainly no normal distribution of — the measurements and characters prevalent in one group and those prevalent in another; in fact, the situation is in general that of plant and animal species, for which reason the above term has been considered most descriptive.

If we consider any one character only, the difference between continuous type and species type systems is simply the difference between a unimodal and bimodal or nonoverlapping pair of distributions, as shown in Diagram 1.

Such bimodality with respect to a single character is found in human beings with respect to eye color, dexterity of hand (right- and left-handedness), color blindness, some kinds of deafness, and so on.

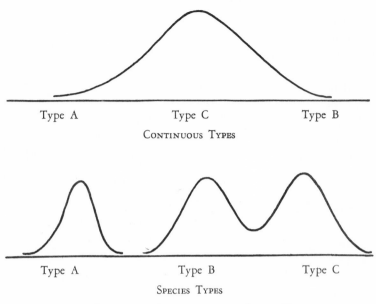

DIAGRAM 1. Continuous and Species Types

When *many* characters are involved in the differentiation of types, however, as is commonly the case if the word "type" is to have its full meaning, it is quite possible to find, even in a true system of species types, that overlap or continuity exists for any one character, while the *patterns* show no overlap or continuity.[1] Mathematically patterns are most easily expressed by ratios, and we then find that these ratios — rather than the original absolute measures — show bimodality or complete absence of continuity in species types.

Such multivariate species types will probably be found, as research becomes more exact, among human races and racial mixtures (i.e., particular historical collections of genes), the

[1] For example, bulldogs and whippet dogs probably form a single distribution in a continuum of size alone but fall into two distinct species types when the ratio $\frac{weight}{height}$ is plotted.

psychotic syndromes, neurotic syndromes, the different forms of mental defect, and imbecility. The last, for example, will show continuity with respect to any one variable — e.g., intelligence — but Mongolian imbeciles will differ discontinuously from, say, cretins, with respect to ratios of intelligence and speed of movement, intelligence and verbal ability, etc., etc. The complete mathematical exploration and expression of species typologies is taken up in Chapter 6, Section 3.

2. SURVEY OF DISCOVERIES AT THE "CLINICAL-EXPERIENTIAL" LEVEL

Uncertain usage of "type." The use of the type conception in psychology has suffered from confusion of the above two meanings. When Jung, for example, described the extravert and introvert types which could be recognized in the consulting room, it was not clear whether these were to be considered continuous or discontinuous types. When the educator of the late nineteenth century discovered individual differences in ability to employ imagery or different sense modalities, the same confusion led to the assumption that species types would exist: that children could be classified as "audiles," "visiles," etc., to receive instruction by different methods appropriate to the predominant imagery. The situation with regard to imagery of the six senses, however, proved to be better represented by Diagram 1 than by Diagram 2, so that it is impractical to segregate in the way envisaged.

Continuous normal types. Apparently most observers of individual personality differences within the range of normality have, however, used the term "type" in its continuous sense.[1] The keen observation of fellow men in their everyday life, over centuries — an observation sometimes genial and sometimes misanthropic — by philosophers, physicians, novelists, and essayists, has yielded a great abundance of type

---

[1] An exception is Max Dessoir, who writes (72): "We take it for granted that an individual . . . can belong only to one type."

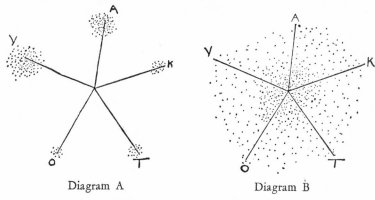

Diagram A   Diagram B

DIAGRAM 2. IMAGERY TYPES

systems, notably with respect to temperament but also in relation to character, intellect, interests, and dispositions. A scholarly conspectus and discussion of the varied fruits of this observational, clinical, and literary approach has been published by Roback (*217*); but since most of these systems, at least in their original form, are of merely historical interest, we shall confine ourselves to a tabular listing of the historical types which have achieved some importance.

TABLE 1

List of the Principal Types from the Experiential, Clinical Approach

1. *Predominantly According to Temperamental Characteristics*

   * Sanguine, Choleric, Melancholic, Phlegmatic
   Hippocrates, 460–370 b.c., developed through Aristotle to Galen, 131–201 a.d.
   Developed into sevenfold classification by Laycock, 1862
   * Muscular, Digestive, Respiratory, Cerebral
   Rostan, 1828
   Hutchinson, 1884
   × Motive, Vital, and Mental Temperaments. Wells, 1869
   * Rachitic, Carcinomatous, Scrofulous-phthisic. Beneke, 1878
   * Gallbladder and Ulcer Types. Draper, 1934

TABLE 1 — *Continued*

2. *Predominantly According to Interests and Character*

The Character Sketches of Jean de la Bruyere, 1645–1696
× Economic, Religious, Aesthetic, Theoretical, Social, and Political.
    Spranger
× Oral-erotic, Anal-erotic, and Genital Types.   Freud
* Inferiority and Socialized Types.   Adler
The "being" man, the easygoing man, the striving man.   Dessoir
× Emotionally Mature and Emotionally Immature.   Willoughby

3. *Predominantly According to Abilities*

Imagery Types.   Visile, Audile, Tactile, Motor
Sensory and Motor Types.   Baldwin
Types of mental defect and aphasia
Types of genius; musical, mathematical

4. *Predominantly According to Disposition*

Assertive, Acquisitive, Amorous, Gregarious, etc.
    (fourteen, corresponding to propensities according to McDougall)
    (*173*)
+ Active *vs.* Reflective.   Jordan
+ Explosive *vs.* Abstracted.   James
+ Unrestrained *vs.* Restrained.   Guthrie
Romantic *vs.* Classical.   Ostwald
+ Subjective *vs.* Objective.   Binet, Stern
+ Stable *vs.* Unstable.   Trotter
Sex Types.   Apfelbach
    Masculine, Feminine, Sadistic, Masochistic
+× Extravert *vs.* Introvert.   Jung
* Sympatheticotonic *vs.* Vagotonic
×+* Cyclothyme — Schizothyme.   Kretschmer, Bleuler, and Kroepelin
× Excited, Inhibited, and Labile.   Pavlov, Serokhtin, Yarmolenko
×* Tetanoid and Basedowoid Eidetic Types.   Jaensch
    (also Integrate-Disintegrate)
× Active-Inactive, Emotional-Unemotional, and Perseverative-Nonper-
       severative. Heymans, Wiersma, and Gross
×* Hyperthyroid, Adrenal, Gonadal, Pituitary, and other hormone types
×* Cerebrotonic, Viscerotonic, Somatotonic.   Sheldon
Eight types of Temper corresponding to combinations of high and low
(1) Urgency (2) Persistency (3) Affectability.   McDougall

5. *Predominantly According to Disintegration and Disease Process*

Psychotic Syndromes
Neurotic Syndromes and Symptoms

TABLE 1 — *Continued*

+ = Predominantly observational variants and predecessors of extravert-introvert distinctions
× = Predominantly based on clinical observation and experiment, with the abnormal
* = Predominantly physiological in basis

3. EVALUATION OF THE CLINICAL-EXPERIENTIAL APPROACH TO "NORMAL" SYNDROMES

Critique of type systems based on uncontrolled observation. The initial discovery or definition of these types has sprung from a variety of methods, has occurred in different epochs, and has been founded on very diverse sets of entangling presuppositions. Some systems — e.g., those rooted in literary characterology, in the quest for correlates of physiological "humors," and in the listing of mental traits supposedly tied up with peculiar physiognomic features—luxuriated in remote classical times. Others — e.g., phrenology, clinical experience with behavior problems, neuroses, etc., ethology (Allport (6)), and experimental studies of special functions — are decidedly more modern.

The typologies which are definitely based on physiological or anatomical approaches are picked out by an asterisk. Another scattered group, joined by the fact that they converge, through very various nomenclatures, essentially upon the same modern concept — which we may temporarily label introversion-extraversion — are picked out by a +. Others, partly experimentally grounded and found deserving of fuller discussion in the chapter subsequent to this, are marked by an *x*.

It is possible to pick out several convergences and unrecognized identities of the kind just mentioned. For certain patterns seem to have arrested attention again and again, despite their entering the stage in different guises. They have been rechristened as many times, by psychologists ignorant of history or intoxicated with the novelty of a fashion in typology.

On the whole, and considering the amount of writing and discussion devoted to the method, the observational approach cannot but be judged disappointing. Firsthand observation of people, in contrast to the more objective experimental and statistical approaches to be discussed in the ensuing chapters, had the potentiality of yielding the outlines of types too subtle to be caught by grosser methods. Instead of leading the way for statistical investigation, however, clinical-type observation has fallen a prey to vociferous, preconceived beliefs, pretentious theorizing, and unrestrained, garrulous invention, especially in the field of applied psychology. Hundreds of types, generally as dichotomies and trinities, are propounded every year in the shop windows of psychological literature. In many cases the authors have not even paused to think that human beings require, beyond the shadow of a doubt, more than two or three categories to describe them! In others the classification according to an alleged type clearly has reference to no more than a single trait. Writers and theorists are many; naturalists are few. The observations of the latter, which might have become the growing points of fine experimental studies, have been so heavily snowed under by congealed verbiage left by the former that one can scarcely hope to disinter them. Nevertheless, as far as the labor seems profitable, we shall extricate and set out those typologies which hold promise for further investigation.

Surviving normal typologies at the clinical-experiential level. By reason of converging observations independently pointing to the existence of some underlying reality, the following types can be set aside from the mass as the best representatives of what can be considered established at the clinical level among "normal" people.

TABLE 2

1. EXTRAVERT

EXTRAVERT	INTROVERT
Interested in outer world and in details	Interested in inner experience, not in ordinary affairs of life
Easy expression of emotions	Inhibited emotions
Sociable	Unsociable
Hasty	Introspective
Frank	Secretive
Natural	Formal
Realistic	Hypersensitive, shy
Confident	Anxious
Orthodox	Independent
Dresses well	Careless about his person
Orthodox emotional responses	Individual or queer emotional responses

2. CYCLOTHYME

CYCLOTHYME	SCHIZOTHYME
Oscillating emotional mood	Steady mood, varying excitability
Sociable, good mixer	Unsociable, reclusive
Responsive	Unresponsive
Good-natured, warm	Cold
Humorous	Earnest
Balanced	Extreme
Objective, realistic	Subjective, autistic
Natural	Formal
Energetic	Inert
Tough	Hypersensitive
	Idealistic

3. ORAL AND ANAL EROTIC CHARACTERS. See (*113*).

4. TETANOID AND BASEDOWOID. See (*129*) (*130*).

5. EMOTIONALLY MATURE. This is viewed as a continuous variable, through which the following features increase or decrease together. (*279*)

"Freedom from narcism and ambivalence, release from egocentrism; the achievement of socialized impulses, of insight; emotional acceptance of the reality principle."

A list of 150 behavior items is listed in (*279*). A similar notion occurs in the concept of a "psychotic age" variable, in which attitudes and interests of psychotics are shown to be such as are tolerable only in infants below 36 months.

4. THE VARIETIES AND DIAGNOSTIC RELIABILITIES OF
   PSYCHO-PATHOLOGICAL SYNDROME DIAGNOSES

Types and syndromes. By contrast with "types" among normal persons, which are not easy to discern or confirm, patterns of traits can often be established with considerable certainty in the more extreme forms which personality traits take among the mentally abnormal. The various patterns found among psychotics (lunatics) and neurotics are commonly called pathological syndromes rather than types; but except for the fact that they may be only temporary personality manifestations, springing from a diseased condition, they belong technically and formally to types. The term "type" as generally used has the flavor of something too permanent and prevalent to be applied to an abnormality or a temporary maladjustment. Nevertheless, in the formal sense, duration, prevalence, or normality are accidental features of a type and the term will be used to cover all situations.

Thus, if we dismiss questions of etiology and subsequent course, a syndrome is nothing more or less than a type pattern. To be precise, it is a clear-cut *species type* pattern, for usually there is no continuous variation of cases between one disease and another or between having and not having a disease. One either has measles or one does not have it. However, *some* mental diseases — e.g., manic depressive disorder or the psychoneuroses — may be like certain vague physical dysfunctions in that they can show gradation into related disorders on the one hand and into normality on the other; the advance of measurement can alone decide this.

Reliability of syndrome classifications. As we have seen, the approach at the unaided, observational level — which we may best henceforth describe as the *experiential, clinical level*, whether it is connected with an actual clinical organization or not — has a small and uncertain yield of really sound typologies applicable to normal persons. On the other hand, in the pathological realm it has yielded a considerable number of seemingly well-established, widely recognized syndromes. These we must set out exhaustively and study closely in this and the following chapter, before going beyond the purely clinical approach.

First, however, the methods and validities of the clinical psychiatric approach must be placed in perspective. There is not good agreement among psychiatrists — even since the substantial tidying wrought by the insight of Kraepelin and Bleuler — regarding some features of the type systems for classifying psychotics and neurotics. Nor is it found that any actual case will invariably fall into one category only or that, even if it belongs in one category only, psychiatrists will agree regarding the category.

There is no doubt that there is still widespread dissatisfaction among psychiatrists regarding the principal clinical syndromes of the present classification. This is not entirely a reflection on the system. In the first place, men lacking in clinical sense are prone to grumble, when their false diagnoses are brought home to them, that the system is faulty. In the second, there is misunderstanding of what a syndrome is — leading, for example, to the erroneous expectation that there can be no intermediate types or, again, that the syndrome is automatically an interpretation as well as a mere description.

Thirdly, there is conflict between one set of extremists who believe they can deal therapeutically with disease processes without any preliminary classifying of the disease syndrome and another set who seem to think that accurate classification is itself interpretation and explanation. Both, in the opinion of the present writer, labor under serious misconceptions. Admittedly symptoms are only symptoms, and not the real inner processes which need to be understood. Yet in science accurate description must precede interpretation. Those who would by-pass the empirical, phenotypic symptom-complexes are presuming on some ultrascientific insight — some royal road to understanding nature — which does not exist. On the other hand, those who are content to stop at classification have allowed the means to an end to usurp the rank of an end.

In view of the vast body of psychiatrists who entertain even vaster doubts about the classification system in pathology which they daily employ, it is amazing that there are so few studies of the validity and reliability of actual diagnoses. One available recent review of the literature on diagnosis challenges the nosology of neuroses and minor forms of psychoses on the grounds that mixed-type diagnoses are all too frequent. In 100 cases followed up in detail over one year "a major revision of the diagnosis had to be made in more than 40 per cent of the patients." Hoch and Rachlin (119) examined records of 5799 cases in New York and found every 13th case of schizophrenia had originally been diagnosed as manic-depressive. They also noted marked variations in the ratio of schizophrenic to manic-depressive diagnoses in the admissions to different state hospital systems.

One has the impression from these inquiries that about half of the error is due to low reliability — i.e., to differences between clinicians or between a clinician's present and past diagnosis of the same case. The rest must be ascribed to low validity — i.e., to error in the textbook picture of the syndrome, including the mistaken perception of a mixed syndrome as a single entity. Otherwise regarded, this is simply the failure to select the true statistical modal point in the distribution of symptoms — that is to say, to select that equilibrium point among possible symptom groupings which is in fact the most frequent. Clearly, however, the validities are much higher for psychotic syndromes than for neuroses and the still vaguer "character neuroses."

Although there are not sufficient studies for us to judge just how valid and reliable the syndromes are (*a*) in the hands of clinicians of different skill and experience, (*b*) with regard to different alleged syndromes, there can be no doubt that they fall far below the standards which would be considered satisfactory in psychometric assessment of psychological variables or in the definition of psychological factors — e.g., "g" or general ability, "F" or surgency factor. However, that is no reason for rejecting clinical evidence *in toto* from a study of this kind. Confused though the picture may be, it nevertheless contains more patient and faithful observation and deals with more personality variables which are real and vital in relation to the total life situation than are yet found in psychometric data. In this survey our aim must be to record the clinical syndromes as such with complete faithfulness, so that they may be used as a basis for more exact psychological research and analysis and become integrated with the factor data later to be described.

List of psychotic and neurotic syndromes. Abnormal personality syndromes are of two kinds: psychotic and neurotic. Psychoses differ from neuroses principally in that in the latter conditions the patient still retains contact with reality. He has insight, is aware of his disablement, and is socially responsible.[1] One might say that in neuroses only part of the personality is affected. There is in general a difference of degree in the disorder of personality produced by psychoses and neuroses; but this is not the essential difference, and certain neuroses may disable the individual, emotionally, socially, and in regard to earning a living, more than some psychoses. In general, neuroses respond to psychotherapeutic treatment more than do psychoses. Most of these differences are differences of degree; but it is generally agreed that neurotic syndromes are not transition stages in incurring or recovering from psychoses, except in rare instances. They are qualitatively different and statistically independent in occur-

---

[1] See Rogerson (*220*) for a recent discussion of possible distinction of neurosis and psychosis. The conclusion is that no single symptom (e.g., intensity of anxiety) other than "contact with the real world" (or insight) will distinguish.

rence.   Mental disorders have been brought into their present classificatory relationships not merely on the basis of the syndrome of symptoms which each displays at its fullest development, but also through taking into account the features which characterize the etiology, course, and prognosis of the disorder — i.e., it is born of longitudinal as well as cross-sectional observation.   The emphasis here, however, will be on careful and detailed description of the typical symptom complexes, by means of which the disorders can be adequately differentiated, granted sufficient skill, even without the aid of developmental observations.   For the present treatise is devoted to the descriptive phase of personality study, and its purpose is deliberately to rule out bias from premature, erroneous generalizations regarding causation, course, and outcome of personality change.   The aim is to establish facts which can be used as strictly independent evidence when aligned later with the findings of developmental, longitudinal studies.   Moreover (though this also may affront the psychiatrist), the present clinical descriptions must be shorn not only of developmental connotations but must also be kept extremely brief and laconic, for they are but one small aspect — one factual contribution — in the total range of data to be reviewed in this book on personality description.

A note on the general setting of these syndromes is, however, in order.   Psychoses are both endogenous and exogenous, organic and psychogenic.   Though most endogenous psychoses are organic, the physiological basis is in some cases too subtle to have become recognized.   Some exogenous psychoses are, of course, organic, in the sense that the provoking environmental influence — e.g., alcohol or syphilis — is organic.   Though we are naturally more interested in psychogenic psychoses, some description will be given also of organic psychoses, for the fact of their physiological correlation throws much light on the organization of the body-mind unit.

The classification of mental diseases as adopted and amended by the American Psychiatric Association is as follows. The few points at which our description of syndromes departs from this classification are indicated in the corresponding syndrome descriptions, occurring in the following chapter.

TABLE 3

CLASSIFICATION OF MENTAL DISORDERS

1. Traumatic psychoses.

2. Senile psychoses.

3. Psychoses with cerebral arteriosclerosis.

4. General paralysis.

5. Psychoses with cerebral syphilis.

6. Psychoses with Huntington's chorea.

7. Psychoses with brain tumor.

8. Psychoses with other brain or nervous diseases.
    (*a*) Cerebral embolism.
    (*b*) Paralysis agitans.
    (*c*) Meningitis, tubercular or other forms (to be specified).
    (*d*) Multiple sclerosis.
    (*e*) Tabes dorsalis.
    (*f*) Acute chorea.
    (*g*) Encephalitis lethargica.
    (*h*) Other diseases (to be specified).

9. Alcoholic psychoses.
    (*a*) Delirium tremens.
    (*b*) Korsakow's psychosis.
    (*c*) Acute hallucinosis.
    (*d*) Other types, acute or chronic.

10. Psychoses due to drugs and other exogenous toxins.
    (*a*) Opium (and derivatives), cocaine, bromides, chloral, etc., alone or combined (to be specified).
    (*b*) Metals, as lead, arsenic, etc. (to be specified).
    (*c*) Gases (to be specified).
    (*d*) Other exogenous toxins (to be specified).

11. Psychoses with pellagra.

12. Psychoses with other somatic diseases.
    (*a*) Delirium with infectious diseases.
    (*b*) Postinfectious psychosis.

TABLE 3 — *Continued*

    (*c*) Exhaustion delirium.
    (*d*) Delirium of unknown origin.
    (*e*) Cardiorenal diseases.
    (*f*) Diseases of the ductless glands.
    (*g*) Other diseases or conditions (to be specified).
13. Manic-depressive psychoses.
    (*a*) Manic type.
    (*b*) Depressive type.
    (*c*) Other types.
14. Involution melancholia.
15. Dementia praecox (schizophrenia).
16. Paranoia and paranoid conditions.
17. Epileptic psychoses.
18. Psychoneuroses and neuroses.
    (*a*) Hysterical type.
    (*b*) Psychasthenic type (anxiety and obsessive forms).
    (*c*) Neurasthenic type.
    (*d*) Other types.
19. Psychoses with psychopathic personality.
20. Psychoses with mental deficiency.
21. Undiagnosed psychoses.
22. Without psychosis.
    (*a*) Epilepsy without psychosis.
    (*b*) Alcoholism without psychosis.
    (*c*) Drug addiction without psychosis.
    (*d*) Psychopathic personality without psychosis.
    (*e*) Mental deficiency without psychosis.
    (*f*) Other conditions (to be specified).[1]

The frequency of occurrence of the psychologically most important of these syndromes is indicated by the figures for a large sample in Table 4.   Naturally the frequency varies with racial and cultural factors.

The choice of syndromes for more intensive description, in the following chapter, is determined by this frequency and by their importance for psychological theory.   As a result, only the disorders listed from thirteen through nineteen on the American Psychiatric Association list are treated in detail.

[1] Noyes, *Modern Clinical Psychiatry*, page 135.

TABLE 4

FREQUENCY OF MENTAL DISORDERS

A comparison among 10 psychoses of first admissions to State mental
hospitals and to private mental hospitals, 1936 [1]

PSYCHOSIS	PER CENT STATE HOSPITALS	DISTRIBUTION PRIVATE HOSPITALS
General paresis	8.1	2.0
Cerebral arteriosclerosis	12.5	4.2
Senile	8.6	5.6
Dementia praecox	20.1	13.6
With mental deficiency	3.6	.8
Alcoholic	4.6	5.3
With epilepsy	2.2	.4
Manic-depressive	11.7	14.6
Involutional psychoses	2.8	4.4
Paranoia and paranoid condition	1.5	2.5
With psychopathic personality	1.7	1.8
Alcoholism without psychosis	5.2	15.8

TABLE 5 [2]

SEX DISTRIBUTION OF MENTAL DISORDERS

PSYCHOSIS	MALE	FEMALE
Involutional	1	2.5
Manic-depressive	1	1.25
Psychoneurosis	1	1.75
Dementia praecox	1	.87
Cerebral arteriosclerosis	1	.60
General paresis	1	.28
Alcoholic psychosis	1	.14

[1] United States Bureau of the Census. *Patients in Hospitals for Mental Diseases:* 1936 (Washington, 1938), page 14 (Table 10).

[2] *Mental Deviants in the Population of the United States.* Nathaniel D. M. Hirsch. Division of Health and Disability Studies, Bureau of Research and Statistics, Social Security Board, Federal Security Agency.

Chapter Three

DESCRIPTION OF THE PRINCIPAL PATHOLOGICAL SYNDROMES, NEUROTIC AND PSYCHOTIC

1. ADAPTATION OF DESCRIPTIONS TO PURPOSES OF INVESTIGATION

Formalizing description. In the space available, having regard to the main objectives of a work on personality description, the numerous pathological syndromes cannot be described with that detailed thoroughness which the psychiatric practitioner would require; nor, on the other hand, can the description be made in terms entirely intelligible to the novice in psychology. The aim has been to give a maximum amount of meaningful description of each syndrome within a brief space and in a form which will (*a*) be thorough from the standpoint of research discussion, (*b*) remind the psychologist of as many angles of the subject as possible, and (*c*) permit ready relation of these syndromes to those described later under the statistical and experimental approaches. Such description has necessitated the use of some technical terms, the ignoring of some debates on interpretation, and the adherence to a stereotyped round of aspects (cognitive, dynamic, physiological) in an attempt at consistent comprehensiveness.

Scope and index arrangement of material. Only the main psychotic syndromes are to be discussed, followed by the most common neurotic syndromes. For the purposes of later comparison with syndromes obtained through quite different methods, notably through correlation of test and questionnaire response items, it is necessary to be able to identify the present syndromes by an index number. All of the syndromes of this chapter have the prefix C, indicating that they are *clinically founded*, and are numbered serially in Roman numerals as they occur here.

It is possible for more than one syndrome to appear in one disease entity. Most clearly this occurs in manic-depressive disorder, where three syndromes can be recognized: (*a*) the manic syndrome, (*b*) the depressive syndrome, and (*c*) a cyclothyme personality make-up which persists constantly with the individual in all states. Index numbers have been given to all three of these, though the third unfortunately is not emphatic enough to have been clinically defined with any exactness. Similarly in the schizophrenias, more than one syndrome has been recorded and indexed.

2. PSYCHOTIC SYNDROMES: SCHIZOPHRENIA AND TRUE PARANOIA

General definition. Schizophrenia describes a group of psychoses having a large, common core, which account for more cases of mental disorder than any other psychotic syndrome. The term replaced dementia praecox, which now tends to be used, if at all, with some specialization toward schizophrenia simplex occurring in early life. There are four principal varieties (sub-syndromes) within schizophrenia: simple schizophrenia, hebephrenic schizophrenia, catatonic schizophrenia, and paranoid schizophrenia. It is doubtful whether a pure paranoia exists independently of paranoid schizophrenia; probably it is a limiting instance of paranoid schizophrenia, with a minimum amount of mental deterioration, but for the sake of caution it is listed separately here.

The central features of schizophrenia are withdrawal from social contacts, dislocation of the usual relations of thought to emotion and of the individual to his external environment. It is characterized by likelihood of onset in early life and by an irreversible, deteriorative course. The essential splitting of mental and emotional processes, the breaking of the normal synthesis of thought, feeling, and conduct, led Bleuler in 1908 to designate this disorder by its present name.

Simple schizophrenia C(I). The common core of schizophrenic symptom syndromes are as follows. The affective life is characterized by irritability; moodiness; rigidity and inadaptability; lack of rapport with others; superficiality; "unreal" momentary emotionality; underlying hatred and anxiety, making most affection ambivalent; sensitiveness and, above all, indifference; apathy and will-lessness, alternating with stubbornness. Schizoids verging on schizophrenia are defined, affectively, as anxious, embarrassed, suspicious, hypochondriacal, and lacking in adaptability.

The sexual and social emotions are perhaps most obviously affected. Sexuality seems underdeveloped, autoerotic, and isolated from true affection. Younger schizophrenics intellectualize love and limit it to the self, while older patients may develop hostility to sexuality or have love objects which are ego phantoms. (*156*)

The patient may complain of his affective emptiness and of feelings of depersonalization and unreality. His affective personality shows marked variability according to the person with whom he is conversing and according to the complexes touched off by conversations. Interests in general are narrow.

In thought and verbal process the schizophrenic shows lack of logical connectedness, bizarre associations, a tendency to understand symbols literally — e.g., he stands on his head because he thinks the world is "all upside down" — and to confuse words with the real objects for which they stand. He uses many neologisms, makes morbid generalizations, and systematically misuses words. The thought process suffers complete obstructions or falls into perseverations. He is aware of a sense of strain in attempting to think, and the thought process shows general impoverishment.

Intelligence tests, especially verbal tests, are done much better than one would expect having regard to the stupidity of behavior. Actual irreversible intellectual deterioration seems less common than was once supposed, except in schizophrenia of very long duration (285). Memory is generally good except for specific blockings and misinterpretations.

Hallucinations are frequent and excite affective responses, amusement, excitement, or anger and violence.

Delusions are usually unsystematized, contradictory, and unrelated (except in paranoid schizophrenia, where they approach the systematic character of true paranoia). Even so they are detectably delusions of reference, with persecution and megalomania predominating.

Physically the schizophrenic is likely to suffer from respiratory infections, shows defective vasomotor functions (cyanosis, overhot and overcold extremities, oedemas), is liable to large and unaccountable fluctuations in body weight, has exaggerated deep reflexes, and frequently shows a variety of exhaustion symptoms.

The schizophrenic is likely to have a history of inability to hold a steady job (cf. the notion of "ambulatory schizophrenia"), of defective affectional relationships, unsatisfactory schoolwork, a poor design for living, and general lack of insight into his own personality.

Catatonic schizophrenia C(II). Here motor symptoms are added to the above and certain mental symptoms are exaggerated as follows. (1) There is constant senseless movement (hyperkinesis). (2) The patient fails to remove his limbs from any position in which they are placed (waxy flexibility, catalepsy). (3) At verbal and other levels there is a similar automatic response, automatic obedience, echopraxia. (4) Stereotyped responses occur widely, in movements, mannerisms, bodily attitudes, along with obviously compulsive phenomena which do not seem to distress the patient as in an obsessional neurosis. (5) A condition of stupor, sometimes with apparent depression, in which the patient speaks little or not at all, uninterrupted for years.   (6) Negativism, a tendency to react directly contrary to others' suggestions or their own impulses, with an appearance of all external interference being unpleasant.   (7) Occasional impulsiveness, usually aggressive or with the quality of buffoonery.   (8) Acute emotional episodes, resembling manic, depressive, or acutely anxious states (though the fresh joyousness of the manic or the single idea of the melancholic is lacking and angry aggression is predominant).

Hebephrenic schizophrenia C(III).   The symptom pattern of this syndrome is somewhat less clear-cut than in others.   Silliness and emotional regression are prominent.   There is more phantasy than true delusion, while childish pranks, mimicry, affectations of maturity, and mannerisms are prevalent.   Manic and depressive states and hypochondria are often found in the early stages.

Kraepelin thought to distinguish several varieties of this commonest form of schizophrenia; namely, stuporose, depressive, circular, agitated, and periodic excited forms.

Paranoid schizophrenia C(IV).   Here delusions and hallucinations predominate, the former being largely ideas of grandeur, of persecution, or of hypochondria.   It can follow an onset of manic, depressive, or catatonic variety, or begin direct.   Catatonia may supervene in severe cases.

Paranoia C(IVa).   The patient shows normal emotionality, will, coherence and clarity of thought, and soundness of perception, but manifests the furtive development of a lasting, immovable delusional system.   Commonly the delusions are of grandeur, of persecution, of litigiousness, or of sexual jealousy (Bleuler says *not* of hypochondria, but see Miller below).   Memory, reasoning power, and emotionality become abnormal only around the defense of the fixed idea.   The paranoiac usually shows a character which would be labeled by such terms as sensitive, obstinate, selfish, egocentric, suspicious, reticent, and, sometimes, passionately jealous, cranky, irritable, self-opinionated, and given to projecting blame on others.

It was once believed that the disorder was chronic and slowly progressive, though with remissions. Actually the disorder is more prevalent than the severe, progressive mental hospital cases suggest and, as Miller[1] points out, it may last from a few weeks (e.g., through organic disorder or as an *ad hoc* dynamic defense device attempting to achieve security in a special situation) to a lifelong rigid maladjustment.

3. PSYCHOTIC SYNDROMES: MANIC–DEPRESSIVE DISORDER AND INVOLUTIONAL MELANCHOLIA

Manic-depressive psychosis C(V). Though manic-depressive disorder is a single disease entity, it is obvious that the syndrome pattern in the manic phase is distinct from, indeed opposite to, that of the depressive phase, so that it is difficult to point to any single characteristic personality syndrome unless it be that of the manic-depressive in "normal" moments.

The disorder as a whole is defined by: (1) Occurrence, at intervals, possibly periodic, of extreme exalted or depressed moods, or a cycle of both. (2) Change in the rate of thought, flight of ideas, or retardation of thought, speech, and decision. (3) Corresponding facilitation or inhibition of motor activity and "centrifugal" functions generally. (4) Delusions and hallucinations are inconspicuous and occur only as "accessory symptoms" to the acute affective disorder.

In the "free intervals" the patient tends to show "a number of characteristics which are found in compulsive neurotic individuals." They are also described as (*a*) more conscientious and (*b*) less morose than pre-schizophrenics. Thompson, R. (*256*), and Kisker (*149*), from an analysis of two hundred cases, consider that the constant core of "manic-

[1] Miller, C. W. (16) 1952, 1941, who adds, "Hypochondria stands in the same relation to paranoia as anxiety does to hysteria."

depressive personality" traits persists through "free intervals" between attacks in two thirds of the patients, but that the remaining third suffer from more purely environmentally determined "episodes" which, if repeated, are nevertheless not functionally related.

Each attack is likely to last from three months to a year (mode at seven months) but may be as long as seven years. The melancholic phase tends to be longer. The latter attack begins with obsessive ideas of past real or imaginary misfortune, with seeking of isolation, and develops into active delusions of culpability (*15*). Physical symptoms — e.g., epigastralgia, neuralgia — are conspicuous at the beginning. Memory for these disturbed phases is poor, especially for the manic episodes, and there is a disinclination to attempt recall. Zilboorg reminds us that the general picture of manic-depressive disorder has "remained totally unchanged since the days of Hippocrates."

The manic syndrome C(VI). The central feature is an affective state of exaltation, euphoria, eagerness, and joyous excitement. Cheerfulness may turn to anger if thwarted and there is a constant instability of emotion, but not in the direction of the depressive group of emotions. The excited, elated emotional phase, however, is often ushered in by a mild, brief depressed state.

Thought shows a too rapid, uncontrolled association of ideas, flighty but not unclear and illogical and often witty or sarcastic. External stimuli readily distract the course of association. Sometimes there is a dreamlike looseness of ideas and logical connections. Memory and orientation to place, time, and identity are sound, but there is no insight into the fact that personality has changed.

Meanwhile the patient is talkative, overactive, unrestrained, and impatient. He meddles in all sorts of matters, shows excessive enterprise, mischief, or facetiousness and may lose a sense of propriety in sexual as well as other matters.

He is subject to fleeting hallucinations. Sleeplessness and some loss of weight accompany the constant excitement.

The depressive syndrome C(VII). The main affect of depression, worthlessness, and fatigue may be colored by dread, anxiety, precordial tension, and various hypochondriacal physical distresses (compare neurasthenia). The patient describes life as colorless, strange, and wearisome, but worries over trifles. His facial expression is anxious, painful, desperate, but immobile.

Thought is slow and difficult, with a great dearth of ideas. It tends to be egocentric but with a little more capacity to see various sides of a question than manics display. Orientation to place, time, and identity is good, except for dreamlike states which are more conspicuous than in mania.

Motor activity is greatly retarded, the limbs feel heavy as lead, speech tends to be monosyllabic, and sentences are unfinished. Decisions require great effort, so that the patient remains vacillating and perplexed.

Delusions and hallucinations are more marked than in mania, being connected with ideas of guilt, remorse, self-accusation, pain, and hypochondriasis (quite different from delusions of persecution, unless the patient's previous character happened to be paranoid and sensitive). Suicidal intentions are common. Sleep, digestion, and sexual potency are impaired.

Special forms of manic-depressive disorder. Various forms of manic-depressive disorder, analogous to the sub-syndrome groups of schizophrenia, have been distinguished, notably by Kraepelin, but there is not yet such general agreement on their nature as with the schizophrenics. Kraepelin's sixfold division is formed by the possible mutations of positive and negative phases of three variables: affect, thought, and motor activity. Commonly clinical observation recognizes only the first three or four of these. (1) *Agitated melancholia:* Anxious depression without motor retardation; i.e., with restlessness. (2) *Manic stupor:* Manic mood of cheerfulness, mischievousness, and destructiveness, but with a dearth of ideas and without motor acceleration (Kraepelin's "Galgen humor" symptom, one of cheerful despair, perhaps belongs here). (3) *Unproductive mania:* Cheerful but with impoverished thought. (4) *Depressive mania:* Overactive, of incoherent thought, with depression. Kraepelin's list also includes (5) Depression with flight and (6) Inhibited mania.

Involutional melancholia C(VIII). It is questionable whether this may not be in fact manic-depressive disorder occurring for the first time late in life. It tends to occur in the late forties for women and the late fifties for men. The syndrome is that of agitated melancholia, with some special emphasis on insomnia, suicidal attempts (more frequent than in any other disorder), narrowing of interests, and some schizoid traits of negativism, stubbornness, and paranoia. About 40 per cent to 60 per cent of cases recover slowly. The disorder is generally founded on a well-marked personality type (narrow-minded, dull, censorious) and is ushered in by a neurasthenic-like phase of irritability, peevishness, insomnia, and weeping spells.

It is argued by some (*29*) that a chronic mania occurring late in life is the manic equivalent of this disorder, in mental content, course of disorder, age of onset, and type of personality affected.

4. PSYCHOTIC SYNDROMES: EPILEPSY, PSYCHOPATHIC PERSONALITY, TOXIC, DETERIORATIVE, AND OTHER PSYCHOSES

Epilepsy C(IX) requires here only a relatively abridged account. It may occur from organic brain disease or ideopathically. There are fits, recurring with varying frequency, which at their most developed form (grand mal) are a sudden onset of tonic and clonic spasms with total loss of consciousness, and in their slightest form (petit mal) are only a momentary stutter or blackout in consciousness.

The particular psychological interest of the epileptic turns on (1) abnormal mental states before and after the fit and (2) a possible "epileptoid personality" in individuals prone to such fits.   Before the fit there is the mental experience of an "aura," which may be an hallucination — e.g., of light, pain, or cold; a disturbance of mood and thought through which the individual's moral conduct becomes abnormal[1]; or a motor symptom — e.g., a typical scream.   After the fit there is a clouded "epileptic twilight" state.

Regarding the character syndrome of epileptics the following traits have been asserted: strong affectivity and moodiness (and therefore some undependability), egocentricity, preoccupation with "righteousness," and a façade of conformity, vanity, retardation and poverty of ideas, perseveration, awkward formation of verbalizations, narrowing of interests and attention to personal matters, accentuation of preferred ideas and moral evaluations (too frequent use of good, bad, beautiful, dreadful), circumstantial, garrulous, anecdotal conversation, fussiness, interest in detail, poorness of memory immediate and remote, susceptibility to transient delusions, sluggish, unvaried speech ("plateau speech"), taciturnity alternating with overfriendliness, and a superficial religiosity.   Kreyenberg (154) characterizes the epileptics studied as "clammy," coarse, familiar, brutal, bigoted, pedantic, egocentric, moody, and troublesome, with more than common addiction to truancy and drinking.   By a questionnaire study aiding clinical observation others have concluded (10) that epileptics show a tendency to withdraw into themselves, to impose various self-limitations, to feel superior in attitudes, feelings, and interests, but to behave in a substandard fashion.

There is no evidence that the above traits are necessarily due to the epileptic fits *per se* (in the above study, however, the siblings did not show the traits) and they are more likely

---

[1] It has been suggested — e.g., by R. Persch — that pyromania is especially likely to occur here, as a substitute for sexual interests.

associated with the social situation created by being liable to fits, with institutional life, with the defects of intelligence which tend to supervene after repeated fits, or with other organic damage from fits. At the present descriptive phase we are not concerned with origin except to tie up the traits with the variable to which they properly belong.

Psychopathic personality C(X). This is a clinically convenient syndrome which has obstinately grown up in the literature at the point whence the notion of "moral imbecile" had been seemingly uprooted.

There is considerable variability of description. Rosanoff describes an antisocial personality, given to malingering or hysteria, parasitism, indolence, gambling, swindling. Elsewhere (*191*) we find the designation "cheerless, discouraged, harmlessly vain, and impulsive psychopaths." Cleckley (*62*) describes an attractive person of good intelligence with no sense of responsibility, ability to follow consistent plan, regard for truth, or sincere shame. Egocentricity, improvidence, inability to show deep affection for a sex object (but charm for women), promiscuity, with impotence and infantilism are added. Menninger (*178*) describes synonymous traits, stressing the intention to exploit and distress others, to dissemble and flatter, and to have no constant loyalties.

Caldwell (*28*) observes in thirty-one cases the same core of delinquency, egocentrism, and irresponsibility and records also lack of judgment, inconsistent worry, and, especially, nomadism and inability to withstand tedium. Another observer (*237*) stresses "affective immaturity," failure of motivation to widen into the adult world, and lack of superego integration (conscience) in the personality. A brief review (*60*) lists autism and egocentricity (Kahn), aggressiveness (Henderson), and emotional instability (Healy). Another (*208*) summarizes the pattern as one of emotional immaturity, impulsiveness, childishness, defective judgment, mood swings, and inability to learn from experience. In the more recent studies it is pointed out that the syndrome can occur at all levels of intelligence.

The syndrome can thus only be considered at present to be a loosely defined conglomeration, still more loosely differentiated from straight defect of character integration, from the character neuroses, and even from that combination of high general emotionality and low intelligence which has been called moral imbecility. Because of the lack of insight, the presumed constitutional elements, and the serious consequences for society, it is probably better classified among the psychoses than the neuroses.

Organic, toxic, and degenerative psychoses. The chief toxic (alcoholic, autotoxic, thyrogenic) psychoses syndromes are set out in the study of physiological correlates of personality in the volume on personality development, being irrelevant here. *General paralysis* C(XI) (Syphilitic psychosis) may, however, be considered best here. It is characterized by breakdown of inhibition, impulsiveness, uncontrolled and elated or despondent mood, delusions (grandiose, persecutory, hypochondriacal), irritability, inconsiderateness, failure of memory, neglect of appearance, transitory confusion, and perseveration. The later stages bring impaired bodily coordination and reflex control.

Senile deteriorative psychoses C(XII). There are three main syndromes: senile deteriorative, Pick's disease, and Alzheimer's disease. They have in common: apathy, narrowing of field of interest and attention, impairment of memory (with pseudoreminiscence), loss of orientation in time, Korsakow's syndrome (defective recent memory), irritability, inability to sleep well or keep awake fully. Symptoms of agitated depression, paranoia, or chronic mania may be interspersed. The Parkinsonian syndrome and Huntington's Chorea C(XIIa), in which physical symptoms, palsy, etc., are conspicuous, are also classed here and share the general picture of deteriorated personality and intelligence.

Arteriosclerosis C(XIII). Principal symptoms are fatigability, emotional instability, forgetfulness, disorientation, drowsiness, and, not invariably, moods of marked anxiety or depression. The patient shows, however, a degree of persistence of insight into his condition which is unusual with so much general deterioration.

Cerebral trauma C(XIV). Chiefly characterized by loss of memory and mental ability, irritability, increased susceptibility to the effects of alcohol, and loss of sense of responsibility; but almost every type of symptom may be manifested — e.g., epilepsy, chorea, Parkinsonianism, narcolepsy, etc. The effects of definite cerebral lesions and tumors are discussed in the volume on genesis of personality. The behavior syndrome resulting from brain injury through encephalitis corresponds very closely to what has been described above under psychopathic personality, and other cerebral traumas may issue in the same general syndrome.

5. PSYCHONEUROTIC SYNDROMES: CONVERSION HYSTERIA, ANXIETY
    HYSTERIA, ANXIETY NEUROSIS, OBSESSIONAL–COMPULSIVE
    NEURASTHENIA, NEURASTHENIA, AND EFFORT SYNDROME

The general nature of the neuroses is so much discussed and the symptoms are so much nearer to those describable by everyday speech that the syndromes can be adequately covered by a straight, brief listing, in a way not possible for the psychoses.

Conversion (classical) hysteria C(XV).

(1) Presence of a physical symptom — e.g., paralysis, anesthesia, loss of voice, not having an organic basis, and without normal neurological signs.

(2) Fits, distinguished from epileptic ones by occurring only in presence of others and with only trivial self-injury.

(3) Tics, contractures, or compulsions.

(4) Other physical conversion symptoms, pains, head-aches, migraine, dermatographies, globus hystericus. (NOTE. No emphasis on pains in digestive tract.)

(5) Peculiarities of overeating, occasional excessive eating, more commonly loss of appetite, cyclic vomiting.

(6) Some degree of splitting of personality, big variation of personality, instability of motives and emotions.

(7) Somnambulism, marked talking in sleep.

(8) Episodic dream states, fugue states for which memory is incomplete.

(9) Complete forgetting of relatively important incidents and remarks, over a few days.

(10) Susceptibility to hypnosis and suggestion, inclined to be superstitious.

(11) Combination of emotionality (especially erotic) with primness and reserve.

(12) Shallow feelings but excessive expression, theatricality.

(13) Vanity, excessive desire to impress and gain attention.

(14) Craving sympathy, avoiding responsibility.

(15) Excessive business, but rather aimless and with lack of persistence of feelings and of efforts.

(16) Elation or offense at trivialities, quick emotional changes.

(17) Simulated foolishness and childishness, inept funni-ness.

(18) Vivid compensatory daydreaming (appearance of absent-mindedness), leading to fabrication of half-believed stories.

(19) Essentially undisturbed complacency (Janet's "belle indifference") in face of grave personal problems.

(20) Generally of good will and well-disposed (unsus-picious).

(21) Sleeplessness.

(22) Overactive autonomic, blushing, trembling, etc.

The "classical" picture of hysteria seems to be in some degree determined by the culture pattern, and it is the impression of clinicians that this neurotic syndrome has become relatively infrequent in the last thirty years. Alcoholism and drug addiction, however, present hysteria as a part symptom with more than accidental frequency.

Anxiety neurosis C(XVI) and anxiety hysteria C(XVII). After an attack of anxiety hysteria has been dispelled by psychotherapy, there sometimes remains a core of symptoms seemingly due to sheer physiological hypersensitivity to anxiety. The latter may be a true neurosis; at any rate it is possible to distinguish this syndrome as an entity in itself which, combined with additional symptoms, becomes anxiety hysteria. Anxiety neurosis can have the following symptoms:

(1) Morbid, excessive feeling of anxiety or dread.

(2) Occasional "fits" (loss of consciousness without convulsions).

(3) Rapid heartbeat.

(4) Palpitation, anginal pain (pseudoangina).

(5) Tremor and twitching of muscles.

(6) Sweating of hands and feet, nocturnal perspiration.

(7) Lack of appetite, dryness of mouth, flatulence, fullness in stomach, nausea.

(8) Breathlessness, sense of suffocation or breathing oppression, asthma.

(9) Constipation and diarrhea coexisting.

(10) Sleeplessness.

(11) Hypersensitiveness to light, sound, etc., "jumpy" nerves.

(12) Depression, irritability, and excitability.

(13) Restlessness and inability to concentrate.

(14) Vasomotor constriction, coldness and blueness of extremities.

(15) Weakness of limbs and blurring of vision.

(16) Frequency of micturition (and of seminal emissions).

In the full anxiety hysteria or phobia there are added to these:

(17) Anxiety, fear, or anguish in certain situations, notably closed spaces — e.g., railway carriages.

(18) Anxiety, fear, or anguish in large gatherings or open spaces.

(19) Fear of insanity or of recurrence of hysterical fit.

(20) Fear of bodily illness or disease.

(21) Exaggerated fear of heights.

(22) Any particular "irrational" fear (fire, cats, opening letters, insects, thunder).

(23) Night terrors (nightmare).

Obsessional or compulsion neurosis C(XVIII). The elements of this syndrome are:

(1) Constant preoccupation with a single topic (usually trivial and felt by the subject to be so).

(2) Obsessive rumination (*folie de doute*) — e.g., speculation about small religious points or, "Why must I breathe?" "What was the first cause?"

(3) Scrupulous compulsions to carry out trivial tasks — e.g., to read notices, to fold up clothes in a particular fashion.

(4) Compulsions to totally unnecessary acts — e.g., to count windows, to utter rhymes or phrases, to touch or step over objects, to wash too frequently.

(5) Fear of compulsion to carry out dangerous, immoral, or destructive acts — e.g., to stab someone, to set fire to something, to mutilate animals, to swear in church, etc.

(6) Obsessive fear of some unlikely danger or of no danger — e.g., of destroying something valuable, of blushing, of dust, of fire.

(7) Obstinacy. Assertive character with insistence on the power of the will, aggressiveness.

(8) Orderliness. Overconscientiousness and exaggerated, detailed thoroughness in general work.

(9) Insomnia (not invariable).

(10) Parsimony.

Averbukh (*12*) says this disorder is likely to occur in individuals with marked affectivity and slowness of reaction. Most observers — e.g., Wittels — note the general character, as having traits of meticulousness, earnestness, aggressiveness, and responsibility. It usually shows itself between the fourth and the twelfth years.

Neurasthenia C(XIX) **and effort syndrome** C(XIXa). Neurasthenia was at one time a "hold-all" category for a number of neuroses now recognized as distinct — e.g., anxiety neurosis. The essential neurasthenia is a nervous fatigue syndrome. As such it may appear in the course of many chronic mental conflicts, including those of psychosis, but it also seems to appear "in its own right" without any features of emotional conflict. The basic symptoms are:

(1) Gets tired very easily physically.

(2) Gets tired very easily mentally.

(3) Unable to make any effort, trembles at thought of any task.

(4) Unable to concentrate; attention easily distracted.

(5) Memory poor.

(6) Interest lacking or quickly disappearing.

(7) Sense of pressure on head, pain at occiput and back of neck, irritable spine.

(8) General malaise, aches and pains, legs heavy.

(9) Irritability, aggressive temper.

(10) Moodiness.

(11) Depression, tearful or dull.

(12) Flatulence, dyspepsia, and disturbances of appetite.

(13) Constipation.

(14) Exaggerated (deep) reflexes.

(15) Poor sleep at night, difficulty in waking in morning.
(16) Hypersensitiveness to bright light, to noise, and to cold.
(17) Sweating of skin and palms of hands.
(18) Nocturnal emissions (and ejaculatio praecox impotence).

More recently, in connection with mental disorders among soldiers, a new syndrome has been described and labeled as "Effort Syndrome C(XIXa)," which has some similarity and probable relation to neurasthenia. Abrahams (*3*) defines effort syndrome as "an abnormal physiological response to effort, with the production of breathlessness, disproportionate or premature exhaustion, palpitations, precordial pain, faintness, dizziness, and blurred vision." Clearly this differs from the neurasthenic syndrome in the prominence of the autonomic overreaction and the absence of reference to debilitation of will and reasoning; but the possibility that closer observation will show relatedness justifies their being linked here.

6. UNCOMMON, BORDERLINE, OR ILL-DEFINED PSYCHOTIC AND NEUROTIC SYNDROMES

Rare psychoses and neuroses. The psychotic patterns are in their main features independent of cultural localization (though it is said that Japanese manics are more polite than others!); but a few disorders are peculiar to race, culture, or climate.

The Malays are subject to Amok and Lattah. The former is a state of extreme introvert, resentful brooding, followed by a fit of excited, murderous, universal destructiveness in which the subject acts regardless of danger to his own life. (Nearest perhaps to paranoid schizophrenia.) Lattah occurs both in Malays and Arabs, usually to individuals in subservient positions, who imitate movement and speech of others (echolalia), usually their masters' (*211*). It differs from hysteria in that the patient shows great resistance, anguish, or anger at the involuntary compulsion. It differs from catatonia in the patient's good contact with his social environment.

Arctic hysteria C(XX). This has a similar pattern of behavior, sometimes with hallucinations, and occurs in very cold climates, especially toward the end of the long winter. The last two disorders are neuroses rather than psychoses.

Imu C(XXI). This is a mental disorder peculiar to the Ainu in Japan (rarely occurring, for example, among the Japanese under the same culture pattern), in which the patient, apparently due to precipitating circumstances of some extreme fear, reacts with panic or with violent aggression. These intermittent fits of loss of control occur in a chronic process of increased shyness, fearfulness, meticulousness, and imitativeness and are accompanied by states of automatic obedience, echolalia, echopraxia, and tics. It is most common in women and is very similar to the Meriachinie of Eastern Siberia, Yann (Burma), Bah-tchi (Siam), Jumping (Red Indians), and Lattah.

Hypochondria C(XXII). This may appear as a feature of psychoses, especially melancholia, but it is considered a possible distinct independent syndrome (*141*). It develops gradually as a fixed set of excessive, morbid interests in disease or health. The individual is plaintive and self-centered, but the remaining personality traits are heterogeneous and undetermined.

Traumatic neuroses C(XXIII). Head trauma may result in neurasthenic and hysteric type symptoms, chiefly increased fatigability, slight ·memory disorder, irritability, sleeplessness, dizziness, headache, subjective paresthesias, anxiety, tremors, and other hysterical symptoms the development of which depends upon the social gain to be had from them. There may also be paranoid symptoms, but they are not central (Tchernoruk, V.G., 11, 1349, 1936).

Psychosomatic neuroses C(XXIV). With the exception of the following special example the neuroses with largely physical expression (of a real kind, distinct from conversion hysteria) are considered under physiological correlates of personality in the volume on personality genesis.

Migraine and allergy syndrome C(XXV). The characteristic unilateral headaches, nausea, and paresthesias of migraine have been linked by a majority of clinicians with the general allergic reactions and these again with certain personality traits. In the first place, it is noticed that the actual attacks of migraine and of allergy can be brought on by similar frustrating situations and have similar psychological associates in the attack period: despondency, irritability, restlessness, drowsiness, feelings of fatigue, states of anxiety, fear, or confusion. Jensen (*134*) finds in the allergic personal make-up chronically rapid pulse, hypersensitivity to glare and noise, poor sleep, chronic indigestion, cold or clammy extremities, visual disturbances, and soreness in the capitis and cervicis muscle groups. Others have pointed out a suspected connection with running away, as a periodic mode of "adjustment," and with compulsive neurotic traits. One observer claims to find a combination of self-absorption and dreaminess with overweening ambition. Russ and De Cillis find the allergic child more ascendant, extraverted, and emotionally unstable, frequently troubled with overanxiety, jealousy, and sibling rivalry.

Enuresis syndrome C(XXVI). Enuresis may spring from many causes, but there is one prevalent type of child with enuretic difficulty in which certain neuropathic traits are evident and in which there is clear evidence of heredity. Hirsch (*118*) shows a significant association of enuresis with delinquency and specifically with the personality traits emotional immaturity, hypersuggestibility, instability ("Everything by starts and nothing long"), and inferiority and insecurity. Ackerson (*4*), Highlander, and others point out correlations with irritability and seclusiveness, restlessness in sleep, delinquency particularly of a kind called "incorrigibility," useless and senseless crime (not for lack of intelligence), destructiveness and sex offenses — i.e., the typical impulsive crimes — temper tantrums, quarrelsomeness, emotional immaturity, instability, inferiority and insecurity, overintense fear reactions, and sex perversions.

Neurotic personality, neuropathic personality, and emotional immaturity. Clinicians disagree as to the existence and nature of a "general neurotic personality," though, as the next chapter shows, the questionnaire designers have proceeded on the assumption that such a syndrome exists. Freud spoke of a psycho-sexual constitution, causing the individual to be prone to neurosis. Psychiatrists of a generation ago had a category of psychopathic inferiority, the description of which fell short of any actual psychosis and generally even of what is now sometimes called "psychopathic personality." The same general set of traits seems to be covered by the notion of "neuropathic inheritance." The characteristics described in these syndromes have an extremely close resemblance to the psychologists' "emotional immaturity," and both of these have some relation to the last two listed above. (Gordon points out a fair correlation of migraine allergy with enuresis and night terrors. Hirsch points out the close relation of enuresis and emotional immaturity.) It is for this reason that the four syndromes are set out here in proximity. The last two syndromes, below, might easily be run together and we refrain from doing so only to avoid the loss of a possible fine distinction.

Neuropathic constitution C(XXVII). Such traits as thumb-sucking continued into late childhood, nail biting, speech impediments, sleep disturbances, crying spells, hypochondria, restless nervous habits (tics), vague but usually noncompulsive fears, enuresis, etc. Stern (244) describes the syndrome in terms of character traits of undue ego-centricity, vanity, inordinate sensitivity, rigidity of personality, deep-rooted inferiority feelings, masochism, anxiety, fear of growing up, withdrawal from emotional ties, inability to put emotions to test of reality, etc. The Freudian concept stresses infantile sexuality and inability to adjust the pleasure principle to the reality principle.

Emotional maturity-immaturity C(XXVIII). Impulsiveness, ego-centricity, dependence on others to an undue extent, suggestibility, guilt and lack of objectivity about one's own impulses, inability and unwillingness to accept responsibility, lack of reality sense about one's powers in relation to actual situations. An extended list is available in Willoughby's questionnaire (279). There is usually an implication in these descriptions that this syndrome is somewhat more environmentally determined than the neuropathic syndrome.

The character neuroses. A more subtle, but not necessarily more vague, set of clinically perceived syndromes are those constituted by the comparatively recently described "character neuroses." Since they are contributed by psychoanalytic practitioners, their description is couched partly in interpretive psychoanalytic terms.

The "as if" personality C(XXIX). Deutsch (73), among others, has described one of the more subtle borderline psychotic syndromes as the "as if" personality. It is akin to "depersonalization" phases occurring in the development of schizophrenia, and is undoubtedly schizoid. The patient, however, may not experience the feeling of emotional emptiness, which is sensed by those who witness the formality and superficiality of his emotional expressions. The individual is plastic, passive, successfully imitating what he does not feel. He identifies readily with others and is adhesive and suggestible to each admired personality for a time. There is a lack of warmth and originality and of super-ego demands. Aggressive tendencies are masked by amiability and negative "goodness."

The fixation-stage character neuroses. The three syndromes which constitute the most important and most commonly described character neuroses are each defined by a "zonal" fixation level of libidinal development. The fixations are at levels prior to the genital level which defines the fully developed, normal (but not necessarily most prevalent) personality, as follows:

The incorporative oral character C(XXXa), presumed frustrated in the early oral stage, is pessimistic, impatient, whining, clinging, demanding in social attitudes, hasty, apprehensive, and given to finding insuperable obstacles even in the smallest undertakings of life.

The aggressive oral character C(XXXb) is unduly hostile, disapproving, envious, malicious, and tends to be constantly ambivalent in his attitudes.

The anal character C(XXXIa) is preoccupied both with autoerotic, narcissistic pleasures and with the social taboos which maintain their suppression. Three traits are outstanding: orderliness (overaccentuated, pedantic interest in cleanliness, reliability, conscientiousness in trivial duties), parsimony (extending to avarice), and obstinacy (extending to defiance, vindictiveness, and irascibility). Others are cruelty, undue resentment at being thwarted, touchiness about encroachments on one's own power, arrogance, alternation of energetic, persistent application and inactivity, difficulty in beginning or in leaving off a task, procrastination, brooding, moroseness, reticence, and aloofness. A related character neurosis picture is that of the *urethral character* C(XXXIb), showing the same meticulous concern about toilet habits, parsimony, and obstinacy and, in addition, impatience, envy, and, especially, ambition.

To the above harvest of clinical vigilance one should certainly add, for completeness, the clinical types of mental defect. When one is studying primarily the normal personality, only the most generalized picture of mental defect is likely to be sufficiently relevant. One may add, therefore, *mental defect* C(XXXII), characterized by inability to learn, difficulty with all abstract ideas, lack of adaptability to new situations, very limited general information, suggestibility, lack of persistence and frequently of dependability, proneness to delinquency, and inability to reason.

7. POSSIBLE INTERRELATIONSHIPS OF ABNORMAL SYNDROMES

Except in the case of certain psychotic and neurotic sub-patterns already mentioned — e.g., the varieties of schizo-phrenia — the above-listed clinical syndromes are normally considered to be independent. Nevertheless, some clinicians maintain that certain syndromes are practically mutually exclusive — e.g., manic-depressive disorder and schizophrenia, epilepsy and schizophrenia, neurosis and psychosis. Others maintain that unbiased observation will reveal the superim-position of two or more syndromes in the symptom complex of one and the same individual — e.g., of manic-depressive dis-order and Huntington's chorea — or true intermediate syn-dromes, such as would be expected for "continuous types" — e.g., there seems to be a continuum from anxiety neurosis through anxiety hysteria to obsessional-compulsive neurosis. Naturally it is extremely important for later analysis of causal connections to know where continuous types and where species types prevail and whether among species types there are many systematic associations.

The encephalographic observation (*133*) that schizophrenic and epileptic E.E.G. patterns appeared at opposite ends of the scale of classification led to the observer's discovery that in the research sample concerned combinations of the two dis-orders occurred less frequently than one would expect from chance. The finding is not confirmed by other investigators (*283*) who studied several instances of epileptics who devel-oped schizophrenia (in spite of the endogenous convulsive therapy!).[1]

---

[1] It will be remembered that the original fallacious observation was the origin of a "true" therapy — shock therapy!

There are some clinical investigations of atypical syndromes.   One of these, for instance (*115*), recognized instances of apparent catatonic schizophrenia in psychoses of syphilitic, toxic, traumatic, and epileptic origin.   They noted, however, that the organic brain disease is differentiated by having a clouded sensorium.   They concluded that there are three types of catatonic syndrome, associated with (1) Cortical damage, (2) Hypothalamic signs, and (3) Psychological symptoms generally.

At the present time, however, clinical observation has very little to offer on these issues, and there are no reliable studies on the relation of the observed frequency of combined syndromes to the frequency that would be expected from chance.

Chapter Four

THE NATURE OF TRAITS

1. FROM CLINICAL APPRAISAL TO MEASUREMENT

Syndromes and traits. Clinical psychology has always taken traits — as descriptive elements — for granted, turning its interests to the syndromes that may be made out of their patterning. When one comes to the end of the clinical approach, however, and begins to follow the penetrations which modern psychological method has made into the subject of personality description and measurement, he is forced at once to take a more sophisticated view about the nature of traits, to enter upon an entirely new vista of concepts and a new discipline of thought.

Need of digression into theoretical treatment. Before the actual findings of statistical and experimental psychology, concerning temperament and other aspects of personality, can be reviewed and integrated, it is necessary, therefore, to devote at least three chapters to the systematic development of a new and precise equipment of concepts regarding traits, syndromes, and other bases for description and measurement. This task also involves developing the more subtle possibilities of personality measurement or comparison implicit in the clinical approach into a more explicit system. We have, in fact, to bridge the gulf between clinical and statistical, psychometric approaches to personality.

2. UNIQUE AND COMMON TRAITS

Confusion over trait concept. Although psychologists use traits quite as freely as the layman in describing personality and even in "measuring" it, no exaggeration is involved in saying that they have not yet arrived at any agreement as to what is meant by a trait. In attempting to solve this problem we must first eschew the current tendency to seek solution through calling traits by other names.[1] The realities of the situation are better brought into clear relief through grappling with the actual difficulties which arise in attempting to measure and predict individual differences in personality response.

Behavior intrinsically measurable. Thorndike once heartened psychometrists with the slogan, "Whatever exists, exists in some quantity and can — at least theoretically — be measured." This we shall take as our first axiom. Unfortunately, the large number of psychometrists who permit themselves to be hastened into shoddy production by the urgencies of applied psychology have taken this remark as a license for devising "tests" at a moment's notice for everything under the sun. They have not stopped to ask exactly what trait they are measuring and have even forgotten the elementary algebraic rule that directly added units must be of the same kind. They have completely neglected the necessity for first discovering the number and nature of the qualitative varieties of traits with respect to which measurement is to be made. They have not stopped to ask by what methods we may investigate the limits and boundaries of the functional unities of behavior — i.e., of traits. In short, in their haste to "measure," they have not asked the simple but crucial question as to whether the traits of different individuals are of the same kind, measurable on the same axis in the same units.

With respect to the last issue, Allport (8) has done a signal service to psychology by insisting, when the tide of wishful

[1] Healy, Bronner, and Bowers (113), page 311. "Nobody seems to know what a trait is, so it appears to us better to use 'characteristic'"!

thinking was all in the opposite direction, that though some traits are virtually common — i.e., similar in all people and present in various degrees in all — others are unique to the individual. To the present writer it seems that one must subscribe to the extreme sense of Allport's argument[1] and admit that *all* traits are in some way unique. However, common racial heredity, common cultural situations, and a common physical environment suffice, with respect to the majority of people in any psychological survey, to insure substantially the same forms, especially among mature adults, in many forms of behavior — e.g., in the nature of character stability, in dominant-submissive behavior, or in radicalism-conservatism. It is therefore feasible to say, with respect to some traits, that different individuals have more or less of the same trait. But we must not forget that this field of uniqueness approaches only asymptotically the state of commonness. (Mathematically, as we shall see later, a common *source* trait is absolutely common, its uniqueness being expressed through additional traits.)

3. THE PRINCIPAL MEANINGS WITH WHICH "TRAIT" IS USED

A trait, whether unique or common, is a collection of reactions or responses bound by some kind of unity which permits the responses to be gathered under one term and treated in the same fashion for most purposes. Before approaching the matter experimentally it seems advisable to see what the long cultural experience and wisdom embodied in language has to say about the nature of this unity. Let us examine the

[1] "Strictly speaking, no two persons ever have precisely the same trait," for "what else could be expected in view of the unique hereditary endowment, the differing development history, and the never repeated external influences that determine each personality?" Let us note, however, in connection with the widespread quasi-philosophical demand for a psychology that will give a unique individual, that uniqueness of the individual does not require unique traits. For we can produce any number of unique individuals by setting up various combinations of common trait measurements — e.g., by equations giving different loadings of the same mathematical "common factors." (See, e.g., Guilford (*100*).)

many senses in which professional psychologists and their gifted amateur predecessors in the last two thousand years have used the term "trait," as illustrated in the very large number of trait terms in the language.

A survey of trait terms, made as a preliminary preparation for the present study (54), shows that there are some six senses in which the concept has been used, but we shall set out to demonstrate that only three of these are psychologically real.

(1) **Dynamic (teleonomic or teleological) trait unities.**   In traits of this kind the behavior manifestations are united by being all directed to a single goal.   The goal is to perform something — e.g., eat, kill, avoid — with respect to some particular object (or class of objects) in the external world or to gain some particular kind of internal satisfaction (the two being generally correlated).

Since the dynamic purposes of the individual are centered upon hierarchies of goals, some subsidiary to others (intermediary goals, means to ends), the trait unities will also overlap, in patterns of *subsidiation*.[1]   There are thus traits corresponding to ergic, innate, biological goals, namely the *disposition* traits, according to which an individual is described as, for instance, timid, amorous, or pugnacious.   There are also traits corresponding to acquired dynamic unities, namely interests, attitudes, and sentiments — e.g., traits covered by such adjectives as patriotic, domestic, radical, sporting.

The trait terms of the second kind, describing such habit systems as sentiments, attitudes, interests — i.e., what can be conveniently and inclusively called "metanergs" (see Chapter 6)[2] — are not nearly so numerous in our speech as might be expected.   Probably this is due to many sentiments being

[1] See Murray (*190*).

[2] Metanergs are all dynamic traits derived from ergs — i.e., from propensities or innate biological drives.   Ergs and metanergs together constitute the total equipment of dynamic traits (*49*).

too personal, too narrow, or too culturally transient to have earned a name. Only those sentiments which are culturally common and important have acquired a name as common traits.

Metanergs are in general centered upon and named after certain objects, as, e.g., in "patriotism," "domesticatedness," or "artistic sentiments," and, as noted above, many of these objects are themselves too specific to the life of one individual to have a general name even when the object is an abstract concept — e.g., differential calculus. There is no name, for example, for a passion for the paintings of Correggio or a deep sentiment for precision in statistics. The ergs themselves, on the other hand, give an innate interest in the generalized goals of sex, safety, food, company, etc., and can receive a common trait label, though not one of an "object" in the sense of a single, literal object. This distinction is tied up with a second difference found between ergic and metanergic dynamic traits, namely that the latter, being centered on particular objects of the real world, which usually affect the organism in more than one respect and are used for more than one purpose, are generally traits involving a *mixture* of ergic emotional qualities. For example, the fatherly sentiment toward a child may involve protectiveness, the desire for company, pride, etc. The true "ergic" trait, on the other hand, is of dynamically unmixed, pure quality — e.g., amorousness, assertiveness — and has to be inferred and abstracted from observations of behavior toward many different actual, environmental objects. In each of these real-object-centered dynamic traits — the metanergs — the ergic dynamic purpose is subtly interwoven with those of other ergic drives, as is illustrated by the diagram on page 109.

In summary, therefore, dynamic traits are collections of behavior manifestations in which all are directed to the same ultimate biological goal, as in ergs, or to some intermediate goal, as in metanergs, the goal being the label of the trait.

(2) **Environmental mold unities.** In these traits the unity *at first* seems to be that of a *common effect, end, or purpose* from the *standpoint of society or the physical environment.* The trait of honesty covers many diverse pieces of behavior which have in common the serving of a certain social end, namely society's need for reliability in its citizens. The physical and general environment itself may also provoke such unities, as when we speak of the trait of being a good fisherman, a skilled cyclist, etc. The existence of a bicycle brings into existence a cluster of trait elements called "being a good cyclist."

However, as will become clearer in the final stages of this presentation, the important fact about an environmental mold unity is not that the habits and systems of response all have the same social purpose or serve the same purpose of physical adjustment.[1] It is rather that, because of this common end, society or the physical world forces (or induces) these diverse habits in the individual *at much the same time, and in much the same degree in the given person, so that they form a single pattern of covarying parts. For this purpose it uses much the same educational and other agencies, in similar manners, with all people, which also aids the similarity of the pattern.* Or, in the terms of one psychological school, the habits have been "rewarded or punished" in common. This common origin, character, age, and fate stamp upon the dynamically distinct habits a unity which will stand out as a pattern of covarying elements when we study individual differences — for the total impress will differ in strength in different individuals — or if we study the rise and decline of habit systems in one individual.

If we look at a list of such traits — e.g., conscientiousness, courage, tactfulness, the Freudian super ego, "charm," destructiveness, superciliousness, humanitarianism, and selfishness — we may suspect that some of them are merely social

---

[1] Society is, in any case, too naïve and ignorant to know the ultimate effect of many kinds of behavior, and so does not train all the habits that could effect any particular socially desired, central goal.

evaluations, or logical or moral categories imposed on functionally disconnected behaviors and present as a unity only in the minds of the spectators. Closer consideration of the situation, however, shows that most of these common verbal unities are likely to have real unity also. This comes secondarily, by reason of the fact that society, which needs the traits it talks about, deliberately molds them in the individual in unitary form.

To repeat the basic proposition: the elements of a social mold trait will covary, in the field of individual differences, because a single external influence — e.g., family, school, national culture pattern — has impressed all of them, as from a single focus. The individual is likely to have more or less of *all* the pieces of behavior which constitute honest behavior according to the degree to which his family and school influences have been successful in producing the impress of that social mold. That is to say, when we consider individual differences, we find that all the pieces of behavior vary in common, as those parts of a pottery design vary in depth of imprint or color together, when the die which stamps them has fallen with varying strength on the different individual pieces of pottery.

Two kinds of environmental mold traits may finally be distinguished: (1) *Conscious environmental mold unities*, in which the need is consciously realized by society, deliberately inculcated by education, and therefore embodied finally as a conscious sentiment in the mind of the individual — e.g., punctuality, patriotism, kindliness to others — and (2) *Unconscious environmental mold unities*, arising from pressures and educative circumstances not planned by society and generally not consciously realized by the individual — e.g., the syndrome of behavior responses which go with poverty, with the countryman's unconscious attachments to the sounds and smells of rural life, the attitudes and skills which develop from following a certain occupation or living in a certain climate, the syndrome of attitudes which arise from being the only child, and so on.

The stuff out of which environmental mold traits are carved is, of course, the constitutional dynamic, temperamental, and ability potentialities.   Since there is no obvious reason why an environmental mold should confine its effects to only one of these constitutional fields, we should not expect to be able to distinguish dynamic, temperamental, and ability environmental mold unities as separate categories.   This reflection casts doubt on the correctness and utility of the above "dynamic trait" category.   For presumably the mold which fashioned a metanerg would in general also create a set of cognitive skills to go with it and even modify temperamental manifestations in conformity with the dynamic purposes.

However, at the moment we do not claim that these usages give independent categories.   The present plan of exposition is to proceed by a series of successive approximations, and to refine current psychological concepts gradually to the final simplified and basis concepts necessary to describing personality.   Consequently we shall admit dynamic traits as a contingent concept, in spite of this suggestion that it is incomplete, and shall put it in perspective as the full scheme is revealed.   In passing, however, it is desirable to point out that any considerable alignment of environmental mold patterns with the natural dynamic connections of dynamic unities can only arise from a culture pattern which is highly sophisticated as to its needs and which educates deliberately, early, and well, teaching the child conscious sentiments as to what behavior is desirable.

(3) **Logical, semantic, evaluative trait unities.**   Anyone surveying the actual use of the term "trait," even in modern psychological studies, is soon compelled frankly to admit that in many cases the term is used to refer to a purely logical division of behavior, having no relation whatsoever to any real structures in the typical organism as it stands functionally

related to its environment. "Mechanical aptitude" may be defined as the degree of success within an arbitrarily selected field of use of particular mechanical appliances; "charm" may mean the capacity to sell vacuum cleaners to lower-middle-class housewives; "quickness" may be defined as sheer chronoscope speed on a tapping key in some arbitrarily chosen set of reactions.

In discussing environmental mold unities it has been admitted that many are, in the first place, purely logical divisions. They constitute "inorganic" — or biologically and sociologically non-existent — divisions of human activity. However, we have also admitted that because the activities have sometimes been acquired at the same age, etc., through a concerted and often deliberate influence by society or the physical world, they may eventually have a real unity in intra-individual and inter-individual calculations and transactions. For example, the set of skills and qualities acquired in many years of driving a streetcar will show positive correlation among any set of inter-individual measurements in a population of drivers and non-drivers, in this and in other ways attaining a real trait unity. But this is a secondary and relatively exceptional development. It is as exceptional as to find a line of latitude becoming an effective international boundary or a natural limit of climate or vegetation.

Incidentally, the ways in which items of behavior are selected and combined in these logical, unreal "traits" may be other than according to logical categories in the strict sense of "logical." They may follow stylistic unities, as in Allport's "stylistic traits," or moral evaluative unities, or any other arbitrary boundaries which the observer cares to lay down for purposes of alleged description or measurement. Examples of such traits are ceremoniousness, altruism, eloquence, equableness, ape-likeness, debonairness. Their unities are imposed only by the spectacles which the observer chooses to wear before his mind's eye.

Though the psychologist can have little use for these purely logical, subjectively defined traits, because they are as unreal in the topography of the personality as political regions are in regard to the topography of land, there are nevertheless occasions on which they have either (*a*) some specific practical value, or (*b*) some degree of potential reality as environmental mold traits, through society "realizing" its ideas in the way described above.[1]   For any truly logical division, in any subject matter whatever, has some functional relation to possible utilities and common purposes, by reason of the nature of logic.   Since logical attributes are related to functions, it may be of value in some circumstances — e.g., vocational selection — to measure sets of organically unrelated habits having some common quality or utility — e.g., a congeries of clerical skills labeled "clerical aptitude" — to fit the individual momentarily to an occupational pattern.   This is a very prevalent practice.   It has persisted, for example, through most of the test construction carried out for military use during the war.   But in most cases it seems shortsighted; for, in the absence of true organic unity, it is unsafe to predict performance in anything but the immediate situation — i.e., the "trait" has no permanence or interchangeability.   Lack of realization of the real nature of trait unities, however, permits many vocational psychologists blithely to make predictions of future "clerical aptitude" (or other logical trait) from an average of a conglomerate of functionally unrelated present measurements.

(4) **Constitutional unities.**   There exist constitutional trait unities which are inherent in the organism — in relation to its

[1] For example: The teaching of a logically bounded set of activities — e.g., mathematics — in school leads to individual differences in regard to an arbitrarily bounded set of habits taken as a whole, which may be said to be a trait of "mathematical ability."   There may be, of course, also some innate ability, a *constitutional* trait, which shows itself largely in mathematics, but this might appear also simultaneously in, say, musical and mechanical ability.   The latter would obviously be a different and more real kind of mathematical ability unity, or mathematico-mechanical-musical ability, than that resulting merely from the pattern of schoolteaching being what it is.

environment — but which are not of a dynamic, teleological kind — i.e., not ergs. Unities of this kind occur in such traits as nervous sensitivity, intelligence, energy, fatigability, speed of motor reactions, excitability, goodness of memory, languidness, constraint, ready recovery from shock, and a number of traits referred to by terms for constitutional abilities.

Obviously, no forms of *finished behavior* are wholly constitutional any more than they are wholly the product of an environmental mold. But there are some in which the constitutional influence is more emphatic, and these (in the absence of refined research to reveal those fainter constitutional patterns affecting only part of the variance in a set of behavior elements), are best utilized as an immediate illustration. The argument is, not that certain observed behaviors are wholly constitutional, but that a certain amount of the variation in these behavior elements is due to constitutional influences and that they vary together as a single pattern because they stem from a single constitutional influence. (In factor analytic terms, part of the variance of these elements springs from a single factor.) Each individual is more or less endowed with this unitary constitutional influence.

Now, as with environmental mold traits, there is no reason why the constitutional pattern should not extend over dynamic, ability, and temperamental characters. For example, the schizothyme temperament or schizophrenic diathesis, which we know to have an appreciable genetic determination, includes effects on dynamic traits and directions of interests, on temperamental reactivity, and on intellectual performances. Consequently it seems that this category should rightly include much of our first contingent category above, dynamic trait unities. Indeed, as will soon become evident, the most basic division of trait unities is into those which are constitutional and those which arise from environmental impress. Within these, if we wish, we can form subdivisions by a cross classification according to modality — temperamental, dynamic, and ability classes — but it will require the thorough investigation of Chapter 6 to discover how true a picture of reality this cross classification according to modalities really is.

(5) **Developmental trait unities.** A special ground for considering a set of reactions to have a unitary trait character, but one not represented in current trait surveys, would seem to be that they all *emerge* together, either phylogenetically, ontogenetically, or at some environmental provocation. A fair number of terms can be discovered covering traits of this kind. The adjectives "infantile," "emotionally mature," "senile," "adolescent" illustrate the ontogenetic usage. "Beastly," "monkey-like," "cave-mannish" illustrate the phylogenetic usage. Here also we could place the psychotic syndromes, for no matter what provokes, for example, manic-depressive disorder, it has, when it emerges, always substantially the same pattern of components, recognized as belonging together by reason of their simultaneous appearance. Simultaneous disappearance is also a ground for trait unity of this kind.

(6) **Other and accidental unities.** There are a few trait terms in common use in which the unity of the parts has none of the above true, functional bases, nor even, seemingly, a mere logical, subjective basis. Indeed, nothing binds the parts together other than the social habit of referring to the various pieces of behavior by one and the same name! If one considers such trait labels as chauvinistic, Falstaffian, Prussian, or bourgeois, he perceives that a real entity once justified putting the cluster of characteristics under a single trait name, but that the term has more or less outlived the integration which constituted the object of its reference and is now applied to some fragmentary thing, faintly, partially resembling the originally existent pattern. It may be, in extreme instances, that, like Zola's description of the Parisian woman, or Kipling's picture of the empire builder, such terms, through constant usage, tend to create or stabilize the type they de-

scribe; just as we have seen that a true logical category, on becoming embodied in an actual occupation or school subject, may produce a true functional unity of skills. But the career of the "historical" syndrome as an environmental mold trait is likely to be more meteoric and more brief than is that of a widely used logical category and in most instances the term represents only the ashes of a once organic whole.

Other trait terms arise by semantic or etymological accident. Others again, like "musty," "flabby," "asthenic," "crippled," "acrid," "lion-like," attempt to smuggle over to personality in a colorful metaphor a pattern which, as a known certainty, exists only in the original. Others seem to conjure up a trait about some stimulus — e.g., a football fan, a seafaring personality, an alcoholic. These are essentially environmental mold traits, largely dynamic, in which the stimulus rather than the goal of the sentiment has been used to label the trait.

In short, there are many historical, semantic, and accidental unities which either resolve into our basic categories or which vanish, and must henceforth be set aside from our main discussion as so many "illusions of unity."

4. COVARIATION AS THE BASIS OF REAL FUNCTIONAL UNITY

The Meaning of Functional Unity. The distinctions between "real" unities and those merely imposed on data by fashions of the mind is in some respects an elusive one and in the last resort can be pursued into remote philosophical fastnesses. For the moment we shall refuse to be led into more remote discussion and shall take our stand, until the end of this section, on the common sense but by no means superficial ground that *the unity of a set of parts is established by their moving — i.e., appearing, changing, disappearing — together, by their exercising an effect together, and by an influence on one being an influence on all.*[1]

---

[1] Note that this does not include any reference to a qualitative similarity, such as is involved in the notion of a perceptual "gestalt."

Fundamental importance of the problem. Actually the problem of establishing functional unities is wider than the field of personality study. Wherever the psychologist makes a measurement, he has as his ideal that the measurement shall represent some single, defined, uniform quality or direction in an established continuum. Whenever the psychologist describes a function with one noun — e.g., a mental set, reaction time, the super ego, frustration tolerance — he implies that he deals with some kind of unity. Experimental psychology, despite its pretensions to some superior methodological standing, shares with the despised qualitative psychiatry the stigma of making unities by fiat, for it has generally not been content to consider its measurements as physical, interactive (58) measures but has labeled them measures of some psychological function — e.g., "rote memory, pitch discrimination." Proving functional unities is thus the most general and fundamental problem in psychology. Unfortunately, real advances in many fields have had to be postponed because the more superficial investigators have pursued the wild geese of colorful clinical and experimental hypotheses instead of coöperating to carry forward these somewhat laborious and difficult morphological determinations of trait unities on the basis of which exact research can alone go forward.

Covariation as the indicator of unity. If the above criterion of functional unity is translated into the language of psychological observation, it implies that a unity can be detected from the fact that the constituent behavior elements in a trait *covary*. That is to say, if we take a number of different individuals and measure them with respect to the elements A, C, K, and T, the person who has a lot of A will also have a lot of C, K, and T, while the person who is low in K will also be low in A, C, and T. In other words, scores in A will *correlate highly* with C, K, and T scores. It does not follow that covariation of measurements as between persons — i.e., of individual differences — is the only kind of covariation to be considered, nor is the product moment correlation coefficient the only expression of covariation to be employed. Covariation means here any kind of *going-togetherness*.

Our preliminary survey above, intended to sift, simplify, and classify the current notions as to what a trait consists in, implicitly used this test: that covariation of parts is the criterion of real unity. Now we shall conclude, without experimental demonstration but on the basis of common sense and of that firsthand observation throughout psychology which is open to all, that the above four real unities, (1) Dynamic, (2) Environmental mold, (4) Constitutional, and (5) Developmental, reduce, as far as essential characters are concerned, to two; viz., (1) *constitutional unities* imposed from within the organism by genetic, mainly hereditary factors and by intrinsic physiological conditions, and (2) *environmental mold unities* imposed by patterns of pressures existing in the external world chiefly, perhaps, in social life. Compared with these differences of ultimate source the differences in the nature of the environmental conditions which cause the unity, or the modality in which unity exists, are extraneous and even accidental. However, this dichotomy, as will be seen more clearly later, applies only to *source traits*, not to mere correlation clusters or *surface traits*.

The two basic and the six conditional unities. The division of traits according to what, for lack of any really good term, we shall call *modality* — i.e., into dynamic traits, abilities, and temperament traits — is independent of the above basic division and therefore can cut across it, making possible six descriptive varieties of traits.

At this stage, however, we shall not inquire as to what is the ultimate basis of the modality division, for it is a subtle one. Suffice it that the division into abilities and dynamic and temperament traits is a conditional one — conditional on certain features of measurement or test situation and the predictive purposes of the psychometrist. (See Chapter 7.)

As constitutional and environmental mold traits appear in nature, they normally subtend all modalities. That is to say, as pointed out above, a single set of covarying elements may include, for example, attitudes, skills, attainments, and even temperamental reactions. The psychometrist, therefore, succeeds in getting unities in one modality alone only by imposing artificial conditions. He abstracts dynamic, temperamental, and ability aspects because they can be used most economically for separate predictions in special conditions and fields of performance. For one modality of traits is frequently irrelevant to a certain class of problems, or can readily be held constant.

How convenient it is in the long run to deal in these three modality abstractions instead of including in every calculation the total constitutional or environmental mold pattern remains to be seen. For the present it seems best to employ them, in which case six [1] kinds of trait unity eventually appear, as follows:

TABLE 6

THE SIX PRIMARY FORMS OF TRAIT UNITY

	CONSTITUTIONAL UNITY	ENVIRONMENTAL MOLD UNITY	
Dynamic Modality	1. Ergs, Needs, Drives (Constitutional Dynamic)	4. Metanergs, Sentiments, Attitudes (Environmental Mold Dynamic)	
Temperament Modality	2. Constitutional Temperament	5. Modified Temperamental Tendencies	
Ability Modality	3. Constitutional Abilities and Capacities (Intelligence, Memory, Musical Ability)	6. Acquired Skills and Information	
		Conscious	Unconscious

[1] Or nine if we concern ourselves with the further possible division of Environmental Mold unities into those consciously and those unconsciously acquired.

Considered in the light of this final simplification, the more numerous, currently entertained "varieties" of trait unity discussed above will be found to reduce themselves readily enough to this smaller number of basic forms. Developmental unities, for example, are special instances of constitutional patterns developing suddenly, or of environmental mold traits suddenly impressed. *Accidental, Semantic Unities* do not concern us here and can be passed on to the student of cultural curiosities, while *Logical Unities*, arbitrarily defining trait boundaries to fit the environment or the psychometrist's immediate purpose, are to be considered forced unities, only of limited value and then only in special tasks — e.g., vocational selection.[1]

It is interesting to note that some psychological theoretical systems, both historical and modern, have proceeded as if there were only one kind of trait unity to be considered, or, if they recognized more, they have considered only one to be of practical importance. Generally this one has been the environmental mold unity (as is implicit, for example, in the theory of recent studies on honesty, suggestibility, persistence, level of aspiration, and aesthetic sense). Actually we should expect this to be the less well-defined or stable of trait unities. If social thought cannot itself agree as to the boundaries of manifestation of such traits — and few philosophers would be found to agree as to the ramifications of "honesty" or "aesthetic sense" over various physical, mental, and moral fields — then it cannot be expected that the trait will be

[1] As suggested in an earlier comment, even in these particular restricted situations it is generally unintelligent to measure a trait in boundaries immediately defined by the need of the situation — e.g., to measure "capacity to withstand the monotony of drill punching," when selecting drill punchers. One knows nothing about the dynamic or constitutional structure of this *ad hoc* "trait" and may discover, after the subjects have had a month's training, that, owing to the trait having become differently structured, one's predictions are amiss and the selectees are not the best workers that could have been chosen. Even apart from this, the logical unity measure is wasteful, because it cannot be applied to any other situation with regard to which the subject may need to be considered at some other time. The use of logical traits would lead to a separate test for each of ten thousand occupations.

formed on an absolutely uniform pattern, in all individuals, by existing education.

5. COVARIATION IN CLUSTERS AND IN FACTORS

Correlation clusters and factor analysis. The covariation of individual differences (or any other observations), which we have shown is the one essential character in a trait unity, can be formulated and operationally studied in two alternative mathematical, statistical ways. The unity of the trait may exist in the form of *a cluster* of elements which mutually correlate above a stipulated degree; or it may express itself as an independent mathematical *factor* which indicates that the elements covary, to a certain extent of their total variance, in some common dimension. A cluster can be readily understood by anyone who knows what a correlation coefficient is — it is just a bunch of trait elements which correlate highly, for all possible pairings of items in the cluster; but to understand what is meant by a factor the rather more technical concepts of factor analysis must be learned.

An unfortunate feature of the present stage of personality research is that relatively few psychologists are prepared to master the technical difficulties of factor analysis and relatively few students, especially in psychiatry, get a training in this aspect of statistics (often of *any* aspect of statistics) before approaching personality study. Yet, since the human mind is certainly no less complex than the finest of engineering structures or the most intricate of man-made machines, the psychologist must be prepared to serve an apprenticeship to mathematics no less difficult than that which the engineer is willing to face. Space compels us in the present treatise to assume from this point on that the student of personality is familiar with the general principles of factor analysis.[1] We

---

[1] He may get the required principles from recent textbooks of psychological statistics, or more fully from Burt (*27*), Holzinger (*120*), Thurstone (*258*), or Thomson (*254*).

shall assume that he knows the sense in which the correlations between many variables may be substantially accounted for by relatively few general factors; the meaning of general, group, and specific factors; the way in which the number of factors is determined by the nature of the correlations; the possibilities of alternative factorial explanations; the spatial representation of correlations by angles and of factors by coordinates and dimensions; the possibility of non-orthogonal factors and the notion that several factors may contribute in differing degrees to the variance of any test or personality variable.

At this point we have stated the argument that there are two mathematical, operational forms in which any kind of psychological unity could manifest itself; namely, the correlation cluster and the factor. If the much-battered verbal symbol "trait" is to have any precise meaning at all, therefore, it must be attached to either or both of these forms. From an incisive survey of the sense in which "trait" is most consistently used in general parlance, one might conclude that, if anything, it is more properly assigned to factors than to clusters: for —

(1) Clusters are themselves often considerably intercorrelated, whereas there is no reason to expect such high and frequent intercorrelation in the influences — temperamental, environmental, and dynamic — which constitute what we call traits; (2) clusters are each concerned with only a few trait elements — i.e., restricted behavior manifestations (three to a dozen, as a rule), in a very limited area — whereas, from the nature of traits as psychologically understood, we should expect the trait to spread its influence very widely into many operationally remote segments of behavior, as a factor does; (3) clusters are simply statements of literal going-togetherness, whereas factors are *analytical* of covariation, being constructible according to various hypotheses. Similarly, by "trait" we normally mean something *interpretive* about the

source of behavior, rather than a merely literal description of behavior. (See page 232.)

Source traits and surface traits. However, both kinds of mathematical representation have their uses and meanings. The cluster, as a simple statement that certain kinds of behavior are observed in everyday life to be closely associated (e.g., as in a syndrome) — an observation unprejudiced by any "explanation" — is also, in many senses of the word, a trait. Therefore it seems best to meet the situation by employing two clearly distinguished definitions of trait paralleling the two mathematical concepts. Thus we shall speak henceforth of two kinds of traits: *Source traits*, corresponding to factors, and *Surface traits*, corresponding to clusters. To decide which are more important for diverse psychological purposes and to appreciate correctly the relation of one to the other, the following essential comparisons of clusters and factors need to be kept in mind.

(1) Surface, cluster traits are likely to be far more numerous than source or factor traits. It is mathematically possible (though so extreme a proportion may be rare in nature) to find a set of two or three hundred trait elements which can be represented on the one hand by, say, a dozen clusters and, alternatively, by no more than two factors. (See Diagram 1.) The object of describing and measuring personality with practicable economy by relatively few variables is not so well achieved by clusters as by factors.

(2) The number of clusters which can be obtained from a set of intercorrelations (a correlation matrix) depends (*a*) on the arbitrary level of intercorrelation fixed as defining a cluster, whereas in factor analysis the number of factors is fixed (or substantially fixed) by the nature of the correlations, (*b*) on the grouping of the variables; in regions of even density of variables, as in Diagram 3, it is not possible to demarcate clusters, except in an arbitrary way. (Thus these 15 variables may be regarded as two clusters, A' and B', or three,

A, B, and C, according to the minimum correlation accepted; the smaller angle, of course, represents the higher correlation.)

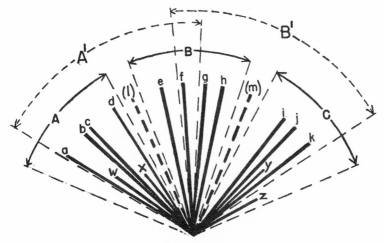

DIAGRAM 3. THE ARBITRARINESS OF CLUSTER UNITIES

(3) On the other hand, and apart from this arbitrariness of the line drawn for admission of elements to a cluster, the cluster method of simplifying the correlation picture is less interpretive and more nearly a literal statement of empirically observed connections. The factors are possible explanations of how the actually existing cluster forms may have originated.[1] Hence research findings expressed in clusters are not lost to later reinterpretation as are mathematical factors, the selection of which, by rotation, is often prejudiced by theoretical interpretations.

---

[1] A helpful analogy here may be found in physics, where we consider, for example, a particle of water involved in a wave form as involved (*a*) in the complex literal wave form existing at a given instant, and (*b*) in a series of distinct, simple, hypothetical, contributing wave forms out of which the literal wave form is created. Similarly, a trait element may figure in only one, or at most two or three, actual correlation clusters or surface traits — it is on the crest or in some intercluster trough — but it is a representative of — i.e., is loaded by — perhaps a dozen different factors or "interpretive" source traits "causing" the clusters.

(4) For the reasons given in (3) it is sometimes contended that clusters are more "real" and less arbitrary than factors — i.e., more likely to correspond to actual functional unities. Such a conclusion is incorrect, for (*a*) if functional unities operate as mathematical factors, which is undoubtedly true in certain instances, the bunching of trait elements in highly intercorrelating clusters is by no means certain to correspond to a single functional unity. It *may* do so, if the trait elements concerned are all highly loaded with the same factor; but in the usual situation of many factors operating at once, the clusters are far more likely to occur in *areas of overlap* of several positively operating factors — i.e., they do not correspond to a *simple* function but rather to the *most complex* possible heaping-up (overlap) of interacting functions.

(*b*) The criterion of "reality" is surely, in part, stability — i.e., permanence of form. (See discussion on trait "reality," page 93.) It remains to be seen whether the clusters appearing in one correlation matrix or psychological situation or sample will turn up as faithfully in other situations as do the factors. If the relationship is as indicated in (*a*), we should expect the factors to be more permanent and more widely useful in predicting behavior. For the particular overlaps and interferences of factors, which throw clusters into relief and even bring about their existence, are likely to be more fortuitous and specific to situations and samples than are the factors (causes) themselves.

(5) Against factors it may be objected that they are not so much existent, tangible, behavior patterns in the individual as influences — however real — which have operated (or are operating) upon him from his constitution or from society. This is true; an environmental mold trait, for example, may correspond precisely to some actual external social influence — e.g., a church pattern — but, whether it has become internalized in the individual's inhibitions or still operates only as long as he remains in that cultural setting, it provides a more

economical, understandable, and sure way of predicting his behavior than by considering a host of clusters.[1] This character of the factor is indeed implied by the term *Source Trait* (or deeper, underlying trait) as contrasted with the *Surface Trait* designation of the cluster.

The statistical patterns known as clusters and factors do not entirely exhaust the mathematical devices by which unitary covariation can be represented. But it seems that they correspond to psychological realities; that well-known syndromes appear as clusters while many traits long since described in verbal terms demonstrably exist as factors. Furthermore, in those few special situations where the real influences at work in producing variation are known and can be controlled, it is demonstrable that these influences can be rediscovered by the mathematical analysis of observed correlations.

If we glance briefly at the known mathematical alternatives at present available, we find only one of any practical use. This is the theoretically possible hybrid between a cluster and a factor; namely, representation by a set of oblique axes, which differ from oblique factors in that there are more of them than there are dimensions to the factor space, which are in fact as numerous as clusters and which are directed through the centers of clusters. This is the cluster as defined by Tryon, and which differs in a rather radical fashion from the cluster as used throughout this treatise. Tryon discovers clusters by correlating the columns of correlation coefficients in a correlation matrix; i.e., the members of a cluster have similar profiles as regards their correlations with all the other variables. The members of such a cluster do not necessarily correlate highly directly with one another.

The nature of this cluster, which, for reasons given on page 82,

---

[1] It might even be argued that the source trait has the virtue of reminding us that *all* traits are really relations between human beings and their environments rather than characters in the individual only.

we shall call a *qualitative cluster*, can best be seen by reverting to the representation of correlations by angles and lengths of lines as in Diagram 3 on page 79. The correlation between two variables is equal to the projection of one line upon the other. Variables *a*, *b*, *c*, and *d* in cluster A have high correlation because they are about equally long and are separated by only small angles. Variables *w* and *x*, on the other hand, though they are well within the angular space of the cluster, are only short lines and therefore do not have very high correlations with each other or with variables *a*, *b*, *c*, and *d*. All six would form a qualitative cluster, in Tryon's sense, but only *a*, *b*, *c*, and *d* would form a cluster in the primary sense of cluster — i.e., as a syndrome. The student familiar with statistical representation will see that all variables occupying the same direction in space will have the same common factor constitution. The shorter ones will have the same relative factor ingredients as the longer ones, but reduced in loading — i.e., as it were, diluted. They will, in other words, be qualitatively similar, for which reason we have suggested the term *qualitative cluster* for Tryon's device. This device, incidentally, suffers from the same arbitrariness of boundaries as does the regular cluster. It is perhaps hardly necessary to remind the student that the length of the variable vector is the length in *the common factor space*. That is to say, variables *w* and *x* in cluster A, or *y* and *z* in cluster C, are shorter than the others because they protrude less into the common factor space; i.e., they have less mean correlation with all the other variables involved. Their shortness in the common factor space means that they must have a large proportion of their variance accounted for by a factor or factors unique to each one of them.

ILLUSTRATION OF FACTORS AND CLUSTERS AS TRAIT UNITIES

The following is an attempt to illustrate in diagrammatic form the relation of clusters, factors, and measured variables or trait elements. It seeks to make the matter intelligible to those insufficiently famil-

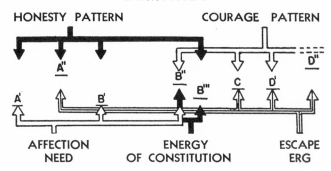

SOCIAL AND PHYSICAL PRESSURES AND DEMANDS

CONSTITUTIONAL PATTERNS IN THE ORGANISM

Definition of trait elements.

A'. Respecting property of friends.
A''. Respecting property of strangers.
B'. Being truthful to friends.
B''. Being truthful to strangers.

B'''. Avoiding exaggeration in relating stories.
C. Facing physical dangers.
D'. Keeping one's head in emergencies.
D''. Magnitude of vegetative n. s. response in fear.

DIAGRAM 4. Traits as Covariation Patterns Due to Factors

iar with factor analysis to follow the above. Further, it illustrates the relationship in a new fashion, extending the meaning, for those already conversant with the factor analytic approach.

The row of eight small bars with letters in Diagram 4 represents eight measured pieces of behavior[1] (for a whole population) which we may call trait elements, or separate, restricted, well-defined pieces of behavior which can be accurately measured — A', A'', B', B'', B''', C, D', D''. The variance in each of these trait-element measures is accounted for by influences from various factors — repre-

---

[1] Those indicated by the same letter, with differing superscript, are logically or stylistically similar kinds of behavior (see key below diagram) which on a priori grounds might be (mis)conceived to belong to one and the same functional unity.

sented by arrows — each of which belongs to a particular factor, in-dicated by a series of arrows linked together. These work variously to raise or lower the individual's endowment in a particular trait element. For instance, both the source trait "Affectionateness" and the source trait "Energy of Constitution" act to increase B '' ("Avoiding exaggeration in relating stories"), while the source trait "Courageousness" tends to decrease it. But in any case they coöperate to increase its variability. (In the diagram the opposition of arrows does not mean that they work in an opposite direction: influences from the environment are placed above, while constitution factors are indicated as coming from below.)

If all the influences operating on any two elements were the same in kind and intensity, these two would vary together — i.e., the individual who had a lot of one would have a lot of the other. This could be represented on the diagram by having both elements on the same level (for we may adopt just here the convention that when elements are drawn at the same level they covary). The influences which cause the elements to group together in patterns, each having elements which covary, are of two kinds: first, external "presses" (to employ Murray's useful concept), arising from uniformities (patterns) in the social or physical environment — i.e., environ-mental mold traits — and, secondly, internal forces arising from the common strength of drives (needs, ergs) or the common source of a variety of constitutional manifestations — i.e., constitutional traits.

As examples of external presses or molds we will take honesty and physical courage, one involved in four and one in three of the be-havior elements here concerned. For a given individual, by reason of his particular life situation and experience, the element of the definite, conscious social pattern of honesty or courage will tend to be impressed upon him with a force (arising from punishments and rewards) which is common to all the elements of the pattern. That is to say, by reason of the social mold alone there will tend to be, as between different individuals, a common variance discoverable in the different elements of the pattern.

Similarly for the internally originating unities, which in this case we have illustrated by two ergs or needs (affection and fear) and one constitutional but non-teleological character (energy). Here, for example, the individual with a strong affectional drive will tend to rate high in all elements which are manifestations of affection, to the extent ultimately manifested by the appearance of a general factor, as discussed in the factorial analysis of the dynamic traits in Chapter 5. The extent to which the variance of a trait is contributed to by the external and internal sources of common variance is indicated in the diagram by the length of the arrows. It is obvious that neither the internal nor the external unity will succeed in expressing itself by bringing about a perfect covariation of the elements in which each is involved. For if some forms of honest behavior are based on affection and some on fear, the individual with an excess of the former will "take" unduly well the parts of the social pattern which fall in the realm of affection motivation, but not those motivated by fear. Similarly, if some timidity expresses itself in lack of courage and some in honesty, the individual who has had an especially good training in courage will not show a good functional unity of all manifestations of the fear erg, for those appearing (negatively) in courage will tend to be masked. In short, *each factor pattern will tend to be obscured and modified by the other factor patterns.* That is, *clusters* of high correlation will not correspond in outline with the realm of influence of *factors*.

The relation of factor influences and clusters can be illustrated yet again, in other terms, by means of the following diagram:

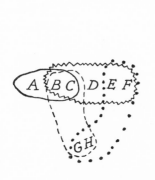

	A	B	C	D	E	F	G	H
A								
B	.2							
C	.2	.8						
D	0	.2	.2					
E	0	.2	.2	.2				
F	0	.2	.2	.2	.6			
G	0	.4	.4	0	.4	.4		
H	0	.4	.4	0	.4	.4	.8	

Known Plan of Factor Overlap   Resultant Correlation Matrix

Factor I   Outline ———— Mean Communality 0.2
Factor II   Outline ᴧᴧᴧᴧᴧ Mean Communality 0.2
Factor III Outline - - - - Mean Communality 0.4
Factor IV   Outline · · · · Mean Communality 0.4

DIAGRAM 5. CLUSTERS AS PRODUCTS OF FACTOR OVERLAP

An instance is taken where eight variables are in part accounted for by four factors. The only assumption made is that the loadings of variables by any one factor are either zero or uniformly high — i.e., there is "plateau loading," as occurs to a considerable extent in simple structure. If a mutual intercorrelation of at least 0.5 is taken as the criterion for belonging to a cluster, there are — as inspection of the correlation matrix shows — three clusters: viz., B–C, E–F, and G–H. These occur only at points of overlap of factors. If the criterion is reduced to 0.3, two clusters run together and one cluster becomes the region of a factor (factor III). "Low" clusters are in general more likely to correspond to factor regions than high, narrow clusters, which are more likely to be regions of overlap — especially in situations such as those of personality measurement, where many factors affect the whole.

6. SOME METHODOLOGICAL DIFFICULTIES IN EQUATING TRAITS TO FACTORS

One must not lose sight of the fact that descriptions of the unitary traits of personality — (1) as clusters or surface traits and (2) as factors or source traits — constitute two equivalent, mutually transformable, alternative and not independent systems. Usually the cluster description of the unitary traits amounts to an intermediate stage on the way to description in terms of factors — i.e., the way to final interpretation in terms of causal influences.

Our position is, therefore, that the discovery of clusters cannot be regarded as an end in itself. Clusters, as attempts at definition of unitary traits, have certain defects — some already discussed in this chapter, others set out systematically elsewhere (57). In general they are not so analytical as factors. We cannot, for example, refer to surface traits as constitutional or environmental mold traits: they are the resultants of both of these. We cannot always clearly separate clusters or know their exact boundaries (57).

In spite of these considerations, some psychologists have reverted to description of personality in terms of clusters because factor analysis also is dogged by a methodological disability. It consists in the inability of the experimenter to make certain that the mathematical factors he gets do indeed correspond to truly functional unities and psychologically unitary source traits. As the mathematical considerations of Chapter 8 will show, a source trait will appear as a factor, but not every factor solution gives the source traits. We have still to develop entirely satisfactory methodological criteria for distinguishing between factors that are merely mathematical artifacts and those which correspond to real psychological traits. Factor analysis yields as many factors as there are dimensions required to represent the directions of variation presented in the observed correlation coefficients. But in the opinion of many statistical psychologists, the particular set of factors or the particular rotation of factor axes which shall take shape in this multidimensional space cannot at present be unequivocally determined and defined by the given data and must be left to arbitrary inclinations on the part of the experimenter. A given pattern of clusters — of surface traits — can therefore at present be accounted for by an immense variety of alternative factors — indeed, an infinite variety within a certain series — only one of which corresponds to the real source traits.

So far the most promising solution to this indeterminacy has been Thurstone's principle of simple structure, which assumes that the most likely solution is that which gives the most parsimonious explanation *with regard to a single matrix of correlations (261)*. Recently another way out of the factor analytic impasse has been propounded, which is derived from the same general scientific principle of parsimony differently. The new "principle of proportional profiles" *(58b) (58c)* proceeds on the assumption that the true functional unities, and these only, will manifest themselves as factors in different, independent, correlation matrices arising from measurements of the same sets of variables under different conditions.

This solution is discussed fully in Chapter 9. At this point we wish only to call attention to the existence of a weakness, a remediable weakness, in factor analysis. But the reader familiar with this criticism should not succumb even for one moment to the misconception that this invalidates the concept of a source trait as a factor.

Traits are abstractions from concrete, "operational" behavior. From the above mathematical discussions it will be clear that trait unities are patterns among responses, or, rather, among habits of responding. Any particular response habit, behavior item, or *trait element* [1] can be employed as a necessary element in defining or measuring traits of many different kinds — indeed, of all kinds. One element may enter into all traits — or practically all — and all traits may enter into the determination of one element, though normally some particular elements can be found which are almost entirely expressions of one trait. For instance, the fact that a child consistently brings home the right change when sent on an errand may be used, along with other correlated trait elements, to deduce (1) a certain level of impress of the environmental mold pattern of honesty (in this and other honesty responses), (2) a certain level of the dynamic trait of acquisitiveness, and (3) something about the constitutional-economic trait of general intelligence, as well as many other traits, though its greatest contribution may be to the measure of honesty.

Statistically [2] and experimentally the situation reduces to this: one deals with a large population of trait elements the majority of which are shared by all traits but among which

---

[1] From this point on we shall use the term "trait element" to describe the restricted behavior elements among which covariation and correlation are observed. For the present a trait element is the structure underlying some limited, clearly definable piece of behavior, operationally describable with a minimum of psychological interpretation — e.g., a disposition to seek large groups, to fatigue readily in muscular activity, to react quickly to visual presentations. Later the implications of the notion of trait element will be looked into at a more philosophical level.

[2] See the final expression of this in mathematical symbols on pages 558–560.

each trait has its own pattern of emphasis. To infer the strength of a particular trait from the weighted sum of certain trait elements one must give attention to certain mathematical principles which are best considered in detail later.

Or, to express this mathematical notion by a simile from art, one might say that the trait elements are like the individual colored threads in a tapestry, or the individual brush marks upon a painting, each of which may be a point of intersection of several patterns and contribute to the perception of the shape of all of them.

Again, the mathematic, formal statement is to be seen as another form of expression of what is commonly expressed by some psychologists in verbal terms, when they say that one and the same piece of behavior may indicate different things in different persons or that a given trait can be seen in all aspects of a person's behavior. For if any one trait element is determined by several source traits, one source trait may predominate in its causation in one person and another in its appearance in a second person, the interpretation depending upon the trait elements that are found associated with the first.

Moreover, it follows that in order to predict any one narrow piece of behavior — i.e., a trait element — it will generally be necessary to measure *all* of the individual's common traits. In practice, of course, behavior in one field — e.g., solving puzzles under conditions of constant motivation — may often be sufficiently well predicted from traits of one modality only — ability in this case — or even one single trait — say intelligence — alone, because one trait can account for most of the variance in some one trait element.

Occasional difficulty in envisaging psychological source of covariation. The importance of discovering true unitary traits — a task often fraught with great theoretical or practical difficulties — resides in the superior power and accuracy of prediction which the knowledge of such unities permits.

This applies both to surface and source traits, but *a fortiori* to the latter. By "prediction" we mean, here and throughout this treatise, the prediction from a trait strength (based on measurements of a few trait elements) of (*a*) how the individual will react in other trait elements of that trait at this moment and (*b*) how he will react in the same trait elements at some future moment.

Current discussion suggests that psychologists have greater difficulty in envisaging a functional unity in the sense of what we have called an environmental mold trait than as a constitutional trait. It seems desirable, therefore, to make a brief digression or expansion to show more convincingly how the mathematical unities of covariation with which we are dealing can be connected with the functional unity caused by environmental influence.

Perhaps the most disturbing doubt regarding environmental mold unity springs from the consideration that in many cases it is only a historical unity — i.e., at some time in the past the individual was subjected to a training situation which developed a pattern of responses A, K, L, and T; but can the psychometrist still predict the strength of, say, T from that of A and K at the present moment?

One must bear in mind that trait elements formed under one environmental influence are likely to have in common other things than the common variance impressed at the time. Habits formed at the same place and the same age are likely to share reactivity to the same stimuli, to show the same amount of functional autonomy after a certain lapse of time, to follow the same curves of extinction, etc. There are probably as yet unknown similarities through coincidence of place and age in habit formation — e.g., similar susceptibility to physiological influences.

Consequently the environmental mold trait has more than a historical unity — i.e., a unity existing at some time in the past. It will tend to persist and function as a unity. But in any case this is not simply assumed; it is accepted in so far as it is proved to exist at the present time by the observed correlations. However, these circumstances argue that the environmental mold trait will, more frequently than the constitutional trait, appear as a less well-defined or more fragmentary factor.

Chapter Five

BASIC METHODS FOR DELIMITING AND MEASURING COMMON AND UNIQUE TRAITS

1. THE MEANING OF FUNCTIONAL UNITY

Stage of the argument. The preceding chapter has attempted to separate the wheat from the chaff among current verbal definitions of the kinds of unity that constitute a trait. It has led (1) to a division into common and unique traits, (2) to the subdivision of common traits into *surface traits* or clusters and *source traits* or factors, (3) to the subdivision of source traits into environmental mold and constitutional traits, (4) to the notion that all unity is based on covariation and that trait unities can accordingly only be experimentally discovered through observations of covariation.

The present chapter takes up this last proposition for an expanded, systematic study. It asks what kinds of covariation can be observed in nature and by what operational methods trait unities can be deduced from observations and measurements of such covariation.

What does the psychologist mean by "real"? It has been pointed out in the first references to factor analysis, and will be developed in practical mathematical terms in Chapter 9, that though source traits will appear in correlation data as factors, not all obtainable mathematical factors correspond to source traits. Indeed, in some circles it has become customary to criticize factor analysis on the false assumption that all factors obtainable by this means are "unreal," "artificial," mathematical entities having no psychological meaning as functional unities.

Our practical standpoint has been in the first place that a unity exists when parts appear together, change together, and mutually influence one another, when viewed in different contexts and from different angles. This is no more than the common-sense viewpoint on real unities. A man who suspects that the elephant he sees in his garden is nothing but the juxtaposition of two tree forms or even an outright hallucination gets up and looks at it from a new direction, waits to see if it moves as a whole independently of his will, and tests its connectedness by other senses.

Even at the beginning, however, we can see that the requirement that a unity shall persist in many kinds of situation will compel us to admit "degrees of reality," for on general psychological grounds it is probable that in some cases covariation will manifest itself only in *some* of the possible covariation situations. In short, with some "unities" covariation of parts will persist into more situations than with others. The notion of "degree of reality," however, so affronts the implicit assumption of a dichotomous "real" and "unreal" in our initial question about factors that this in turn must be examined.

The accusation forces us into an examination of the psychologists' meaning of "real," an examination which must partake of the depth, if not the hairsplitting, of philosophy and which will prove fruitful for methodology and the design of experiment.

The philosophers' view of "reality." In order to travel, if possible, ahead of the philosopher, instead of limping in the trail of his past errors, the psychologist would do well to ask what philosophy has so far had to say about "real" unities. Plato and his earlier successors admitted grades of reality, but modern philosophy will hear only of the existent and the non-existent. For Plato a thing is real if it "exerts power"; for Aristotle the real is the "independent"; for Descartes it is that which has "perfection" or "completeness."   All of these admit degrees!

Modern philosophers, however, make "real" synonymous with "existent."   Since an entity, be it matter or consciousness, either exists or does not exist, the possibility of degrees of reality is denied.

Whether we decide to speak of the "reality" of a functional unity or to use some term to which philosophers are less allergic, the conclusion seems unavoidable that functional unities must be recognized to exist in some hierarchy of reality, meaning thereby something more subtle than mere existence, as the older philosophers implied.   To this continuum we might apply instead the labels "degrees of independence," "efficacy," [1] or "completeness."

The notion of degrees of efficacy or completeness of a unity is best illustrated by considering unity in *any* class of objects before turning specifically to the more subtle data of psychology.   We observe that among unities some will be split up by a change of situation, some will be more universal in their manifestation, more permanent, and in short of greater total *utility* as a reference idea.   Thus, if we consider physical objects, a railway engine is more of a unity than is an engine wheel of a train, simply because it is less frequently incorporated in larger units or broken down into smaller ones.   Similarly in the hierarchy of psychological variables the

---

[1] The question has actually wider meaning than with respect to covariation. When we throw items into a group — i.e., into a unity — our grouping has degrees of "reality" according to the essentiality of the attribute in which they resemble one another. A botanist, for example, may classify plants according to major aspects of structure, so that those which are grouped together do indeed have a common fate in most situations. But for the purpose of decorating a beauty chorus the mere color may be more important than this "essential" structure, and flowers of a common color will share a common fate.   In psychology we have to consider the basis on which trait unity is established from the standpoint of its aptness to the greatest number of purposes in which trait unities are used.   This amounts to saying that covariation must occur in as many different kinds of observation — e.g., of individual differences, of growth increments, of fluctuation within one individual — as possible, for the trait to have greatest "efficacy."

"psychologically meaningless" mathematical factor has a lowly and local reality: it functions as a single predictor of many performances in the conditions in which that particular correlation matrix was established. But such factor traits as an aggressive disposition, hyperthyroid temperament, or general mental ability have a higher level of reality or utility, for they appear as unitary factors of predictive value in a great variety of situations and could manifest themselves as factors in many different correlation matrices obtained variously from clinical, experimental, psychological, and physiological data.

The task of psychology, therefore, seems to be to seek the most widely useful, efficacious, *influential* functional unities — i.e., those appearing in all or most circumstances of covariation and offering the most economical set of factors for prediction when psychology is considered as a whole. The present writer would hazard a guess that the frequency distribution of "reality" or "utility" of factors, though continuous, will be found to be bimodal, so that most will be either ephemeral and entirely local mathematical factors or else factor traits of very substantial functional reality.

"Real" thus means primarily *influential*, or often recurring in different situations. However, apart from a trait unity's degree of reality in this sense it may also have a specially enhanced reality or utility in regard to some particular reference system. For example, though the sociologist, the psychologist, and the physiologist may possess a considerable number of factors of common utility, some will have greater reality so long as we stick to one system. The sociologist, for example, may find it convenient to work with a factor of "good citizenship" (*111*), which is a compound of what the psychologist finds as two factors: intelligence and character integration. And the physiologists may break down the psychologist's general intelligence factor into brain mass, oxidation efficiency, and other factors more frequently in common use in separation in their field. The present discussion should also be considered in connection with "second order factors" on page 516.

2. SYSTEMATIC PRESENTATION OF THE THEORETICALLY POSSIBLE COVARIATION DESIGNS

Previous limitation of sources of correlation data. We have spoken of real functional unities as being those factors or groups of covarying elements which appear in *most* circumstances of covariation. What are these circumstances? Up to the time of writing, practically all factor analytic and cluster studies aimed at discovering unitary traits have dealt with only one kind of covariation. They have implicitly assumed that covariation can exist only with respect to individual differences, measured at a given time — i.e., with respect to the simultaneous departure of different kinds of individual measurement from the mean of a group (of people in tests).

The present contention is that for a variety of important purposes — notably for uncovering the degree of reality of a trait; for providing independent correlation matrices for determining rotation by parallel proportional profiles (see Chapter 9); and to aid in determining trait modalities (see Chapter 7) — *covariation must be conceived and studied not only in this one "dimension" but in every theoretically meaningful and practically possible sense.* These senses seem never to have been systematically explored.

The covariation chart. Omitting the trial-and-error approaches which led to the present formulation, we may present the results most succinctly by means of Diagram 6, which we may call a *covariation chart*. This presents a system of rectangular coördinates in three dimensions, reproduced below in perspective and arbitrarily truncated at some indifferent distances. The coördinates do not represent continua,[1] but

---

[1] It is necessary to stress this, and to point out in particular that *OC* is not a time axis. The occasions of testing need not be separated by equal intervals of time or even be in temporal sequence. *OC* is a series of *occurrences* of test-person events, with some changing external or internal conditions which distinguish the events.

in each case a population of points arranged in serial order, equidistantly but in no immutable order. Along *OA* lies a series of persons, a_1, a_2, etc.; along *OB* lies a series of (personality) tests, b_1, b_2, etc.; and along *OC* a series of occasions of testing, c_1, c_2, etc.

Now a correlation coefficient, assessing covariation, can be calculated between any two series of test measurements matched in some way item for item. Consequently a correlation coefficient is represented in the diagram by any pair of parallel (and in some cases non-parallel) lines of equal length (in terms of points). Apart from diagonal lines, which may momentarily be set aside as relating to comparatively rare, esoteric, experimental designs, and non-parallel lines, which are largely psychologically meaningless, there are primarily six possibilities of correlation, represented by the pairs of parallel lines one can draw rectangularly in each of the three

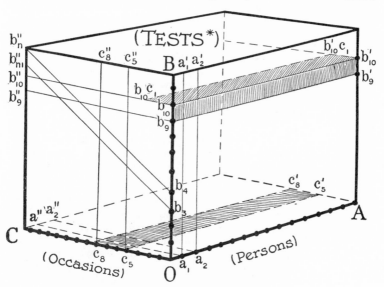

* Strictly, "Varieties of Measurement."

DIAGRAM 6. THE COVARIATION CHART

planes (and other lines parallel thereto). These lines need not, of course, begin at an edge or even at a face of the parallel-epiped shown in the diagram; but for ease of illustration we shall take as representative of each of the six possibilities a pair of parallel lines starting off from an edge and in fairly close proximity. For the sake of later discussion each possibility of covariation study will be given a name, the forms in the same plane being put under a generic title.

TABLE 7 (I)

Six Designs of Covariation Using (*A*) Literal Measurements

A 1. Static Covariation. (Test-person variation. Time constant.) This is called static because it deals with measurements taken on only one occasion, as in a snapshot. The paired lines lie in the plane OA–OB (and others parallel). The two possibilities are:

    1 *a*. *Static correlation (and analysis) of tests.* One correlates a series of persons on any two tests. This is the commonest of all correlation procedures and has been called R-technique. (*27*)(*242*) It is illustrated by the lines b_9b_9' with $b_{10}b_{10}'$, giving a paired series of persons' scores on the tests b_9 and b_{10}. (Also by any pairs of lines, adjacent or separated, parallel to these in this plane or in parallel planes.)

    1 *b*. *Static correlation (and analysis) of persons.* One correlates a series of test scores with respect to two persons at a time. This has been called Q- or P-technique. (*27*)(*242*) It is illustrated by the lines a_1a_1' with a_2a_2', etc.

A 2. Monovariate Covariation. (Person-occasion variation. Test constant.) Here the variation is with respect to any one test and lies in the plane of one test only — i.e., in OA–OC and planes parallel thereto. The two possibilities are:

    2 *a*. *Monovariate correlation (and analysis) of occasions.* One correlates the scores of a series of persons with respect to any two administrations of the same test — i.e., the single correlation is a reliability or consistency coefficient in form. Illustrated by lines c_5c_5' with, say, c_2c_2'. Factor analysis would yield *uniformities or groupings of occasions.* In so far as these are related to stimulus situations, the analysis would throw light on dynamic trait outlines. It would in general throw light on problems of social psychology — e.g., on moral or other similarities in the historical sequences of group life. For uniformity with the existing nomenclature this can be called O-technique.

TABLE 7 (I) — *Continued*

2 *b*. *Monovariate correlation (and analysis) of person relationships.* One pairs any two individuals with regard to scores on a series of occasions of application of one kind of test. The correlated persons are represented by lines a_1a_1'' with a_2a_2''. The factors from such correlations would be factors in persons — i.e., types — in relation to reaction to experimental influence, maturation, or learning.

A 3. INTRA-INDIVIDUAL COVARIATION.[1] (Test-occasion variation. Person constant.) Here differences between persons are not involved. The variation is that of time and test within one person. The lines lie in the plane *OB–OC* (and others parallel thereto). The two possibilities are:

3 *a*. *Intra-individual correlation (and analysis) of test-mutation relationships.* One pairs the scores of one person with regard to a series of applications of any two tests, as represented by the line system b_1b_1'' with b_2b_2''. A common factor would represent a unity among certain performances in relation to fluctuations produced by physiological, environmental, or other influences, or merely by time changes. This seems to be especially important in the investigation of dynamic trait unities and of unique traits generally. (*52*)

3 *b*. *Intra-individual correlation (and analysis) of occasions.* The scores (or rank orders) of a series of tests given to one person are correlated with the same series given on another occasion. The factors would be positions of equilibrium of the total personality with respect to different occasions. This is the mathematical device required for the objective study of multiple personality, in regard to the slighter manifestations of such equilibrium positions in "normal" persons. The typical correlation is represented by the line system c_5c_5'' with c_8c_8''.

These six designs necessarily exhaust the theoretical possibilities for absolute scores — i.e., if the correlated measures are literal measurements. But further designs, of great practical importance and clear psychological significance, emerge if one considers covariation in which the individual measurements employed are *differences* or *ratios* of absolute measurements. To be meaningful, the differences or ratios have to be those between systematically paired scores. That is to say, they lie between paired, parallel lines in the diagram. Consequently the new designs obtainable can be exhaustively ex-

---

[1] If, as seems likely, Stephenson's term "Q-technique" becomes adopted for 1 *b* above, it would be convenient to adapt Burt's term "P-technique" to refer to this analysis within the single person.

plored by substituting a *strip* for each line in the first set of designs, the strip being bounded by the two sets of scores between which differences are taken.

A strip, developed from any one line, may lie in either of two planes, at right angles. There are, it is true, other possibilities geometrically, but they are psychologically meaningless. One could, for example, let the differences lie along the length of a line, as when one correlates one series of people on two tests, the score attached to one person being the difference of his score from that of the next person; or one could allow the two correlated strips to be other than parallel. Confining the exploration to the more widely meaningful situations, one would find, on account of the two strips possible for each line, twelve possibilities in place of the six based on absolute measurements. They are outlined with great brevity in Table 7 (II).

TABLE 7 (II)

Twelve Designs of Covariation Using (B) Differential Measurements

B 1. Static Covariation of Differences. This is analogous to A 1, with the edges of the strips in OA–OB.

1 *a*. *Test increment correlation among tests*. One correlates increments in test scores, as between two occasions, for a series of persons on any two tests. The factors will be developmental functional unities — of learning, maturation, or physiological influence, according to the experimental design. Typical strip $b_{10}b_{10}'bc_{10}bc_{10}'$, taken in conjunction with a parallel strip.

1 *b*. *Test difference correlation among tests*. One correlates two scores for a series of persons, each score being the difference between test X and test Y in one series and test U and test W in the other. The strips will lie in the plane of OA–OB.

1 *c* and 1 *d* are the technique equivalents of 1 *a* and 1 *b*.

B 2. Monovariate Covariation of Differences. Analogous to A 2.

2 *a*. *Monovariate correlation of occasions as occasion differences*.

2 *b*. *Monovariate correlation of occasions as test differences*. A factor here would run through a set of occasions in which persons' differences as between two performances tend to be alike. It is a likely design for exploring dynamic traits.

2 *c*. *Monovariate correlation of persons respecting person differences*.

2 *d*. *Monovariate correlation of persons respecting test differences*.

TABLE 7 (II) — *Continued*

B 3. INTRA-INDIVIDUAL COVARIATION OF DIFFERENCES. Analogous to A 3.

3 *a. Intra-individual correlation of tests respecting test differences.* This leads to the discovery of those differences of performance between tests which are functionally associated.

3 *b. Intra-individual correlation of tests respecting person differences.* If the differences in both tests are with respect to the same second person, this design might be used to explore the hereditary similarity of identical and fraternal twins with respect to maturation and learning processes.

3 *c. Intra-individual correlation of occasions respecting person differences.*

3 *d. Intra-individual correlation of occasions respecting differences of occasion.* Factors in these last two designs will be unities among occasions, in the life of a single individual and with respect to his differences from other persons on a series of tests or from his own score on these tests on another occasion. The latter may be one standard occasion or a different occasion for the two series. Indeed, throughout the present twelve different series the difference can be from the same or from two different standards for the two series of differences involved in the correlation.

3. THE PRACTICAL RICHNESS OF THE FORMULATED THEORETICAL COVARIATION SCHEME

Discussion of further possible designs. While it has to be admitted that the above eighteen designs do not *absolutely* exhaust the resources of data for covariational analyses, they certainly leave designs only of an altogether lower order of originality and independence, scarcely one of which has any meaning for practical research issues. These residual correlatable series consist chiefly of (1) the paired series of measurements constituted by various oblique parallel pairs of lines through the parallelepiped, (2) lines in further but secondary dimensions which might be introduced into the figure. A new dimension would be one whereby a person or a test is systematically modified through a series of changes made continuously in one direction; e.g., a test might be given under increasingly speeded conditions or to persons increasing in fatigue or years of age. As indicated in the footnote on page 96, the occasions could not be distinguished from one another unless they differed in conditions additional to those which constitute the test situation. The original scheme can handle such modifications, by means of the "occasions" axis, if they occur only in test or person but not in both. But for changes carried out simultaneously — e.g., one test applied to one person, the test or the person being simultaneously modified in two directions to create two parallel series — a new axis, perhaps most simply viewed as a new "occasions" or "conditions" axis, is needed. With one exception, however (that constituted by bb_{n-1}'' with b_1b_n'', and discussed below under dynamic sequences or subsidiation within a dynamic trait), these additional variants are meaningless or valuable only for recondite issues or esoteric, specialized problems.

Origins of customary limitations of correlation. Historically it is clear that the needs of particular experiments have dictated the directions of development of correlation techniques. Indeed, at no point has there appeared in the literature any broad view of the theoretical possibilities of correlation sources. For instance, the incontinent improvisations of applied psychology in the psychometric field led historically to a great concentration on covariation in the OA–OB plane of Diagram 6. There followed such competitive keenness on the technical punctilio of methods in this realm, that it is little wonder psychologists failed to look around and recognize the larger universe of possibilities in which they stood. Even when other directions of correlation were employed, there was no attempt to employ covariation to detect manifestations of the same unities in different situations. Factor analysts have concerned themselves almost exclusively with the plane OA–OB; experimental psychologists have crept gingerly over parts of the plane OA–OC; while clinical psychologists have dealt freely, though without any mathematical method or accuracy, with covariation in the plane OB–OC. These groups of psychologists proceeded as if each operated through some remote, methodological approach quite unconnected with the other.

The present theoretical approach tries to transcend the viewpoint of custom and to reveal, in a single system of thought, the gamut of possible covariation observations, used and unused, on which inferences about psychological entities may be based. One sees, in the light of this formulation, that the R- and Q- techniques, on which the extant factor analyses of abilities and personality factors have solely depended, are but the visible part of an iceberg. It is true that some of these submerged possibilities do not correspond to convenient or practicable experimental procedures, while others belong to social psychology rather than the study of the individual. The majority, however, are designs each of which points to some entirely original experimental approach or even to some novel psychological concept. Indeed, the parallelepiped of Diagram 6 is a treasure chest of suggestions for effective new research approaches, any one of which will long defy exhaustion by the industrious experimentalist.

The designs which apply particularly to the delineation of trait structure in the individual, and which offer themselves as sources of supply for the independent correlation matrices[1] needed to determine rotation of axes by means of the principle of parallel proportional profiles, are as follows:

A 1 (*a*) Static correlation of tests. (R-technique)
A 1 (*b*) Static correlation of persons. (Q-technique)
A 3 (*a*) Intra-individual correlation of test mutations. (P-technique)

---

[1] The principle of proportional profiles for guiding rotation of axes to positions corresponding to real functional unities has not yet been described, and cannot appropriately be described, until the strictly mathematical discussions of Chapter 9 are taken up. But the general principle can be quite clearly stated at this point — that more than one type of covariation has to be observed to confirm the persistence of a covariation pattern in different situations — and in the light of that principle it is already obvious that correlation matrices from diverse sources of observation need to be obtained.

B 1 (*a*) Test increment correlations among tests. (S-technique)

B 1 (*c*) Test increment correlation among persons.

Apart from the Q-technique equivalents, A 1 (*b*) and B 1 (*c*), which may not be adequately independent, these matrices are independent yet comparable. They deal with functional unities which manifest themselves by common variation of elements (*a*) in occurrence in a population, (*b*) in growth, and (*c*) in day-to-day fluctuation within one individual. Further matrices, which would yield factors comparable only in some respects — e.g., only with respect to hereditary, constitutional contributions [1] — are as follows:

B 3 (*b*) Intra-individual correlation of tests respecting person differences.

B 2 (*b*) Monovariate correlation of persons respecting person differences.

The following may be expected to yield factors relating in special ways to the factors in the above sets of matrices.

B 1 (*b*) Test difference correlation among tests.

B 3 (*a*) Intra-individual correlation of tests respecting test differences.

The correlations of occasions (O-technique) are presumably also capable of yielding contributory matrices, aiding in the confirmation of factors, if the occasions are associated with specific provocations to dynamic or temperamental traits.

4. THE METHODS SPECIALLY APPLICABLE TO DISCOVERING DYNAMIC TRAITS, UNIQUE OR COMMON, AND FLUCTUATING TRAITS GENERALLY

Specialization of further development. Space forbids adequate illustration of each of the avenues of covariation study

---

[1] For example, the designs B 1 (*b*) and B 3 (*b*) could be used with a series of twin pairs, correlating the differences of the twins with respect to certain tests. The trait unities which are products of environment will then appear as factors, whereas those which are constitutional will presumably not manifest themselves in the differences of identical twins.

briefly defined in the preceding conspectus. The importance of one or two, and their previous neglect by research workers, justifies, however, an expanded treatment of them in the rest of this chapter.

At this point the reader whose main interests are practical and who wishes only to acquire the minimum theoretical background necessary for intelligent use of the actual factors and source traits of the preceding four chapters may be advised (if he has grasped the argument thoroughly up to this point) to omit the rest of this chapter and the whole of Chapter 7. Nevertheless, the subsequent arguments are essential to a complete theory of personality measurement and are very important for the development, by further research, of fields of practical knowledge about personality beyond those at present garnered into our last four chapters.

The exploration of dynamic traits. For many aspects of personality diagnosis and treatment, notably the psychiatric, no traits are of greater importance than those which we have called dynamic. Yet clinical psychology has been innocent of any attempt at a methodology and systematic theory which would make possible the operational and experimental delimitation and measurement of dynamic traits. The present section and the one following describe the development of criteria and research methods for dealing with dynamic traits.

First, through common observation, we notice that it is a characteristic — not the most essential or unique characteristic, however — of dynamic traits to fluctuate from day to day in response either to (*a*) internal physiological conditions or (*b*) the changes in press of general external stimuli (provocations). Temperamental and ability traits may also fluctuate, but seemingly much less.

We are proposing that correlations should be carried out on longitudinal observations, therefore — i.e., according to the schemes which have been classified as A 3, B 3, and to a lesser extent B 1 (*a*) in the covariation chart. The simplest situation is that in which a variety of narrow functions (trait elements) are measured in one individual on each of a series of days, with the effect as shown in Diagram 7. Correlation

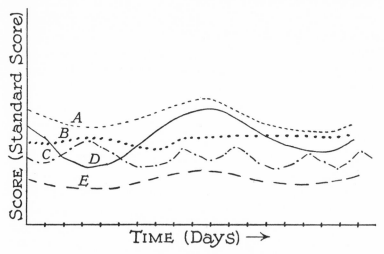

DIAGRAM 7. BEHAVIOR OF TRAITS IN TEMPORAL COVARIATION

of temporal series for each pair of tests will then give a correlation matrix from which those tests varying together will be found to share a common factor. Thus the possession of a common factor by tests A, D, and E, showing temporal relations as in the following diagram, will be revealed by correlation. Of course, as the discussion of Chapter 7 on modalities will show, it is only under special conditions that the elements of one modality — e.g., dynamic modality — are separated from the total factor in all its modality aspects; but these conditions very frequently hold in psychometric measurement and we shall suppose that they are maintained, to select dynamic responses, in the present method of experiment.

The mathematical manifestations of goals and equivalents.
There are two other important ways, however, in which
dynamic trait behavior differs from that of other traits and
in a more absolute sense than with respect to the amount of
fluctuation. (1) The behavior of a dynamic trait persists
until a goal is reached and then ceases, or alters. (2) Certain
forms of behavior act as "equivalents" — i.e., as alternate
manifestations of the same drive — so that as one becomes
more prominent the other declines. That is to say, in any
temporal series correlation they will tend[1] to be *negatively*
correlated. Such relations do not exist with abilities or temperament traits.

The fact that *negative* correlation may actually indicate that
two behavior manifestations belong to one functional unity
is not widely realized. To bring out more clearly this peculiarity of the dynamic trait we shall explore here in a specific
illustration the relationships involved. First we shall see
what mathematical relationships exist when there is "dynamic equivalence" between two kinds of behavior, and secondly what mathematical relationships indicate goal-directed,
subsidiated behavior — i.e., we shall take (2) above first.

Equivalence, and the subsidiated structure normally found
in dynamic traits — i.e., the hierarchy of purposes of which
habitual responses are a part — can be expected to reveal
themselves in several distinct approaches to covariation.
They will appear in *Static Covariation* experiments ("equivalence" being shown by opposite-sign loadings in group factors) and in various *Intra-Individual Covariation Designs and in
Test Increment Correlation between Tests*.

Let us consider first static covariation. We shall begin by
assuming a dynamic structure of known pattern and shall then
proceed to find out what correlations this would produce. ·

---

[1] They will not usually be actually negatively correlated, for the negative relation
is offset by the positive one, due to their sharing the major fluctuations of the total
underlying drive.

In Diagram 8 we take the simplest population for illustrating a correlation — namely, a population of two persons. The diagram represents, for each person, a basic drive, which first becomes invested in two major directions of distinct discharge and later ramifies into still more numerous interest investments. In the later investments some drives run together again or even join with products of entirely different basic drives, as in many common sentiments.

Let us suppose that the first individual is endowed with a strength of drive — e.g., sex drive — of 20 units and the second with 10. In the course of ontogenetic, individual development let us suppose that in each case some of the drive takes infantile fixation forms, α (left branch), and some β (right branch) moves on to more adult expression, and that their strengths are, respectively, 6 and 14 for the first person and 5 and 5 for the second. In adult life let us suppose these directions of expression have ended in the actual, detailed, overt interest investments A, B, C, D, E, F, and G. The problem is that of deducing the underlying dynamic structure merely from the *observed* measurements A, B, C, etc., made perhaps by the obstruction method or any other method of measuring the strength of interests which permits a rating or scoring of individuals.

Let us suppose the resulting measurements are those shown at A, B, C, D, etc., in the diagram. The approach to the full, complex problem is best made by considering first the situation at the simplest division of the dynamic stream — namely, where the measures α and β are obtained. α and β will tend to show (1) a negative correlation by reason of being complementary and (2) a positive correlation by reason of springing from a common total. The magnitude of the observed correlation, and whether it is negative or positive, will depend on whether, on the one hand, the (environmental?) forces determining the variations of degree of infantile fixation, or, on the other, the (hereditary?) circumstances determining the variations in natural endowment in the total drive

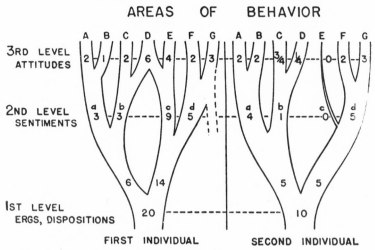

DIAGRAM 8. CORRELATIONS TO BE EXPECTED IN DYNAMIC TRAIT MANIFESTATIONS

strength in that population, are greater, and by how much. Consideration of the diagram will show that if the numbers at α and β are correlated for a whole series of subjects, and if from the correlation is partialed out the correlation of α and β with the original strength of the drive $(\alpha + \beta)$, the resulting correlation should be -1.

An examination of measurements at a "higher" level of development — i.e., when the original drive has become invested in still more alternative manifestations — will not yield so simple a mathematical analysis, as a glance at A, B, C, and D shows. However, one may deduce that the intercorrelation of these four measures could be factored into a positive general factor, a bipolar (i.e., positive and negative) general factor,[1] and two bipolar group factors, as shown in Diagram 9.

[1] The term "bipolar factor" has been used by Burt (27) for a factor that has as many negative as positive loadings. In this case it would be negative in a and b and positive in c and d — i.e., negative in A, B, C, D and positive in E, F, G. The next positive factor (group factor I) would be positive in a and negative in b. From this pattern of superposed factors we can deduce the underlying branching structure.

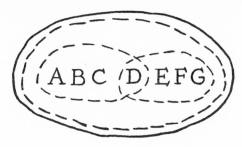

DIAGRAM 9. FACTOR PATTERNS IN DYNAMIC TRAIT MANIFESTATIONS

Behavior measurements, dynamic structure, and factor pattern. The above examples are of course much simpler than most that would be found in nature. The picture at the third level of complication and development comes nearer to most actual examples. Normally we have no direct access to the lower levels of the structure. They may — and probably did — exist as actual behavior manifestations in the earlier life of the subject and could be tapped by special clinical techniques even in adult life. But what the psychometrist has to deal with is a series of actual behavior manifestations. He is like a plumber who is given no map of the underlying connections but is asked to deduce, from the rates of flow from many faucets — and their mutual interferences — what conduit system exists.

For purposes of illustration the above diagram has been simplified, it should be noted, in a number of ways. In the first place it deals only with those trait elements common to all subjects and it assumes that the only structure which matters is common structure. In the second place, it takes account of comparatively few recombinations of secondary drives (as of A'' and B' in Diagram 10), whereas in real life the number of trait elements which are overdetermined by two or more converging purposes must be considerable. Thirdly, it involves in the diagram only one propensity, erg or basic biological drive, whereas in life most trait elements would be overdetermined by several of these also. Taking into account these changes, we should expect any factorial analysis of correlations of individual differences in dynamic trait elements to yield general (or almost general) factors corresponding to the main drives, bipolar group factors corresponding to bifurcations into sentiments or instinctual fixations, and various specific factors corresponding to the objects, attitudes, and interests of the final behavior pattern.

Now the same pattern of correlations and the same factors — excepting the first general factor — should be obtained from analysis of temporal, longitudinal covariation, either intra-individual or on group mean performances. If one piece of behavior repeatedly appears when another disappears (or, less drastically, waxes when another wanes) — e.g., a trait element of sociability and a trait element of interest in the opposite sex — then a negative correlation will be found between them and further analysis will show them to be affected oppositely by the same bipolar factor and to be, therefore, "equivalents." Of course, in experiment one need not wait for the daily conditions of life to produce fluctuations: one can deliberately block some outlet for expression and provoke the appearance of equivalents in emphatic form.

5. THE DETERMINATION OF SUBSIDIATION SEQUENCE
   OR TELEOLOGICAL CAUSATION [1]

The approach through temporal sequence. Let us consider next the operational determination of goals, dynamic

[1] As stated elsewhere (page 174), it is not supposed that "teleological causation" is more than a mere description of a *phenomenon* in psychology. It is not intended as a final category. Probably the surface teleological causation is ultimately to be interpreted as an arrangement of physical, "efficient" causalities. Notice, however, that as an *observed* relation it is precisely the opposite to ordinary physical causality. In establishing the latter we find out which one, among a great variety of events, *invariably precedes* the event in question — e.g., lightning is considered the cause of thunder because lightning, more consistently than any other event, precedes thunder. On the other hand, if a child's trait of abuse against another tends to be invariably *followed* by his hitting the second child, we conclude that the abuse is part of a dynamic trait — pugnacity — directed to damaging the other child.

sequences, or teleological causation. Here we seek to uncover the dynamic subsidiation pattern in a different way: we map the structure by, as it were, moving *along* the branches. Or, if we return to our hydraulic analogy, the plumber now attempts to discover the conduit structure by squeezing a pipe at one point and observing at what places farther on the flow is affected.

In any purposive sequence or "subsidiation" of behavior we are accustomed to say that each piece of behavior is done "for" some more remote end. A man acquires, say, a trait element of "punctuality at one's job" because he does not want to lose his job, he wants to keep the job because he wants to get married, and so on. The test of the purpose of a trait element is to find which one, out of many items, alone invariably follows the first.[1] In spite of the fact that we are constantly concerned in daily life with testing the real motives of the people we meet, notably those of hypocrites and neurotics, the basic operational test is seldom explicitly understood, even by psychologists.

Consider Diagram 10, which is essentially Diagram 8 placed on its side to emphasize the temporal sequences of behavior events, and which is somewhat simplified by omission of bifurcations. Here are illustrated three "equivalents" for a common dynamic need of expression. If we consider the equivalent sequences A′, etc., and A″, etc., our proof that A′ lies on the subsidiation path to D′ and not to D″ is that the appearance of A′ is apt to be followed by D′ and not by D″. This is not, generally, an all or nothing phenomenon. Instead we may find that an unusual *amount* of A′ is invariably followed by an unusual amount of D′ (rather than an unusual amount of D″, though D″ actually appears). If a boy takes the quickest route home from school whenever he eats an unusually large dinner afterward, we may conclude that his

---

[1] This could be achieved, if people were honest and omniscient, simply by reiterating "What for?" to every answer.

behavior is a manifestation of hunger. Or, more obscurely, if a child is more prone to temper tantrums on the afternoons of those days when he spends the evenings unduly close to his mother, we may conclude that the tantrums are somehow part of the drive to gain affection.

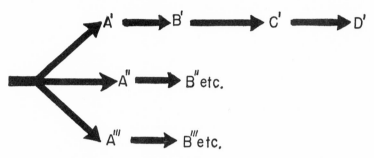

DIAGRAM 10. DYNAMIC SUBSIDIATION AND EQUIVALENCE

The technique for discovering dynamic subsidiation — i.e., for connecting behavior with its proximate or remote goals — therefore becomes as follows: One takes two or more behavior manifestations in a supposed behavior sequence and measures them on a series of occasions constituted by the repetition of the supposed behavior sequence. One then correlates the series (presuming circumstances produce differences among the occasions). A high correlation of two performances indicates that they belong to the same subsidiation path to a common final goal.

For example, one might take, on one hundred days, the performance of a rat (*a*) on the activity wheel in the morning and (*b*) in running a maze to reach food in the afternoon. An appreciable correlation indicates that both share a certain drive — hunger — which fluctuates from day to day. By taking a large number of performances, especially with deliberate daily alteration of incentives, one could find which performances are and which are not part of the same dynamic sequence. Here again a performance farther back in the sequence, satisfiable by either of two equivalents, would show itself by an intermediate size of correlation with either of the subsidiation sequences A′ and A″.

How, then, is the final goal to be discovered, by which the whole subsidiation chain is named (in the above instance "hunger")? It might be argued that the final goal or incentive in any subsidiation sequence will identify itself by being the temporarily last detectable correlated item in a series of performances correlated with respect to occasions. But this conclusion is not entirely safe. All the behaviors that arise from hunger cease when the rat is fed — i.e., they are the correlated items standing out from among all items that preceded the feeding, and it might be supposed that the feeding is recognizable (if we did not know, on general grounds, that it was the goal) by being the last correlated item in the series. But this is not the whole story. There are behavior items following satiation that are also a function of — i.e., correlated with — the final performance of eating. Indeed, there seems to be no point short of death at which any drive is wholly quiescent and without influence. The proof that a piece of behavior is the final goal achievement would seem to be (1) that it is *more* correlated (in crescendo form) with items that precede it than with those that follow it — i.e., the relation is a relative one — and (2) that its mean correlation, within the group of correlated items forming the subsidiation sequence or trait, is higher than that for any other item. In factor analytic terms this can be interpreted by saying that the vigor of the goal behavior — i.e., the measurement of the performance at the goal — is more highly *loaded* with the general factor which delimits and constitutes the dynamic trait in question than is any other behavior falling on the subsidiation path to the goal. For the correlation of these other behaviors with their final expression is likely to be attenuated by all chance slips between the cup and the lip, by the intrusion of various other motives into the sequence, and by the imperfections in the perception of cues and incentives remote from the final goal.

The difficulty or undue abstractness which some may experience in the above propositions may tempt the less-determined student to believe that the easier, intuitive path, such as is used in everyday life and seemingly in clinical practice, is quite sufficient. It may be necessary, therefore, to challenge this common view very explicitly, by emphasizing that the present contention states that the unities which constitute traits, and the purposive connections in behavior, can be established scientifically *only* by such observations of covariation and sequence (covariation of occasions) in behavior. It is, of course, true that in daily life we establish teleological sequences by other "methods." For instance, we ask a man to tell us for what more remote purpose he carries out an act, or we judge as observers from the formal, stylistic similarity of the supposed "equivalent" behavior, as when we say that a man who kicks a chair really wants to punch his opponent's head. Yet we do not trust either of these cheap methods, introspective or intuitive, even in routine practice, beyond a certain point. The hysteric cannot say why he suffers from impaired vision, nor can the psychological observer intuit whether a man who is pounding the piano does so to express aggressiveness, lust, or fear. In the end, dynamic, teleological causality has to be established like any other causality, by proving covariation in a temporal sequence. This becomes more clearly evident if one turns to the study of animal motivation. The psychoanalytic method of free association, as it proceeds along a chain of situations, is a loose, unstatistical, and unchecked application of the sequential method.

6. THE METHODS OF DELIMITATION AND MEASUREMENT OF UNIQUE TRAITS

Unique traits too important to be abandoned. Much of the methodology worked out above for common traits applies equally to unique traits. The above form of intra-individual correlation is *the* primary method for investigating functional unities in the individual, especially dynamic unities.

Before exploring the techniques in more detail it is necessary to examine the notion of unique trait as such, to see whether any modifications have become necessary in the simple verbal notion with which we started.

Clinical psychology especially asserts the importance of unique traits. Any studies on dynamic traits, such as interests, in regard to scholastic and occupational prediction is bound to emerge with the conclusion that dynamic traits cannot be ignored; and dynamic traits tend especially to be unique, peculiar to the individual adaptation and history. A psychometry which ignored individual, unique traits would not only be one addicted to crude outlines of personality but also would miss the very flesh on the skeleton outline constituted by common traits.

Therefore, in spite of the great theoretical difficulties and the irrelevance of the whole subject to the psychometrist whose practical problems are those of mass, approximate, personnel prediction, we shall devote these sections to its intensive study. A psychology which neglects the most individual traits cannot help much in the future of a society the first tenet of which is respect for individuality.

A first analysis suggests two kinds of uniqueness. The verbal approach from which we took our start can lead readily to the notion that there are two kinds of uniqueness: (*a*) Uniqueness of pattern — i.e., the individual has the same trait elements as other persons, but in unique proportions. (*b*) Uniqueness of dimension — i.e., the individual may have an entirely new trait element not possessed by others in any degree whatever. In parentheses one should point out here that for practical purposes a unique trait does not have to be *absolutely* unique — i.e., the only instance in the universe.

A trait that is *rare* enough to defy common trait-measuring devices has to be treated as a unique trait.

At the outset it is necessary to distinguish between the notion of a unique trait and that of unique units of measurement; indeed, this discussion soon forces us to an explicit treatment of the whole problem of units of measurement.

The trait elements which may enter into the pattern of a common or unique trait — except in sense (*b*) above — are themselves common traits measured in common units, for we measure them as common traits and neglect any peculiarities. Such trait elements might be: reaction time, number of strangers spoken to in a day, length of time in seconds a person remains silent, lateness to appointments, acceleration in warming-up period in games, magnitude of psychogalvanic reflex to pain, etc.

Any single trait element has its variance accounted for by several factors — i.e., it is a part of several covariance patterns.[1] For this reason we may well ask whether uniqueness in the first of the above senses (pattern) is not illusory. If we take any configuration[2] whatsoever of common trait elements, can this not be accounted for and reproduced by a suitable combination of common factor patterns?[3] Mathe-

[1] This last statement, of course, applies to factors or *source* traits. It has no mathematical meaning with regard to representation by surface traits.

[2] The term "configuration" will be distinguished from pattern in this discussion as follows. A configuration means a shape (set of relationships) in a single concrete instance. A pattern means a pattern of covariation — i.e., the elements and their loci of movement with respect to a population of instances.

[3] Perhaps before dealing with the *real* mathematical difficulties it would be profitable to help those unfamiliar with the mathematical foundations to overcome certain *misconceptions* which have grown up about past mathematical findings.

As an illustration let us recall what happened when such careful experimenters as Hartshorne and May (*111*) found distinctly low correlations between different measures of honesty. As a result, apparently, of having expected perfect correlation (when corrected for attenuation), they and others concluded disappointedly that there were no general traits but only specific stimulus-response consistencies. This conclusion, so devastating to psychology as a simple predictive science, seemed in harmony with the results of the previous decade showing negligible transfer of training.

Allport rejected this conclusion through one of the possible logical loopholes, arguing that the specifists had not disproved trait unity; instead they had only

matically there is no doubt; the answer is "yes" — if the case in question has been included in the population from which the factors were established.   Any set of actual trait element quantities can be reproduced by a particular combination of factors, and *every* individual is a unique combination of factors.

Consider a simple physical example: the representation of the individuality of human hands, in so far as it concerns finger lengths.   The shape of the hand can be defined by measures for each of the five digits (trait elements) or alternatively

proved that they themselves had been engaged in an uninspired search for the wrong instances or kinds of unity.

That, for example, the highly aggressive man would not be equally aggressive in all situations nor the honest man equally honest in all is precisely what would be expected from the superimposition and interaction of several factors, operating on the same trait elements — e.g., the overlap of environmental mold and constitutional patterns.   For two men equally aggressive by constitution might be unequally affected by an environmental mold, so that the various situations (trait element measures) of aggression would not rank them in the same order.   Incidentally, the absence of perfect correlation seemed to blind the specificists to the fact that in the large-scale Hartshorne-May research substantial positive correlations of trait elements were nevertheless found.   The correlations are entirely consistent with a general factor being at work, but not one which accounts for *all* the variance of any one trait element.   The difficulty vanishes if one thinks of unity in terms of source traits — i.e., factors instead of surface traits only.

Actually most clinical discussion seems to confuse two ways in which a trait has some specificity to a situation.   The writers mistakenly invoke specificity both because *all* people show a trait — e.g., dominance unequally in different situations — and because one person reacts to apparently the same situation differently on different occasions.   First, the general traits at work are modified in each particular trait element by reason of the interaction just discussed.   Secondly, since the factors as measured in factor analysis are on the basis of situations of a *certain standard strength* of provocation (usually the average found in everyday life), it is obvious that the predicted reactions in any particular trait element situation must take account further of *changes functionally dependent on* the strength of the stimulus situation.   X may be unusually aggressive regarding trait element *a* because the situation of *a* is unusually strong in his life.   This may seem very obvious but is frequently overlooked in discussions on specificity and uniqueness.

One must be on guard against considering specific factors — i.e., factors specific to one trait element — to be the same as uniqueness.   True, the specifics — i.e., the variance unaccounted for by common factors or communality — will be greater when the population concerned is rich in individuals with unique traits, for no amount of common variance can then account for all the differences in trait elements.   But this seems to be only a matter of incompleteness of research.   In time this specificity can be resolved into specific factors which are truly common to all persons and certain new dimensions of variation which exist only in certain individuals.

by perhaps two or three mathematical factors (abstract source traits) — plus five specific factors — by which the lengths of the five digits can best be predicted.[1] Thus there is one extensive sense in which "uniqueness" is used which resolves itself into a *unique combination of common traits or factors* both general and specific. It is contended by the writer that there is a tendency among some psychologists to fall back too readily, either in theory or practice, upon the "necessity" for defining by unique traits when common traits could be used. Recourse to unique traits is often nothing more than a lack of imagination in envisaging how the trait elements in question could be embodied in a common trait. On the mathematical level it is a failure to bring into a correlation matrix such psychological variables as will increase the communality — i.e., for lack of which too much of the variance has to be left outside general or group factors.

Mathematically the presence of many unique patterns — i.e., the absence of obvious, powerful common surface traits — would seem to imply lower correlations of trait elements, lesser variance absorbed in general factors and more in specific factors. But specific factors are just as much common traits as are general or group factors. Incidentally it will be seen in our final analysis of personality data that only about half the variance (individual difference) in all personality traits can be accounted for by general factors. There seems to be no

[1] The extent of the uniqueness permitted by factor analysis is sometimes not realized by its critics. First, the individual has a unique amount of any one common factor. Secondly, he has a unique position in an *n*-dimensional space, when *n* factors are required. Thirdly, he may have uniqueness in any one measurement through a specific factor or error variance which may be considered either as specific to the individual or the test. For instance, when one defines a common trait (a correlation cluster or factor) by the set of trait elements which "go together" most consistently to constitute the factor, cluster, or syndrome, it is not unusual to meet the objection, among those who stress uniqueness, that in actual fact no individual ever has this exact syndrome of trait elements in the typical, proportional strengths. This is true; but the strengths of the trait elements are determined by *all* the common factors, and the uniqueness which the critic claims to be unrepresented in the mathematical picture is in fact represented by the unique combination of factor endowment in that individual, accounting for the unique pattern of trait element strengths.

guarantee that the behavior which is accounted for by specific factors — i.e., that part of a trait element not accounted for by general factors — is, psychologically, absolutely the same for all persons; though in the behavior dimension measured it is. This point is somewhat subtle, better reëxamined after further reading; it amounts to saying that we know the character of something of which we have many measured aspects (the general factor) but not much of the character of that of which we have only one measurement (the trait element).

The upshot of this discussion would seem to be that, except for the possible uniqueness of the specific factor character just discussed, the first kind of uniqueness posited in the clinical approach does not really exist. It is reducible to unique endowment in common traits. Beyond this spurious "uniqueness of pattern," however, exists the second uniqueness — of dimension. To take an extreme example: a human being might be born with direct sensitivity to waves of radio frequency. This would introduce an entirely new trait element, or set of trait elements — a dimension of measurement not existing for other human beings.

This second and unquestionable sense in which a trait can be unique we may call an *intrinsic unique trait*, because its very trait elements are unique. Of course, the physical units in which the new trait element is measured will not be unique; they belong to the common environment of all people — e.g., if a human eye became sensitive to infra red, its sensitivity could be measured in common *physical* units.

The two problems which arise in connection with all traits must now be cleared up in respect to the intrinsic unique trait, as follows: (1) How can the form of the traits, its boundaries and functional unitariness, be determined? and (2) How can its quantity be measured?

The issues involved are most readily grasped by returning to the same physical analogy used in discussing the first kind of uniqueness — in the form of a human hand. Intrinsic uniqueness would here correspond to the appearance of a sixth finger — an entirely new trait element not existing in the pattern of other hands.

First let us note that it is impossible either (*a*) to produce any inter-individual correlation: functional unity can be shown, if at all, only by intra-individual correlation — i.e., that the finger is a part of the functional unity of the hand can be shown only by the simultaneous waxing and waning of its strength along with that of the other fingers — or (*b*) to measure the finger in normative units — i.e., we cannot say whether a sixth finger or a capacity to see infra red is strongly or poorly developed; we have no standards.[1]

Unique traits: their boundaries and measurement units. In practice the problem of unique traits boils down to the discovery, delimitation, and measurement of *rare* traits — principally dynamic traits and largely rare interests and symptoms. To set up, in any personality-assessment scheme, the frame of almost infinite categories required to meet possible rare traits is impractical. The psychologist must depend on alert observation to spot such traits. Nevertheless, a limited list

---

[1] The mathematically sophisticated may object that as soon as a single further instance of a six-fingered man is discovered, the trait ceases to be unique (and it is practically impossible to find a psychological trait element that does not recur a few times in nearly two thousand million persons). If another is found, a new continuum can be set up, and the two men concerned can be measured in the standard scores of their "population" from a common average in a common trait. From this simple instance the logical mathematician may next proceed to argue that the same is really possible when there is only one case — by assuming that all the other persons have a sixth finger of zero dimensions. Between this zero and the single positive quantity a scale of six-fingeredness can be erected and correlations worked out with the lengths of the other fingers. From this mathematical viewpoint the unique is only the extreme instance of the common; it is the unusual score appearing still farther out on the tail of the distribution; it is an asymptote of the normal.

But this is a barren mathematical and logical victory, for in practice nothing is gained. The normative measurement is in a dimension uninhabited and desert, depending for its meaning on the frail thread of a single individual score. The correlations, even if carried out as a tertachoric correlation, is worthless on so skewed a population (one above average, the rest below), and even if it were relied upon the new dimension might prove to be irresolvable into the existing common factors and require largely a new factor dimension for its own representation.

covering possible areas of important unique behavior might be helpful; for it must never be forgotten that whether we deal with common or unique traits their presence and true outlines cannot be discovered unless the requisite variables (trait elements) are made available.

As for boundaries, that behavior which cannot be correlated and brought within the functional unity of a general factor can only have its limits defined as a "logical trait unity." The meaning of a trait is normally defined by its functional unity — e.g., it is the set of correlated reactions associated with a pyknic physique. When one cannot be certain of the functional unity, one can only take all those pieces of behavior which fit into no known functional unity and define them "logically" — i.e., by certain boundaries in terms of physical and social effects. However, whenever intra-individual correlation, followed by factor analysis, can be applied, a true delimitation of the function unity of the intrinsic unique trait is possible.

Nevertheless, its units of measurement cannot be normative (except with respect to the comparatively useless standardization in terms of the range of its fluctuation in that one individual) and must remain in terms of what we have called in the following section "interactive" units.

Obviously the investigation of certain aspects of unique traits — e.g., their nature-nurture ratio — presents greater problems than for common traits, even when they are well delimited and measured.

7. ARE TRAIT ELEMENTS DEFINABLE AS COMMON TRAITS OF CONSISTENT CHARACTER?

Possible hidden assumptions in trait elements. Throughout this chapter the assumption has been made that any trait can be broken down into "trait elements." This could be attacked on two grounds: (1) From the viewpoint of doctrinaire Gestalt theory that a whole cannot be broken down into and reconstituted from parts, and (2) from the ground of the above discussion, arguing that *some uniqueness will enter into each individual's measurement even on a very narrowly, operationally defined trait element*. For example, it may be said that the "talkativeness in company" of the maniac is not the same as that of the hysteric, that a physicist's skill in using a slide rule is not the same kind of skill as that of a psychologist with the same instrument, that the irritability to noise of the hyperthyroid temperament is not the same as that of the neurasthenic, and so on. This uniqueness we may call the *organic character* of the trait element.

With regard to the intrusion of Gestalt theory, whatever may be true of sense perception (where wholes can be considered points of arrest in hierarchies of relations), the fact remains that here we start with actual measurements of trait elements and the wholes undoubtedly arise as systems of relations among them.

To examine further and develop the difference between the *actually measured trait dimension* and the possibly unique *specific factor character* adumbrated in the last section, we shall call that which we actually measure, in the same way for all persons, the *literal trait element* — e.g., a reaction time in seconds to a note of pitch 250, etc. The whole behavior involved in the trait element, and of which our measurement is an attempt at measuring the most salient dimension, we shall call the *organic trait element*. Our aim now is to clarify the extent to which our measurements and methods of investigation succeed in defining the organic character of common traits and unique traits.

Research begins by measuring only the literal trait element. But when the factor (pattern) is discovered to which certain trait elements contribute, their own nature becomes illuminated by the whole which they have created and to which they belong. If "talkativeness" is found highly contributory to the hypomanic syndrome, future measurements of this trait element, *for the estimation of that particular syndrome*, can be made more efficient by reshaping the measurement of the trait element a little to make it a measure more of *that particular kind of talkativeness which is part of the hypomanic syndrome.* That is, we shape the *literal trait element* to align it with, and make it a better measure of, the *organic trait element.*

In short, the personality research psychologist has to proceed here by a method of "successive approximations," using relatively vague, shifting, or blindly guessed landmarks and refining them until he finds those which are very highly loaded with the one factor that interests him. This need to sketch in broadly and roughly before settling on final, precise trait elements is the reason why the research in this book begins with widely sampled ratings rather than test performances in a narrow field.

However, those who advocate searching *always* for the organic trait element forget that for many purposes this is not desirable. For the purpose of estimating simultaneously, from one battery of measurements, several different factors, we cannot refine any literal trait element in the direction of "organic-ness" as required by any one factor. The variance of one trait element contributes to *several* factors. In practice one may need to retain, in one battery, elements that have optimum utility for measuring several factors at once. Then the trait element must be retained in its original form, in greatest simplicity, and with its clearest, most stable, and most practical "logical" definition.

It is in applied psychology, where some one factor needs to be measured by a particular test battery, that we can expect most refinement of trait elements toward the meaning of one factor, as has occurred in the evolution of intelligence test subtests. Moreover, even in general and theoretical work, it is often advantageous to discover trait elements which are almost exclusively measures of one factor, for thereby one can most surely discover and define the nature of the factor. Concentration on the organic type of trait element helps to define the nature of factors; concentration on the literal trait elements helps most to delimit their boundaries.

Concerning the "width" of trait elements. Any clearly, logically, and operationally defined trait element can be used to give measurements for factor analysis. But there are good reasons for preferring a trait element that is narrow in definition to one that is wide and inclusive. In applied psychology, this falls in with the aim of having trait elements that are organic; for such a trait element must be very specific in intent, in fact directed to the essence of a source trait quality, in order to contribute powerfully to the measurement of a single source trait. Secondly, in pure psychology, one cannot so readily establish the essential nature of a factor on a basis of blurred, vague trait elements as on those of very definite, limited behavior character. Thirdly, the discrepancy between the literal and the organic trait element becomes greater with a broader behavior manifestation.

Rating studies especially have suffered from this carelessness over trait elements, and the widespread lack of realization of how accurate good rating can be is partly due to this cause.

By what touchstone can we test the optimum size and nature of trait elements? The experimental work of Thomas, Loomis, and Arrington (253) indicates that by trial and error it is possible to arrive at fairly generalized behavior units that still have great consistency. Elsewhere (54) the present writer has advocated splitting behavior elements — e.g., splitting "sociability" into "sociable-gregarious" and "sociable-not-shy" — until the sub-traits correlate with each other to the level of their own reliability coefficients.

In the psychologist's search for graspable unities, for firm entities from which to start, he seems to have the same experience as the physical and biological scientists. Wholeness and unity can be found by proceeding far enough in either direction — downward to the cell and the electron, upward to the star or the organism. One can achieve some sort of consistent atomicity in the trait element that is so narrow as to be covered by a single measurement or in the organic functional unity of the broad factor or syndrome.

Shrewd clinical observation must be the best guide to the "absolute size" of behavior sections at which one can most readily strike these natural "smaller" units. The experimenter searching for certain syndromes is in the position of the radio listener desiring some melody from the ether; he has first to find the wave length of the stuff in terms of which the larger configuration may be perceived. In most psychological work the temptation will be overwhelmingly toward making the trait elements too large, for few persons will have the time and patience to split supposed unitary trait elements again and again until the split correlation reaches the level of a split-half consistency coefficient.

Trait elements are bounded by logical, physical definition. Though it is mentioned in the above discussion, we shall re-emphasize here that though the common traits which emerge from studying trait elements have unities of a true, organic (social mold or constitutional) kind and can be defined and normatively measured in appropriate units, the trait elements themselves are, at least in the beginning, *logical traits* (in the sense of section 3 above). That is to say, the behavior in question has to be defined purely by its performance character and delimited by some arbitrary, logical limits in the mind of the experimenter.[1] The experimenter defines a trait element of "mechanical aptitude" or "frustration tolerance" or "honesty" or "perseveration" by performance in a particular logically delimited situation. Out of these arbitrarily

---

[1] For example, the rate of tapping against a given spring resistance is a logically precisely defined performance, but is practically meaningless from the standpoint of the biological and social functions of the organism. However, it may turn out to belong to some larger functional unity the biological and social meaning of which will be deducible from the logical nature of the other trait elements heavily involved in the latter.

chopped-up bits of behavior, functional, organic trait unities may or may not appear, like designs in a mosaic.

When they *do* appear, the known, logical characters of the elements — i.e., of those elements which turn out to be heavily loaded with the factor in question — are the principal basis for deducing the essential character of the functional trait unity emerging as a pattern. This has been obviously the procedure in most factor analysis of abilities, where "intelligence" and "spatial ability" have been named from the character of the trait elements which play the largest part in them. These "logical trait" elements are the stable dust out of which transient,[1] organic psychological unities are defined, and to which their definition and measurement may have to return from the realm of living normative measurement. The "logical trait unity" which was rejected, on a number of cogent psychological grounds, as the standard form for describing, delimiting, and measuring the major traits of personality, thus becomes, from another aspect and considered at the level of the trait element, the veritable cornerstone of personality description.

8. THE DURABILITY OF TRAITS, AS ORGANISM-ENVIRONMENT
   RELATIONSHIPS

Duration and consistency of trait manifestations. Some appreciable duration, relative to the individual's life span, is normally implied in the term "trait"; yet it is almost impossible arbitrarily to fix the duration necessary for a trait. A mental set of an hour's duration, which gives an actor certain consistent modes of behavior in a play, does not give him those traits as a person; nor does a brief alcoholic capacity for being inordinately amused establish a trait of silliness as a regular characteristic.

---

[1] Transient because the covariation patterns change with the cultural design and the racial mixture of the population.

The possibility of instantaneous traits. A trait is normally a mental structure deduced from a continuous — or, more commonly, an intermittent — set of behavior manifestations, remaining recognizably consistent over some period. But if a piece of behavior repeats itself only once, in an unmistakable pattern, it can theoretically justify the deduction of a trait *structure* and the assignment of a label. On the basis of inter-individual difference measurements and factor analysis, a trait could be picked out even from instantaneous observations of behavior, dealing with manifestations which never again repeat themselves. But, though such a structure would have the "causal" (explanatory) properties of a trait, and the unity of quality and function which go therewith, we should not usually call it a trait. The explosion of an armor-piercing shell is characteristically different from a high explosive shell, and ballistic experts may deal with this as equivalent to a "trait" of the shell. In dealing with human beings, however, we are not interested to any extent in something which never happens again and which cannot be used to predict later behavior. The issue may seem an academic one, for there may in fact be no pieces of behavior found to exist which do not repeat themselves, granted the same circumstances (the latter being normally implied in "consistency"); but it clarifies the trait concept to bring this possibility into the open. Usually the psychologist gets more interested in traits which last with great stability and over longer periods of life, for these are more useful in prediction and in most applied psychological work. Yet there are traits — e.g., those of a manic period or a fugue state — which it is important to study and delimit even though they are brief.

Trait consistency. Just what degree of consistency — i.e., what reliability or consistency coefficient — one should demand in behavior manifestations to justify a trait is also an arbitrary matter, best left for discussion when more data have accumulated on trait consistency. (Note that some discussions (*8*) on "trait consistency" are not discussions of true, statistical consistency as implied by "consistency" or "reliability" coefficient, but of prediction from one form of trait manifestation to another — i.e., of what we have dealt with under covariation and factor analysis.)

The mutability of common and unique trait forms. It is in the very nature of both common and unique traits that they slowly change their forms, so that even if perfectly measured they should not give perfect repeat consistency coefficients. For a trait, as is repeatedly stressed in this book, is not a characteristic of the individual, inherent in the individual, but a relationship between the individual — or, rather, his group — and some real (or formerly real, or phantasy) object. It can be defined, as we have seen, only in terms of both organism and environment. Since both the constitution of the organism and its social and physical environment are constantly changing, no trait, unique or common, is unchanging. One cannot find personality traits (other than logically defined trait elements themselves) in terms (defined in the population of any single culture) of which Shakespeare and Diogenes, an Eskimo, a modern American, and an Australian Black can all be measured and accurately compared.

Only the slowness of cultural change, with respect to things important to human nature — e.g., family, religion, social competition, sexual inhibitions, group patriotism, etc. — and the still greater stability of man's genetic constitution, make it possible and worth while to spend time and effort in locating the great common trait functional unities and devising scales for their measurement.

The defining and quantifying of traits, especially the most common and most important, in normative units which change with the population and in terms of environmental objects which change with the cultural pattern, may nevertheless introduce some error when a common trait is measured and employed some time after the moment at which it was first born as a scientific datum.

Once a trait is established as a functional unity, it achieves, in the literature and in practice, a certain life of its own. In tests it becomes measured by a relatively small number of "token" sub-tests, which at some time in the past have been found the best indicators among a larger battery. Later, these tests may mislead, either because the factor loadings themselves have changed with some changing cultural pattern or because psychological discussions have lost sight of all the other variables which also play their part in defining the factor. It becomes primarily a verbal symbol — e.g., "general intelligence," "verbal ability."

Psychometry must not lose sight of the necessity for preserving the definition of source traits in terms of the exact, "logical" *trait-element* performances of the original researches which established those trait unities. Consider, for example, that a factor analysis of a large number of musical-appreciation test performances made fifty years ago yielded two general factors, and that a brief battery of reference tests was made for them and standardized for a large population. Today we should have no means of interpreting historically preserved records of scores on this reference battery, unless the original loadings of the larger group of tests had been preserved, for in the present population these reference tests would relate themselves very differently to whatever factors of musical appreciation exist with regard to choices in modern music.

It is convenient and economical to think in terms of organic trait unities and normative units, but the psychologist must descend periodically to reëxamine the stuff of logically, physically defined performances — existing in the trait elements — out of which the trait is made.

Chapter Six

SYSTEMATIZATION OF DESCRIPTION AND MEASUREMENT SCALES

1. THE ALIGNMENT OF VERBAL AND MATHEMATICAL DESCRIPTION

Covariation patterns and verbal symbols. Beginning with current practices of personality description, we have, so far, (*a*) attempted to arrive at the essential covariation patterns which can be found in behavior to constitute trait unities, and (*b*) systematized the methods of investigation by which these trait unities may be found.

To complete the theoretical clarification required for the correct use of unitary traits, we need now (*a*) to develop the theory of measurement of the unitary traits so far delimited — i.e., to deal with the nature of units and scales — and (*b*) to systematize the present chaos of verbal usages in conformity with the mathematical patterns of trait unity revealed by covariational investigation.

The verbal clarification can advantageously be carried out as early as possible. First one may ask, Do the two languages — those of verbal and mathematical symbolization — have a sufficiency of suitable parallel, equivalent terms? Let us examine the verbal equipment.

2. THE HIERARCHY OF TRAIT, TYPE, FACTOR, CLUSTER, SYNDROME, AND TRAIT ELEMENT

Sources of concepts. In general use, flowing in from experimental, psychiatric, and statistical streams of practice and research, is to be found an apparent superfluity of terms for describing patterns and characteristics of personality. Research and practice would be greatly aided if general agreement could allot to each of these expressions a definite position in a hierarchy [1] of concepts, or some such specialized use. Although there appears to be a definite position for "trait" in this hierarchy, somewhere above "trait element" and below "syndrome," general usage seems to have destined it also to function as the generic term covering all personality manifestations. For, as indicated in the preceding chapter, terms such as "personality characteristics" are too unwieldy. Table 8 will most succinctly summarize the hierarchical plan implicit in current usage.

Criteria for division of the hierarchy. Current practice does not provide any means of drawing a sharp line at any level — e.g., between a syndrome and a trait. Nor will the principle of greater "qualitative difference of the parts" help, for quality is too subjective a notion. In actual fact, what is called a trait by one investigator at one time is called a syndrome by another elsewhere. The situation reminds one of early navigators, who called islands continents and vice versa. The

[1] Among the various terms used to describe different kinds and classes of traits it is possible to recognize some kind of hierarchy based on the "width of reference" of traits. Terms such as "trait elements" are very narrow and specific in the behavior they describe. Others, such as "syndrome" or "type," are wider, blanket terms, occupying a higher level in the hierarchy and being inclusive of many different trait elements.

The notion of "width" or "area" implicit in this generally accepted reference to wider and narrower traits seems to have many hidden connotations and has never been thoroughly examined as to its theoretical credentials. We may illustrate it by citing as a trait element some special aspect of sociability — e.g., a liking to be on crowded streets — or of mechanical aptitude — e.g., the ability to foresee the directions and speeds of rotation among cogwheel gears — and we may contrast this with a syndrome such as that of extraversion, which covers all kinds of skills, social-behavior patterns, mood changes, and speeds of reaction. In the first place, the decision that the syndrome is wider resides in a purely qualitative judgment of the observer that certain kinds of behavior are more unlike and remote than others. It is clear that this judgment does not rest on anything we have so far explicitly defined — e.g., it has nothing to do with whether a trait is unique or common, an environmental mold or a constitutional trait.

TABLE 8

THE HIERARCHY OF TRAIT TERMS

Traits (or *General Traits*, or *Personality Characteristics*) (A comprehensive term for *Structure Deduced from Behavior*)	*Syndrome*, or the character of a *Type*,[1] or *Trait Configuration*	Toward Widest Reference
	Trait or *Symptom* (Normal) (Pathological)	↑ ↓
	Trait Element[2] (Operational unity, "atomic unit of behavior")	Toward Narrowest Reference

"importance" of the pattern is also no criterion, for this is distorted too readily by immediate social urgencies or even fashions.

Perhaps the real basis of present practice is not comprehensiveness of manifestation but comprehensiveness *beyond what common sense would expect.* If a particular tempo runs through all behavior, this does not astonish the observer and he calls it a trait. But if a person simultaneously acquires a change in cognitive endowment, an alternation in dynamic purpose, and a transformation of temperamental emotionality — as, for example, in general paralysis — the pattern is called a syndrome. Ascribing the distinction of syndrome, trait,

[1] The equating of type with syndrome rather than trait is justified by the fact that both are required to subtend a wide modal variety of personality traits — i.e., they are both used as high-level, broad unities. With increasingly appropriate use of the term "syndrome" there is little utility left in the notion of type — except to describe an individual endowed above some arbitrary level with a syndrome. It would seem to be erroneous to use it to describe anyone above a certain level in a single trait. Occasionally "type" is used for a comparatively small collection of traits, as in Jaensch's T and B types, but even so the qualitative variety is great.

[2] It is noteworthy that these levels are represented with great difference of frequency in terms of actual examples in the dictionary. There are two or three thousand trait terms, but very few terms corresponding to trait elements, presumably because they are too narrow and numerous to be usefully employed in the general handling of personality problems.

Psychological literature, following medical literature, has developed considerably the representation of the upper end of the hierarchy, with many syndrome labels, and is beginning to develop also in the opposite direction, to provide examples of trait element definition.

and trait element (or symptom) to the number and variety of distinct *modalities* or aspects of behavior involved seems at present as far as one can go in analyzing the hierarchical basis at the verbal level. As we shall see later, the modality character can be given operational recognition and is no longer subjective. But temporarily the final arbiter of hierarchical position can remain common usage of terms, as dictated by common convenience and sometimes, alas, by common misconception or failure of insight.

The possibility of mathematical criteria of trait breadth and hierarchical position. Failing any simple verbal, qualitative basis for precise, hierarchical systematization, it might seem that a mathematical basis could be found, having the advantages both of objectivity and of representing with exactitude many different degrees of hierarchical station.

The factors of factor analysis are called general, group, and specific factors, according to whether they enter into (load), respectively, all, some, or one only of the trait elements measured as variables in a given experiment — i.e., in a given matrix. The prospects of equating these three levels of factor to the three levels of trait breadth in personality do not seem immediately promising, in view of the difficulties which have met the corresponding task in the far simpler realm of abilities, where, for example, the abilities which one psychologist calls group factors appear to another so narrow as to be properly called "specifics."

In fact, the breadth of a factor in terms of the sheer number of variables it covers depends entirely on the prior choice of variables in the particular matrix concerned. A factor may be a group factor in one "social circle" of variables and a general or specific factor in another. A general factor is, of course, something which must appear in every test anyone may care to put forward to challenge its generality. At the opposite extreme a specific factor is one which no one can find in any other test. It is a historical fact that psychologists have never applied any such severe test to their general and specific factors. Even if they did they would not get unequivocal answers, for it would be difficult to distinguish between a "trace" of a factor and none at all. Probably many psychological source traits now regarded as group factors would be found in traces in every conceivable performance.

Apart from instances where the above principles give relatively clear-cut decisions, meaning can only be given to the hierarchy of factors — i.e., to the order of *width* of source traits — by providing some further principle by which a sample of variables can be considered wide or narrow. That criterion has to be found in the culture pattern itself. A set of mechanical aptitude measurements may yield a "general factor" in the matrix, but we know that it is only a group factor because our culture provides a great variety of other performances in which this factor plays no part. It is argued in Chapter 8 that language provides a standard of sampling and that a complete "personality sphere" may be built by taking all symbols for human behavior tendencies from the dictionary — for the dictionary is the mirror of our civilization. A factor is a general factor only if it appears in all of a representative sampling of these traits. It is a specific if it appears in one. Otherwise it is a group factor of a width which can be relatively precisely calculated in terms of the fraction of the total cultural pattern in which it appears.

Incidentally this approach permits us to make a major division in the hierarchy of factors, at the general factor level itself, by distinguishing between those general factors that run through all modalities and those which are "conditional source traits" (factors) restricted to either dynamic or temperamental or ability manifestations only. (See Chapter 7 on modality.)

3. MATHEMATICAL PATTERNS IN RELATION TO CLINICAL, VERBALLY DEFINED PATTERNS

The mathematical meaning of type and syndrome. Our main task at this point is, as indicated, to rivet in correct alignment two reference systems which have obstinately ignored each other in modern psychology — the flexible verbal system of describing personality differences, due largely to clinicians, and the more subtle, mathematical system due to psychometrists and statisticians.

A syndrome, or the collection of characters constituting a type, is clearly in the first place a correlation cluster — i.e., it is an instance of a "surface trait."

Because clinical observation is not capable of detecting with certainty a low degree of correlation, the items which belong on the fringes of a cluster (especially if it is an "attenuated" cluster, with a minimum correlation of no more than, say, .40) will not usually be recognized and included in the corresponding syndrome or type.

Reference to the preceding mathematical discussion of clusters and factors will remind the reader that a cluster can be accounted for by the overlap of several factors or by high loadings of one factor only. In the latter circumstance, the trait elements which define the surface trait will be exactly the same as those used to define the source trait, for the source trait has here made an "outcrop" on the surface. However, if, as later chapters indicate, at least a dozen factors are needed to explain even half the variance of personality trait elements in general, it will be rare for a single factor to account for much of the variance of any set of trait elements. In short, it will rarely happen that the correlation due to a single factor is enough to make trait elements stand out in a well-defined surface trait.

If verbal equivalents are wanted for the discussion of these mathematical possibilities, it may suffice to call the syndrome produced by factor overlap a *composite syndrome*, that due to a single factor an overt *source trait syndrome*, and the elements in a cluster which are not recorded clinically a *syndrome fringe*. By the same approach the group of elements most highly loaded in a factor or source trait which has too little variance to manifest itself to the clinical eye might be called a sub-merged source trait syndrome.

The evidence of the succeeding four chapters suggests that the varieties of schizophrenia, conversion hysteria, somato-tonia (*231*), and the cluster of traits normally called "good character" are instances of *composite syndromes*, whereas Bleuler and Kretschmer's schizothyme tendency, the cluster investi-gated and labeled "dominance" by Maslow (*166*) and that dis-covered and labeled "surgency" by the present writer (*40*) are *overt source trait syndromes*.

The problem of species type. It will be evident that in the above verbal-mathematical dictionary the "type" concept we have matched mathematically is the *continuous* and not the *species type*. At this point we must digress a little to clarify the mathematical form of the species type which was intro-duced in a preliminary way in Chapter 2, if the matched verbal and covariational forms in this section are to be complete. Especially we must look more closely at the methods by which it is to be discovered.

One species type (see page 18) differs from another by (*a*) non-continuous or bimodal distinction with respect to any one trait element, and (*b*) non-continuous distinction with respect to pattern (ratio) of trait element measures, and pos-sibly (*c*) possession of some totally new dimension — i.e., a trait element unique to itself. Clearly it is theoretically possible to have types partly continuous and partly species types in character — i.e., with trait elements, some con-tinuous in distribution, some discontinuous, and with some parts of the pattern (some ratios) continuous and some dis-continuous. For example, some traits of the schizophrenic — e.g., his spelling ability — may fall well within the normal

distribution; others — e.g., his hallucinatory tendencies —
may form a new mode beyond the normal. Similarly some
parts of the pattern — e.g., the ratio of intelligence to verbal
ability — may be continuous with those found among normals; others — e.g., the ratio of subjective to objective interests — may fall right outside the normal curve.

Since the genes of heredity are discrete influences, producing
discontinuous mutations, it seems reasonable to conclude that
any sets of characters, normal or abnormal, which depend
largely for their existence on a single gene, will act as a species
type pattern. (The reason, presumably, that most syndromes,
such as that of intelligence, do not do so is that they arise
from a summation of many genes and the sharp, step-like increments to be expected from gene combinations are smoothed
out by environmental influences.) Species types may exist
also with respect to the ideal profiles for various occupations,
as we shall see in Chapter 12.

Almost certainly species types will become more in evidence
as research employing measurement expands more boldly into
the clinical field. Nor need we expect such types to be rooted
only in constitutional traits. Intercultural comparisons and
opinion studies, etc., are already revealing what are essentially
species types in terms of environmental mold traits.

The detection of species types. The discovery of species
types requires:

(*a*) Examination of the measurements on many variables to
detect cases of bimodality or discontinuity of distribution.

(*b*) The correlation of these variables by statistical devices
suited to a discontinuous distribution (1) with each other,
by means of the mean square contingency coefficient or similar
device, and (2) with other variables by biserial correlation
coefficient.

(*c*) Examination of the correlation matrix for clusters and
factors. It would seem that Q or P technique — i.e., the
correlation of persons — would be especially valuable for

picking out types, as Stephenson (*243*) has pointed out. In the case of species types we should expect some sets of persons with intercorrelations very near unity and sharply distinguished from the others with which there is moderate or zero correlation — i.e., there should be step-like changes in the size of the correlation coefficients among various individuals. The existence of non-overlapping ratios — i.e., patterns — requires such correlations. The matter requires further mathematical and experimental investigation, to decide precisely what magnitudes of correlation may be expected with the elements of true species types and how the factors involved in the species type manifest themselves in associated "continuous" traits. Although this device does not appear to have been used by the physical anthropologist, it is the technique for investigating the existence and nature of racial types. Two problems exist here: (1) What types are found? and (2) How well does the profile of a given individual fit a particular pattern? The latter, as vocational selection, is left to Chapter 12.

Mathematical and verbal equivalents. Although our survey did not have as its aim to judge which method of representation is superior, some observations on relative utility naturally arise. It is evident that every clinical pattern or verbal concept can receive a mathematical formulation. The converse trade cannot always be made and we have had to suggest new clinical terms. In Table 9 on page 140 the results of the attempt to match symbols are set out in brief tabular form. The nature of the relationship is such that it cannot be simply represented by a one-to-one lexicon; so the table cannot be understood without the above discussion.

Most verbal, clinical entities prove to be compounds of mathematical statistical entities. For this reason, and also because the latter permit quantitative treatment, the statistical concept seem destined to prevail in research and, in the end, in clinical and general psychological practice. But the verbal symbols necessarily have a wider popularity in discussion and are more deeply rooted in the modes of observation of clinical psychology. Psychological progress requires, not that we choose between them, but that we bring them together. It is suggested that the refinement of terminology proposed here will help make this possible and will at the same time raise the level of technical understanding and precision of communication possible in verbal, clinical discussion and description.

TABLE 9

MATHEMATICAL EQUIVALENTS OF VERBAL TRAIT TERMS

MATHEMATICAL ENTITY	SUGGESTED VERBAL EQUIVALENT	PARTICULAR FORM OF MATHEMATICAL PATTERN	SUGGESTED VERBAL EQUIVALENT
Correlation cluster	Surface trait	1. Items in a cluster	Syndrome
		2. Items in a cluster from several factors	Composite syndrome
		3. Items in a cluster from one factor	Overt source trait syndrome
		4. Items low in correlation in a cluster	Syndrome fringe
Factor	Source trait	1. Items highly loaded with the factor	Factor syndrome
		2. Items insufficiently loaded to be in syndrome	Factor fringe syndrome
		3. Items in a factor having insufficient variance to appear overtly as a syndrome	Submerged factor syndrome

Wherever the term "syndrome" appears above, the expression "type" can be used for the group showing that syndrome to a defined degree. Whether it is a continuous type or a species type can be decided only by considerations too complex for representation in Table 9.

4. CONCERNING THE DEGREES OF "ABSTRACTION," "INFERENCE," AND "REALITY" IN TRAIT, FACTOR, AND OTHER TOOLS OF PERSONALITY DESCRIPTION

The role of armchair analysis. In the preceding chapter we became involved, willy-nilly, in what bordered on philosophical dispute concerning the relative "reality" of various forms of trait unity. Here we are forced again, by certain dangerous implications latent in loose popular discussions of personality, to clear up a jungle of uncertain theoretical assumptions and to take up a definite position, even though another excursion into philosophical issues be demanded.

Recently an eminent psychiatrist, doubtless concerned only to remind callow students that no actual psychosis is ever "true to type," asserted: "The syndrome itself has no real existence. Only a patient with a real personality, which is itself the psychosis, exists." [1]

The psychologist as arbitrator. The present generation of psychologists, having recently made good their escape from the apron strings of philosophy, are perhaps rightly suspicious of being re-involved in purely verbal entanglements.[2] But in

---

[1] Macfie Campbell, a psychiatrist of renown, observes similarly: "A psychosis cannot be abstracted from the patient for study, although some workers seem not only to extract psychoses but chop them up into syndromes and symptoms, and use them as counters with which to play complicated games." The chemists, it may be pointed out, play similar "complicated games" with the patient's physiology!

[2] Many of these classically "important" psycho-philosophical issues are best totally rephrased or even ruthlessly by-passed and ignored. But, on the other hand, many time-consuming experiments and much confusion and waste in applied psychology could have been saved by less slipshod, ready-made theory and by greater prior attention to clear conceptualization. In so complex a subject as that of personality-in-relation-to-its-universe one cannot hope to "get by" with conventional oversimplifications and the ignoring of some very broad issues of a philosophical nature.

A philosopher would recognize at once that these technicians are blundering in the trail of an ancient philosophical dispute between realism and idealism or, alternatively,

the present instance the psychologist who stands between several once independent disciplines and who has to weave his science out of their relationships is called upon to negotiate between the clinician who sees realities only in the way crassly expressed above and the statistician who is equally convinced about the reality of his abstract concepts.

All traits are real. When applied to traits the question of reality is exactly on the footing of the question as to whether an average is more or less real than the measurements which go into it, a melody more or less real than the notes which compose it, or a human being more real than that collection of visual and other impressions, in the minds of many people, from which he is inferred. In this matter we shall take the view that whether a particular event is a brass instrument or a printed word or an idea in consciousness can have no relevance with respect to estimating its reality, except that, on the whole, elements of consciousness and behavioral events are less stable and consistent than "brass impregnable," while conscious events suffer from the special disability that there can be no satisfactory evidence (collective witnessing) of their reality.

To speak of relative reality of personality characteristics is therefore pointless — in any defensible meaning of reality. A syndrome *exists* as much as a given individual with a psychosis exists. Both exist only as inferences from sensory data. But the provocation of the discussion has this much value: that it calls attention to the differences in the degree of abstraction — in the amount of inference involved — characterizing various trait concepts. It is evident that at no

in nominalism and realism. At the various extremes we encounter Plato's view that only ideal "types" exist; Berkeley's view of the world as the ideas of a single mind; and the "realism" implicit in such recurrent scientific fashions as "operationalism." True operationalism is, of course, as old as science. It appears clearly, for example, in Newton's laws of motion or whenever science uses ". . . is that which . . ." But the recent revivalists have been as shortsighted in applying the principle as in failing to notice that it is not new.

phase of personality description do we define a trait as a literal, tangible operation in behavior. The trait is something less transient than the actual behavior events, though its whole existence and nature are inferred from repeated transient events. It is an empirical concept. It is a convenient construct or entity, which we call a "mental structure" and by reason of which the particular behavior sequence in question reappears repeatedly in a consistent and recognizable form. The trait is an abstraction in the further sense that usually it is an abstraction from the behavior of many men, not one only. For the trait of "laughing at being tickled" or "having rapid handwriting" has its character as an average of the behavior of many. Thirdly, not only does the trait abstract from the concreteness of time, place, and person, but it abstracts also by some degree of interpretation, however small, in so far as it usually goes beyond the operational definition. The trait element involves the least interpretation and comes nearest to being a construct defined literally by the behavior events. But even there language allows interpretation to creep in. We say that the man laughs: we do not describe the spasmodic lung movements and facial contortions in precise physical terms alone. Life is too short to be pedantically operational. But the psychologist should certainly be ready at any moment to cash the verbal check at the bank of literal operational definition.

Relative abstraction and interpretation in traits occurring at different hierarchical levels. The smallest behavior variable which it is practicable to take into account in studying personality — the trait element — is thus already an abstraction from concrete events. But it is an abstraction only of the first order — a structure based on repeated observed behavior.

Cluster and factor are also structure, not behavior; but they involve further abstractions, of two kinds, according to whether we define them merely by enumerating a collection of traits or as some underlying entity. In the first case we refer to the "syndrome" or "factor syndrome" as in the right-hand column of Table 9, whereas if we refer to some essential character of the whole we should strictly speak respectively of surface trait and source trait as in the left column. The abstraction involved in using "syndrome" is simply that the pattern of traits referred to may never exist in any actual person. It is an *average* — a statement of the probable level of endowment in a certain set of traits, as calculated by the regression coefficients from the given cluster correlations. An individual will sometimes be "unduly" low on one or another of the traits in the cluster or factor syndrome, due to the operation of other clusters or factors involving the same variable. Such deviations are understood in the notion of probability implicit in the abstraction "syndrome."

The abstraction in surface and source trait concepts. At the outset it was said that the surface trait is a descriptive device and the source trait an interpretive concept. But the statement must be qualified by admitting some degree of inference even in describing the essential surface trait. Consider the cluster A, B, C, etc., in Diagram 11.

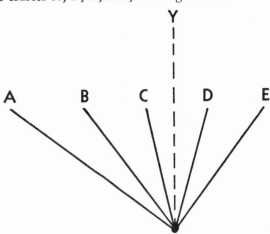

DIAGRAM 11. AMOUNT OF ABSTRACTION IN GIVING UNITARY CHARACTER TO A SURFACE TRAIT OR A QUALITATIVE CLUSTER

Clearly, when we think of a surface trait cluster — e.g., schizothyme temperament, Mongolian imbecility, or a "well-educated mind" — we tend, for economy, to think of some central entity or "underlying character" which is not any one of the constituent traits but which would be represented by Y, the centroid line in the cluster. Such a "most centroid character" can be abstracted from the circumscribing traits even when the cluster is a "composite syndrome," and it involves some interpretive abstraction. This use of an axis — of *a most central character* — applies also to the qualitative clusters of Tryon. (See page 82.) The true cluster, however, abstracts both for qualitative character (direction) and level of saturation.

By contrast the factor involves greater abstraction,[1] for it has the right to be considered interpretively as something beyond phenomena. It may be some historical influence, or something outside psychological observations altogether — e.g., a physiological substance or a sociological institution. Indeed, among the relatively few factors so far soundly established a good proportion have readily been assigned fairly remote interpretations. Thus Spearman's "g" became "cortical energy" and "w" (our "G") has been considered character integration or dynamic balance of the sentiments, while Kretschmer has related our A factors to genes which influence body build.

Naturally, in some circumstances the causative factor thus

---

[1] It is argued by some workers with clusters (*225*) that the description of personality by clusters has this advantage over description by factors — that it calls attention more readily to interesting individual departures from the typical form of a common trait. For example, if a person has four out of six traits in a cluster well developed, but has two others conspicuously lacking, one is provoked to look for a cause of this anomaly. But it is equally true of factor representation that departure from a calculated expectation can be noticed. However, many anomalies in the form of a cluster cease to be anomalies in factor representation, for as more factors enter into the determination, the endowment in any variable becomes more completely predicted. In the end an "anomalous" trait endowment provokes one to look into a specific factor influence. With this last understood, the factors completely define the traits — which is more than can ever be hoped from clusters.

inferred from many concrete measurements may itself be a concrete thing — e.g., in psychology a physiological hormone producing a psychological syndrome, or in astronomy a planet behind the irregularity of movements of another planet. But this return to "reality" is nonetheless an abstraction from the first concrete observations — i.e., it is "abstract" as far as the first set of data is concerned.

Indeed, here, as in so many branches of science, the path to abstraction does not lead away from concreteness and "reality." It actually widens the realm of reference and relevance of a measurement, makes prediction more powerful, and gives greater control over the concrete.

Consideration of the nature of the "reality" of trait forms, and of the degree of their abstractness as concepts, is thus not necessarily a sterile philosophical trade in verbalities. It reminds even the busy worker in applied psychology of the true meaning of his measurements and of the circumstances and limits of prediction. He realizes, for example, that an individual's possession of one trait in a cluster syndrome does not infallibly indicate the presence of others; that the definition of a trait element always refers only to those aspects of behavior which are common to a population; and that the essential character of an "interpretive" source or surface trait may frequently appear rather remote from the behavior appearing in any particular constituent element.

5. MEASUREMENT SCALES: IPSATIVE, NORMATIVE, INTERACTIVE

Validation and standardization. Modern psychometry is seldom defective in its standardization procedures, which are pursued with great thoroughness. But their precision is futile and their thoroughness an absurdity if the validation is poor. In actual fact, validation all too frequently in applied psychology has been poorly conceived and sadly unimaginative, for there has been far too little attention to the question, "Is there a unitary trait to be measured here?"

Consequently the present treatise gives by far the greater part of its space to discovering what is to be measured. Nevertheless, we must turn now from validation to standardization, in fact to the theory of standardization in its broadest sense — i.e., to consideration of the scales and units in which measurement may be expressed.

For even when measurements are made in truly conceived directions there sometimes arise subtle difficulties with respect to the continuum employed and there is danger of misinterpreting the meaning of scale units in certain unusual trait dimensions. From some current happenings one may well suspect that in the coming age of psychometric applications, when few persons' lives will be unaffected by psychological diagnoses, a new peril will stalk the social life of the individual — namely, the half-trained psychometrist, unaware of the real nature of the various measurement scales or of the true relativity of his units to the social and moral norms of his day.

Behavioral and introspective measurement. Psychological measurement has been based upon two distinct kinds of observational data, introspection and behavior. Any kind of seemingly introspective observation among humans that could be arrived at equally well with an animal subject — e.g., reports of absolute or differential thresholds — is really to be regarded as a behavior measurement, in which the verbal response is simply a substitute for grosser behavior. *True* introspective "measurement" occurs when we record as a measurement a person's statement, say, that one fifth of his total interests lies in gardening, or that one sound is twice as voluminous as another, or that his nervousness in high places is above average — e.g., rating 3 — whereas his nervousness in social situations is only average — e.g., rating 2. If he merely relates to the experimenter that one line seems longer than another, this is not introspection; he could react equally by pressing a key.

Normative, ipsative, and interactive scales of measurement. The observations of data on which measurement can be imposed are thus of two kinds — introspective and behavioral. The forms of measurement scale and unit in terms of which either of these forms of observations may be quantified seem to be, principally, three — normative, interactive, and ipsative. Only two of these appear to have been commonly recognized in textbooks and the newcomer needs some more detailed introduction.

These three forms of scale unit may be briefly defined as follows:

(1) **Interactive measurements** are the foundations of all others. Here the measurement is "raw" score — i.e., a performance reckoned in units of the physical world — e.g., seconds (reaction time); energy (basal metabolic rate); number of words recognized (scholastic test); number of friends visited in one week ("sociability"); etc.

(2) **Normative measurements** are performances which have become transformed into figures which express the achievement relative to other human beings, and, typically, relative to the population of the social group of which the subject forms a part. Naturally this brings additional meaning into the measurement; but it also drops out meaning — that given by the immediate physical units of the original interactive score. An IQ, a percentile score on an aptitude test, or a score expressed relative to a standard average performance are normative measurements. Normative measurements are obviously only possible after standardization has been applied to interactive measurements made on a whole population.

(3) **Ipsative measurements** are, like normative scores, derived values, arising from the comparison of interactive scores. But in this case the measurement is expressed relative to *standards existing in the individual* instead of in his group. An ipsative measurement is represented by the percentage which a man remembers of what he once committed to memory; by

his ratings of the relative vividness of his imagery; by changes in his visual acuity in the dark; by a measurement of interests through recording the fractions of his own total income spent on various objects or by experiments in which an animal's eagerness for food is measured in terms of his drive to escape shock.

The possibilities of interactive measurement. The choice of the term "interactive," instead of "physical," "absolute," or "objective," arises from the need to remind the psychologist that this measurement, alone among mental measurements, attempts to deal with the energy exchanges or "interaction" between the subject and his environment. It contains the possibility of measuring literally *what he does to his environment* and thus of incorporating the science of mental measurement with social psychology, physiology, and an integrated prediction system concerning man and his environment.

The striking possibility which arises here is that in its interactive terms psychological measurement might eventually be reduced to and incorporated in the centimeter-gram-second units of the physical sciences. If vitalism becomes banished from the sciences, as a false partition separating biological and physico-chemical processes, should it not also be banished from the measurement systems? The answer seems to be, first, that psychology could not accomplish this until the sciences which it integrates — e.g., sociology, economics, physiology — do the same. Secondly, there is likely to be an insuperable intrinsic objection to such an ultimate reduction: almost certainly the highest biological and psychology units — e.g., the IQ, the strength of a drive, the potency of a vitamin — cannot be expressed in C.G.S. units without a simultaneous *statement of the form, pattern, or system in which the energy expresses itself* — i.e., our units imply structure as well as quantity.

Relative utility of different measurement bases. At present these attractive developments potential in interactive measurement must remain speculative possibilities. The interactive measurement even now, however, has the advantage of being independent of changes of population and the vagaries of cultural change. If, for example, we are told that Shakespeare when nine years old achieved a 96th percentile score on the County of Warwick Vocabulary Test, this would be less informative to us today than if we were told the actual number of words in his vocabulary — i.e., his interactive score. But the normative score would nevertheless in turn be, for most purposes, more informative than the ipsative score. For the latter would tell us only that his vocabulary score was one standard deviation above the average of all his other school performances, or that his vocabulary at the time in question was 73 per cent of his vocabulary at twenty-one.

The relationships between these measurements are summarized in Table 10. Here the three varieties of measurement scale unit are applied to the two sources of observation — introspective and behavioral — producing the six basic theoretical possibilities of measurement scale. Psychologists have at some time or another employed every one of these kinds of units in their attempts to express results in figures. It will be contended below, however, that *some* of these scales do not deal with observations which in any full sense of "measurement" can be given quantitative form. They may yield ordinal numbers, indicating ranks, but they cannot yield units which can be added, multiplied, or otherwise manipulated.

To those ipsative measurements which are based on introspective observations, the individual attempts either to express one sensation or feeling in terms of another ("Ratio Solipsistic") or to express an interest or drive in terms of his total interest or drive ("Fractional Solipsistic"), the term "solipsistic" is given. This term, borrowed from philosophy, reminds one that no one else can "look in" on this measurement, to check it. It is in a universe of its own.

At least two important fields of psychology have taken

solipsistic "measurements" and attempted to use them as absolute or normative measurements. Psycho-physics (*244a*) has treated solipsistic "Ratio" measurements as valid absolute measurements (Stevens's extensive scale), and the personality studies which rest on questionnaires and self-ratings have taken both kinds of solipsistic measurements and freely converted them into normative measurements, as we shall see in Chapter 10.

If we accept a logical and consistent behaviorist position, such solipsistic "measurements" can only be accepted as gross approximations, vitiated by systematic and chance errors of unknown extent. Except in the highly artificial sense of a formal system, in which we make rules and conditions to fit

TABLE 10

The Relationships of Measurement Scales

Nature of Reference System	Source or Nature of Raw Data	
	Behavioral (dimension of external worlds)	Introspective (dimensions of consciousness)
In terms of literal dimensions of observed happenings	Interactive or Absolute	↑ False Absolute
In terms of the population of measurements in a group of persons	*Normative* 1. "Simple" Normative 2. "Ratio" Normative 3. "Ipsative" Normative 4. False Interaction Normative	False Normative
In terms of a population of measurements within the individual	↓ *Ipsative* 1. "Simple" Ipsative 2. "Ratio" Ipsative 3. "Fractional" Ipsative 4. "Normative" Ipsative	Solipsistic 1. "Ratio" Solipsistic 2. "Fractional" Solipsistic

our desires — for example, a system of non-Euclidian geometry — these are not true measurements. For this reason two categories in our diagram are labeled "false absolute" and "false normative," indicating that such measurements are misleading, while the third of the introspective categories bears the label "solipsistic," which indicates at once its limitations.

Attention may be called to the fact that the order of derivation of one measurement form from another is not the same in introspective and behavioral data. As the arrows in the diagram indicate, the former *begins* with the ipsative-type measurement, from which others are derived, whereas the behavioral measurements are all founded primarily on interactive measures.

Secondary measurement scales. A consideration of psychometric practice shows that some of the six divisions in Table 10 (four of which are scientifically respectable) manifest subcategories. These result from further manipulations of the scores, giving units still more remotely derived from the primary data. They are, in some cases, in such widespread use that it would be negligent to pass on without examining them critically and getting their relationships into perspective.

Ipsative measurement breaks down into several forms. (1) *"Ratio" measures*, in which the person's present score is expressed in relation to and in units of some present or past score of the same person — e.g., Vincent curves in learning. (2) *"Fractional" measures*, in which the score is expressed relative not to one score but to the total sum of the individual's endowment in that modality or field — e.g., interest measured objectively as a fraction of his total objectively measured interest. (3) *"Simple" Ipsative* measurements, in which the various measurements of the individual in some one dimension — e.g., his various interest scores or a series of daily measurements in some function — are expressed in standard form — i.e., in relation to the mean and standard deviation of his measurements. (4) *"Normative" Ipsative* measurements, in which scores which have first been expressed in simple normative form — i.e., relative to the group — are then reëxpressed finally in ipsative form. The utility of the last form of scaling, as Burt (27) and Stephenson's (243) Q-technique procedures (the correlation of persons instead of tests) show, is that it permits ipsative scoring of interactive scores which are themselves not directly comparable — i.e., not in the same scale units or even modality — and which have to be reëxpressed in a common normative dimension of "degree of eccentricity" before they can be compared ipsatively.

Normative measurements have parallel subdivisions to these. In addition to the well-known "simple" normative measures there are (2) *"Ratio" normative measurements*, in which the individual's interactive score is expressed in a new unit relative not to the total group but to a group standard or representative — e.g., that of the average or modal man, or to some authoritarian standard. Such scales are comparatively rare in psychology, but common elsewhere. The yard was such a standard, when it was the length of the king's arm. Some measures in industrial psychology — e.g., Bedeaux units — are expressed thus as fractions of the output of the average man. (3) "Ipsative" normative measurements are the converse of normative ipsative measurements — i.e., they are measures which have first been expressed ipsatively and then reëxpressed finally in normative form. Both first came into use most explicitly in connection with Q-technique, but ipsative normative measures are used, less consciously, in other fields.

Ipsative normative measurements permit the normative scoring of responses which could not be readily scaled normatively directly from interactive measurements. For example, aesthetic preferences, or just noticeable sensory differences, can be scaled ipsatively and then rescaled normatively. Again, the strengths of drives, in animals, are commonly measured by measuring the urgency of one drive against that of another — i.e., by ipsative measurement. The scores of a series of animals, with respect to one drive, may then be expressed normatively by "ipsative normative" scaling. The remaining category, "false interactive normative," is discussed below.

General aspects of the primary scale systems. It is perhaps unnecessary to emphasize that measurements in any one of these scale forms must lie in a single continuum of a well-defined nature. Sometimes the nature of the continuum will not be simple. For instance, as Burt (27) and Stephenson (243) show, it is possible to express simultaneously an IQ, a measure of scholastic achievement, a reaction time, and a bodily dimension in the same normative ipsative scale. The measure is then one in the continuum of "the individual's departure from normality."

Incidentally, it may settle possible queries in the mathematical reader's mind to state at this point explicitly that in the present initial survey of this field the difference between measuring and ranking in these continua is not considered important enough to justify digressive discussion or the complicating of the above schema by further subdivisions or labels for ranking. If positions in a continuum can be measured they can be ranked — though the converse is not true — and the choice of ranking or direct measurement depends on the fineness of instruments. What can only be ranked but not measured does not concern our study of measurement — except where it is possible to assume normal distribution, in which situation ranks (percentiles) and normative measures, granted a large enough sample, are mutually transformable.

The above schema of scale forms apparently exhausts the possible foundations of mental measurement, but not the possible superstructures. Normative ipsative and ipsative normative are but two of many possible "hybrids" derived from normative and ipsative forms. (From the same foundation of interactive measures the scores on these two conversely derived scales do not, incidentally, converge to make identical scales.) Each derived scale will have its own distribution, properties, and character or "dimensions" of units. It would be academically interesting, but at present not relevant to any known personality-measurement problem, to explore farther divergent derivatives from these foundations.

Fashionableness and utility of various scale forms. A survey of current psychometric practices reveals, first, that there is a great predominance of normative measurements in all fields; secondly, that there is a tendency for different branches of research and applied psychology traditionally to segregate to themselves particular forms of scale measurement. Thus interactive measurements are most common in animal study, solipsistic in psychophysics, ipsative in learning, and normative and false normative in education and guidance work.

It will show also that psychological measurements in any one field are of a very motley kind and often deceptive as to their real nature, appearing, for example, to be interactive when they are really ipsative — e.g., many measures in experiments on learning and forgetting are really ipsative; many measures in personality appear as interactive and true normative when they are really false normative — e.g., the majority of neurotic questionnaires and some interest and attitude measures are false normative.

The value of explicitly realizing to what scale system a given psychological measurement belongs is that one is safeguarded against improper manipulation or interpretation of the measurements and enabled to put them in a form most apt to the purposes in view. Usually, obvious differences in origin and modality, or the actual terms of the units, suffice to remind the psychological statistician when he is being tempted to mix scales, but not invariably. It would probably be helpful in most applied psychology to have measurements of every variable expressed in all three primary scale units.

6. THE UNITS OF UNIQUE AND COMMON TRAITS

Scales for common and unique traits.. By definition a unique trait is one with respect to which a population cannot be measured. Consequently it is a sharp distinction between unique and common traits that the former cannot be measured in the units of a normative scale. Nor can it be measured on a normative-ipsative scale, though it can be measured in a ratio-ipsative scale, derived directly from interactive measurements.

A unique trait is most readily measured in the units in which all traits can basically be measured — namely, the units of an interactive scale. Here the units are of a physical nature and have to do with a logically, objectively definable performance in what is therefore essentially a physically defined continuum. The performance is, for example, to depress a key in response to a light and is measured in seconds; or it is to cross out e's in a page of print and is measured by the number of e's struck out per minute; or it is a unique interest, as of the French count who took live lobsters promenading at the end of a blue ribbon, and is measured by the number of lobsters taken out per day or the number of lobster-yards traversed.

"Logical trait unities" — i.e., trait divisions arbitrarily cut out of the organic structure of behavior, in *ad hoc* fashion, for the purposes of immediate vocational selection, etc., and which we have discarded[1] (Chapter 4) as lacking the scientific utility and meaning of a true functional trait unity — may also be measured — if they *must* be measured — in these

[1] Briefly to recapitulate the position on logical trait unities, we may repeat (1) that the functional trait unity will not be a logical unity — e.g., a temperamental trait of "speed of response" may appear in and be measured by some speed responses but not by others, which, on any "logical" classification of responses (including any classification according to occupational requirements) would appear to belong in the same trait. What will be included has to be decided by the correlation methods of trait-unity investigation outlined in Chapter 5. (2) We can in general expect the composition of the functional unity to change somewhat, in terms of constituent logically defined performances measured in interactive units, as we pass from one end of the normative scale to the other.

"logical," interactive units. Though no human, biological, or social influences fashion a unified trait of "ability to align gun sights accurately at low oxygen pressures, plus good middle-ear efficiency, plus good spatial thinking," it may be desirable to measure this mixture as it stands, in a single combined score, as a measure of "fighter pilot aptitude," because time does not allow research into the real functional unities which operate in juxtaposition in this situation.

In such special circumstance the psychometrist may for expediency put the sum of this hodgepodge of interactive measures in a normative form. Yet this is false, because there is no true psychological continuum here, but only a continuum in a highly artificial mathematical composite. The combination of abilities at one part of the logically defined performance scale will have quite different meaning, in terms of functional unities involved, from that obtaining at some other point. Without analysis into personality factors the measurement is predictive only in that sample and for that week. Such procedures and interpretations, unfortunately, are not uncommon, even where not dictated by urgency and expediency, in the less responsible fields of applied psychology. Such measurements constitute the "false interactive-normative" scale in Table 10. They are so labeled because they are normative in a relatively meaningless and internally inconsistent continuum — a continuum such as one might obtain by averaging together a man's stature, his metabolic rate, and his intelligence, when such a combination runs athwart all the natural, existing directions of correlation.

Of course, the true, functionally-integral common traits also depend ultimately on those logically defined, physical, interactive dimensions and units in which their illegitimate brethren — the less useful and satisfactory unique and logically defined traits — are alone expressible. Both the definition of the trait and its measurement unit hark back to the particular trait elements which, by their salience in the pattern, demarcate and fix the common trait. This was pointed out at the end of the preceding chapter, in saying that only through the logically defined behavior of the trait elements can the psychological character of the common trait factor be recognized, understood, defined, and safely preserved in records.

Nevertheless, once the true functional unity is isolated, it is usually best measured in normative units. These are, of course, based on a composite — frequently a weighted composite — of trait-element interactive raw scores. In any really refined measure in normative units the composite may need to be adjusted or reweighted for different ranges of the distribution — according to the changes of intercorrelation and factor pattern at widely different levels of endowment. This is shown very clearly, for example, by the measurement of intelligence as a common source trait. The trait element constituted by a form-board performance may be heavily weighted in general intelligence at a six-year level but not in the composite that gives the intelligence measure where the normative score is around fifteen years of mental age. There is every reason to believe that personality source traits will behave in the same way. The trait element — i.e., interactive measurement — composition which defines trait boundaries *and* units of measurement, will change both with the development through age and development toward extreme ranges of score within the same age group. For example, the pattern of traits for assessing degree of mania may be somewhat different from those for assessing degree of hypomania, and may differ somewhat with the age of the patient.

Chapter Seven

THE PREDICTIVE CONVENIENCE OF CONDITIONAL MODALITIES AND OTHER TRAIT SUBDIVISIONS

1. TOWARD A COMPLETE EQUIPMENT OF CONCEPTS

Remaining problems. Before exploring those mountain ranges of accumulated experimental results which occupy the remainder of this treatise, the psychologist needs to be equipped for his expedition with yet one more set of theoretical instruments. The psychometrist more immediately interested in applying the results along limited, conventional lines may, however, be well advised to skip this chapter on a first reading.

The position so far consolidated may be summarized by the following diagram:

Intrinsic Unique Traits — — — *Common Traits*

Surface Traits — — — *Source Traits*

Constitutional Traits — — — *Environmental Mold Traits*

Dynamic Traits   *Ability Traits*   *Temperament Traits*

Our remaining problem is that represented by the last step in the above analysis — namely, the clarification of the meaning of the "modality" distinctions and the development of experimental methods for discovering the "modality" of different trait unities. This introduces important developments in the use of source trait factors in behavior prediction. We shall also set out to develop a clear and valid terminology for dealing with those smaller divisions of trait forms — e.g., special kinds of dynamic traits and special kinds of abilities which so frequently need to be referred to with precision and good common understanding in the transactions of psychometrists, clinicians, and educators.

What is the role of modality distinctions? From the very infancy of psychology it has been customary, and therefore presumably useful, to distinguish traits with respect to at least three categories of quality or modality.[1] But most psychologists would be extremely puzzled to supply any precise operational definition of modality on a scientific level appropriate to the context of exact and practical mental measurement in which such modality terms as "ability," "temperament," and "dynamic trait" are confidently used. Our task is to ask (*a*) what modality is, and (*b*) why it is useful.

In Chapter 4 a method of determining dynamic trait unities has been given — the method of intra-individual correlation — which distinguishes these unities from others. We have to explore this further and bring modality — the last refuge of unrealized implications in psychological description — into the light of logically defined conditions and consequences.

If we achieve a clear, formal, operational basis for the distinctions, it may well be that these formal characters will in turn suggest new, as yet unsuspected, trait classifications, having predictive usefulness as great as the modality categories already familiar to common sense and general usage.

---

[1] "Modality" is a term which elsewhere — e.g., in regard to sensation — usually implies a more radical difference than exists here. We shall use it temporarily for lack of a better term; but it will be suggested later, when the investigation has clarified certain issues, that the expression "conditional modality" is better.

2. FACT AND FALLACIES IN THE ACCEPTED, COMMON–SENSE
   CLASSIFICATION OF TRAIT FORMS

The accepted varieties of trait forms. By "trait forms" are meant the smaller subdivisions, much more restricted than the broad modality groupings, into which psychological experience has found it convenient to classify the multitudinous instances of trait unities. It would help subsequent discussion if the reader would hold in the background of his mind the following population of trait forms most commonly recognized and used by psychologists. The list is practically exhaustive, but includes a number of overlapping terms.

TABLE 11

A LIST OF MINOR TRAIT FORMS [1]

Abilities	Ideologies	Somatic (Autonomic)
Achievements	Illusions	Reaction Patterns
Accomplishments	Inhibitions	Symptoms
Ambitions	Interests	Talents
Aptitudes	Knowledge	Tastes
Attitudes	Mannerisms	Temper
Beliefs	Manners	Temperamental
Capacities	Motives	Energies
Character Qualities	Needs	Temperamental
Complexes	Phantasies	Tendencies
Conflicts	Phobias and Fears	Tempos
Convictions	Prejudices	Unconscious Fixations
Defense Mechanisms	Propensities	Vices (Evaluative)
Desires	Repressions	Virtues (Evaluative)
Dispositions	Sensitivities	Will Qualities
Habits	Sentiments	
Ideals and Values	Skills	

The conventional modality classification. On the basis of current usage, built upon insight and pragmatic truth, these trait species can be classified into trait modalities, in a preliminary way, as follows:

[1] This list is built up from a survey of modern writers' usage of terms, principally from Allport (*6*), McDougall (*173*) (*174*), Kantor (*140*), and Roback (*217*).

TABLE 12

A CONTINGENT LIST OF MODALITY DIVISIONS AND SUBDIVISIONS

A. *Abilities or Cognitive Traits* (First Modality)	1. *Native, Potential Capacities or Aptitudes*
	  a. Discriminatory: Intelligence, the inherited aspects of musical aptitude, number aptitude
	  b. Retentive or Controlling: Memory, the inherited aspects of general and special retentive capacities
	  c. Effector or Motor: The inherited aspects of motor skills, drawing ability, mimicry, dancing
	2. *Achievements or Skills* (Environmental Mold Traits)
	  a.
	  b. } The acquired elements in *a, b, c* above
	  c.

B. *Temperamental, Constitutional Traits* (Second Modality)	1. *Temperament:* Excitability, Emotionality, Speed of Response, Fatigability, Sensitivity 2. *Temper:* Perseveration, Impulsiveness, Smoothness of Dynamic Flow. Conceivably these also have environmental mold as well as hereditary patterns.

C. *Dynamic, Conative or Motivational Traits, Synonymous with Interests* (Third Modality)	1. *Disposition, Needs, Total Ergic Balance* } Constitutional
	  a. Appetitive, viscerogenic ergs
	  b. Non-appetitive ergs
	2. *Sentiments and the Ego Structure: Character* } Environmental Mold
	3. *Attitudes*
	4. *Complexes and Unconscious Fixations*

Other psychologists would add a category for describing reflexes at the somatic level, including neurological data as such, reaction times, handwriting pressures, manner of digestion, style of walk (claiming that how a man hiccoughs is as important for personality description as when he hiccoughs!). These responses at the somatic level are in a sense a part of the man's personality, but of such little social consequence in themselves that, except for aesthetic reasons or scientific completeness, one would not include them.

Some false leads in modality definition. Certain current misapprehensions are best set aside before undertaking constructive examination. In the first place, it cannot suffice to define temperament as McDougall, in the wake of popular practice, has done, by calling it the inherited aspect of personality, or that aspect of mental life which is correlated with physiological conditions. For all mental life is correlated with physiological conditions and many traits besides temperamental ones are largely inherited; e.g., general intelligence or the dynamic manifestations of an inherited psychosis — e.g., a manic depressive disorder. In any case, it would seem that modality distinctions should really depend on some more immediate character of the trait than is concerned in its origin or remote associations. The particular nature-nurture ratio, or the nature of the physiological or anatomical associations which secondary and prolonged research studies may show a trait to possess, are characteristics which are usually established long after the modality of the trait is known through more immediate criteria.

Secondly, it seems to be commonly overlooked that the unity of a trait — of a source trait or mathematical factor — may normally extend over, and be inclusive of, a pattern the parts of which are of more than one modality. This is true both of constitutional traits and environmental mold traits. A gene which causes the covariation visible in a constitutional trait may, as far as can be seen from present biological knowledge, affect simultaneously cognitive, temperamental, and dynamic aspects of behavior. For example, the Mendelian dominant responsible for Huntington's chorea influences at least both temperamental and ability responses. Similarly, a single environmental mold trait — e.g., the pattern of elements affected by repressiveness of family discipline — may produce covariation at once in dynamic, temperamental, and other manifestations of behavior. That the factors commonly found in factor-analytic research appear to be generally of only one modality is a state of affairs which can readily be traced to preselection of variables occurring unconsciously in the conventional experimental design.   A more adventurous use of factor analysis seems to lead to very different results (*274*) (*58a*).   The discussion below leads to the conclusion that most of the unities so far produced by the factor-analysis method are indeed the artificially truncated forms of naturally wider patterns of covarying elements.

No actual behavior is of one modality only.   A third dangerously misleading assumption in current discussion is that any single piece of behavior [1] can be said to have a modality.   The error in this mode of thought can be readily seen from several considerations, of which two may suffice.   First, in a factor analysis of, say, a dozen behavior variables the total variance of each element is usually accounted for not by one factor but by all or most of the factors — some of which are of one modality, some of another.   That is to say, the same measurement — e.g., speed of completing a task — is a measure partly of ability, partly of temperament, partly of effort arising from the strength of a dynamic trait.   True, in estimating a source trait or factor, it is usual, in practice, to pick out a few variables the greater part of the variance of which is accounted for by the factor in question — e.g., an intelligence test may be made from half a dozen sub-tests with highest "g" loading. Here it is *approximately* correct to consider certain behavior measures as a measure of one factor and one modality, but it is theoretically inadmissible to consider any piece of behavior as a pure manifestation of one modality.

The fallacy of considering modality to be demonstrated in pure form by a certain piece of behavior can be seen also from

---

[1] To avoid tiresome circumlocutions, we may speak at times of elements or patterns of *behavior* when strictly the reference is to elements or patterns of *mental structure* — the mental structure which accounts for the episodic appearance of the observed behavior in question.   The trait or trait element is, of course, the mental structure rather than the behavior from which it is inferred, but we can let one stand for the other without confusion in the present context.

first principles. Clinical psychologists have sometimes been led by the seeming logic of their observations to the curious conclusion that since *all* behavior is dynamic or purposive there can be no traits that are not dynamic traits. It is indisputable that abilities and temperament traits manifest themselves only in the course of dynamic behavior, as the "how" and the "when" of a behavior sequence directed to some satisfaction. They are, in other words, abstractions from dynamic behavior — i.e., from an observed piece of behavior directed to a goal. They are concerned with the *way* in which the organism reaches the goal and cannot have a life of their own apart from activation by, and representation in, behavior directed to a goal.

Yet a moment's reflection will show that the dynamic trait, as distinct from the "dynamic behavior," is also an abstraction, an abstract relation determined by the question "Why?" The dynamic trait consists of a set of subsidiation relationships, a statement either that certain pieces of behavior are equivalent or that they form a sequence of mediate goals to a common final goal. It is a pattern which abstracts from all aspects of behavior only what is relevant to relationships of this dynamic, telic kind.[1] *All* behavior, in fact, can just as truly be said to manifest ability as to manifest motive: all modalities are present, ready to be abstracted.

3. THE FORMAL CHARACTERS OF MODALITY IMPLICIT
     IN CURRENT USAGE

Is the specific character in the measurement form or the circumstances? Although it must be accepted that the measure-

---

[1] These alternative abstractions, and the way in which they stand out by virtue of the direction of the observer's curiosity or by intrinsic prominence as determining factors, may be illustrated by the reactions to an alleged murder. The legal inquirer is principally concerned to examine the act of shooting from the standpoint of its motive — i.e., of the dynamic goal sequence. A ballistics expert, if he finds that the shooting has been done at four hundred yards, is principally impressed by the ability aspect. The psychiatrist, if the motivation has been shown to be weak and the ability unquestionable, in turn becomes interested in the temperamental aspects which cause a man to become so excitable on trivial provocation.

ment of any one variable cannot measure one modality and trait only, but instead contributes simultaneously to the patterns of several traits of different modalities, the experimenter interested in distinguishing modalities has to be particularly attentive to those variables which prove to be highly loaded with, and substantial measures of, one factor trait. From them he may hope to pick out and generalize about the characteristics which distinguish a measurement mainly of one modality.

At once the question arises: "Does the modality characteristic lie in the form of measurement or in the design of the situation in which the measurement is made?" Even apart from the suggestions offered by existing temperament or ability tests, it seems an inevitable theoretical conclusion that either form of definition of the measurement may be employed. Alterations in either may affect the modality of the measurement. Ability, temperament, and dynamic trait measurements may be given their specific character either by measuring different aspects of a certain performance in the same field or by sticking to one and the same fixed dimension of performance repeated in three different settings of the field. There is no more antagonism in these two approaches than in deciding to move either the rule or the map in measuring, say, degrees of latitude where the rule must lie in a north-south direction.[1]

Modality is more obviously defined by the field characters. However, the more promising avenue for discovering what differentiates measurements of different modalities seems to lie in the direction of altering the field characters of the situation in which one and the same measurement is made. For in actual fact we do not vary the character of psychological measurements very much, nor do we have much systematic knowl-

[1] For example, an ability may be measured by the total time for a certain performance, a temperament trait by the acceleration shown in that performance. Alternatively, traits of both modalities may be measured by total time of performance, but under two different conditions of the field governing the performance.

edge of the effects of varying these measurement forms.   The great majority of psychological measurements are simply measures of speed or of errors, and are interpreted according to the nature of the situation in which they are measured.

Now the nature of the field characters which distinguish the three modalities seems to be analyzable — if one surveys current, conventional practice and whatever is implicit in common discussion — as follows:

(1) Dynamic traits are measured best by those variables the measures of which change most in response to change of incentives in the situation.

(2) Abilities are measured best by those traits the measures of which change most in response to changes in the complexity of the path to the goal.

(3) Temperament traits are measured best by those variables the measures of which change least in response to any change in the field.

Before undertaking to interpret these definitions in terms of more precise experimental and statistical operations, it is necessary to clarify some more general perspectives.   In the first place, the above must not be misconstrued as an attempt to avoid the task of definition by bartering unknowns in behavior for equally arbitrary, undefinable features of the field — e.g., by leaving incentives undefined.   Nor does it slip into circular definition, defining dynamic traits as those affected by incentives and incentives as those objects which affect dynamic traits.   Actually the mere shifting of the crux of definition from behavior to the field characters as commonly understood *would* constitute some slight advance, for agreement about and recognition of the latter is more widespread; but it is our intention also to proceed to independent and basic definitions of the field characters themselves.

Another general observation on the nature of modality deserves attention — namely, that if there are only three modalities, then any one of them can be defined by exclusion of the other two, if the latter become fixed by intrinsic characters. In practice we shall see that temperament can thus be conveniently defined as a residual measurement.[1]

Statement of the "Discrimination Range" hypothesis. At this stage, however, we shall assume that we know what is an incentive and what is a complexity and that our task is to arrange the situation so that a time or error measure will become largely a measure of only one modality — dynamic or ability. Let us illustrate the next step by experimental situations representative of animal and human studies in this field. We shall consider a population of rats tested on a series of mazes, A, B, C, etc. Let the total time for maze A be A′. Let the number of errors (errors in spite of proper cues) be A″, and let the ratio of time for the second half to that for the first half of the maze be A‴.

There appear to be fundamentally two ways in which the variables which measure predominantly a trait of one particular modality can have their modality recognized.

First, we may plot the relation of the mean performance (and the standard deviation) on some one variable (any one maze, in this case) against some measure of either (*a*) complexity or (*b*) incentive magnitude, as these aspects become continuously, separately varied. Thus, if the complexity of maze A is increased steadily from the simplest possible structure to the most complicated and confusing, we may expect, on general psychological grounds, that variations in the score A′ or A″ will at first reflect differences of ability very little but that later, in the more complex maze, the total time will come more and more to be a measure of ability. At the beginning, when the maze is very straightforward, A′ will be a measure largely of strength of drive, and perhaps also of

---

[1] Theoretically the matter could be approached in two ways: (1) By considering as temperament measures any variables in which two groups differ after they have been equated for abilities and dynamic traits. (2) By considering as temperament measures any measures which do not change, in a given group, when incentives and complexities in the field are changed — i.e., by equating people or by equating the field.

some temperament quality. Similarly, at the upper extreme of complexity, the test will cease to be a measure of ability, because its insightful solution will lie beyond the range of the population's ability and the trial-and-error behavior will become again expressive of drive strength or some temperamental persistence. There will be, therefore, some middle range in which the change of the mean A' or A" score with change of complexity will be greatest. The whole will form an ogive curve, the steep portion of which we may call the ability discrimination range and the two flatter portions of which may be called ranges of ability irrelevance. In the ability discrimination range the variable A can be considered largely an ability measure.

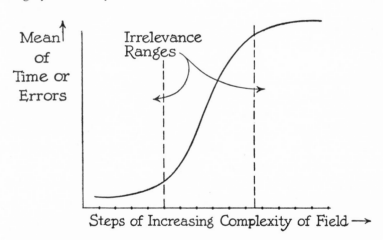

DIAGRAM 12. PREDOMINANT MODALITY DEFINED BY PREDOMINANT RESPONSIVENESS TO PARTICULAR CIRCUMSTANCE

Note that it is neither possible nor necessary to argue that the experimental increments of complexity are equal units. They constitute only a series of changes of unknown intrinsic value. Whenever the curve rises steeply, the tests of that region have become measures of ability. The superposition of dynamic and ability curves at right angles will generate a surface, which offers the most complete picture of the relationships here discussed.

The ability discrimination range needs to be considered in regard to (*a*) the curve for the individual, (*b*) the curve for the mean of the group, and (*c*) the curve for the standard deviation of the group. Without digressing into this finer treatment here, we shall merely indicate that we proceed on the assumption that the situation is the same for the individual and the group mean score — both will change most rapidly in the range where the score becomes the best measure of ability — and that the dispersion of scores within the group will tend to be greatest in the middle range of difficulty; i.e., the dispersion curve will show a maximum where the ogive shows its steepest part.

To obtain next the measure which is largely a measure of a dynamic trait, we keep the maze complexity constant in one of the irrelevance ranges of difficulty and vary the incentive continuously until we discover the part of the ogive curve for A′ or A″ against incentive strength in which there is the greatest change of performance with change of incentive. The lower irrelevance range for complexity is the more practicable range in which to hold the complexity, for if we hold it in the upper level of difficulty no upward variation of the incentive will produce any appreciable change of the score (except perhaps in errors). In other words, when the maze is easy, differences in performance become largely measures of difference in strength of motivation. Similarly, the best irrelevance range with respect to incentives is the upper one.

It may be objected that the "irrelevance range" method is unnecessary; that once we know what is an incentive and what is a complexity we measure differences in abilities when incentives are fixed and complexities varied, and differences in dynamic trait strength when complexities are held constant and incentives varied, at any level of either. The latter is true, but it deals only with relative strengths of motive in an animal or group with changing incentives. We are concerned rather with the conditions under which a standard test and test performance, with fixed complexity and incentive, become interpretable as a measure of *individual differences* of ability or drive strength, either between different animals or the same animal with different internal states.

Statement of the "Shifting Pattern" or "Interchangeable Factor Loading" method. The second method by which it is proposed that the predominant modality in any variable can be discovered is as follows. The measures A', A'', A''', B', B'', B''', etc., are taken (at no matter what degree of complexity or strength of incentive) and intercorrelated for the group. The combinations of the given maze complexities and incentives in the experiment are then altered, so that the incentive offered with maze A is now offered with maze B, or some such systematic recoupling, and the intercorrelations recalculated. When both matrices are factor analyzed we may expect to find that certain factors have recognizably similar loading patterns attached to the complexities while others have loadings which adhere in a recognizably similar pattern to the incentives, following them around no matter with which maze they are coupled. The former will be ability factors and the latter dynamic factors (while the variables which most purely represent each modality of measurement will be those with the largest saturations from factors of that modality).

Naturally, in practice, one would not proceed blindly, hoping that good measures of each modality would just "happen." Rather one would work on some hunch in designing the situations of the measurements so that each modality would be well represented. For example, A'' seems likely to measure discriminative ability, while the acceleration measurement, A''', seems likely to measure temperament. But such special measurement forms, arbitrarily invented on a hypothesis, have to await the verdict of the experimental results to confirm their success as comparatively pure modality measurements.

A further technical possibility would seem to be the use of the first method as it were within the framework of the second. The correlation between two variables will increase as their scatter increases (Karl Pearson's selection formula) and especially as the variance of that influence which is common to them increases. Consequently that "discrimination range" which exists somewhere in the middle of the range through which one varies a complexity or an incentive could be detected indirectly by the correlation coefficient. One would need to vary the complexity in two test situations until the correlation between them reaches a maximum. They are then measures of ability. Afterward, reverting to the ability irrelevance range in the two situations, one manipulates the incentives until a maximum correlation appears. They are then measures of dynamic traits.[1] Unfortunately, except in so far as there is a general factor in abilities and in incentives, the converse situation — i.e., absence of correlation — does not prove absence of common modality. It might arise when both are abilities, but unrelated abilities.

Both of the above principles are implicit in present practice — for example, in intelligence tests. In the first place, the psychometrist does not begin to give a test until he is sure that the motivation has shifted into the upper flat portion of the curve, the region of "irrelevance," where the attention to testing is so adequate that slight differences of concentration are not enough to affect performance. For the same reason

[1] With appropriate modification these methods could be employed not only with person-test correlation — the plane *OA*, *OB*, of Diagram 6 — but also through the other available planes. For example, one could present a single maze to a number of animal subjects on a number of occasions — one aspect of the maze, say the incentive, being continuously varied through the series of occasions. On factorizing the correlations between occasions, the factor with the larger loadings on the middle range of occasions could be taken as a dynamic factor. Again, one could give all mazes to one subject on a series of occasions, varying, say, the incentive with different occasions. The factor which increased with greater variation of the incentive (the complexity being constant) would be the factor (from correlation of the mazes) of a dynamic character. Unfortunately it would not be entirely safe to generalize that the variable which proved to be the most saturated measure of a dynamic trait in this individual would be so in all individuals.

These variants of the second method could be matched by the variants of the first method, in which the "ratio of mean score change to mean situation change" would be worked out for a single individual, or as between many individuals on one occasion (becoming then the standard deviation variant already indicated).

the general factor extracted from measurements under these conditions is considered an ability factor, not a dynamic or temperamental factor.   But under special conditions the same test could be used as a measure of effort.   Again, it is generally realized that if the degree of complexity of the tests is much increased or much decreased, passing into the "ability irrelevance" range, the saturation with the general factor becomes much reduced and other factors come into prominence.   Indeed, it is but a special instance of the general proposition that one and the same test measures quite different factors at different times, depending on its difficulty in relation to the subject's level of ability, the nature of the incentive situation, etc.

4. THE FORMAL, OPERATIONAL IDENTIFICATION OF INCENTIVES AND COMPLEXITIES

Common sense cannot always distinguish incentives and complexities.   The proposed shifting of modality recognition to put the weight of evidence on recognition of field characters is itself sufficient in practice to give a basis of modality definition.   For in animal studies the situations are simple — an odor of cheese and a degree of hunger are an incentive, while an extra turn in a maze or some overt cue is a complexity.   Similarly in human studies the generality of our own experience makes introspection sufficiently enlightening.   Yet it will not have escaped the analytically-minded reader that our task is not complete until we have given some operational means of recognizing what things in the field have the character of "complexities" and what have the character of "incentives."   Even in practice, guided by the sharpest intuition, the distinction is occasionally difficult.   When a boy sets out to solve a wire puzzle or a young man to woo and win a coy young woman, it would be hard to say which features of the stimulus are incentives and which difficulties.[1]

[1] In child-guidance practice it is often difficult to prove whether the individual's failure — e.g., in socialization — is really due to lack of some ability or to lack of interest.   To find objective methods of modality distinction is, in short, no mere academic problem.

Now the recognition of that part of a situation — that goal or goal symbol — which constitutes the incentive proves to be essentially the same as the task of disentangling the elements of a dynamic trait, as discussed in Chapter 5. There it was shown that the ramifications of a dynamic trait can be mapped (1) by cross-sectional, static correlation studies, in which the sharing of a common goal by various behavior elements is indicated by a common factor, while behavior "equivalents" (*190*) are indicated by bipolar factors weighting the equivalents with opposite signs, and (2) by longitudinal studies with either a group (Design B 1 (*a*)), or an individual (Design A 3(*a*)) which will reveal the course of "subsidiation" or "teleological causation"[1] in a series of behavior manifestations. (See page 111.)

Mapping a subsidiation sequence and a goal. If we assume that behavior in any situation depends on some goal which may be called a "final incentive" (the attainment of which is indicated by the cessation of behavior) and certain intermediate, subsidiated "incentive symbols" which the organism by learning or innate endowment has come to look upon as encouraging signals, the task of recognizing the goal is the same as that of tracing dynamic subsidiation, for the trail of subsidiation leads up to the final goal. Of course, one may pursue the inquiry only up to some convenient subsidiary goal or goal symbol when that suffices for the practical problem at hand. For example, a man may be avaricious both because of some ultimate goal of security and some ultimate goal of ambition, but for some purposes the making of money may be

---

[1] The reader is again reminded that "teleological causation" is not meant to be more than a descriptive term. Most teleological causality in psychology can doubtless be reduced in the end to physical causality; but meanwhile it is more nearly correct, as far as description of immediate psychological observation is concerned, to say that a piece of behavior is caused by what follows it. Physical causation is operationally established by invariable sequence — i.e., A is established as the immediate "cause" of B if it, and it alone, is invariably among the immediate antecedents of B. Teleological causation means here simply the establishment of an invariable sequence *in the opposite direction*.

considered a goal in itself and attention need then be given only to the subsidiation processes leading up to this goal. Most dynamic traits presumably form a *network* of converging and diverging subsidiation chains, ultimately converging on the biological goals of the propensities or ergs.

The means by which the subsidiation paths and the final incentive can be discovered by objective scientific methods have already been fully discussed in Chapter 5, Section 5, dealing with the operational criterion of a dynamic trait unity. It is concluded there that the behavior at the final goal is better recognized by its high factor loading with the factor common to all the variables in the subsidiation sequence than by its being the last item (temporally) in a chain of correlated items loaded with the same factor.

The determination by these methods of the physical, or at any rate environmental, object which constitutes *the goal or incentive* presents the primary step to the whole course of clarification of modality characters. For therefrom the conditions in the environment which are complexities can be immediately defined by exclusion. *Any alteration of the field which is not an alteration of incentives is an alteration of complexities.* This is a broad definition, awaiting further inner structuration — e.g., into complexities affecting perception and complexities affecting execution; but any narrower definition would not cover all that is meant by "abilities." With this we reach the end of our search for logical foundations; for the definition of "incentives" and "complexities" enables dynamic and ability traits to be recognized, whence temperament traits can be defined by exclusion.

5. THE UTILITY OF MODALITY DISTINCTIONS IN GIVING
   "CONDITIONAL FACTORS"

The confusion of ability and temperament endowment. The above formal distinctions can now be examined (*a*) as to their effectiveness in handling some practical difficulties which arise when deciding on modality, and (*b*) to throw light on the question of the actual utility of making modality distinctions.

In practice perhaps the most frequent difficulties arise in distinguishing temperament traits, both from abilities and from dynamic traits. Since both temperament traits and abilities measure the "how" of a piece of goal-directed behavior, it is not surprising that some alleged ability measures, fashioned in the belief that abilities are what makes an organism able to reach its goal, turn out to measure also temperament traits! For example, there are many tests in which temperamental quickness of response contributes to the ability score.[1]

An interesting topical instance of this uncertainty about temperament factors is that of the "F" factor of *fluency of association*, for years regarded by most English psychologists, including the present writer, as a temperament factor (*41*) and recently appearing in Thurstone's ability analyses as a "W" factor of verbal fluency ability (*262*). Again, this common "how" character led the present writer in an earlier approach (*52*) to classify ability and temperament factors together as "constitutional economic" or "constitutional non-dynamic" factors, the feasibility of which testifies to the reality of the generic relatedness of these modalities. Before clarifying the situation, we must explore some further facts.

Some inconsistencies in the definition of ability. Although the factor analytic discovery of unitary traits has been carried on far more vigorously and extensively in the field of ability than with respect to traits of other modalities, it seems to have led to very little speculation as to what is really meant

---

[1] The confusion of ability traits in practice extends even to confounding them with dynamic traits. Success in an occupation may be contributed to by the possession of those (dynamic) sentiments which make a good character. If abilities are falsely defined as *what leads to success*, character becomes an ability. This definition would make abilities depend too much on the goal, so that what is an ability in one purpose is a disability in another. Thus the man of good character has a disability where success in shady transactions is concerned.

by an ability.   The unities have been defined operationally, but the modality of the test variables, among which psychologists have searched for these unities, has had its boundaries defined only by intuition.

Of the two or three current definitions of ability, explicit or implicit in present practice, there are two — one of which has just been mentioned — which are inconsistent with the basic operational definition we have adopted and which are likely to mislead both research and such practical applications as personnel selection.

First one encounters the notion that although both abilities and temperament traits are "interchangeable" — i.e., employable in the service of or in association with a great variety of dynamic traits — abilities alone can be employed *at will*, and that temperament traits admit of no control.   It is true that a schoolboy can deliberately give an impression of having poorer arithmetical ability than he actually possesses, but we must note that he does so by refusing the goal itself — that of excelling.   That he cannot hide a temperament trait so easily in a temperament test is due, in the first place, to his not knowing by what signs the examiner is estimating temperament.   He could score high or low at will on a speed or fluency or perseveration test, if he knew in which direction this would influence the interpretation of temperament.   Secondly, he faces the more systematic difficulty that temperament traits tend to show themselves in almost all dynamic traits, not merely in those operating in a field of a given complexity.   It would show even in the subject's accepting or refusing the given test goal;   indeed, he would have practically to refuse to manifest *any* kind of behavior in order to withhold demonstrations of his temperament characteristics.

Another distinction which appears to be a dangerous half truth is that already mentioned.   It is the simple and widespread definition of ability as that *which makes an organism able to reach its goal*.   This criterion of success would clearly include many temperament traits, as indicated above, and also many purely physical measurements — e.g., the body weight would be an "ability" in boxing.[1] Moreover, it would lead to many characteristics described as abilities in one situation being described as disabilities in another,[2] for many temperamental and physical characters — e.g., sensitivity to pain, muscular bulk — would behave in this way. It would become impossible to define an ability without defining a goal at the same time, and confusion would arise from the different labelings, now as an ability, now as a disability, of the same tendency. Indeed, by suitable manipulation of the difficulties to be faced almost any kind of dynamic or temperamental trait can be made an "ability" in this sense.

On the other hand, one cannot be entirely certain — experiment alone can decide — as to whether the different, more fundamental concept of ability proposed in their treatise would entirely eliminate the possibility that the same skill would sometimes appear as an ability, sometimes as a disability. However, we suggest that the definition of ability as a "contributor to success," now being discussed, should be regarded as a secondary aid to the main definition — i.e., it should be considered a desirable feature of an ability trait that its factor loads *positively* most performances (when scored in a positive direction).

Confusions of temperament and dynamic traits. Perusal of the literature indicates that temperament traits are in fact also confused, secondarily, with dynamic traits. This arises, first, because some kinds of temperamental excitability, ardor, emotionality, or rapidity of acceleration of performance can be

[1] Also such purely physiological advantages as being able to digest a greater variety of foods, being more resistant to cold and germs.

[2] Conceivably exceptional endowment in color vision might impair a man's night vision, and sensitivity to high-frequency notes in noise might impair a rat's performance in conditions of noise. Otherwise, however, there is always a high or a low, a good or a bad, in ability scores — which distinguishes ability from temperament traits and from dynamic traits, except when "good" or "bad" is used in a moral sense in relation to the goals of dynamic traits.

mistaken for great strength in the particular drive which happens to be operating. The proof that mistakes can occur in practice is shown by the fact that one of the classical temperaments — the choleric — is certainly what we should nowadays call a disposition (pugnacity) and therefore a dynamic trait. Again, some writers, describing extraversion or surgency of temperament, refer to the sociability there manifested as if it were a dynamic trait in its own right — a direction of interest — rather than a permissive manifestation, through temperament, of a dynamic trait which is present, as a repressed interest, also in desurgent temperaments.

The effectiveness of the present operational definition in getting at the essence of temperament and separating it in a clear-cut fashion from other aspects of behavior is best judged by looking at a comprehensive list of qualities which have at

TABLE 13

LIST OF TEMPERAMENT TRAITS IN GENERAL USE

High-strungness, tenseness *vs.* ready relaxation
General emotional reactivity
Excitability
Overintensity *vs.* phlegmaticness
Expressiveness, vivacity *vs.* reserve
General susceptibility to inhibition *vs.* poor restraint
Proneness to physical activity
General energy (total output)
Spiritedness, restiveness
Zest, ardor, enthusiasm, urgency
Fieriness, headstrongness
Irritability
Smoothness *vs.* unevenness of emotional flow
Sensitivity to noise, shock, etc.
Hardness, unresponsiveness *vs.* sensitivity of sympathetic response
Susceptibility to fatigue
Susceptibility to drugs

Depth of sleep
Introspectiveness
Autism, subjectivity of perception
Tolerance of monotony
Tolerance of physical pain
Tolerance of excitement and adventure
Tolerance of personal conflict and of constant association with other people
Tolerance of internal mental conflict
Proneness to dissociative amnesia
General speed of response
Fluency and breadth of association
Speed of change of mood (brooding, resilient, or mercurial)
Motor and sensory perseveration
Rigidity, routinizing *vs.* flexibility of habit and attitude
General level of optimism or anteversion

various times and places been considered representative of temperament.

About these qualities as a whole one can observe: (*a*) that they are formal and applicable to any variety of drive — i.e., they have no specific, restricted dynamic drive quality; (*b*) that they are concerned with time and energy relationships rather than with discriminatory processes, as with abilities; (*c*) these relationships are describable principally by such terms as reactivity, variability, susceptibility, tolerance of stimuli, etc.; (*d*) in mathematical analysis many of these relationships can be resolved into temporal acceleration and deceleration measures or acceleration and deceleration in relation to continuous change in strength of dynamic provocation. The latter may more specifically refer to "temper" within the area of temperament, for temper has centered on the notion of quickness of rise and fall of *all* dynamic responses in relation to stimulus strength, rather than absolute strength of the final dynamic response; (*e*) that they are in many cases not dependent on the measurement being made in connection with any particular incentive or complexity condition.

In common-sense estimates of temperament and dynamic traits we readily recognize that an emotional, expressive person can give a momentarily false impression of strength in the particular drive being observed. Normally we wait to observe other drives, make from all of them a general estimate of temperament, and allow for that henceforth in estimating any particular drive. The ultimate test of temperament resides in the question: "Is the behavior interchangeable, manifesting itself with any and all kinds of dynamic (or ability) traits?" Our criterion seems to place one trait which could be dynamic — namely, "general energy or total dynamic drive" — among temperament traits. General custom, it may be pointed out, is at any rate in agreement with this decision. Whether this is to be considered a dynamic or a temperament trait is a rather academic question at present; there are borderline cases in all systems.

The practical gains from modality classification. So far it is not particularly evident what psychology gains from classifying traits under modality labels. First, we reply that any system of classification, on no matter what superficial but consistent features, offers *some* small advantage, in subdividing traits into smaller groups for separate study, etc. But the psychologist, whether in applied fields or in theoretical issues, maintains modality distinctions so obstinately, in spite of his inability to make any explicit claims for their utility, that one suspects a more functional and fundamental utility than the mere intellectual grace of orderly classification.

Let us now look squarely at a fact so far only emphasized in passing; that a factor or source trait, such as is usually obtained from static correlations of individual differences or correlations of increments, in *a wide variety of variables*, may include within itself, simultaneously, characteristics that are temperamental, dynamic, and of the nature of ability. In short, under general, unspecified, natural conditions of trait-element sampling a source trait is *not* of any one modality alone. This becomes quickly evident whether one studies environmental mold traits or constitutional, genetic patterns. For example, both training as a soldier and the inheritance of manic-depressive tendencies induce patterns which are made by a common variation in abilities as well as in attitudes and temperamental responses.

The factors obtained in most reported test and experimental situations, however, are in fact different from those obtained in more wholistic and naturalistic collections of variables, such as that of the present personality research set out in Chapter 9, in that they do not subtend this diversity of modality. In most experiments (*a*) the range of variables is deliberately restricted, and (*b*) certain conditions are kept constant, or, at any rate, *in an irrelevance range* where individual differences are no longer important. Consequently, factors of a single modality, obtained under these conditions, are properly to be considered as *conditional factors*. They are to be contrasted with the factors in variables from naturalistic life situations of the organism chosen to include a wide assortment of variables, each measured under no peculiar conditions. The latter might be called *naturalistic or wholistic factors*. Conditional factors are derived from naturalistic factors by "squeezing out" certain modality areas; they are restricted segments of the larger factor. In view of this relationship and of the objection raised earlier to the use of the term "modality," it may be most satisfactory to refer to temperament, ability, and dynamic forms as *conditional modalities* — i.e., as groupings possible only among conditional factors or conditional source traits.

Now the advantage of using conditional modalities — i.e., of factors each restricted to one modality — is that they can operate as independent, interchangeable predictors, and such that all of one modality become automatically held constant (ruled out) when certain conditions are held constant.

Of course, in the simplest sense, *all* factors are independent entities, which can be recombined in various groupings to predict people's performances in various kinds of situation. For example, when we have isolated factors of intelligence, verbal ability, and musical ability and know the endowments of many individuals in each, we can proceed to predict when we know the independent weights with which these factors enter into each situation concerned.

Sorting factors into modalities, however, tells us more about their possible combinations and interchangeabilities. Certain conditions do not merely rule out one particular trait, but can be trusted to rule out *all* traits labeled as of a certain modality. In a naturalistic situation — i.e., those with the minimum of special conditions, as in real life performances — (1) a wide range of factors operate and need to be taken into account in predicting any one performance, and (2) the factors have each an ability, temperamental, and dynamic aspect.

For example, (1) a man's success at some aspect of his job cannot be reduced to abilities alone, as can some psychometric performances, and (2) any one factor — e.g., that from his college training (factor K in Chapter 9) — will have aspects of ability, character, and temperament. But the prevalence of special conditions reduces the utility of naturalistic factors.

By contrast, the performances in certain special conditions can (1) use factors truncated to one modality only, and (2) recombine the resulting fractional factors in special ways.

The meaning and utility of conditional factors may now be made clearer, after the above preparatory discussion, by stripping the relations down to their bare mathematical form. For simplicity we shall illustrate by only two factors, F_c and F_e, which will be representative, however, in that they symbolize respectively constitutional and environmental mold (c and e) traits and, in their conditional forms, both dynamic (d) and ability (a) modalities. For simplicity also we shall take only five variables or trait elements, though decidedly more would be desirable in any actual experiment. Of these five, a and b will be largely dynamic in character, d and e largely measures of straight abilities, and c representative of those variables which are about equally of both modalities. Their general nature, as described briefly below, is that of variables which might be taken from everyday-life observations and

TRAIT ELEMENT OR VARIABLE	FACTORS AND FACTOR LOADINGS								
	(1)			(2)			(3)		
		F_c	F_e		F_c^a	F_e^a		F_c^d	F_e^d
Amount of literature read per month	a	.2	.6	a^a	.0	.0	a^d	.2	.6
Visits to needy friends	b	.0	.8	b^a	.0	.0	b^d	.0	.8
Success in college studies	c	.5	.7	c^a	.3	.5	c^d	.4	.5
Intelligence test	d	.9	.0	d^a	.9	.0	d^d	.0	.0
Musical performance	e	.3	.4	e^a	.3	.4	e^d	.0	.0

psychometric data to include in wholistic factors. Instead of adding further algebraic symbols for the loadings, we shall take actual figures, such as might reasonably make sense in such an experiment; the formula can readily be universalized when required.

According to the arguments above, the conditional dynamic factors F_c^d and F_e^d will cease to have any appreciable loadings in the ability variables d and e, while the conditional ability factors F_c^a and F_e^a will no longer have these loadings in the dynamic trait elements a and b possessed by the original wholistic factors F_c or F_e. It is important to notice, however, that the variables are themselves modified, as well as the factors; so that the last sentence really refers to the modified a, b, etc., variables, as represented by a^a, b^a, etc., and a^d, b^d, etc.

Since a and b were, in the original situation, practically pure dynamic trait elements, the over-all modification of elements for the extraction of the dynamic factors scarcely affects them and a^d and b^d remain substantially the same variables as a and b. Similarly, d^a and e^a are measurements made in approximately the same conditions of performance as for d and e, though very different from those of d^d and e^d. With respect to these variables of the same modality, therefore, the loadings of the appropriate conditional factor are substantially unchanged from those of the wholistic factor. One sees at once that the conditional factor, as stated in the general discussion, becomes simply a truncated wholistic factor, obtained by dropping from the contributory elements of the latter any variables which are not largely of the required modality. The loadings of these variables fall practically to zero in the conditional factor because the conditions imposed shift the modality influence in question into the irrelevance range.

Once experiment has revealed which elements become deprived of loadings by modality conditions, the experimenter may deliberately omit the test elements concerned from any future battery for the assessment of the given factor. The history of progress in measuring, for example, the intelligence general factor shows that experimenters in fact rejected large numbers of essentially dynamic and temperamental trait elements partly by actual experimental verdict and partly by common sense or intuition. Prior insight, of the latter kind, was probably vindicated in the majority of instances, but, as a glance at the general ability factor in personality, B in Chapter 12, will show, this practice has blinded most psychological thinking up to the present time to the fact that the wholistic general ability factor B includes such dynamic traits as conscientiousness and persistence.

The role of conditional factors will be still more clear if we consider finally the prediction of the actual performance of an individual, x, in each of two representative trait elements, a and c.

From wholistic factors we have:

$$a_x = .2\,F_{cx} + .6\,F_{ex} + \text{loadings in all other wholistic factors}$$
$$\text{in personality;}$$
$$c_x = .5\,F_{cx} + .7\,F_{ex} + \text{loadings in all other wholistic factors}$$
$$\text{in personality;}$$

and correspondingly for c, d, and e.

From conditional factors we have:

$$a_x^d = .2_{cx}^d\,F + {}_x.6\,F_{ex}^d + \text{loadings on all other dynamic factors}$$
$$\text{in personality;}$$
$$c_x^d = .4\,F_{cx}^d + .5\,F_{ex}^d + \text{loadings on all other dynamic factors}$$
$$\text{in personality;}$$

and correspondingly for b, d, and e, and for the prediction of the ability trait elements from the ability factors.

In the first place, the subscripts and superscripts of these equations remind us that the individual's endowment in a particular factor is estimated in general from a different set of trait elements in the case of the conditional factor, F^d, from the set used in the wholistic factor, F, or another conditional factor, F^a. For example, an individual's endowment in general intelligence, "g," as estimated from summing the subtest scores of an intelligence battery, is not quite the same as his endowment in the "General Intelligence in Personality" factor, B (Chapter 10), which is a wholistic factor, admitting differences in motivation endowment.   Consequently, wholistic and conditional factors representing the same source trait cannot in general be substituted for one another in equations.

Similarly, we may illustrate the modification of the variables themselves, to which we have already referred and which render them likewise, in general, non-interchangeable.   Thus c^a in the above equations is "Performance in college studies when motivation is held at so adequate a level for all subjects that no individual differences arise from gross differences in motivation." c^d equals "Performance in college studies when the studies are at such a low level of complexity that differences are no longer accounted for by differences in aptitudes." College performance is most commonly used as a variable in various calculations in the form of the wholistic trait element, c, which means "Performance in college studies when the levels of difficulty and incentive are those commonly obtaining in present-day colleges."   One should note, in passing, that the loadings of the dynamic trait elements in the dynamic factor, or of the ability trait elements in the ability factor, do not become unity,[1] because, of course, there may be many other conditional factors besides the one now discussed which also account for fractions of the variance of the trait elements under the conditions of irrelevant incentive or irrelevant complexity.

The special value to psychology of the conditional factor concept now becomes apparent.   Whereas the equation for the wholistic factor predictions applies to only one situation — that in which the measurements were taken — with fixed incentives and fixed complexities, the conditional factor equations can be systematically modified and recombined to meet

[1] The relations of the loadings in the table on page 183 are to be regarded as illustrative, not accurate.   More precise theoretical analysis and practical confirmation is necessary before the relations of wholistic to conditional loadings can be fully worked out.

those changes in incentive and complexity level which often occur *independently* in real-life situations. The *factors* (as endowments), it will be remembered, represent in the equation what the *individual* brings to the situation; the *loadings* represent *functions of the situation*, indicating how influential the particular factor is in the situation. For example, an equation might say that "g," general mental capacity factor, loads arithmetic 0.6 and ability to play tennis only 0.2, indicating that the former situation is of a higher complexity, making greater demands upon this factor. Now it should be possible, by investigation, to arrive at the loadings needing to be prefixed to the conditional factors in order to adjust the influence of each to the particular strength of incentive or degree of complexity obtaining in the total situation at the time of the required prediction. This adjustment to changing incentive and complexity cannot be made with the wholistic factor, for the composition of the factor alters (i.e., the variables needing to be used in its estimation alter), producing different weightings respectively of the ability, dynamic, and temperament elements involved together, and the factor as a whole is applicable only to a situation in which all aspects are simultaneously fixed.

What we may call the *conditional factor pattern* or conditional factor regression equation is thus a more adaptable and widely useful instrument than the wholistic factor pattern. In the equation for predicting a given variable score for a given individual the wholistic factor can be replaced by three conditional factors, each with a distinct, appropriate loading. (The conditional factors normally predict the conditional variables; hence some modification of mathematical function remains to be worked out here.) It follows that the wholistic factor (as a weighted sum of variable scores) is the sum of the conditional factors, each being weighted according to the role of incentive strength or complexity in the situation in which the wholistic factor was calculated. Thus, in the above example, if we weight the dynamic and ability factors equally

(0.5 to each), we can sum them to get the wholistic factor for predicting a, b, c, etc. That is to say, as indicated in the general discussion, the conditional factors can be regarded as truncated segments, from which the wholistic factor can be rebuilt.

The above mathematical statement is the equivalent of the clinical generalization that any ability (or temperament manifestation) may be the servant of practically any dynamic trend. By reason of generation by the same gene a certain talent may appear in company with a certain temperament (i.e., correlate with it, in a population of individual differences); or, again, a certain environmental mold may always produce a particular skill simultaneously with a particular dynamic character attitude. In either instance, however, these components of the same wholistic factor can function with independent strengths and in new combinations with other traits.[1] Among these combinations, of course, is that representing the original wholistic trait, but with different weightings of the dynamic and ability parts thereof. Our general approach, equating "functional unity" with covariation (Chapter 4), arrived at the conclusion that the covariation pattern which persisted in more situations of correlation was the truer or more efficacious unity. By this touchstone conditional factors represent truer functional unities than wholistic factors.

What sets of conditions may create conditional modalities? Modality classification of personality traits, we have concluded, is essentially classification according to conditions surrounding measurement of the trait elements from which the factors are extracted. The question next arises: "Do modalities at present recognized utilize all, or even most, of the useful and practicable restrictive conditions that could be imposed? In general it is clear that the measurement of factors under limiting conditions is likely to be a useful procedure

---

[1] For example, if we consider the environmental mold trait of being trained as a soldier, the skill in shooting, acquired along with a habit of obedience to authority, may later be employed in the service of some quite different dynamic trait.

only if the conditions are simple, independent, able to be readily set up and defined in experiment, and *such as occur widely in real life*.   At first sight it is not at all obvious that the conditions of sufficient incentive or irrelevance of complexity of field which experimentally distinguish the measurements of ability and dynamic trait modality are conditions which exist widely in the real world — or, at least, widely enough to justify modality distinctions having the importance which in psychology they have come to possess.   We measure a pure ability modality trait — general intelligence — under conditions of approximately equal and adequate motivation. But are there any conditions in life outside the examination room where this will be repeated?

More close scrutiny indicates that there are indeed many situations in real life where people have adequate and approximately equal desire to succeed, and vary in performance according to abilities, and others where what they do depends more on their dynamic make-up than on any capacity to do what is required.   There are, for example, scholastic performances, from the nursery school to the university, in which the dynamic and temperamental factors remain tolerably constant, so that the gamut of conditional factors which we call abilities can profitably be considered alone.   On the other hand, there are problems of conduct, such as appear in the police court or in psychoanalytic consultation, in which individual differences in abilities or temperament traits seem relatively unimportant and where one operates largely in a universe of dynamic traits.   The naturally prevalent conditions, it will be noted, are such as rule out not one trait but a whole class of traits — a whole modality — so that it is profitable to know the modality of traits and to think in terms of modality.

Having analyzed out the fundamental nature of the traditionally accepted modality divisions, we are in a proper position to ask whether there may not be conditions applicable to measurement which have not been previously employed to give conditional factors and which might yield novel modalities of traits quite as useful as those stumbled upon in psychological history.   One can conceive, for example, measurements made under conditions in which the training has reached for all a level of saturation — i.e., the top of a plateau — or in which age, heredity, sex, or other characteristics of the population are held constant, or in which a particular level of fatigue has been brought about, or in which only perception through one sense organ is involved, and so on almost indefinitely.

Factor analysts have, indeed, frequently set out deliberately to hold certain variables or dimensions — e.g., age, training, speed of performance — in a condition of irrelevance, in a majority of researches done up to the present time.   Spearman, for example, in his classical researches into the nature of the general ability source trait, always insisted that in child populations variance in age, and sometimes education, should be excluded, because it produced "spurious correlation" — e.g., of the individual's score on a classification or analogies test and the number of molars he possesses.   However, many other instances of restrictive conditions are due to nothing more than a lack of understanding of the true role of statistical methods in research, and to a naïve transfer of the viewpoints of experimental method into problems that are actually more efficiently handled by statistical method.   A hybrid method, in which one controls as many variables as possible through experimental design and treats the rest statistically, is undoubtedly the best approach to many investigations.   But in the factor analysis of factors operative *in situ* in everyday life, within the totality of the social organism, the extraction, definition, and measurement of various specialized conditional factors would seem to be generally pointless and wasteful.   After all, the predictive situations in which one wants to use factor measurements are usually those of everyday life — i.e., situations in which practically nothing can be artificially held constant. Factors assessed from the trait elements of restricted situations are then more or less seriously inaccurate. Effective prediction in the general, unrestricted situation requires use of a larger number — if possible all — of the factors operative in that situation, and they must be uniformly wholistic in derivation. The exception to this seems to be the conditional modalities, since in everyday life incentives and complexities frequently vary, or can be made to vary, independently in a given situation.

The present volume cannot encompass any larger digression into "conditionality" or into working out the mathematical details of conditional factor combination. Suffice it that a first survey of the possibilities of other special conditions than those of modality — e.g., of those listed above — suggests that no new modalities are created as fundamental as those already known. Mainly these new conditions suggest subdivisions within the modality of ability, notably into *retentive* and *plastic* (acquisitive) abilities, and independently into *perceptual-discriminative abilities* and into *executive abilities*, such as will be listed more fully below. Alternatively, though memory is commonly considered an ability trait, this analysis suggests that it might, in so far as the retentive power proves independent of complexity, be given a conditional modality of its own. There is much to be said for instituting this fourth modality, for memory phenomena are far wider than abilities — i.e., cognitive performances.

The specific nature of measures highly saturated in one modality. Modality is seemingly defined fundamentally by the conditions under which a performance is measured rather than by character of the performance itself. Nevertheless, it is worth while to pause momentarily and see whether, after all, there may not be some qualities — which might be found by inspecting the trait elements heavily loaded by factors of one modality — characterizing the modality performance itself.

In the main the net of inspection catches nothing. As said already, time and errors measure — e.g., with a rat in a maze — ability, drive, or temperament. However, errors seem used somewhat more frequently than time, both with animals and men, to measure abilities.

Furthermore, just as the temperament modality differentiates itself from dynamic and ability traits by a somewhat more fundamental character — independence of the environment — than distinguishes either of these from the other, so, in practice, most temperament measures have been devised with characteristics which depart most clearly from those time and error measures commonly employed with these other modalities. Among temperament measures one finds a predominance of measures, such as perseveration or oscillation (*204*), which are ratios or measures of acceleration or of change — i.e., they cancel out the direct effect of the drive or ability by the comparison of two performances employing the same drive or ability. But the comparative infancy of attempts at discriminating modalities objectively does not permit more than these guesses at the trends which differentiate the characters of the measures employable to distinguish modality in the general situation (indeed, we have so few measures made in a general situation). The basic differentiation of modalities therefore rests on definitions of *situations of measurement*.

6. DYNAMIC TRAIT FORMS AND SUBDIVISIONS: ERGS AND METANERGS

The value of the concepts "erg" and "metanerg." Having dealt with the division of traits into modalities, we are now prepared to handle the descriptive classification *within* modalities — i.e., in each of the three main trait form groupings. We shall begin with dynamic traits. A glance at any clinical textbook will show that the varieties of dynamic trait forms necessary in practice are considerable. However, the following list describes the chief categories now in use.

TABLE 14

LIST OF DYNAMIC TRAIT FORMS IN GENERAL USE

Interests	The Censor structure
Needs, appetites, drives, ergs	Fixations
Complexes	Regressive trends
The Ego ("Will"), and its Defense Mechanisms	Attitudes and Sentiments
The Super-ego structure	Tastes

The common character which brings these into the community of dynamic traits is, as agreed upon in the above discussion, that they all evidence sequences of behavior which aim at a goal (the goal being some specific relation of the organism to its internal and/or external environment) and which decline or disappear in the period immediately after the goal is reached. Our present purpose is to see whether this modality admits of any useful subdivisions.

The goals are of two kinds: innate and acquired. This is no place to enter into the unnecessary arguments and misconceptions about innate goals which have to be recorded in the history of psychology during the past thirty years. Although there is comparatively little irrefutable *experimental* evidence of ergic goals in man, equivalent to the instinctive goals of animals — except at the appetitive, viscerogenic level — there are great ranges of empirical evidence of their existence. Opposition to the theory of propensities, coming largely from a narrow, pedantic school of reflexologists who fail to cope with 90 per cent of the legitimate data of psychology, presents merely an egregious example of that scientific atomism which fails to see the wood for the trees. With space for only one of the many arguments for ergs, we may perhaps best point to the fact that the social pattern cannot be made responsible for creating ergic behavior, since it is actually opposed to ergs. The uphill, thorny path along which education struggles in its persistent efforts to train human beings away from such goals as those of aggressive destructiveness, sexuality, pride, excessive food seeking, etc., shows clearly the potency of such hidden goals.

However, since few of these goals are actually realized in the original, innately-prescribed manner, they have to be discovered and defined indirectly — not by the goals and stimuli to which we *do* acquire reactivity, but by the goals and stimuli to which the human being *can be or could be most easily trained to react*.

Clinical psychology assumes that these needs are of different strength in different persons and that, by abstracting a need from its many different behavior manifestations, we can arrive at a source or factor trait — a "need," drive, or erg — which can be scored for each person. The whole analysis, for example, in Murray's *Explorations in Personality* depends on this assumption. Experimental psychology, with the exception of a few animal experiments, has, on the other hand, tried to get along without a clear, theoretical, quantitative treatment of specific drives in animals or of ergs in man.

The methodology for investigating dynamic traits developed here — notably P-technique — provides for the first time an operational means of investigating the nature and magnitude of specific needs, propensities, or ergs.

The "general factors" obtained mathematically in the analysis of dynamic trait elements outlined in Chapter 4 will in general be dynamic constitutional traits, which are these *innate* drives, whereas the less pervasive factors evidenced in the environmental mold dynamic traits will correspond to the *acquired* dynamic goals. Because of the literary associations of the word "instinct," which is appropriately applied only to the lower animals, and the awkwardness of the term "propensity," as well as the loose connotations which have gathered around such terms as "drive," "urge," "tension," etc., the unspoiled term "erg" has been put forward elsewhere (49) by the present writer to apply to a more precisely defined concept of innate drives in man. The term "metanerg" — that which is developed *beyond* (meta) ergs — then applies to all the *acquired* dynamic reactivities derived from ergs — i.e., to dynamic environmental mold traits, such as sentiments, complexes, attitudes.

The definition of erg. The term "erg" has the advantage not only of being uncontaminated by the popular connotations of other drive terms, and of being unscarred by the vagaries of preoperational psychological writings, but also of being more readily declined into the adjectival and adverbial forms "ergic" and "ergically." An erg may be defined as *"an innate psychophysical disposition which permits its possessor to acquire reactivity (to attend) to certain classes of objects more readily than others, to experience a specific emotion therefrom, and to enter on activity which ceases more completely at the attainment of one specific goal than at other (putative) goals. The goals satisfactions may be defined either externally by the particular relation between the organism and an environmental situation, or internally, by some physiological condition. There are, further, innately preferred ways of behaving in reaching the innately preferred goals."* (Page 110, 50a.)

The ergs of man, appetitive and non-appetitive, of which there seem to be about twenty, can be investigated in ways suggested by the above definition. The innately provocative situation can be explored by determining gradients of difficulty in acquiring attention to certain situations. The goals can be located by trying many alternative final situations to see which best brings cessation of activity, as well as by factoring, in the manner described, to find the element with the greatest loading. The preferred paths to the goal may be revealed by studying *the relative difficulty of learning* of a variety of forms of behavior leading to the goals of striving thus determined. Owing to the great plasticity of human ergs, in contrast to those of the lower animals, education may apparently shift not only the paths to the goals but even the goals of ultimate satisfaction themselves (e.g., art for coition and religion for hunger; for great artists have sometimes been impotent, and men have starved themselves to death in hungering for heaven). This greater plasticity makes the empirical determination of the structure of ergs in man very difficult.

Ergs, like all source traits, are abstractions. The strength of an erg — e.g., of such a constitutional dynamic unity as the hunger, sex, or aggressive drives — has to be inferred by abstraction from many actual metanergs. It is the factor measure obtained by weighted addition of the many sentiment trait-element scores appreciably loaded with the factor. Thus in the case of the assertive, power-seeking erg, these metanergs will be sentiments, complexes, and interests generally having some quality of power-seeking in the total satisfaction which each metanerg offers — e.g., an interest in political activity, in stern morality, or an attitude in favor of dominance of one's country over other countries. Metanergs themselves could be subdivided according to their position in the total subsidiation sequence culminating in ergs, so that the strength of an erg would be inferred from a collection of sentiments and the strength of each sentiment from averaging a greater array of attitudes and opinions.

An essential fact sometimes lost sight of in measuring the strength of ergs (i.e., the "disposition") of an individual is that ergic "strength" is always relative to (*a*) the cultural pattern and (*b*) the individual's position. Sex and self-assertion are ranked high — i.e., have powerful manifestations in our cultures because they are the most frustrated, not because they are intrinsically strong. If thirst were equally frustrated, its manifestations would be equally persistent and widespread. When the measurement of dynamic traits becomes more developed, a clear theoretical appreciation of the necessity for correcting a measurement against "norms of satisfaction" will have to be formulated if behavior predictions, with change of the individual's environment, are to be accurate.

Ergic span. In this connection it is useful to introduce a notion of "ergic span" between any two goals in a subsidiation sequence. It is the distance — in terms of behavior events or other units yet to be defined — between the intermediate and the final goal reaction. For example, if a rat is trained to press a lever to get a token which is then exchanged for a pellet of food, there is an ergic span between the lever-pressing and picking up the token, and between picking up the token and taking it to exchange it for food.

The notion of ergic span can be very useful in clinical discussions and calculations. For example, one would need to take note that the greater the ergic span the greater would be the temptation to short-circuit behavior and the greater the neurotic strain in maintaining the subsidiation. But its interest for the present discussion of morphology and trait naming lies in the fact that it permits a grading of metanergs, from those having goals most near to the ergic goal to those most remote, "artificial," or "civilized."

It reminds us further that if we cut all the ramifying subsidiation chains at a fixed ergic span from their common ergic goal we have to infer the strength of the erg from these many actual, overt manifestations — manifestations which tend to increase in number as the ergic span is extended backward from the goal. Indeed, from the moment of birth, the strength of any given erg can only be determined as an inference from behavior scattered in many metanergs over a wide field. It requires great clinical skill in those who, as in Murray's experiments (*190*), would infer the trait strength, without factor-analytic aids, from these many manifestations.

7. DYNAMIC TRAIT SUBDIVISIONS: THE TRAIT FORMS "COMPLEX," "SENTIMENT," AND "ATTITUDE"

Sentiments and attitudes. Of metanergs, or "secondary[1] dynamic traits," the most frequently encountered in general

---

[1] "Secondary drive" or "dynamic trait" is not so satisfactory a term as "metanerg" because it has been tied up with the gratuitous assumption that non-appetitive ergs are derived, by secondary processes, from appetitive ergs, and because it is cumbersome.

discussions of personality are those in which there is consciousness of the object on which the dynamic purposes are directed. These we call sentiments and attitudes.

Common discourse, as has been shown more fully elsewhere (49), distinguishes these two notions in the following ways. The sentiment structure is deeper, more widely ramifying in the personality, usually established earlier, and accompanied in its functioning by more emotion. The attitude is more transient (though not to be considered a mere momentary stance, akin to a physical attitude) and emotionally more superficial. It arises from the impact of a sentiment upon a particular situation — e.g., a man has a sentiment of affection toward his son and as a result of his son's success in, say, a progressive school acquires a favorable attitude toward progressive education. An aroused attitude may be expressed in verbal opinion, as in an attitude test, but an aroused sentiment may express itself also in powerful emotional action which would be uncommon in an attitude. Change of environment or the impact of new facts may alter an attitude, readily molding it to be a consistent "go-between" between the new facts and the sentiment from which it derives; but the sentiments change only slowly, unless there is some major upheaval of personality.

It is clear that the general trend of usage is to make what is essentially a *quantitative* difference between the labels "attitude" and "sentiment," a relation most aptly defined by calling the attitudes the twigs and the sentiments the boughs of the dynamic ramification — i.e., the attitude is farther in the subsidiation chain from the ergic source. The difference thus refers to the conative pattern structure, to the amount of loading with emotion or drive, and to the sequence of dynamic dependence or subsidiation. The order of *cognitive* complexity and importance is in general precisely opposite to the order of dynamic strength — i.e., what is emotionally narrow, specific, and faint is most likely to be intellectually complex, and what is emotionally powerful is most likely to be intellectually simple. A man's sentiment to his home is perhaps massive but simple; his attitude to the gold standard or the use of the "look-and-say method" in teaching reading is complex but emotionally much weaker. The greater the ergic span from the erg source, the greater the intellectual complication, the less the dynamic investment.

The term "attitude" gets used, in addition, in an entirely general, formal way to mean any structure — conditioned reflex, mental set, attitude, sentiment, complex — which implies the possibility of recurrent dynamic action in regard to some particular stimulus. This parallels the generic use of "trait," and, as with that term, the context must indicate whether the generic or the specific use is intended; but the term "interest" could with advantage supplant the generic use of "attitude." The use of "attitude" to mean an entirely temporary mental "stance," under immediate control of the will, is best met rather by the term "mental set."

Complex and sentiment. The usage of a decade ago distinguished "complex" from "sentiment" comparatively readily by the following criteria. (1) The sentiment lies in the conscious mind; the complex is repressed in the unconscious. (2) The sentiment is generally in good accord, dynamically and logically, with other conscious sentiments, particularly with the ego ideal, while the complex is in conflict with these. With this goes the implication that the emotional attachments constituting the complex are socially disapproved, humiliating, and immoral. (3) The complex is dynamically less well integrated, within itself and with other complexes. (4) The complex frequently involves only one or two ergs, whereas a sentiment is generally formed of the ramifications of several.

But when the "unconsciousness" of the complex is examined more closely, one has to admit that only *some* of the several distinct meanings of "unconscious" are involved and that in some senses the sentiment must also be called unconscious. In the sense that the ultimate ergic (and generally biological) goal is not known by the subject, most sentiments and complexes are alike unconscious, differing only in degree. If the tendency of the obsessional neurotic to peep inside old shoes were as socially approved as his raising his hat to ladies, it would never occur to him that he was more conscious of the purpose of the latter than of the former. In fact, he is probably equally unaware, unless he stops to reason, of the sexual goal of both. However, it may be granted that there is generally more teleological awareness with the sentiment and fewer gaps in the true understanding of the relationship of its behavior to other pieces of behavior.

Consequently, with regard to the alleged greater consciousness of the sentiment one must disagree with the earlier formulation of McDougall and maintain that all sentiments are to some extent unconscious. They frequently derive directly from complexes in the id — e.g., as reaction formations — and generally, in their normal formation, spring from the unconscious ergs of the id. They differ from complexes in degree of consciousness in the following respects. (*a*) The individual can see several steps farther ahead regarding the goal of the sentiment behavior. (*b*) There is no point at which he encounters a wall of repression when he deliberately tries to bring the objectives of the behavior more fully in consciousness. (*c*) There is clearer consciousness of the personal historical origin of the sentiment. (*d*) There is less resistance in admitting the logical connections of the sentiment ("logical" as judged by the impartial observer) with other dynamic systems and other feelings from the same root.

Varieties of sentiments and complexes. No very complete exploration has yet been made of the possible sub-varieties of sentiments and complexes and the natural ways of classifying them. Complexes have been classified, by implication, according to the level of psycho-sexual development of the libidinal ergs at the time fixation takes place, and according to the erotogenic zones involved. This fixes at the same time the object of the complex — e.g., the narcist's own body, the mother image, the brother, etc. — defining it as we define a sentiment. There is, however, this difference from the sentiment, that in the latter the true object of the dynamic system is the same as its overt object, whereas the overt attachments of the complex are symbolic substitutes. There is little point in classifying complexes according to the overt object — i.e., the particular symptom attachments, which are too individual for general classification.

The sentiments, on the other hand, because they refer to real objects, a great many of which are of emotional importance to all people, can be (except for unique traits) classified on a common basis. A beginning of such classification has been made by Murray, with his study of environmental "press" — i.e., objects which commonly acquire sentiment interest, attitudes, or valence. These are: the family, individual members of the family (notably parents), the school, the gang, hobbies, occupations, the church, the nation. These are the unities corresponding to which one would expect to find environmental mold unities in the covariational study of the dynamic behavior elements. It is conceivable that these structures could be fruitfully classified, for the purposes of research and applied psychology, according to whether the pattern is established predominantly by fear, by affection, or by the emulation of good example. Again, they could be classified according to the age at which they normally appear and have their greatest influence. But no useful classificatory system has yet been adequately explored and accepted.

There is a great and untouched field of research open here for whosoever will map out, with interest tests (preferably using interactive rather than solipsistic measurements) and using static, mutational, and sequential correlational analyses, the normal development of sentiments and attitudes. For lack of norms in this field many erroneous conclusions — e.g., regarding emotional development, abnormality of interest, etc. — are drawn daily in clinical work and education. It is in this field, also, that unique traits are most important.

These brief definitions of dynamic trait forms are not complete without a summary of the final, more precise meanings which can usefully be assigned to interest, character, and disposition. By "interests" we mean *all* dynamic cathexes of objects, concrete and abstract, real and subjective. An individual is interested in things *to which he attends, whether the attention be connected with attraction or aversion, with sentiments, attitudes, or complexes, with ergs or metanergs, with material or subjective objects.* The term "interests," in psychology, does not refer to the objects of interest themselves, but to the psychoneural structures which, when they function, cause the individual to attend to the objects.

Character or **character integration** refers to the manner in which the drives are organized in relation to one another. By many persons it is also understood to mean the consequent relation of the total system of drives to some set of external principles — e.g., religious or moral beliefs, a social code, or a philosophical system, or even only to the particular code in which they themselves believe. It happens that good dynamic integration, on the one hand, and good orientation to the moral code of the culture in which one is brought up, on the other, tend strongly to go together. But the psychologist, who is not in a position to judge moral values or weigh the relative goodness of culture patterns, defines character simply as *good integration of dynamic traits* — i.e., perseverance and freedom from maladaptive impulsiveness — *in relation to the attainment of those cultural goals which the individual has accepted, whether or not they are in his own culture pattern.*

Disposition defines the hierarchical relationship with regard to the energies expressed in the different drives. If we say, e.g., that a person is of an assertive or amorous disposition (or both), we mean that these drives predominate in responsiveness, energy, and frequency of action over other drives. To measure a person's disposition is therefore precisely the same as measuring the relative strength of a particular erg, by the methods described above. As we have seen, it involves abstraction and summation from a host of actual, metanergic trait manifestations. Disposition is usually regarded as an aspect of personality which is almost as stable and constitutional as temperament.

Dynamic traits schematized. The position arrived at by the above discussion regarding the provisional system of nomenclature by which the dynamic traits of personality can best be handled may be summarized as follows.

Dynamic Traits or Interests
{
(1) *Ergs*, or *Constitutional Dynamic Unities*. Commonly summarized as "*Disposition*"
{
(1 *a*) Appetitive Ergs ("Viscerogenic Needs")

(1 *b*) Non-Appetitive Ergs (Needs, Drives)
}

(2) *Metanergs* (or *Dynamic Environmental Mold Unities*) Integrated as *Character*
{
(2 *a*) Complexes — Symptoms (Unconscious Metanergs)

(2 *b*) Sentiments — Attitudes (More Conscious Metanergs)
}
}

8. ABILITY TRAIT SUBDIVISIONS

Perceptual and effector abilities. A preliminary, common-sense classification of abilities into discriminatory, retentive, and effector abilities and into innate and acquired patterns has already been attempted in Section 2. The discussion of ability modality has refined the general concept of ability and suggested that the retentive abilities might conceivably stand on their own, as a fourth modality. Pending further research we shall acknowledge the greater divergence of retentive capacities but not separate them from the ability modality.

Despite the uncovering of unitary abilities in considerable numbers and with great certainty, by more extensive factor analyses than have been made in any other field, the question of classifying and subdividing abilities has received as yet very little attention. Among the true abilities — those other than retentive capacities — we shall argue that the above-mentioned division is basic; i.e., into *Perceptual, Discriminatory Abilities and Effector, Motor Abilities*. Most abilities of importance in everyday life are combinations of effector and perceptual skills, but some are by nature largely of one kind, while *all* can be made largely of one kind by altering the situation appropriately. An ability is made predominantly a perceptual ability by reducing the response complexity during its measurement until no one fails by reason of being slow or making errors in the motor response. For example, this condition is met in a vocabulary test where one has simply to underline with a pencil words chosen with intellectual difficulty. On the other hand, in an effector ability measurement the cues as to the intended action are simple, but the execution of the behavior offers the chief opportunities for failure.

The systematic procedure for separating these two aspects of ability seems to be entirely analogous to that required for separating modalities. One varies the conditions, one at a time, to find a range in which a certain condition becomes practically irrelevant. In this case one begins with high complexity of the motor response and simplifies it until no more improvement occurs with any further executive simplification. Maintaining this low level of complexity of the motor response one varies the perceptual cues until, for the group of subjects concerned, one enters the range of maximum change of performance per unit change of perceptual complexity.[1] The converse procedure leads to a pure test of motor skill.

Classification according to realm of complexity. Both perceptual and effector abilities can be classified, and indeed *are*

---

[1] It is quite possible that popular assumptions as to whether the "bottleneck" in the flow of efficient performance lies in the sensory, perceptual-discriminatory apparatus or in the effector, motor apparatus, in any given case, are quite erroneous. Experiment alone can decide what crucial factor sets the limit to performance.

most commonly classified, according to the field of complexity; i.e., according to the material of the field, in which they show themselves — e.g., words, mechanical contrivances, bodily dexterity, mathematical symbols. The subdivisions most valuable here will be those into which abilities *naturally* group themselves, and it has been the main concern of the pioneer wave of factor analysts to discover these particular natural divisions. Probably in the end the array of discovered and well-confirmed factors among abilities will be so great that some secondary, perhaps hierarchical principle will have to be invoked to classify and index them.

This classification according to field and material, which at the present stage of factor analysis yields the particular list of group factors set out below, has to be superimposed, as a second dimension of subdivision, upon the duality already existing, as shown in Diagram 13 on the following page.

Retentive and plastic abilities. Here, as already pointed out, we deal with abilities recognized only by *changes* in the primary response abilities, discriminatory and effector. The writer is inclined to believe that in the end it will be found most nearly correct to consider these measures as measures in a fourth modality. If plasticities and retentivenesses could be matched, as trait unities, with true abilities — e.g., retentiveness in the verbal field having the same boundaries as verbal ability — the case for such separation would be destroyed; but so far the evidence is against such specificity of retentiveness (even when powerful dynamic trait influences are allowed for), and even learning rates, into which retentiveness enters in a minor way, cease to be exactly the same in grouping as abilities.[1]

However, if we proceed for the time being on the accepted

[1] The factor analyses of learning by Woodrow (*281b*), Wherry, and others show some discrepancy between ability factors and factors of increments in ability; but they also show, more saliently, the existence of identities of pattern. At the moment, therefore, one cannot generalize as to whether retentivenesses are aligned with abilities.

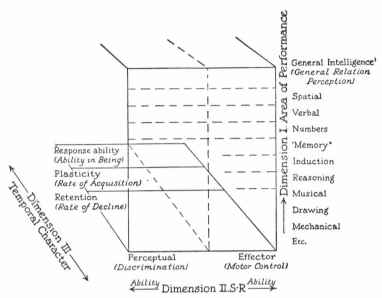

DIAGRAM 13.   CLASSIFICATORY SCHEME FOR ABILITIES

classification of these tendencies as abilities, the most complete scheme for ordering abilities seems to be as in Diagram 13.   This takes account of three principles of classification: (1) According to area[1] or qualitative character — e.g., mechanical aptitude; (2) According to temporal character, (*a*) "Ability in being," (*b*) Acquisition or plasticity, and (*c*) Retention of abilities; and (3) According to a Perceptual *vs.* Effector dichotomy — i.e., stimulus-response dimension.

The distinction in (2) between "plasticity" and "retentiveness" is perhaps a fine one.   Logically they could be distinct — plasticity would express inertia to new influences, and retention would express inherent slowness of fading (paralleling friction and inertia in physics).   Whether the independence logically possible here and in general among the sixty forms of ability indicated by the chart actually exists remains to

[1] Only some ten unities of area are listed here, representative of the rather fuller list from the complete exploration in Chapter 11.

be decided by experiment. There may well be fewer functional unities, but we do best to begin by assuming their multifarious independence, in which case we can recognize today some sixty known abilities (see chart).

Some apparent confusions in describing abilities. In current discussions of abilities one finds divisions according to "speed," "power," "goodness," "level," etc., as if the same ability could be measured according to many different aspects.

These are not so fundamental as the above dimensions. They raise the question, however, of how many ways an ability can be tested in terms of manifestations. One might ask first, for example, can a certain response be made *at all* — e.g., color blindness? Again, can a discrimination be made between two stimuli? How *well*, in some motor sense, can this response be made? Can certain objects be recognized?

Such approaches, in all their variety, nevertheless reduce in the end to the two basic kinds of measurement discussed before — time and errors — in the framework of categories in Diagram 13. Time and error measurements permit assessing an ability respectively as to *speed* and to *goodness;* but it does not follow that in correlation these will prove functionally independent. In intelligence tests of children (under the instruction to work fast), for example, these do not give independent abilities. Speed and goodness can readily be parts of a single ability measurement, as can be seen if we fix a goodness level for all subjects and measure their speed in reaching it, or, conversely, allow all persons the same time and compare their goodness levels. The review of established unitary ability traits set out in Chapter 9 shows, however, that some researchers who have thought in terms of "speed factors" as distinct from "ability factors" have isolated speed factors which, on reëxamination, are found to be ability factors under a new guise. Occasionally, in a certain field, one factor may appear predominantly in speeded items and only very faintly in goodness measurements, or vice versa.

Another source of current confusion in ability classification lies in our inheritance of a set of vague and largely useless verbal labels, about the preciser use of which there is no agreement — namely, aptitude, ability, talent, skill, and attainment. These could conceivably be made serviceable terms by making "aptitude" refer to a native ability factor — i.e., *a constitutional source trait;* "skill" to *an environmental mold source trait;* "attainment" to the "ability in being" — i.e., to *a surface trait*, whether from innate or environmental sources, from a factor or an overlap of factors; and "ability" either to the above gamut generically or to *the capacity to acquire capacity* in that field, as a result of both aptitude and present skill. But there is no sign of such simplification yet appearing in current verbal usage.

Chapter Eight

THE PRINCIPAL SURFACE TRAITS
DISCOVERED THROUGH BEHAVIOR RATINGS

1. DEFINING THE OBJECTIVES OF INVESTIGATION

The actual findings concerning common surface traits.
Equipped with the methods and definitive concepts of the last few chapters, the psychometrist is now in a position profitably to take hold of the actual data. The remainder of this book is accordingly devoted largely to the results of using such tools for the investigation of the actual surface and source traits, syndromes and facters, in terms of which personality can best be described and measured.

Naturally, the study will deal first and mainly with common traits. Following the necessary sequence of investigation, it will begin by examining the description of personality in terms of surface traits — i.e., clusters — before turning to interpretation in terms of source traits. The present chapter will survey the whole field of surface traits, as established by statistical and experimental methods in contrast to clinical (Chapter 3) methods.

Compromises forced by the scantiness of research data. The objectives of investigation must from now on always be a compromise between those which would be planned in a co-ordinated, large-scale research using the improved methods and categories just described and those which are actually possible with the resources of present researches. For example, the final description of personality by surface traits should properly be a cataloguing undertaken systematically with respect to (*a*) the modifications of common trait patterns which exist in different cultural and racial groups; (*b*) changes of common trait patterns through taking population samples of different age levels; (*c*) changes of trait patterns in various other extreme groups — e.g., the highly intelligent, the physically defective. Systematic recording of the *modifications* of source traits at various critical age levels should be part of any complete survey, for the whole study of personality development depends upon accurate cross-sectional pictures for different ages. But the present study can only hope to sketch in, faintly and suggestively, the modifications due to age.

On the whole, with present resources of data, it can hope to be reasonably complete only for the culture patterns of the Atlantic democracies and for those major traits which are relatively persistent throughout adolescence and middle life.

Postponement of analysis into modalities. At this stage no interpretation of the actual surface traits discovered will be attempted. Even when the analysis of the clusters into factors is pursued later, there will seldom be sufficient evidence, from the application of such ancillary methods as those defined in the preceding chapter, to decide definitely whether the trait pattern is dynamic, temperamental, constitutional ability, or environmental mold in type. Nor can one hope, with present data, to make any subclassification in categories such as temperamental traits, sentiments, complexes, or character formations. The first aim must be unprejudiced, empirical description of trait patterns.

2. THE CHOICE OF OBSERVATIONS ON WHICH TO ESTABLISH PATTERNS

Ratings, objective tests, and self-ratings. It is the ideal of a science of personality description to build its traits upon a foundation of objective test measurements, as has been done to a very large extent in the analysis of abilities. The data offered by researches at present available are constituted by three kinds of observations: (1) Ratings of observed behavior in general life situations by more or less skilled judges (including "Time Sampling"). (2) Measurements on actual tests and experimental situations. (3) Self-ratings on inventories or questionnaires or as recorded by an interviewer.

The relative validities (and reliabilities) of these methods will come up for discussion at various points in the next few chapters. Here it is enough to point out that though (2) is the soundest and (3) the most fraught with systematic errors, (1) is in some respects the most important and is likely to remain so for years to come. For though objective tests are most reliable, they have as yet been devised to measure only narrow functions, in a few specialized regions of personality, whereas ratings by observers cover great stretches of personality and in respect to those traits which are definitely of social, occupational, moral, and personal importance. The human judge abstracts the essentials from masses of behavior observation, sometimes with bias but in a way that no machine measurement or statistical device can yet accomplish.

Of course, objective tests may eventually escape, as some do now, from the criticism that they are restricted to measuring only what they literally measure in the test situation. They may instead become valid referents for wider behavior in real life, as a result of previous special proof of correlation with wider behavior in real-life situations — as, for example, an electroencephalogram may be used as an indicator of epilepsy or a fluency test as a measure of surgency. But in this case they cannot be more reliable than the rated or time-sampled behavior for which they stand as a referent. In this connection it must be kept in mind that the rated or sampled behavior in the research which established the test as a referent will usually be far more careful and reliable than what passes for "rating" in most situations in applied psychology.

Behavior ratings as the foundation of perspective. Most work on the definition of personality variables has to proceed by successive approximation. It defines a behavior trait approximately, investigates its relation to other traits and to its own parts, and, on the basis of the structural findings, returns to defining the essence of the trait by more refined, restricted definition of behavior.

As we have pointed out when speaking of the nature of trait elements, the individual trait is fully understood only by taking account of the patterns of traits in which it stands and of which it forms part. (See Chapter 5, Section 7, on organic and literal trait elements.) This pattern may be a universe of objective measures or a universe of rated traits. The latter at present has an advantage because (*a*) it will be a very long time before a sufficiently wide variety of personality aspects are simultaneously presentable in objective measurements to give meaning to the patterns (factors), and (*b*) the meanings obtained are more relevant to practical problems, because the ratings relate more directly to the fields of real-life behavior in which we wish to predict. Indeed, it seems likely that *objective measures will at first grow up within, and take their initial validities and meanings from, a framework of ratings.* These ratings will act as a builder's scaffolding to shape the growth of research in real objective test measurements. Within this building frame the solid articulation (by correlation) between test measurement and more laboriously, objectively rated or sampled real-life performance can be worked out.

Consequently, both the limitations of available data and the need for building a perspective to guide further research dictate that the first system of traits for describing personality shall be established *in terms of rating variables.* The findings by behavior ratings are thus the substance of the next two chapters, after which questionnaire and objective test data respectively will be studied.

The efficiency of rating. Much has been written and demonstrated about the reliabilities and validities of ratings

(*40*), (*152*), (*157*), (*250*), (*232*), (*269*). As employed in the most routine situations these are undoubtedly significantly lower than for tests, but with the special precautions which are sometimes taken in research it is possible to raise both to a very satisfactory level. The precautions include:

(1) Having the subjects ranked instead of rated and ranked within small groups only. This is less artificial and also more thorough, insuring actual paired comparisons with respect to the behavior studied.

(2) Having judges who are (*a*) skilled in judging, (*b*) not related to the subjects in any official capacity but preferably peers of the subjects, (*c*) really intimate with all aspects of the subjects' lives. This last requires that the group to be ranked shall be small (and preferably residential), say not more than twenty subjects.

(3) Avoiding halo and stereotype distortions (*a*) by fore-warning and training the judges to avoid prejudiced attitudes, (*b*) by having the subjects ranked on one trait at a time, (*c*) by multiplying the number of judges, preferably to include those seeing the subjects from more varied angles. This last modification may end by requiring all members of a group to rate all members. As the present writer has shown (*55*), the consistency coefficients obtained when the estimates of one half of a group are correlated with the other half (pooled ratings) are extremely good, rivaling those found with objective tests ($+ 0.9$). (See also Carter.)

(4) Having the trait elements to be rated very clearly defined in terms of a series of actual behavior manifestations, and having the judges observe the subjects for the same amount of time in the same situations.

3. THE CHOICE OF ACTUAL TRAIT ELEMENTS IN TERMS OF WHICH TO ESTABLISH PATTERNS

The factor-analytic quandary. The choice of trait elements is conditioned from the beginning by the important consideration that the *surface traits* which are established will normally themselves have to stand as material for a later *factor analysis into source traits*.

Now the structure of *factors* which is extracted from a correlation matrix depends partly, with respect to the definition both of the number and the nature of the factors found, upon the choice of the trait population which forms the foundation of the original correlation matrix. The introduction of extra traits will usually mean the emergence of one or two new factors, the modification of existing factor meanings, and the extension of some factors from specific factors to group factors. For factors originally appearing in only one or two traits may find expression also in some of the newcomer traits, while factors which covered the whole of the original matrix may fail to cover everything in the extended matrix. This matter of "factor perspective" is enlarged upon in the next chapter.

Consequently one cannot hope to analyze the factors of personality by dovetailing together, as an aerophotographer puts together many consecutive photo maps, a large number of separate researches, each factor analyzing one restricted aspect of personality. Further discussion will show that such merging can be done to some extent with surface, cluster traits but not readily with factors.

The outstanding need in personality research today, therefore, is the provision of a broad, perspective-giving factor foundation for all later small researches undertaken in restricted or special areas. This requires a truly comprehensive research, taking into account, in a single factor analysis, all aspects of personality. Within the perspectives of such a research, which could succeed in setting out the major factors adequate for describing of the greater part of known individual differences of personality, it would be possible later to plan restricted researches and to elaborate local factors resulting from more microscopic examination of behavior in a particular field. The theoretical difficulties, and the arduous practical labor of a factor-analytic study on so wide a basis, have hitherto prevented its realization, but an attempt to handle the problem is presented here and in the following chapter.

The concept of the personality sphere. The first and greatest theoretical difficulty in the path of this enterprise consists in finding a basis for deciding when the chosen population of traits is truly comprehensive. In what way can one insure that all aspects of personality are taken into account in the trait-element list?

This is a question of such rich philosophical implication that it stuns the imagination. Yet the answer may be extremely simple. Human nature, its vagaries and consistencies, have been so important a topic of human interest for such countless centuries that it would be strange if language had not yet developed reference symbols for all aspects having any importance. It is true, as Allport has so interestingly shown (6), that language is constantly developing new trait terms. It is also true, as the present writer discusses more fully elsewhere (54), that different languages sometimes appear to have noncomparable terms, though closer inspection shows that the new terms correspond either to true culture-trait novelties or else to subdivisions of terms present in the other language.

Language vocabulary on the whole, however, appears almost to have reached a plateau in its development of symbolism for personality traits. Examination of most of the novel terms in any generation shows that they are mainly creatures of fashion, essentially synonymous with ten to twenty terms already in use for the trait concerned (54). There is very little in human nature today that can be better described by the words invented in the past four hundred years than by the words which Shakespeare used.

A small minority of trait terms, corresponding to new aspects of personality rendered important by changing social structure and mechanical invention, or created by new environmental molds, really represent something new. Such traits can be exemplified by air-pilot skill, the trait of being a good democratic leader, and perhaps by certain syndromes of nervous exhaustion connected with the pace of modern life.

Throughout the above discussion it is implicit that language covers all aspects that are important for other human beings. It is likely that language neglects some traits which are relevant only to the physical world or to animals. If machines had tongues they might rate human beings according to certain machine-handling traits which do not issue in results observable by or important to other human beings, while among dogs there might well be terms much concerned with the way human beings use their feet. Language, in short, is not guaranteed to cover *all* aspects of personality behavior, but all aspects which have social and material importance for humanity.

This is the justification for taking language as the basis for the personality sphere. The personality sphere may be considered to present a complete surface, constituted by many small "trait areas," each trait area defined by a trait term and abutting on traits most closely resembling it, the whole constituting an endless but finite continuum of behavior meaning. If trait character is represented by direction as in factor-analytic representation, the sphere must be considered as one in n-dimensional space. There is no guarantee, in the axioms of this formal system, that the trait terms in languages will be absolutely evenly distributed over the spherical surface. Intercorrelation must decide the actual closeness of different trait-term areas. However, it is part of our assumption from the study of language that no large area is completely neglected by vocabulary and that all dimensions of personality receive some representation.

A comprehensive list of basic trait elements. Recourse to the dictionary, to provide the actual trait sphere, reveals some four thousand trait terms in most modern, developed languages (*6*). Allport and Odbert have listed some 4500 trait terms in the English language. By throwing together terms which any average user of the language would consider synonyms, we found that the list can be reduced, however, to about 160 terms. These comprise a kind of Basic English for the complete description of personality.

In the research in which the reduction was carried out (*54*) we desisted from reducing the list farther by any mere inspection of meaning, and kept many terms separated which on logical grounds could well have been thrown together. The "trait element," with which covariational research begins, must be a unitary piece of behavior. If there is the slightest doubt about considering two trait terms as identical in meaning, therefore, it is best to keep them apart and leave the verdict to the correlation coefficient. Only the correlation of actual behavior can decide whether two near-synonyms can be considered two measures of the same thing. For this reason the basic trait list below errs on the side of multiplying variables. It lists, for example, two varieties of the trait "sociability": "Gregarious" (liking to be in company) *vs.* "Self-Sufficient" and "Adventurous" (liking to meet new people) *vs.* "Shy"; also two varieties of "emotionality" and several forms of "assertiveness." However, it remains questionable whether this list can be considered a list of *trait elements* rather than *traits*, in the sense of the definition of our system. We should like to believe that all are narrow enough for trait elements, but by the standards of Chapter 4 and of the tests and measurements section (Chapter 11) we cannot consider specificity to have been attained. Rather they are a compromise, constituting the smallest elements which it is practicable to pursue with present research resources, but still, in the commoner sense of the term, traits.

To the 160 concepts derived entirely from the dictionary were added, in our basic trait list, all terms which have been used in technical psychological description, including (1) the trait fragments formed from breaking down all well-known type classifications, normal and abnormal; (2) the unitary abilities found by the last twenty years of psychometric research; (3) the principal interest categories as used in measuring interests; and (4) a number of special psychological concepts such as frustration tolerance (Rosenzweig), level of aspiration, sthenic emotionality (Burt), disposition rigidity (perseveration), etc. Some modern psychologists may be astonished to hear that these concepts were found so well represented in the common dictionary-derived concepts that the addition of the above four sources only raised the total number of variables from 160 to 171. Of course, some of the psychological variables from the abnormal field indicated more extreme behavior than that connoted by the dictionary terms, but they could be considered as lying farther out on the same "meaning continuum." Indeed, in the end the *interest categories* turned out to be the only real additions, for the trait lists of the dictionary are, for some reason, short on interests. A number of technical psychological variables are too wide to be equated with any one dictionary trait. Others — e.g., schizothyme — are too interpretive to be trusted as such for a groundwork of personality observation.

Throughout, our aim has been to provide a list of *descriptive variables*. Most of the 171 traits in the following standard basic trait list are in the form of a pair of polar opposites. Most dictionary terms arrange themselves in opposites as naturally as in synonyms. Definition by polar opposites has very great advantages in rating. When opposites are not given, raters tend to put in their own. Since one trait logically has several different orders of opposites, depending on the field of reference, the axis of the continuum then "wobbles." But if the opposite is to form a maximally useful bipolar continuum, it is very important that it should be a true opposite psychologically as well as logically. Masochism is the logical opposite of sadism, but a psychologist might argue that an individual could in fact be high in both sadism and masochism — i.e., in algolagnia. Most dynamic traits should have as opposites a term denoting a zero amount of that trait. As with synonyms, if one proceeds cautiously, desisting from matching as opposites whenever there is doubt, the correlations can be trusted later to throw true opposites into line. Consequently, dynamic and some ability and temperament traits were not given opposites. (The rating opposite to high gluttony (hunger) is low gluttony, not disgust and dislike of food.)

Each variable label is a term chosen from many synonyms collected in that group. A few of these synonyms, not the closest but those chosen to stake out the limits of meaning of the trait category concerned, are set out alongside each of the polar opposites in the list below, in order that each variable may be adequately defined and "standardized."

4. A LIST OF VARIABLES CONSTITUTING THE COMPLETE "PERSONALITY SPHERE"

TABLE 15

PERSONALITY VARIABLES COMPRISING THE COMPLETE PERSONALITY SPHERE

First Condensation from Unabridged Dictionary and Psychological Literature Fields

TRAIT OR VARIABLE	OPPOSITE OF TRAIT OR VARIABLE (IF ANY)
1. ABILITIES. INTELLIGENCE. Capacity to perceive relations, insight, quickness to learn, adaptability in problems.	
2. ABILITIES. SPECIAL ABILITIES. DRAWING. Facility in graphical representation.	
3. " " " " " " " "	MATHEMATICAL. Thurstone's N or number ability.
4. " " " " " " " "	MANUAL DEXTERITY. (See Cox's M factor.)
5. " " " " " " " "	MECHANICAL APTITUDE. Facility in constructing and understanding machinery.
6. " " " " " " " "	MUSICAL APTITUDE. (See Seashore.)

TABLE 15 — *Continued*

Trait or Variable	Opposite of Trait or Variable (if Any)
7. ABILITIES. SPECIAL ABILITIES.	PHYSICAL STRENGTH AND ENDURANCE.
8. " " " " " " " "	LOGICAL ABILITY, REASONING. Thurstone's I, etc.
9. " " " " " " " "	SPATIAL, VISUAL ABILITY. Thurstone's S and Kelley's factors.
10. " " " " " " " "	VERBAL APTITUDE. Thurstone and Spearman's V factor. Facility in right use of words.

11. ALERT ——————————— ABSENT-MINDED
   Observant, vigilant, omniper-   Dreamy, indefinite, depersonalized.
   cipient.

12. ACQUISITIVE
   Greedy, grasping, covetous, money-minded, mercenary.

13. AFFECTED ——————————— NATURAL
   Theatrical, pretentious, foppish.   Sincere in manner, pretenseless.

14. AFFECTIONATE ——————— FRIGID
   Loving, fond, comradely, subli-   Cold, indifferent, cool.
   mated sex attraction.

15. AGOROPHOBIC
   Nervous out in the open, terrified of space.

16. ALCOHOLIC
   Addicted to getting drunk, fond of intoxication.

17. AMBITIOUS ——————————— UNAMBITIOUS
   Aspiring, self-improving.   Lackadaisical.

18. AMOROUS ——————————— LUSTLESS
   Erotic, amative, lascivious, carnal,
   lustful.

19. ANALYTICAL
   Casuistical, hairsplitting, penetrating.

20. ANTEVERT ——————————— RETROVERT
   Oriented to the future, forward-   Retrospective, oriented to child-
   looking.   hood and family.

TABLE 15 — *Continued*

Trait or Variable	Opposite of Trait or Variable (if Any)

21. ARGUMENTATIVE
Altercative, contentious, factious, disputatious.

22. ARROGANT ——————— HUMBLE
Insolent, proud, supercilious,   Meek.
scornful, snobbish.

23. ASCETIC ————————— SENSUOUS
Abstinent, abstemious, Calvinis- Pleasure-seeking, self-indulgent,
tic.   epicurean.

24. ASSERTIVE ———————— SUBMISSIVE
Ascendant, dominating, aggres- Self-abasing, obedient, deferential,
sive, emulous.   diffident.

25. AUSTERE ————————— PROFLIGATE
Stern, dignified, severe, strict,   Licentious, abandoned, debauched.
Spartan, chaste.

26. AUTOCRATIC
Domineering, dictatorial, tyrannical, presumptuous, bullying.

27. BOASTFUL ———————— MODEST
Blustering, vauntful, grandilo- Unassuming, demure, coy.
quent.

28. BROODING ————————— UNREPINING
Mopey, sulky, moody, moony.

29. CAUTIOUS ———————— RECKLESS
Circumspect, wary, careful, pre- Rash, unwary, dashing, careless.
cautious.

30. CHARMING
Magnetic, pleasurable personality, sweet.

31. CHEERFUL ———————— GLOOMY
Euphoric, gay, exalted, happy,   Depressed, sad, melancholy,
lighthearted.   suicidal.

32. CLEAR-THINKING ———— INCOHERENT
Incisive, does not lose head if   Confused, disoriented, disturbed in
excited.   judgment.

33. CLEVER
Agile, adroit, deft, facile, sharp-witted.

34. CLAUSTROPHOBIC
Nervous in small enclosed spaces, afraid of being hemmed in.

TABLE 15 — *Continued*

Trait or Variable	Opposite of Trait or Variable (if Any)
35. CONCEITED ——————— Self-complacent, self-important, vain, cocky, pompous.	SELF–DISSATISFIED Self-disdainful, self-loathing, self-accusing.
36. CONSCIENTIOUS ——————— Active super ego, dutiful, principled.	CONSCIENCELESS Unscrupulous, expediential, remorseless.
37. CONSTRUCTIVE Creative, happy in building and making.	
38. CONTENTED ——————— Adjusted, satisfied, not allergic to monotony.	DISSATISFIED Discontented, wistful, nostalgic, craving excitement.
39. CONVENTIONAL ——————— Orthodox, conforming, prim, decorous.	INDIVIDUALISTIC Iconoclastic, dissenting, unpredictable in outlook.
40. COÖPERATIVE ——————— Helpful, willing, assistful.	OBSTRUCTIVE Saboteurish, refractory, ill-wishing.
41. COURAGEOUS ——————— Brave, plucky, physically courageous.	COWARDLY Pluckless, flinching, giving way to fear.
42. CURIOUS ——————— Inquisitive, snoopy, wondering, nosy.	UNENQUIRING Incurious, searchless, unwondering.
43. CYNICAL ——————— Misanthropic, nihilistic, sneering.	IDEALISTIC Noble-minded, lofty.
44. DEBONAIR Jaunty, dapper, natty.	
45. DEFENSIVE Self-justifying, having chip on shoulder.	
46. DUBITATIVE ——————— Doubting, hesitant, vacillating, folie de doute.	DECISIVE Decided, succinct, sees in black and white.
47. EASYGOING ——————— Happy-go-lucky, good-natured, lacking exacting interests.	PERNICKETY Unteasable, strained, short-tempered, rigorous.
48. ECCENTRIC Queer, unpredictable, quixotic, cranky, faddy.	

TABLE 15 — *Continued*

Trait or Variable	Opposite of Trait or Variable (if Any)
49. EFFEMINATE ———————— MASCULINE Womanish, girlish.	Virile.
50. EGOTISTICAL ———————— ALTOCENTRIC Narcissistic, egocentric, incapable of object love.	Thinking of others.
51. ELOQUENT ———————— INARTICULATE Fluent, oratorical, ranting.	
52. EMOTIONAL I ———————— UNEMOTIONAL Emotionality in all varieties of emotion.	Burt's general emotionality factor.
53. EMOTIONAL II —(Burt's ——— UNEMOTIONAL sthenic-asthenic factor) Emotionality in sociability, assertiveness, anger, sex.	Opposed to emotionality in tenderness, submissiveness, disgust, fear.
54. ENERGETIC-SPIRITED ——— LANGUID Chipper, forceful, high-spirited.	Listless, languorous, spiritless.
55. ENERGETIC–INDUSTRIOUS —— INACTIVE–INDOLENT Diligent, active, strenuous, tireless.	Fatigable, hypokinetic, idle, lazy.
56. ENTERPRISING ———————— SHIFTLESS Initiative-having, eager to undertake.	Helpless.
57. ENTHUSIASTIC ———————— APATHETIC Zestful, ardent, zealous, avid.	World-weary, desireless, resigned.
58. EVASIVE ———————— FACING LIFE Equivocating, excusatory, escapist.	
59. EXCITABLE ———————— PHLEGMATIC (as unexcitable; Thrillful, volatile, marked autonomic response.	see No. 76) Stolid, impervious, immobile.
60. EXTRA-PUNITIVE ———————— PRAISEFUL Censorious, faultfinding, critical, scolding, nagging.	Complimentary, eulogistic.
61. EXHIBITIONIST ———————— SELF-EFFACING Self-displaying, eager for admiration.	Not show-off, not craving recognition.

TABLE 15 — *Continued*

Trait or Variable	Opposite of Trait or Variable (if Any)
62. FAIR–MINDED Fair, just, non-partisan.	PARTIAL Prejudiced, biased.
63. FASTIDIOUS Squeamish, prudish, dainty, over-nice.	COARSE Slatternly, slovenly, crude.
64. FLATTERING Sycophantic, unctuous, fawning, oily.	
65. FORMAL Ceremonious, ritualistic, impersonal.	CASUAL Spontaneous, informal, offhand.
66. FRANK Straightforward, candid, boldly direct in manner.	SECRETIVE Guarded, non-committal, disingenuous.
67. FRIENDLY Accommodating, obliging, affable, bland.	HOSTILE Surly, disagreeable, ill-willed.
68. GENEROUS Indulgent, liberal, magnanimous.	TIGHT–FISTED Mean, stingy.
69. GENIAL Convivial, cordial, hospitable, neighborly.	COLD–HEARTED Inexpansive, infestive.
70. GLUTTONOUS Overfond of eating, gourmand, piggish.	
71. GRATEFUL Appreciative, thankful.	THANKLESS Ingrateful, inappreciative, ungracious.
72. HABIT–BOUND Stereotyped, in a rut.	LABILE Unroutinized, youthful.
73. HARD Hard-hearted, callous, harsh, unfeeling.	SOFT–HEARTED Sensitive to feelings of others.
74. HEADSTRONG Self-willed, fiery, urgent-tempered.	GENTLE–TEMPERED Conciliable, ruly, passionless.
75. HEARTY Boisterous, vibrant, noisy, tumultuous.	QUIET Mild, gentle, milquetoast.

TABLE 15 — *Continued*

TRAIT OR VARIABLE	OPPOSITE OF TRAIT OR VARIABLE (IF ANY)

76. HIGH–STRUNG ——————— RELAXED
Tense, intense, hypertonic, hectic, taut.   Calm, serene, reposeful, inexcitable, phlegmatic (as unexcited; see No. 59).

77. HONEST ——————— DISHONEST
Upright, principled, truthful, incorruptible.   Cheating, thievish, rascally, lying.

78. HURRIED ——————— LETHARGIC
Hustling, hunting disposition, pursuing competition.   Leisurely, unhurried, no press of activity.

79. HYPOCHONDRIACAL
Concerned with half-imaginary illnesses, malingering.

80. IMAGINATIVE ——————— DULL
Fanciful, visionary, mentally fruitful.   Literal, unimaginative, plodding.

81. IMITATIVE   NON–IMITATIVE
Apish, plagiaristic, quick to copy.   Inemulous

82. IMPULSIVE (TEMPERA- ——— DELIBERATE
MENTALLY)
Impetuous, precipitate, hasty.   Level-headed, judicious, self-restrained.

83. INDEPENDENT ——————— DEPENDENT
Self-reliant, self-helping, self-sufficient.   Dependent, passive, clinging.

84. INFLEXIBLE (EMOTION- ——— ADAPTABLE (TO CHANGE)
ALLY)
Rigid, conservative, die-hard.   Elastic, flexible, pliant, low P.

85. INHIBITED ——————— INCONTINENT
Restrained, constrained, restricted movement.   Free, expresses emotions easily.

86. INTERESTS WIDE ——————— INTERESTS NARROW
Emotional response to many things.   Emotional response narrow and restricted.

87. INTERESTS, SPECIAL, AESTHETIC.
General aesthetic, poetry, decoration.

TABLE 15 — *Continued*

Trait or Variable	Opposite of Trait or Variable (if Any)

88. INTERESTS, SPECIAL, ARTISTIC
Specifically with respect to painting, art, architecture.

89. " " " " ECONOMIC
Commerce, business.

90. " " " " HOME AND FAMILY
Domestic, children, immediate circle, house.

91. " " " " MUSIC
Playing or listening.

92. " " " " PHYSICAL ACTIVITY
Athletics, sports, travel.

93. " " " " POLITICAL
Nationalistic, patriotic.

94. " " " " RELIGIOUS
In religious beliefs and systems.

95. " " " " SOCIAL
People, meetings, social entertainments.

96. " " " " THEORETICAL   Endocathective.
Intellectual, scholarly language, literature, philosophy.

97. " " " " TECHNICAL   Exocathective.
Mechanical, scientific, interest in manual construction.

98. INTUITIVE ——————— LOGICAL
Implicit thought and emotion,   Explicit, detached thought.
intraceptive.

99. INTROSPECTIVE
Looking into the self (core of introversions in strict sense).

100. IRRITABLE ——————— GOOD–TEMPERED
Crabbed, choleric, querulous,   Slow to anger.
hot-tempered.

101. JEALOUS
Envious, rivalrous.

102. KIND (BY DISPOSITION) —— RUTHLESS
Benevolent, pitiful, maternal,   Uncharitable, mean-spirited.
protective.

TABLE 15 — *Continued*

Trait or Variable	Opposite of Trait or Variable (if Any)

103. KIND (ON PRINCIPLE)
Christian, humanitarian, humane, considerate.

104. LAUGHTERFUL ——————— MIRTHLESS
Jestful, flippant, jocose, face-   · Laughterless, unamused.
tious.

105. LEADING (NOT DOMINEERING)
Managing, leading democratically, didactic, proselytizing, controlling persuasively.

106. LOYAL ——————————— FICKLE
Faithful, stanch, single-hearted,   Inconstant, never strongly
true.   attached.

107. MATURE (IN EMOTIONAL — INFANTILE
DEVELOPMENT)
Frustration tolerant, accept re-   Not self-objective, ignored subjec-
sponsibility.   tive in others.

108. MEMORY GOOD ————— FORGETFUL
Recollective, retentive.   Amnesic, aphasic.

109. MISCHIEVOUS
Impish, wanton, playful, larksome, puckish, frolicsome.

110. MULISH ————————— REASONABLE
Obstinate, negativistic, con-   Tractable, teachable.
trary, perverse.

111. MYSTICAL ——————— APOLLONIAN
Superstitious, metaphysical,   Matter-of-fact, classical, unsenti-
Dionysian, soulful.   mental.

112. ·NEUROTIC
Showing mental conflict and general symptoms, unstrung, nervous tics, easily startled.

113. OPINIONATED ————— TOLERANT
Bigoted, narrow-minded, fanat-   Open-minded, liberalistic.
ical, cliquish.

114. OPTIMISTIC ——————— PESSIMISTIC
Sanguine, hopeful.   Hopeless, panic-mongering, de-
spairful.

115. ORIGINAL ——————— BANAL
Resourceful, inventive, ingen-   Notionless, platitudinous, poverty
ious.   of ideas.

TABLE 15 — Continued

Trait or Variable	Opposite of Trait or Variable (if Any)
116. PATIENT —————— IMPATIENT Forebearing, long-suffering, in- frustrable.	Overhasty, restive.
117. PAINSTAKING —————— SLIPSHOD Neat, thorough, accurate, thoroughgoing, prompt.	Lax, careless, slovenly, amateur- ish, procrastinating.
118. PEDANTIC —————— DISORDERLY Precisionist, fussy, doctrinaire, sterile, punctilious.	Inexplicit, vague, unacademic.
119. PERSEVERING —————— QUITTING Persistent in motive, determined, tenacious.	Faltering, flagging, lacking grit.
120. PHANTASYING Deluded, living in imaginary world, hallucinated, excessive fiction or drama.	
121. PHYSICALLY ACTIVE Need of physical exercise, excessive physical energy.	
122. PIOUS —————— WORLDLY Devout, saintly, spiritual.	Materialistic, impious, secular.
123. PLAINTIVE Lamentful, greedy for affection, cry-baby, sighful, grumbling, sup- pliant.	
124. PLANFUL —————— PLANLESS Prudent, foresighted, purpose- ful, provident, designful, scheming.	
125. POISED —————— AWKWARD Self-assured, nonchalant, hav- ing savoir-faire.	Self-conscious, unsure, stilted.
126. POLISHED —————— ROUGH Urbane, smooth, refined, cour- teous.	Bluff, curt, abrupt, rude, gruff.
127. PRACTICAL —————— UNREALISTIC Capable in emergencies, efficient in practical matters.	Not grappling with everyday mat- ters.
128. PUGNACIOUS —————— PEACEABLE Truculent, quarrelsome, mili- tant, destructive.	Pacific, not belligerent.

TABLE 15 — *Continued*

Trait or Variable	Opposite of Trait or Variable (if Any)
129. RELIABLE —————————— Trustworthy, dependable in general.	UNDEPENDABLE Unpredictable, not steadfast.
130. RESERVED —————————— Reticent, seclusive, Olympian.	INTRUSIVE Expansive, outgoing, intimate, adhesive.
131. RESILIENT —————————— Buoyant, effervescent, ebullient, frisky.	DEPRESSIBLE Not readily recovering from emotional shock.
132. RESPONSIVE —————————— Accessible, sympathetic, commiserative, movable.	ALOOF Shut-in, indifferent, no social rapport.
133. REVERENT —————————— God-fearing, contrite, penitent.	REBELLIOUS Ribald, aweless, defiant, disrespectful.
134. SADISTIC —————————— Cruel, spiteful, malevolent, murderous, bloodthirsty.	MASOCHISTIC Seeking suffering.
135. SARCASTIC Sardonic, mordant, satirical.	
136. SELF–CONFIDENT ————— Confident, assured.	SELF–DISTRUSTING Self-uncertain.
137. SELF–CONTROLLED Self-commanding, stoic, self-mastering, self-disciplined.	
138. SELF–DECEIVING Self-deluding, self-escaping.	
139. SELF–PITYING Martyr-like, self-immolating.	
140. SELF–RESPECTING High ego ideal, self-revering, attending to standards of selfhood.	
141. SELFISH —————————— Egoistic, self-interested, uses people, parasitic. (Egotistic is elsewhere.)	SELF–DENYING Selfless, considerate, chivalrous.
142. SENSITIVE —————————— Feelings easily hurt, offendable.	TOUGH Thick-skinned, insensitive.

TABLE 15 — *Continued*

Trait or Variable	Opposite of Trait or Variable (if Any)
143. SENTIMENTAL ——————— HARD–HEADED	
Slushy, maudlin, romantic.	Unromantic, not easily sentimental.
144. SERIOUS ———————— FRIVOLOUS	
Sober, earnest, grave, solemn.	Light-minded, giddy, rattlebrain.
145. SHREWD ——————— NAÏVE	
Calculating, cunning, astute, crafty.	Innocent, simple, un-Machiavellian.
146. SLANDEROUS	
Calumniating, vituperative, detractory.	
147. SLEEPS WELL ————— SLEEPS POORLY	
Deep sleeper.	Insomniac.
148. SLOW (TEMPERAMEN- ——— QUICK TALLY, MOVEMENT, REACTION)	
Sluggish, slow-witted, torpid, retarded.	Quick of apprehension (not g), nimblewitted.
149. SOCIABLE I ——————— SHY	
Fond of meeting people, good mixer.	Bashful, hermitish, feeling of social inadequacy.
150. SOCIABLE II ——————— SELF–SUFFICIENT	
Gregarious, congregative, companionable.	Exclusive, self-contained, need of seclusion, solitary.
151. SOPHISTICATED ————— SIMPLE–HEARTED	
Blasé, subtle, wordly-wise, tortuous.	Childlike, guileless, ignorant.
152. SOUR	
Sullen, sulky, embittered, dour.	
153. STABLE EMOTIONALLY ——— CHANGEABLE	
Persistent in temper, constant, steady.	Chameleonic, mercurial, fitful, erratic, temperamental.
154. STRONG IN PERSONALITY	
Impressive, easily dominating, well-knit.	
155. SUBJECTIVE ——————— GUIDED BY REALITY	
Autistic, theoretical, a prioristic.	Objective, pragmatic, not deceived by wishful thinking.

TABLE 15 — *Continued*

Trait or Variable	Opposite of Trait or Variable (if Any)

156. SUGGESTIBLE
Hypnotizable, impressible, easily influenced.

157. TACTFUL ——————————— TACTLESS
Discreet, politic, sensitive of Undiplomatic.
   others' feelings.

158. TALKATIVE ——————————— TACITURN
Profuse, voluble, vociferous, Terse, incommunicative, silent.
   flight of ideas.

159. TEMPERATE ——————————— EXTREME (IN SCHIZO-
   THYME SENSE)
Balanced, moderate, equable, Tragic and heroic emotionality,
   Platonic.   intemperate.

160. THOUGHTFUL ——————————— UNREFLECTIVE
Reflective, studious, meditative. Incogitant, thoughtless, hasty.

161. THRIFTY ——————————— CARELESS WITH GOODS
Parsimonious, frugal, niggardly. Spendthrift, extravagant, thrift-
   less.

162. TIMID (DISPOSITION) ——— ADVENTUROUS
Fearful, apprehensive, faint- Love of risk and chance, bold,
   hearted.   daring.

163. TREACHEROUS
Traitorous, treasonable, deceitful, sly, dissembling.

164. TRUSTFUL ——————————— SUSPICIOUS
Credulous, humbugable, gulli- Skeptical, distrustful, agnostical.
   ble, trusting, unsuspecting.

165. VERSATILE
Jack-of-all-trades.

166. VINDICTIVE ——————————— UNRESENTFUL
Grievance-bearing, vengeful, Forgiving, reconciliatory.
   rancorous, litigious.

167. VIVACIOUS
Lively, animated, expressive of face and gesture.

168. WANDERING ——————————— SETTLING DOWN
Vagabondish, unable to stay Belonging.
   still, gypsy-like, runabout.

169. WITTY ——————————— HUMORLESS
Humorous, waggish, quipsome,
   esprit.

TABLE 15 — *Continued*

Trait or Variable	Opposite of Trait or Variable (if Any)
170. WISE ——————— FOOLISH	
Sage, sagacious, wordly-wise, owlish, sensible.	
171. WORRYING ——————— PLACID	
Anxious, stressful, agitated, fretful, alarmist.	Untroubled, airy, fatalistic.

5. THE MANNER OF INTEGRATING RESULTS FROM DIVERSE RESEARCHES

The goals of cluster research collation. The evidence of trait clustering shortly to be examined is not all founded on correlations from the above trait list. It is compiled from fourteen different researches, each using a different and limited list of variables; but with extremely few exceptions (variables which are not really personality traits) all the variables used in these studies can be found in the above trait list.

From these fourteen researches some 130 clusters were catalogued. Many of these "phenomenal" clusters are obviously likely to be mutually confirmatory rediscoveries of clusters already found in one or another of the parallel researches. To determine the number and the nature of the independent clusters, *paired comparisons were carried out in every possible way among the 130,* and clusters showing considerable overlap in their entourage of constituent traits were thrown together as a single match.[1] In this way the 50 *nuclear* clusters of the chart beginning page 246 were obtained.

Technical problems in collation of clusters. The collation of findings from these different researches could not be carried out with mechanical certainty because of the following circumstances:

---

[1] In two of the largest researches — that of the Harvard Psychological Clinic (*225*) and that of the present writer (*54*) — this judgment of similarity on the basis of content could be assisted by knowledge gained from further research, showing the actual intercorrelations among the clusters.

(1) Different investigators have used different correlation standards for admission of traits to clusters. The variations of standard are not great (0.4 to 0.6); and one may note that even if the same numerical standards had been adopted the situation would not have been improved, for differing variabilities of groups, reliabilities of estimates, etc., would normally cause one and the same cluster to have a different mean intercorrelation in different researches. Instead of taking a rigid arithmetic standard in judging equivalence, we have allowed for population selection effects, or, failing that, have assumed investigators have about the same standard when they get about the same percentage of the randomly sampled traits into clusters.

(2) Some have taken rather atypical traits or groups, or groups limited in personality variety — e.g., graduate students or college faculties — and have thus found esoteric clusters not present in the general population, while missing more fundamental patterns of human nature. However, the striking fact about these anomalous studies is that the majority of their clusters *are* the same as in other researches.

(3) The populations have been of very different ages. Ideally a presentation of empirical clusters would prepare parallel charts, one for each age level, to reveal modification of clusters, for it is likely on general clinical grounds that the form and constitution of clusters would change with age. Similar separations would need to be made with respect to population sampling by social class, intelligence, etc. But the first need in cluster research is to establish the patterns which persist over most settings of human nature and most ages.

That most clusters retain recognizable identity or continuity over critical age and sex transitions is shown in Tryon's observations (*226*) with boys and girls of different ages and by Sanford's and Horn's data comparing children and university students, as well as by the close similarity of many of Sanford's (*225*) clusters for children and the present writer's clusters for mature adults. Tryon found the following type of cluster modification with age and sex.

TRAITS FALLING IN TWO RECOGNIZABLY SIMILAR CLUSTERS (TWO INSTANCES)

(1) FOR BOYS 12 YEARS	(2) FOR BOYS 15 YEARS	(1) FOR BOYS 15 YEARS	(2) FOR GIRLS 15 YEARS
Daring	Daring	Restless	Restless
Leader	Leader	Talkative	Talkative
Active in games	Active in games	Attention-getting	Attention-getting
Friendly	Fights		Bossy
			Fights
(Nuclear Cluster CB 1–2 on chart)		(Nuclear Cluster CA 1 on chart)	

(4) As stated above, different trait lists have been used out of which to establish clusters. Clusters, or parts of clusters, are missing from some researches for no more mysterious reason than that the grist has not been available in the mills of the original trait list. Here, too, one meets the difficulty arising from the use of different but synonymous terms or of the same terms somewhat differently. For example, *Good Follower* in AA 11 (McCloy) seems to be the same as *Loyal* in AA 14 (Cattell), while *leading* in CA 53 (Cattell) becomes (*a*) *Desire to Impose Will on Others* in CA 51 (McCloy), (*b*) *Need Dominance* in CA 54 (Sanford-Murray), and (*c*) *Leader* in CA 52 (Williams). Two particularly ambiguous terms are " aggressive " (sometimes pugnacity, sometimes energy, sometimes assertion) and "sympathy" (sometimes kindness, sometimes sensitive, gregarious responsiveness). This last defect of procedure is the most serious source of indeterminacy (and the least likely to be accidentally illuminating) in cluster definition.[1]

---

[1] The need for some more standardized, comprehensive trait list, of the kind presented above, and for the definition of traits by bipolar opposite pairs of terms, is grievously evidenced by these researches. It is interesting to find that in the cluster-classification process a syndrome which was not recognized in one form was often recognized easily by the psychologist in its obverse form, indicating the practical value of bipolar definition.

The trait-population problem reaches its climax in dealing with those researches in which the investigator has been interested in only one pet cluster and has packed the original list with traits likely to fall in or near this cluster, while neglecting to take bearings on a sufficient number of other important points of the behavior compass.

(5) If there is much difference in reliability of rating or measurement among the various traits, or among the various researches using the same traits, the attenuating effect of low reliability will have reduced the intercorrelations of variables to the point where some will no longer reach the standard required for admission to a cluster.

6. PHENOMENAL CLUSTERS, NUCLEAR CLUSTERS, AND PERSONALITY SECTORS

The relativity of clusters. Before the results of combining cluster findings from different researches can be understood, without danger of misinterpretation, it is necessary to go more deeply into the nature of clusters than the presentations of Chapters 4 and 5 permitted. In any typical correlation matrix, whether of ability or personality variables, one rarely finds the ideal "textbook" clusters consisting of entirely separate groupings of variables. Instead there is a ragged network of high-correlation linkages. Therein one variable appears in as many as three or four clusters, and any one cluster may appear to be built up of several overlapping clusters.

The typical situation when a matrix is searched for clusters [1] is instanced by Diagram 14. Let us suppose that a variable is admitted to a cluster on condition that its correlations with each and every other member exceeds [2] $+ 0.5$. Then we may

[1] The actual techniques of cluster research are described in detail in a special article (57).

[2] The criterion for entry might almost equally well be an *average* correlation with other cluster members to exceed a certain figure, or an average correlation exceeding a certain *ratio* to the general level of the matrix, as in Holzinger's B coefficient criterion (120); but the great majority of cluster studies have actually used the above criterion.

find four "phenomenal" clusters: (1, 2, 6, 7, 11, 15), (1, 2, 7, 9, 11, 12, 15), (1, 2, 5, 7, 11, 13, 15), and (1, 2, 5, 7, 8, 15). By "phenomenal cluster" we mean a literal cluster, in which

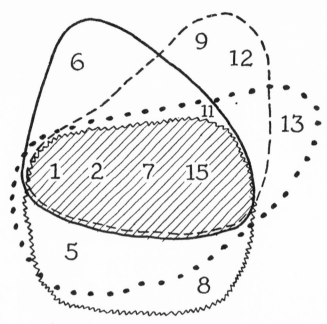

DIAGRAM 14. Phenomenal and Nuclear Clusters

each variable satisfies the given requirements, the whole cluster being staked out without regard to its possible trespass on other clusters. In all data known to the writer it happens that these phenomenal clusters do not arrange themselves randomly among the variables but tend to converge on certain "nuclei" — (1, 2, 7, 15) in the diagram above. It is economical, therefore, to deal with "nuclear clusters" (1, 2, 7, 15) and to consider the other variables involved as different "appendages" to the nucleus — namely (11, 12, and 9), (11, 13), (5, 8), (11, 5, and 6) — which can be recorded alongside the nucleus.

Questions of the independence of clusters and the status of nucleus and appendage are closely tied up with the arbitrary level of correlation accepted for admission to a cluster. The relativity is precisely the same as that which bothers the cartographer trying to decide to which land masses the terms "hill" and "mountain" should properly be applied. A matrix which yields, in a certain area, two entirely distinct clusters when a high level of correlation is demanded by the criterion may yield only one large cluster when the criterion is slightly lowered — as two islands merge into one with the falling of the tide.

The problem arising from this fact can be grasped more comprehensively if correlations are represented spatially as cosines. The reader should turn back to Diagram 3, page 79, where for simplicity the correlations are assumed to fall in two dimensions. In a research having eleven variables ("a" through "k" in the diagram) and a minimum correlation of 0.75 for admission to a cluster, there are three clusters, A, B, and C. If the criterion is lowered to 0.40 there are two clusters, A' and B', overlapping. If, retaining the first criterion level, the variables are now increased by adding "l" and "m," correlating as shown, there arises a series of continuously overlapping clusters, such that only by some very arbitrary decision is it possible to arrive at separate clusters, A, B, and C. From consideration of this last situation, it will become evident that one could conceivably add together a number of clusters, each showing a definite overlap and partial identity with its neighbor, to form a cluster so wide that the later additions would actually have negative correlations with the first members — i.e., the cluster would subtend more than a right angle. Nothing so extreme as this actually happened with our data; but in some intensively studied areas of behavior the "cluster angle" of a continuous constellation of variables often becomes fairly wide, getting equivalent to a minimum correlation (for "belonging") of no more than 0.2.

The real danger of getting a "continuous arc" of variables, having no natural point of division, as well as the inescapable arbitrariness based on diverse minimum correlation levels (angles of inclusion), should be borne in mind when some psychometrists insist that the cluster is far more "real" and less arbitrary than the factor! In short, although the cluster claims modestly to be only a surface, or *descriptive* (rather than an *interpretive*) trait, it does not avoid certain errors of abstraction and interpretation, at least to the extent present in, say, any map projection. It singles out arbitrarily certain features and it does not record others. It simplifies the correlation matrix but at the cost of some arbitrary misrepresentation. If and when finer grades of cluster description are required, it should not be difficult to work out something akin to the Holzinger B-coefficient which will pick out clusters showing concentration of traits *relative to the surrounding topography*.

Conglomerate nuclear clusters and personality sectors. The findings of all published or otherwise available cluster researches were matched, according to the trait contents of the clusters, as indicated above, with due regard for the need to avoid wide angle clusters of the kind discussed and with alertness to the danger of forming purely arbitrary cluster boundaries. In most researches the clusters finally recorded for publication are essential nuclear clusters. Whenever clusters from different researches showed substantial overlap in one half or more of their variables, they were listed here as a probable single cluster, the slight differences in manifestation being considered traceable to different research circumstances.

These confirmed clusters may be called *conglomerate nuclear clusters*, to distinguish them from the *apparent nuclear clusters* of a single research, though they are still *nuclear clusters* and the final catalogue lists them simply as such. The trait variables set down to define the conglomerate cluster nucleus are those that are most frequently repeated in the overlapping apparent nuclear clusters. For example, in nuclear cluster

CA 1, the trait "argumentative" (or bossy-talkative) occurs in all five of the contributory apparent nuclear clusters (page 251), while "self-effacing" and its opposite appear in four out of five. These, therefore, appear at the head of the nuclear cluster list and less common variables at the foot. When the trait appears in *all* clusters, the magnitude of the average correlation with other members of the cluster decides the rank order of the trait in the nuclear cluster.

The chief generalized findings from this collation of various researches may be summarized as follows: (1) Clusters from diverse researches *do* tend to confirm each other and converge on fairly well-marked nuclei; (2) a few researches, with low cluster correlation standards, have published clusters — e.g., Maslow's "Dominance" syndrome, Sheldon's "Somatotonia" — stretching, without indication of natural divisions, over two or three nuclei — i.e., they have been considered one continuous cluster because of defective, unduly low correlation criteria; (3) though distinct nuclear clusters are everywhere readily distinguishable, they nevertheless make some loose contact with one another, seeming in this respect to go together in gregarious "groups" of nuclear clusters.

The structure of personality variables suggested by this last finding creates descriptive problems closely analogous to those encountered in descriptive astronomy. Traits are unevenly gathered together in constellations which we call clusters and, secondly, many clusters in turn bunch in "universes" of clusters. Our terminology therefore needs the flexibility of astronomical terminology, for some of these universes contain many nuclei, others only one or two; some are very remote from neighboring universes, while others are so close that the division is barely perceptible.

For the flock or "universe" of cluster nuclei, related by having some common variables in their appendages or nuclei, the term "sector" or "aspect" of personality is suggested as best corresponding to common usage and the spatial picture of correlations. Sectors are naturally discrete, irregular regions of high trait density on the surface of the multidimensional personality sphere.

Eighteen out of the twenty sectors which emerged were flocks of nuclear clusters showing definite natural limits where they "petered out." They did not subtend so wide a region of behavior (or so wide an angle of correlation) that any opposition arose between the character of the clusters fringing opposite boundaries. But two regions, A and C, extended more than could be tolerated, having regard to the necessity for logical consistency among the psychological variables in a single sector. In other words, the angle of the sector had become too wide. Region A, as indicated in another connection, began with character trustworthiness and finished with something nearer temperamental stability. Sector C began with uncomplicated self-assertiveness and ended with insecure self-defensiveness with distinct maladjustment. In both of these too extensive sectors some relatively faint dividing cracks were eventually found, so that the unduly large A cluster was split into AA, AB, and AC; and the sector C into sectors CA and CB, partly on logical grounds. No data are available to indicate definitely the width of the typical sector, but from indirect evidence one may estimate that it is about 75°, corresponding to an r of about 0.26 between the least correlated (most outlying) of the constituent nuclear clusters.

The scheme of representation and conceptualization at this stage has to be a fairly elastic one. The situation needs to be met as was met a generation ago the problem of mapping stellar distributions. The concepts and nomenclature must at once place in proper perspective the particular pattern described but must also accommodate to local anomalies of perspective and distribution. The notions of sector, cluster nucleus, and phenomenal cluster seem to meet these conceptual requirements. Naturally there will be big differences of size among the representatives of any one concept. Some sectors contain many nuclei; others, as yet, only one or two. In some — e.g., the F region — the nuclei are very closely packed, in others highly discrete and disparate.

The sectors, like the nuclei, have been arranged so that those with the closest resemblance are in immediate contiguity and labeled by consecutive letters of the alphabet. From the *"character"* quality of AA there is transition to the *"realism-emotional integration"* of AB, thence to the *"balance-frankness-optimism"* of AC, and so through the typical borderline cluster B 1, straddling both sectors, to the purely *"intelligence-rooted"* qualities of B. (The frequency with which intelligence and character integration are found to correlate would lead us to expect such a smooth bridge here.) Similarly, the *"daring and social boldness"* of CB pass, with a barely perceptible break in cluster quality, into the pure *"sociability and friendliness"* of D. Any really pervasive continuity of sectors is acknowledged, as indicated, by a master letter spreading over the sectors concerned, as in AA, AB, and AC.

It is noticeable that where sectors make contact (as by some cluster which could almost equally be either) the actual "transition cluster" bridges not only in one direction but in several. Thus G 1 (Austerity-Thoughtfulness-Stability) grades not only into AA 1 (Self-control-Loyalty-Fairminded-ness-Reliability) but also into B 2 (Gentlemanly-Disciplined Thoughtfulness) and into E 3 (Deliberateness-Seriousness-Reserve). Also there are linkages other than at the boundaries of sectors, breaking the apparent continuity of regions, notably through obvious psychological cousinship of CA 3 and F 6, of CA 1 and E 1, and of AC 2, D 5, and F 7. In short, it is not possible, in other than a rough manner, to arrange sectors in a linear continuum, or even in the richer relationships representable by the two-dimensional continuum of the surface of a literal sphere. The nature and relationships of clusters are such that the nuclei can be shown only in a multidimensional surface, as the theory of the trait sphere (*54*) has always required and as the findings of factor analysis (which deals with the same material as cluster studies) demonstrate.

7. A CATALOGUING AND AN APPRAISAL OF
AVAILABLE RESEARCH DATA

List of contributory researches. As already indicated, the research data are based on diverse population and trait samples, so that certain precautions have to be observed in combining the results. In order that the reader may assign proper weight to the various findings and perhaps draw conclusions provocative of further research from noticing correlated divergences of findings and samples, it seems worth while to describe the foundation of each research in a few evaluative observations.

The researches are listed in alphabetical order of authors, with notes on (*a*) subjects, (*b*) traits, (*c*) method of rating, and (*d*) source of rating.

* *Ackerson*, L. (*4*). 1000 girls and 2000 boys, 6–16 years. Traits checked present or absent, on basis of extensive, clinical, social, or police records.

Cattell, R. B. (*40*). (Not present research but former temperament research, labeled "Temperament–Research" in ensuing list.) 62 male college students. Rated by four fellows in residential "house." 48 traits, mainly temperamental, some characterial. Ranked on each trait on separate occasion.

Cattell, R. B. (This is the main source of data referred to in the preceding and the present chapter, undertaken especially for the solution of problems raised here, and referred to in the chart of clusters by the name of the author without addition. It is described in more detail in (*54*)). 100 adults, chosen (*a*) to be in the "settled age" period of 25–55, (*b*) to be more representative than student populations, including unskilled laborers, artists, business and professional men and women.

Traits: the complete basic trait list of 171 bipolar traits, described above. Each marked "comparatively strongly present" or "rather below aver-

---

* These trait studies are not strictly cluster studies, but are included because the data have such special virtue that it is considered worth while to approximate to the clusters in them by secondary, and necessarily rough, examinations of the correlations, rather than discard the data. In each study we are given a set of traits which correlate highly with one particular trait, without proof that they correlate highly among themselves. Ackerson's comprehensive work is particularly valuable because it deals with recorded behavior (according to clinic, police, and social worker) of really adequate numbers of children and gives such extensive intercorrelation lists that the cluster formation can be almost completely determined.

age," by two intimates of the subject. Tetrachoric intercorrelations. The clusters were found by an entirely blind and mathematical process, permitting no operation of prejudices about the nature of cluster syndromes (*54*).

Flemming, E. G. (*89*). 71 high school girls, 46 traits, rated by teachers.

* *Jones, E.* (*137*). 145 men business executives and teachers. Rated by associates. Brief but comprehensive trait list.

Maslow, A. H. (*165*) (*166*). 60 women college students. Rated at interview, after selection by questionnaire, as to presence or absence of traits.

Maurer, K. M. (*169*). 50 children of 4–6 years. Traits checked present or absent by one judge. 50 traits reduced from very wide dictionary lists.

McCloy, C. H. (*170*). 31 college students. Rated by one another. 43 traits, largely characterial.

* *Olinick, S. L.* (*197*). 60 adults, mainly professional class. Traits checked present or absent, by an intimate acquaintance of each. 173 traits chosen from Allport-Odbert list.

Sanford, R. N. (*225*). Labeled in chart, because Sanford's established clusters are in terms of Murray's (*190*) trait list and concepts. 43 boys and girls, 5–14 years of age. Rated by adult judges over a period of three years. 35 traits, 34 of which were purely ergic (*49*) in character.

Sanford-Horn-Murray, in Horn, D. (*122*). Extension of Sanford-Murray inquiry to college students, establishing four of Sanford's twenty clusters essentially in same terms for adults. 28 university students. Rated by several judges in clinical study. 11 traits from Sanford-Murray list.

Sheldon, W. (*231*). 33 students and faculty. Rated by one judge. 50 traits clinically sifted from 650 in temperamental field. Repeated with 100 students, conditions of rating not stated, to fix intracluster relationship of variables.

Tryon, C. M. (*266*). 170 12-year-old boys, 170 12-year-old girls, 169 15-year-old boys, 181 15-year-old girls. Rated by classmates. 18 traits of varied character.

Williams, H. M. (*278*). 53 3-year-old children. Rated by experienced adult judges. 30 traits taken from Berne Scale.

Details of personality cluster chart construction. The exhaustive intercomparison of 130 phenomenal clusters, as described above, led to the formation of 50 nuclear clusters, falling into 20 personality sectors, but with the majority falling in the first ten sectors. The roundness of these numbers is purely fortuitous and later research may modify the number of nuclear clusters if not the number of sectors.

The present aim has been not only to chart and systematize clusters but to make the classification such that it will form a convenient framework for the addition of fresh material and permit of continuous adaptive growth. A first requisite for this aim is that one avoid the prejudiced interpretation and classification which would come from affixing names, especially interpretive names, to the nuclei and sectors. As the ensuing discussion indicates, many of these clusters are clearly old friends from the clinic, the classroom, or the laboratory, such as the syndromes of paranoia, neuroticism, somatotonia, cyclothymia, extraversion, dominance, etc. The temptation to leap to an interpretive label of this kind is considerable, because it is briefer, more colorful, and seemingly more technical than literary trait terms. But it is highly desirable to separate clearly the descriptive and interpretive steps of personality research, and the present project deals with the description of personality only. For, in the opinion of the writer, the too facile and premature interpretation which has prevailed in this field has aborted the enterprise of exact observation. It has left psychology with a set of popular syndrome concepts, such as extraversion, neuroticism, and anal-erotic character, so battered and warped by the superficial interpretations of the market place that they might as well be thrown away.

The general structure of cluster and sector is such that the notation which suggests itself as most practicable for indexing is something akin to the Dewey decimal system of library classification — i.e., one fitted to permit constant growth. Instead of using numbers throughout, however, it seems best to indicate the sector by letter, since sectors, judging by the number already recorded, are not likely to extend beyond the alphabet.

The nuclear cluster is identified by a number within a sector — thus, D 1, D 2, D 3, etc. — and the actual, historical, phenomenal clusters by an additional decimal point — thus, D 1.1, D 1.2, etc. — indicating the cluster converging on the nucleus D 1. The order of these clusters within the nuclear group is a chance arrangement, there being no basis, except perhaps historical order of discovery, for any other. Each *phenomenal* cluster is labeled further by the name of its discoverer — thus, *D 5.1 Tryon* — to facilitate reference to the original research and conditions of its isolation. The phenomenal clusters isolated by the present writer and published in a recent research, which are more numerous than others and need further identification, have in addition a member in brackets giving their index number in the list there published.

Each sector and cluster nucleus indexed in the manner just described is also defined by a triplet of terms aimed at maximum literal description of the behavior concerned in that region. Although the writer believes adjectival trait terms are better, these traits are given in noun form, to follow general practice, which has favored hypostatizations. But the actual list of traits by which the nucleus is eventually anchored is set out in adjective form immediately below the title.

The terms in which this final nuclear definition in all that has appeared in the various phenomenal clusters is expressed are translated where necessary into the standard basic list of 171 trait terms already described. The reasons for putting weight on this particular trait list and its constructs in our final summary, rather than on the trait material of other researches here listed, are as follows: (1) It covers all trait terms, including those in various specialized systems. (2) The terms are themselves standard dictionary terms, having widely understood meanings, widely stabilized in language. (3) There is a more considerable literature of clusters already in this trait system than in any other. It is a system of clusters (54), moreover, with the following special utilities: (*a*) they are based on a more typical, adult population than most; (*b*) they are unbiased by theories, being based on purely blind mathematical treatment of variables; (*c*) the structural relationships among the clusters are systematically known through further intercorrelation studies on clusters themselves (58). This gain of perspective, whereby clusters are put in their proper mutual relationships and whereby the outlines of sectors are better known, together with its insurance against the omission of any important possible clusters, is perhaps the most valuable of all gains from the use of the basic list. The practical contribution of the latter is further attested by the finding that the 69 clusters based on the 171 traits involved (54) cover decidedly more sectors than are subtended by any other cluster researches, and open up regions of type and syndrome description not previously suspected. It actually increases the number of sectors from 11 (from the cumulative results of previous researches) to 20. At the same time all of the older 11 sectors are confirmed. Indeed, 28 of the original 31 nuclei within these sectors, which are based on all previous researches, are rediscovered in the single research on this wider trait foundation, while 19 new cluster nuclei are added.

TABLE 16

A CHART OF THE PRINCIPAL NUCLEAR AND PHENOMENAL CLUSTERS AND
PERSONALITY SECTORS

SECTOR OR REGION A

CHARACTER–PERSONALITY INTEGRATION OR DEVELOPMENT
v.
MORAL CHARACTER DEFECT, NEUROSIS, PSYCHOSIS

1. SECTOR AA. FINENESS OF CHARACTER
v.
MORAL DEFECT, NON-PERSISTENCE

CONGLOMERATE NUCLEAR CLUSTERS	APPARENT NUCLEAR OR PHENOMENAL CLUSTERS
Nuclear Cluster AA 1	*Overlapping, Apparent Nuclear Clusters in AA 1*
Integrity, Altruism	
v.	*AA 1.1. McCloy*
Dishonesty, Undependability	Integrity (Having), Good Follower, Fair, Characterful, Self-Denying, Trustworthy. (And other traits described as "passive but constructive virtues.")
Nuclear Traits	
Honest — Dishonest	
Self-Controlled	*AA 1.2. Flemming*
Self-Denying — Selfish	Fair, Good Judgment, Honest, Idealistic, Intelligent, Understanding
Loyal — Fickle	
Fair-Minded — Partial	*AA 1.3. Cattell (39)*
Reliable — Undependable	Stable Emotionally — Changeable
	Thoughtful — Unreflective
	Self-Respecting —
	Self-Controlled —
	Reliable — Undependable
	— Suggestible
	(Practical — Unrealistic)
	AA 1.4. Cattell (40)
	Dishonest — Honest
	Fickle — Loyal
	Infantile — Mature
Nuclear Cluster AA 2	*Overlapping Clusters in AA 2*
Conscientious Effort	*AA 2.1. Cattell (13)*
v.	Clear Thinking — Incoherent
Quitting, Incoherence	Persevering — Quitting
	Independent — Dependent
	Painstaking — Slipshod
	Conscientious — Conscienceless

TABLE 16 — *Continued*

Nuclear Traits	*AA 2.2. Sanford-Murray*
Persevering — Quitting Pedantic (Orderly) — Disorderly Painstaking — Slipshod Conscientious Thoughtful	Need Blamavoidance, Need Order, Deliberation, Conjunctivity, Endurance, Need Achievement, Need Counteraction, Need Understanding, Need Construction (Called "Conscientious Effort")

AA 2.3. Olinick

Conscientious, Courteous, Neat, Thoughtful, Aggressive, Practical, Earnest

AA 1-2. Flemming

This extends over AA 1 and AA 2.

Dependable, Industrious, Loyal, Modest, Neat, Sincere, Tolerant, Unselfish

2. SECTOR AB. REALISM, EMOTIONAL INTEGRATION
v.
NEUROTICISM, EVASION

Nuclear Cluster AB 1	*Overlapping Clusters in AB 1*
Realism, Reliability *v.* Neuroticism, Changeability	*AB 1.1. Cattell (21)* [1] Practical — Unrealistic Reliable — Undependable 　　　　— Neurotic Self-Controlled Loyal — Fickle
Nuclear Traits Practical — Unrealistic Reliable — Undependable 　　　　— Neurotic 　　　　— Worrying Loyal — Fickle	*AB 1.2. Cattell (53)* Unrealistic — Practical Quitting — Persevering Suggestible — Undependable — Reliable Subjective — Guided by Reality

AB 1.3. Ackerson

Overlaps also with AB 2.

Sensitive, Worrisome, Depressed, Changeable, Finicky Food Habits, Lacking Initiative, Nervous Symptoms, Bossy, Inferiority Feelings, Spoiled Child

---

[1] These numbers refer to the cluster numbers in the original published cluster explorations (*40*) and (*54*).

TABLE 16 — *Continued*

Nuclear Cluster AB 2	*Overlapping Clusters in AB 2*
Practicalness, Determination	*AB 2.1. Cattell (12)*
v.	Self-Deceiving —
Daydreaming, Evasiveness	Evasive — Facing Life
	Unrealistic — Practical
Nuclear Traits	Dubitative — Decisive
	Acquisitive —
— Self-Deceiving	
Facing Life — Evasive	*AB 2.2. McCloy*
Decisive — Dubitative	Aggressive, Initiative (Having), Convic-
Enterprising — Shiftless	tion (Having), Decisiveness (Having)
— Phantasying	

Nuclear Cluster AB 3	*AB 2–3.1. Ackerson*
Neuroticism, Self-Deception,	A cluster overlapping AB 2 and AB 3.
Emotional Intemperateness	Daydreaming, Masturbation, Depression,
v.	Fantastic Lying, "Queer" Behavior,
	Absent-Minded, Irresponsible, Inferiority
	Feelings
Nuclear Traits	*Overlapping Clusters in AB 3*
Self-Deceiving —	*AB 3.1. Cattell (8)*
Neurotic —	Self-Deceiving —
Hypochondriacal —	Hypochondriacal —
Depressed — Cheerful	Neurotic —
Emotionally Intemperated —	Plaintive —
Balanced	Self-Pitying —
Absent-Minded — Alert	Extreme — Temperate
	(Emotionally intemperate)

Nuclear Cluster AB 4	*Overlapping Clusters in AB 4*
Infantile, Demanding,	*AB 4.1. Cattell (38)*
Self-Centeredness	Infantile — Mature (Emotionally)
v.	Hypochondriacal —
Emotional Maturity, Frustration	Self-Pitying —
Tolerance	Exhibitionist — Self-Effacing
	Unself-Controlled — Self-Controlled
	AB–C 1. Ackerson
	"Personality Total" extends through
	AB 2, AB 3, AB 4, AC 1, and AC 2.
	Incipient Psychosis, Defective Conduct
	Total, "Queer," Depressed, Contrary,
	Jealousy of Siblings, Worrisome, Inferi-
	ority Feelings, etc.

TABLE 16 — *Continued*

3. SECTOR AC. BALANCE, FRANKNESS, OPTIMISM

v.

MELANCHOLY, AGITATION

Nuclear Cluster AC 1	*Overlapping Clusters in AC 1*
Agitation, Melancholy, Obstinacy	*AC 1.1. Cattell (56)*
v.	Self-Pitying —
Placidity, Social Interest	Hypochondriacal —
	Pessimistic — Optimistic
Nuclear Traits	Worrying — Placid
Depressed — Cheerful	(Habit-Bound — Labile)
Hypochondriacal —	*AC 1.2. Ackerson*
Worrying —	Depressed, Crying, Sensitive and Worri-
Habit-Bound — Labile	some, Psycho-neurotic, Daydreaming,
Sensitive — Tough	Hatred, Jealousy of Sibling, Changeable
Seclusive — Sociable	Moods, Seclusive

Nuclear Cluster AC 2	*Overlapping Clusters in AC 2*
Balance, Frankness, Sportsmanship	*AC 2.1. Cattell (Temperament Research (40))*
v.	Emotionally Balanced, Temperate
Pessimism, Secretiveness,	— Extreme
Immoderateness	Frank — Secretive
	Optimistic — Pessimistic
Nuclear Traits	Generous — Tightfisted
Frank — Secretive	*AC 2.2. Flemming*
Generous — Tightfisted	Frank, Generous, Good-Natured, Good
Temperate — Emotionally Extreme (schizoid)	Sport, Natural, Unaffected
Easygoing —	

4. SECTOR B. INTELLIGENCE, DISCIPLINED MIND, INDEPENDENCE

v.

FOOLISH, UNDEPENDABLE, UNREFLECTIVENESS

Nuclear Cluster B 1	*Overlapping Clusters in B 1*
Emotional Maturity,	*B 1.1. Cattell (6)*
Clarity of Mind	Mature — Infantile
v.	Clear-Thinking — Incoherent
Infantilism, Dependence	Independent — Dependent
	Spatial, Visual Thinking Ability
Nuclear Traits	— Neurotic
As in B 1.1, opposite	— Undependable

TABLE 16 — *Continued*

Nuclear Cluster B 2	*Overlapping Clusters in B 2*

Nuclear Cluster B 2

Gentlemanly, Disciplined
Thoughtfulness
v.
Extraverted, Foolish,
Lack of Will

Nuclear Traits

Thoughtful — Unreflective
Wise — Foolish
Persevering — Quitting
Austere — Profligate
Polished — Rough

Overlapping Clusters in B 2

B 2.1. Sanford-Murray

Need Counteraction, Endocathection
(Called "Counteractive Endocathection")

B 2.2. Cattell (5)

Thoughtful — Unreflective
Wise — Foolish
Austere — Profligate
Independent — Dependent
Polished — Rough
Reliable — Undependable

B 2.3. Cattell (15)

Thoughtful — Unreflective
Theoretical Interests —
Logical Ability, Reasoning —
Planful — Planless
Wise — Foolish
— Suggestible

B 2.4. Cattell (16)

Thoughtful — Unreflective
Polished — Rough
Analytical —
Interests Wide — Interests Narrow
Sophisticated — Simplehearted

Nuclear Cluster B 3

Creativity, Self-Determination,
Intelligence
v.
Narrowness of Interests,
Fogginess

Nuclear Traits

Original — Banal
Constructive —
Interests Wide — Interests Narrow
Independent — Dependent
Persevering — Quitting
Intelligent —

Overlapping Clusters in B 3

B 3.1. Cattell (2)

Original — Banal
Interests Wide — Interests Narrow
Versatile —
Independent — Dependent
Constructive —
Intelligent

B 3.2. Sanford-Murray

Creativity, Endurance, Need Counteraction, Need Order, Need Construction
(Called "Orderly Production")

TABLE 16 — *Continued*

Nuclear Cluster B 4	*Overlapping Clusters in B 4*
Intelligence, Penetration, General Talent *v.* Lack of "g"	*B 4.1. Cattell (3)* Intelligent, Clear-Thinking, Logical Ability, Reasoning, Clever, Spatial, Visual Ability, Mathematical Ability, Analytical
Nuclear Traits As in B 4.1	*B 3-4.1. Flemming* Cluster extending over B 3 and B 4. Clever, Cultured, Original, Talented, Well-Informed, Wide Interests

SECTOR OR REGION C

SELF-ASSERTION, VENTURESOMENESS, CLAMOROUSNESS
v.
GENERAL INHIBITION, MODESTY, TIMIDITY

5. SECTOR CA. EGOTISM, ASSERTION, STUBBORNNESS
v.
MODESTY, SELF-EFFACEMENT, ADAPTABILITY

Nuclear Cluster CA 1	*Overlapping Clusters in CA 1*
Crude Social Assertion, Exhibitionism *v.* Modesty, Obedience to Authority	*CA 1.1. Tryon* Restless, Talkative, Attention-Getting (Bossy), (Fights), (Unkempt) *CA 1.2. Sanford-Murray* Need Blamavoidance, Need Deference (Called "Willing Obedience")
Nuclear Traits Exhibitionist — Self-Effacing Argumentative — Talkative — Taciturn Boastful — Modest Arrogant — Humble	*CA 1.3. Cattell (1)* Arrogant — Humble Exhibitionist — Self-Effacing Conceited — Self-Dissatisfied Headstrong — Gentle-Tempered Argumentative — Assertive — Submissive Autocratic — Boastful — Modest *CA 1.4. Cattell (4)* Exhibitionist — Self-Effacing Treacherous — Extrapunitive — Praiseful Talkative — Taciturn Argumentative — Boastful — Modest

TABLE 16 — *Continued*

CA 1–2.1. Maurer

Cluster overlapping CA 1 and CA 2, and some of CA 3.

Talkative, Domineering, High-Strung, Forward, Active, Persistent, Obstinate, Noisy, Independent, Plucky

---

Nuclear Cluster CA 2	*Overlapping Clusters in CA 2*
Stubbornness, Pugnacity, Clamorousness	*CA 2.1. Sanford-Murray*
v.	Need Defendance, Need Rejection, Need Autonomy, Need Blamescape, Need Aggression, Need Retention, Need Acquisition, Need Dominance, Projectivity (Called "Aggressive Self-Defense")
Tolerance, Self-Effacement	
Nuclear Traits	*CA 2.2. Cattell (34)*
Extrapunitive — Praiseful	Extrapunitive — Praiseful
Pugnacious — Peaceable	Opinionated — Tolerant
Self-Pitying —	Pugnacious — Peaceable
Mulish — Reasonable	Self-Pitying —
	Exhibitionist — Self-Effacing
	Mulish — Reasonable

Nuclear Cluster CA 3	*Overlapping Clusters in CA 3*
Rigidity, Despotism, Egotism	*CA 3.1. Cattell (27)*
v.	Inflexible — Adaptable
Adaptability, Friendliness, Tactfulness	Extrapunitive — Praiseful
	Hostile — Friendly
Nuclear Traits	Opinionated — Tolerant
	Egotistic — Altocentric
Inflexible — Adaptable	Flattering
Extrapunitive — Praiseful	*CA 3.2. Flemming*
Tactless — Tactful	Adaptable, Considerate, Not Easily Excited, Pleasant Voice, Sympathetic, Tactful
Hostile — Friendly	
Ruthless — Kind	*CA 3.3. Cattell (10)*
Defensive —	Extrapunitive — Praiseful
Acquisitive —	Treacherous —
(Infantile — Mature)	Acquisitive —
	Thankless — Grateful
	Defensive —
	CA 3.4. Sanford-Murray
	Need Blamavoidance, Need Abasement (Called "Guilt and Remorse")

TABLE 16 — *Continued*

CA 3.5. *Cattell* (*Temperament Research* (40))
Mature (Emotionally) — Infantile
Kind on Principle —
Good-Natured —
Tactful — Tactless

Nuclear Cluster CA 4	Overlapping Clusters in CA 4
Dictatorial, Shrewdness	CA 4.1. Cattell (47)
v.	Autocratic —
Naïve, Unassertiveness	Shrewd — Naïve
	Boastful — Modest
Nuclear Traits	Assertive — Submissive
As in CA 4.1, opposite	(Austere — Profligate)

Nuclear Cluster CA 5	Overlapping Clusters in CA 5
Assertion, Rivalry, Conceit	CA 5.1. McCloy
v.	Eagerness for Admiration, Self-Esteem
Modesty, Unassumingness	(Conceit), Desire to Impose Will on Others
Nuclear Traits	CA 5.2. Williams
Leading —	Ascendant, Rivalrous, Leader, Independent of Adults
Conceited — Self-Dissatisfied	
Assertive — Submissive	CA 5.3. Cattell (32)
Autocratic —	Conceited — Self-Dissatisfied
Self-Confident — Self-Distrusting	Leading —
Exhibitionist — Self-Effacing	Boastful — Modest
	Self-Confident — Self-Distrusting
	(Headstrong — Gentle-Tempered)
	(Hurried — Lethargic)
	CA 5.4. Sanford-Murray
	Need Dominance, Need Aggression, Need Acquisition, Need Autonomy, Need Recognition, Need Cognizance, Need Defendance, Need Exhibition, Need Excitance, Intensity (Called "Ascendance")

Nuclear Cluster CA 6	Overlapping Clusters in CA 6
Eager Self-Assertion	CA 6.1. Sanford-Murray
v.	(There are insufficient elements in this cluster to locate it with confidence. It seems most likely an appendage of the CA sector.) Need Achievement, Intensity (Called "Undisciplined Achievement")
Lack of Ambition	

TABLE 16 — *Continued*

6. SECTOR CB.   BOLDNESS, INDEPENDENCE, TOUGHNESS

v.

TIMIDITY, INHIBITION, SENSITIVITY

Nuclear Cluster CB 1	*Overlapping Clusters in CB 1*
Energy, Boldness, Spiritedness	*CB 1.1. Cattell (33)*
v.	Energetic, Spirited — Languid
Apathy, Timidity, Languor	Self-Confident — Self-Distrusting
	Enthusiastic — Apathetic
Nuclear Traits	Independent — Dependent
Energetic, Spirited — Languid	(Physical Activity Interests)
Enthusiastic — Apathetic	(Debonair —)
Alert — Absent-Minded	
Debonair	*CB 1.2. Sanford-Murray*
(Strong Personality —)	Need Passivity, Need Harmavoidance
(Quick — Slow)	(Called "Passive Timidity")
(Bold — Timid)	
(Independent — Dependent)	*CB 1.3. Cattell (44)*
Clusters extending over CB 1 and CB 2	Alert — Absent-Minded
	Energetic, Spirited — Languid
	Quick — Slow
	Strong in Personality —
	CB 1.4. Cattell (28)
	Energetic, Spirited — Languid
	Vivacious —
	Assertive — Submissive
	Hearty — Quiet
	Debonair —
	CB 1–2.1. Sheldon (Somatotonia)
Nuclear Cluster CB 2	Assertive, Dominating, Competitive,
Independence, Cleverness, Confidence	Energetic, Adventurous, Bold, Coura-
v.	geous, Not Sensitive, Unrestrained, Noisy,
Timidity, Dependence, Languidness	"General Extravert Qualities"
Nuclear Traits	*CB 1–2.2. Tryon*
Independent — Dependent	Daring, Leader, Active in Games,
Clever —	(Friendly), (Fights), (Humor about
Versatile (Technical Aptitudes)	Jokes)
Self-Confident — Self-Distrusting	*CB 1–2.3. Olinick*
Alert — Absent-Minded	Independent, Proud, Active, Sociable,
Energetic, Spirited — Languid	Leader, Adventurous
	Overlapping Clusters in CB 2
	CB 2.1. Cattell (26)
	Independent — Dependent
	Technical Interests —
	Mechanical Aptitude —
	Versatile —
	Self-Confident — Self-Distrusting

TABLE 16 — *Continued*

CB 2.2. Sanford-Murray

Need Succorance, Need Harmavoidance, Projectivity (Called "Timid Dependence")

CB 2.3. Cattell (43)

Bridges clusters CB 1 and CB 2.

Independent — Dependent
Clever —
Alert — Absent-Minded
Energetic-Spirited — Languid
(Adventurous — Timid)
(Quick — Slow)

Nuclear Cluster CB 3	*Overlapping Clusters in CB 3*
Lack of Restraint, Adventurousness	*CB 3.1. Ackerson*
v.	Bashful, Apprehensive, Lack of Initiative, Seclusive, Inferiority Feelings, Follower, Irregular Sleep, Listless, Sensitive and Worrisome
General Inhibition, Fearfulness	
Nuclear Traits	*CB 3.2. Sanford-Murray*
Timid — Bold	Need Infavoidance, Need Harmavoidance, Anxiety (Called "Timid Withdrawal")
Shiftless — Enterprising	
Submissive — Assertive	*CB 3.3. Cattell (46)*
Worrying —	Inhibited (in general) — Incontinent
Shy — Sociable I (Forward)	Timid — Adventurous
Inhibited — Incontinent	— Gluttonous
	Submissive — Assertive
	(Uninquiring — Curious)

Nuclear Cluster CB 4	*Overlapping Clusters in CB 4*
Poised Sociability, Inertia, Toughness	*CB 4.1. Sheldon (Cerebrotonia)*
v.	Mental Overintensity, Fast Reactions, Inhibited, Shy, Not Sociable, Poor Sleep, Not Habit-Bound, Sensitive, "General Introvert Qualities"
Introspectiveness, Sensitivity, Haste	
Nuclear Traits	*CB 4.2. McCloy*
Tough — Sensitive	Cool-Headed, Resourceful, Poised, Self-Controlled, Sociable
Lethargic — Hurried	
Poised — Awkward	*CB 4.3. Cattell (60)*
— Introspective	Introspective —
Sociable — Shy	Sensitive — Tough
Relaxed — High-Strung	Hurried — Lethargic
(Slow — Quick)	(Cautious — Bold)
	(Taciturn — Talkative)

TABLE 16 — *Continued*

(Easygoing — Short-Tempered)
(Clear Thinking — Incoherent)

Ill-defined clusters in this area

CB 1–3–4.1. Maslow (Dominance)

A cluster covering most of CB sector, but principally CB 3 and CB 4. Admixture of traits from Sector A.

Self-Confident, Self-Assured, Socially Poised, Leader, Relaxed, Extraverted, Hypnotizable, High Self-Esteem, Tendency to Use People, Freer Personal Expression, Love of Adventure and Novelty, Shy and Quiet, Embarrassable, Self-Conscious, Inhibited, Envious, Distrustful, Conventional, Modest, Honest and Reliable, Neat and Prompt, Faithful, Conservative, More Religious, More Polite

CB 1–2–4. D. 1. Jones, E.

A cluster running on into the D sector. Sympathetic Appreciation of Others' Difficulties, Confidence in Bearing, Cheerful and Optimistic, Energetic, Good Mixer, Clever in Repartee, Fluent

Nuclear Cluster CB 5

Smartness, Assertiveness, Independence

v.

Unsophistication, Submissiveness, Reverence

Nuclear Traits

As in CB 5.1, opposite

Overlapping Clusters in CB 5

CB 5.1. Cattell (41)

Sophisticated — Simplehearted
Independent — Dependent
Intelligent —
Assertive — Submissive
(Impious — Reverent)

7. Sector D. Sociability
v.
Timidity, Hostility, Gloominess

Nuclear Cluster D 1

Sociability, Adventurousness, Heartiness

v.

Shyness, Timidity, Reserve

Nuclear Traits

Sociable (Forward) I — Shy
Sociable (Gregarious) II — Seclusive
Adventurous — Timid
Social Interests —
Intrusive — Reserved

Overlapping Clusters in D 1

D 1.1. Cattell (49)

Social Interests —
Sociable I — Shy
Curious — Uninquiring
Adventurous — Timid
Intrusive — Reserved

D 1.2. Olinick

Extends beyond this nuclear region; e.g., into CB 1.

Sociable, Sympathetic, Active, Independent, Economical, Witty, Adventurous

TABLE 16 — *Continued*

	D 1.3. Cattell (51)
	Sociable I — Shy
	Responsive — Aloof
	Social Interests —
	Sociable II — Seclusive
	Hearty — Quiet
	(Intrusive — Reserved)

Nuclear Cluster D 2	*Overlapping Clusters in D 2*
Sociability, Sentimentalism, Warmth	*D 2.1. Cattell (45)*
v.	Responsive — Aloof
Independence, Hostility, Aloofness	Sentimental — Hardheaded
	Affectionate — Frigid
Nuclear Traits	Genial — Coldhearted
Responsive — Aloof	— Sour
Affectionate —	*D 2.2. Olinick*
Sentimental —	Sensitive, Sincere, Aloof, Independent,
Social Interests —	Domestic, Critical
Home and Family Interests	*D 2.3. Sheldon (Viscerotonia)*
Dependent — Independent	Love of Comfort, Relaxed, Slow, Gregari-
Friendly — Hostile	ous, Needing Sympathy, Easily Expressed
Frank — Secretive	Feelings, Even-Tempered, Amiable,
(Genial — Coldhearted)	Social, Personality Interests
(Tough — Sensitive)	*D 2.4. Cattell (29)*
	Secretive — Frank
	Aloof — Responsive
	Sadistic —
	Formal — Casual
	D 2.5. Cattell (30)
	— Social Interests
	Sour —
	Slanderous —
	Brooding — Unrepining
	Aloof — Responsive
	D 2.6. Sanford-Murray
	Need Affiliation, Need Nurturance, Need
	Deference (Called "Social Feeling")

Nuclear Cluster D 3	*Overlapping Clusters in D 3*
Interest in Group Life,	*D 3.1. Sanford-Murray*
Liking to Participate	Need Rejection, Need Seclusion, Need Re-
v.	tention (Called "Self-Sufficiency")
Self-Sufficiency	

TABLE 16 — *Continued*

Nuclear Traits	*D 3.2. Williams*
Sociable II — Seclusive Coöperative — Obstructive Responsive — Aloof Dependent — Independent	Participating, Coöperative, Interested in Group

---

Nuclear Cluster D 4	*Overlapping Clusters in D 4*
Personal Attractiveness, Sociability, Pleasure-Seeking, Frivolity (Extraversion) * *v.* Earnestness, Asceticism, Mirthlessness (Introversion)	*D 4.1. McCloy* Cheerful, Fond of Large Gatherings, Concentrating on Pleasure *D 4.2. Tryon* Popular, Good-Looking, Friendly, (Enthusiastic), (Humor)
Nuclear Traits	*D 4.3. Flemming* Athletic, Good Personal Appearance, Beautiful, Smiling, Sociable
(Attractive Personal Appearance) (Popular — Unpopular) Cheerful — Gloomy Sociable — Seclusive Laughterful — Mirthless Mischievous (Playful) — Sensuous — Ascetic Frivolous — Serious (Physical Activity Interests)	*D 4.4. Sanford-Murray* Need Sociability, Need Play (Called "Good Fellowship") *D 4.5. Cattell (Temperament Research (40))* (Surgency — Desurgency) Cheerful — Gloomy Natural — Formal Sociable — Unsociable Humorous — Earnest Adaptable — Conservative
* Broad Cluster, constituting the nearest reality to the classical concept of *extraversion-introversion*.	*D 1-2-3-4-5.*[1] *Maurer* Extending over all nuclei of D. Sociable, Cheerful, Amenable, Responsive, Resourceful, Enthusiastic, Curious, Happy, Frank

---

Nuclear Cluster D 5	*Overlapping Clusters in D 5*
Cheerful, Enthusiastic, Witty *v.* Coldhearted, Sour, Mirthless	*D 5.1. Tryon* Enthusiastic, Happy, Humor about Jokes (Humor about Self)

[1] D 4 and D 5 cannot be fused, for in Tryon's data and again in Cattell's data both clusters appear from the same population of traits. Also, sociability is absent from D 5.

TABLE 16 — *Continued*

Nuclear Traits	*D 5.2. Cattell (19)*
Cheerful — Gloomy	Genial — Coldhearted
Enthusiastic — Apathetic	Cheerful — Gloomy
Optimistic — Pessimistic	— Sour
Laughterful — Mirthless	Optimistic — Pessimistic
Witty, Humorous —	Enthusiastic — Apathetic
	Laughterful — Mirthless

8. Sector E.   General Emotionality, High-Strungness, Instability
v.
Placidity, Deliberateness, Reserve

Nuclear Cluster E 1	*Overlapping Clusters in E 1*
High-Strungness, Impulsiveness, Anxiety	*E 1.1. Cattell (22)*
v.	Excitable — Phlegmatic
	Highly Strung — Relaxed
Apathy, Relaxation, Deliberateness	Hearty — Quiet
	Hurried — Lethargic
Nuclear Traits	Impulsive — Deliberate
	Vivacious —
High-Strung — Relaxed	
Impulsive — Deliberate	*E 1.2. Cattell (52)*
Hurried — Lethargic	Highly Strung — Relaxed
Emotional — Unemotional	Hurried — Lethargic
(Worrying — Placid)	Sleeps Poorly — Sleeps Well
(Excitable — Phlegmatic)	Impulsive — Deliberate
(Vivacious —)	Irritable — Good-Tempered
	E 1.3. Sanford-Horn-Murray
	Impulsivity — Deliberateness
	Projectivity — Objectivity
	Emotionality — Placidity
	Intensity — Apathy
	Disjunctivity — Conjunctivity
	High Anxiety — Low Anxiety
	Transcience — Endurance
	(Intraception — Extraception)
	(Called "Anxious Emotional Expressiveness")

Nuclear Cluster E 2	*Overlapping Clusters in E 2*
Sthenic Emotionality, Hypomania, Instability	*E 2.1. Cattell (37)*
v.	Emotional — Unemotional
Self-Control, Patience, Phlegm	Impulsive — Deliberate
	Excitable — Phlegmatic
	Impatient — Patient
	— Self-Controlled

TABLE 16 — *Continued*

Nuclear Traits	(Irritable — Good-Tempered)

Emotional — Unemotional
Impulsive — Deliberate
Irritable — Good-Tempered
Unself-Controlled — Self-Controlled
(Impatient — Patient)

(Irritable — Good-Tempered)
(Emotional II (Sthenic Emotionality) —)
(Hearty — Quiet)

E 2.2.   Ackerson

Emotionally Unstable, Moody, Temper Tantrums, Violence, Nervous Symptoms, "Queer," Staying Out Late Nights, Object of Teasing, Neurological Defect, Encephalitis

---

Nuclear Cluster E 3

Intrusiveness, Frivolity, Neurotic Instability
v.
Deliberateness, Seriousness, Reserve

Nuclear Traits

As in E 3.1, opposite

Overlapping Clusters in E 3

E 3.1.   Cattell (20)

Intrusive — Reserved
          — Self-Controlled
Impulsive — Deliberate
Frivolous — Serious
Neurotic —
(Self-Pitying —)
(Changeable — Stable Emotionally)

Nuclear Cluster E 4

Generally Emotional, Dissatisfied, Intense
v.
Content, Placid, Temperate

Nuclear Traits

Emotional — Unemotional
Impulsive — Deliberate
Extreme — Temperate
Dissatisfied — Contented
(Enthusiastic (Ardent) — Apathetic)

Overlapping Clusters in E 4

E 4.1.   Sanford-Murray

Need Exhibition, Need Excitance, Need Cognizance, Need Recognition, Need Sex, Need Succorance, Need Exposition, Need Blamescape, Need Defendance, Projectivity, Impulsivity, Emotionality, Change. (Called "Sensation.")

E 4.2.   Sanford-Horn-Murray

(Impulsivity — Deliberateness)
Change — Sameness
Emotionality — Placidity
Intensity — Apathy
(— Need Passivity)
(Called "Placid Immobility.")

E 4.3.   Cattell (25)

Extreme — Temperate
Emotional — Unemotional
Dissatisfied — Contented
Alcoholic —
Self-Deceiving —

TABLE 16 — *Continued*

9. SECTOR F.   GRATEFULNESS, FRIENDLINESS, IDEALISM
v. SADISM, SLANDEROUSNESS, SUSPICIOUSNESS
(BENIGN CYCLOTHYME *v.* HOSTILE SCHIZOTHYME)

Nuclear Cluster F 1	*Overlapping Clusters in F 1*
Gratefulness, Easygoingness, Geniality *v.* Hardness, Vindictiveness, Coldheartedness	*F 1.1. Cattell (11)*
	Grateful — Thankless
	— Slanderous
	Softhearted — Hardhearted
	Unresentful — Vindictive
Nuclear Traits	Easygoing — Short-Tempered
	— Sour
As in F 1.1, opposite	Genial — Coldhearted

Nuclear Cluster F 2	*Overlapping Clusters in F 2*
Gratefulness, Kindness, Christian Idealism *v.* Hostility, Cynicism, Selfish Withdrawal	*F 2.1. Cattell (54)*
	Grateful — Thankless
	— Sadistic
	Self-Denying — Selfish
	Kind on Principle —
	Unresentful — Vindictive
Nuclear Traits	(— Self-Pitying)
Grateful — Thankless	*F 2.2. Cattell (14)*
Idealistic — Cynical	Grateful — Thankless
Self-Denying — Selfish	Curious — Uninquiring
Friendly — Hostile	Friendly — Hostile
	Softhearted — Hardhearted
	Idealistic — Cynical
	F 2–3.1. Cattell (9)
	Perfect overlap of F 2 and F 3.
	Grateful — Thankless
	— Treacherous
	Kind — Ruthless
	Friendly — Hostile
	Softhearted — Hardhearted
	— Jealous
	Generous — Tightfisted
	— Slanderous

Nuclear Cluster F 3	*Overlapping Clusters in F 3*
Friendliness, Generosity, Coöperativeness *v.* Hostility, Meanness, Obstructiveness	*F 3.1. Cattell (24)*
	— Agorophobic
	Friendly — Hostile
	Generous — Tightfisted
	— Jealous
	Coöperative — Obstructive

TABLE 16 — *Continued*

Nuclear Traits

Friendly — Hostile
Generous — Tightfisted
Coöperative — Obstructive
— Phobic

Nuclear Cluster F 4	*Overlapping Clusters in F 4*
Cynicism, Suspicion, Dishonesty	*F 4.1. Cattell (50)*
v.	Cynical — Idealistic
Idealism, Trustfulness, Respecting Self and Others	Suspicious — Trustful
	Dishonest — Honest
	Slanderous — Praiseful
Nuclear Traits	— Self-Respecting
As in F 4.1, opposite	

Nuclear Cluster F 5

Obstructionism, Cynicism, Unstable Hostility

v.

Idealism, Affection, Sensitive Consideration

Nuclear Traits

Obstructive — Coöperative
Cynical — Idealistic
Ruthless — Kind
Headstrong — Gentle
(Self-Distrusting — Self-Confident)

Overlapping Clusters in F 5

F 5.1. Cattell (18)

Obstructive — Coöperative
Cynical — Idealistic
Extrapunitive —
Hostile — Friendly
Self-Distrusting — Self-Confident
(Headstrong — Gentle-Tempered)
(Habit-Bound — Labile)

F 5.2. Cattell (62)

Idealistic — Cynical
Gentle-Tempered — Headstrong
Home and Family Interests —

F 5–6.1. Williams

A cluster subtending F 5 and F 6, and possibly some of Sector A.
Affectionate, Polite, Sympathetic, Socially Controlled, Sensitive

---

Nuclear Cluster F 6

Benign Emotional Maturity

v.

Slanderous, Jealous, Self-Pitying Infantilism

Overlapping Clusters in F 6

F 6.1. Cattell (17)

Jealous —
Thankless — Grateful
Slanderous — Praiseful
Treacherous —
Self-Pitying —
Infantile — Mature

TABLE 16 — *Continued*

Nuclear Traits	
Jealous —	
Slanderous — Praiseful	
— Kind on Principle	
Infantile — Mature	

Nuclear Cluster F 7	*Overlapping Clusters in F 7*
(Paranoid schizoid	*F 7.1. Cattell* (35)
v.	Sarcastic —
Trusting cyclothyme)	Sadistic —
Sadism, Vindictiveness, Suspicion	Vindictive — Unresentful
v.	Irritable — Good-Tempered
Good-Tempered, Unresentful,	Suspicious — Trustful
Complaisant	*F 7.2. Cattell* (55)
	Sadistic —
Nuclear Traits	Lethargic — Hurried
Sadistic —	Shrewd — Naïve
Sarcastic —	Sarcastic —
Vindictive — Unresentful	Vindictive — Unresentful
Suspicious — Trustful	
Shrewd — Naïve	

10. Sector G. Liveliness, Instability, Verbal Expressiveness

v.

Reserve, Quiescence, Naturalness

Nuclear Cluster G 1	*Overlapping Clusters in G 1*
Austerity, Thoughtfulness, Stability	*G 1.1. Sanford-Murray*
v.	Need Play, Need Exposition, Impulsivity,
Playfulness, Changeability,	Change (Called "Lively Self-Expression")
Foolishness	*G 1.2. Maurer*
	Grave, Meditative, Cautious, Careful
Nuclear Traits	*G 1.3. Cattell* (7)
Austere — Profligate	Austere — Profligate
Thoughtful — Unreflective	Wise — Foolish
Deliberate — Impulsive	Deliberate — Impulsive
— Mischievous	Thoughtful — Unreflective
Stable Emotionally — Changeable	Reserved — Intrusive
Reserved — Intrusive	Stable Emotionally — Changeable
(Serious — Frivolous)	Serious — Frivolous
(Cautious — Reckless)	

TABLE 16 — *Continued*

Nuclear Cluster G 2	*Overlapping Clusters in G 2*
Verbal Skill, Interesting Ideas, Inquisitiveness *v.* Narrow Interests, Absence of Flattery *Nuclear Traits* As in G 21, opposite	*G 2.1. Cattell (42)* Verbal Aptitude — Curious — Uninquiring Interests Wide — Interests Narrow Flattering —

Nuclear Cluster G 3	*Overlapping Clusters in G 3*
Eloquence, Affectedness, Amusing Conversationalism *v.* Self-Effacement, Inarticulateness, Naturalness *Nuclear Traits* Exhibitionist — Self-Effacing Eloquent — Inarticulate Original — Banal Affected — Natural Debonair — Flattering —	*G 3.1.[1] Flemming* Amusing, Entertaining, Interesting in Conversation *G 3.2. Cattell (31)* Eloquent — Inarticulate Exhibitionist — Self-Effacing Treacherous — Flattering — Imitative — *G 3.3. Cattell (23)* Affected — Natural Exhibitionist — Self-Effacing Talkative — Taciturn Debonair —

Nuclear Cluster G 4	*Overlapping Clusters in G 4*
Creativity, Wit, Emotional Color *v.* Dullness, Banality, Stability *Nuclear Traits* Original — Banal Clever — Witty — Constructive — Enterprising — Shiftless Vivacious Talkative — Taciturn (Changeable — Stable Emotionally) (Curious — Uninquiring)	*G 4.1. Sanford-Murray* Creativity, Need Understanding, Need Exposition, Change, Intensity (Called "Colorful, Intelligent, Self-Expression") *G 4.2. Flemming* Competent, Has Individuality, Lively, Sense of Humor, Witty *G 4.3. Cattell (64)* Enterprising — Shiftless Original — Banal Witty —

[1] Some interpretation of G 3.1 is involved, since it is in terms of effects on the observers rather than traits.

TABLE 16 — *Continued*

11. Sector H. Imaginative Intuition, Curiosity, Carelessness
v.
Thrift, Inflexible Habit, Smugness

Nuclear Cluster H 1	*Overlapping Clusters in H 1*
Thrift, Tidiness, Obstinacy	*H 1.1. Olinick*
v.	Obstinate, Thrifty, Tidy (Exact)
Lability, Curiosity, Intuition	*H 1.2. Cattell (61)*
Nuclear Traits	Habit-Bound — Labile
Habit-Bound — Labile	Logical — Intuitive
Thrifty — Careless	Thrifty — Careless over Property
Logical — Intuitive	(Uninquiring — Curious)
Pedantic — Disorderly	

Nuclear Cluster H 2	*Overlapping Clusters in H 2*
Creativity, Curiosity, Intuition	*H 2.1. Sanford-Murray*
v.	Creativity, Need Sentience, Need Under-
Stability, Insensitiveness	standing, Endocathection, Intraception,
Nuclear Traits	Change (Called "Sensitive Imaginative
Constructive —	Creation")
Curious — Uninquiring	
Introspective —	
Intuitive — Logical	
Changeable — Emotionally Stable	

12. Sector I. Bohemian, Disorderly
v.
Persevering, Pedantic

Nuclear Cluster I 1	*Overlapping Clusters in I 1*
Profligacy, Planlessness, Friendliness	*I 1.1. Cattell (48)*
v.	Profligate — Austere
Austerity, Hostility, Perseverance	Disorderly — Pedantic
Nuclear Traits	Planless — Planful
As in I 1.1, opposite	Friendly — Hostile
	(Quitting — Persevering)

TABLE 16 — *Continued*

13. SECTOR J. AESTHETIC INTERESTS, THOUGHTFULNESS, CONSTRUCTIVENESS

Nuclear Cluster J 1	*Overlapping Clusters in J 1*
General Aesthetic Interests, Thoughtfulness, Constructiveness	*J 1.1. Cattell (36)*
	Artistic Interest —
Nuclear Traits	General Aesthetic Interests — Thoughtful — Unreflective
General Aesthetic Interests —	Constructive —
Musical Ability —	Musical Ability —
Thoughtful — Unreflective	(Ambitious — Unambitious)
Constructive —	*J 1.2. Cattell (63)*
	Musical Ability —
	General Aesthetic Interests —
	Musical Interests —

14. SECTOR K. PHYSICAL STRENGTH, ENDURANCE, AND COURAGE
v.
PHYSICAL INACTIVITY, AVOIDANCE OF DANGER

Nuclear Cluster K 1	*Overlapping Clusters in K 1*
Title as above	*K 1.1. Cattell (57)*
	Physical Strength and Endurance — Claustrophobic
Traits opposite in K 1.1	Courageous — Cowardly
	(Physical Activity Interests —)
	(Physically Energetic and Active —)

15. SECTOR L. AMOROUSNESS, PLAYFULNESS
v.
PROPRIETY

Nuclear Cluster L 1	*Overlapping Clusters in L 1*
Title as above	*L 1.1. Cattell (58)*
Nuclear Traits	Amorous — Lustless
	Eccentric —
As in L 1.1, opposite	Mischievous —

16. SECTOR M. ALCOHOLISM, REBELLIOUSNESS, CARELESSNESS
v.
PIETY, REVERENCE, THRIFT

Nuclear Cluster M 1	*Overlapping Clusters in M 1*
Title as above	*M 1.1. Cattell (59)*
Nuclear Traits	Alcoholic —
	Worldly — Pious
As in M 1.1, opposite	Rebellious — Reverent
	(Selfish — Self-Denying)
	(Careless with Property — Thrifty)

TABLE 16 — *Continued*

17. Sector N. Curiosity, Wide Interests
v.
Limited Interests

Nuclear Cluster N 1	*Overlapping Clusters in N 1*
Title as above	*N 1.1. Cattell* (65)
Nuclear Traits	Curious — Uninquiring
As in N 1.1, opposite	Wide Interests — Narrow Interests
	Political, National Interests —

18. Sector O. Hypochondriacal, Taciturn Retroversion
v.
Eloquence, Interest in Future

Nuclear Cluster O 1	*Overlapping Clusters in O 1*
Title as above	*O 1.1. Cattell* (66)
Nuclear Traits	Antevert — Retrovert
As in O 1.1, opposite	Eloquent — Inarticulate
	— Hypochondriacal

19. Sector P. Asceticism, Eccentricity
v.
Comfort-Loving Conventionality

Nuclear Cluster P 1	*Overlapping Clusters in P 1*
Title as above	*P 1.1. Cattell* (68)
Nuclear Traits	Ascetic — Sensuous, Comfort-Seeking
As in P 1.1, opposite	Individualistic — Conventional
	Eccentric —
	(— Plaintive)

20. Sector Q. Inflexibility, Wandering
v.
Adaptableness, Ease of Settling Down

Nuclear Cluster Q 1	*Overlapping Clusters in Q 1*
Title as above	*Q 1.1. Cattell* (69)
Nuclear Traits	Inflexible — Adaptable
As in Q 1.1, opposite	Wandering — Settling Down

8. SUMMARY AND PRELIMINARY INTERPRETATION

Results. A survey of 130 apparent nuclear clusters, established in 14 independent researches, has shown that they fall fairly clearly into 50 confirmed *nuclear clusters*, which gather in 20 topologically and psychologically distinct regions or *sectors*, on what has been called (54) the *personality sphere*. In a minority of instances the boundaries of clusters or sectors are not sharp, and some two or three clusters from past researches using rough criteria each sprawl over two or three nuclei.

Speculation. In closing this descriptive phase we shall speculate briefly on the relations of certain clusters to each other and to historical syndromes. Freer discussion and speculation can more safely be enjoyed when the actually observed clusters are first preserved in the above index system against the sclerosis of premature naming and the insidious assault of implicit interpretation. As already noted above, one notes that a majority of the clusters established by correlation procedures seem actually to be old friends of the clinic and the laboratory. AB 3 appears to be the syndrome of general neuroticism pursued in questionnaires; AB 4, the clinical picture of conversion hysteria; AA 1, the psychopathic personality; AC 1, constitutional, agitated melancholia; and E 1 and E 2, two varieties of hypomania.

The schizoid pattern appears to be actually split up into several facets. F 4 and F 7 are clearly two developments of paranoid personality; AB 1–2, AC 2, and E 3 indicate the pre-psychotic schizophrenics; P 1 suggests the hermit-eccentric schizothyme; and Q 1 presents a glimpse (a pattern fragment, albeit a nuclear fragment) of what has recently been called the ambulatory schizothyme.

Experiment and test results also link up with these clusters. B 4 reflects the main test results of Spearman's general ability factor, the personality associates of which ramify throughout the B sector. Spranger's aesthetic type, as measured by the Allport-Vernon study of Values, seems to have the pattern of J 1. The fairly remote divergence of F 6 and B 1 may indicate that Willoughby's Measure of Emotional Maturity should be oriented to two sorts of measurement. The six nuclei found in the CA sector suggest a revision, along similar lines, of Allport's Ascendance-Submission measure. The vague entity measured by many extraversion scales is perhaps the whole of the sector D, with its five distinct patterns, of which we shall allow D_4 to inherit the title extraversion-introversion. Thurstone's antevert-retrovert measure is given new content (hypochondria with retroversion) by O 1. The concept of the "general inhibition" of personality, suggested alike by animal studies and philosophical generalizations, is given form by CB 3, but the similarly founded notion of "dominance" does not receive support as constituting a true surface trait.

Physiological-constitutional unities also appear, as in E 4, which is clearly Burt's "general emotionality" syndrome (25), CB 1–2, which is Sheldon's "somatotonia," and CB 4 which suggests a "hyperthyroid hypersensitivity" syndrome.

The subtler adjustments which escape broad typology (though not the psychologist in the consulting room) are also represented, and there are patterns which suggest that correlation technique is capable of revealing less crude syndromes than those required to arrest clinical attention. F 3 seems a central variety of obsessional compulsive personality; CA 1 presents the standard description of inferiority overcompensation; while H 1 is clearly the character neurosis of the anal erotic character.

The outlook for research. That correlation-cluster analysis is capable of yielding, without any conspicuous absentees, the principal syndromes known to the clinical-experiential approach, but in more exact form, gives confidence in the method and its other results. Research can proceed, now that the main framework of surface traits is plotted, to define each with increased precision and to inquire into the causes of variation among phenomenal clusters. A complete cartography of clusters will require, further, that we extend the survey into the realm of smaller clusters; for our research into the total personality sphere did not gather into the chart clusters constituted by only two or three traits.

Other directions of advance lie in the comparison of these clusters with those obtained experimentally in animal research — e.g., in dominant and submissive types. Again, a most important field of research is opened up — directed to stabilizing surface traits and encompassing their objective measurement — by correlation studies intermixing objective measurements with ratings. Finally, by this more precise and more objective definition of surface traits the way is opened to more exact studies than have hitherto been possible regarding nature-nurture and developmental studies of personality.

Nevertheless, the greatest interest attaches, not to the more exact establishment of long-suspected syndromes, but to the discovery of many entirely new patterns in sectors of personality hitherto unobserved.

Chapter Nine

THE PRINCIPAL SOURCE TRAITS DISCOVERED
THROUGH BEHAVIOR RATINGS

1. FOCUSING FACTOR ANALYSIS IN RELATION TO TRAIT RESEARCH

The necessary assumption of statistical training. The resolution of the complete surface-trait picture of the preceding chapter into an equally comprehensive framework of source traits is to be understood only by a grasp of the general theory of factor analysis.

So far our basic hypothesis, as stated in Chapter 4, is that a single influence or source trait will manifest itself in correlation data as a mathematical factor. In any factor analysis, however, only *one* of the possible alternative mathematical solutions will yield factors corresponding to the real source traits. We have assumed that devices can be produced to insure the discovery of this unique solution. It is necessary now to fulfill this promise in a thorough technical appraisal of the situation.

Some knowledge of statistics, especially in relation to correlation and factor analysis, has been assumed from the beginning of this book. Since no one can hope to gain a real understanding of so complex a universe of events as that of personality without the use of such technical devices as factor analysis, it is absolutely necessary now to enter on a proper survey of its use in this field. We shall assume that the groundwork is understood. The reader unfamiliar with the subject should, therefore, at this point turn to one of the excellent introductions to factor analysis — e.g., (27), (120), (254), (261) — for otherwise he will be reduced to accepting, without insight or proof, the validity of the arguments and procedures advocated.

The present quandary of factor analysis. We propose to concentrate only on that aspect of factor analysis which has to do with deciding between alternative solutions.   We shall ask: "What are the alternative solutions?" and "What principles exist to guide the choice?"

Let us see the problem in its full setting. Psychology shares with most biological and sociological sciences an onerous "embarras de richesse" in that all the influences in which it is interested tend to act at once, in the situations which are worth observing. Except in the few problems that can be brought into the laboratory it faces too many variables, and too many influences behind these variables, for piecemeal investigation. Its most potent method of attacking the tangle is to work out correlation coefficients between the inconveniently multitudinous variables abounding in the subject and to seek some smaller number of "behind the scenes" or underlying variables, known as factors, of which the more numerous variables may be considered lesser representatives or, at any rate, functions. In quite a variety of sciences and situations real causal entities or influences are known which produce correlations among a larger number of more superficial or trivial variables, operating as factors among these lesser variables. Thus, in psychology, we have temperament factors in the form of hormones, each changing, in covariation, a set of symptoms; or we have drives, or external training influences, each responsible for changes in a whole variety of surface traits.

The scientific application of factor analysis to unearth basic causes and influences is, however, at present crippled by the fact that any set of correlations can be very variously interpreted. A given set of factors will resolve into one and only one set (matrix) of correlations between variables; but, proceeding in the reverse direction, from the correlations of variables to factors, many sets of possible factor systems, each mathematically sound and satisfactory, can be arrived at from any one correlation matrix.

Faced with this methodological difficulty of choosing the "meaningful" factors, researchers have taken one of two attitudes. Some have been content to find only mathematical factors, not troubling about their corresponding to any psychological or physiological entity, but glad to have a set of predictive variables decidedly less numerous than the individual trait measurements with which it would otherwise be necessary to work. Between the possible sets of mathematical factors they make a choice on grounds of mathematical or test-procedure convenience. The factors they adopt have an "as if" reality — i.e., one can predict behavior in many (but not all) situations as if a single trait or real influence of that kind were at work.

On the other hand, the researcher may demand more than convenience. If he is primarily a psychologist and a scientist, he will want to find the set of factors which corresponds to a set of psychologically real influences, because he is interested in understanding the psychological meaning of his predictions and because he is curious to gain truth for its own sake. In that case he may (1) devise possible ways of overdetermining the analysis of the given correlation matrix so that only the one set of true factors will emerge, or (2) start from the opposite shore and propound, on psychological grounds alone, a hypothesis about what source traits are operative in the variables. Then he will see if these factors correspond to any of the possible mathematical factors found in the matrix. This latter procedure is a very common and respected one in science. Typically the researcher invents a hypothesis and tests it against measurements. But, unfortunately, in the present situation this scientific habit of working is far from being a happy one. For, in the first place, personality study has so few other reliable avenues for arriving at, or even suspecting, the basic source traits, that hypotheses are likely to be erratic. In the second place, the mathematical solutions to any set of correlations are so numerous and varied that unless the hypothesis can be stated in very precise quantitative terms the "proof" of it is easy — so easy as to be worthless.

Yet a disillusioned acceptance of merely mathematically convenient factors is not only scientifically, but even practically, less convenient than the use of the true factors, if they could be obtained. For the purely mathematical economy of having a few factors rather than many variables is an economy which holds *only in relation to one matrix and one prediction situation*. In another matrix, using a considerable number of the variables from the first, quite different mathematical factors may be obtained. On a population of high school students and for predicting school success, thirty tests may be resolved mainly into three "ability" factors, A, B, and C. The same tests, mixed with ten others, and applied to college students, may resolve into four factors, D, E, F, and G. The experimenter may find the first three of these mathematically more convenient and just as "psychologically defensible" as A, B, and C. If analyses are repeated in a few more situations, we may soon have more factors listed in the various researches than variables! So that it might have been better to establish scholastic, occupational, and other associations and predictive values round the variables rather than the factors — a conclusion which some psychologists do not hesitate to adopt. Despite the enormous obstacles, true research is compelled to return to the attempt to direct factorization toward obtaining real psychological influences and functional unities.

Possible aims of factor analysis. Burt (*27*) points out that factor analysis can serve three distinct purposes: (1) Suitably improved, it may offer causal interpretation, of the kind we now seek in source traits, which is demanded alike by scientific curiosity and the greatest convenience of applied psychology; (2) it offers economical statistical prediction for applied psychology in any one research even though through purely artificial mathematical factors; and (3) less ambitiously it offers aesthetic and scientific satisfaction by providing a basis, other than a semantic one, for systematic description and pigeonholing of traits, even though the classification may be in part arbitrary or relative to a particular matrix.

2. THE VARIETIES OF TRAIT PATTERNS OBTAINABLE FROM DIVERSE FACTOR-ANALYTIC SYSTEMS

Historical origin of factor analysis. If the psychologist addresses himself to the general problem of finding a true psychological interpretation through factor analysis, the first constructive step that can be taken is the elimination of certain mathematically possible factoring *systems* (not merely individual solutions) which are, psychologically, impossible or highly improbable.

Various mathematical systems of factor analysis have been intensively developed in the past twenty years, largely due to the works of Spearman (*235*), Burt (*27*), Thurstone (*261*), Kelley (*145*), Thompson (*254*), Stephenson (*243*), Holzinger (*120*), Hotelling (*124*), Tryon (*267*), and many others. We may first glance at the historically developed systems and then at the theoretical possibilities.

Alternative factorial systems. The earliest and perhaps the simplest system was (1) Spearman's "two factor" analysis into a general factor common to all variables in the matrix and a number of specific factors, one peculiar to each variable. This analysis can be carried out only where correlations are largely positive, as occurs in most matrices measuring abilities only, and also when the special tetrad difference criterion (*235*) is satisfied by the correlations.

(2) Resolution into a general factor, positive in all variables, as in system (1), plus a number of nonoverlapping exclusively positive *group factors* subtending several but not all tests, plus specific factors. This is Holzinger's *Bi-Factor Analysis System (120)* and is also most useful with abilities, where the correlations are practically all positive.

(3) Resolution into a series of (overlapping) general or group factors, plus specifics. This results from Thurstone's centroid method *(261)*. If the result is unrotated or haphazardly rotated, the signs of the loadings will be both positive and negative. With abilities, when rotated for simple structure, the factors are virtually wholly positive.

(4) Resolution into a series of general factors which are as numerous as the original variables (and therefore require no specifics to complete the picture), but with the greater part of the variance accounted for by the first few factors. This is the "principal component" method [1] of Hotelling and Kelley *(124)*, *(145)*, which has also been independently developed by Burt *(27)*.

(5) Resolution into a general factor (positive) and a series of *bipolar general factors* each having as many negative as positive saturations — i.e., acting about equally in both directions, plus specifics. This system, essentially the centroid system above (3) without any rotation, has been developed chiefly by Burt *(27)*, who points out that certain aspects of personality, notably emotional expression, are most likely to be represented by factors acting positively in some traits and negatively in others. Its factors are the *differences* of factors in the centroid rotated analysis.

Systems conceived as combinations of certain possibilities. The above systems represent the possibilities which have been

---

[1] It differs significantly from any of the above systems in that it employs a weighted summation of the correlations of the individual variables (weighted in proportion to the loadings) in determining the factors. (Weighted by reason of using covariances instead of correlations, and still further weighted, in Kelley's system, by psychological judgments as to the importance of each variable in the total personality.)

actually realized in practical mathematical procedures. It is worth while to ask how far they reproduce the theoretically conceivable combinations of factor forms, since for certain psychological purposes almost any combination of factor forms might sometime be required. The primary conditions, which may be varied, are: (*a*) the factors — general, group, and specific; (*b*) the signs of the factors — all positive, all negative, equally or unequally positive and negative; (*c*) the presence or absence of overlap among the group factors. Each of these three aspects of the factor system presents a possible viewpoint from which factor systems can be classified, and various writers at various times have made one aspect predominant. For example, the available systems — which, incidentally, do not equal in number the theoretically possible combinations — have been classified as general factor methods and group factor methods (Burt (*27*)), as one, two, and three factor methods (Holzinger (*120*)), and as positive factor methods (Thurstone's rotated centroids) or positive and negative factor methods (Thurstone's unrotated or Burt's[1] Bipolar Factor Method).

All the above systems, including even Spearman's two-factor analysis, can be considered as special instances of (and can, at least theoretically, be derived from) Thurstone's centroid method, though historically they did not appear in that way.

[1] Burt amplifies his distinction (*27*, page 296):

"I shall call those methods which proceed by analyzing the correlation matrix taken as a whole 'general factor' methods, and those which partition the correlation matrix into suitable sub-matrices, and then analyze them separately, 'group factor methods.' With the former all the factors after the first have *negative as well as positive saturation coefficients;* with the latter, the factorial matrix has a large number of *zero saturations* in each column, and for the rest contains only *positive saturations.*

"Under the heading of general factor methods may be placed those used by Spearman, Holzinger, Kelley, Thurstone (before rotating), and Stephenson. Under the heading of group factor methods may be placed Holzinger's bifactor method, Thompson's alternative analysis of artificial correlation-tables obtained from dice and cards, Stephenson's procedure when analyzing correlation between persons, and my own early efforts when demonstrating group factors in educational abilities and in emotional traits."

Further mutations of the above theoretical possibilities can be made by (*a*) working with factors which, instead of being entirely independent of one another — i.e., orthogonal in the geometrical picture — are to some extent themselves correlated — i.e., oblique; (*b*) working on the assumption that factors do not interact in simple additive fashion or have linear relations to the variables, but that they affect variables by mutual multiplication or according to some logarithmic or other relation.

Psychological arguments for the choice of a factor system for personality variables. The choice of a factor system *may* be determined, within certain limits, by the nature of the correlation matrix itself. There are some patterns which cannot be obtained from some matrices — for example, one can get a resolution into a general and specific factor only if the tetrad difference criterion is met by the relations between the coefficients. Again, one cannot get a general factor and positive group factors from a correlation matrix with practically as many negative as positive correlations.[1] In technical mathematical terms, the number of factors which can be obtained from a correlation matrix *is equal to the rank of the matrix*.

What, then, are the limits generally set by the actual nature of the correlation matrices found in psychological work? The correlation matrix for our personality variables (available from study *58a*) offers correlations which are probably typical of those which will generally be obtained in matrices using widely sampled personality traits. They fall into no simple pattern and are almost as frequently negative as posi-

[1] If the matrix permits analyses into two or three different factor-combination patterns, it is always possible, as Burt has shown (*27*), to convert a set of measurements in one of these factor systems fairly readily into those of any other. For example, the loadings on a set of bipolar factors (Burt (*27*), page 309) are nothing more than the weighted differences of the loadings on a set of positive group factors from the same matrix.

However, though it is good to know that a set of valuable data is not irrevocably lost by being expressed in an unsuitable factor system, it is desirable to have it factorized in the most appropriate way from the beginning and if possible in factors corresponding to the real psychological influences in the situation.

tive. After all, most of the bipolar traits could just as easily have been rated positively from one end as from the other. There is no "generally good" or "generally efficient" direction in personality traits, unless the traits are in some narrow region or the experimenter has a narrow mind. Further, it is not possible, by "reflecting" certain variables — i.e., exchanging the poles of negative and positive scoring — to make the matrix as a whole predominantly positive. The matrix, in short, is not favorable to a resolution into patterns (1) or (2) or certain forms of (3) as listed above (two factor, bifactor, or wholly positive group factor structures).

As for the presumed nature of personality, which must be the primary guide, it is clear, from the discussions in Chapters 4 and 5 on the nature of traits, that *a fairly large number of general factors and overlapping group factors are to be expected,* corresponding to constitutional (temperamental, ability, and dynamic) traits and to environmental mold traits. Presumably, temperament traits will affect practically all trait elements, as also will such a constitutional trait as general intelligence. Since environmental mold influences are directed more frequently to restricted areas of behavior — or even to developing specific skills or responses — we should expect group and specific factors from these. Except in abilities we should not expect either general or group factors to be wholly positive — first, because of the "chance" direction of our bipolar variables; secondly, because various dynamic and temperamental influences are frequently in conflict — i.e., operating in opposed directions; and finally because any one of them can confidently be expected from general psychological experience to aid some behavior expressions and reduce others. Furthermore, we should expect the division between general and group factors to be relative rather than absolute; for even a restricted trait may exert some *slight* influence on all behavior — i.e., the division of methods into general factor and group factor methods is not a very practical one.

Thurstone's multifactor centroid method, with rotation, alone gives the flexibility in the number, sign, extent, and nature of overlapping of factors required to meet the possible demands of this probable personality structure. But for the moment we accept it without the further special modification involved in his "rotation into simple structure." Burt's bipolar factor method is almost as convenient, but might need some rotation, for there is no special need to believe that the *first* general factor will be wholly positive or that the subsequent factors in the series would arrange themselves in the "genealogical" [1] pattern required by this form of analysis.

Our general knowledge of personality structure demands further that factors be allowed to be sometimes oblique; for the general factors of constitutional temperament — e.g., two endocrine gland influences — are not likely to be entirely independent, nor are many of the environmental mold patterns — e.g., those of the church and social class — likely to be entirely unrelated, for they operate within the organic unity of a society.[2]

The indicated plan, therefore, seems to be a centroid analysis followed by some rotation, even to oblique axes where necessary. This *could* meet the needs of personality forms.

[1] I use the term "genealogical" here to describe the "necessary relationships" of sign which in Burt's system exist as a pattern among subsequent factors in the series, as illustrated by the following example.

Traits	Factor I	Factor II	Factor III	Factor IV
A	+	+	+	−
B	+	+	+	+
C	+	+	−	−
D	+	+	−	+
E	+	−	+	−
F	+	−	+	+
G	+	−	−	−
H	+	−	−	+

[2] A well-known instance of correlation between two inherently quite different factors is that between general intelligence and character integration, which has been repeatedly found to approach + 0.6.

Whether in fact it *will* do so and yield factors corresponding to realities depends on the principles followed in rotation, which must now be discussed intensively.

3. PRINCIPLES FOR DETERMINING THE CHOICE OF FACTORS

Restriction of the problem. The centroid method, being the most flexible and easily adapted to yield whatever factor structure is formed by the real functional unities in psychological data, will be taken as the general starting point. The focus of controversy concerning the use of this method turns, however, on the choice of criteria for determining the rotation of axes.

In proceeding we shall remind the reader that we have rejected one of the two major approaches normally approved by scientific method — namely, that of inventing a hypothesis about the particular factors expected and attempting to discover a factorization to match it — because in this field almost any hypothesis could be so "confirmed." Instead, we seek general guiding principles for the mathematical analysis itself which will lead to a unique solution. Naturally there is nothing to prevent one from starting off with a hypothesis to be checked against this *unique* empirical finding, but the solution stands in its own right.

Survey of available principles. There are some seven independent and not necessarily conflicting principles now available, of which three have not been so far generally employed and of which only two — simple structure and proportional profiles — are of major importance. Most are equally applicable to orthogonal and oblique axes solutions. It seems to the present writer, however, that the only entirely satisfactory principles are those which *do* have this character of being applicable also to oblique solutions. For it is part of the general flexibility required in any factor-analytic system that it shall be able to yield oblique factors. As indicated above, there is no guarantee that the source traits in personality, and the social, physical, genetic, and physiological influences which produce them, are entirely independent. For example, the combination of social stratification and assortative mating almost certainly produce some correlation between the genetic source traits of general mental capacity and general emotional stability (see Diagram 19). For all we yet know, there may very occasionally be quite marked departure from orthogonality, and our whole system of choosing factors should be able to adapt to this.

(1) **Rotation to agree with clinical and general psychological findings.** The axes are centered on some well-known syndromes or some sets of variables, each known to be highly involved in a psychological unity. If the syndrome is known only from cross-sectional studies, this procedure amounts to nothing more than putting axes through clusters, for a syndrome may be merely a correlation cluster or *surface trait*. The alignment of source traits with surface traits manifests the radical weaknesses discussed under the cluster principle, No. 3 below. However, a syndrome may be more than a cluster: it may have its true functional unity as a source trait witnessed by developmental and other observations. In this case there is no fallacy but there is also no discovery, except in so far (*a*) as the factor reveals the influence of the source trait in trait elements not clinically recognized in the gross syndrome, and (*b*) as such fixation assists in the realization of principle No. 4 below.

(2) **Rotation to agree with factors from past factor analyses.** As advocated and practiced by Reyburn and Taylor (*215*), this involves rotating an orthogonal system to get as many as possible of the factors to agree with previously established factors in independent researches. The factors of earlier researches have sometimes been established as single general factors, by concentrated research in a particular field — e.g., intelligence, perseveration, surgency, using tests deliberately devised to measure what on clinical or general psychological

grounds is expected to form a functional unity in that field. Consequently these more intensive and insightful researches on single factors are felt to be sufficiently established to anchor the rotations of the more dispersed multifactor research. A powerful objection to this principle is that it may merely perpetuate psychologically fallacious concepts guiding the pioneer analyses.

(3) **Rotation to put axes through the center of clusters.** This is a special case of (1) above. It may be done either by picking out the outstanding correlation clusters in the original correlation matrix or by considering the clusters which exist in any two-factor space — i.e., in the projection on a single plane when the number of factors is known and the variables are plotted in space of the appropriate dimensions. The following comments apply substantially to both of these related procedures. If there are two factors operating fairly evenly, in a positive way, in a certain matrix, the original observed clusters are likely to occur in the regions of overlap of the two factors. There the shared variance (communality) is higher. From this point of view a cluster is more likely to be a region of overlap — i.e., high communality — than to be the heart of a factor. On the other hand, most factors do *not* distribute themselves with even loadings over the variables they load, and a cluster then represents the variables with the highest factor loadings. (For example, in a matrix satisfying the two-factor theory we put the axis through the center of the most highly intercorrelating bunch of variables, for those have most "g.") However, both possibilities exist and there is no guarantee that a salient cluster is anything more stable than a province of overlap of two or more real, functional factors.

Further, it can be even more radically objected against this somewhat popular practice that many clusters are sheer artifacts produced by the experimenter's more or less deliberate choosing of obviously psychologically related tests.

Frequently, moreover, he may be unaware of the existence of some important psychological variables which, if brought into the matrix, would fill the empty spaces between his clusters and demolish their claim to individuality and diagnostic worth as determinants. Actually the simple structure principle (see (6) below), at least when used with orthogonal axes, tends to produce some relation between axes and clusters, but this is only a secondary result of a primary aim of over-all simplicity.

(4) **The principle of orthogonal additions: rotation to agree with successively established factors.** In an n-dimensional orthogonal system, if the position of $n - 1$ axes is known from previous sources of evidence, the position of the nth axis is automatically established. One begins, therefore, with tests which, apart from specific factors, measure only known factors, or even a single known factor. "Known" means here, "known to correspond to a real functional entity" — e.g., general mental capacity, hyperthyroidism, manic-depression. By trial and error, guided by psychological insight, one then attempts to add variables to the matrix which will introduce, apart from specifics, only one new factor. When the new factor is determined a further set of variables can be added, introducing one more new factor the position of which in turn becomes fixed by the earlier factors.

In this way, starting with one factor of known position, it should be possible, theoretically, by successive additions to fix the rotation of a most complex multidimensional factorization. Indeed, in a relatively inexplicit and planless fashion this principle has been employed in practical research problems, as the history of establishment of factors during the past twenty years shows. For example, Garnett's "c" factor (95), later refined into the concept of the surgent temperament (40), was first established as the second factor in a set of variables in which Webb's general character integration factor "w" was taken as the prior, confirmed, functional unity.

This in turn was first established as the second factor in a system in which "g," the first factor, was considered known.

The defect of this method is that it depends on orthogonal axes. If the first factor, used as starting point, happened really to be the least orthogonal of any factor in the system, there would ensue a considerable systematic error in the positions of all the other factors, in addition to the errors due to each departing a little from the mean orthogonal position.

(5) **The principle of expected profiles: rotation to produce loading profiles congruent with general psychological expectations.** It is possible that on general psychological grounds one could validly conclude that certain *kinds* of traits should manifest certain general forms of factor-loading pattern in certain samples of variables. One would then rotate to get the maximum number of factors giving loading profiles — i.e., factor patterns (*120*) of the kind required. The different kinds of traits most likely to have consistent, characteristic profiles are those distinguished earlier as temperamental, ability, and dynamic source traits, and these expected profiles might be subdivided further according to whether they arise from constitutional or environmental mold traits. To make a detailed defense of particular, definitive views as to what these profiles are is not within the scope of this treatise, but one may hazard that environmental mold traits — e.g., honesty, politeness, and, especially in the field of ability, certain dexterities and skills — would tend to be group factors and to have all-or-nothing loadings, because they are imposed by education deliberately, in a few trait elements, and neglected elsewhere. That is, they would appear essentially as group factors in any general sample of trait elements or as general factors showing what we might call "plateau loading" — i.e., either very high or very low loadings. By contrast, constitutional, temperamental source traits would be expected to manifest themselves more uniformly in all trait variables, as a general factor and a rather even one at that.

According to this principle, therefore, one would rotate to get profiles of loadings having relationship to the nature of the source traits (factors) as shown by the nature of the trait elements in which the factor tends to appear most heavily. For example, a factor showing bigger loadings in temperament traits than any other would be adjusted in rotation to give a smooth profile, while a factor looming large in skills should show sharp "plateau loading." The profiles expected will obviously depend also on the choice of variables. If, for example, they are all of one kind — e.g., temperament variables — so that the factors will be all of one kind, this principle will give no assistance.

(6) **The principle of "simple structure" relative to the given correlation matrix.** Thurstone has answered the question, "What is there intrinsic to the statistical data which will provide a basis for solution?" by taking his stand on the existence of simplicity and parsimony in nature.

From the dawn of science it has been usual to guide the choice between hypotheses, when no crucial experiment could lend its aid, by the "principle of parsimony" — i.e., assuming that the simpler explanation is more likely to be correct. Newton's *Natura est simplex* was a formal scientist's statement of the principle originally propounded by the scholastic logician, William of Occam (Occam's "razor"). It directs the scientists to accept the simplest hypothesis, requiring fewest explanatory assumptions.

Simple structure supposes essentially that the correlations are to be explained by the fewest possible factors per variable. It asks that there be no one factor in every variable; no variable with a loading from every factor; a general maximizing of zero loadings. Reyburn and Taylor (*215*) have criticized the criterion, saying that one should look for simplicity and parsimony not with respect to all matrices in which the variables occur. Thurstone has never denied this desideratum, but the principle and practice of rotation for simple structure pay attention *to only one correlation matrix at a time* and aim at conditions defined with respect to that matrix only. It is claimed that simple structure produces factor invariance — i.e., similar loading profiles for factors in different studies. In short, if "simplicity" is produced for several matrices at once, that is a secondary consequence of having found the true functional unities by simple structure in each separate matrix.

4. THE MOST FUNDAMENTAL PRINCIPLE: PROPORTIONAL PROFILES

More extended consideration will be given to the most basic principle, as follows:

(7) **The principle of proportional profiles or "simultaneous simple structure."** This begins with the same general scientific "principle of parsimony" that forms the premise of Thurstone's simple structure, but arrives at a different formulation of the meaning of the principle in the field of factor analysis. The present writer maintains that the principle of parsimony should not demand "Which is the simplest set of factors for reproducing this particular correlation matrix?" but rather "Which set of factors will be most parsimonious at once with respect to this and other matrices considered together — especially when the correlations emanate from many diverse fields of psychological observation — e.g., applied, social, and physiological psychology?" The criterion is then no longer that the rotation shall offer fewest factor loadings for any one matrix, but that it shall offer fewest dissimilar (and therefore fewest distinct total) loadings in all the matrices together.[1] This is the essential origin of the new principle.

This formulation depends on the consideration that the *real*

[1] Simple structure does not preclude this condition, but it does not demand it as the *primary* condition. Thurstone writes: "It is fundamental criterion for a valid method of isolating primary abilities that the weights of the primary abilities for a test must remain invariant when it is removed from one test battery to another test battery" (*261*). But this is expected to follow from simple structure instead of conversely.

psychological functional unities are bound to appear as possible mathematical factorizations in *many* different kinds of situation, whereas the mathematical factors which are artifacts will only stand the test of fitting the matrix in which they happen to appear.

But when one asks more precisely, "What exactly is the nature of the agreement required for 'proportional profiles'?" the answers have to be carefully qualified.

Regarding the derivation of the factors which have to agree, it is clear that to require agreement in factors and factor loadings among correlation matrices derived from the same or similar test variables on the same or similar population samples is an empty challenge. No new source of rotation determination is introduced, for such matrices will differ only by sampling errors and there will be an infinite series of possible parallel rotations in the two analyses. The new and special condition is that the two matrices should be such as to contain the same factors but that in the second matrix at least one factor should be accentuated or reduced in influence by the experimental or situational design, so that all its loadings are proportionately changed, producing a correlation matrix different from the first.

The changes of design or circumstance which can be introduced are broadly of two kinds: (*a*) distortion of the factorization by special selection of the population, or by altering all the trait-variable measurements in some systematic fashion; (*b*) changing the trait measurements from measures of static, inter-individual differences to measures of other sources of difference in the same variables.

The first, which seems to the present writer a less satisfactory[1] approach, would have, on more detailed examination,

---

[1] It might be difficult to reduce the variance of a factor as a whole — as distinct from that of particular variables — when one does not know beforehand what the factor is. As Thurstone has shown recently ("The Effects of Selection in Factor Analysis," *Psychometrika*, 1945, 10, 3), univariate selection generally alters the angles between factors, which would upset the method of proportional profiles.

the following subvarieties: (1) differential selection of the two populations with respect to those features which are likely to constitute a functional unity — e.g., more or less age-selected, more or less of normals and psychotics, males and females, hyper- and hypo-thyroids, etc.; (2) change in form or method of scoring of the tests — e.g., increasing the level of difficulty, administering under speeded or unspeeded conditions, administering before and after practice periods; (3) allowing the same tests to be associated with different supplementary tests in different matrices has also been suggested, but except in special circumstances would not be a determiner of rotation in the sense required here. Some of the early work of Spearman, and more recent work by Guilford, Woodrow, Wherry, and others, shows clearly that method (2) does produce modifications of factor emphasis while retaining the same factors.

The second source of matrix difference requires the gathering of measurements in ways not hitherto generally envisaged in factor-analytic studies of personality. These diverse sources of correlation data have been reviewed systematically in Chapter 6. Among the most practically important for the present purpose are (in addition to the usual (1) Static Covariation), (2) Test Increment Covariation — i.e., S-technique, correlating *changes in score* of individuals through time or experimental influence; (3) Intra-Individual Covariation — i.e., P-technique, the analysis of correlations between series constituted by many successive measurements of a set of variables in one person; (4) Intra-Individual Covariation of Differences and the differences of scores in related pairs of individuals — e.g., twins. These and their various modifications and extensions provide in all an ample source of matrix variations.

The argument for "proportional profiles," as a means of determining rotations, now runs as follows: (*a*) If one is dealing with true functional unities (unitary traits), they should show themselves alike in static, mutational, incremental, intra-individual, and other situations of covariation. (*b*) Owing to the modifying circumstances, however, the factors will be present in different amounts, so that the loadings of a set of variables a, b, c, d, $\cdots$ n by factor A in the first matrix will appear reduced or increased — in the same proportion for each of the variables[1] — in the modified factor A_1, in the second matrix. For if a factor is one which corresponds to a true functional unity, it will be increased or decreased *as a whole*.

Consequently it should be possible to find a position in the rotation of the factors from the first matrix which will give, for each factor, a profile of loadings, "similar" — i.e., proportional — to those obtainable from some rotation of the second matrix. Mathematically, the following questions now arise: (*a*) Is it possible to discover — other than by the insuperably long process of trial and error — the two positions (one in each matrix) between which this relationship holds? (*b*) Will this matching be unique — i.e., will there be only one position in both at which such matching is possible? The problem is like that of rotating two or more cylinders on a combination lock to find the one position in which all will "click." And (*c*) can it be shown that such a solution is *not* possible for any two factor matrices taken at random?

The solutions can be presented either geometrically or through matrix algebra. As they have been set out in detail in two papers elsewhere (*58 b*)(*58 c*), we shall not do more than indicate them here. It can be shown that (1) in the normally occurring numbers of variables and factor, sets of purely random loadings can never be brought into this special relationship; (2) the position is uniquely determined; (3) the number of variables required to fix the rotation is $2n + 1$, when n is the number of factors; (4) with artificial data, which have alone been available since the principle was

---

[1] Closer examination may require the conclusion that though the loadings of A_1 are all functions of the loadings of A, the function may not be one of simple linear proportion. Throughout this first exposition we shall assume for simplicity that all the loadings of A_1 are the same linear function of all the corresponding loadings of A.

Factor Loadings from First Correlation Matrix   Factor Loadings from Second Correlation Matrix

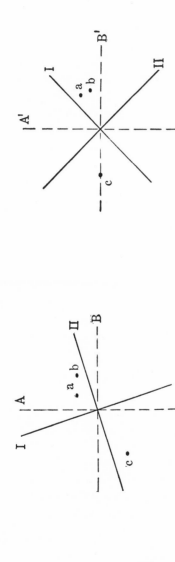

DIAGRAM 15.   Parallel Proportional Profiles for Two Factors

In the second diagram the loadings on the first factor, I, are increased by a third and those on II are reduced by a half. The positions of a, b, and c were first plotted by means of the unrotated factor matrices with results shown by AB and A'B'. Each coördinate system was then independently rotated to find the only "real" factor position — that in which such relationships of loadings alone exist.

published, the proportional profiles and the simple structure methods tend to the same rotation.

However, the present method could be used successfully when, for lack of any inherent simple structure in the data, the simple structure method cannot be used. For example, there are no grounds for denying the possibility that some general factors exist which enter to such an extent into all variables that no hyperplane of zero loadings could be found to fixate them by simple structure. Factors B and D in our data (Chapter 10) were difficult to fix in this way. Consequently, the new principle, if the mathematical difficulties connected with its practical operation can be overcome, offers certain advantages over and above that of basic theoretical soundness. Unfortunately, until mathematical improvement is brought about, the labor of solving so many simultaneous equations must prohibit use of the method when many factors are involved.

In outline the mathematical solution is as follows: We take a factor system f and another, f′, which are the unrotated centroid factorizations obtained from the two correlation matrices on the same variables in the two given situations. Each constitutes a system of projections of the same variables on the same number of axes. Let us suppose that we know the solution positions, $\bar{f}$ and $\bar{f}'$, in which the projections on $\bar{f}'$ stand in certain ratios to those on $\bar{f}$. The matrix of direction cosines by which the system f is to be multiplied to carry it into the desired position $\bar{f}$ we shall call A and the matrix for the $\bar{f}'$ transformation B. Thus, in matrix rotation,

$$(1)\ \bar{f} = f \cdot A \qquad \text{and} \qquad (2)\ \bar{f}' = f' \cdot B$$

The transformation from $\bar{f}$ to f′ can also be represented by a matrix multiplication, O — a diagonal matrix in which each term represents the ratio of the projections on one axis of $\bar{f}$ to one axis of $\bar{f}'$.

$$(3)\ \bar{f}' = \bar{f} \cdot O$$

Then the total transformation from the given f to the given f' may be represented in matrix rotation as follows:

$$f \cdot A = f' \cdot B \cdot O^{-1}$$
$$\text{whence } f = f' \cdot B \cdot O^{-1} \cdot A^{-1}$$

The solution for A, B, and O, which gives the required "psychologically meaningful factor" loadings $\bar{f}$ and $\bar{f}'$, requires the use of sets of simultaneous equations, which are quite harassingly numerous when more than three factors are involved. However, further study by mathematicians may suggest less onerous methods of handling these solutions in practice.

Until the special difficulties connected with oblique axes and variable error in the given data have been smoothed out, the method cannot be put into routine form for handling research data. Consequently no results of its application can be published here. This consummation, with its certainty of rotation toward true functional unities, must also wait upon the collection of precise correlation on the same sets of variables measured under different conditions. Fortunately, the agreement of factors from different factorizations using Thurstone's already practicable principle of simple structure is so unmistakable, even though approximate and occasionally lacking, that we may in the meantime put considerable faith in it as a means of arriving at that same goal of true functional unities which is sought by the new method. The criticism that in practice there is no adequate criterion as to how far the goal of simple structure has been attained is now being met by a number of empirically derived devices. (See, e.g., (*58 d*).)

5. PRINCIPLES OF DESIGN IN THE PRESENT, MAJOR
   ORIENTING FACTOR-ANALYSIS EXPERIMENT

Combining the findings of factor-analytic researches. Our purpose in the remainder of this chapter is to list and evaluate the results of factor-analytic research to date. To integrate the findings into a reliable, comprehensive list of the major real source traits of personality, it will be necessary also to describe in particular a major factor-analytic experiment carried out specially for this integrative purpose. Thereby we shall finish with a survey of source traits comparable to that carried out for surface traits in the preceding chapter.

The combination of factors from different researches, however, presents special difficulties, discussed below. Before attempting this combination we shall describe the experiment which provided the framework for that whole integration.

The necessary primacy of rating data. To formulate the results of the preceding chapter's discussion as to whether the variables employed should be ratings or objective-test measurements or questionnaire data and self-ratings, we may conclude:

(1) In the initial phases of personality study, when it is especially important to get perspective and discover the major factors of personality, before splitting them by secondary dimensions, it is not safe to depend on test or questionnaire items. Only the total vocabulary of personality description, confirmed by centuries of utility, can be certain to provide the total personality space and to occupy the complete "personality sphere."

(2) Despite the somewhat inferior reliability of ratings, as usually made, they can, by the special care possible in research situations, be made satisfactory.

(3) Ratings analyze out aspects of behavior which simply cannot be assessed, even by the most ingenious of objective-test devices, at the present time; and

(4) Ratings can deal with aspects of behavior which have the greatest practical importance in those situations in which the results of factor analyses of personality will most frequently be used.

However, later work will aim to intersperse objective-test variables among the rated variables.

The variables of the main factor analysis. The 62 clusters originally obtained (54) from, and very substantially representing, the 171 basic traits still constituted too large a trait population to be practicable for a factor analysis by anything less than a regiment of workers. Consequently clusters were first combined, wherever there was overlap, into nuclear clusters which were substantially those of the list in the preceding chapter prior to the addition of clusters from other researches. By such condensation the variables were eventually reduced to 35, as listed in Table 17. The effect upon the ultimate factor analysis of condensing the trait variables into clusters will be to reduce the number of dimensions relative to the factor space which might have been obtained from the original trait variables, for each cluster itself has at least two dimensions.   But we would argue that the factors we obtained would be the major ones, giving perspective relative to *the main structure of personality*, whereas *the dimensions lost through considering any one cluster as a point (or line) will be relatively small and "provincial."*   Indeed, it would seem that, once perspective is gained, the picture can be filled out later by local factor studies, in the region of each cluster.[1]

This reduction of clusters to single variables can, of course, be carried out by mathematical treatment, obtaining for the individual a composite score in the cluster from his scores in the constituent trait elements.   Holzinger describes precise ways of getting the "center" of a cluster and refers to the factor pattern obtained — as here — from clusters as a "reduced pattern."

TABLE 17

DESCRIPTION OF THE 35 ESTABLISHED CLUSTERS USED AS VARIABLES [2]

POSITIVE POLE	NEGATIVE POLE
1. Self-assertive	Self-submissive
Boastful	Modest
Assertive	Submissive
Conceited	Self-critical, dissatisfied
2. Intelligent, analytical	Unimaginative, stupid
Intelligent	Stupid
Clear-thinking	Incoherent, confused
Clever	
3. Wise, mature, polished	Dependent, silly, incoherent
Independent	Emotionally dependent
Reliable	Undependable
Mature	Emotionally immature, irresponsible

[1] See footnote 1, page 132.

[2] The cluster title, it will be noticed, is sometimes distinctly wider in reference than the three actual traits listed here would seem to justify — notably in clusters 5, 14, 15, 21, 33. But it must be remembered that there are usually at least six traits in the cluster. Our aim has been to represent as accurately as possible, by the title and traits in combination, the general character of the cluster. Occasionally, where the three highest traits would give a misleading impression in this respect, slightly lower but less overlapping traits on the cluster correlation list are allowed to represent the cluster here.

TABLE 17 — *Continued*

Positive Pole	Negative Pole
4. Changeable, frivolous	Thoughtful, stoic, reserved
Unreflective	Thoughtful
Impulsive	Deliberate
Profligate	Austere
5. Neurotic	Not generally neurotic
Self-deceiving	Realistic
Hypochondriacal	
Nervous, specific neurotic symptoms	
6. Hard, cynical	Kindly, gentle, idealistic
Thankless	Grateful
Hostile	Friendly, understanding
Hardhearted	Softhearted
7. Willful, egotistic, predatory	Mild, self-effacing, tolerant
Extra-punitive (blaming mistakes on others)	
Headstrong	Gentle-tempered
Exhibitionist	Self-effacing
8. Rigid, tyrannical, vindictive	Adaptable, friendly
Extra-punitive	
Inflexible (emotionally)	Adaptable (to change)
Hostile	Friendly
9. Surly, hard	Good-natured, easygoing
Thankless	Grateful
Hardhearted, embittered	Softhearted
Short-tempered	Easygoing
10. Demoralized, autistic	Realistic, facing life
Unrealistic	Realistic, practical
Quitting	Persevering
Subjective, evasive	Facing life
11. Strong-willed, conscientious	Indolent, incoherent, impulsive
Persevering	Quitting
Painstaking	Slipshod
Conscientious	Conscienceless
12. Intellectual	Simple, undisciplined mind
Thoughtful	Unreflective
Analytical	
Wide interests	Narrow interests
13. Insecure, infantile, hostile	Mature, kind, tactful
Easily jealous	
Thankless, unappreciative	Grateful
Self-pitying	

TABLE 17 — *Continued*

Positive Pole	Negative Pole
14. Antisocial, schizoid	Outgoing, idealistic, coöperative
Cynical	Idealistic
Obstructive	Coöperative
Timid, withdrawn	Adventurous
15. Cheerful, enthusiastic, witty	Unhappy, frustrated, dour
Genial	Coldhearted
Optimistic	Pessimistic
Enthusiastic	Apathetic
16. Active, neurotic, creatively un-stable	Self-controlled, rigid, conventional
Intrusive	Reserved
Impulsive	Deliberate
Neurotic	
17. Character neurosis, psychopathic	Emotionally mature
(Neurotic, irritable, uncon-trolled)	Balanced
Fickle	Loyal
Dishonest	Honest
18. High-strung, expressive, driven	Phlegmatic
Highly strung	(Unexcited and unexcitable)
Hurried	Lethargic
Vivacious	
19. Spiteful, tightfisted, superstitious	Natural, friendly, open
Hostile	Friendly
Obstructive	Coöperative
Secretive	Frank
(Irrational, obsessive fears)	
20. General emotionality (with maladjustment)	Unemotional
Emotional (in all ways)	Unemotional
Dissatisfied	Content
Excitable	Phlegmatic
21. Ascendant, expressive, widely in-terested	Retiring, quiet, narrow
Energetic, spirited	Languid
Self-confident	Self-distrustful
Debonair	
22. Responsive, genial, sentimental	Aloof, cold, misanthropic
Responsive	Aloof
Genial	Coldhearted
Social interests	Brooding (not an opposite)

TABLE 17 — *Continued*

Positive Pole	Negative Pole
23. Facile, foppish, affected	Inarticulate, natural
Exhibitionist	Self-effacing
Eloquent	Inarticulate
Flattering	Natural (not an opposite)
24. Hostile, paranoid	Trustful, good-tempered
Sadistic	Not sadistic
Suspicious	Trustful
Mulish	Reasonable
25. Aesthetic interests, independent mind	
General aesthetic interests	
Musical ability and interests	
Independent	
26. Restlessly, sthenically, hypomanically emotional	Calm, self-effacing, patient
Emotional	Unemotional
Excitable	Phlegmatic
Impatient	Patient
(Sthenically emotional — [Burt])	
27. Infantile, demanding, self-centered	Emotionally mature, adjusting to frustration
Infantile	Mature emotionally
Self-pitying	
Exhibitionist	Self-effacing
28. Changeable, characterless, unrealistic	Stable, integrated character
Changeable	Stable emotionally
	Self-respecting
Unself-controlled	Self-controlled
29. Psycho-physically vigorous, alert	Neurasthenic
Alert	Absent-minded
Energetic, spirited	Languid
Quick	Slow
30. Adventurous, lusty	Generally inhibited, timid
Incontinent	Inhibited
Gluttonous	Queasy
Curious	Uninquiring

TABLE 17 — *Continued*

POSITIVE POLE	NEGATIVE POLE
31. Sociable, hearty	Seclusive, shy
Sociable (forward, gregarious)	Shy (and seclusive)
Responsive	Aloof
Hearty	Quiet
32.	Melancholic
	(agitated/involutional)
	Hypochondriacal
Optimistic	Pessimistic
Placid	Worrying
33. Tough, solid, talkative	Introspective, sensitive, scared
	Introspective
Tough	Sensitive
Lethargic	Hurried
34. Imaginative, introspective, constructive	Set, smug, thrifty
Labile	Habit-bound
Intuitive	Logical (precise)
Careless of material things	Thrifty
35. Smart, assertive	Simplehearted, meek
Sophisticated	Simple
Intelligent	
Assertive	Submissive

The population sample and the ranking method employed.
Regarding the choice of population, it is enough to point out that
our aim from the beginning has been to determine the patterns of
personality in a *typical adult population.* Consequently, as in the
preparatory study (54), we took pains to obtain a more average,
varied, and less academic sample, socially and geographically, than
has unfortunately appeared so commonly in researches in this field.
Further, in response to the requirement of greater accuracy in this
final stage of the research, the following additional conditions were
insured in regard to population and rating.

(1) All subjects were of one sex, male, to avoid complications in
rating and in extraction of factors such as would result from lack of
sex homogeneity, but were otherwise as representative as possible
of a full population range of personality and background.[1] It

[1] Regarding the nature of the population, it is sufficient to record that eight of
the groups were squads of soldiers, the members of each of which had known one
another at close quarters and in various situations, over several months. The remaining five groups were business and professional men, artists and artisans, intimate
acquaintances, over a long period, of those who rated them.

would seem desirable also to have the group highly homogeneous as to age, for we aim at a cross-sectional study and it is likely that factors continually change with the age of the human sample and the development of personality. However, these changes are unlikely to occur so rapidly in our "mature" group (mean age 30.2 years) as in the groups of adolescents or children commonly studied. Since it was impossible to get subjects confined to an age range of a year or two, we therefore accepted any within the range of maturity.

(2) The number of subjects was increased to over 200 (208, to be precise), resulting in comparatively small standard errors for correlation coefficients and permitting the factor analysis to be carried further.

(3) In order to combine the advantages of large numbers with the great gains in real reliability of ratings resulting from working with small intimate groups, the large group was divided into thirteen small groups of sixteen men each. The ratings and correlations were made independently for each of these groups and the coefficients were then averaged, via the "z" function, to obtain the correlation matrix for the factor analysis.

The experimenter who aims to get average humanity rated by intelligent judges finds himself in combat with a natural law: that birds of a feather flock together, so that intelligent, trained minds rarely have in their circle of intimate acquaintances as many as sixteen persons of average ability. In some cases we trained judges in average social groups; in others we directed trained persons to study more average persons.[1] The result was a group geographically well sampled from America (also from Britain), but more urban and socially more middle class than the ideal we had in mind. Never-

---

[1] Two raters from each group independently rated their fellows. When the reliability was found to exceed 0.60, the two ratings were averaged to get the final rating of each man; when it fell below this, the raters were set to work again, after some further discussion of the nature of the cluster concerned, until adequate agreement was reached. It was interesting to discover that judges had no more difficulty in rating for clusters than with respect to single traits. Indeed, it was our impression that the reliability of the ratings was greater than for single traits under the same conditions. If this is found to be true, it would seem to endorse the reality of the particular clusters which our preparatory research claimed to have established; for no reliability could result from the rating of a collection of traits which were not mutually well correlated.

Since no actual units of measurement exist for personality variables, it seemed reasonable to suppose that in our groups the endowments in these variables were approximately normally distributed. The rating rank order (dependent ultimately on paired comparisons) was therefore converted into actual scores (one to five) by a transformation assuming normal distribution.

theless, the range and level were decidedly more true than in most researches we have studied. The mean age of the population was 30.2 years, with the median at 29.

The product-moment correlation matrix thus worked out (on scores 1, 2, 3, 4, and f) for the thirty-five cluster variables is shown in the Appendix, Table 2.

Outcome of the factor analysis. The details of this particular centroid analysis have been set out sufficiently elsewhere (*58 a*). It yielded eleven, twelve, or thirteen factors, the exact point for the cessation of factoring being somewhat differently indicated by McNemar's (*177*) and Tucker's (*262*) criteria. Thurstone suggests that the process of rotation will "squeeze out" unnecessary factors as residual factors. Consequently he does not place any emphasis on criteria of the number of factors. But neglecting such criteria is not entirely satisfactory, as simple structure may leave alternative rotations. Our first rotation eliminated the thirteenth factor and left the twelfth as virtually a residual, but we retained the last, here and in the publication elsewhere (*58 a*), because it made some sense and had a slight variance left in it.

Our rotation, which we shall call the alpha rotation, was directed by the following principles and goals: (*a*) To obtain simple structure — in practice, with this material, this goal amounted to getting for each factor a hyperplane in which at least *one third* of the variables had virtually zero loadings — i.e., 0.09 or less. With the first trial rotation *none* had such a hyperplane. By the third, over-all rotation a hyperplane appeared for nine of the twelve factors. (*b*) To have every factor loading some variables positively and others negatively; for our bipolar variables had been oriented at random and there is no reason why a factor should load wholly positively or wholly negatively such a randomly oriented set of variables. It is necessary to stress this break with the traditional practice of getting positive loadings which has, quite properly, arisen in the field of ability factorizations. (*c*) To avoid factors which are *too* oblique, say over 0.5, and aim at approximate orthogonality. However, simple structure and (*b*) above had priority over this, and in fact we did not find that following (*a*) and (*b*) alone resulted, in the end, in anything but mildly oblique factors.

It is necessary to stress that the rotations were carried out "blindly" according to these scientific principles. To guard against prejudice from any existing historical views about personality structure, the variables were always represented by identification numbers only and were maintained incognito throughout the six months of experimentation with rotation positions.

The whole system was rotated three times, using Thurstone's as yet unpublished analytical method of successive approximations. Then individual axes were adjusted several additional times. B and L did not give good hyperplanes. (B later turned out to be the intelligence or "g" which we might expect to enter into so many variables that few would remain free to form a hyperplane.) The greatest difficulty, however, was found with D, which was rotated a dozen additional times. This is of special interest in view of the fate of D in the beta rotation.

In the end, two distinct rotation positions were found which offered acceptable simple structure. The first, which we have called the α factorization, is simple structure within the full twelve-factor space. The second, called hereafter the β factorization, aimed at simple structure regardless of the indicated factor space, and actually finished with seven factors. These alternatives are discussed below, the α rotation being finally considered the preferred solution. The results of the alpha rotation, in terms of (*a*) the factor loadings of the 35 variables and (*b*) the angles among the factors, have already been published elsewhere (*58a*) and the present text will therefore not repeat the extensive tables required. (For reasons of economy the factor structure has not been set out additional to the factor pattern; nor are the transformation matrix from the centroid factors, and the variance due to unique factors and error, systematically recorded here.)

The naming and interpretation of these factors will be postponed until after the review of all other factor studies, now to be presented, in the next section.

6. CATALOGUE OF AVAILABLE FACTOR–ANALYTIC STUDIES OF PERSONALITY THROUGH RATINGS

Particulars supplied in catalogue. The following researches are listed in alphabetical order of their authors. For ease of later reference, the factors in each are numbered serially. Under each research is listed the size and nature of population and the conditions of rating.

Burt (25). 500 normal children, 124 delinquent and neurotic children rated and analyzed by r-technique. 11 children measured by time sampling, analyzed by q-technique.

Factor (1) General emotionality
" (2) Sthenic emotionality
" (3) Optimism — Pessimism
" (4) Sex; curiosity

Cattell (41). 62 male students, rated each by four coevals on 48 traits, mainly of character and temperament. The following were not established at the time as factors but as very wide clusters.

Factor or Cluster (5) Will-character
" " " (6) Surgency
" " " (7) Maturity
" " " (8) Adjustment

(The results of the present research are listed here for catalogue completeness)

Factor or Cluster (9) *A.* Cyclothyme *v.* Schizothyme
" " " (10) *B.* Intelligence
" " " (11) *C.* Mature Character *v.* General Emotionality
" " " (12) *D.* Sthenic Emotionality
" " " (13) *E.* Dominance *v.* Submissiveness
" " " (14) *F.* Surgency *v.* Melancholy
" " " (15) *G.* Integrated Character *v.* Character Neurosis
" " " (16) *H.* Charitable Cyclothyme *v.* Obstinate Schizothyme
" " " (17) *I.* Anxious Emotionality *v.* Tough Poise
" " " (18) *J.* Neurasthenia *v.* Vigorous Character
" " " (19) *K.* General Education *v.* Boorishness

Factor or Cluster (20) *L.* Surgent Cyclothyme *v.* Paranoid
"   "   "   (21) *M.* Residual Factor

Chi (59). 100 11–12-year-old school children rated by teachers on 26 mainly school important traits.

Factor (22) Initiative Industry

Garnett (95). Same data as Webb.

Factor (23) Will-character
"   (24) Cleverness or "c" factor

Kelley (146). Young children rated by teachers on 8 traits.

Factor (25) Puritanism
"   (26) Rugged Individualism or Ascendance

Koch (153). 50 nursery-school children, rated by time-sampling on 9 varieties of "activity."

Factor (27) Maturity or Physical Strength
"   (28) Nervousness or Emotionality
"   (29) Spontaneous Activity or Aggression

Maurer (169). 1. 50 children 4 to 6 years old. Check ratings by one woman on each child, chosen by the rater. 50 traits boiled down from very catholic dictionary lists.

Factor (30) Enthusiasms, Sociability
"   (31) Cautious, Resourceful
"   (32) Grave, Persistent

Maurer (169). 2. 71 high school girls, all in some respect leaders, but of varying degrees. Rated by teachers and by coevals on 46 quite varied traits.

Factor or Cluster (33) Leadership

McCloy (170). *a.* Fresh data from 31 students in American college, rated by one another on 43 traits, mainly of character. Multifactor analysis with rotation. *b.* Same data as Webb.

a. Factor (34) Will-character ("socialized")
"   (35) Positive attitudes ("surgency")
"   (36) Positive action tendencies ("dominance")
"   (37) Individual tendencies ("poise")
"   (38) Tends to merge with group (obverse of 37)
b. "   (39) Will-character
"   (40) Positive attitudes
"   (41) Positive action tendencies
"   (42) Individual qualities
"   (43) Tends to merge with group (obverse of 42)

McDonough (172). 50 boys and girls, aged 13 years, rated by teachers on 33 varied traits.

Factor (44) Will-character
"   (45) Sociability
"   (46) Emotionality
"   (47) Cheerfulness

These factors have been rotated for simple structure by Brogden (20 b), resulting in the following factors:

Factor (44 a) Goodness of Behavior
        "   (45 a) Sensitivity to Social Disapproval
        "   (46 a) General Ability in Personality
        "   (47 a) Gregariousness

Moore (185). 367 psychotics, rated by psychiatrists and nurses on records of behavior with respect to 41 symptoms or traits. The factors are not independent, but oblique. The two depression factors correlate 69, the euphoric manic correlates negatively with them and the destructive manic very slightly negative. There was also a general ability factor.

Factor (48) Destructive Manic
        "   (49) Euphoric Manic
        "   (50) Retarded Depressed
        "   (51) Agitated Depressed
        "   (52) Catatonic
        "   (53) Kinetic — Uninhibited
        "   (54) Deluded Hallucinated

Reyburn and Taylor (213). Webb's data reëxamined in multo-factor analysis.

Factor (55) Will-character
        "   (56) Charity
        "   (57) Surgency
        "   (58) Social Sensitiveness

Sahai (224). Over 100 children rated by elders on mainly temperamental traits. Adolescents (separate) also rated by elders.

Factor (59) Cyclothyme temperament

Studman (246). 40 adult psychotics, rated by psychiatrists on 21 varied traits.

Factor (60) *a.* Will-character
        "   (61) *b.* Will-character with group factor
        "   (62) Manic syndrome

Thurstone (260). 1300 adults, each check rated by a friend, on 60 very varied traits.

Factor (63) Self-important, cynical
        "   (64) Magnanimous character
        "   (65) Patient, Earnest
        "   (66) Will-character
        "   (67) Capable, Frank

More recently (1945) this study has been carried further by Thurstone and subjected to rotation. The factors, not yet published, are described below and will be referred to serially as follows: (63) A, (64) B, (65) C, (66) D, (67) E, (67 a) F, (67 b) G, (67 c) H, (67 d) J, (67 e) K, (67 j) L, (67 g) M.

Webb (274). 200 students, average age 21 years; 140 boys, average age 12 years. Rated by trained judges among elders, on 90 traits of varied nature, but with predominance of character traits.

Factor (68) Will-character or "W." General intelligence factor also appeared.

Williams (278). 53 pre-school children aged 3, rated on 50 traits from Berne scale by experienced adult raters.

Factor (69) Proto Will-character
    " (70) Approach Withdrawal

Koch (153 *a*). 46 nursery-school boys and girls 21–58 months rated on 38 forms of behavior (many nervous habits) in 400 half-minute time samples by two trained observers.

Factor (71) Social extraversion
    " (72) Even temper; low sympathetic reaction

" (73) Tension	Factor (76) Hypersensitiveness
" (74) Femininity	" (77) Conscientiousness
" (75) Ear-nose manipulation	" (78) Immaturity
	" (79) Alertness *v.* Autism

Hart and Jenkins, et al. (110 *b*). 300, 10–16 yr. delinquent boys: 25 traits.

Factor (79 *a*) Group stealing	Factor (79 *d*) Street gang
" (79 *b*) Temper-assault	" (79 *e*) Aggressiveness
" (79 *c*) Ego-compensation	" (79 *f*) Prominence

Eysenck, H. J. (83 *a*). 700 neurotic male adults rated by psychiatrists as to presence or absence of some 33 neurotic traits and 6 circumstances from the case history.

Factor (80) General Emotionality or Personality Disorganization
    " (81) Hysteria — Dysthymia
    " (82) Neurasthenia
    " (83) Psychological Conflict *v.* Shiftlessness

These factors have since been re-rotated for simple structure by Cattell (58 *g*), with the following result:

Factor (80 *a*) Stable Character *v.* Personality Disorganization
    " (81 *a*) Sensitive, Anxious Emotionality
    " (82 *a*) K factor or General Intelligence
    " (83 *a*) Surgency *v.* Melancholia

Howie (126 *a*). 16 personality and ability traits rated and measured on 295 boys. Rotated.

Factor (84) Intelligence — Quickness
    " (85) Cheerfulness, Bodily activity
    " (86) Character, Popularity
    " (87) Nervous, Timid, Excitable
    " (88) Dominance

7. PROBLEMS ON COMBINING FINDINGS FROM DIVERSE FACTOR ANALYTIC RESEARCHES

The "confirmation" of factors. The 70 factors listed in the catalogue almost certainly represent, in many instances, the same factor rediscovered many times. Indeed, in compiling our final list of factors for the description of personality we can only be satisfied with source traits which *have* been confirmed by at least two independent discoveries. Since the principle of rotating for proportional profiles has not yet been applied — and cannot be applied, until there is large-scale organization of research in this field — we must content ourselves with factors the soundness of orientation of which is vouched for by simple structure alone. There is reason to expect that these orientations will be substantially the same as those from proportional profiles. However, to decide if and when one factor *does* confirm another is a task beset by a few theoretical and many practical difficulties.

Practical difficulties. The naturally independent course of pioneer researches in this field leaves us with the following obstacles to their clear collation:

(1) Diverse factor systems have sometimes been used in analyzing the correlation.

(2) In spite of using a common criterion in rotation, generally that of simple structure, the absence of a precise criterion of simple structure leaves room for some differences of orientation in different researches. This weakness is especially obvious, as Eysenck has pointed out (*83b*), where simple structure has been attempted with too few variables — e.g., among attitudes.

(3) The same, probably minor, distortions, readily technically explicable, exist here as in cluster data. They arise from differences of sample, of precise trait definition (e.g., "sociable" apparently means all things from gregarious to altruistic), of mode of trait assessment (by equals or superiors), of homogeneity of population, etc.

If the labor of re-rotating so many published factorizations had not been quite beyond our resources, we should have assured ourselves by independent experimental rotation, before collation, that simple structure had been reasonably attained in each case. It is regrettable, in view of the large investment of research time in a factor analysis, that there seems so far to be only one (*836*) published instance of one researcher critically examining the simple structure put forward by another, and only three instances (Brogden (*20 a*), Reyburn (*215*), and the present writer (*58 z*)) of past published centroid analysis being rescued for collation with later work by simple structure rotation. However, it must be admitted that in some researches, fortunately the less important, re-rotation could not have been satisfactorily carried out, even if we had had time, because of the insufficiency of the published data *or because the experimenter had not extracted all the centroid factors*, without which the rotated loadings would be incomplete and the loading patterns distorted.

Fortunately, with the additions from the above re-rotations, the great majority of results are in terms of centroid factors rotated for simple structure. As regards another but small sub-group of data, that collected by the Kelley-Hotelling principal component analysis, experience has shown that it yields the first few factors (which take most of the variance) in a very similar form to the centroid factors and generally "identifiable" with them. Transformation from bi-polar factors is also not difficult.[1]

Regarding the second difficulty there is also a fortunate practical outcome — namely, that despite its inability, theoretically, to meet the whole range of circumstances, simple structure *does* tend to give the same factors in different researches. In only about one in five of the instances where parallelism of loadings between certain factors was likely and expected did we fail to find it.

The problem of missing variables. A difficulty provoking more explicit discussion of theory is that which arises from the dissimilarity of the population of *variables* used in different researches. Practical clinicians have sometimes objected sharply to critical findings of meticulous but absent-minded statistical psychologists, pointing out that if the appropriate variables are not used in a research it is no wonder that the factor which might appear in such an investigation is not found. (They have sometimes gone further and said that one can only get out of factor analysis what one puts in, implying that nothing new is discoverable; but this implication is false, for the analyst may use variables containing many more factors than he consciously believes them to contain.)

What one finds in the available personality researches is

---

[1] Burt writes (27): "Bipolar factors denote the corresponding principle of 'Dichotomous' classification, while the corresponding group factors (rotated centroid) deducible from them denote the corresponding principles of 'manifold' or coördinate classification." The positive and negative loadings of the bipolar factors are weighted *differences* between the loadings of corresponding rotated centroid positive factors.

that a moderate majority of the studies have at least *some* overlap in their lists of variables; but that, even when studying the same field — e.g., temperament — one research manifests a considerable number of variables not appearing in the other. Before concluding that one inquiry fails to confirm the factor found in another, this elementary fact of "absence of material" must be taken into account. (The presence of *one* common variable is, of course, not enough, for the factor concerned becomes merely a specific and, as such, unrecorded.) Unless this absence of required variables is noticed the integration may overlook certain factors, considering their existence disproved, or may admit a distorted interpretation of others (as has been pointed out similarly for clusters).

Again, in researches with quite different variables — i.e., no overlap — it is entirely possible that the factor high in variables a, c, f, in the first, is the same as that present in r, u, w, in the second. But we have no means of knowing this without a third, overlapping research. In short, the number of actual unitary traits covered by present research could well be decidedly fewer than the present disjointed and repetitive catalogue of research findings permits us to conclude.

More commonly we encounter in present researches the situation of Table 18, representing two researches in which

TABLE 18. A PROBLEM IN FACTOR IDENTIFICATION

	a	b	c	d	e	f	g
Factor in Research I	.3	.4	.7	.3	.2	unused	unused
Factor in Research II	.3	.4	.7	unused	unused	.1	.2

variables a, b, and c are common and d, e, on the one hand, and f, g, on the other, are unique. Where there are five or six, rather than three, common variables one can usually conclude that the two factors are the same and accordingly include both d, e and f, g in attempting as complete a description as possible of the factor.

However, one must bear in mind that it is *theoretically possible for two factors to have exactly the same loading profile and yet be independent,* providing their loadings are low — i.e., so that together they do not give a variance on any trait element of more than one. It is of course hard to conceive two influences alike in *all* their effects — at *some* variable they would normally part company, manifesting distinctive loadings. In any case, it may be said, any research which uses *a, b,* and *c* would get both of the factors influencing them, so that though doubt might arise in their matching with the pair from some other research with *a, b,* and *c,* no doubt would exist, in ideally correct researches, that there are two factors in the picture.

Unfortunately we have to distinguish two distinct fields of discussion here: (*a*) the problem of matching factors when the factors are based on ideal researches and simple structure rotation and (*b*) the problems in inadequate and inaccurate material. One must remember it requires three variables to fix the communalities defining one factor and five to define two factors. In the practical task of matching factors we frequently encounter researches in which not enough, or barely enough, variables are involved to define some particular factor. Add to this the difficulties arising from inaccurate measurement and defective population sizes and one will see that the presence of a distinct general factor akin to the first, in a small set of variables, is often not clearly established until other variables are brought in which involve it more grossly.

Further, we have to note that later more intensive research often "splits" what was first considered a single factor into two. For example, four factors were first found in the region of musical ability, but later study revealed as many as eight (*142*). This can only arise through an alteration of rotation, brought about in the light of fuller knowledge and the use of more variables giving new dimensions and new hyperplanes. No truly established factor is ever "split," so that in pure factor theory this difficulty does not exist; but through practical imperfections it has frequently happened that the variance first ascribed to one factor has later been split between two "coöperative" factors — i.e., factors with very similar loading pattern. For example, our factors A, H, and L have been mistaken in previous researches for a single cyclothyme factor; C and G for a single character factor; and B and K for a single intelligence-education factor. The practical and theoretical handling of factor "fission" is dealt with more definitively in Chapter 12, page 523.

Consideration of these technicalities will show that the matching of factors from different researches, as carried out below, could be no casual process of merely checking off lists of variables recorded as high in the factors concerned. It required attention to the above difficulties and possibilities and was guided especially by (*a*) the profile of loadings, (*b*) the fact that if a factor in research A is matched by one in research B it cannot also be matched by another in research B, (*c*) the relative "magnitude" of factors — i.e., whether they contribute much or little to the total variance of traits.

8. DESCRIPTION OF THE TWELVE PRIMARY SOURCE
   TRAITS OF PERSONALITY

The factors are listed in the order of diminishing variance as found in the main, perspective-giving research which is described in Section 5 above and with more technical detail elsewhere (*58 a*). The highest five to seven clusters, out of thirty-five, are listed to describe each factor and below it are added the factors from other researches which appear to confirm it. A note is then added on the ways, if any, in which these other factorizations add to the picture given by the main factor study.

Considerable attention has been given to the naming and indexing of these factors, since a system which will stand for some time is required. The index letters are capitals, to avoid confusion with the small letters which have been used generally in indexing abilities. The writer ventures to suggest that this distinction — using small letters for ability factors which, apart from "g," are quite limited in area, and capitals for the broader factors in personality as a whole — offers a convenient general convention. Experience might show, further, that this amounts to using capitals for wholistic factors (Chapter 6) and small letters for conditional factors.

Similarly, it would help to bring order into the matching and mapping in this field if letters of the alphabet were used in an order corresponding to the "importance" (Mean contribution to variance of an adequate sample of traits from the personality sphere) of the factors, instead of representing the initial letter of some name the experimenter temporarily attaches to the factor. For names are likely to be temporary, different according to the field of work of the researcher, and not based on real understanding of the nature of the factor, for a long time to come.

The present titles, given additional to the letters, are an attempt (1) to give maximum *literal description*, avoiding premature interpretation, (2) to provide historical continuity with sound clinical observation or experiment (but not theories) of the past. In conformity with the individual trait list, the titles are *bipolar*. Experience shows that psychologists are frequently unable to recognize a type pattern in its obverse form: the bipolar system reminds one of both aspects of any major source trait.

The attempt at full interpretation of these factors is postponed to Chapter 12, where factors from all sources of observation are brought together.

FACTOR A

CYCLOTHYMIA — v. — SCHIZOTHYMIA

Evidenced by factors 8, 9, 45, 58, 59, 64, 72, 79 *f.   Cattell* (*9* or A).

(Variables above .34: Mean Contribution 0.069)

(14) −59 OUTGOING, IDEALISTIC, — *v.* — ANTISOCIAL
           COÖPERATIVE   SCHIZOID
           (Idealistic)   (Cynical)
           (Coöperative)   (Obstructive)
           (Adventurous)   (Timid, withdrawn)

(9) −51 GOOD–NATURED,   — *v.* — SURLY, HARD
           EASYGOING
           (Grateful)   (Thankless)
           (Softhearted)   (Hardhearted,
           (Easygoing)   embittered)
                              (Short-tempered)

(19) −49 NATURAL, FRIENDLY, — *v.* — SPITEFUL,
           OPEN   TIGHTFISTED,
                          SUPERSTITIOUS
           (Friendly)   (Hostile)
           (Coöperative)   (Obstructive)
           (Frank)   (Secretive)
                          (Irrational)

(8) −46 ADAPTABLE,   — *v.* — RIGID, TYRANNICAL,
           FRIENDLY   VINDICTIVE
           (Adaptable (to change)) (Extra-punitive)
           (Friendly)   (Inflexible
                            emotionally))
                          (Hostile)

(15) 44 CHEERFUL, ENTHU- — *v.* — UNHAPPY, FRUS-
           SIASTIC, WITTY   TRATED, DOUR
           (Genial)   (Coldhearted)
           (Optimistic)   (Pessimistic)
           (Enthusiastic)   (Apathetic)

(24) −41 TRUSTFUL,   — *v.* — HOSTILE,
           GOOD–TEMPERED   PARANOID
           (Not sadistic)   (Sadistic)
           (Trustful)   (Suspicious)
           (Reasonable)   (Mulish)

In each factor (from *58a*) the five or six highest correlating varia-bles out of 35 are alone listed.   The numbers in parentheses are the numbers of the variables as listed in Table 17 and in the original study (*58a*).   The numbers next to these are the loadings with the factor.

Where the sign is negative, the verbal labels have already been appropriately reversed (relative to the original variable list to which the sign actually applies). Above .34 means that the next highest loading, beyond these six, is .34 — i.e., there is a drop from .41 to .34.

McDonough 47 a
Affectionate
Sympathetic
Sociable
Cheerful
Contented
Unself-conscious
Humorous

Sahai — (59) —
Natural
Generous
Coöperative
Frank
Balanced
Emotionally expressive
  (and sociable)
Warmhearted
Trustful
Tendency to enjoy good things of life
Varying emotional mood
Humorous

Reyburn and Taylor — (58) —
Corporate spirit
Kindness on principle
Trustworthiness
Impulsive kindness
Conscientiousness

Hart and Jenkins — (79 f) —
Not popular (boy leadership)
Destructive
Seclusive
Homosexual

Burt's factor 3, now under F below, could belong almost equally here.

Except for some dominance traits *Williams's — (70) —* under H could also go almost as well here.

Thurstone — (63) —
Jealous
Spiteful
Suspicious
Grasping
Stubborn
Disagreeable
Domineering

Cattell — (8) —
Generous
Frank
Tactful
Objective
Balanced
Optimistic
Emotional

Koch — (72) — (Schizoid pole)
Pouting and sulking
Indirect attack
Active physical attack
Flitting from task to task
High P.G.R. deflection
Good P.G.R. recovery
(Opposite: "Evenness of temper back of drive")

This has also strong resemblance to general emotionality, C Factor, especially in the evidence of high sympathetic system reactivity and in the marked similarity to 79 *b*, also found among children. It is temporarily placed here because another Koch factor is now under C and because, as with 79 *b*, there are also schizoid elements not found in the adult C minus pattern.

FACTOR B

INTELLIGENCE, GENERAL MENTAL CAPACITY — v. — MENTAL DEFECT

Evidenced by innumerable T factors (see Chapter 11) but few BR factors — namely, 10, 46 *a*, 64, and probably 82 *a* and 84. *Cattell* (*10* or B).

(Above .39: Mean Variance Contribution .063)

(2)	.52	INTELLIGENT, ANALYTICAL (Intelligent) (Clear-thinking) (Clever)	— *v.* — UNIMAGINATIVE, STUPID (Stupid) (Incoherent, confused)
(11)	.47	STRONG–WILLED, CONSCIENTIOUS (Persevering) (Painstaking) (Conscientious)	— *v.* — INDOLENT, INCOHER-ENT, IMPULSIVE (Quitting) (Slipshod) (Conscienceless)
(4)	−43	THOUGHTFUL, STOIC, RESERVED (Thoughtful) (Deliberate) (Austere)	— *v.* — CHANGEABLE, FRIVOLOUS (Unreflective) (Impulsive) (Profligate)
(28)	−42	STABLE, INTEGRATED CHARACTER (Stable emotionally) (Self-respecting) (Self-controlled)	— *v.* — CHANGEABLE, CHARACTERLESS, UNREALISTIC (Changeable) (Unself-controlled)
(12)	.41	INTELLECTUAL (Thoughtful) (Analytical) (Wide interests)	— *v.* — SIMPLE, UNDISCI-PLINED MIND (Unreflective) (Narrow interests)
(3)	.41	WISE, MATURE, POLISHED (Independent) (Reliable) (Mature)	— *v.* — DEPENDENT, SILLY, INCOHERENT (Emotionally dependent) (Undependable) (Emotionally immature, irresponsible)

The identification of this factor as "intelligence and its personality associates" was checked by correlating the items in this pattern with an actual intelligence test, on 108 subjects. Of the 6 (out of 35) variables correlating most highly with the objective test, four were the same as above and two were items which had been in the above with very slightly different orientation of the hyperplane. They were:

		Correlation with (g) test
(2)	Intelligent, analytical	.40
(12)	Intellectual	.31
(11)	Strong-willed, conscientious	.30
(29)	Psycho-physically vigorous, alert	.29
(3)	Wise, mature, polished	.26
(35)	Smart, assertive	.24

No comment is called for here, except to point out that the objective test endorses the rather surprising appearance of *(11)* *strong-willed, conscientious,* and other "character" variables as expressions of the general intelligence factor.   This association of the more consciously developed character qualities with general mental ability as the core, in a single factor, is overwhelmingly demonstrated again by a special investigation on the point *(58 e)*. Other research examples are:

Thurstone 64
Systematic
Precise
Hard-working
Persevering
Conscientious
Dependable

McDonough (46 a)
Intelligence
Lack of credulity
Tendency to be active (in school)
Independence

Eysenck 82 a
Repeated unemployment
No group membership
Lacking initiative
Pursuit of unskilled occupations
Narrow interests
Apathy, mental slowness

Howie 84 is probably mixture of this and K
Intelligence test
Initiative
Mental Activity
Exam results
Common Sense

FACTOR C

EMOTIONALLY MATURE STABLE CHARACTER — v. — DEMORALIZED GENERAL EMOTIONALITY

Evidenced by 1, 11, 23, 34, 39, 44, 55, 60, 65, 68, 77, 79 *b*, 80.   *Cattell* (*11* or C).

(Above .35 Mean Variance Contribution .049)

(10) −.42 REALISTIC, FACING   — *v.* — DEMORALIZED,
                      LIFE   AUTISTIC
               (Realistic, practical)   (Unrealistic)
               (Persevering)   (Quitting)
               (Facing life)   (Subjective, evasive)

(28) −.38 STABLE, INTEGRATED — *v.* — CHANGEABLE,
                  CHARACTER   CHARACTERLESS,
                                    UNREALISTIC
               (Stable emotionally)   (Changeable)
               (Self-respecting)   (Unself-controlled)
               (Self-controlled)

(26) −.38 CALM, SELF–EFFACING, — *v.* — RESTLESS, STHENIC,
                  PATIENT   HYPOMANIC
               (Unemotional)   (Emotional)
               (Phlegmatic)   (Excitable)
               (Patient)   (Impatient)
                                   (Stenically emotional — [Burt])

(17) −.38 EMOTIONALLY   — *v.* — CHARACTER NEUROSIS,
                  MATURE   PSYCHOPATHIC
               (Balanced)   (Neurotic, irritable, un-
               (Loyal)   controlled)
               (Honest)   (Fickle)
                                      (Dishonest)

(27) −.37   EMOTIONALLY   — *v.* — INFANTILE, DEMAND–
             MATURE, ADJUSTING   ING, SELF–CENTERED
             TO FRUSTRATION
             (Mature emotionally)   (Infantile)
             (Self-effacing)   (Self-pitying)
                                      (Exhibitionist)

(4) −.36 THOUGHTFUL, STOIC, — *v.* — CHANGEABLE,
                  RESERVED   FRIVOLOUS
               (Thoughtful)   (Unreflective)
               (Deliberate)   (Impulsive)
               (Austere)   (Profligate)

(20) −.36 UNEMOTIONAL

(Unemotional)
(Content)
(Phlegmatic)

Burt — (1)
Proneness to emotional manifestations of:
  Anger
  Assertiveness
  Sociability
  Curiosity
  Joy
  Sex
  Disgust
  Tenderness
  Sorrow
  Fear
  Submissiveness

Studman — (60)
Trustworthiness
Conscientiousness
Unselfishness
Self-control

McCloy (*own data*) 34
Trustworthiness
Sportsmanship
Thoroughness
Character
Loyalty
Respect for rights of others
Resourcefulness
Integrity

Reyburn and Taylor (55)
Perseverance — *v.* — abandoning through changeability
Perseverance — *v.* — abandoning through obstacles
Trustworthiness
Conscientiousness
Kindness on principle

−*v.* — GENERAL EMOTIONALITY (WITH MALADJUSTMENT)
(Emotional (in all ways))
(Dissatisfied)
(Excitable)

McDonough — (45 a)
Lack of searching for sympathy
  "   "   forwardness
  "   "   quarrelsomeness
  "   "   conceit
  "   "   irritability
Self-control
Truthfulness
Lack of impulsiveness
  "   "   expressiveness (excitement and impulsiveness)
Stability
Religiousness
Lack of emotionality
Generosity (kindness, thinking of others)

Koch — (77)
Persistent effort
High skin-resistance level
Does not refuse and ignore adult suggestions
Participates in formal group work
Does not cry and whine
Does not attack others
Is not attention-getting
Does not have respiratory mannerisms

Hart and Jenkins (79 b)
Temper tantrums, assault
Emotional instability
Delinquent siblings
Negativism, inferiority
Truancy
Overprotected in home

McCloy (*Webb data*) 39
Trustworthiness
Conscientiousness
Kindness on principle

Freedom from anger	Unreadiness to become angry
Freedom from sudden oscillations of mood	Absence of eagerness for admiration
	No offensive manifestations of self-esteem
Webb 68 and Garnett 23	Mental work on studies
Perseverance — *v.* — Willful change-ability	
Perseverance in face of obstacles	*Thurstone 67*
Kindness on principle	Frivolous —
Trustworthiness	Peevish —
Conscientiousness	Fickle —
	——— Grasping

Possibly, especially among children, the high general emotionality can be mistaken for energy (see Koch's "Lack of Drive" with stability). It may at any rate be associated with high sympathetic reactivity. McDonough's factor is classified here, and not as its originator, Brogden, views it, because of the clear variety of emotionality displayed and because, like C, it has a high positive correlation with G and because it is the second biggest factor. Incidentally, here and in 1 and 39 there is a clear tendency for general emotionality in children to show itself more in pugnacity and self-assertion (or display) than is found in adults. This might lead to a misclassification under E, Dominance. (See euphoric and non-euphoric mania.)

FACTOR D

HYPERSENSITIVE, INFANTILE, STHENIC EMOTIONALITY — v. — PHLEGMATIC FRUSTRATION TOLERANCE

Evidenced by 12, 31, 46, 48, 79 *c.* *Cattell* (*12* or D).

(Above .23 Mean Contribution .039)

(27) 50	INFANTILE, DEMANDING, SELF–CENTERED	— *v.* —	EMOTIONALLY MATURE. ADJUSTING TO FRUSTRATION
	(Infantile) (Self-pitying) (Exhibitionist)		(Mature emotionally) (Self-effacing)
(26) 41	RESTLESSLY, STHENICALLY HYPOMANICALLY EMOTIONAL (Emotional)	— *v.* —	CALM, SELF–EFFACING, PATIENT (Unemotional)

(Excitable)   (Phlegmatic)
(Impatient)   (Patient)
(Sthenically emotional —
[Burt])

(28) 34   CHANGEABLE,   — *v.* — STABLE INTEGRATED
CHARACTERLESS,   CHARACTER
UNREALISTIC
(Changeable)   (Stable emotionally)
(Unself-controlled)   (Self-respecting)
     (Self-controlled)

(5) 26   NEUROTIC   — *v.* — NOT GENERALLY
     NEUROTIC
(Self-deceiving)   (Realistic)
(Hypochondriacal)
(Nervous, specific neurotic
symptoms)

(1) 24   SELF–ASSERTIVE   — *v.* — SELF–SUBMISSIVE
(Boastful)   (Modest)
(Assertive)   (Submissive)
(Conceited)   (Self-critical, dissatisfied)

Moore — (48)
Non-euphoric manic
Irritable
Temper tantrums
Destructiveness

(This should perhaps be under C,
resembling C minus in children, but
also has resemblances to E.)

Hart and Jenkins (79 c)
Attention-getting
Overaggressive bravado
Homosexuality (active, passive)
Inferiority and compensation
Enuresis
Negativism
Sibs not delinquent

Maurer — (31)
Cautious — Bold
Responsive — Unresponsive
Careful — Reckless
Direct
Keen
Resourceful, noisy, earnest

Thurstone — 67 g
Careless
Ingenious
Unconventional
Awkward
Impetuous
Courageous
Headstrong
(This factor might also be inter-
changed with the Thurstone factor
under J below.)

There is some doubt about elation: it probably has a low loading;
for Studman's factor is a general manic factor, such as seems the
result of D and F together (see Chapter 12) while Moore's factor
clearly separates euphoric and non-euphoric manic. We believe that

McDonough's 36 and Burt's 1 and Reyburn and Taylor's 56 could almost as readily have gone under E.   Their emphasis on anger and assertion favors transfer; the other qualities do not.

FACTOR E

DOMINANCE (HYPOMANIA) — v. — SUBMISSIVENESS

Evidenced by 2, 26, 32, 36, 41, 49, 62, 63, 69, 71, 79 *e*, 167.   *Cattell* (*13* or E).

(Above .27 Mean Variance Contribution .036)

(1)   .39   SELF–ASSERTIVE   — *v.* — SELF–SUBMISSIVE
                (Boastful)   (Modest)
                (Assertive)   (Submissive)
                (Conceited)   (Self-critical, dissatisfied)

(7)   35   WILLFUL, EGOTISTIC,   — *v.* — MILD, SELF–EFFACING,
                PREDATORY   TOLERANT
                (Extra-punitive [blaming   (Gentle-tempered)
                mistakes on others])   (Self-effacing)
                (Headstrong)
                (Exhibitionist)

(35) .34   SMART, ASSERTIVE   — *v.* — SIMPLE–HEARTED,
                                                             MEEK
                (Sophisticated)   (Simple)
                (Intelligent)   (Submissive)
                (Assertive)

(33) .31   TOUGH, SOLID,   — *v.* — INTROSPECTIVE,
                TALKATIVE   SENSITIVE, SCARED
                (Tough)   (Introspective)
                (Lethargic)   (Sensitive)
                                                        (Hurried)

(8)   .29   RIGID, TYRANNICAL,   — *v.* — ADAPTABLE, FRIENDLY
                VINDICTIVE
                (Extra-punitive)   (Adaptable [to change])
                (Inflexible [emotionally]) (Friendly)
                (Hostile)

(9)   .28   SURLY, HARD   — *v.* — GOOD–NATURED,
                                                            EASYGOING
                (Thankless)   (Grateful)
                (Hardhearted, embittered) (Softhearted)
                (Short-tempered)   (Easygoing)

Williams — (69) (Three-year-olds)
Does not respect others' property
Does not respect social ownership
Does not obey
Selfish
Does not conform socially
Not kind
Self-defensive
Ascendant
Not sensitive
Leads
Teases
Rivals others
Does not depend on an adult
(This might go partly under C)

Maurer — (32)
Grave
Domineering
Persistent
Active
(Negatively in Happy)

Moore — (49)
Euphoric manic
Irritable
Temper tantrums
Destructiveness
Euphoria
(Moore's Retarded Depression. 50 possibly belongs here rather than with J, while this might be with F.)

It seems appropriate to include here a syndrome which, though it is only a cluster, is of special interest because established in chimpanzees (167).

Maslow — (167)
Preëmpts all or most of a limited food supply
Frequently mounts subordinate (regardless of sex)
Frequently bullies
Is never bullied
Initiates most fighting
Never cringes under aggression and is rarely even passive
Almost never flees
Is likely to be more active
Is likely to do more grooming
Is likely to initiate more play

Kelley — (26)
Mastery
Praise
Individualism

Burt — (2)
Proneness to displays of:
  Assertiveness
  Sociability
  Anger
  Curiosity
  Sex

Howie — (88)
Dominant (on A–S test)
Not self-conscious
Poor exam results (but not low IQ)

Hart and Jenkins (79 e)
Aggressiveness (in stealing)
Absence inferiority feelings
Absence passive homosexuality
Absence furtive stealing
Active homosexuality
Destructiveness

Studman — (62)
Energetic
Elated
Expressive
Self-confident
Independent
Unstable in emotion
Quarrelsome

Reyburn and Taylor — (56)
Readiness to become angry
Occasional extreme anger

Negative (increasingly) in:
  Tenderness
  Disgust
  Sorrow
  Fear
  Submissiveness

Koch — (71)
Conversing
Trying to boss
Verbal attack
Showing off
Laughing and smiling
Participating
Not given to playing alone

Thurstone — (66)
Craft
Satisfied
Haughty
Grasping
Self-important

Eagerness for admiration
Bodily activity in search of pleasure
Fondness for large social gatherings
Increasingly negative in:
  Impulsive kindness
  Trustworthiness
  Conscientiousness
  Kindness of principle
  Ready acceptance of sentiments of
    associates
  Ready recovery from anger

McCloy — (*own data*) (36)
Aggressiveness
Initiative
Decision
Self-confidence
Ability to discipline others

McCloy — (41)
(Considered similar by McCloy, but
  this may be questioned by reason
  of the first item)
Desire to be liked by associates
Desire to excel in chief interests
Desire to impose will on others
Self-esteem (offensive)
Degree of corporate

Of the additional factors 32 is less clearly matched than others. They bring into the syndrome the following traits: initiative, disobedience, decisiveness, desire to be liked by associates, corporate spirit but unwillingness to conform, teasing and bullying, tendency to be somber or unhappy, absence of kindness and sensitiveness. There is, however, disagreement over lethargy *v.* activity, presumably because some researches have interpreted activity as initiative or athletic activity (which our research indicates belong to dominance), whereas others have considered it as hurriedness or restlessness (which go on the submissive pole above).

FACTOR F

SURGENCY — v. — AGITATED, MELANCHOLIC DESURGENCY

Evidenced by 3, 6, 14, 24, 30, 42, 47, 51, 57, 73, 78, 81.   *Cattell* (*14* or F)

(Above .27 Mean Contribution — 0.033)

(15)   37   CHEERFUL, ENTHUSI-   — v. —   UNHAPPY,
                  ASTIC, WITTY   FRUSTRATED, DOUR
                  (Genial)   (Coldhearted)
                  (Optimistic)   (Pessimistic)
                  (Enthusiastic)   (Apathetic)

(32)   34   OPTIMISTIC   — v. — MELANCHOLIC,
                                               (AGITATED,
                                               INVOLUTIONAL)
                  (Optimistic)   (Hypochondriacal)
                  (Placid)   (Pessimistic)
                                               (Worrying)

(31)   32   SOCIABLE, HEARTY   — v. — SECLUSIVE, SHY
                  (Sociable (forward,   (Shy [and seclusive])
                   gregarious))   (Aloof)
                  (Responsive)   (Quiet)
                  (Hearty)

(33)   31   TOUGH, SOLID,   — v. —   INTROSPECTIVE,
                  TALKATIVE   SENSITIVE, SCARED
                  (Tough)   (Introspective)
                  (Lethargic)   (Sensitive)
                                               (Hurried)

(22)   30   RESPONSIVE, GENIAL, — v. — ALOOF, COLD,
                  SENTIMENTAL   MISANTHROPIC
                  (Responsive)   (Aloof)
                  (Genial)   (Coldhearted)
                  (Social interests)   (Brooding [not an
                                                opposite])

(24)   —29   TRUSTFUL,   — v. — HOSTILE, PARANOID
                  GOOD–TEMPERED
                  (Not sadistic)   (Sadistic)
                  (Trustful)   (Suspicious)
                  (Reasonable)   (Mulish)

(34)   28   IMAGINATIVE,   — v. — SET, SMUG, THRIFTY
                  CONSTRUCTIVE,
                  INTROSPECTIVE
                  (Labile)   (Habit-bound)
                  (Intuitive)   (Logical [precise])
                  (Careless of material   (Thrifty)
                   things)

Burt 3 (Some resemblance to A)
Decreasing positive in emotions of:
    Joy
    Tenderness
    Curiosity
    Assertiveness
    Sociability
Increasing negative in emotion of:
    Fear
    Disgust
    Anger
    Sorrow

Garnett 24
Cheerfulness
Desire to excel
Quickness of apprehension
Originality
Gregariousness
Intense influence in group
Corporate spirit
Bodily activity
Tact
Rapid mental work
Desire to be liked
Soundness of common sense
Impulsive kindness

Maurer 30
Enthusiastic
Cheerful
Sociable
Happy
Keen
Talkative
Responsive
Curious
Resourceful
(Negatively)
Meditative
Grave

Moore 51
Depressed
Previous history of attacks
Fearful
Insane relatives

Reyburn and Taylor 57
Positive in:
    Gregarious (large groups)
    Sense of humor
    Cheerful
    Corporate spirit
    Bodily activity
Negative in:
    Conscientious
    Occasional extreme depressions

Howie 85
Bodily activity and excitability
Cheerfulness
No fearfulness
No self-consciousness
Initiative

Koch 73
Nervous habits
(Oral, pedal, corporal, limited and
    corporal mass)
Possible autoerotism
Constipation
Lack of persistent effort
Tension

Cattell 6
Cheerful
Natural
Sociable
Humorous
Adaptable
Gregarious
Quick of apprehension
Hasty
Forward
Responsive
Verbose

Eysenck 83 *a*
Apathy, retardation
Anxiety, nightmares
Depression
Hysterical conversion symptoms ab-
    sent (i.e., negative loading)

Koch 78 Possibly belongs here, though not precisely because it occurs in young children and cor- relates with immaturity (age).

Pines and whines

Nervous habits of hair- and scalp- pulling

Refuses and ignores adult requests

Not given to *verbal* attack

Absence of pedal and corporal bodily activity (nervous)

McCloy (Webb's data)[1] 42

Cheerfulness

Readiness to recover from anger

Fact

Degree of corporate spirit

Fondness for large social gatherings

Mental work on pleasures

Thurstone 65

Solemn

Pessimistic

Suspicious

The additional factors add to the syndrome: sense of humor, quickness of mental operations, tact, originality, interest in bodily activity, readiness to recover from anger, mental work on pleasures, resourcefulness, common sense, and lack of gravity. Cheerfulness, sociability, and resource seem to be the keynotes.

FACTOR G

POSITIVE CHARACTER INTEGRATION — v. — IMMATURE DEPENDENT CHARACTER

Evidenced by 5, 15, 25, 66, 79 *a*.   *Cattell (15* or G).

(Above .25 Mean Contribution .032)

(3)	35	WISE, MATURE, POLISHED (Independent) (Reliable) (Mature)	— *v.* — DEPENDENT, SILLY, INCOHERENT (Emotionally dependent) (Undependable) (Emotionally immature, irresponsible)
(11)	33	STRONG–WILLED, CONSCIENTIOUS (Persevering) (Painstaking) (Conscientious)	— *v.* — INDOLENT, INCO- HERENT, IMPULSIVE (Quitting) (Slipshod) (Conscienceless)
(10)	−31	REALISTIC, FACING LIFE (Realistic, practical) (Persevering) (Facing life)	— *v.* — DEMORALIZED, AUTISTIC (Unrealistic) (Quitting) (Subjective, evasive)

[1] We cannot accept the fourth match by McCloy of his own data with Webb's. His factor in the Webb data is very distinctly like F; that in his own data seems to be more like our factor I.

(17) −29 EMOTIONALLY MATURE
(Balanced)
(Loyal)
(Honest)

− v. − CHARACTER NEUROSIS, PSYCHOPATHIC
(Neurotic, irritable, uncontrolled)
(Fickle)
(Dishonest)

(4) −27 THOUGHTFUL, STOIC, RESERVED
(Thoughtful)
(Deliberate)
(Austere)

− v. − CHANGEABLE, FRIVOLOUS
(Unreflective)
(Impulsive)
(Profligate)

(27) −27 EMOTIONALLY MATURE, ADJUSTING TO FRUSTRATION
(Mature emotionally)
(Self-effacing)

− v. − INFANTILE, DEMANDING, SELF–CENTERED
(Infantile)
(Self-pitying)
(Exhibitionist)

(28) −27 STABLE, INTEGRATED CHARACTER

(Stable emotionally)
(Self-respecting)
(Self-controlled)

− v. − CHANGEABLE, CHARACTERLESS, UNREALISTIC
(Changeable)
(Unself-controlled)

Cattell 5
Webb's first five and then:
Energetic
Tactful
Mature
Steady emotional mood
Confident
Pedantic

Thurstone 76
Determined
Persevering
Hard-working
Systematic
Grasping
Ingenious
Crafty
Self-reliant

Kelley 25
Honesty in schoolwork
Regard for property rights
School drive
Loyalty
Mastery
Fair play

Eysenck (80 a) (Here or in "C")
Badly organized personality
Personal history of abnormality
Abnormality in parents
Consistently depressive or hypomanic
Schizoid, seclusive
Upset by wartime separation
Weak, dependent personality
Poor muscle tone and posture

Howie 86
Perseverance
Continuity of interest
Popularity
Freedom from anger
Common sense
Self-consciousness

Hart and Jenkins (79 *a*)
Group stealing
Gang activity
Aggressive stealing
Submissiveness
Delinquent siblings

This is not placed with confidence, for the population is anomalous to the others. Within delinquents, however, it associates with defective moral environment and absence of temperamental causes.

There is, naturally, a fairly sharp difficulty in distinguishing the factors that match G from those that match C. Factors 34, 39, 5, 23, 68, 25, and 55 could almost as well be placed in either. However, 5 and 25 are placed here because they stress energy and perseverance. The additions to the syndrome are few and narrow — namely, readiness for hard work or studies, regard for property rights, tact, resourcefulness, and physical courage.

FACTOR H

CHARITABLE, ADVENTUROUS CYCLOTHYMIA — *v.* — *OBSTRUC-*
TIVE, WITHDRAWN SCHIZOTHYMIA

Evidenced by 7, 16, 52, 70, 76. *Cattell* (*16* or H).

(Above .22 Mean Contribution to Variance — 0.30)

(6) —.32 KINDLY, GENTLE,   — *v.* — HARD, CYNICAL
            IDEALISTIC
            (Grateful)   (Thankless)
            (Friendly,   (Hostile)
             understanding)   (Hardhearted)
            (Softhearted)

(14) —.32 OUTGOING, IDEAL-   — *v.* — ANTISOCIAL, SCHIZOID
            ISTIC, COÖPERATIVE
            (Idealistic)   (Cynical)
            (Coöperative)   (Obstructive)
            (Adventurous)   (Timid, withdrawn)

(19) —.31 NATURAL, FRIENDLY, — *v.* — SPITEFUL, TIGHT-
            OPEN   FISTED, SUPERSTITIOUS
            (Friendly)   (Hostile)
            (Coöperative)   (Obstructive)
            (Frank)   (Secretive)
                                   ([Irrational, obsessive
                                    fears])

(22) +.27 RESPONSIVE, GENIAL, —v.— ALOOF, COLD,
SENTIMENTAL MISANTHROPIC
(Responsive) (Aloof)
(Genial) (Coldhearted)
(Social interests) (Brooding
[not an opposite])

(30) +.24 ADVENTUROUS, LUSTY —v.— GENERALLY IN-
HIBITED, TIMID
(Incontinent) (Inhibited)
(Gluttonous) (Queasy)
(Curious) (Uninquiring)

(24) —.24 TRUSTFUL, —v.— HOSTILE, PARANOID
GOOD–TEMPERED
(Not sadistic) (Sadistic)
(Trustful) (Suspicious)
(Reasonable) (Mulish)

(21) +.23 ASCENDANT, —v.— RETIRING, QUIET,
EXPRESSIVE, NARROW
WIDELY INTERESTED
(Energetic, spirited) (Languid)
(Self-confident) (Self-distrustful)
(Debonair)

Cattell 7
Mature — v. — Willful
Good-natured — v. — Spiteful
Kind on principle
Tactful

Williams 70
Participates
Interested in group
Coöperates
Sociable
Critical
Maternal
Leads
Seeks approbation
Ascendant

Thurstone 67 *d*
Friendly   Accommodating
Cheerful   Awkward
Congenial   Satisfied
Tolerant   Frank
Careless   Generous

Koch 76 (possibly obverse of H)
Pouts and sulks
Plays with fingers
Not compliant
Not given to genital play
Not aggressive
Not attention-getting
Not flitting from task to task
High skin resistance

Moore 52
Mutism
Negativism
Refusal of food
Stereotypisms of attitude

The matching in these instances is less confidently made than for previous factors. McCloy's 42 could be almost as well placed here as under F. Moore's psychotic factor might be considered the extreme of the low loading in this factor.

FACTOR I

SENSITIVE, IMAGINATIVE, ANXIOUS EMOTIONALITY — v. — RIGID, TOUGH, POISE

Evidenced by 4, 17, 37, 67, 74. *Cattell* (*17* or I).

(Above .20 Mean Contribution to Variance = 0.019)

(6)   −.38   KINDLY, GENTLE   — v. — HARD, CYNICAL
             IDEALISTIC
                 (Grateful)   (Thankless)
                 (Friendly,   (Hostile)
                   understanding)   (Hardhearted)
                 (Softhearted)

(34)   .29   IMAGINATIVE,   — v. — SET, SMUG, THRIFTY
             INTROSPECTIVE,
             CONSTRUCTIVE
                 (Labile)   (Habit-bound)
                 (Intuitive)   (Logical [precise])
                 (Careless of material   (Thrifty)
                   things)

(27)   .28   INFANTILE,   — v. —   EMOTIONALLY
             DEMANDING,   MATURE, ADJUSTING
             SELF–CENTERED   TO FRUSTRATION
                 (Infantile)   (Mature emotionally)
                 (Self-pitying)   (Self-effacing)
                 (Exhibitionist)

(5)   .27   NEUROTIC   — v. — NOT GENERALLY
                                                 NEUROTIC
                 (Self-deceiving)   (Realistic)
                 (Hypochondriacal)
                 (Nervous, specific
                   neurotic symptoms)

(3)   −.26   DEPENDENT, SILLY,   — v. — WISE, MATURE,
             INCOHERENT   POLISHED
                 (Emotionally dependent)   (Independent)
                 (Undependable)   (Reliable)
                 (Emotionally immature,   (Mature)
                   irresponsible)

(20) .25 GENERAL EMOTION- — *v.* — UNEMOTIONAL
ALITY (WITH MAL-
ADJUSTMENT)
(Emotional [in all ways])   (Unemotional)
(Dissatisfied)   (Content)
(Excitable)   (Phlegmatic)

McCloy (own data) 37
Athletic ability
  (the profession of the group rated)
Poise
Not a good follower
Alertness
Not coöperative
Popular
Not high in integrity

Possibly *Burt 4*
Decreasingly positive in emotional
    expression of:
  Sex
  Curiosity
  Joy
  Disgust
Increasingly negative in:
  Fear
  Tenderness
  Sociability

Thurstone 67 a
Stern —
Unnatural —
———— Grasping
———— Impetuous
———— Submissive

Howie 87
Excitable
Fearful
Not given to anger
Not popular
Self-conscious
Low common sense
Low bodily activity

Thurstone 67
Capable
Frank
Self-reliant
Courageous

Koch 74
High skin resistance level
Sex (masculine)
Acting silly and swaggering
Genital manipulation
Laughing and smiling
Negative:
  Hair and scalp manipulation
  Trying to boss

Eysenck 81 a
Hypochondriasis
Fatigue, effort intolerance
Dyspepsia
Fainting fits
(Sexual anomalies — negative; i.e.,
  absent)
Poor muscle tone and posture
Hypochondriacal personality
Somatic anxiety

Past research has rarely caught this factor, and the above matches are tentative and assume some interpretation. However, they are in part based on personal observation of individuals highly positive in I and one consequently made with more confidence than the paper list of traits would permit alone.

The additions generally agree in the core of poise, capability, and self-reliance. "Popularity" creates a problem in that the most altruistic qualities appear at the non-poise pole. Observation, however, suggests that in some curious sense popularity does go to the poise pole, especially in groups where masculinity or rugged individualism is part of the socially approved pattern. Tension and nervous restlessness are stressed in the obverse.

FACTOR J

NEURASTHENIA — v. — VIGOROUS, "OBSESSIONAL DETER-MINED" CHARACTER

Evidenced by 18, 22, 35, 40, 50. *Cattell (18 or J).*

(Above .17 Mean Contribution to Variance = 0.018)

(11) −.26 INDOLENT, INCO-HERENT, IMPULSIVE   — v. — STRONG–WILLED, CONSCIENTIOUS
(Quitting)   (Persevering)
(Slipshod)   (Painstaking)
(Conscienceless)   (Conscientious)

(35) −.24 SIMPLE–HEARTED, MEEK   — v. — SMART, ASSERTIVE
(Simple)   (Sophisticated)
(Submissive)   (Intelligent)
   (Assertive)

(3) −25 DEPENDENT, SILLY, INCOHERENT   — v. — WISE, MATURE, POLISHED
(Emotionally dependent)   (Independent)
(Undependable)   (Reliable)
(Emotionally immature, irresponsible)   (Mature)

(29) −.23 NEURASTHENIC   — v. — PSYCHO–PHYSICALLY VIGOROUS, ALERT
   (Alert)
(Absent-minded)   (Energetic, spirited)
(Languid)   (Quick)
(Slow)

(2) −.22 UNIMAGINATIVE,
            STUPID
            (Stupid)
            (Incoherent, confused)

— *v.* — INTELLIGENT,
            ANALYTICAL
            (Intelligent)
            (Clear-thinking)
            (Clever)

(10) .20 DEMORALIZED,
            AUTISTIC
            (Unrealistic)
            (Quitting)
            (Subjective, evasive)

— *v.* — REALISTIC,
            FACING LIFE
            (Realistic, practical)
            (Persevering)
            (Facing life)

(30) −.19 GENERALLY IN-
            HIBITED, TIMID
            (Inhibited)
            (Queasy)
            (Uninquiring)

— *v.* — ADVENTUROUS,
            LUSTY
            (Incontinent)
            (Gluttonous)
            (Curious)

(21) −.18 RETIRING, QUIET,
            NARROW

            (Languid)
            (Self-distrustful)

— *v.* —   ASCENDANT,
            EXPRESSIVE,
            WIDELY INTERESTED
            (Energetic, spirited)
            (Self-confident)
            (Debonair)

Koch 79 (also has resemblance to H)
Daydreaming
Plays alone
Does not comply
Poor recovery of skin resistance
Does not laugh and smile
Freedom from digital and corporal
  nervous habits

Chi 22
Initiative
Mental alertness
Accuracy
Promptness
Independence
Industry
Persistence
Originality
Emotional balance
Facing reality
Leadership

McCloy (own data) 35
Energetic
Lack of leadership
Healthy
Not modest
Hard-working

McCloy (Webb's data) 40
Originality of ideas
Quickness of apprehension
Belief in own powers
Desire to impose will
Intensity of influence on intimates

Moore 50
Depression — Retardation
Depressed
Retarded (slow)
Neurasthenic
Suicidal

Thurstone 67 c
Quiet
Bashful
Reserved
Awkward
Calm
Tidy
Pessimistic
Submissive

Again there is a fair amount of doubt, first because McCloy's matched factors do not match very well and because they do not match too well with our main syndrome. McCloy's 40 has some resemblance to F. Moore's factor, however, gives a likely extreme of this "neurasthenic" type syndrome. Thurstone's factor under G has some resemblance to J. In view of this uncertainty, we cannot safely use these matches to expand the boundaries of the syndrome.

FACTOR K

TRAINED, SOCIALIZED, CULTURED MIND — v. — BOORISHNESS

Evidenced by 19 and factors in educational measurement. *Cattell* (*19* or K).

(Above .16 Mean Contribution to Variance = 0.13)

(12)   .30   INTELLECTUAL

(Thoughtful)
(Analytical)
(Wide interests)

— *v.* — SIMPLE, UNDIS-
CIPLINED MIND
(Unreflective)
(Narrow interests)

(11)   .23   STRONG–WILLED,
CONSCIENTIOUS
(Persevering)
(Painstaking)
(Conscientious)

— *v.* — INDOLENT, INCO-
HERENT, IMPULSIVE
(Quitting)
(Slipshod)
(Conscienceless)

(35)   .22   SMART, ASSERTIVE

(Sophisticated)
(Intelligent)
(Assertive)

— *v.* — SIMPLE-HEARTED,
MEEK
(Simple)
(Submissive)

(25)   .18   AESTHETIC INTERESTS,
INDEPENDENT MIND
   (General aesthetic
     interests)
   (Musical ability and
     interests)
   (Independent)

(14) −.18   OUTGOING, IDEAL-   − *v.* − ANTISOCIAL, SCHIZOID
ISTIC, COÖPERATIVE
   (Idealistic)   (Cynical)
   (Coöperative)   (Obstructive)
   (Adventurous)   (Timid, withdrawn)

(33) −.17   INTROSPECTIVE,   − *v.* − TOUGH, SOLID,
SENSITIVE, SCARED   TALKATIVE
   (Introspective)   (Tough)
   (Sensitive)   (Lethargic)
   (Hurried)

Thurstone 67 f
Refined —
Reserved —
Tidy —
――― Awkward
――― Careless

With the exception of the Thurstone factor, there is no record of the appearance of this pattern in past BR researches; but it evidently corresponds to a social mold trait from good education and home background and is discernible in actual test data (Chapter 11).

FACTOR L

SURGENT CYCLOTHYMIA − *v.* − *PARANOIA*

Evidenced by 20 and 67 *e.*   *Cattell* (*20* or L).

(Above .18 Mean Contribution to Variance = 0.07)

(15)   .22   CHEERFUL, ENTHUSI- − *v.* −   UNHAPPY,
        ASTIC, WITTY   FRUSTRATED, DOUR
     (Genial)   (Coldhearted)
     (Optimistic)   (Pessimistic)
     (Enthusiastic)   (Apathetic)

(9) .19 GOOD–NATURED,   — *v.* — SURLY, HARD
EASYGOING
(Grateful)   (Thankless)
(Softhearted)   (Hardhearted,
(Easygoing)   embittered)
                             (Short-tempered)

(14) −.18 OUTGOING, IDEAL–   — *v.* — ANTISOCIAL, SCHIZOID
ISTIC, COÖPERATIVE
(Idealistic)   (Cynical)
(Coöperative)   (Obstructive)
(Adventurous)   (Timid, withdrawn)

(8) −.16 ADAPTABLE,   — *v.* — RIGID, TYRANNICAL,
FRIENDLY   VINDICTIVE
(Adaptable [to change])   (Extra-punitive)
(Friendly)   (Inflexible [emotionally])
                             (Hostile)

(24) −.16   TRUSTFUL,   — *v.* — HOSTILE, PARANOID
GOOD–TEMPERED
(Not sadistic)   (Sadistic)
(Trustful)   (Suspicious)
(Reasonable)   (Mulish)

(6) −.16 KINDLY, GENTLE,   — *v.* — HARD, CYNICAL
IDEALISTIC
(Grateful)   (Thankless)
(Friendly and   (Hostile)
understanding)   (Hardhearted)
(Softhearted)

(22) .16 RESPONSIVE,   GENIAL, — *v.* — ALOOF, COLD,
SENTIMENTAL   MISANTHROPIC
(Responsive)   (Aloof)
(Genial)   (Coldhearted)
(Social interests)   (Brooding
                          [not an opposite])

Thurstone 67 e
Cynical
Eccentric
Unconventional
Talented
Ingenious
Pessimistic
——— Religious

Except for the above lone instance, this has not appeared in previous BR researches. It resembles the other cyclothyme-schizothyme factors, A, F, and H, especially A, from which it differs in stressing kindly — *v.* — cold, hard qualities. It is matchable in questionnaire data and in the clinical picture of paranoia.

The only Behavior Rating factors remaining unmatched from previous studies are two in Moore's studies of psychotics, which, dealing with deteriorated conditions, were not likely to separate from our "normal" populations. There is, however, some slight resemblance of 53 to the I factor.

Factor M.   Pathological "Uninhibited or Kinetic" Syndrome.
Evidenced by 53.

> *Moore 53*
> Stereotypism of actions
> Destructiveness
> Talking to voices
> Giggling

Factor N.   Pathological "Deluded Hallucinated" Syndrome.
Evidenced by 54.

> *Moore 54*
> Auditory hallucinations
> Bizarre delusions
> Other hallucinations
> Stereotypisms of words
> Disorientation in space

9. RESOLUTION OF ALTERNATIVE FACTORIZATIONS

Difference of principles governing factorizations. The rotation of the data in the major research underlying this book resulted in twelve factors (of which one is possibly a residual factor), as set out in Section 8 above. A search was made for any reasonably stable alternative rotation which might need to be considered as representing an alternative mode of psychological explanation.

An alternative becomes possible only if we modify somewhat our principles of search, which we could do as follows: (1) We could seek a more "severe" simple structure [1] — i.e.,

[1] We are very greatly indebted to Dr. Thurstone, the originator of simple structure, for his help in this rotation of our data. Our final result embodies a possible simple structure solution as viewed by his Chicago laboratory.

one which would "block in" the total variance roughly with the fewest factors in the simplest possible way. This means that we neglect the fainter suggestions of hyperplanes, and refuse to consider those psychological possibilities of unilateral and coöperative factors discussed in Section 4 of Chapter 12. In short, we accept only obvious hyperplanes through the middle of nebulae of points. All factors then stand or fall by an unmodified, gross mathematical test of over-all simple structure. (2) We could give up the attempt to retain the eleven or twelve factors suggested by the criteria of the original centroid factorization, and allow the rotation to "squeeze" out, as mere residuals, any factors which could be dispensed with as far as reproducing the original correlations is concerned.

Two alternative simple structures were actually discovered, which have been called β_1 and β_2, because they resemble each other pretty closely and differ from the above — hereinafter called α factorization — in giving seven factors instead of twelve.

As they have been examined elsewhere (*58 d*) and as the considered conclusion is that they are not as scientifically satisfactory as the α rotation, they will not be set out in detail here. It has been shown also that the more "severe" simple structure referred to under (1) above, in which a hyperplane (section) is formed always by taking the long axis of any elliptical swarm of variables that appear in the diagrams, can be distinguished from the simple structure based on "natural" hyperplanes by a relatively simple test. This test consists in dividing the number of near-zero projections (within ± 0.05) for all factors by the communality for all traits, yielding a higher value for better simple structure. Other indices also have value, notably the ratio of ± 0.05 to ± 0.10 projections, which, as a diagram will show (*58d*), tends to be higher for a natural simple structure than when a large number of near-zero loadings are obtained by drawing the hyperplane section down the long axis of an ellipse, without regard to more local configurations.

The nature of the beta factors. The transformation from the α to the β factorizations, which required about as many more rotations as had already been made, occurred mainly through the running into a single factor of what have been called elsewhere (*58b* and page 530) "coöperative" factors — i.e., similar factors with similar patterns of loadings. However, some other redistributions of variance also take place, as will now be indicated.

Except for one factor the β factorizations result in qualitatively the same factors as the α factorization. One finds in both β_1 and β_2 the α factors A, B, C, F, and also a new factor labeled M but considerably resembling the J factor of α. In addition, I is found again in β_1 and E, and in G, β_2. The coöperative factors A, H, and L have coalesced, as also have the factors G and C in one case and B and K in both cases. The A factor in one β rotation has a good deal of the old E in it; i.e., the schizoid trend is accompanied by more dominance than before. Except for a rise in the saturations of E and a fall in the saturations of F, the order of importance in α and β rotations is little different. B accumulates rather more variance. C takes a slight turn toward more pure "general emotionality" (as distinct from "character") in the β rotations. A factor N appears in one β rotation which has a surgency-like quality, with high loadings in cheerful, talkative, absence of aesthetic sensitivity, freedom from neuroticism and emotionality. Similarity of intercorrelations of factors is not noticeably preserved in the different factorizations, except that large correlations, like that of B with C and B with K, tend to persist.

Resolution of alternative factorizations. Alternative factorizations, as we have seen, normally reproduce the correlations equally well. The purely mathematically minded may therefore prefer the β factorization, asking, "Why use twelve factors when seven will suffice?" The psychologist, on the other hand, may at first doubt the reality of factors if they can be so transformed. He may be reassured, since the different systems agree in the main on the factors A, B, C, E, F, G, and I, to believing in the psychological substantiation of these, but might doubt D, H, J, K, and L.

Our own verdict is to accept the α rotation as the fundamentally correct one, for the following reasons: (1) Criteria of the centroid analysis point to twelve factors. (2) When examined in detail the results of the method of finding simple structure there used are better (*58i*). (3) Other researches, when all their contributions are considered, require twelve major factors to account for these findings. (4) The β factorizations actually *do not* reproduce the correlations so well. The variance that has been sloughed off in apparent "residual factors" actually adds up to a good deal. A "residual" may affect only three or four variables out of thirty-five above 0.10; yet this, it appears, cannot be regarded as error variance, and it would seem wise to reject fewer factors as residuals than current practice presumes to do. Larger populations and more accurate and insightful variables, however, can alone achieve the definition of these lesser factors.

Chapter Ten

THE PRINCIPAL SOURCE TRAITS BASED ON SELF-INVENTORIES

1. SELF-INVENTORY DATA: THEIR VALIDITY, RANGE, AND MANNER OF ORGANIZATION

The meretricious questionnaire. Because of the extreme ease with which data can be gathered by questionnaire methods, especially on that atypical minority of studious, docile, and intelligent humanity which sits in university classrooms, the inquirer into personality structure encounters an abundance of self-inventory "findings." They receive a prominence out of all relation to their scientific value.

As a temporary "stopgap," while personality research becomes organized, the questionnaire has its place. But as a serious approach to discovering the structure of personality it represents the nadir of scientific inventiveness and subtlety. Lured by the machine-like ease of scoring, and blinded by their lack of clinical sense, many workers and educational psychometrists are at present under the delusion that the measurement of personality can be thus artlessly dragged in by questionnaires at the tail end of the mental-test procession and handled by the same simple mechanical conceptions. So we get even "personality quotients"; traits on a continuum of good and bad, efficient or inefficient; simple additive totals to predict "success"; and other naïve imitations of ability testing.

The abuses practiced by those who typically seize upon the questionnaire are no argument, however, against its proper research use within the true limits of its validity. Those limits, as indicated, are so sharp that the factor findings in this material must be kept entirely separate from that on other foundations, at least until the period of integration is reached. Actually there has been astonishingly little research to discover the relation of questionnaire results to objective observations on behavior of the kind referred to in the questionnaire items. Instead there has been a great deal of easy, implicit assumption that behavior looks as it feels. Yet, as Allport, Huntley (*126 b*), Vernon, and Wolff (*280 a*) have clearly shown in studies of expressive movement (stylistic traits), the individual is normally very unreliable in recognizing his own gait, voice, etc. It is unfortunate that these studies of stylistic — i.e., mainly temperamental — source traits have not been continued into other kinds of factors; but at least it is certain, as we shall see later, that the matching of internal questionnaire factors and external behavior factors is systematically more difficult than those who so confidently predict from questionnaires in guidance and personnel work imagine.

Strictly the observations by questionnaires live in a world of their own, conditioned by systematic errors springing from (1) lack of self-knowledge on the part of the subjects — i.e., lack of correct appreciation of their own behavior;[1] (2) distortion of responses by such factors as dishonesty, carelessness, or ulterior motivation generally in the test situation; (3) lack of any true measurement continuum in which normative measures could be set up; as indicated in Chapter 6, these responses are really solipsistically based (As in introspective "measures" generally, there is no true ground for the subject's judging himself above or below average.);[2] (4) Even

[1] As the work of Sears (*230*), for example, shows, a considerable proportion even of intelligent students do not place themselves in the same half of the distribution as they would be placed according to the behavior ratings by their associates.

[2] It may be objected that *some* of the items in questionnaires are not of the type which ask the subject how shy he is. They ask instead about some objective and specific piece of behavior. These are not solipsistic; they are merely judgments of behavior by a biased judge. But most have concealed solipsistic measurement involved.

lack of understanding, in the least intelligent quarter of the population, of what the questions and words mean.[1]

Nevertheless, the data have considerable value and interest (*a*) as preliminary guides to direct further researches using objective methods; (*b*) for consulting-room practice and appreciation of the introspected side of human life generally, in showing how certain syndromes "feel" from the inside — i.e., revealing how a well-known behavior syndrome will commonly be subjectively reported. When we match questionnaire with behavior factors we may consider it as a matching of "interiors" with "exteriors." (*c*) as a rapid means of exploring the further traits likely to occur on the fringe of some known source or surface trait, preliminary to objective testing; (*d*) special diagnostic value may lie in the measured discrepancies between the questionnaire responses (as responses) and the true behavior measurements.

Organization of the data. Like most of the lower forms of life, the self-inventory is very prolific! P. E. Vernon, in his survey of verbal methods of assessing personality (*269*), observes: "It is probable that a hundred or more of such tests have been published. But the great majority are simply modifications or extensions of three prototypes: Woodworth's *Personal Data Sheet*, Freyd-Heidbreder's *Introversion-Extraversion* test, and Allport's *Ascendance Submission* test."

The aspects of personality to be covered here include not only "personal inventories" on neuroticism and adjustment, but also on disposition (ascendance, dominance, self-sufficiency), on temperament (extraversion, cyclothymic tendency), on emotional maturity, on interests and on values.

---

[1] The only situation in which a questionnaire would have complete validity would be with a person of complete integrity and complete self-knowledge — and such a person would scarcely need a personality test. Its next best use is in research with research-devoted subjects, and the validities obtained in this situation should not be uncritically presumed in applied psychology. However, despite this unreliability and the treacherous "precision" of its scoring, especially with unusual subjects, the applied psychologists seem determined to use the questionnaire — and may be expected to continue for a decade or more.

Because the data have been built up, however, in three fairly distinct fields by somewhat distinct methods, it has seemed most appropriate to list the phenomenal data and the integration of data in three sections, each with its own numbering system, as follows:

(1) Indexed QP = Questionnaire factor in Personal Adjustment and Temperament
(2) Indexed QI = Questionnaire factor in Interests
(3) Indexed QA = Questionnaire factor in Attitudes

Not *all* questionnaire-type data have the limitations described in the introductory paragraphs. It is possible to treat the responses in questionnaires in two ways: (*a*) *literally*, as statements of fact about the individual, as in most questionnaire work; (*b*) *symptomatically*. Here one simply correlates the response with some outside performance and uses it as an index or symptom of that performance, without regard to its literal meaning. For example, the questionnaire asks, "Would you enjoy being a sailor in a submarine?" If the subject replies "Yes," one does not assume that he would in fact be happy as a sailor in a submarine. One observes, perhaps, that good librarians as opposed to bad librarians more frequently answer "No" to this question, and one uses it empirically as an index of librarianship interests or temperament.

This audaciously empirical but non-naïve use of the questionnaire is rare (it occurs in Strong's test (*245*)). Such "symptomatic" questionnaire findings are temporarily included here. In fact, it seems most consistent to include here also some data that run over into objective measures or which are derived by techniques not purely of a self-inventory type. For the questionnaire scores have been related to such objective data as college success, physiological findings, sex, intelligence, which nevertheless can be organized only about the questionnaire measurements. The techniques have been modified in the direction of objectivity also in such devices as

Thurstone's attitude measures and Kelley's use of word associations.

2. CATALOGUE OF DATA CONCERNING NEUROTICISM, INTROVERSION, SUFFICIENCY, ASCENDANCE, HYPERACTIVITY, ETC., QUESTIONNAIRES

Original scope and purpose of the questions. The intention of designers of questionnaires has usually been to measure some single tendency; but occasionally they have believed, on clinical or *a priori* logical grounds, that the general tendency could be split into subdivisions, and the questionnaires have been sorted out to give a separate score for each subaspect of the personality trend.[1] These prejudged divisions have not affected the subsequent analysis into factors except (*a*) by restricting the questions to certain aspects of personality and so limiting the number of factors which could be obtained and (*b*) by providing, in instances where single items are not used, the single variables which are to be intercorrelated. The effect of the last will be evident from the next subsection.

The available studies, in the strictly personality questionnaire data with which we shall deal in this and the next section, are those of Darrow and Heath (*71*), Flanagan (*88*), Guilford and Braly (*101*), Guilford and Guilford (*102*), (*103*), (*104*), (*105*), Layman (*159*), Mosier (*187*), Perry (*201*), Reyburn and Taylor (*214*) (*215*), Stagner (*239*), and P. E. Vernon (*268*). The majority of these are restricted to less than the whole of the range of personality aspects listed at the head of this section. They intercorrelate yes-no responses on the various items, using a tetrachoric correlation coefficient (assuming responses are really normally distributed and cut into a yes-no

---

[1] For example, the Bernreuter has six scales: neurotic tendency, self-sufficiency, introversion-extraversion and dominance, self-confidence (not self-conscious), and sociable as opposed to solitary. Cattell (*46*), the Minnesota Multiphasic Test designers, and Humm and Wadsworth (*127*) have shaped rating scales and questionnaires on the assumption that the syndromes of neuroses and even psychoses — e.g., anxiety hysteria, obsessional neurosis, epileptoid personality, cyclothyme constitution — are present in lesser degree as integral syndromes among "normals."

dichotomy) or a coefficient based on the coefficient of contingency. Some correct for the effect of correlated errors (*88*). A few correlate whole blocks of items, as indicated in (*b*) on the preceding page.

The intercorrelation of questionnaire subdivisions. Before studying the factor-analytic results, one should face the salutary experience of glancing at the intercorrelations between the various questionnaires and subdivisions of questionnaires in order to appreciate adequately their arbitrary character. Rarely have psychologists descended to such levels of irresponsibility and scientific naïveté as when they supplied businessmen and school counselors with these "measures" of "independent dimensions of personality"! The results are too well known to need more than a few typical illustrations.

Guilford and Braly (*101*) showed that there was practically no agreement between the results of introversion-extraversion scales designed by different authors. Newcombe (*192*) (*193*) found no self-consistency among extravert-introvert items. Kruger (*155*) found the intercorrelations between the component sections of the Humm-Wadsworth scale quite different from those stated by the authors. Vernon, surveying many findings (*269*), averaged four major researches showing that in the Bernreuter the introversion measurement correlates 0.93 with the neurotic tendency measurement, the latter 0.81 (negatively) with Dominance, and the Dominance measurement − 0.67 with the introversion measurement. He adds that a survey of forty experiments in the literature shows that in such tests as generally designed, the alleged measures of introversion correlate on an average with neuroticism to the same extent as any two neuroticism tests correlate with one another — namely, 0.36 ± 0.10! Stagner (*239*) found the following correlations of the separate measures of the Wisconsin Scale.

		1	2	3	4
Emotionality	1		.57	− .31	.31
Introversion	2			15	.38
[1] Persistence	3				.04
Seclusiveness	4				

[1] For some reason Wang's "w" factor was considered in this scale as a measure of "inferiority"!

Perry (*201*) found considerable intercorrelations in the Bernreuter, Laird, Ascendance-Submission, and other questionnaires. He carried out a factor analysis and obtained one general factor, presumably of "general neuroticism," running through all plus a second factor of dominance and self-sufficiency.

Vernon points out that in eighteen experiments with the Allport Ascendance-Submission test there was an average correlation of + 0.30 between introversion and submissiveness or, alternatively, psychoneurotic tendency.

Clearly the natural unreliability of self-ratings questionnaire testing has here been still further exaggerated by the lack of clarity and critical insight in the designers themselves when setting up their "unitary traits" or syndromes. Obviously these categories of the market place cannot be accepted as the true functional unities.

List of factors as first isolated — i.e., "phenomenal" factors. As stated, the data for analysis in this section have been limited by practical applications to neuroticism, ascendance, introversion, self-sufficiency, and hyperactivity items, as judged loosely by popular concepts. To facilitate the final discussion and assembly of the factors from diverse researches, each factor now to be listed and briefly described will be given a serial number.

Flanagan (*88*), with 305 eleventh-grade boys measured on 125 Bernreuter items, intercorrelated the four Bernreuter subdivisions. Using a principal components analysis he found three factors, but the last was unimportant, accounting for only 4 per cent of the variance. They were:

(1) Factor I, "Self-Confidence." Distinguishing the "self-confident, socially aggressive, well-adjusted, thick-skinned" individual from the "self-conscious, shy, emotionally unstable." It loaded heavily the Neurotic Tendency, Introversion, and Submissiveness and, to a lesser extent, social dependence (opposite self-sufficiency).

(2) Factor II, "Sociability." Distinguishes the "social" person from the "independent" aloof person. It loaded largely the self-sufficiency measurement and, to a slighter extent, introversion and neuroticism — i.e., it implies independence but not aggressiveness.

(3) Factor III, "Dominance." This loaded almost entirely the dominance measurement.

McCloy Layman (*159*) tested 276 students on 67 personality items chosen from a preliminary list of 782 from very varied personality questionnaires. Using a centroid analysis, she obtained twelve factors, agreeing among repeated factorization of small matrices, which, after rotation, are as follows: Some 45 items had a loading of .5 or more for one factor *only* — i.e., were relatively "pure."

(4) Factor 1. Sociability (*a*) Gregarious needs.
(5) Factor 2. Sociability (*b*) Feelings of social inadequacy.
(6) Factor 3. Sociability (*c*) Social initiative.
(7) Factor 4. Sociability (*d*) Social aggressiveness.
(8) Factor 5. Independence or Self-sufficiency.
(9) Factor 6. Impulsive action.
(10) Factor 7. Changeability of interests.
(11) Factor 8. Emotionality. *A*, Moodiness.
(12) Factor 9. Feelings of Inferiority — *v.* — Self-confidence.
(13) Factor 10. Emotionality Factor. *B*, Sensitivity or excitability.
(14) Factor 11. Emotionality Factor. *C*, Emotional introversion.
(15) Factor 12. Inability to meet demands of reality.

Martin (164a) "Factors in choice" not usable here, but noteworthy for research.

Mosier (188) tested 500 male college students on 39 of the 42 most discriminative items in the Thurstone inventory. A centroid analysis yielded eight factors, rotated to the following positions:

(16) Factor 1. Cycloid tendency.
(17) Factor 2. Depressive tendency.   G's (S)
(18) Factor 3. Hypersensitivity.
(19) Factor 4. Inferiority.
(20) Factor 5. Social introversion (Self-consciousness in intimate, face-to-face situations).
(21) Factor 6. Platform self-consciousness.
(22) Factor 7. Cognitive defect (Resulting personality frustration).
(23) Factor 8. Autistic tendency (Schizothyme).

Darrow and Heath (71) tested four groups of college men and women, selecting twenty to thirty from each with well-marked questionnaire scores, on the Thurstone Neurotic Inventory and the Northwestern Introversion-Extraversion Scale. No factor analysis was performed, but the questions were thrown into what are essentially clusters (the "nuclear clusters" of our Chapter 5) by a rather unusual but significant and interesting procedure.

The experiments were concerned with physiological correlates of personality, chiefly P.G.R. and blood pressure data of a varied kind.

They proceeded to bunch the questionnaire items which correlated with the same physiological pattern. They also bunched physiological reactions which lined up with the same personality items, and brought in further personality items which correlated with these physiological items. By cross reference and repeated examination of this kind they arrived at ten personality item clusters, as follows: (1) Sleep difficulties; (2) Health group number 1 — Somasthenia (digestive, heart, anemia troubles); (3) Socially inactive make-up (withdrawing); (4) Health group number 2 — Neurasthenia (weakness and undue awareness of bodily processes); (5) Depressive tendency (low spirits and loneliness); (6) Anxiety (phobias, worries); (7) Hypersensitivity (insecurity-inferiority); (8) Excitability (impulsiveness); (9) Paranoid tendencies (distrust, persecution); (10) Orientation toward reality (daydreaming).

These clusters were found not to be entirely independent and it is clear that one cannot assume them to be factors. Darrow and Heath grouped them in overlapping groups each corresponding to a larger syndrome. From an inspection of the indicated intercorrelations and from their own regrouping scheme, the present writer considers the following to be the indicated larger groupings, probably acceptable as factor groupings:

(24) Factor 1. Melancholy Agitation. This is the most clearly marked of all constellations, appearing in higher intercorrelations of Depressive Tendency, Anxiety, and Hypersensitivity, but to some extent in all.

(25) Factor 2. Called "Neurotic Constellation" by Darrow and Heath. An intercorrelating set including the above but extending more widely to Depressive Tendency, Anxiety, Hypersensitivity, Health 2 (Neurasthenia), and Social Inactive Make-up (Withdrawing).

(26) Factor 3. Sleep difficulties with Somasthenia.

(27) Factor 4. Neurasthenia with Excitability and a slight correlation of these also with Social Inactivity (Withdrawing tendencies).

(28) Factor 5. Paranoid tendency with Excitability and with Depressive tendency. Called Hyper-reactivity when Hypersensitivity and Extraversion are added.

(29) Factor 6. Social Inactivity (Withdrawal) with Somasthenia and, to a lesser extent, Neurasthenia. Called Hyporeactivity by Darrow and Heath.

Guilford and Guilford (*102*), (*104*), (*105*) tested 930 men and women students with 36 "typical" items from introversion-extraversion questionnaires. They found[1] five centroid factors as follows:

(30) Factor 1. (S) Social Introversion. (Shy, modest, slow.)

(31) Factor 2. (E) Emotional immaturity or dependence. (Insecure, daydreaming, emotional.)

(32) Factor 3. (M) Masculinity or Dominance. (Masculine sex, dominating, steady.)

(33) Factor 4. (R) Carefreeness. (Rhathymia.) (Meticulous, deliberate *vs.* free and easy.)

(34) Factor 5. (T) Intellectual Leadership. (Thinking Introversion.) (Intellectual, independent, not submissive.)

The Guilfords labeled the factors S, E, M, R, and T and pointed out that the two last were not so well defined. Later (1939) they continued the research with 89 items, expanded by addition of more material likely to define the R and T factors, on 610 men and 390 women students. The following centroid factors were found:

(35) Factor 1. (D) Depressive tendency. (Depressed, worrying, introspective.)

(36) Factor 2. (R) Rhathymia. (Carefree, unintellectual, loving excitement.)

(37) Factor 3. (LT) Liking thought. (Intellectual, considerate.)

(38) Factor 4. (S) Shyness. (G. considers same as (30) and Mosier's factor.) (Shy, deliberate, overconscientious.)

(39) Factor 5. ( ) (Unnamed. Saturations low and indefinite.) (Practical, not a theorizer, loves excitement but not impulsive.)

(40) Factor 6. (T) Thinking. (Analytical, not practical.)

(41) Factor 7. (A) Alertness. (Not retiring, alert to surroundings and people's feelings.)

An eighth and ninth factor were also found but with low saturation. The Guilfords next took 24 items out of 100 touching "hyperactivity" and administered to 600 students. There were eight factors, but only two had highly significant saturations (*104*).

(42) Factor 1. (N) Nervousness. (Easily startled, insomniac, uses up energy too readily.)

---

[1] By Thurstone's early technique, they found eighteen factors, of which the first were (1) a tendency to fear the environment and shrink away from it, (2) an emotional sensitiveness to the environment, (3) impulsiveness, and (4) interest in self (*103*). Recomputing the coefficients as tetrachoric correlations and using Thurstone's centroid method, then newly appeared, the Guilfords obtained five factors, as above.

(43) Factor 2. (GD) General drive. (Quick, talkative, happy, active, impulsive.)
(44) Factor 4. Variety-loving. (Likes change, talkative.)
(45) Factor 5. Active, but capable of relaxation. (Quick, gets excited, can relax, fastidious.)
(46) Factor 6. Restlessness. (Nervous habits, eats rapidly, insomniac.)

Reyburn and Taylor (*214*) tested 115 students with the first ten items from the Freyd-Heidbreder neuroticism questionnaire and obtained four factors. They rotated the axes to a discriminating position and one which placed them in agreement with previously known factors, namely "w," "c," and "p" (see Chapters 7 and 9), the last being fixed by a perseveration test given to the students at the time.

(47) Factor 1. (w) Will-character. (Perseveres, prefers working with others; is not self-pitying, worrying, or suspicious.)
(48) Factor 2. (c) Surgency-Desurgency. (Takes prominent part in social affairs; does not get easily hurt nor lose head in excitement.)
(49) Factor 3. Sociability. (Makes friends easily, takes prominent part in social affairs.)
(50) Factor 4. Perseveration. ("p" test; careful of others' feelings; easily hurt. Prefers to work alone.)

These research workers next reanalyzed (*215*) two researches by the Guilfords (*104*) (*105*). Their work is noteworthy because they to some extent succeeded in two aims: (*a*) to bring the questionnaire factors into line with those of behavior ratings, and (*b*) to rotate the Guilford studies in such a way as to obtain the same factors from the two matrices. They produced four factors having the same loadings for the same test items in both matrices and, in addition, four factors specific to the first matrix and two factors specific to the second, as follows:

(51) Factor 1. (Common) (w) Will-character. (Not wanting change of work, not worrying, not depressed, not impulsive.)
(52) Factor 2. (Common) (c) Surgency. (Carefree, impulsive, not overconscientious, craves excitement.)
(53) Factor 3. (Common) Flexibility. (Quick, not pausing to deliberate, able to produce rapidly.)
(54) Factor 4. (Common) Tension. (Cannot relax, overconscientious, easily distracted and fatigued.)

(55) Factor 5. Sociability. (Guilford's S.) (Forward socially, not depressed.)

(56) Factor 6. Alertness. (Alert, considers things and people around.)

(57) Factor 7. Liking Thinking. (Slightly different from Guilford's LT.) (Interest in problems, introspective, not happy-go-lucky.)

(58) Factor 8. Interest in Action. (Prefers athletics to intellect; practical, not theorizer.)

(59) Factor 9. Nervousness. (Like Guilford's N.) (Distractible, insomniac, nervous habits.)

(60) Factor 10. Inhibition. (Does not hurry, get excited, relax, sleep too well.)

P. E. Vernon (269) tested 100 men and women teachers on nineteen variables from the Boyd adjustment questionnaire. A rotated centroid analysis gave the following four orthogonal factors:

(61) Factor 1. (A general factor.) Self-depreciation and neuroticism. (Depression, instability, lack of self-confidence.)

(62) Factor 2. Carefreeness. (Freedom from worries and tenseness, lack of definite interests and responsibilities, unintegrated thinking.)

(63) Factor 3. Scrupulousness. (Not unstable, not unable to concentrate, obsessionally careful and self-controlled.)

(64) Factor 4. Neuroticism factor, different for men and women. (Women: phobias, instability. Men: Persecutory, suspicious, inability to concentrate.)

Whisler (276) tested 126 male and female undergraduates with question items of a most varied kind, finding six factors which he named as follows:

(65) A. Acceptance of Conventional Ethical Principles.

(66) B. Enjoyment of Momentary Pleasures.

(67) C. Interest in Conflicts and Controversies.

(68) D. Energetic, Independence.

(69) E. Participation in Casual Social Relationships.

(70) F. Criticalness and an Interest in "Truth."

Kling (151) tested 808 college students with 160 questionnaire items dealing with (1) clinically defined neurasthenia, (2) gastrointestinal disorder, (3) symptomatic allergy, (4) clinical allergy, (5) allied allergic symptoms, and (6) manic traits. Four factors can be deduced from the table of positive intercorrelations he obtained.

Factor (71). Common to all six fields.

Factor (72). Common to all fields except the manic.

Factor (73). Common to gastrointestinal symptoms and the three allergies.

Factor (74). Common only to neurasthenia and the gastrointestinal group.

Also a group factor in the allergies.

Thorndike, R. L. (257 a). 594 men and women college students on 70-item questionnaire from Kling and using same divisions. The following are deduced from his correlations, but do not cover all possible factors.

Factor (75). Common to neurasthenic and allergic fields.

Cluster (76). Allergy and inferiority-inadequacy responses.

Pallister (200). 209 college women, 200 questionnaire items dealing with withdrawal, shyness, lack of optimism or will, and neurotic symptoms.

Factor (77). General Approach-Withdrawal.

Jasper (131). 100 students, 40 questionnaire statements on personal and general optimism.

Cluster (78). Depression-Elation.

Stagner and Krout (238). 100 college students on questionnaire. Three major and two minor clusters.

Cluster (79). Conversion or somasthenic syndrome.

Cluster (80). Forgetfulness and daydreaming.

Cluster (81). Anxiety (worrying remorse, suspicion).

Here also must be listed T (16) from the data of the next chapter, as: Factor (82). Feeling of adequacy.

Brogden and Thomas (20 a).

Factor (83). Intellectual independence.

Factor (84). Gregariousness.

Factor (85). Liking for prolonged speculative considerations of problems, with social inhibition.

Factor (86). Emotional need for close friendship or family ties.

Factor (87). Intellectual leadership.

Gibb (96 c). 42 neuroticism items (Martin) on 100 students.

Factor (88). Depression or Cyclothyme.

Factor (89). Emotionality.

Factor (90). Sociability — *v.* — Shyness.

(Factorization not carried further.)

3. ORGANIZATION OF THE PRINCIPAL SOURCE TRAITS IN THE REALM OF "ADJUSTMENT"

To arrive at what may be considered the reasonably well-established solipsistically based factors or clusters, by critical comparison and combination of the above ninety phenomenal factors, is not possible by any mechanical procedure. The judgments made must take into account (*a*) that some correlations are based on items, some on blocks of items put together on logical grounds, some on clusters; (*b*) that the factor rotations might have been somewhat differently arranged, with very little dispute, in several researches; (*c*) that the size of populations, of item lists and other aspects of reliability require different weights to be given to the findings of different researches; and (*d*) that the populations of traits — i.e., of questionnaire items — are often widely different and sometimes subtly different. In short, the same problems arise as in the previous work of reaching the "observed behavior" factors, plus some new to this situation.

The aim here has been to put together factor syndromes identified by considerable item overlap, to add on representatives of the fringe of associated traits indicating the extent of the factor, to avoid as far as possible employing "interpretation" of items, and to refrain from throwing factors together when any doubt exists.[1]

---

[1] Naturally one never throws into one identity two factors from the same research! Moreover, since several factors may appear only as different loadings of the same items, mere identity of items (often only indicating the employment of the same trait population) does not indicate identity of factor. In the case where Reyburn and Taylor reanalyzed Guilford and Guilford's matrix, we have listed some factors from both researches — where the factors seemed very similar, but have otherwise accepted the simplified factors of the former experimenters. The speculation encountered in previous literature as to the relatedness or identity of factors from different researches agree in the main with ours, but there are some alarming instances of quite different interpretations. In one case a researcher considers a certain factor from his second research identical with one from his first. By taking into account the items and their saturations, especially in the light of later researches, the present writer identifies the factor in the first research with a different one in the second! Again, another researcher identifies a questionnaire factor with the present writer's behavior-based "surgency" factor, but the present writer cannot support this identification.

The order of arrangement is such as (1) to list first the factors which have been most repeatedly found and which are most securely established by size of population, method, etc.; (2) to list in close contiguity in the number sequence those factors which resemble each other and which in later research, or by other analyses, might be regarded as having something in common. When these two intentions conflict, the latter is followed.

The items listed under each factor are those having a saturation usually of 0.4 or more, but occasionally extending into the 0.2–0.4 range. Those with the highest saturations, in all the contributory researches, are placed highest in the item list.

TABLE 19

DESCRIPTIVE LIST OF QUESTIONNAIRE FACTORS

Factor QP. I. Shyness (Cluster D 1).[1] Also called "social introversion," "social inactivity," "S," "withdrawal approach," and obverse of "self-confidence." This is the best-established of factors, occurring as factors (1), (6), (20), (29), (30), (38), (55), and (90) above. (38) shows some overlap with the will-character factor QP IX, and others a little overlap with the autism factor QP V.

1. Troubled with shyness.
2. Keeps in background on social occasions — e.g., does not take responsibility for introducing people.
3. Has difficulty in, and dislikes, starting conversations or meeting new acquaintances.
4. Does not make new friends easily.
5. Prefers to read about a thing rather than experience it.
6. Is not forward in a social group, but is inclined to keep quiet and in the background.
7. Has feelings of inferiority.
8. Is self-conscious in the presence of superiors.

[1] As in some instances the resemblance of the questionnaire factors to behavior clusters in Chapter 9 was very striking, we noted these resemblances by the appropriate index number, as shown.

TABLE 19 — *Continued*

9. Has feeling of being watched by others in the street.
10. Is not much in touch with what goes on around him.

(Also: Has not been active in organizing clubs, teams, or other such groups; not self-confident; not self-confident about abilities, limits acquaintance to a select few, is not impulsive; interests do not change quickly; not prevented from sleeping by run of ideas; considers self rather nervous; is bothered by being watched when at work, is inclined to be slow and deliberate in movement, does not crave excitement, does not adapt readily to new conditions, situation, is not subject to fits of the blues, is over-conscientious, may allow people to crowd ahead of him in line without protest, does not express emotions readily; feelings readily hurt; cannot make up mind till time for action is past.   Probably also the following: Does not get interested in people met, mother is a dissatisfied person; finds it necessary to watch health carefully; is frequently bothered by indigestion; has had heart trouble; has had anemia, prefers intellectual to athletic competition; has general "somesthetic" complaints.)

(77) above is a factor which spreads also in Q II, III, and VI, due to different bases of analysis.   Pallister found (77) to correlate + 0.26 (significant) with verbal ability, also slightly with defective health, with languages and literature at college as opposed to choice of mathematics, with being eldest child as opposed to only child, with being Catholic or Jewish rather than Protestant or Socialist, with choice of occupations involving science rather than business occupations.   Factor (77) has items involving, in the approach side, optimism and will-character, as well as those central to Q I.

QP. IIa. General Emotional Hypersensitivity (Cluster AB 1 or E 1).   Also called "emotional immaturity," "hypersensitivity," "neurasthenic-excitability," "dependence, emotionality," "desurgency," "gregariousness" (inverted), and "social inadequacy."   Is constituted by factors (15) (and possibly 13), (18), (27), and (48). Has some overlap with III and also with schizoid traits list.

1. Feelings are hurt easily.
2. Often gets excited and is easily rattled in exciting situations.
3. Is easily upset.
4. Has frequent ups and downs in mood.
5. Is inclined to worry over possible misfortunes.
6. Expresses his emotions readily and replies "No" to "does consider himself as emotional as the average person."

TABLE 19 — Continued

7. Cannot stand criticism.
8. Indulges in self-pity.
9. Prefers working with others (from 48).
10. Does not take prominent part in social affairs.

(Also: Daydreams frequently, considers self a nervous person, is easily discouraged, has "neurasthenic" symptoms: constipation, dizziness, shooting pains, unpleasant sensations from the body.)

Apparently closely related to this, though possibly also with III or IV, are certain sets of allergic symptoms, contingently given as a separate cluster as follows.

Cluster QP. (IIb.) Allergy-Hypersensitivity-Inadequacy. Evidenced by (27) and (76). Related to IIIc below.

Questionnaire responses of hypersensitivity, inferiority, withdrawal, and "neurasthenia."

General allergic responses. The highest saturations of allergic cluster are in angioneurotic oedema and catarrhal conjunctivitis, the lowest in sinusitis and respiratory conditions.

QP. III. Melancholy Agitation (Cluster AC 1). Also called "cycloid tendency," "depressive tendency," "emotionality," and "moodiness." Factors (11), (89), (some resemblance to (12)), (16), (35). This factor has been considered by some to be the same as II above and by others the same as IV below. Factor (11) has fairly marked overlap with (IV). Factor III lacks the sensitivity running through II and the loneliness and neuroticism of IV. Mosier's research (*187*), moreover, has a factor for each of these three from the same matrix.

1. Is often just miserable (for no reason at all).
2. Has frequent ups and downs of mood (experiences many pleasant and unpleasant moods).
3. Worries over possible misfortunes.
4. Is frequently in low spirits (spells of "blues").
5. Frequently is meditative and introspective (daydreams frequently).
6. Is not carefree.
7. Has difficulty in making up mind.
8. Cannot relax.
9. Frequently feels grouchy.
10. Mind wanders and useless ideas bother him.

TABLE 19 — Continued

(Also: Swings from happiness to sadness; is inclined to be suspicious of the motives of others; troubled by inferiority and self-consciousness; touchy on various subjects; compulsion to do a job several times before leaving.)

This factor seems to be the nearest to that called neurasthenia in researches involving somasthenic and allergy variables, though the "neurasthenic" pattern there found also resembles Q IV and further research will be necessary to find which is most involved. Contingently we shall list here (26), (74), and (79). Consisting of:

Somasthenic tendencies: bodily debility, fatigue, digestive disorders.

Sleeplessness and restlessness of sleep.

Gastrointestinal disorders of certain kinds.

Dizzy spells, headaches, feeling of suffocation, intestinal pains.

Here also it seems appropriate to list two related, but, judging by their appearance in the same matrix, independent factors, as follows:

QP. IIIb. Allergy-Debility.
Evidenced by (73). An influence common to the allergies and to gastrointestinal disorder.

QP. IIIc. Neurasthenia-Allergy.
Evidenced by (72) and (75). An influence common to the above neurasthenic traits, gastrointestinal disorders, *and* the allergies.

This factor may be closely related to II*b*, above.

QP. IV. General Neurotic Maladjustment. (Clusters AB 3, AC 1). Also called "depressive tendency," "emotionality," "self-depreciation and general neuroticism," and "melancholic tendency." Factors (10), (17), (24), (25), (61), and (88). Mosier notes (*187*) that essentially this variable was found by Bridges, Garrison (*96*), and Slawson to be most diagnostic in differentiating delinquents and non-delinquents, and also that it characterizes psychotics generally. Vernon (*269*) finds it the biggest general factor in neuroticism. In Darrow and Heath's work it also appears to be the most general factor. For this reason and because, reading between the lines, one sees the behavior of a person who has given cause to be shunned, to be remorseful, to feel discouraged, we call it general neurotic maladjustment. There is probably much more in the nature of generally poor personality integration needing to be included in the symptom list.

TABLE 19 — *Continued*

1. Frequently in low spirits (depressed, or fits of the blues).
2. Lonesome, even with others.
3. Has frequent periods of feeling lonely.
4. Frequently feels remorseful or grouchy.
5. Often just miserable (easily moved to tears).
6. Gets discouraged easily (and lacks self-confidence).
7. Feels not adjusted to life.
8. Often in a state of excitement.
9. Suffers from instability of mood.
10. Has difficulty in making friends.

(Also: Afraid of falling when on a high place; frequently troubled by nightmares; finds difficulty in speaking in public; is uneasy in tunnel or subway; worries over humiliating experiences; is easily moved to tears; feels self-conscious when reciting in public.)

QP. V. Schizoid Asthenia (Cluster AB 2). Also called "autistic tendency," "social inadequacy." Factors (23) and (80) and perhaps (14). Not yet very well defined. Has possible relation to III.

1. Daydreams frequently.
2. Has periods of loneliness.
3. Is burdened by sense of remorse.
4. Is self-conscious over personal appearance.
5. Troubled by ideas running through head at night.
6. Lonesome even with others.
7. Has feeling of being watched on the street.
8. Is bothered by some useless thought.

(Also: Forgetfulness and poorness of memory organization.)

QP. VI. Confident Self-Assertion (v. *Inferiority Sense*). (Spreads over several clusters of CA and CB sections, especially the latter.) Also called "dominance," "social aggressiveness," "self-confidence," "inferiority sense," "feeling of inferiority," "confidence," "masculinity." Factors (3), (12), (19), and (32). (Also T. XVIII or (82).) It is possible and even probable that later research will reveal two or three factors here. Layman's data indicate two; and Guilford's masculinity factor is clearly "off center" in regard to other factors, seeming to be a sex factor only. However, it has seemed most practicable at present to set down one rather sprawling factor. Its associated traits are often similar to those for I, but there is ample proof that it is an independent factor.

TABLE 19 — *Continued*

1. Does not lack self-confidence.
2. Does not keep in background on social occasions.
3. Self-confident about abilities.
4. Is not easily discouraged — e.g., when opinions of others differ.
5. Is prepared to complain to waiter if served unsatisfactory food in a restaurant.
6. Is not troubled by feelings of inferiority.
7. Likes to sell things or to solicit funds for cause in which interested.
8. Does not find it difficult to get rid of a salesman.
9. Is not troubled by shyness.
10. Is not self-conscious in the presence of superiors.

(Also: Does not complain that mind wanders badly and is not absent-minded; is not easily rattled; does not work by fits and starts; has organized clubs, teams, etc., on own initiative; is more interested in athletics than in intellect; has never kept a personal diary; does not find it difficult to speak in public; makes up his mind easily; introduces people at a party; takes lead to enliven a dull party; does not feel reluctant to meet most important person at a party; does not feel self-conscious at having to start discussion among a group of people; is more frequently of masculine sex.)

QP. VIb. Hypomanic Aggressiveness. Called "aggressiveness." Factor (7) is shown to be independent of VI by Layman's study. It has some resemblance to XVIII but closest superficial relation here, as far as three items can show.

1. Do you ever try to argue or bluff your way past a guard or a doorman?
2. Do you ever upbraid a workman who fails to have your work done on time?
3. Do you ever heckle a public speaker?

QP. VII. Group Deference. Also called "platform self-consciousness" and "social inadequacy." Distinct from I or VI, but not yet well-defined, being found only twice: Factors (5) and (21). As its first discoverer (Mosier) points out, there are persons who are good mixers who nevertheless find it very difficult to speak in public. The Layman factor (5) has even closer ties with I and is listed separately here (but Layman also has an I factor). But the Layman factor is very broadly established.

TABLE 19 — *Continued*

Mosier: 1. Finds it difficult to speak in public.
2. Suffers from stage fright.
3. Is self-conscious when reciting.
4. Hesitates to volunteer in class.
5. Is self-conscious with superiors.

Layman: 1. Do you feel embarrassed when you have to enter a public assembly after everyone else has been seated?
2. Do you feel self-conscious in front of strangers or in a large crowd?
3. Do you often have difficulty in thinking of an appropriate remark to make in group conversation?
4. Does it bother you to have people watch you at work even when you do it well?
5. Are you troubled with the idea that people on the street are watching you?

QP. VIIIa. Self-sufficiency (v. *Gregariousness*) (Cluster D 3 and probably D 4). Also called "sociability" and "independence." Factors (2), (4), (49), (68), and (84); Brogden's confirmation of Layman is pretty definite here. Layman has two factors in this area, one called gregariousness and one independence. Their soundness of establishment suggests that two really exist, but owing to the difficulty of distinguishing them on item content they are listed here as VIII*a* and VIII*b*.

1. Becomes so absorbed in creative work that does not notice lack of intimate friends.
2. Do you care much for parties or dances?
3. Prefers travel in company of a guide to the adventure of traveling alone.
4. Do you like to be with other people a great deal?
5. Is not more interested in athletics than in intellectual affairs.
6. Do you enjoy taking part in many social affairs?
7. Finds books more entertaining than companions.
8. Does not enjoy getting acquainted with most people.
9. Usually enjoys spending an evening alone.
10. Does not prefer to work with other people.

(Also: Daydreams frequently; slow in making decisions; feels lonesome with others.)

TABLE 19 — *Continued*

QP. VIIIb. Independent Self-sufficiency. Evidenced by (8) and (83). This factor is also similar to V, III, and, in a lesser degree, to XXII.

1. Prefers to do own planning alone rather than with other people.
2. Prefers to work things out in own way rather than to accept suggestions from others. (Also: Tends to be a radical.)
3. Understands a problem better by studying it out alone than by discussing it with others.
4. Daydreams frequently.
5. Feels lonesome with other people.
6. Is considered to be critical of other people.
7. Does not want to be with people a great deal.
8. Prefers to make hurried decisions alone.
9. Gets as many ideas at time of reading a book as from discussion of it afterward.
10. Does not make friends easily.

(Except possibly for the second item, Whisler's (68) seems likely to belong here. As follows:

Much enjoyment in working with materials and in making things.

Much interest in politics.

As a spectator is indifferent to conflicts of personalities and violations of conventional codes of behavior.

Prefers stability in type of associate.

Thinks problem of free will vital.)

(Also: Does not take a prominent part in social affairs.)

QP. IX. Will-Character (Cluster AA 1). Also called "variety-loving" (opposite). Factors (10), (47), (51), and (65). This, and factors X and XI, show some overlap, so that it is likely that some restructuring will have to be carried out in this area — e.g., (44) might almost as well be here as in XI.

1. Is persevering and stable. (Also: "Finds his interests do not change rapidly.")
2. Prefers working with others.
3. Does not desire constant change of work.
4. Does not worry about possible misfortunes.
5. Is not suspicious of others' motives.
6. Does not indulge in self-pity.
7. Is not impulsive (is self-controlled).

TABLE 19 — *Continued*

8. Is slow and deliberate in manner.
9. Is not easily hurt.
10. Does not suffer from depressions.

QP. X. Obsessional-Inflexible Will-Character (Cluster AA 2, also perhaps CB 3, G 1, and H 1). Also called "inhibition," "rhathymia" (carefreeness) negatively, "impulsive action," and "scrupulousness." Factors (9), (33), (60), and (63). Factor (9) has some relation also to XI.

1. Is not impulsive. (Is self-controlled.)
2. Is scrupulously correct.
3. Is persevering and stable.
4. Usually plans his work before he begins it.
5. Is very particular about his dress and personal property.
6. Is inclined to be considerate of other people's feelings. (Also: Does not say things on the spur of the moment which he regrets later.)
7. Is able to concentrate well.
8. Does not daydream.
9. Is not easily disturbed by distractions.
10. Does not relax easily.

(Also: Does not sleep too well; in a spectator situation much affected by whether right triumphs; feels the problem of "the duty of the individual to society" to be vital; thinks much about the effect of one's actions on others; places evaluation of person of opposite sex largely on probable satisfactoriness as a mate; is inclined to worry over possible misfortunes; does not "think about self much of the time"; is slow and deliberate in movement; does not gobble his food; does not perspire easily in exciting situations; does not hurry unnecessarily; does not like to see people clean fingernails in public; does not waste time between jobs.)

QP. XI. Relaxed Independence (Cluster CB 4 and I 1). Also called "rhathymia" and "carefreeness." Factors (15), (36), (52), (62). Opposite of (81) Anxiety.

1. Is carefree.
2. Is happy-go-lucky.
3. Does not worry.
4. Is impulsive.
5. Is not overconscientious.

TABLE 19 — *Continued*

6. Craves excitement.
7. Prefers athletics to intellectual activities.
8. Is unconcerned with what others think.
9. Is not tense. (Can relax.)
10. Has few definite interests and responsibilities.

(15) seems to be the obverse of this. But since there are only three items by which to identify it, it could possibly belong to II or XIII. It is, however, ruled out from II (unless called II*b*) because Layman's research already has a factor there. It is as follows:

1. Is bothered if he has an unfinished job on his hands.
2. Is often in a state of excitement.
3. Gets "rattled" easily in exciting situations or at critical moments.

(Also: Is talkative; does not integrate his thinking thoroughly; is not slow and deliberate in manner; is not easily distracted.)

QP. XII. Variety-loving (Cluster B 2 or G 1). This factor disappears in Reyburn and Taylor's rotation of Guilford's results. It could be easily submerged in XI or others of this group — e.g., IX — and cannot be considered at all a well-substantiated factor. Factors (44) and (66).

1. Likes a position with varied tasks.
2. Is not slow and deliberate in movement.
3. Is talkative.
4. Is easily disturbed by distractions.
5. Likes to be waited on.
6. Enjoys verbal expression, use of language very highly.
7. Prefers to work with people rather than things.
8. Worries frequently.
9. Gets enjoyment in doing or saying shocking things.

QP. XIII. Nervous Anxiety and Instability (Cluster E 2). Also called "nervousness" and "sleep difficulties with somasthenia." Factors (26), (42), (59).

1. Is easily startled.
2. Suffers from insomnia.
3. Is easily distracted.
4. Suffers from nervous habits and restlessness.
5. Is frequently bothered by indigestion.
6. Talks or walks in sleep.

TABLE 19 — *Continued*

7. Is annoyed by people cleaning fingernails in public.
8. Is inclined to express emotions easily.
9. Is inclined to "doodle."
10. Feels that he uses more energy than most in getting things done.

(Also: Is not happy-go-lucky; is made uncomfortable by changes of work; cannot relax in repose; feels fatigued on waking; ideas run through head so that sleep is difficult; finds it necessary to watch his health carefully; has suffered from heart trouble or anemia.)

QP. XIV. High-strungness (Cluster E 1). Also called "tension." Note some resemblance of XIII and XIV to II. Factor (54).
1. Does not stop to think things over before acting.
2. Is overconscientious.
3. Cannot relax easily.
4. Is easily distracted.
5. Feels that he uses up more energy than most in getting things done.

QP. XV. Paranoid Schizothyme (Cluster F 5, also F 4 and most of F sector). Also called "paranoid trend and excitability" and "perseveration." This is practically the least-established factor, constituting items put together partly on logical grounds, and is listed here rather than at the end only to be in proximity to similar material. Factors (13), (28), and (50).
1. Thinks most people are self-seeking or malicious.
2. Dislikes many people.
3. Does not usually trust people or[1] prefers to work alone.
4. Believes found fault with more than he deserves[1] or feels easily hurt.
5. Gets easily rattled.
6. Often in a state of excitement.
7. Gets upset easily.
8. Has a high perseveration score on a "p" test. *(214)* (Objective variable.)

---

[1] These are the factor 50 items considered equivalent.

TABLE 19 — *Continued*

QP. XVI. Speed and Flexibility (Most nearly the CB sector). Also called "flexibility." Factor (53). Well-defined loadings.

1. Is not slow and deliberate in movement.
2. Rushes from one activity to another without rest.
3. Is quick in action.
4. Can turn out much work in short time.
5. Does not analyze motives of others.
6. Is not often in meditative or introspective mood.
7. Does not think things over before acting.
8. Does not discuss serious problems with friends.
9. Eats more rapidly than most, even when there is time.
10. Is talkative.

QP. XVII. Liking Thinking (Clusters B 2 and B 4, possibly G 1 or J 1). Also called "thinking." Factors (40), (57), (70), and (85).

1. Is introspective.
2. Analyzes motives of others.
3. Is interested in complicated problems.
4. Is interested in problems generally.
5. Discusses life's serious questions with friends.
6. Ponders over the past; is meditative.
7. Is not wholly carefree.
8. Is not happy-go-lucky.
9. Prefers intellectual to athletic activities.
10. Is not practical, but theoretical.

(Also, from (70): Criticalness or alertness in regard to propaganda; likes having a small "social gallery"; decrease in daydreaming in past five years; thinks problem of free will is vital; frequently thinks about the meaning of life; thinks much about the effect of one's behavior on others.)

QP. XVIII. Intellectual Leadership (Cluster B 3 or CB 5). Also called "thinking introversion." Factors (34) and (87) and some resemblance to (37), (67).

1. Is not more interested in athletics than in intellectual matters.
2. Generally prefers to lead in group activities.
3. Prefers to work alone rather than with others.
4. Inclined to study motives of others.
5. Prefers to work things out in his own way.

TABLE 19 — *Continued*

From (67)

6. Thinks the problem of "whether the modern industrial and machine age limits and dulls most people's appreciation of beauty" is vital.
7. Dislikes being waited on.
8. Is critical or alert to propaganda.
9. Thinks the problem of "whether the use of force in settling disputes is justified" is vital.
10. Enjoys moderately strong cold winds.

(Also: Thinks the problem of waste versus efficiency in the economic and social system is vital.)

QP. XIX. Extravert Alertness (Cluster CB 2 and perhaps CB 1). Factors (56) and (41). Also called "alertness" and "extraversion." (Jung, Conklin.)

1. Keeps in close touch with things going on around him.
2. Is more alert than the average person to his surroundings.
3. Is concerned as to what other people think.
4. Is considerate of other people's feelings.
5. Does not remain in background on social occasions.

QP. XX. Interest in Action (Cluster K 1). Factor (58). (Possibly opposite of (85).)

1. Becomes easily absorbed in athletics.
2. Prefers athletics to intellectual affairs.
3. Regards himself as practical man, not a theorizer.
4. Would rather do things than read about them.

QP. XXI. Frustrate Determination (Cluster B 3 and possibly AB 1). Also called "cognitive defect" and "obsessive or compulsive." Factor (22).

1. Depressed by having low marks in school.
2. Bothered by some useless thought.
3. Touchy on various subjects.
4. Hesitates to volunteer in class.
5. Must do a thing several times.
6. Below group median in mental test. (Objective variable.)

QP. XXII. Rigid, Lonely, Power Seeking. Also called "participation in casual social relationships." In the present writer's judgment this has relation to V but is kept separate pending further research. Factor (69).

TABLE 19 — *Continued*

1. Thinks rarely about the meaning of life.
2. Little enjoyment of spicy and highly seasoned foods.
3. Is concerned to see conventional codes of behavior violated.
4. Prefers to work with people and no enjoyment in working with materials.
5. Much interested in politics.
6. Increased daydreaming in last five years.
7. Is much different from intimate friends in interests, likes, etc.

Factors XXIII, XXIV, and XXV might be added to the above out of serial factors (14), (25), and (45) respectively. The last, "*Active but Capable of Relaxation*," disappears in the Reyburn and Taylor (*215*) analysis and is judged doubtful. No. (25), *Neurotic Constellation*, is established on the basis of rough clustering and seems, moreover, to be essentially a wider outcropping of (24) — i.e., Factor IV, General Neurotic Maladjustment. No. (14) is given by a single item, but unequivocally; viz., "Do you have difficulty in starting conversation with a stranger?" It is, however, different from I, for it appears independently in the same matrix. All other serially numbered factors of the original research list, except (86) are accounted for in the above twenty-one main factors. There are probably fewer ultimate factors, but, it will be remembered, doubtful matches are separated, possible resemblances being noted.

4. CATALOGUE OF QUESTIONNAIRE DATA ON INTERESTS
   AND VALUES

The supposed factors in interests. The development of objective interest tests has been so recent (*45*) (*248*) that the bulk of work on analysis of interests is bound to rest at present on questionnaire data. The suggested classification of interests — i.e., the functional unities supposed on general observational grounds — spring from two entirely different sources: (*a*) the study of vocational, occupational interests for purposes of applied psychology, and (*b*) a more general view of the human being in his total libidinal cathexes or interest investments. Data have been accumulated far more rapidly in the former field.

In the former field the suggested unities have been occupations and groups of occupations; in the latter they have ranged from the six "types" of Spranger and the Allport-Vernon questionnaire to the fifteen sections and five aspects [1] of the present writer's objective tests (*46*).

Available research findings. A considerable group of researches is now available showing the relation of interest measurements to other variables — e.g., to scholastic and occupational success, training, etc. (*245*). But there are still relatively few serious inquiries into the soundness of the unitary interest scales employed as the pillars for this bridging of fields.

The difficulties of getting a few clearly established findings from a survey of this scant and uneven material are increased by the diversity of the measurement foundations. Several of the "interest" measures are partly attitude measures. Some are partly subjective, partly objective. It is important to note in this connection that though Strong's Interest Blank, on which a good portion of the following findings are founded, is superficially a questionnaire measurement, it is actually essentially an objective measurement. For the responses, as is well known, are not treated at their face value. Instead, the measures have been established simply by recording what responses a person in a given occupation actually makes (without regard to their superficial, cognitive meaning).

---

[1] These divisions are as follows:

I. Direct activities with emotion in action
1. Travel
2. Sport
3. Commercial

II. Detached and unemotional interests
4. Mechanical
5. Scientific
6. Things of the mind

III. Interest with projected emotion (aesthetic, religious)
7. Rural, naturalistic
8. Religious
9. Literary
10. Artistic and musical
11. Decorative
12. Sensual pleasures
13. Sex

IV. Sexual and sensual

V. Social, human, home attachments
14. Social
15. Home

However, because of the limited data it was not deemed desirable, in getting a view of the situation as a whole, formally to separate these varieties of data. Nor has it seemed desirable to separate cluster and factor data, as in preceding chapters. For in this field factors are seldom chosen to be orthogonal and are commonly directed by clusters. In the final summary we have listed the few well-established factors and indicated the possible development of further factors out of these by "clusters or sub-factors" — i.e., cross groupings within the factors.

As throughout the book, the discovered "phenomenal" clusters and factors are first listed, in this section, with serial numbers attached, and these serial numbers are used for reference in grouping them in the deduced "minimum" list of necessary factors set out in the following section.

Thurstone (259) carried out a multiple-factor analysis, rotating axes, of eighteen Strong vocations (derived from the Interest Blank) with 287 male students. He arrived at four factors.

(1) 1. Scientific interests.
(2) 2. Language interests.
(3) 3. Business interests.
(4) 4. Interest in people.

He found that there were appreciable specific occupational interest factors left over.

Gundlach and Gerum (106) studied fifteen Strong occupations. Members of a varied committee of judges first classified the occupations on *a priori* grounds, and arrived at the following divisions: Technical occupations (Bookkeeping to Dentistry), Intellectual (Mathematics and Science), Creative (Artistic, Musical), Physical Skills (Games and Recreations), and Social. Although there was marked consensus of opinions, the groupings were later found to bear little relation to the observed correlations. From a relatively brief study of these correlations the present writer finds the following clusters:

(5) 1. *"Practical Business Activity."* Journalist, Advertiser, Real Estate (and zero or negative, Teacher, Minister).
(6) 2. *"Scientific."* Engineer, Architect, Doctor, Chemist, and less clearly, Psychologist.

(7) 3. *"Spiritual Guidance."* Teacher, Psychologist, Minister.

(8) 4. *"Concrete Transactions."* Purchasing Agent, Architect, Engineer (negative, Minister, Life Insurance).

(9) 5. *"Clerical."* Life Insurance, Real Estate (negative, Chemist and Psychologist).

(10) 6. *"Independence."* Lawyer, Journalist, Doctor.

(11) 7. *Non-aesthetic interests.* Lawyer, Journalist, Certified Public Accountant.

(12) 8. *Personal-Social.* Personnel Man, Teacher.

(13) 9. *Precision interest.* Architect, Public Accountant.

Abernethy (1) gave 44 questions testing either interest in people or interest in thought and things of the mind to 400 adults, students, and older people. Social interests had a very low negative correlation with thought interests among the students; but among adults the supposed "alternative" interests were actually quite independent.

Carter, Pyles, and Bretnall (36) studied the vocational interests of 133 high school boys (12–19 years old), using the Strong Interest Blank. The correlations among 18 of the 24 variables which were the same as in Thurstone's study agreed with the latter study to the extent of 0.77. They obtained four factors, and these factors also correlated highly in their saturations with those of Thurstone (259) — i.e., they were easily mutually identified. This agreement of child and adult results is of considerable interest. The factors also agreed on an eighteen-item and a twenty-four-item matrix analysis. Specific factors were found to be more important with older subjects and of very little importance in regard to the interest of children. Four scales — namely, Minister; Y.M.C.A. Secretary; Schoolman; and Personnel Manager — differ in their intercorrelations for children and adults. These are the items which Strong found to correlate most highly with interest maturity.[1]

The final factors are:

(14) 1. Interest in people.

(15) 2. Interest in science.

(16) 3. Interest in language.

(17) 4. (Possibly) Aversion to business and intellectual interests (Farmer, Artist).

---

[1] This correlation with age suggests marking these off as an interest-maturity factor, No. 31 on our list.

The fourth factor in this study was not so consistent, nor did it stand out with such significant loadings, as Thurstone's fourth factor, with adults. On the other hand, "Interest in people" was more important.

Lurie (*163*) studied Spranger's value types by the method of factor analysis, using 144 items, 24 for each of the six interest-value measurements, on 203 male and female students of eighteen and nineteen years of age. He obtained seven factors which he rotated, when necessary to oblique angles with one another, to give factors with maximum high loadings and maximum zero loadings — i.e., passing centrally through clusters. Four of these covered most of the ground dealt with by Spranger's six categories, three of which proved difficult to distinguish empirically. The factors were:

(18) 1. Social interests and altruism (corresponding to Gladstone's "Interest in people").

(19) 2. "Philistine," go-getting, utilitarian (economic, political, and negative aesthetic).

(20) 3. Theoretical, corresponding to Thurstone's "Interest in science" and Whisler's "Criticalness and interest in the truth."

(21) 4. Religious interests, more for doctrine and practice than mystical unity with the cosmos.

Lurie points out that most researches have found a high correlation of Spranger economic and political interests and a negative one of these with aesthetic interests, so that the wide factor (18) seems well justified.

This research includes in addition to true interest items a number concerned with beliefs, opinions, and ideals — i.e., with the category of attitudes. The remaining factors are mainly concerned with these; they are often oblique to them and contribute relatively little to the variance. They are:

(22) 5. Open-mindedness. (Possibly radicalism-conservatism or church-anti-church.)

(23) 6. Practicability. Positive in some economic, political, and social scores, negative in some aesthetic and religious.

(24) 7. Conventional or spectatorial aestheticism, loading aesthetic interests but not aesthetic ideals and somewhat negative to ideals generally. Lurie considers it a "social pressure" factor.

Thorndike (*257*) studied the likes and dislikes of 116 college graduates for a miscellany of interests, 16 in number, covering such things as interest in reading fiction, in games, music, occupation, politics, travel — i.e., corresponding roughly to the Cattell list (*46*) above. When "general liking for everything" was partialed out, the inter-correlations were all low. The following "liking" clusters were observed:

(25) 1. Social intercourse, including talking.

(26) 2. Utility.

(27) 3. The world of ideas.

(28) 4. Music.

(29) 5. Outdoor sport.

The "general factor" partialed out was not actually a general liking but might be called

(30) 6. Dislike of sedentary games and of one's job.

As might be expected, the most extensive and soundly based data on the intercorrelation of occupational interests is that gathered by the author of the vocational interest blank himself. Strong (*245*) intercorrelated 38 occupations on a population of 285 college seniors.

Classifying first according to clusters (in each of which the members must have a mean correlation of 0.60 with others), he arrived at the following "functional unities":

(32) 1. Artist, Psychologist, Architect, Physician, Dentist.

(33) 2. "Science." Mathematician, Physicist, Engineer, Chemist.

(34) 3. Production Manager.

(35) 4. Aviator, Farmer, Carpenter, Math-Physical Science Teacher, Printer, Policeman, Forest Service.

(36) 5. "Handling People for Their Presumed Good." Y.M.C.A. Secretary, Y.M.C.A. Physical Director, Personnel Manager, School Superintendent, Minister, Social Science Teacher.

(37) 6. Musician.

(38) 7. Certified Public Accountant.

(39) 8. "Office Activities." Purchasing Agent, Office Worker, Accountant, Banker.

(40) 9. "Selling." Real Estate Salesman, Life Insurance Sales-man, Sales Manager.

(41) 10. "Language." Lawyer, Author-Journalist, Advertising Man.

(42) 11. President of Manufacturing Concern.

These eleven clusters can have far more weight put upon them than the nine tentatively suggested above by the present writer, both by reason of data and care of analysis. It is noticeable, however, that in most instances there is agreement, as far as the occupation lists are common.

Strong (*245*) carried out four factor analyses, each on an occupation list increased by two or three more items. He arrived at five factors, instead of four as found by Thurstone, but two of the five were not well marked. The agreement of the different analyses (correlation of factor loadings) was good on most factors. After rotation, they appear as follows. IV fits badly with the Thurstone set.

(43) Factor 1. "Science."

(44) Factor 2. Unnamed (items given in IV below).

(45) Factor 3. "Things *v.* People" or "Language."

(46) Factor 4. "Working with People for Their Presumed Good."

High	Low
Minister	President
Social Science Teacher	Purchasing Agent
School Superintendent	Production Manager
Musician	Engineer
Y M.C.A. Secretary	

(47) Factor 5. Unnamed.

High	Low
Personnel	Mathematician
Sales Manager	

Ferguson, Humphrey, and Strong (*86*) tested 93 male students on both the Vocational Interest Blank (eight items only) and the Allport-Vernon values. They obtained five factors, as follows:

(48) 1. Thurstone "language" factor, with high aesthetic, high theoretical, and low economic values.

(49) 2. Thurstone "people" factor.

(50) 3. Thurstone "science" factor, with high theoretical and low political values.

(51) 4. No Thurstone factor. High religious, high social, and low aesthetic.

(52) 5. No Thurstone factor. High political, low economic values.

Sarbin and Bordin (*226*) investigated the Strong occupational clusters listed above and found the following had outstanding associations on the Allport-Vernon measures:

(53) Group I, High theoretical and aesthetic, low economic and political.

(54) Group II, High theoretical, low political.
(55) Group V, High religious.
(56) Group IX, Low theoretical.

Brogden (*20 a*). Intercorrelation of 60 items on the Allport-Vernon Interest Values Test with large adult population.

(57) Aesthetic interests (excluding fine arts) *v.*
(58) Fine arts, culture-for-its-own-sake *v.* Practical living concerns
(59) Spiritual, cultural, ideal, dramatic values (Quixotism) *v.* Matter-of-fact humanitarianism
(60) Moral "churchgoing" religion *v.* Untied emotional interests
(61) Enlightenment, education *v.* Approval of interests, ignorant, aggressive solutions
(62) Charitable, humanitarian, socialistic service *v.* Individual business enterprise
(63) Science *v.* (arts, business, athletics, politics)
(64) Liberalism, rationalism, serious thinking *v.*
(65) Analytical, theoretical, curiosity (emphasis on psychology) *v.*
(66) Aggressive, hard-boiled, materialistic, adhering to "rugged individualism" *v.*
(67) Residual — possibly an abstract, theoretical interest *v.*

Among the studies on the fringe of this area which need to be recorded are the correlations with items of the last section, notably the finding by Roberts and Flemming of Bernreuter "Dominance" significantly related to Religious Interest values and that of Sisson and Sisson (*245*) showing that higher aesthetic interest values go with higher Bernreuter introversion. Also the role of sex differences in interest must be noted, as a possible general factor syndrome. Finch and Odoroff (*87*) and Carter (*36*) have listed such differences on the Strong Blank and shown that they are quite well developed before the age of fourteen. In general, however, they do not reach the magnitude of a new factor. Indeed, the masculinity-femininity correlates − .83 with III below as the interest maturity correlates − .81 with II, and intelligence .90 with III, so that these do not require separate listing.

5. ORGANIZATION OF PRINCIPAL SOURCE TRAITS AMONG INTERESTS AND VALUES

List of interest factors from combined researches defined. The findings of vocational interest analysis are relatively definite and well-confirmed. The chief difficulty lies in bridging from these to the analyses, themselves scattered and patchy, on the broader field of life interests generally. Since there is no reason to believe that the social and theoretical factors of the Allport-Vernon and similar studies are any different from those of the vocational interest studies, we have brought them into the same field of reference. After combining wherever possible, the less well-defined or established factors, such as occur when one research has not included the data that have been the grist of another, are listed separately.

It seems to the writer that in this field the choice of titles for factors has not been particularly illuminating.[1] Most are best defined, in fact, as bipolar factors, for it remains true that they are as well defined by their negative as their positive loadings. This we must expect, for by the dynamic nature of interest, the positive and negative loadings of a factor properly represent alternative and opposing expressions.

TABLE 20

Descriptive List of Interest Factors

QI. Ia. Sociable-Activity v. Detached Creative Interests. Also called "social interests," "interests in people," "altruism," "social intercourse, variety, and travel." Factors or clusters (4), (12), (14), (18), (25), (36), (47), (49), and perhaps (56) and (64).

Defined by: Among Strong's occupational interests —

High	Low
Vacuum-cleaner Salesman	Artist [2]
Office Clerk	Doctor
Y.M.C.A. Secretary	Physicist
Personnel Worker	Mathematician
School Teacher	Journalist
School Superintendent	Architect

[1] Dissatisfaction with titles is fairly widespread. Strong (*Vocational Interests of Men and Women*, 1943, page 316) observes: "The names given by Thurstone to his four factors . . . do not fit so well . . . the (extended) factors extracted in later analyses based on a larger number of occupations."

[2] The items at the top of these lists are in general the more saturated, respectively, with the positive and negative factor loadings.

TABLE 20 — *Continued*

Among Lurie's items —

Liking to teach labor relations.

Believes science should increase sum total human happiness.

Likes the magazine *Social Forces*.

Would like son at college to engage in social and fraternal activities.

Would spend fortune in anonymous charitable gifts.

Would like most a series of lectures on "A life of service."

And others.

Among Thorndike's items —

Interest in politics.

Interest in welfare work.

Interest in talking with old friends.

Interest in making new acquaintances.

Interest in travel and sightseeing.

QI. Ib. Guiding People for Their Own Presumed Good v. Being Coldly Objective, is a new sub-factor, cluster, or reorientation of axis in this region suggested by (12), (36), (42), (46) and involved in —

High	Low
Y.M.C.A. Secretary	Purchasing Agent
Personnel Worker or Personnel Manager	President of Manufacturing Concern
Social Science Teacher	Engineer
Y.M.C.A. Physical Director	Production Manager
Musician	

IIa. Thoughtful Interest in Understanding Nature. Also called "interest in science," "theoretical interests," "criticalness and interest in the truth." Factors (1), (5), (60), (9), (15), (20), (32), (33), (43), and perhaps (65).

Defined by: Among Strong's occupations —

High	Low
Architect	Office Manager*
Physician*	Banker*
Artist*	Sales Manager*
Physicist*	Accountant*
Dentist*	Life Insurance Salesman
Chemist	Real Estate Salesman

* Exclusive to Strong's analysis.

TABLE 20 -- *Continued*

High	Low
Psychologist	Advertiser
Engineer	Journalist
Farmer	Lawyer
Schoolman	

Among Lurie's items —

Would prefer (among various subjects) to teach algebra.

In *Time* magazine would turn to section on science.

Would read magazine *Scientific American*.

Would like son at college to join debating society.

If moneyed man, would endow scientific laboratory.

Would like lecture on postulates of scientific method.

Interested in life of Galileo, Aristotle.

Would like a mate able to offer intellectual companionship.

In Allport-Vernon data —

(50) and (54) by high theoretical and low political values.

Five less well-marked sub-factors are suggested by clustering or alternative factor orientations encountered here, as follows:

QI. IIb. Altruism and Theoretical Interests.

(5) High in Teacher and Minister, low in Advertiser, Journalist, and Real Estate Agent.

IIc. Concrete Scientific Interests.

(6) High in Engineer, Architect, Chemist.   Perhaps also (63).

IId. Exploratory Scientific Interests.

(9) High in Chemist, Psychologist; low in Insurance Agent, Real Estate.

IIe. "Science as an Art" Interest.

(32) High in Artist, Psychologist, Architect, and Physician.

IIf. Precision (Mechanical?) Scientific Interests.

(33) Mathematician, Physicist, Engineer, Chemist.   Perhaps also (67).

QI. IIIa. Verbal Persuasion vs. Practical Control of Materials. Also called "interest in language" or "things *vs.* people." Factors and clusters (2), (7), (8), (16), (35), (41), (45), (48), and perhaps (58).

Defined by: Among Strong's occupations —

High	Low
Advertising Man*	Carpenter*
Psychologist	Purchasing Agent

* The starred items are exclusively in Strong's analyses.

TABLE 20 — *Continued*

High	Low
Lawyer*	Math.-Science Teacher*
Minister	Engineer
Journalist*	Policeman*
School Superintendent	Real Estate Salesman
Life Insurance Salesman*	Chemist*
School Teacher	Aviator
	Printer*
	Forest Service
	Accountant*
	Farmer

Among Allport-Vernon data —

(48) and (53) by high aesthetic and theoretical and low economic (and political, less definitely) values.

Three strong sub-factors or alternative orientations are suggested by the clusters.

IIIb. Guidance (also called "humanitarian"). (7), (34), (46). This has some resemblance to II*b*.

High in Teacher, Psychologist, Minister, Y.M.C.A. Secretary; low in Production Manager.

IIIc. Interest in Materials.

(8) High in Purchasing Agent, Architect, Engineer.

IIId. Verbal Skills. Also called "competitive" interests. (41). Present in the starred variables above, principally —

Advertising Man, Lawyer, Author-Journalist.

QI. IVa. Philistine Go-getting v. Aesthetic Interests. Also called "business interests," "Philistine, go-getting," "utilitarian," "economic-political non-aesthetic," "accounting," "orderly-systematic." Factors (3), (11), (17), (19), (44), and perhaps (57).

Defined by: Among Strong's occupations —

High	Low
Certified Public Accountant	Farmer
Lawyer	Artist
School Superintendent	
Purchasing Agent	
Life Insurance Salesman	
Accountant	

TABLE 20 — *Continued*

Among Lurie's data by —

Would like to teach (*a*) Advertising, (*b*) Recent Political Theory but *not* (*c*) Modern Poetry.

In *Time* magazine would turn to (*a*) "Business and Finance" and (*b*) "National Affairs" but *not* (*c*) "Modern Poetry."

Would read magazine *National Business* but not *Saturday Review of Literature.*

Would like son at college to (*a*) take part-time job (unneeded) or run for campus office, but *not* join poetry society and write.

If moneyed man, would invest in industry or use in campaign as a political candidate but *not* to endow a symphony orchestra.

Would attend lectures on "Budgeting a Reduced Income" or "Dictators and Their Exercise of Power," but *not* on "Architecture in Relation to the Other Arts."

Is attracted by career of diplomat and congressman.

Would above all like to be considered ambitious, a leader, and aggressive.

Relatively uncertain sub-factors or clusters suggested:

IVb. Interest in Sharp Practices. (11). High in Lawyer, Journalist, Certified Public Accountant.

IVc. Business Accountancy. (38). High in Certified Public Accountant.

IVd. Called *"Office Activities."* (39). High in Office Worker, Purchasing Agent, Accountant, Banker.

IVe. Musical Interest. Constituted by (Thorndike) by interest in making music and in listening to music (28) and Strong's (37).

QI. V. Socialized Religion v. Irreligious Aesthetic Interests. Also called "religious interests." Factor (21) and probably (51), (55), and (59).

Defined by: Among Lurie's data —

Would like to teach "Comparative Religion" and to read magazine sections on Religion.

Is attracted to careers of missionary and minister.

Would encourage child to seek career in theology.

Would most like to be considered reverent, high-minded, and an idealist.

If moneyed, would donate to a church.

In magazine would turn to article on "The New Paganism."

In Allport-Vernon data —

(51) by high religious, high social, and low aesthetic values.

TABLE 20 — *Continued*

QI. VIa. Practical Citizenship. Also called "utility," "practicality." Factors (23), (26), and perhaps (60).

Defined by: Among Thorndike's items —

(26) Interest in reading non-fiction.
Interest in reading fiction.
Interest in one's regular job.
Interest in politics.
Interest in welfare work.

VIb. Socialized Philistinism. Perhaps relatively distinct from VI*a*. Factor (23) and perhaps (66).

Defined by: Among Lurie's data —

(Some economic, political, and social items as follows:)

Believes scientific research should increase wealth.

Believes education should teach people to be busy and productive.

Believes governments exist to foster industrial production.

Believes a man can best spend his leisure making extra money.

Admires most in history Croesus, Robert Fulton, and Henry Ford.

VI*b* is known to have appreciable correlation with I and IV, while VI*a* appears likely to have correlation with them. Factor (52), High political and low economic values, on the Allport-Vernon Scale perhaps distinguished these two aspects of VI, as a factor at right angles to it.

QI. VII. Dilettantism. Also called "conventional or spectatorial aestheticism."

Defined by: Among Lurie's data —

Factor (24).

Would like to teach Modern Poetry, to read about Art and the *Saturday Review of Literature*.

Would like son at college to join poetry society and write.

If moneyed, would endow symphony orchestra.

Would not be attracted by career of musician or portrait painter.

Would not encourage child to career of literature or of social worker.

Does not particularly want to be considered altruistic, loyal or likable, a connoisseur, talented, or artistic.

This factor has appreciable correlation with I, II, IV, and VI.

QI. VIII. Intellect, Literature, Drama Recreations. Also called "interest in world of ideas and fancy."

Defined by: Among Thorndike's data —

TABLE 20 — *Continued*

(27) Interest in reading non-fiction.
Interest in reading fiction.
Interest in theaters and movies.

This could be the obverse of IV, but seems also related to II. At present is best left as independent cluster. Note resemblance to (59).

QI. IX. Interest in Sports. Defined by Thorndike's Cluster (29), Outdoor Sports.

The remaining interest factors are relatively ill-defined and speculative.

QI. X. Interest in Independent ("Free Lance") Career. Defined by cluster (10): Strong's vocational group, Lawyer, Journalist, Doctor.

QI. XI. Interest in Precision Activities (?). Cluster (13): Occupations of Architect and Public Accountant.

QI. XII. Interest in Action and Variety. Cluster (30): Dislike of sedentary games and of one's job, but above average rating for enjoyment of everything else.

QI. XIII. Social Interest Maturity. Defined by: interest in the Strong occupation items in cluster (31).

Minister
Y.M.C.A. Secretary
Schoolman
Personnel Manager

QI. XIV. "Selling." Strong's cluster (40), which seems to fall between Language III and Business Interests IV.
Defined by:

Pattern of:

Real Estate Salesman
Life Insurance Salesman
Sales Manager

Largely because the researches on interest have been dominated by two particular published tests, each having a limited view of the total field of human interest, the definition of factors among interests is less satisfactory than in any other field. The above matchings are to be considered decidedly tentative — suggestions for the principal factors to be studied by any comprehensive future research rather than a statement of proved entities. When in doubt, we have split factors instead of pooling, so that it is likely that research will match many factors left separate above. The probable relations, possibly identities, among factors are indicated by their bearing the same number and by cross references on resemblance. The present writer is inclined to believe that the Brogden research, yielding eleven factors, is the most likely statement of the number of important factors in this field.

Perspective in regard to these factors is likely to be reached, however, only when researchers (1) use true measures of interest (45) instead of merely asking subjects what they are interested in, and (2) take a naturalistic survey of existing human interests instead of beginning with *a priori* or very limited categories (e.g., occupations). For example, true measures would almost certainly yield immediately a general factor of "total interest" which the present methods are incapable of revealing. Markedly schizoid or depressive patients, and to some extent all persons mentally or physically ill, show a definite narrowing of total interest or libido investment. There is every reason to believe that variations in total interest exist through the whole range of normal personality also. Consequently, even after intelligence has been eliminated as a source of variation, a single general factor in interests would be expected. Apart from this, because of the individuality of dynamic connections, we should expect specific rather than group factors to account for the major part of the variance in interest measurements.

6. CATALOGUE OF DATA ON ATTITUDE FACTORS

The nature of attitude measurements. Attitudes are distinguished from interests in that they are defined not only by the object and the strength of the attitude, but also by the *direction*, in dynamic, feeling (i.e., orectic) terms. Some confusion is bound to arise in this field at the moment because these characteristics of an attitude have not been taken into account in many current attitude scales. The *strength* of an attitude — i.e., the amount of interest or concern behind it — is strictly an interest measure. The *direction* or *dynamic quality* is a measure of orientation of a vector. Most existing attitude tests measure only the orientation through the 180° plane between approval and disapproval, but there are many other planes which are important for prediction; e.g., curiosity-incuriosity, acquisitiveness-lack of acquisitiveness. In fact, as the discussion of Chapter 7, Section 7, shows, the attitudes, like all metanergs, are most simply resolved into the dimensions of ergs. The principal point to bear in mind in retaining clarity here is that what is referred to as the "strength" of an attitude on many published attitude scales is actually a statement of vector *direction*.

There is naturally a little overlap between the data of this and other sections, but in the main it is confined to true attitude rather than mere interest measures and to specialized attitudes rather than personality traits, which *could* be called "generalized attitudes" and so confused with true attitude measurements. Most of the data concern social attitudes, and, as anthropologists and sociologists are comparatively unaware of the value which the psychologists' development of factor-analytic techniques would have for their social analyses, the data available from sociological studies are very meager, though attitude and opinion studies are themselves multitudinous. Indeed, there are only three well-confirmed factors to report, yet in the nature of things there is no reason why these social mold traits should not be very numerous.

The available research findings. *Lentz* (*160*) (*161*) tested 579 college students on 190 questionnaire items, divided among the following fields: Education, Religion, Government, Sex, Non-Social Matters, and General Matters, and each having what might be considered a more and a less conservative possible response, as follows:

(1) Voters should disregard the party and vote for the man.
   Women in general are not as intelligent as men.

There is no probability that the artificial production of milk substitute will do away with the cow.

Much more energy should be expended in conserving what mankind does know than in discovering what it does not know.

The intercorrelations of the five sections, scored for conservatism, were all positive, the median attenuation-corrected coefficient being .73. Lentz considers that this confirms Murphy's earlier report of a "general conservatism" trait, extending through liberalism-conservatism in both intranational and international affairs.

The same worker set out to explore the wider limits of the trait (*161*). Using 409 sixteen- to forty-three-year-old subjects (median 22), more widely scattered than previous groups educationally and geographically, he applied 3000 test items, using thirteen different techniques — e.g., preference, joke rating, picture rating, opinionnaire, etc. Taking the highest and the lowest quartile groups in score on the above questionnaire conservatism, he found the further associations listed below in the combined summary (2).

Dexter (*74*) separated 267 women students on the Lentz questionnaire into conservative and radical groups. She found the radicals significantly:

Cluster (3) 1. More intelligent.
2. Better informed.
3. Slower in measured speed of movement and of decision.
4. More introvert, more self-sufficient, more dominant, and more given to feelings of inferiority on the Bernreuter categories.
5. Less frequently from small towns.
6. Not different in regard to size of family, income, emotional stability, or intensity.

Carlson (*31*) tested 215 undergraduates with Thurstone's attitude scales to Prohibition, Pacifism, God, Communism, and Birth Control. The following cluster was obtained:

Cluster (4) Agnostic attitude to religion.
Pacifist inclinations.
Pro-Communist views.
Criticism of Prohibition.

He notes that his results confirm the earlier indications of Vetter, Folsom, and George, in showing a general trait of conservatism-radicalism and in showing it to be positively correlated to intelligence.

He found that a single general factor, however, was not enough to account for the correlations and finally analyzed the results in three factors, as follows:

	(5) "Intelligence"	(6) "Radical-Conservative"	(7) "Religious"
Intelligence	.59		
Pro-Communist Attitude	.53	.53	
Conventional Religious Belief	− .29	− .42	.35
Pro-Pacifism Attitude	.62	.10	− .06
Pro-Birth Control	.33	.15	− .34
Pro-Prohibition	.06	− .56	.03

The Thurstones (*261*) made a wider study on similar material, using eleven attitude scales on 380 students. Two factors were found sufficient to account for the correlations, as follows:

(8) Radicalism

   High in belief in
      Evolution
      Easier Divorce
      Communism
      Birth Control
      Intelligence

   Low in belief in
      Church and God
      Sunday Observance

(9) Nationalism-Internationalism

   High in
      Patriotism
      Opposition to Pacifism

   Low in
      Communism

Eysenck (*82*). Tests of artistic preference and of radicalism-conservatism.

Factor (10). Radicalism, non-academic art, and extraversion.

Eysenck (*83 b*). 694 adult-members of a variety of social and political societies measured on 32 opinion statements, on a six-point scale on each. Unrotated factors, as follows:

Factor (11). Radicalism *vs.* Conservatism.

Factor (12). Rational-scientific *vs.* Sentimental, emotional.

Factor (13). Freedom from interference *vs.* Fondness of coercion.

Factor (14). Residual factor.

Ferguson (*84*) (*85*). 185 college students, ten attitude scales, later confirmed on 178 students elsewhere.

Factor (15).   Religionism.
Factor (16).   Humanitarianism.
Factor (16 *a*).   A supposed residual.
Cason (37), *Harsh* (*110 a*).   507 (reduced 341) questions on common annoyances; population 200.
Factor (17).   Annoyance over appearance of others.
Factor (18).   Annoyance over violation of mores or morals.
Factor (19).   Annoyance over claims to superiority in others.
Factor (20).   Annoyance over unintentionally disagreeable acts.
Factor (21).   Annoyance from personal sensitivity.
Here also must be listed T (23) from the data of the next chapter, as:
Factor (22).   Radicalism.
Carter, H. D., Conrad, H. S., and Jones, M. C. (35).   100 school children.   Wide variety of "annoyance" in everyday-life items.
Factor (23).   General sensitivity to annoyance.
Factor (24).   Annoyance mainly at untidiness.
Factor (25).   Personal annoyances.

7. ORGANIZATION OF PRINCIPAL SOURCE TRAITS AMONG ATTITUDES

List of factors in attitudes.   As Eysenck (*83 b*) has pointed out, some dubious procedures have been followed identifying the factors in this field; e.g., finding simple structure with insufficient population of variables, naming a factor "religion" when the loading on religion is actually less than in the "conservation" factor, counting intelligence as a general factor in one study but ignoring it in another.   There is almost as much lack of clarity as in the realm of interests, and partly because of the same restriction of field of observation; but in this case it can be resolved with more confidence and completeness.

The present writer would suggest that again part of the confusion arises from attempts to name as "attitude factors," in terms of too specific social attitudes, factors among attitudes which are probably the same basic personality factors as were encountered in the last chapter.   There is no reason why these broad factors should align directly with social and political prejudices [1] and attitudes. From the relatively small contribution which the discovered factors make to the variance (from 3 to 31 per cent) one can conclude that several more appreciable factors remain to be found when the area of attitude study is widened, which would make them correspond better in number with the known personality factors.

TABLE 21

Q.4. Ia. Radicalism vs. Conservatism (About 30 per cent of variance). Evidenced by 1, 2, 3, 4, 5, 8, 10, 11, 15 rotated, and 22. It is defined by the following approximate order of diminishing saturation:

R. favorable to:

Belief in evolution
Belief in communism or economic reform
Belief in pacifism or international control of power
Loadings .075 to 0.4 in birth control
Loadings 0.75 to 0.4 in eugenics
(Also: Non-academic art, sexual freedom, humane (less retributive— more reformative) treatment of criminals, greater equality of the sexes)

C. favorable to:

Regard for the church and its orthodox position
Belief in God conceived as a personal being
Belief in Sunday observance
Belief in more censorship of behavior generally
Belief in one's country "right or wrong"
(Also: Belief in prohibition of alcohol)

The T factor (22) from the next chapter includes

Attitude favorable to the Constitution	.71
Attitude favorable to Communism	.63
Time required for judgment (Thermal lag report)	.58

Conservatives are:

More opposed to change
More favorable to convention, tradition, routine — e.g., church attendance, anti-feminism
Less intelligent
Less well-informed

---

[1] The reader will note that throughout this study we have not attempted to distinguish those attitudes which are prejudices — e.g., the so-called "religious, racial, food, and political prejudices" — from attitudes in general. No scientist as such can say whether the value judgment in an attitude is justified or unjustified; so that the use of the term "prejudice" in the social sciences implies that science is being employed for propaganda.

TABLE 21 — *Continued*

Quicker in measured speed of movement and decision (See also T (22) above)

More antagonistic to science, especially its future activities

More prudish on sex

More inclined to moralize

More timid

More inclined to smooth sailing in personal and social contacts — more opposed to argument

Less introvert, less self-sufficient, less dominant, and less given to inferiority feelings as measured by four Bernreuter sections

Less tolerant and sympathetic of the underdog

More capitalistic

More athletic in interests

More inclined to take their adventures vicariously

Less aesthetic

More frequently from small towns

Lentz (161) supplies a differentiating list of admired (and known) personages for radicals and conservatives, revealing, e.g., that R's admire significantly more poets and explorers, C's more military leaders and perhaps athletes.

QA. Ib. Fundamentalist Religious Beliefs. Evidenced by 6 and 15. This factor is listed here because in some rotations it is claimed to be independent of Radicalism-Conservatism. As is implied by labeling it *Ib*, however, the present writer is inclined to agree with Eysenck that it is largely the same as I*a*.

> Belief in orthodox, authoritarian religion
> Opposition to birth control

If it is distinguishable from I*a*, it is so by its negligible loadings in Prohibition and Pacifism and small loadings on Communism.

QA. II. Hard-headed, Rational vs. Sentimental, Emotional. (About 11 per cent of variance.) (After title suggested by Eysenck.) Evidenced by 9, 12, and 16. Defined by high loadings roughly in the following order:

R. favorable to:	S. favorable to:
Resort to war; dependence on military power of one's own country	More humane, less retributive treatment of criminals
Right of the individual to abortion	Abstemiousness
Maintenance of capital punishment	Vegetarianism
Socialism (less: communism)	Non-smoking

TABLE 21 — *Continued*

R. favorable to:

Sexual freedom
Utilitarian ethics
Sterilization of the unfit
Patriotism which puts one's country
   first
Rationalism

S. favorable to:

Preservation of landscape
Anti-vaccination
Humaneness to animals
International language

QA. III. Personal liberty vs. Coercion. (About 6 per cent of variance.)
Evidenced by 13.

P. favorable to:

Sexual freedom
Freedom of speech
Birth control
Nudism
Divorce reform

C. favorable to:

Abstemiousness
Communism
Non-smoking
Prohibition of vivisection

QA. IV. Violence vs. Gradualness. Evidenced by (16*a* rotated), possibly
(14).

V. favorable to:

War
Communism
Capital punishment

G. favorable to:

Birth control
Humane treatment of criminals

The last two factors are poorly defined compared with I and II. It is
probable that intelligence is a general factor among attitudes, but although
it loads Factor I considerably there is doubt as to whether it can be considered (experimental error apart) as identical with I.

Because they are not yet confirmed or on a sufficiently wide basis,
the eight annoyance factors (17), (18), (19), (20), (21), (23), (24),
and (25) are not set out in the Roman numeral system here.

8. POSSIBLE RELATIONSHIPS OF FACTORS FROM DIVERSE
    QUESTIONNAIRE FIELDS

The possibilities of cross identification. Our exploration
has revealed some 22 factors in the realm of adjustment and
neurotic inventory data; 14 major factors and clusters, with
certain sub-clusters, in the realm of interests or values; and
possibly 5 factors (apart from the "annoyance" factors)
among attitude measurements.

Any attempts to bridge these fields, in the attempt to discover identities and reduce the given 40 factors to a smaller number, are bound to be speculative, especially since it would be our aim in this chapter and at this stage to put together factors only *by the intrinsic nature of the questionnaire data* and without aid by the more comprehensively founded factors known from objective ratings and measurements. However, the attempt is worth making, for the items which have to be compared show some resemblances if not identities, and occasionally, as in Whisler's research (*276*), we have factors established simultaneously in data from all fields, by reason of the deliberately miscellaneous character of the original item list.

Suggested identities. Careful scanning of the actual item loadings, the patterns, the known independencies and associations of factors, will suggest the following possible mergings of factors from the three fields. Naturally these identifications cannot be considered as established, but they are strongly indicated and suggestive for immediate further research. In two or three instances only is the similarity so marked that we seem justified in proceeding later on the assumption of identity.

In the list below the equivalent factors are placed on the same level. Where a factor on one side resembles two on the other side these are placed in contiguity, so that the fact that this item has a choice of alternative matchings will not escape notice. Occasionally, as notably in the radical-conservative factor among attitudes, one factor looks as if it might be psychologically equivalent to a composite of factors. This, of course, is psychologically quite conceivable. Radicalism-conservatism may be the result of a temperament factor in combination with an interest factor and an intellectual factor.

The mathematical theory also permits. In one medium we may tend to choose variables, because of the greater "spacing" in that field, which yield as a first-order factor what would only be found as a second-order factor from among several factors in another. Alternatively viewed, we can say that we have omitted from the factorization in the first field those variables which, in the second, create communality for additional factors.

On the other hand, it would also seem possible that the dimensions within the item field chosen for attitudes will not be so numerous as those among interests or personality traits, so that one factor in the attitude field will split up into several only when the personality items are added. The relative "breadth" of the factors isolated by the alternative choices of items — neurotic responses, occupations, or attitude scales — would seem, from the comparisons below, to be sometimes greater in one, sometimes in another, but essentially of the same "order" in all. The occupation interest groupings are perhaps somewhat narrower than others and the attitude groupings, at least in the one outstanding instance, wider.

TABLE 22

EQUATING OF FACTORS FROM DIVERSE QUESTIONNAIRE DATA

FACTORS IN PERSONAL ADJUSTMENT-NEUROTICISM ITEMS	FACTORS IN INTEREST AND VALUE ITEMS AND SCALES	FACTORS IN ATTITUDE SCALES
Q.P.	*Q.I.*	*Q.A.*
*I. Shyness	I. Sociable-Activity	
*VIII. Self-sufficiency vs. Gregariousness	III. Verbal Persuasion vs. Practical Control	
VII. Group Deference		
XXII. Rigid, lonely, power-seeking		Ia. Radicalism-Conservatism
*VI. Confident Self-assertion	IV. Philistine Go-getting	
XIX. Extravert Alertness	V. Socialized Religion	Ib. Conventional Religion

TABLE 22 — *Continued*

Factors in Personal Adjustment-Neuroticism Items	Factors in Interest and Value Items and Scales	Factors in Attitude Scales
Q.P.	*Q.I.*	*Q.A.*

X. Obsessional, Inflexible Will-character

Possibly:

V. Socialized Religion

Ib. Guidance of People for their own Presumed Good

VIa. Practical Citizenship

VIb. Socialized Philistinism

XI. Interest in Precision Activities

XX. Interest in Action —— IX. Sports Interest and/or

*XI. Relaxed Independence

XII. Interest in Action and Variety and/or

VII. Dilettantism

III. Liberty *vs.* Coercion

*XII. Variety-loving

*XVII. Liking Thinking —— IIa. Interest in Understanding Nature

XVIII. Intellectual Leadership

IIb. Altruism and Theoretical Interests and/or

X. Interest in Independent Career

II, IV, and V? Emotionality and Withdrawal

—VIII. Intellect, Literature, Drama Recreations

IX. Will-character —— XIII. Interest Maturity

Only the starred equivalences can be called identities with any degree of confidence, and in four of these, notably the first and the second, there seems to be some doubt as to whether the two factors on one side may not be somewhat differently combined in the two equivalent factors on the other side.

At this stage of research, therefore, with question marks so numerous, it is certainly not worth while to set out any full or final definition of the extended factors such as would be obtained by these combinations. Research is proceeding under the present writer to obtain by experiment the real matching in this field. The preceding speculative attempt reduces Q factors from about forty to thirty, but the surer path of large-scale factorization may well show them to be different outcroppings of a distinctly smaller list of nuclear factors.

Chapter Eleven

THE PRINCIPAL SOURCE TRAITS DISCOVERED
THROUGH OBJECTIVE TEST MEASUREMENTS

1. NATURE OF THE DATA AND PLAN OF PRESENTATION

The limitations of test data. The substratum of observations on which the trait unities now to be surveyed depend is distinguished in two ways: (1) The behavior is produced in artificial "test situations" instead of in the ordinary situations of life. (2) It depends on literal measurement instead of ratings. The first character is the more essential, for by time sampling and other devices the observations of behavior that remains socially *in situ* can also be given the character of objective measurement, though no such research happens yet to be available in factor-analytic studies.

At present, therefore, the founding of personality observations on the rock of actual measurement is somewhat dearly paid for by the ensuing limitation of observations to very restricted and sometimes quite unimportant manifestations of personality, such as are hardly likely to fall in the same universe as those considered in preceding chapters.

However, "miniature situations," time sampling, projection, dynamism (*58 a*), and other personality-testing techniques now being developed may make available, in another decade, such an array of objective data on more important aspects of personality as will permit a truly wide integration of the analyses of this chapter with those of preceding chapters.

Plan of presentation. As usual, the procedure will be first to list very briefly the researches included, the factors discovered being merely named and numbered for later reference. The factors will be listed in full only at the second stage, when they are set out in their presumed correct classification, with essentially identical factors brought together under one heading.

The present material, however, requires some slight modification of the cataloguing procedures followed in preceding chapters. In the first place, an enormous preponderance of the original researches are concerned with abilities, and these are not so important for personality study *per se* as to justify the actual researches being individually listed and numbered. Secondly, far more of the present researches, even in the true field of personality, are concentrated on the delimitation of a single factor. We have not listed in the preliminary catalogue all such one-factor researches. Instead, the truly exhaustive account of such factors has been postponed to the secondary, classification and integration stage of presentation. The initial catalogue, therefore, deals only with the more important and extensive researches, in personality as such.

The role of abilities in personality. In some psychological writings it has become almost customary to omit abilities when studying personality. They very rarely enter, for example, into psychoanalytic literature. Sometimes this omission seems to express the disgust of the psychologist at the extremely narrow, cut-and-dried conceptions of ability which have prevailed among those who have studied abilities most, namely the educational psychologists, who are seemingly unaware that they have mistaken the classroom for the world. Beyond the stereotyped and artificial motivation conditions of the classroom it is readily seen that abilities, instead of being the only "powers" to be measured, are indeed nothing but tools and specific habit skills variously ordered about at the behest of more fundamental personality traits.

Vocational guidance and selection are prone to deal with abilities and achievements as the only solid ingredients in the individual and the only indisputable coinage for the transaction of predictions of performance. They set out to perform simple sums with these alone — very much as a college dean's office does in the more mechanized colleges to see if certain numbers and varieties of credits add up to an "education."

When a good novelist describes a character with the greatest realism and insight, so that the individual's success in his career, his adjustment in marriage, and his whole destiny follow with inescapable necessity, he does not seem to find it necessary to tell us at the beginning the hero's performance on a standard arithmetic speed test or the percentile level of his attainment on the graduate record examination in biology. Neither does a man in ordinary conversation, when giving a thumbnail sketch of a personality to help a prospective employer, find himself, as a rule, mentioning more than the level of general intelligence and one or two outstanding aptitudes. These may occasionally be introduced, moreover, as sometimes happens when one speaks of musical and artistic aptitudes, more to indicate the general nature of temperament and personality than for their own sake.

However, it would be a mistake for the pendulum to swing from the pedantic excesses of educational psychometrists to the equally erroneous perspective of those psychotherapists and others who omit abilities from personality description and prediction. For this latter course can be charged with more serious faults than mere lack of catholicity and comprehensiveness. Abilities may be integral parts of more important personality traits. They may be the simplest and clearest manifestation through which some dynamic trait can be observed and measured. Although a few of the most important abilities — e.g., general intelligence — may be largely constitutional and purely cognitive traits, one must not be deceived by a name into forgetting that many tests classified in applied psychology as measures of cognitive abilities must also be measuring dynamic and temperamental traits. McDougall made a rather remarkable argument for even general intelligence being a dynamic "will" trait (*175*), and though we must reject this (for there is enough evidence that general ability, musical ability, and perhaps drawing ability and a few others are largely innate), there is ample indication that many skills are the outcome of persistent and sometimes unconscious and symbolic dynamic expressions. For example, one can readily point to clinical instances in which high mechanical aptitude has appeared as a masculine protest, arithmetical skill as an obsessional symptom, verbal ability as an oral erotic expression, or precocious reading skill as an escape from social maladjustment.

The dynamic determination which can sometimes be detected in apparently quite deep-seated "natural aptitudes" can usually be seen quite obviously at work in mere attainments. The measurement of an attainment, however great its apparent accuracy, is really only as accurate as the psychologist's predictive powers with respect to the future of the dynamic trait of which it forms a part. For these reasons there is much to be said for using wholistic source traits (see Section 5, Chapter 7) rather than conditional modalities — i.e., for considering in all cases the personality traits which are naturally associated with certain abilities.

Two recent studies (*58 e*) (*58 f*) reveal significant correlations between the personality source traits of Chapter 9 and certain specific abilities. They show, in addition to the inclusion of perseverance and conscientiousness in the wholistic general ability factor, that wholistic factors F, H, E, and J have a role (in that order) in drawing ability; that B, G, and K have a role (in that order) in both verbal and mathematical ability, and that verbal ability, in addition, has loadings in factors I (positively) and F (negatively); i.e., the tendency to "neuroticism" and "introversion" is instrumental in high verbal ability.

Such connections will doubtless be revealed now with increasing frequency. The task of personality prediction is to take them properly into account. In short, abilities must be considered not only because they are in themselves a necessary completion of the description of a personality, but because they appear as manifestation of, or interlock with, dynamic and general personality traits.

2. CATALOGUE OF RESEARCHES USING OBJECTIVE PERSONALITY TESTS

Serially numbered list of "phenomenal" factors. As indicated, the foundations of the ability factors are given separately in the next section. The experimental foundations of the factors and the listed "phenomenal" factors themselves are as follows:

Hargreaves (108). 151 children; 18 tests of four kinds: imagination, completion, intelligence, reproduction.
Factor (1). Fluency.
Factor (2). Speed.
Factor (3). Memory.
Bernstein (16). 130 children; 20 tests, speeded and unspeeded, mental performance, perseveration.
Factor (4). Perseveration, unrelated to speed.
Flugel (90). 80 children, 12 years old; 8 kinds of mental work.
Factor (5). Oscillation.
Philpott (204). 120 children (?); 10 kinds of mental work.
Factor (6). Fluctuation or oscillation.
Hartshorne and May (111). 850 children Grades V to VIII, in three different communities; tested some 24 tests and questionnaires dealing with honesty, persistence, foresight, social service, ethical knowledge.
Cluster or Factor (7). Moral character integrations.
Cattell (41). 62 university students; tested on a variety of perseveration and speed tests.
Cluster or Factor (8). Perseveration.
Cluster or Factor (9). Fluency and speed.
Crutcher (65). 83 children, 6–17 years; 6 tests aimed at measuring persistence.
Factor (10). Persistence and various group factors (intelligence, determination, perseveration, specific abilities).

Howells (*126*). 97 students; 10 tests, distressing or fatiguing situations — e.g., electric shock, pinching, bearing heat.

Cluster or Factor (11). Persistence as endurance.

Ryans (*222*). Deduces from researches of others a general factor of persistence, as "continuous release of energy," "drive," or "endurance" rather than will alone. This is the same as experimentally shown in maze by Morgan and Hull (*186*).

Factor (12). Persistence as drive.

Thornton (*258*). 189 college students; 30 tests.

Factor (13). Willingness to withstand discomfort.

Factor (14). Plodding, willingness to spend time.

Factor (15). Physical strength and masculinity.

Factor (16). Feeling of adequacy (a questionnaire factor).

Factor (17). Mental fluency and verbal speed.

Rethlingshafer (*212*). 38 college students; 30 tests of inhibition, persistence, perseveration.

Factor (18). Keeping at a task once started.

Factor (19). Mental inertia or perseveration.

Factor (20). Willingness to endure discomfort.

Factor (21). Controlling desire to escape unpleasant situation.

Factor (22). Intelligence — speed.

Factor (23). Radicalism-Conservatism.

Factor (24). Natural tempo or fluency.

Cummings (*66*). 18 women students; 4 tests, ball and slot, matching grays, judging character.

Factor (25). Variability.

O'Neil (*198*). 550 subjects (university students, children and delinquent children, separately); 8 tests, varied: persistence, careful work, resistance to distraction, and maintenance of effort.

Factor (26). Will-Character.

Factor (27). Inhibition.

Factor (28). Speed.

Notcutt (*194*). 50 primary school teachers; 22 tests of sensory, motor, and associative perseveration, speed and fluency of association. Also three questionnaires and a "g" test.

Factor (29). Motor perseveration.

Factor (30). Fluency and speed.

Brogden (*20*). 100 boys, 12 years old; 30 performance tests, ten questionnaires, in the realm of character.

Factor (31). "W" or will-character.

Factor (32). Honesty.

Factor (33).   Persistence.
Factor (34).   General intelligence.
Factor (35).   Achievement and certain attitudes.
Factor (36).   Self-control, inhibition, or duty.
Factor (37).   Well-behaved, compliant to moral code.

The researches of Lankes (*235*), Wynn Jones (*235*), Yule (*284*), Jasper (*132*), Rangacher (*209*), Pinard (*205*), (*206*), Stephenson (*240*), (*241*), Shevach (*233*), and others in the field of perseveration are described under perseveration, below.

Factors (38) through (47) are factors of motor perseveration.

Holzinger and Swineford (*121*).   145 children; tested on 24 tests, largely of cognitive performance.   Found four factors, only two of which may be of interest to personality study.   These are oblique factors.

Factor (48).   Speed.
Factor (49).   Memory.

Thurstone (*262*).   1154 children; 60 tests of cognitive performance. Of the ten factors discovered, three have interest, possibly also for personality, as follows:

Factor (50).   W.   Word fluency.
Factor (51).   M.   Memory.
Factor (52).   V.   Verbal ability.

Brintnall (*19*).   19 subjects; 3 scores on maze performance.

Cluster (53).   Persistence and confidence in success.

Carpenter (*33*).   250 boys and girls in Grades I to III; 14 tests of large-muscle movement.

Factor (54).   Strength.
Factor (55).   Velocity.
Factor (56).   Ball-handling dexterity.

Walton (*271*).   55 girls; tested for oscillation or arithmetic performance.

Factor (57).   Oscillation.

Madigan (*164*).   117 adults; given 29 tests of mental and motor speed, memory, fluency, perseveration.   Four factors, of which three are of special interest to personality, as follows:

Factor (58).   Oscillation.
Factor (59).   Perseveration.
Factor (60).   Motor and (some) mental speed.

McCloy (*171*).

Factor (61).   Muscular strength.
Factor (62).   Velocity of movement.

Line and Kaplan (*162*). School children; cognitive tests in field of intelligence and association.

Factor (63). Intelligence — speed (g).

Factor (64). Speed-alertness.

Asch (*11*). Tests of tapping, color naming, etc.

Factor (65). Variability or oscillation (in learning efficiency).

Entwhistle (*80*). 60 girls, 12–16 years; tests of addition, subtraction, multiplication, and division.

Cluster (66). Oscillation. (Proof that same oscillations run through diverse material.)

Harrison (*109*). 50 male undergraduates, 15–29 years; 13 measures of speed and personal tempo. Harrison is not responsible for the following clusters, which are tentatively picked out by the present writer from Harrison's correlation matrices.

Maximal Voluntary Speeds	Involuntary Tempos
Cluster (67). Rhythm.	Cluster (72). Rhythm.
Cluster (68). Ideomotor.	Cluster (73). Ideomotor.
Cluster (69). Perceptial-Dexterity.	Cluster (74). General.
	Cluster (75). Body Tempo.
Cluster (70). Finger Dexterity I.	Cluster (76). Limb Tempo.
Cluster (71). Finger Dexterity II.	

Frischeisen-Kohler (*93*). Several thousand subjects of all ages; 4 or 5 tests.

Cluster (77). General Tempo.

McNemar (*178*).

Factor (78). Speed factor other than intelligence.

Slater (*234*). 450 children; tests of intelligence, also of perseveration and fluency.

Factor (79). Natural Tempo in Intelligence Tests.

Burri (*24*). 51 students; 8 tests of alternation or perseveration. Two minor factors also found.

Factor (80). Perseveration, especially in motor sets.

Factor (81). Perseveration in mental as opposed to motor performance.

Allport and Vernon (*7*). 20 subjects, aged 20 to 60; 20 tests of various tempos.

Cluster (82). Rhythm Tempo.

Cluster (83). Verbal Tempo.

Cluster (84). Drawing Tempo.

Kelley and Krey (144).

Factor (85).   Speed in Mental Performance.

Factor (86).   Memory.

In addition to the above there are studies, too numerous for such preliminary listing, but recorded at the appropriate points in the ensuing sections, which indicate only clusters rather than factors, or which evidence significant positive correlations of only three or four variables.

Cattell (53).   60 children, 40 women undergraduates; 6 tests, of fluctuation in the self-concept, deeper sentiments, superficial attitudes, mood, general information, and recent memories.

Cluster (87).   Fluctuation of attitudes.

Gould (98).   82 students; 6 unrelated tasks.

Cluster (88).   Aspiration level.

Gardner (94).   51 adolescents (students) on digit-symbol tests.

Cluster (89).   Level of aspiration.

Herrington (116).   11 young men; 4 tests, each administered twelve times a day, and three personality traits, rated.   The following factors are not set out by Herrington but are extracted by the present writer from Herrington's correlation matrix.   In view of the small numbers they are highly tentative.

Factor (90).   General Metabolic Activity.

Factor (91).   Pulse, Respiration, B.M.R., or Sympathetic Activity.

Factor (92).   Pulse, Activity-Level.

Factor (93).   Circulatory Variability (apparently two factors).

Darling (68).   58 children; 6 personality ratings, 10 physiological measures.

Factor (94).   Cholinergic Activity.

Factor (95).   Attention-Alertness.

Factor (96).   Motor Activity.

Factor (97).   Sympathetic Reactivity.

Cattell (38).   10 subjects; 600 observations.

Cluster (98).   Low electrical skin resistance, high alertness, activity, and anxiety.

Darrow and Heath (71).   100 undergraduates; tested on questionnaire and twenty physiological-response measurements.   The groupings here are not exactly those of Darrow and Heath, but adapted from them by the present writer, as in the preceding chapter, except for (10).

Cluster (99).   ((24) and (25), and Q IV in the preceding chapter.) Neurotic Constellations.

Cluster (100). ((26) of preceding chapter.) Somasthenia and sleep difficulties.

Cluster (101). ((27) of preceding chapter, and Q II.) General Emotional Hypersensitivity. (Neurasthenia with excitability.)

Cluster (102). ((28) of preceding chapter and Q XV.) Paranoid Excitability and "Depression."

Cluster (103). ((29) of preceding chapter and Q I.) Shyness. (Social inactivity and somasthenia.)

Cluster (104). Hypersensitivity, Anxiety, Excitability, and Manic-Depressive Tendency.

Johnson (136). 30 women students; 4 tests and various subjective reports on depression, etc.

Cluster (105). Depression-Euphoria.

Jaensch, E. R. (129), and Jaensch, W. (130). Several hundreds of subjects examined on imagery, skin texture.

Cluster (106). T-type.

Cluster (107). B-type.

Kretschmer (154). Many hundreds of subjects. Bodily measurements and various perceptual, speed, and dexterity tests.

Cluster (108). Schizoid-Cycloid.

Oates (196). 100 children on 12 tests of June Downey battery.

Factor (109). General Emotionality (or Fluency of Association).

Factor (109a). Repressed *vs.* Unrepressed Disposition.

Brackett (17). 29 children, 18 to 48 months; 24 five-minute measures of behavior (by observations).

Cluster (110). Tendency to laughter.

Cluster (111). Tendency to crying.

Cattell (50). 49 normals, 46 psychotics, 50 delinquents; on nine cursive miniature situation traits, largely in the realm of character.

Cluster (112). Integration of Character Responses.

Cluster (113). Forceful Leadership.

Sanford (225). 39 children, aged 7 to 14 years. Projection tests of phantasy in story completion, similes, picture interpretation.

Cluster (114). Strong Character.

Cluster (115). Ego Defense.

Cluster (116). Anti-Social.

Cluster (117). Self-Assertion.

Cluster (118). Social.

Miller (182). 39 children, 7 to 14 years; tested on bodily measurements, growth, hormone excretion, B.M.R., etc.

Cluster (119). Parasympathetic Response.

Cluster (120).   High Metabolism — Advancing Osseous Development.

Cluster (121).   Advanced Muscle, Hormone Excretion, and Osseous Development.

Cluster (122).   Coördination.

Cluster (123).   Physical Strength.

Cluster (124).   Large Build — Pituitary Syndrome.

Dudycha (77).   307 students; measured on punctuality in various situations.

Cluster (125).   Punctuality.

Andrews (10).   300 students; measured on response to 90 jokes.

Factor (126).   Derision — Superiority.

Factor (127).   Reaction to Debauchery.

Factor (128).   Subtlety.

Factor (129).   Play on Words and Ideas.

Factor (130).   Sexual.

Factor (131).   Ridiculous — Wisecracks.

Eysenck (82a).   50 male and 50 female subjects; about 30 years of age, tested on 60 jokes.

Factor (132).   General Funniness (comic).

Factor (133).   Clever, Complex *vs.* Simple funny.   (Wit.)

Factor (134).   Humor, superior adaptation.

Thurstone (262a).   60 varied perceptual tests given to 190 undergraduate students; 12 oblique factors as follows:

Factor (135).   Perceptual closure, against distraction.

Factor (136).   Susceptibility to optical illusions.

Factor (137).   Reaction time.

Factor (138).   Alternation of perspective.

Factor (139).   Manipulation of two configurations.

Factor (140).   Speed of perception (and dark adaptation).

Factor (141).   "G" or general ability.

Factor (142).   Shape *vs.* color-texture perception.

Factor (143).   Speed of judgment.

Factor (144).   Tests in Rorschach.

Factor (145).   Gottschaldt figure responses.

Eysenck (83).   16 adult subjects, 89 jokes rated.

Factor (146).   General sense of humor.

Factor (147).   (Bipolar factor.) Sexual jokes and extraversion *vs.* non-sexual.

Factor (148).   (Bipolar factor.) Complex jokes and introversion *vs.* simple jokes.

Factor (149).   (Bipolar factor.) Personal *vs.* Impersonal jokes.

Gibb (96b). 200 men and women students of 17 tests mixing questionnaires and objective tests of fluency, perseveration, intelligence, and clerical ability. Orthogonal "simple structure" obtained.

Factor (150). Emotional Instability E.

Factor (151). Concentration in clerical field A.

Factor (152). Verbal Fluency V.F.

Factor (153). Pictorial Fluency P.F.

Factor (154). Confidence C.

Factor (155). Solitariness and Perseveration $(-)$ 5.

Cattell and Luborsky (58i). One hundred jokes reduced to 13 clusters, used as variables on 50 students.

Factor (156). Aggression against civilized decency *vs*. Whimsy.

Factor (157). Gallic wit.

Factor (158). Sex.

Factor (159). Derision, masculine assurance.

Factor (160). Subtle, light humor.

Factor (161). Play on words.

Freeman and Katzoff (92a). Some 10 variables derived from a small number of measurements, mainly P.G.R., voice, nervous movements.

Factor (162). Control.

Factor (163). Arousal.

Factor (164). Anxious emotionality.

Wenger (275b). 62 children on a wide variety of physiological variables (but not biochemical). Wenger's earlier study *(275a)* is suggestive, but owing to the small number of subjects (6 boys) is not set out here.

Factor (165). Autonomic function.

Factor (166). Muscular tension.

Factor (167). Residual or indefinable.

Some extensive, as yet unpublished, studies of physiological response patterns have also been made in the Army Air Force, with results in general agreement with the factors emerging from an over-all view of the published researches.

Woodrow (281b). All 5th, 6th, and 7th grade children in a small town, tested on various achievements and IQ. Measures of *increment* of performance from year to year.

Factor (168). Ability to improve in arithmetic problems and fundamentals.

Factor (169). Ability to improve in reading, vocabulary, English.

Factor (170). Ability to improve in vocabulary and spelling (less clear).

Factor (171). Ability to improve generally and score on intelligence test (almost a residual factor).

Carroll (34). 42 tests of verbal abilities administered to 119 students.

Factor (172). *A.* Fluency. Speed of word association with restrictions.

Factor (173). *B.* Rote learning. (M) Paired words.

Factor (174). *C.* Verbal Ability. Richness of linguistic responses. (Vocabulary, grammar.)

Factor (175). *D.* Speed of articulatory movements.

Factor (176). *E.* Fluency. Association speed, without direction other than syntactical corrections.

Factor (177). *F.* Facility and fluency in oral speech.

Factor (178). *G.* Verbal ability or fluency. Description, similes, speed of reading.

Factor (179). *H.* Facility in naming or giving symbols to stimuli.

Factor (180). *J.* Verbal ability (Analogies, Morpheme recognition.)

Eysenck (83c).

Factor (181). Overall physical size.

Factor (182). Girth.

3. THE PRINCIPAL SOURCE TRAITS AMONG ABILITIES

Terseness of summary. To give a fair summary in brief of so great a volume of research as has been accomplished in the field of abilities, without taking somewhat dogmatic short cuts, is very difficult; for, as with personality factors, various workers have obtained different factors according to the system of factorization which they adopt or different clusters according to the kinds of test which they used to make up the original pool of tests.

Concerning what has roughly been called "intelligence," an interpretation of the apparently conflicting Spearman, Thomson, and Thurstone viewpoints will be assumed according to arguments stated in more detail elsewhere (*51*). According to this interpretation it is most economical and best in accordance with a wide range of facts to analyze abilities into one general ability and a number of group factors, the latter corresponding to the primary abilities discovered by Thurstone.

TABLE 23

Descriptive List of Ability Test Factors

Factor T. I. General Ability. Phenomenal — i.e., independent re-search — factors are too numerous to list. This general factor has high saturations in such performances as understanding mathematical and grammatical relationships, judging synonyms and opposites, drawing inferences, perceiving complex relationships in perceptual material, etc.

Special aptitudes and abilities. Group factors and clusters in the realm of abilities have been located as follows.

Factor T. II. Verbal Ability. A group factor was established by Brown and Stephenson (*23*) and a corresponding primary ability by Thurstone (*262*). It has twice been confirmed among educational abilities by Burt (*26*) and independently by Moore (*184*), Schiller (*227*), and Holzinger and Swineford (*121*) and m...y be considered one of the best-established restricted abilities. Car oll (*34*) has made a finer analysis of some 42 tests of verbal abilities, resulting in sub-divisions of the group factors previously identified in verbal performance. Thurstone's V factor of verbal ability was found in company with a memory factor M and a factor of verbal fluency W. Carroll's work confirms M but splits V into three factors C, J, and G, and splits W into A and E. These may roughly be defined as follows: C is stock richness of vocabulary, J ability to handle semantic relations, A is fluency with high restriction on the conditions of production, E is fluency with no restrictions. To these, three new factors were added: F, facility and fluency in oral speech; H, facility in attaching appropriate names to stimuli, and D, speed of articulatory movements. Woodrow's factors (169) and (170) seem to show V and W appearing in *gains* of performance from year to year.

Recent independent analysis (*135*) seems to confirm two of these finer factors, that of fluency (W or A and E) and that of selection of responses (J). The former factor is listed in this chapter among the personality factors below. Verbal ability is likely to prove one of the first clear illustrations of the above-discussed interrelation of cognitive and conative traits, for the verbal fluency factor (W or A

TABLE 23 — *Continued*

and E), as shown later in this chapter, is related to surgent temperament, while the speed factor, D, described later, may be the general temperamental speed factor in its verbal context. Gibb confirms W (152) and finds a factor of pictorial fluency also (153). See Fluency.

Factor T. III. Mechanical Ability. As first demonstrated by Cox (*63*), there is a clear group factor in understanding (but not necessarily in manipulating) mechanical contrivances and connections. It is more marked among, and higher, in boys than in girls, and is almost certainly a "social mold" trait due to training. Burt (*26*) and others have confirmed this factor. It may be a combination of a special factor with the spatial factor.

Factor T. IV. Spatial-Visual Ability. This has been isolated by Thurstone (*262*) as S factor and is apparently the same as El Koussy's (*79*) K factor and Alexander's (*5*) "practical ability" and Schiller's spatial ability (*227*). A recent study of five form-board performances, the wiggly block and intelligence test (*81*) found a common spatial ability factor. It was tested as well by two- as by three-dimensional problems and was found to predict also success in descriptive geometry.

Factors T. IVa, IVb, and IVc. These are perceptual-ability factors isolated in Thurstone's extensive and thorough study of perceptual powers (*262 a*), but not yet confirmed or viewed from fresh angles by other researches. They are: *IVa* (*135*) *Ability to get closure* (Gestalt) in incomplete data, despite distractions; *IVb* (*136*) *Ability to allow for optical illusion effects; IVc* (*139*) *Ability to control configurations* (*visual*) *flexibly*, for one's own purposes, instead of being dominated by them. This may be the obverse of perseveration.

Factor T. V. Dexterity. The factor of general dexterity is slight to negligible, but restricted dexterities, notably manual dexterity, have been shown to exist by Cox (*63*), Spearman (*235*), Burt (*26*), and others. Larson analyzed the somewhat related matter of gymnastic-athletic performance and found the primary components to be: dynamic strength, static dynamometer strength, gross bodily coördination and agility, motor educability, motor explosiveness, and abdominal strength. Cluster (122), consisting of coördination, flexibility, balance, accuracy of large-muscle movement, small-muscle movement, grace of movement, and infrequency of extraneous movements, evidently belongs here, possibly as Larson's third factor.

TABLE 23 — *Continued*

Va. Motor Steadiness has been shown to be a general manual-performance factor correlating with marksmanship (*128*).

Factor T. VI. Numerical Ability. Called by Thurstone N factor. This appears to be the same as the arithmetical ability discovered earlier by Spearman (*235*), Rogers (*219*), Schiller (*227*), and Collar and Burt (*26*), who were explicit in indicating that the ability did not appear to be a general mathematical ability (which seems to be, from preliminary indications, a complex affair) but a facility in dealing with figures and arithmetical computation. It is well confirmed by the recent work of Goodman (*97*). Woodrow's factor (*168*) of *gains* in arithmetical ability appears to be somewhat wider than N factor.

("Perceptual ability," Thurstone's P factor, an ability to recognize and deal with visual forms, has not been confirmed by recent studies, notably that of Goodman (*97*), and has temporarily been set aside by Thurstone from his list of primary abilities.)

Factor T. VII. Deductive or Reasoning Ability. Spearman and Burt demonstrated that what they called *Logical Ability* involves a group factor additional to "g." Thurstone's more recent work finds this same primary ability, as D factor.

Factor T. VIII. Induction or Generalizing Ability. Thurstone also shows that an inductive, generalizing ability is distinct in what has generally been called logical ability, and calls it I factor. Goodman's recent work confirms it (*97*).

Factor T. IX. Musical Ability. Seashore's researches showed a considerable group factor in musical ability, independent of the general factor of intelligence and indubitably innate. This independence has been frequently confirmed, notably by Ross (*221*), who showed, as would be expected from theory, that exceptional musical performance requires high "g" as well as high musical ability. Finer analyses of musical ability have been made by Seashore, Drake (*75*), Karlin (*142*), and others. Drake found more than one factor, the chief among them being "memory for auditory items" (or "ear-mindedness"), "pitch-intensity," and "intensity-time." Karlin found eight interpretable factors, in a very extensive test battery, as follows: frequency integration, loudness judgment, auditory integration, auditory resistance, speed of closure (not restricted to this sense modality), general span (also not restricted to hearing), and two memory factors (Factors IX *a* to *b*).

TABLE 23 — *Continued*

Factor X.   Drawing Ability.   Curiously enough, there are no adequate researches showing the existence of a group factor here.   But general drawing ability is known to be one of the abilities least correlated with intelligence, and therefore almost necessarily an independent group or general factor.

Factors Xa and Xb.   Aesthetic Appreciation.   The researches of Eysenck (*82*) indicate an ability not accounted for entirely by intelligence and capable of being split into at least two capacities.

Factor T. XI.   Concerning memory or retentivity, the evidence is still not clear.   Thurstone finds clear evidence of a primary ability, M, or memory, present in tests of memorizing "word numbers" and "initials."   Spearman summarizes several researches (*235*) to show that ability to commit to memory becomes increasingly independent of "g" (Factor T. I) as the data change from connected sentences to word-number associations, disconnected words, and rote memory generally.   Woodrow (*281*) very clearly showed retentivity — e.g., in acquiring mental and motor skills — to be independent of intelligence.

The work of Carey (*30*) agrees with Thurstone (*262*) and with the evidence of Factors (3) and (49), in pointing to a general retentivity factor, which manifests itself as much in language as in sensory qualities and as much in visual as in auditory material.   There is also some evidence indicating group factors covering verbal, nonverbal, and various sense modality data, but not differentiating immediate and delayed recall.   A more detailed analysis is that of Carlson (*32*) showing eight factors, three covering visual varieties of memory and the rest defying easy definition; but this remains unconfirmed.

It is unfortunate, from the standpoint of the study of personality, that this "cognitive" capacity has not been more definitively investigated; for the close relationship between memory trends and dynamic and temperamental traits, so clearly evident in clinical work, would make comparison of the findings in the two fields particularly fruitful for understanding the total personality.

All in all, therefore, we must recognize some fifteen to twenty ability factors to be established by present research. The above enumeration lists the eleven more basic ones, omitting some less confirmed perceptual factors, minor dimensions, or those factors which have cropped up in ability researches but which seem to be primarily temperament measures and, as such, to be included in sections below. If minor factors — so-called "subdivisions" — are included, about twice the above number of ability factors can be recognized.

Unpublished research and general clinical experience[1] already indicate some systematic relation of these abilities to wider personality traits. For example, spelling disability has often been noted with conversion hysteria; number facility with schizoid and analerotic character; verbal ability with introspective, sensitive, unsociable traits; and general emotionality and sociability with artistic and drawing abilities. But the systematic bridges between abilities and personality have still to be built.

The mode of measuring abilities in which they are considered exclusively as "speed" capacities — i.e., the powers which have loosely been called "quickness" as opposed to "capacity" — are considered together under Section 6 dealing specifically with Speed, Tempo, and Fluency, but it seems very likely that we shall finish by perceiving speed and ability factors to be in many cases different aspects of one and the same source trait.

4. THE SOURCE TRAITS OF PERSISTENCE, WILL–CHARACTER, PLODDING APPLICATION, AND INHIBITION

Range of research exploration. Because character is so important a variable in applied psychology, there have been more experimental attempts to measure it by test situations than have been made with any other variable.

[1] Reik, for example (*Thirty Years with Freud;* 1941), observes: "Experience bears out that there is a kind of functional relationship between literary and oratorical gifts. Master stylists are seldom good speakers; ability to express oneself in one form seems to hamper expression in the other." This might well be due to the imposition of Burt's sthenic-asthenic emotionality bi-factor upon a general-verbal factor — i.e., high verbal ability with the sthenic factor gives oratorical skill, with the asthenic loading stylistic skill. Clinical experience is replete with such observations of ability-temperament overlap.

They have chosen tests mainly, but by no means exclusively, in two fields — persistence qualities and honesty-dependability — both of which are prominent in the general will-character factor discovered in terms of ratings. However, practically all extensive studies have found not one factor but several — generally five or six — as follows. As usual, one finds little consistency in the labels used by the various researchers, so that the factors have to be equated by close scrutiny of the loadings and types of test used.

TABLE 24

Descriptive Lists of Test Factors

Factor T. XII. Honesty-Integrity. Found in factor (32) and in cluster (7).

1. Not Cheating on Coördination Test	.63
2. Maller Honesty Test	.59
3. False Book List Statements	.55
4. Overstatement Test	.53
5. Questionable Character Preferences Test	.34

It is possible that this factor is much wider in influence than specific honesty, and the notion "general integrity" is contingently attached to it, meaning "general guidance of behavior by principles of altruism."

Hartshorne and May stressed the specificity of the habits they studied, ignoring the very considerable generality as evidenced by the correlations. The correlations of tested honesty with other variables were as follows.

With "Integration" (Consistency of moral responses)	.78
Coöperativeness (test)	.39
Persistence (test)	.37
Inhibition (test)	.35
Intelligence (test)	.34
Information (test)	.29
Good Citizenship (Knowledge test)	.27
Emotional Stability (rated)	.20
Foresight (test)	.32

Of the correlations among twenty-four tests (situational) of honesty, helpfulness, coöperation (sharing), persistence, inhibition (to temptation and distraction), all but three are larger than zero by a statistically reliable amount.

TABLE 24 — *Continued*

When ranged in four groups — Honesty, Service (Coöperation), Inhibition, and Persistence — for intercorrelation, the highest *r* was 0.487 between Inhibition and Honesty and the lowest 0.083 between Service and Persistence, with a median at 0.32.

So far as the writer knows, no factor analysis of Hartshorne and May's extensive and valuable data has yet been made. The clustering observed covers factors I and II of the present exposition, and suggests that there may be, in addition to these two factors, a single persistence-honesty factor running over the area of both. The Hartshorne and May data, however, even at a casual inspection, indicate that there are "group factors" distinguishing respectively Honesty-Inhibition and Persistence (our factors I and II). For the present these cluster data may be regarded mainly as supporting factor I, but also factor II and possibly indicating a factor common to both.

Factor T. XIII. Active-Reliable Will-Character; Conscientious Thoroughness. Evidenced by factor (31), cluster (7), factor (26) and perhaps (151)

Resists suggestion, regarding use of words and interpretation of pictures manifesting independence	.53
Conscientious in carrying out instructions in detail	.37
Questionable Character Preferences Test	.31
Perseveration Test I	— .46
Perseveration Test II	— .34

(Also, if (151), thoroughness and accuracy in clerical tasks)

O'Neil's factor (*26*) seems to cover both this and the next two factors below, but in diminishing relatedness from the first to the third. Its saturations lie in the following, in adults:

Persistence on the recording dynamometer
Accuracy (Conscientiousness?) in sorting cards
Retarded tracing of e's (Downey inhibition test)
Confidence in a choice made
Difficulty (insuggestibility, consistency) in reversing a choice once made
Decisiveness of choice made (records of preferred, conflicting, indifferent)

and in the following in children:

The first three of the above performances
Dot-dash concentration test
Persistence on an insoluble maze (Hull)

TABLE 24 — *Continued*

Maintenance of maximum effort in dividing words in a jumbled passage (Hartshorne and May's Story Resistance Test)

Factor T. XIV. Determined Will-Character: Self-Sufficient, confident persistence in face of discomfort. Evidenced by factors (11), (13), (20), (36), and (53). There is most doubt about (36), the items of which are listed separately.

Average strength of maintained grip	.79
Time S will endure painful pressure stimulus in presence of experimenter	.69
Time maintaining handgrip above fixed dynamometer reading	.55 to .67
Time S will endure painful electric shock	.62
S's self-rating on persistence	.42
Time S can hold breath	.41
Willingness to risk and take punishment to improve a test score	
Unwillingness to gamble for an increase of score	
Ascendance on Allport-Vernon A–S	.44
High grades in courses	.44
(But negligible *r* with intelligence)	
Radicalism in religion, etc.	
Male sex	
Oldest rather than youngest in family	
Slimness of body build	
Extreme tallness or shortness	

From (36) we obtain:

Translates slang terms into precise English rather than other slang words, when asked to define them	.55
Indicates preference for duty at cost of pain or discomfort	.50
Prefers better to "questionable" reading	.44
Shows high self-sufficiency on questionnaire	.40
Solves geometrical figure problems	.32

Factor T. XV. Masculine Toughness and Doggedness. Evidenced by factors (15) and (21).

Male sex	1.00
Strength of maximum dynamometer grip	.78 to .89
Height	.60 to .84
Weight	.59 to .70
Time S will endure shock	.61
Time on increasingly difficult material	.46
Motor inhibition on Downey test (writing very slowly)	.47

TABLE 24 — *Continued*

Time S will hold breath	.40 to .47
Time S will endure painful pressure	.47
Time of maintained grip	.40
Rate of fluctuations on ambiguous figures	.31
Time taken to read three paragraphs	.30

Factor T. XVI. Smooth, Unwilled Dynamic Momentum and Absorption. Evidenced by factors (10), (12), (14), (18), (27), (28), and (33).

Time spent on task of building possible words from set of letters	.80
Time on attempting to disentangle story from jumbled print	.51 to .76
Time spent on task with increasingly difficult material	.69
Numbers of words made from six letters	.48 to .55
Lack of decline in latter half of adding test	.53
Freedom from distraction from a task by interpolated irrelevant pictures	.49
Lack of decline in the above, first to last	.58
Lack of "oscillation" in adding performance	.52
Tendency to continue when interrupted	.44
Number of "no" answers concerning recurrence effects	.44
Zeigarnik Ratio	.41
Motor inhibition (Downey: slow writing)	.3
Grades in schoolwork	.37
Perseveration (p test) score	.33 to .36
Time S holds breath	.26 to .32

(Perhaps also: Time spent in sorting cards, time on volitional choice (28).)

The above characteristics are taken from (14), (18), (27), and (33), which agree very well in items and loadings. (10 and (12), showing persistence in tasks, drive, momentum, and tendency to keep on, seem to be essentially the same, and suggest the factor is the most outstanding persistence factor in small children. The clusters found by Cushing and by Chapman (described by Ryans (*222*)) also appear to be of the same nature as this persistence-as-momentum.

This factor is of considerable interest in that it bridges the will-character and perseveration groups and is a vitally important landmark in the current attempts to discover the relation of these two kinds of factors. It also ties up very definitely with oscillation. It has been called by its various discoverers "persistence," "persistent drive," "inhibition," "lack of value of one's time," "willingness to spend time on a task," "habit of keeping on at a task," and "plodding momentum." The title given above is an attempt

TABLE 24 — *Continued*

to do justice to these suggestions and to describe the essence of this primitive and unwilled but integrated dynamic momentum and absorption in a task.

Factor T. XVII. Mental Liveliness from Good Home Background, or, Mental Initiative, Especially in Verbal Acquisition. Evidenced by factor (35).

Knowledge of slang vocabulary and of general vocabulary	.55 to .60
Willingness (on questionnaire) to face discomfort for sake of duty	.47
Good ethical choices in story situation	.44
Interpreting proverbs test (Otis)	.42
Grades in schoolwork	.40
Good reading preferences	.36

That this is not merely a general intelligence factor is shown by the extraction of an independent intelligence factor from the same matrix, and by *r*'s of only about .35 with intelligence test material.

Factor T. XVIII. Confident Self-Assertion (Opposite to Inferiority Sense). Evidenced by factor (16). (Also Q. VI.)

Score on Wang questionnaire on persistence qualities — e.g., in an argument do you find it hard to give in?	.67
Score on Allport-Vernon A–S test	.56
Self-rating on persistence	.56
Self-rating on self-confidence	.51

This factor falls among test material, but is obviously a questionnaire factor and is labeled to identify it with the obviously corresponding Q factor. It is interesting that among test material on persistence this questionnaire factor fails to align itself with any actual persistence tests.

Factor T. XIX. Passive Compliance, or Adjustment to Conventional Code. Evidenced by factor (37).

S, on questionnaire, indicates he would not cheat in a variety of situations	.56
Score on social adjustment in Woodworth Inventory	.44
Indicates ethical idealism and helpfulness to others, on opinionnaire	.41
Indicates compliance with social, parental authority as an ideal	.30

This again stands out as a questionnaire factor, seemingly immiscible with the real test situations in the same correlation matrix. Neither this nor factors XVII and XVIII above clearly prove themselves to be will-character factors in the narrower sense, but they are retained here contingent upon further clarification by research.

5. THE SOURCE TRAITS OF OSCILLATION, VARIABILITY,
   OR FLUCTUATION

Varieties of fluctuation. The kinds of variability which have interested experimenters have been, superficially, very diverse. Some have been interested in reversible perspective; some, in momentary variations of performance on output or errors, measured for magnitude or for frequency; and some, in slower fluctuations, over weeks, in learning or attitudes.

Those studies which deal with performance measured at intervals of a few seconds are unanimous in finding a general factor.

Factor T. XXa. "*O or Oscillation.*" Evidenced by factors (5), (6), (25), (57), (58), (65), and (66). The factor shows itself in the variability between successive five or ten second periods of performance in prolonged activities of the following kinds.

> Adding
> Subtracting
> Multiplying
> Dividing
> Naming colors
> Tapping
> Judging length by reproducing an arm movement
> Judging to drop a ball into a slot
> Judging matching of shades of gray
> Judging personal characteristics (rating)
> Counting dots
> Picking out letters
> Identifying segments of figures
> Writing down numbers

No continuous performances have yet been tried in which the fluctuation tendency did not display itself. That it is practically identical with what used to be called "fluctuation of attention" is shown by Madigan's finding that as the periods of measured performance are extended from 5 seconds to 20 or 30 the validity (group factor correlations) and the reliability fall toward zero. The intercorrelations of fluctuation in diverse performances are fairly high (.35 to .50) for brief tests of this kind. The reliabilities, split half or separated by several days, are of the order 0.8, and show that oscillation is very characteristically at a certain level for each subject. Madigan (*164*) finds that practice does not affect oscillation; Flugel (*90*), that it increases slightly as the subjects reach higher levels of performance. Madigan shows that, by scoring oscillation as deviation from a mean, higher validities and reliabilities are obtained than by subtracting the performance of each period from its immediate neighbor. Philpott has shown (*204*) that the curves of oscillation of performance follow mathematical laws. Hollingworth and Ash find rate of fluctuation in reversible perspective is increased by fatigue and by practice.

Less systematic evidence. Many studies exist, too numerous to mention, showing positive correlations — i.e., clustering — in lieu of proof of a true factor in oscillation. Hertzman (*117*) studied the relation of variability on the Thurstone substitution test and concluded that the variability of an individual is an "important variable in the description of patterns of mental organization." Porter (*207*) experimented with reversible perspective and found the rate was a highly reliable individual attribute, though different figures had different rates.

Other variability factors. Philip (*203*) showed that in high-speed continuous work there are periodicities distinct from and far longer than the variabilities measured in the "o" factor. Weber (*275*) found some evidence of individual constancy with regard to a week-to-week variability of test performance. Many researches on other problems — e.g., Gatewood, Guilford, and Hunt on schizophrenia — have noted correlations by the way with this day-to-day variability, but none has established such variability as a factor or explored its relation to "o."

Its existence as a cluster is shown by the work of Cattell (*53*), measuring day-to-day and month-to-month fluctuations of attitude scores, on 40 children and 50 adult students. The day-to-day and month-to-month fluctuations seem to be the same. Because of its tentativeness and because it has the same relation to certain character landmarks as has the "o" factor, the cluster and possible factor here is best labeled as if it were identical with or related to the "o" factor as follows.

Cluster T. XXa. Fluctuation (possibly Oscillation). A tendency to vary from day to day and month to month in various performances and especially in magnitude and direction of attitudes. Evidenced by cluster (88).

> Variation in sentiments
> Variation in attitudes
> Variation in mood reported by subject

Further characteristics related to oscillation and fluctuation. The most striking correlation that has been found here is between "o" — T. XX and the "w" factor and T. XX*a* and the "w" factor. Cummings (*66*) found *r*'s of — .32 between "o" and will, thoroughness and adhesion to principle, of + 0.29 with surgent traits (opposite of introversion). Walton (*271*) (*272*) found "o" decreasing in children, with age and mental age, and significantly correlated (— .46 to — .75) with "steadiness of character." Madigan (*164*) found "o" higher in children than in adults. Porter found rate of reversible perspective slightly correlated positively with "social introversion" on a questionnaire. Mukergi found oscillation greater in a group than an individual situation and greater in girls than in boys. Oscillation is reported less for those making higher scores.

Regarding fluctuation over longer periods, Weber found more variable subjects higher on Ascendance. Gatewood, Guilford, and Hunt found schizophrenics significantly more variable than normals. Cattell (*53*) found correlations of attitude fluctuation to be — .53 to — 0.98 with ratings of will-character factor "w," 0.03 to 0.61 with surgency, and 0.13 to 0.30 with general emotionality; and concluded that long-term fluctuation of dynamic structure, of the kind measured here, was essentially a direct indicator of degree of character integration. The correlations of "o" with character integration and stability are lower than those of fluctuation, suggesting that these two factors are related but not identical.

Factor T. XXb. Fluctuation of Visual Percepts. Evidenced by 138. Shown in alternation (involuntary) of ambiguous prospectives and of retinal rivalry. There is as yet no proof that this is related to the general "o" factor above.

6. THE SOURCE TRAITS OF SPEED, FLUENCY, AND TEMPO

Origins of factors. The factors and clusters discovered in this area of behavior spring largely from studies on power-versus-speed in intelligence tests and other aspects of cognitive abilities; partly from investigations of temperament itself;

and to a lesser extent from studies of athletic performance. It is now possible, with some confidence, to relate the factors from the first two areas; but the last remains isolated and can be related only by inference.

The "logical trait" boundaries of the concepts in this field may briefly be described as follows: (1) Fluency means speed of spontaneous productivity or of reproduction through association, granted that no demand is made upon discriminatory power — i.e., that individual differences are not due to differences in judgment. (2) Speed means speed of repetitive performance or selective, discriminatory performance where all the content is perceptually given. (3) Tempo means natural speed or rhythm (Maximum rhythm would be considered a speed measurement) — i.e., basal speed when no urgent incentive is operating.

From the debate on speed and power in relation to intelligence tests, clarified by the work of Spearman, Kelley, Bernstein, Boring and Peak, Thorndike, Ruch and Koerth, Thurstone, Lorge, Tryon, and others, emerge the following guiding principles:

(1) In tests largely of intelligence, speed and power are not separate factors (*a*) when all the subjects are of the same chronological age and (*b*) when the subjects deliberately set out to work as fast as possible.

(2) Speed under willed action, however, must be distinguished from temperamental preference for working at a certain tempo, in the kind of situations which testers as such have neglected to observe.

(3) After about 25 years of age, willed speed on intelligence tests declines, but power does not. The two are in this respect separable factors.

(4) As Hargreaves (*108*), Kelley (*143*), Line (*162*), and Holzinger (*120*), in particular, have shown, a speed factor, in willed, speeded-test situations, can be clearly distinguished from intelligence if tests of an easy or repetitive nature are in-

cluded. It is this factor which we shall first set out, relegating the personality factors of "intelligence-speed" or "g" ((1), (2), immediately above) to the abilities, as Factor I, above.

Factor T. XXIa. Speed of Judgment and Ideomotor Skills. Evidenced by factors (2), (9), (48), (60), (64), (78), (85), and (143). Speed of response, *when aiming at speed*, in —

> Simple code substitution
> Sorting cards for color, form, etc.
> Decoding simple code
> Adding (Simple, serial)
> Indicating recognition whether numbers same or different
> Social judgments
> Counting groups of dots
> Distinguishing letters (Perceptual speed)
> Solving easy word analogies
> Simple same-opposite tests
> Numerical puzzles (What numbers add and multiply to *x*?)
> Simple arithmetical problems
> Speed of writing
> Speed copying figures

This is almost certainly the same as the cluster shown in the earlier work of Garrison (96), in such activities as cancellation, tallying, sorting, and vocal reading, which was found, in all clearly ideomotor manifestations, to be independent of "g," and possibly the same as Harrison's cluster — 68 — below. It is perhaps revealed in its most clear-cut form in Thurstone's speed of judgment factor — 143 — which is high also in sorting-decision performances generally. Tinker (264) also summarized evidence showing a "motor habit," speed cluster independent of "intelligence speed" or "g." Dubois (76) also found evidence of a small general speed factor through tests in which the level of performance demanded was not at all exacting.

Cluster T. XXIb. Ideomotor Skills. Evidenced by cluster (68).

> Speed multiplication
> Speed reading
> Speed cranking
> Speed card sorting

Whenever the variety of speed tests has been great, however, the results — e.g., the recent findings of Harrison (109) or of Adams, Dowd, Lanier, Buxton and Humphreys, or other researches summarized by Foley (*91*) — clearly indicate that *no single general factor accounts for maximal speed* in all performances and the above factor must, accordingly, be considered one of several possible group factors in this field.

Harrison (*109*) took a wide variety of movements and performances — e.g., card sorting, tapping, body bending, head turning, counting, reading, turning a crank, making decisions. The mean intercorrelations, as in Adams's and other studies, were only about $0.15 \pm .09$. Practice and habituation do not raise the correlations or bring about a general factor; indeed, Buxton and Humphreys found they increased specificity. The actual speed is, of course, susceptible to practice and this was found by Line and Kaplan to distinguish factor XXI from the "intelligence-speed" factor.

Factor XXIb. Speed of Perception, or "Alertness." Evidenced by 140 and present in:

> Span of visual peripheral vision
> Speed of dark adaptation
> Speed of completion of partial "Gestalts"
> Speed of completion of mutilated words
> Speed of social judgments

This factor, which seems a kind of perceptual "alertness" and which may be related to fatigue, is shown by Thurstone to be quite independent of the reaction time factor (XXIVa), the judgment factor (XXIa), and fluency XXVII, with which one might be inclined qualitatively to associate it. It affects somewhat spatial ability and reasoning.

How many restricted group factors are needed to account for speed performances must remain, with present research data, speculative. All researches agree in finding highest correlations among most similar performances, and in finding considerable consistency in the individual's speed within such restricted regions.

That the available researches have already struck the most important speed factors seems, however, a reasonable expectation. For the present, therefore, we can deal with some confidence with (1) speed of judgment and ideomotor performances, XXIa, (2) speed of reaction time, XXIVa, (3) speed of bodily movement, XXII, (4) maximal rhythm, XXIIIa, (5) fluency or speed of mental output and association, XXVII, (6) various factors of natural tempo, XXIX, and (7) perceptual speed, XXIb.

In the last analysis one might expect the boundaries of speed factors to be the same as ability factors, since abilities are always measured in terms of speed and errors and the errors are often a function of speed. Thus we should expect speed factors corresponding to intelligence, verbal comprehension, drawing, arithmetical processes, manual dexterity, etc. This is to some extent true. Evidently research will get clearer results when researchers are clearer as to what they mean by speed in distinction from ability. This is not the place to discuss the basis of a valid absolute distinction; but a line can be roughly drawn, in existing researches, between those which employ a test situation in which the task to be performed is on the threshold of discriminatory power and is often performed wrongly and those in which the task is well within the individual's capacity to execute it and so easy as to be virtually insusceptible to error.

Evidence which is indubitably on the latter basis is rare. Such as it is, it points to broader factors than among abilities and notably to the one above, which at least covers arithmetical, verbal, and other performances. Whether group factors corresponding to the ability boundaries could still be detected within this more general speed remains to be seen.

The following factor, a speed factor among deliberately speeded large-muscle movements, may or may not be related to the above, but is temporarily given separate labeling.

Factor T. XXII. Velocity of Bodily Movements (Athletics). Evidenced by factors (55) and (62).

It is not our business, in a personality study, to pursue motor speeds or skills as such in the fastnesses of detailed research. But we may point out that the work of McNemar (*178*), M. L. Jones, J. W. Cox, and others, considered in conjunction with the above, indicate factors additional to the above, as follows: (1) Physical muscular strength, (2) Skill in ball games, (3) General dexterity, and (4) *Manual* dexterity or motor skill.

The clusters from Harrison's correlations of speed and other sources, which later research may indicate to be speed factors, are listed for completeness here; but they must be regarded as distinctly tentative.

Cluster T. (XXIIIa). Maximal Rhythm. Evidenced by factor (67).

> Speed tapping
> Speed patting
> Speed turning crank   Mean inter r = .48.
> Speed card sorting (less clearly)
> Speed finger dexterity (less clearly)

Cluster T. (XXIV). Perceptual-Dexterity. Evidenced by cluster (69).

> Card sorting
> Substitution (symbol in a passage of print)
> Tapping
> Finger dexterity (less clearly)

Cluster T. (XXIVa). Reaction Time Speed. Reymert's *(216)* early work showed considerable positive intercorrelation of reaction-time speeds with various senses and various muscle sets. This also correlated with a number of other speed measures. Harrison's study indicates that reaction time does not fall into any of the other clusters. Thurstone's factor 137 confirms this separation of sheer reaction time from the more ideational performance speeds.

Cluster T. (XXV). Finger Dexterity I. Evidenced by cluster (70).

> Writing
> Finger dexterity
> Card sorting

Cluster T. (XXVI). Finger Dexterity II. Evidenced by cluster (71).

> Writing
> Finger dexterity
> Reading

Factor T. XXVII. "Fluency of Associations" (under restrictions). Evidenced by factors and clusters (1), (9), (17), (24), (30), (50), and Johnson's factor in *(135)*. When Hargreaves *(108)* partialed out the speed factor from his correlations, he found remaining — principally in tests demanding a ready, spontaneous flow of indiscriminate words, images, etc. — another substantial factor, which was not "g" or perseveration. This factor, which, following Hargreaves, has generally become known as "Fluency of Association" or sometimes "c factor" or "verbal fluency," has since been separated out a number of times, usually from speed tests, sometimes from ability tests (imagination), and sometimes from character-personality tests.

Verbal Ability: very easy same-opposites and mixed sentences	0.71
Speed of Reading (natural, or, less definitely, maximum)	0.5 to 0.6
Producing words beginning with a given letter, or other *slightly controlled* association	0.5 to 0.6
Producing associations to pictures, as a story	0.5 to 0.6

Producing associations to ink blots	0.5 to 0.6
Free association (number of words, or median reaction time)	0.5 to 0.6
Word-building speed (out of six letters)	0.59
Natural tapping rate	0.54
Finishing sentences or brief unfinished stories (amount and speed)	0.5 to 0.6
Finishing drawings (completing objects out of a few vague lines)	0.5 to 0.6
Amount read on a story with jumbled printing	0.38
Time reported negative after image lingers	0.34
Tendency to continue task when interrupted	0.34
Magnitude of resistance drop on P.G. Reflex	0.30

The problem now arises of determining the relation of this factor — so prominent in temperament researches — to the fluency factors found in the field of abilities. Thurstone's word-fluency factor, W (discussed under T. II above), has the following high loadings:

All r's above 0.5

Words (per minute) beginning and ending with a given letter
Words (per minute) beginning with a given letter
Words (per minute) having four letters and beginning with a given letter
Words (per minute) beginning with a certain syllable
Words (per minute) ending with a certain syllable
Finding rhymes for words
Finding synonyms for words (easy)

Thurstone's analysis proves definitely that this factor does not enter into size of recognized vocabulary or other measures of sheer verbal comprehension.

As the wider temperamental associates of fluency were naturally not included in Thurstone's ability study, they did not appear in the factor saturations.

Apart from these systematic findings the factor has also been encountered in other fields, notably in studies of reading ability and disability, by Bear and Odbert (*14*) and by Traxler (*265*). With intelligence and vocabulary held constant, significant correlations, .10 to .48, were found in the cluster: speed of free association, speed-controlled association, speed of reading continuous or discontinuous material.

However, as we have seen under III, fluency is already known to involve five factors: (1) a factor of fluency of verbal association when associations are in some way restricted by given conditions (A), (2) a factor of fluency with no restrictions (E), (3) a factor of verbal fluency, notably present in word series and pictures, (4) a

factor of pictorial fluency notably present in free drawings and seeing things in ink blots, and (5) a factor of facility and fluency in
oral speech. It seems very likely, however, that Gibb's (3) and (4)
can be identified respectively with (1) and (2); for the real difference of the pictorial and verbal tests in question may be the relative
lack of guiding restrictions in the former.

At present, therefore, it is most likely that we have to deal with
four factors in this field of ready, fluent association and reproduction,
as follows:

1. *Fluency of Association under Restrictions.* This is probably the
substantial core of the crude factor XXVII recorded above, in two
groups of manifestations. It is the A factor (72) of Carroll and
largely the W factor of Thurstone. It manifests itself for certain in
verbal and probably in other material where definite restrictions
are put upon the channels of fluency — e.g., easy opposites, "beginning with a certain letter," reading speed, rhyming, fitting into a
picture. It is probable that this factor is most involved with the
temperament (surgency) association. (See, e.g., the negative correlation with "neuroticism-depression" in 966.)

T. XXVIIa. Fluency of Association with Minimum.Direction. This
is Carroll's E factor (176) and probably Gibb's pictorial fluency
(153). It manifests itself particularly in:

> No. of words per minute expanding
> on a theme or topic.
> No. of relevant words per minute
> describing a picture.
> Production of poetic similes.

and probably
> No. of new objects made by pencil
> strokes on a line.
> No. of objects seen in ink blots.

The general character is that of fluent productivity of ideas with
a minimum of external stimulus or control. According to 966, this
also has some positive correlation with perseveration.

T. XXVIIb. Fluency and Facility in Oral Speech. Evidenced by
(177).

> No. of relevant words in describing a picture.
> Percentage of relevant words in describing a picture.
> Memory for general meaning of a paragraph.

Carroll suggests these measures are partly determined by ease and
confidence in coherent spontaneous expression of ideas in speech in
the experimental situation.

T. XXVIIc.   Verbal Speed. Evidenced by factor (178). This was considered by Carroll a possible third and minor element in V factor; but seems to the present writer more closely related to speed and fluency measures.

> Rating on goodness of picture description.
> Rating on goodness of theme enlargement.
> Maximum (and normal) speed of reading.
> Speed of handwriting.

At present the relative contributions of these factors (their mean variance) in the general field of fluency defined by "logical trait" boundaries cannot be more than very approximately estimated. The nature of the variables suggests that the main fluency factor — that first encountered, e.g., in temperament studies — was actually T. XXVII. In a varied fluency battery Gibb's study gives T. XXVII about 30 per cent greater contribution to the variance than T. XXVII*a*, while Carroll's study likewise gives the former a significantly greater contribution than the latter to the variance of 42 tests.

Accordingly we shall consider this the main fluency factor, but research on the fluency associated with surgent and cyclothyme temperament needs to explore also the role of the three lesser factors.

Tempo. A good deal of research has been done on the temperamental implications, environmental determination and inheritance of "personal tempo." Many writers — among them F. Broun, Frischeisen-Kohler, Guttman, Meumann, and Wu — have conducted research on these influences or built extensive psychological theories of temperament on the basis of general personal tempo. But until recently no one had stopped to prove that such a general personal tempo exists.

The results of Frischeisen-Kohler point, with no great statistical clarity however, to a cluster in such activities as natural speed of tapping with the hand, tapping with the foot, and the preferred speed in a metronome when listening to it. Wu used rhythms, reading, writing, and counting. No single general factor could be found, though there were at least two strongly correlated clusters (tapping and writing being the centers). All observers agree in finding that the individual has great consistency of tempo in any one field of manifestation — i.e., there are real preferred rates and ranges — and that rhythms with small movement amplitude are faster than with large amplitude.

One cannot assume, however, that all "involuntary" basal speeds, even in the same realm of behavior, are the same. Miles (*180*) found that rhythmic performances had a greater range of individual difference than non-rhythmic, though the two proved to be related. Slater (*234*) found a preferred speed of doing untimed intelligence tests, which in intelligence-test performances acted as a general factor and one quite distinct from either "g" or verbal ability. However, in such a case one cannot be sure that the usual habit of working quickly in any test situation is not upsetting basal speed. In short, the line between maximal speed and natural speed is not always easy to draw, and this may account for the appreciable correlation which, as we shall see, is characteristically found between them.

In discussing tempo it seems that a warning should be issued about the much-investigated reversible perspective test, sometimes employed as a measure of oscillation, sometimes of speed or tempo. The correlations of r.p. speed with the latter are just significant and negative, and with oscillation they are almost negligible; i.e., it is not a good tempo measurement.

The following clusters of natural tempo are tentative and based largely on the two most definitive researches, that of Allport and Vernon (*7*) and that of Harrison (*109*). The latter had the most wide range of performance yet studied. Though the intercorrelations were practically all positive, the mean for the ten individual tests varying from .10 to .41, Harrison was not able to conclude that a single general factor ran through the tests. The pool of speeds correlated significantly with individuals' self-estimates of how fast they were in everyday life.

Allport and Vernon (7) obtained an average *r* of .17 for their fourteen very varied natural tempo tests and again could not conclude the existence of a general factor. We have identified their clusters where possible with those of Harrison as follows.

Cluster T. (XXIc). *Ideomotor Tempo, called Verbal Speed by Allport and Vernon.* Evidenced by (73) and (83).

1. Reading	
2. Counting	Good agreement of Allport
3. Handwriting	and Vernon and Harrison.
4. Tapping	Average .46.
5. Blackboard handwriting	

Cluster T. (XXIIIb). *Rhythm Tempo, called Rhythmic Speed by Allport and Vernon.* Evidenced by (72) and (82).

1. Finger and hand tapping	
2. Leg tapping	Average intercorrelation =
3. Patting	0.76 (Allport and Vernon).
4. Counting	
5. Stylus compression	

Cluster T. (XXVIII). *Drawing Tempo, called Drawing Speed by Allport and Vernon.* Evidenced by (84).

1. Drawing figures, etc., on paper	Average intercorrelation =
2. Foot drawing	0.58 (Allport and Vernon).
3. Blackboard drawing	

Cluster T. (XXIX). *General Tempo.* Here we merge Harrison's broadest cluster, which has the very varied items (1) to (6), with the general clusters of Broun and Frischeisen-Kohler — i.e., factors (74) and (77).

1. Cranking
2. Tapping
3. Body bending
4. Patting
5. Speed decision
6. Card sorting

Cluster T. (XXX). *Body Tempo.* Evidenced by (75).

1 Head turning
2. Body bending
3. Arm raising

Cluster T. (*XXXI*). *Limb Tempo.* Evidenced by (76).

    1. Arm raising
    2. Walking

Relationships of speed, fluency, and tempo factors. That there is some relation between natural tempo and the maximal speed patterns with respect to area — i.e., pattern — factor loading is suggested by the three instances above in which the tempo factor has been given the same number as the speed factor, the factors being qualified as "a" and "b." Such a parallelism is suggested also by our discussion above on speed and ability measurements (for even the natural tempo must be determined by specific resistances corresponding to lack of ability in the task). And it is borne out by the finding of Harrison (*109*) that a significant correlation exists between maximal and voluntary tempos (.37 $\pm$ .00). Adams's results definitely indicate, and Harrison's suggest, that the clusters are better defined, and that the rates are more individually consistent, at maximal speed.

Batteries of speed or fluency tests have constantly been found to have a slight (0.10 and 0.30, respectively) positive correlation with "g," and, as few experimenters measure the pure factor, some of the low correlations of speed and fluency measures with various other variables may be interpreted as merely due to "g" contamination. Line found (*162*), however, a slight positive r of the above speed factor (XXI*a*), apart from intelligence, with children's school performance. He also found the speed factor higher in the younger, brighter members of a class and those with fewer misdemeanors.

The great interest of these speed, tempo, and fluency factors for personality, which justifies the somewhat detailed study of their ability roots here, is that they are among the most direct indicators of temperament. To study them only where they outcrop among abilities is to reckon only with the visible part of an iceberg, ignoring their massive importance for the total personality.

Allport and Vernon (7) have emphasized this in terms of the personality diagnostic value of expressive movement. The present writer has emphasized it by pointing out that on clinical grounds the high fluency of the "f" factor seems to be precisely the same as the high surgency ("extraversion") of the "F" factor (Surgency, Chapter 9), and by proving that a high correlation (0.6 to 0.7, uncorrected for attenuation) exists between the surgent temperament (factor F) and measures of fluency (41). This correlation has been confirmed several times in diverse groups since its discovery (47); also, less directly, by lower r's (-0.24, Notcutt (194)) between fluency and questionnaire "introversion."

Although higher correlation of temperament is found with fluency than pure speed measurements, it is still possible that speed alone correlates somewhat with the main surgency factor [1] (41). Between most actual test batteries of speed and fluency there is a low positive correlation (0.3 Cattell, 0.28 Notcutt), because it is extremely difficult to find a test involving fluency but not speed. However, in some instances of correlation with temperament it is now fairly certain which is responsible for the correlation. Indeed, in one research, the important theoretical and practical consequences of which seem to have passed unnoticed, the *difference* between speed and fluency seems to be of paramount significance. This is the research of Studman (246), who showed that in simple depression and mania both speed and fluency are abnormal (low in d, high in m), but that in agitated melancholia fluency measures remain low while speed is unduly high.[2]

Evidently the fluency, speed, and tempo performances spring from different factors of personality and hold great promise for the measurement and understanding of the temperament

---

[1] A contrary indication lies in the fact that Negroes score significantly higher than whites on fluency, yet not so high (Klineberg) on maximal speed tests. The relation of fluency to natural tempo may, however, be much greater (positively) than to maximal speed. This expectation has not yet been subjected to testing.

[2] In conjunction with footnote 1 this suggests that speed is will, fluency a matter of temperament.

factors involved. For example, their measurement may throw light on whether surgency is a matter of high energy endowment or poor inhibition, or may help clarify the physiological basis of cyclothyme-schizothyme and surgency tendencies.

First, however, we need to define the test factors, as such, more completely, and to achieve this it is necessary to convince psychologists that these are not factors merely within the realm of ability — still less only of verbal ability — but factors which need to be pursued experimentally in their relatively remote manifestations.

7. THE SOURCE TRAITS OF PERSEVERATION, DISPOSITION RIGIDITY, OR FUNCTIONAL AUTONOMY

History of perseveration concept. Although the term "perseveration" was first coined by Neisser in 1894, speculation about the phenomena which this term covers has been ancient and perennial. The tendency for behavior to repeat itself, once started, maladaptively, has long been commented upon by psychiatrists, and a long line of writers — William James, Otto Groos, Muller and Pilzecker, Heymans and Wiersma — have made "mental inertia" of central importance in understanding personality. Generally the argument has been that high perseverators should be introverts, but the theory has also been confidently propounded that the stability which high neural perseveration or "secondary function" gives to disposition would cause the higher perseverator to be of firmer character. The experimental investigation of perseveration which begins with Heymans and Wiersma, and with Spearman (235), who gave the phenomenon its first precise definition as "mental inertia," has destroyed most of these theories.

Experimental evidence on perseveration. The manifestations of perseverative tendency which have been brought under experimental surveillance illustrate by their variety the different senses in which perseveration has been understood. They include sensory perseveration, motor perseveration, perseveration of feeling, and many things which have only the most superficial resemblance to what was originally defined as perseveration.

Three questions have to be asked of these tests: (1) Do they correlate positively? (2) Have the correlations the relationships which would be expected if a single general factor of perseveration is operative? and (3) Is this general factor quite different from intelligence and other known factors, and clearly perseverative in character?

Much disagreement has arisen about the answers to these questions, but the perseverative tendency is so important for personality that the present position must be briefly delineated even though our present concepts are not sufficiently established to be immediately applicable to routine practical psychometry. The majority of investigators — Lankes (*235*), Wynn Jones (*138*), Bernstein (*16*), Pinard (*205*) (*206*), Stephenson (*240*) (*241*), Cattell (*42*) (*43*) (*44*) (*47*), Clarke (*61*), Darroch (*70*), Rangachar (*209*), Howard (*125*), Notcutt (*194*), Zillig (*286*), Burri (*24*), and others — find positive intercorrelations and some evidence of a general factor or two general factors. A few, such as Biesheuvel (*18*) and Walker, Staines, and Kenna (*270*), obtain results which are only partly compatible with this finding. And a minority — Jasper (*132*), Shevach (*233*), Hargreaves (*108*), and Hamilton (*107*)— fail to find evidence of any perseveration factor. Of the last, only the two first named can be considered based on a sufficient population. Moreover, it is precisely these negative researches which have included as "perseveration" tests certain forms of response — e.g., time of dark adaptation, reaction time, tapping rate, retentivity (delayed versus immediate recall) — which no careful student would have considered proved manifestations of perseveration. It is advantageous, of course, in the exploration of perseveration, for each new research to include a few far-fetched varieties; but it is scarcely desirable to have *all* tests of this kind, to state beforehand that they *are* perseverative, and to conclude that the absence of correlation disproves the existence of perseveration!

On *a priori* grounds perseveration tests have been divided up into sensory perseveration (e.g., speed of flicker fusion), motor perseveration (interference measured in switching from one performance to another), associative perseveration (as in Jung's repetition of association words or in persistence of ideas), and orectic perseveration (tendency to finish a task once started; persistence of moods). The evidence of the above experiments is that positive correlations exist only among instances of motor perseveration, though occasionally the flicker test of sensory perseveration [1] has fitted in with them. Recent research, summarizing, (*58k*), proves a single general factor through the motor tests and others, and it is certain, through reference tests (Wynn Jones) and direct correlation with "g," that the correlations are *not* due to intelligence, speed, fluency, or other well-known general factors.

In 1935 the present writer pointed out that the notion of perseveration as "inertia" had a double meaning and that the motor tests which best measure whatever "p factor" is present among them are to be distinguished by what was there called "creative effort" character rather than by being mere "alternation" tests. This means that the temporal relations of the two "interfering" performances in a p test are unimportant; the important thing is that one activity (the X performance) — e.g., writing capital S's — shall be an old-established habit and that the other activity (the Y activity) shall be a "creative effort" situation — i.e., a task of equal complexity but breaking new ground; e.g., writing capital S's backward. This distinction has been generally accepted by later researchers, and Walker, Staines, and Kenna (*270*) have gone so far as to deny that p factor in the sense of simple inertia (in quickly switching over from any X to any Y activity) exists.

[1] See controversy, Biesheuvel (*18*) and Wynn Jones (*139*).

In a recent, more extensive, review (*58k*) of the data and theory than is possible here, the writer has shown that the only assured manifestation of perseveration is as *disposition rigidity* — i.e., as difficulty in new relative to old tasks, when the new tasks are not difficult by reason of complexity ("g" saturation). Anderson (personal letter), Darroch (*70*), and Walker (*270*) have shown that a proper rescoring of alternation tests, which gets rid of disposition rigidity influences, leaves no evidence of a "mental inertia" factor *per se*. Other results — e.g., Notcutt (*194*) — show, however, a slight trace of a factor in the mere process of shifting suddenly back and forth between two equally old (or new) tasks.

The theory now propounded (*58k*) is that "perseveration" as measured in a test is $(D-W)$, where D is inherent disposition rigidity and W is the marshaled force of the ego — the will — trying to overcome this lag or rigidity. A secondary, as yet unproved hypothesis is that W, being dependent on integration of inherently refractory dispositions, is itself an inverse function of D; so that the measure remains largely a function of a single D factor. Indeed, the view that we are basically measuring disposition rigidity reconciles several past concepts and findings — e.g., that though tests have a large constitutional and even racial determination they also correlate with individual history of personality integration (being youngest child, being neurotic or delinquent); that some slight loading is found also in pure alternation tests of "mental inertia," that perseveration as "tendency to complete unfinished tasks" correlates positively or negatively with "p" measurement according to whether a minor habit or the whole will is concerned. Wrong orientation in the initial researches was partly due to forgetting that it was not perseveration which needed explanation but rather absence of perseveration — i.e., why a mental process ever changes. It arose also from being misled by loose, figurative uses of the term "perseveration" into including all manner of superficially similar repetition or inertia behavior.

Out of the obscurity of these too broad or loose notions experiment finally leaves the following more definite tendencies: (1) A factor of *disposition rigidity*, manifested, so far as we know, most clearly in motor performances, as a resistance to willed change of old established habits, but perhaps slightly manifested in interference with switching of any kind. (2) Two, or perhaps more, lesser factors in the general realm of what has, without undue looseness of definition, been considered perseveration.

Factor T. XXXII. *Disposition-Rigidity.*

For a comprehensive and detailed description of the tests, suitable for practical work, it is necessary to turn to a handbook of mental testing (46). The following is only a reminder of their nature.

Evidenced by factors (4), (8), (29), (38), (39), (40), (41), (42), (43), (44), (45), (46), (47), (59), and (80). It manifests itself most definitely in (1) *"creative effort"* tests of the following kind:

Difficulty — i.e., relative rate of production — in writing familiar letters; e.g., e's, beginning at end opposite from usual, compared with the usual way.

Difficulty in similar reversals of familiar numbers.

Difficulty (relative speed) in performing any simple habit in an unfamiliar way, with or without interference with the old way — e.g., reading words printed backward, turning right at the word "left."

(2) Less saturated, in *"alternation"* tests, as follows:

Difficulty in writing aA, bB, cC, as compared with abc, ABC.

Difficulty in writing HIHIH, compared with HHH and III.

Difficulty in alternately adding and subtracting numbers as compared to continuous adding or continuous subtracting.

Difficulty in alternating one pattern on a piano keyboard with another.

Difficulty in alternating word associations from verbs to adjectives, compared with either continuously.

(3) Possibly also in sensory and other perseveration, as,

Seeing fusion to gray at a low revolution rate on a "flicker" dial

Burri (24) showed that though correlations can be analyzed into a single general factor, they can also be analyzed into two general factors and possibly three or four. The second factor, having about half the saturation of the first (which was itself positive in all perseverative activities), was as follows:

Factor T. XXXIII. Mental vs. Motor Perseveration.[1] Evidenced in factor (81).

Positive in alternation on adding, subtracting, adjectives, verbs; negative in alternation of triangles, S's, figures.

Possibly a third important factor in the field of perseveration is that of "clinical perseveration" found by Rethlingshafer, as follows:

Factor XXXIV. Clinical Perseveration or Ego Rigidity. Evidenced by factor (19).

Disturbing after-effects of a slower rhythm upon the natural tapping rhythm	.76
Total time spent in making words from given letters	.58
Longest trial of maintained grip	.49
Natural tapping rate	.43
Absence of reported recurrence effects	− .40
Number of words constructed from six letters	− .31

This cannot be factor T. XXXI in a wider context; for p tests were included, yet did not correlate with it. The present writer has attempted to show (*41*) that the greatest subjective report of "recurrence" effects (introspected perseveration) of a certain kind (mental sets) occurs not with high p score but high w score individuals — i.e., perseveration is felt most by those who bring the will to bear most violently on the natural rates of the organism, as an athlete may report more shortness of breath than a sedentary worker. The above may be such an "ego-rigidity" and may relate to melancholia or other manifestations of super ego pressure.

The personality associates of perseveration. The importance of measuring p factor resides, of course, not in the thing immediately measured, but in the personality traits which have been found empirically to be associated with it. By perseveration or p-factor we shall mean factor T. XXXII variously diluted; for even in the researches guided by recent improvements it has been impossible to reach any very high saturation. Walker, Staines, and Kenna have speculated, with good grounds, that disposition rigidity manifests itself also in the warming-up response to a task, in the effectiveness of a mental set or expectancy, in retroactive inhibition, in the tendency of unconscious motives — e.g., completion

---

[1] A second factor in p-tests was also found in (*58k*), loading reading and fluent performance as opposed to alternation.

motives — to work themselves out, and in transfer of training (positive and negative). These relations are unconfirmed, but the relations which *have* been found are compatible with them.

Pinard showed that children showing problem behavior occur with undue frequency among very high and very low perseverators (*205*). Stephenson and Studman (*240*) found more character disintegration among psychotics with extreme, and especially with high, p scores. The present writer confirmed earlier findings of a negative correlation [1] (about 0.4) between p score and w^2 factor, but showed that the relation is curvilinear so that both very high and very low perseverators are in fact rated as unreliable, delinquent, and lacking in persistence of motive. The relation found for children, adolescent students, and adults is as represented in the diagram; but, of course, the correlation is so low that the prediction from p score to character (for any individual case) is not very reliable.

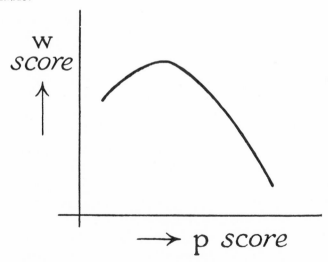

DIAGRAM 16. RELATION OF CHARACTER INTEGRATION TO p MEASUREMENT.

[1] Notcutt (*194*) fails to find this correlation, but his subjects were self-rated.
[2] W is the earlier approach to our final C and G factors, combined.

Regarding the difference between the form of character defect of high and low extremes, it is still difficult to draw a clear picture. If, as we suspect, p factor is a measure of the interactions of a constitutional temperament factor and a character integration level, the apparently mixed nature of the recorded differences, some temperamental and some characterial, would be readily explained.

Low p scores have consistently been found, by Stephenson (*241*), Pinard (*206*), and others for manics and hysterics, while very high p scores have been usual among melancholics, deteriorated schizophrenics, and psychotics rated high for sensitiveness, suspicion, and paranoid and obsessional trends. Eisenson (*78*) found somewhat significantly higher p scores for stutterers than non-stutterers. Higher p scores have also been found for those rated higher in general emotionality (*47*) — our C factor. Determined, face-to-face leaders and people who "get things done" have repeatedly been found to fall in the moderately or very low p-score brackets.

A curious triangular relationship, which has been found to hold in more than one investigation, is as follows: (1) In college subjects low p's choose most frequently mathematics, handwork, and science; high p's history, languages, drama, and religion. Low p's show more dominance; high p's more resignation (*44*). (2) Lower p scores are found, in the same culture group, among anthropometric Mediterranean racial types (*44*) (*209*). (3) As between Nordic and Mediterranean physical types in the same culture group, the former more frequently choose science, mathematics, and physically active pursuits (impersonal interest); the latter languages, drama, and religion (personal-emotional interest (*198a*)). The former, McDougall argued (*175a*), show more mental independence to the culture pattern, the latter more resignation to it. The way in which the pattern of (3) independently confirms that deducible from (1) and (2) is very striking, especially when more details are taken into consideration than can here be listed.

From the rating studies of Cattell (*41*) and Pinard (*205*), the following were taken as most reliably distinguishing the personalities of extreme high and low p-score cases.

CHARACTERISTICS OF

Low Perseverators	*High Perseverators*
Prone to action in dissatisfaction. Assertive; active.	Resigned, but often seeking expression in tortuous ways — hence sometimes deceitful, cruel, spiteful, unpredictable.
Insistently assertive. High tension. Hence nagging, restless, fussy.	Quiet, slow, more emotional and "deep" in general.
Enterprising, self-reliant. Openly individualistic. Tend to be natural leaders.	More skeptical and pessimistic. Conservative in habits.
Not affected by emotional scenes. Inconsiderate, tough.	Sensitive emotionally.
Irritable, selfish, silent, anxious, *tense*.	Rebellious in theoretical outlook, serious, shy, and solitary.
Tends to be interested in mechanical, scientific, and mathematical matters.	Tends to be interested in history, languages, and humanities.
Decisive and impetuous. Ability to grasp situations whole. Good taste and definite style in dress, voice, music, etc.	Absent-minded. Impressed by one thing at a time. Drifting to decisions. Dreamy. Sentimental. Careless of detail. Slovenly in dress.
Dreams very little.	Greater tendency to dreaming (in sleep).
Liable to short periods of acute restlessness and crises of intense emotional dissatisfaction.	Liable to long periods of depression or gentle melancholy.
More interested in scientific, business, and practical matters.	More interested in religious, historical, and language subjects.
	Neurotic symptoms of a general nature more prevalent.
Makes good use of relatively low IQ. (In social status, responsibility of occupation, etc.)	Fails to make best use of intelligence in any ordinary sense. Negligent of external demands.
Systematic, precise, planful.	
In general, character is defective because of "immaturity," naïveté, superficiality of emotions, and self-will.	In general, character is defective because of excessive deep inhibitions, emotionality with general discouragement and lack of integrated driving power.

The picture, as already suggested, appears to be partly one of temperament, partly one of character. The low perseverator is temperamentally more "high-strung," less deeply emotional, and of a more insistent temper. In character he is more disciplined, integrated earlier, and with a more exacting super ego.

Substantiation of any one part of the nexus of qualities which go with the perseveration factor is in general scientifically defective. Data have been admitted which might not have met the standards of significance which have been demanded elsewhere in this book. Some of the personality correlations, for example, have been with p tests which were not of high validity or reliability. But the writer, from considerable clinical experience with these tests, and from study of the interrelationships of the published findings, judges that the trend of the results is so consistent that much would be lost by omitting those parts of the picture — so valuable for the guidance of further research — which do not at the moment satisfy rigid statistical criteria.

8. PSYCHOSOMATIC FUNCTIONAL REACTION PATTERNS

Present treatment of psychosomatic factors. The descriptive study of personality would be guilty of pedantic and unprofitable restriction if it failed at least to indicate the possible physiological and somatic segments of personality factors. Conventionally we think of temperament source traits as having the closest connection with physical measurements and of traits associated with physical measurements as being the most constitutional and hereditary. But none of these three judgments is, of course, more than roughly true. Other than temperament, traits can have well-marked physical associations — e.g., intelligence; not all physical associates are constitutional and not all constitutional (congenital and inborn) traits are hereditary.

Two broad classes of somatic associations can be considered: (1) Functional — mainly physiological — and (2) Structural — mainly morphological, having to do with physique and physical heredity. Though a sharp line could be drawn logically between (1) and (2) and between them and the purely psychological factors, one cannot do so in the research data, for psychological variables have been correlated in mixed populations of measurements in both cases. Accordingly we shall make a relative and arbitrary distinction between (1) pure T factors having to do solely with psychological measurements, (2) T (SF) or *Somatic-Functional*, physiological factors, and (3) T (SS) *Somatic-Structural* factors, using morphological, but also in some instances physiological variables or having to do with constitutional proneness to "physical" diseases.

Somatic-functional, physiological factors. This section will review the physiological factors, but entirely empirically, without resort to physiological principles or preconceptions.

Incidentally we shall not attempt to deal with the important clusters or factors which might be expected in relation to "endocrine types." The fact is that these types are more discussed than worked upon. They exist only at the clinical level of observation, or inferentially from animal measurement. No definite factors based on measurement have been established, and even the clinical picture is vague as far as personality is concerned.

The application of correlation and factor-analysis techniques to physiological and somatic measurements is less developed than in the field of psychology. Of the clinically well-established syndromes none is sufficiently relevant to general personality study to be listed. Of those few syndromes, principally of autonomic nervous-system reactivity, which definitely have personality traits included in the total picture, some are now established in terms of measurement as definite factors or clusters. These we shall now consider, for their importance for personality study, even when the variables included are largely physiological, is great.

On account of the variety of techniques used, the failure to observe precautions necessary in designing satisfactory factor analyses, and the high percentage of findings presented as clusters — i.e., syndromes — rather than as factors, we experienced great difficulty in presenting reliable conclusions sharply distinguished from mere indications. The first two or three factors are tolerably clear; the remainder are only fragments of the "shape of things to come." They are set out in moderate detail in order to offer that perspective and guidance which research in the unstructured realm of meeting of psychological and physiological variables so badly needs.

Factor T.(SF)I. *Metabolic Activity or General Autonomic Activity.* Evidenced by (90), (120), (165), possibly (103), (163).

Basal metabolic rate   (Also, from (12), B.M.R. per unit weight or height; B.M.R. per unit creatinine excretion; advancement of osseous development in children.)
Pulse rate
Systolic and diastolic blood pressure
Body temperature (at tongue but not at finger) .... (lesser loading)
Magnitude of P.G.R. deflection .... (lesser loading)
Possibly, salivary output

In personality traits high ratings on: activity level, aggression, drive, vigor in athletics and physical tempo, excitable speech and pressure for expression in social situations, energy and enthusiasm in work, greater professional success among those equal in intelligence.

Possibly identical with this is Freeman and Katzoff's "Arousal" (163):

Magnitude of P.G.R. deflection
Recovery of resistance level (P.G.R.) during distraction from a prolonged nocive situation

and (the obverse of) Darrow and Heath's *Social Inactivity with Somasthenia or Hyporeactivity and Its Physiological Associates.* Evidenced by (103).

Small P.G.R. resistance recovery in three seconds   .25
Small galvanic reaction to shocks
Few spontaneous P.G.R. reactions in anticipatory period

Tendency larger blood-pressure reactions after shock
Tendency higher minimum resistance

Although it would be a mistake to identify this factor with P.G.R. magnitude alone, since XXXVII and XXXVIII*b* also involve the latter, the following seem to describe relationships important in this factor.

Brown (*20*) found appreciable correlations of P.G.R. with

Soundness of bodily constitution
Desire to excel (overtly expressed, especially in games, social situations)
Rapidity of decision

Here, although we already have a Darrow and Heath cluster above (but opposed in direction to this) we can probably add the pattern they found (*71*) in individuals who had large P.G.R. reactions and small blood-pressure reactions to stimuli. These were more well-adjusted than the opposite, particularly in responses to the following questionnaire items:

Can sit still without fidgeting
Never had strong desire to run away from home
Makes friends easily
Does not often feel "just miserable"
Does not think things go wrong through no fault of self
Seeks most important person at a reception without embarrassment

Cattell (*39*) has summarized the remaining evidence, in conjunction with some original findings, as follows:

P.G.R. correlates positively with

Cheerfulness of temperament (also low in psychotic depression)
Emotionality (slightly) (Mirk (*183*), however, obtained an *r* of 0.67.)
Forcefulness of character (also low in hebephrenics)
Absence of fatigue or intoxication
Goodness of general health and vitality
Possibly with school success, when IQ is held constant

The ratio $\frac{\text{P.G.R. to Sensory Stimulus}}{\text{P.G.R. to Ideational Stimulus}}$ has been found to be significantly higher in conversion hysterics than normals, and in normals than in anxiety hysterics.

There is some suggestion that the P.G.R. correlates with good committing to memory, and, therefore, in terms of individual differences, with the memory factor, T. XI above. (Notably rote memory (Brown (*21*)) and with quickness of reaction time (Mirk

(*183*)). All in all, the P.G.R. is clearly an index of "extravert vigor." The present writer has suggested that the essential correlation is with cortical suppression of conative, orectic impulses — i.e., with dynamic conflict rather than emotional experience as such (*39*). Most of the above work shows the P.G.R. to be very consistent for the individual over short intervals and fairly consistent over long intervals, especially if the subject remains in the same state of health and adjustment. Greenwald (see (*21*)) shows other P.G.R. characters as well as the "response quotient" to have high reliability.

The "sthenic" qualities above seem essential to the present factor; the emotional and neurotic qualities, on the other hand, to factors T.(SF)II and, especially T.(SF)IV*b*.

The existence of a general factor of autonomic efficiency-stability is in accordance with the Danielopulu studies (*75a*), while the earlier, criticized studies of Eppinger and Hess (*75a*), finding independent vagotonic and sympathetionic influence, are reconciled when regarded as secondary factors II and III (—) below.

Factor T.(SF)II. Sympathetic, Adrenergic, Tension. Evidenced by (91), (97), (166). Observe relation to emotionality pattern as described in *283a*. A broad, somewhat "thin" pattern.

Pulse rate
Respiration rate
B.M.R.
P.G.R. magnitude minus systolic blood pressure
Low resistance P.G.R.
P.G.R. magnitude
Systolic blood pressure
Body temperature, muscle tension, and salivary pH belong either here or in a distinct factor splitting from this.
High personal activity level as in T.(SF)I but less so

Factor T.(SF)III. Thyroid v. High P.G.R. Resistance Syndrome. Evidenced by (92),[1] (95), (98), (119), and perhaps (167), a set without adequate overlap and having resemblance to the factor above and below, but seeming to have an additional character.

> Low P.G.R. skin resistance
> Flushing
> B.M.R. (or oxygen consumption)
> Skin-stroking response (Dermatographia persistence)
> Sweating

[1] This contains only pulse rate and activity level.

Odor
Acne
Palpable thyroid
Pulse rate
Low lymphocyte count

And on the psychological side:

Low Absolute Resistance	High Absolute Resistance
Alertness, activity	Sleepiness, passivity, but not fatigue
Easy expression, excitement	Boredom, unhappiness, suppression
Neurasthenics, "nervous temperaments"	Hysterics, "suppressed temperaments"
Basedow's disease	
Feeling of anxiety and depression	Feeling of confidence and physical well-being

Low resistance in daytime (as here) seems to be associated with unusually high resistance in sleep and with more frequent deflections than usual. It is suggested (38) that resistance is most nearly proportional to the fraction: $\dfrac{\text{Available reserves of energy}}{\text{Extent of release of energy taking place at the time in consciousness}}$

In relation to this factor we have to consider Darling's (94), Cholinergic or Parasympathetic Activity, as follows:

Psychogalvanic reflex magnitude minus systolic blood pressure magnitude	.80
Psychogalvanic reflex magnitude alone	.70
Systolic blood pressure	− .72
Conductance (low actual P.G.R. resistance)	.30

No personality variables out of six used gave good correlation, but those high in this factor reported as more alert and uninhibited.

This could be the negative aspect of T.(SF)III', but the absence of P.G.R. magnitude and blood pressure in the former and relative low rank of conductance in this suggests separate recording. Also Darling's (96), as follows:

Loadings

Manic confidence cheerfulness-activity as opposed to "Inhibited"	.57
Hyperactivity	.58
Conductance (low "actual" or "constant" resistance on the psychogalvanic reflex)	.29

Two sound researches agree in indicating two independent factors in what may roughly be called the "thyroid" field. Both are characterized by tendency (1) to low resistance on P.G.R., (2) to large P.G.R. deflections, (3) low systolic (or diastolic) blood pressure, (4) some behavior tendency to overactivity. They are distinguished, however, by greater emphasis in what we are inclined to call the true thyroid pattern (T.(S)III) on pulse, B.M.R., low lymphocyte and high dermatographia, while the other shows more loading on low resistance, on alertness and hyperactivity, and on pupillary diameter. The latter we are inclined to identify with Darling's (96), relegating (94) to the hyperthyroid, but the reverse is not impossible. All we know for certain is that there must be two factors here, requiring more distinction — T.(SF)III above and

Factor T.(SF)IVa. Nervous Disposition. (High strung.) Evidenced by (96) and (167).

> Low P.G.R. resistance
> Large P.G.R. deflection
> Low systolic (and diastolic blood pressure)
> Large pupillary diameter
> Alertness, hyperactivity

This is possibly the same as:

Factor T.(SF)IVb. Reactive P.G.R.; Hypersensitive temperament v. Somesthesia, sleep difficulties. Evidenced by (100), (104), and (164). We have followed the unusual procedure of putting two clusters from one research together; but they correlate negatively and can be considered opposite aspects of one factor. This is not well defined and might, as the suffix indicates, be subsumed in the two preceding factors.

Big resistance drop in two minutes' anticipation (also initial to minimum)
Many spontaneous deflections in anticipatory and interim periods
Small resistance recovery to shocks
Big P.G.R. recovery to shocks

The syndrome correlated positively but low (.15) with questionnaires on anxiety, hypersensitivity, excitability, and manic tendency (extraversion); and negatively (about .18) with sleep difficulties and somasthenic tendencies. This agrees with (164) loadings in frequency of nervous movements, self-rating on anxiety, neuroticism, variability of mood, and actual variability in P.G.R. resistance.

There is insufficient overlap of employed variables to decide whether this is the same as *Factor T.(SF)IVc. Circulatory Variability.* Evidenced by (93).

> Variability of pulse rate
> Variability of respiration rate
> Variability of systolic blood pressure

The pool of these correlates .51 $\pm$ .23 with the Activity Level, and about the same with the absolute physiological level (the three above factors combined).

Factor T.(SF)V. Maladjustment-Emotionality v. Control Blood Pressure Reactivity.

Again we put two correlated clusters of the Darrow and Heath study together (99) and (101) in the belief that they indicate a single factor and one not yet described. Also (162).

Small P.G.R. deflection to conditioned or to direct stimulus
Small (reaction recovery) quotient — i.e., poor return to pre-stimulus level
Large resistance rise in two minutes of rest from stress
Large blood pressure rise to stimulus or threat
Questionnaire emphasis on neurotic maladjustment, emotional excitability

With this we place Freeman and Katzoff's "Control" (*162*) (on the opposite pole).

> Large reaction-recovery ratio on P.G.R.
> Few bodily movements before and after stimulus
> Good recovery of voice level after emotion
> Rating for goodness of adjustment

Cluster T.(SF)VI. Paranoid Excitability and Depression (Q. XV. Paranoid Schizothyme) and Physiological Associates. Evidenced by (102).

Small or negative blood-pressure change after shocks .20
Low initial resistance on P.G.R.
Low final (minimum) resistance on P.G.R. after stressful experiment

Cluster T.(SF)VII. Physical, Muscular Strength. Evidenced by factors (15), (54), (61) and cluster (123).

> Strength
> Energy output
> Large-muscle movements

Factor T.(SF)VIII. Lateral Muscle Endurance. Adequately established in Cureton's study (*66a*).

Factor T.(SF)IX. Endurance in Limb Locomotive Muscles. As above.

Factor T.(SF)X. Endurance of Arm Extension Muscles. As above.

Factor T.(SF)XI. Endurance in Running. As above.

Several T.(SF) factors additional to the above are tolerably established — e.g., one loading low P.G.R. resistance, body temperature, salivary pH; another loading blood sugar level, low body temperature, variability of tidal air in lungs, diastolic blood pressure; another loading temperature and oxygen consumption; but as these have no demonstrated psychological associates they are not recorded.

In the field of cardiovascular efficiency three studies (*158a*)(*171a*) (*188a*) agree in indicating 9 factors, 5 concerned mainly with blood pressure, 3 with pulse, and 1 with respiration. An overall study orienting these fragmentary physiological studies is greatly needed.

Cluster T.(SS)IXc. Rheumatic Fever and Heart Disease Constitution. Heredity in rheumatic heart disease is well established (16*a*), (75*a*), (234*a*). Draper finds a physique in acute rheumatic fever cases of slenderness, small, narrow or long narrow faces, long jaw wide at gonia, long limbs, tendency to asymmetry and irregular teeth and palate, broad shallow chest. This has resemblance about equally to IX and to VIII, involving the "length factor" in both.

Dunbar finds significant associations with cardiovascular disease, extreme nervousness, diabetes (less), generally poor health record, especially pelvic, but also respiratory and gastrointestinal disorders and probably allergy.

Psychologically: Low educational level, sociable, talkative, adventurous. Rheumatic fever and arthritis group show excess of early neurotic traits, temper tantrums, nightmares, nail biting, tics, finickiness and schizoid traits of shyness, sensitive withdrawal. Both have conflicts in regard to authority.

Cluster T.(SS)Xa and Xb. Diabetic Constitutions. The high hereditary determination in diabetes has recently been shown by Dupertius to be associated with two syndromes: (X*a*) the mesomorphic build (VIII), insulin sensitiveness, blood sugar instability, faulty muscle-sugar combustion relationship; severe onset of disease; (X*b*) endomorphic build, insulin-resistant, signs of anterior pituitary disorder, mild onset in adult life.

Dunbar (77*a*) finds significant association with nervousness and insanity, to a lesser extent cardiovascular disease, slightly with accident proneness and less than any group with disease generally.

Psychologically: Better than average education, intelligence, social status. Schizoid, paranoid make-up, with depression. Temper tantrums, phobias, nightmares, restlessness, vacillation, emotionality, concern over sexual adequacy.

Cluster T.(SS)XI.   Infantile Paralysis Constitution.   Draper brings evidence of the greater proneness to infantile paralysis in the following cluster: Internal eyefolds (Mongoloid); central incisor spacing; large central incisors; black spots in skin; long eyelashes; marked hyperextensibility of joints; flat nose bridge, wide-set eyes.

Cluster T.(SS)XII.   Migraine, Allergy, Neurovascular Instability. Bray (16a) considers migraine along with asthma, hay fever, and angioneurotic oedema as a generally inheritable allergic diathesis. Draper finds migrainous women to be distinguished by narrow body build, least evident in the face, most in the pelvis, and by an extremely small subcostal angle.   The possibility of some generalized vascular instability in migraine, with accompanying temperamental tendencies, is frequently noted.

Cluster T.(SS)XIII.   Androgyny Ratio.   A cluster of variables which indicate relative masculinity or femininity of build is described by both Draper and Sheldon.   It is surprising that this cluster, accurately measured (possibly an index of endocrine balance), has never been correlated with German's psychological equivalent (T.XXXV).

Cluster T.(SS)XIV.   Hypertensive Cardiovascular Disease.   Dunbar (77a) finds in this group a very high incidence of nervousness and a somewhat significant incidence of diabetes and perhaps accident proneness.   Also pneumonia, gastrointestinal, major operations, allergy, and obesity.

Psychologically: Obsessive compulsive, aggressive behavior, better intelligence than education, low neurotic record in childhood (and mainly temper, nail biting); excessive use of coffee, cigarettes, alcohol; some athletic interests; ambitious.

Other clusters and factors.   The factorial analysis of anthropometric data is still in its infancy.   The studies of Eysenck and of Cohen suffer from having stopped at two or three factors and possibly also from striving for orthogonal factors.   The more recent, as yet unpublished study by Thurstone gives at least five factors and these may bridge the gap between the sensitive but unreliable clinical approaches above and more exact but blind statistics.   The surprising feature so far revealed by the factorial studies is that if a depth (anterior-posterior) factor exists at all independently of a general "magnitude-of-body-cross-section" factor it must be very small. The main factors are those of overall size, girth, head size, and possibly two others.

Factor T.(SS)XIV. Overall Size. Evidenced by (181) and other studies. This may be the main element also in the cluster "large build — pituitary syndrome," though this was found among children. Evidenced by (124), a cluster among clusters.

Cluster of physical strength (123)	Mean r
Cluster of large build	about
Cluster of parasympathetic response (119)	.38
Cluster of high metabolism — advancing osseous development (120)	

Factor T.(SS)XV. Girth v. Linearity of Build. Evidenced by (182) and others unpublished.

This loads all body cross sections, but most highly *breadth of chest.* It seems to indicate that the distinction between Mesomorph and Ectomorph is only one of degree and that, as Kretschmer finally decided, a division in Pyknic and Leptosome is sufficient. Eysenck further shows that this single factor correlates as highly with schizoid traits as do estimates of the separate clusters.

Factor T.(SS)XV. Head Size. Evidenced by a factor in Thurstone's study, influencing head dimensions alone.

Cluster T.(SS)XVI. Basedowoid or B-Type Temperament. (Integrate.) Evidenced by (129).

Fluctuating imagery, memory images, eidetic images, not clearly separated and largely eidetic in nature
Can voluntarily modify visual imagery with ease
Experiences synaesthesia
Color in images like original
No physiological reaction to calcium
Finer structure of skin capillaries under microscopic examination
Large, luminous eyes and other "hyperthyroid" characters
Greater responsiveness of sympathetic nervous system

Personality traits associated:

Frank, lively, alert, generally good-natured, emotional, changeable, rapid mental associations. Artistically inclined but in good contact, and well integrated with reality. Plastic.

Cluster T.(SS)XVII. Tetanoid or T-Type Temperament. (Disintegrate.) Evidenced by (129).

Little imagery, or no imagery at all. None eidetic.
Persistent, prolonged after images

Cannot modify visual images, produce or remove them, and is sometimes bothered by them

Color in images not like original

Positive physiological reaction to calcium (Parathyroid deficiency)

Coarser structure of skin capillaries, under microscopic examination

"Strained" muscle tensions in face and tetanoid tendency in general

Small eyes

9. PSYCHOSOMATIC, STRUCTURAL, CONSTITUTIONAL PATTERNS

Data available for extending meaning of clusters. The chief patterns known in the realm of physical characteristics come from physical anthropology and clinical medicine. Until two or three years ago factor-analytic technique had not been applied here, and even today the majority of the patterns recognized are clusters few of which are founded on actual measurements and still fewer of which are the results of true correlation of statistical material. Nevertheless, because of indirect evidence there is not the slightest doubt about the existence of most *as clusters*. What is in doubt is *the magnitude of the correlation in the clusters and the interrelations of the clusters*.

The oldest clusters are those of racial physical type. Since crossing breaks up these clusters, they cannot be due to single genes; but whether a race is generally defined by a collection of two or three genes or two or three hundred is unknown. Ideally, contingency coefficients or coefficients of association should be worked out among gene manifestations to determine the intensity of the associations — i.e., the magnitude of mean r — which are now crudely and inadequately defined by the concepts of race and subrace (or national mixture).

Correlation of personality traits with racial anthropometric patterns has the greatest importance for the social psychological problem of predicting group cultural emergents. Moreover, since these patterns have greater permanence than cultural patterns, they have, in enhanced degree, the predictive efficiency for defining the individual that any cluster possesses.

To say that a man is an Eskimo at once defines not one but a host of physical variables.

It must be the ultimate aim of psychology to relate increments in various behavior potentialities to single genes, not merely to the gene-complex which we call a race. But the initial exploration is best guided by seeking behavioral associates of these physical clusters, and the growth of a true science of genetic psychology has so far been held up through the unfortunate neglect of indications in this field.

Anthropometric syndromes. For an exhaustive description of racial patterns the reader is referred to textbooks on anthropometry. The following are salient clusters of most practical importance for research.

Cluster T.(SS)I. Negro physique. Dolicocephalic; long limbs relative to trunk; black, frizzy hair; thick lips; broad, low-bridged nose, dark skin; dark eyes; specific peculiarity of heel structure.

Scores on intelligence tests at a statistically significant lower level than average of a mixed population. Scores on culture free tests too recent to justify conclusion as to amount of difference due to environment.

Cluster T.(SS)II. Mongolian physique. Brachycephalic; limbs short relative to trunk; straight, black hair; dark eyes; yellowish skin; low hirsutism; "Mongolian" epicanthic fold on eye; broad, flat-bridged nose; tendency to shorter stature.

Intelligence test scores not significantly different from Europeans. No other dynamic trait or temperamental differences yet clearly demonstrated.

Cluster T.(SS)III. Nordic physique. Dolicocephalic, light (blue or gray) eyes, fresh complexion; narrow nose, moderate bridge; blond hair, wavy to straight; tall, rather narrow figure.

There is evidence of higher mental ability in this group and the Jewish group than in other groups sampled in America; but it is uncertain how far this is due to sampling. The most interesting and significant difference, however, is a temperamental one. The cluster of "low disposition rigidity, interest in science, mathematics, and practical studies, high emotional integration" which has been reviewed on page 440 and contingently labeled "low p complex" distinguishes significantly this group from Mediterranean (T.(SS)VI) and possibly from Near Eastern (T.(SS)V) and Alpine (T.(SS)IV). McDougall's studies suggest also schizoid traits and dominance in the total cluster.

Cluster T.(SS)IV. Alpine Physique. Brachycephalic, brown-eyed, brown, straight-haired, short, broad build, low bridge to nose, medium complexion.

Cluster T.(SS)V. Near Eastern Physique. Brachycephalic, straight at back, hair dark and curly, brown eyes, brownish skin, very prominent nose and rather full lips, marked hirsutism, middling height, thickset. This and the Mediterranean constitute two principal components in Semitic-speaking peoples.

Cluster T.(SS)VI. Mediterranean Physique. Dolicocephalic, short, slender, relatively long legs, dark, sleek curly hair, dark eyes, rather narrow but shorter nose; rather greater fullness in fleshy parts than in Nordic; olive complexion.

In general mental capacity the samples of this group which have been measured (in America) are below the average of the other European groups. See also (207a). The existence of a genetic temperament difference tied up with these physical characters is strongly indicated by the data discussed on page 440; but its full extent and significance have not yet been explored.

The following clusters represent a trinity of recognized physical types which have come up through Rostan (221a), Kretschmer (154), and Sheldon (231a), which in no case have been subjected to even as much correlation as the racial types (which at least have been correlated with regard to a geographical gradient). It is asserted by these clinicians that the types are not identical with racial types; though the descriptions of VII, VIII, and IX below correspond strikingly to Alpine (IV), Nordic III, and Mediterranean (VI). At any rate, no correlation with eye, hair, or skin coloring has been commented upon, so that these are possibly independent variables in the race complexes. However, Sheldon has not studied and demonstrated these physiques outside the above race groups, while Kretschmer agrees that the *frequency* of these physiques is markedly different in the three races, giving the matching indicated. The descriptions are Sheldon (231a) supplemented by Kretschmer, there being no contradictions in their observations.

Cluster T.(SS)VIII.   Endomorphic or Pyknic Physique (or Digestive type).   Evidenced by (*154*) and (*231a*).

Large girth in relation to height (greatest weight and greatest lower chest measurement (*154*) "central concentration of mass" (*231a*)).
Roundness and softness of body outlines — no muscle or bone
Facial width great, and as large at bottom as top
Short, tapering limbs, small hands and feet
Head large and round
Bones small
Skin smooth and velvety
Tendency to "central" type of baldness.   Hair fine
Small genitalia

The psychological variables associated with these are, according to Kretschmer, the cyclothyme temperament (Factor H −) and according to Sheldon "Visceratonia" (Cluster D.23).   Other researches indicate correlations around 0.3 with these traits as a cluster.   More precise factorial research may indicate higher correlations with the underlying factor.   Kretschmer's study includes the following behavioral variables:

Slower tapping rate
Convex ergograph curve, with less sudden onset of fatigue
Notices color rather than form in tachistoscopic exposures
Is not so well able to analyze, to confine attention deliberately to one aspect
Has better diffuse attention (notices more things)
P.G.R. resistance returns to normal more completely following stimulation period

Cluster T.(SS)VIIa.   Gall Bladder Disease Physique.   Draper has shown that the typical gall bladder patient departs from the average as follows.   Weight over height ratio large; broad face, round head, large chest circumference, short trunk (thickset); roundness and softness of features; subcostal angle broad; short fingers, broad palms; arms fairly long for height; square jaws and small gonial angle — i.e., jaw horizontal to head.

The resemblance to the pyknic is so striking that we have classified it VII*a*, pending further research on the identity.

Cluster T.(SS)VIII.   Mesomorphic, Athletic (or Respiratory type) Physique.   Evidenced by (*154*) and (*231a*).

Tallest of three, slender but broad chest and broadest shoulders.   Rugged, prominent musculature and bones.   Notably trapezius muscle, supraorbital ridges, cheekbones and jaw.   Middling weight

Distal massiveness of limbs

Ratio of transverse to anterior-posterior diameters greater than in ectomorph and especially than in endomorph

Face large relative to head, sloping forehead

"Strong" nose, lips rather thick

Skin thick, elastic, and with large pores, wrinkling heavy and coarse because of deep attachment

Hair coarse, tendency to frontal baldness

Well-developed genitalia

Sheldon relates these variables to the psychological cluster CB1.2.1, but Kretschmer relates to Schizothymia Factor A—. The cluster is partly A—, partly E (Dominance) factors, but the exact factorial relationships remain to be worked out.

Cluster T.(SS)IX. Ectomorphic, Asthenic (or Cerebral type) Physique. Evidenced by (*154*) and (*231a*).

Short, thin

Small, delicate bones and thin, stringy muscles

Trunk relatively short

Rounded shoulders, carried forward, producing clavicular hollow

Fingers, toes, neck, long, slender

Head slight, small facial mass, triangular (pointed chin), low bridge to nose, bulbous or upright forehead, dolicocephalic

Skin thin and dry, not elastic. Epidermis sloughing off; wrinkles even in youth; only loosely fastened

Heavy hirsutism; baldness rare; hair tends to grow forward and to be recalcitrant

Genitalia, moderate development

Sheldon considers the psychological segment of this cluster to be Cluster CB4 (Cerebrotonia), while Kretschmer considers it to be Factor H— (Schizothymia). The evidence is positive for both but does not yet permit factorial resolution. (CB4 seems to be H— and E— factors.)

Sheldon has suggested and used 18 anthropometric measures for the defining of these three — e.g., height over cube root of weight, face breadth, neck thickness — clusters, but so far no intercorrelations of these have been analyzed to substantiate the clinical syndromes. He considers that the clinical evidence shows them to be "independent variables within certain limits"; but the factorial picture, as set out above (*181*), (*182*), and Cohen's study, is at present not entirely compatible with Sheldon's descriptive scheme.

Syndromes of constitutional disease proneness. A short cut to detecting constitutional patterns, in lieu of the longer path of assiduous clinical observation and very refined physiological anatomical correlation work, is to look for evidence of hereditary proneness to certain physical or mental diseases and to collect the associations in physique which become evident. Such lines of exploration will later, of course, need factorial consolidation.[1] Already there are several suggestive indications of personality patterns being associated with such constitutional diatheses.

Below we list the physical diseases or disease groups already shown to have so definite a hereditary pattern in them that temperamental associates might profitably be sought in further research. First one listed those in which a somatic structural cluster has simultaneously been demonstrated.

One such cluster has already been placed above (VII*a*).

Cluster T.(SS)IXa.   Stomach Ulcer (perhaps also phthisis) Physique. Draper (*75a*) has shown that both peptic and duodenal ulcer patients diverge from the average in the following respects:

Narrow heads; narrow faces with pointed chin; large gonial angle — i.e., jaw pointing downward; narrow chests, average stature but low ratio of weight to height, small crania, arms short.

This description is also that of the classical phthisical patient, though there is no recent evidence; but above all it is the same as the ectomorph above and is classified accordingly IX*a*.

Draper has also noted some mental characteristics, notably: inner sense of insecurity based on actual or supposed physical inferiority or gynic emphasis; mother dependence, fear of loss of mother surrogate; jealousy and aggression; guilt and fear (related to sex) and compensatory striving.

Our contingent conclusion is that this cluster is essentially a schizoid pattern (Factor A) associated with essentially leptosomatic physique.

Cluster T.(SS)IXb.   Pernicious Anemia Physique. Draper's measurements show this group to belong to the same leptosomatic pattern but with these definite modifications: extreme (of all groups tested) wide subcostal angle; very short face, wide interpupillary space.

[1] Diseased conditions, like personality manifestations, should permit the same division into constitutional and environmental mold factors, pointing respectively to a

Personality traits associated:

Reserved, morose, conscientious, anxious, restrained, serious, persevering, directed by the will, austere, given to reflection. Theorist. Slow. Hard, harsh. Rigid. Psychophysical functions not well integrated.

10. MISCELLANEOUS SOURCE AND SURFACE TRAITS: IN MINIATURE SITUATIONAL, EGO DEFENSE, AND OTHER OBJECTIVE TESTS

The remaining factors to be listed. For the most part the factors or clusters now to be surveyed are less well-defined, soundly established, or clear in meaning than those already listed and it is necessary to note that the treatment is more speculative. They are, however, not less important, and several, notably those in wit and projection, in miniature situations, and in physiological responses are likely to be the growing points of extensive explorations of personality factors in the next decade.

Here, at the conclusion of the survey, it is necessary to explain why a few apparent factors are not listed. First, the sex-difference factor — the cluster of differences associated with difference of sex — has been omitted because any proper study of it would require a book in itself, to weigh various kinds of evidence and to separate subclusters or factors due to biological, environmental, and culture-pattern influence. We shall record this, for completeness, as an unanalyzed cluster.

Cluster T. (XXXV). Masculinity-Femininity. For the evidence of this clearly defined cluster the reader is referred to the recent and comprehensive book by Terman (*252*).

Factors of Aspiration, Depression, Laughter.

Cluster T. (XXXVI). Level of Aspiration. Evidenced by clusters (88) and (89).

The cluster is constituted by correlated difference scores seemingly in almost any performance. The differences are those between the subject's actual score and the "level of aspiration" score which he considers he expects to reach, knowing the task in question.

source in the organism, as in anemia and diabetes, or to an outside impress, as in occupational diseases, nutritional disorders, etc.

Gould (*98*) obtained *r*'s of .04 to .44 (median .29) between levels of aspiration scores on six unrelated tasks, while Gardner's (*94*) correlations were higher. Frank, in a review of the whole field (*92*), states that correlations range from .25 to .70. Heathers (*114*) agrees that generality in the trait has been established but sums up the evidence by saying: "Generality in the level of aspiration is in part a function of objective similarities in the situations within which the aspirations are set." Although studies have not yet reached the exactitude of factor analysis, one can thus conclude that if there is a general factor it must be supplemented by group factors.

The wider implications suggested by the title seem scarcely justified in view of the artificial nature of the experimental situation, which is unlikely to tie up with the individual's self-regarding sentiment. McGehee (14, 2475) has raised the question whether the discrepancies are really only measures of poorness of judgment, but something was found to remain when this was eliminated. Those with low ability tend to have large positive discrepancies, and those with high ability show little discrepancy or even underestimate their performance. This requires a second factor to be subtracted before the new differences can be handled as "level of aspiration."

Such impurities of the measure may account for the present uncertainty as to the wider associates of the measurement. Sears (*229*) concludes that "aspiration level fits into the more general reaction patterns of the individual and probably forms part of a cluster of associated personality attributes." Gould and Kaplan (*99*) found insignificant correlation of L.A. with grades, dominance measures, or IQ, and Gardner (*94*) also found negative results. Such variables as self-confidence, ambition, subjectivity, wishful thinking *vs*. realism, caution, and modesty, have been suggested as related. Self-sufficient subjects have been found to have higher scores than those more socially motivated, as also have those scoring higher on tests of subjectivity (*94*). The few suggestive significant associations have been found not with level of aspiration but with rigidity of that level when faced with unexpected success or failure. Schizophrenics, notably paranoids, show high rigidity; manic depressives show more mobility. Men have significantly higher level of aspiration scores than women.

Cluster T. (*XXXVII*). *Depression-Euphoria.* Evidenced by cluster (105). The cluster established by Johnston deals with traits differentiating two states in the same set of individuals, rather than two types among different individuals. But since there is every reason to believe that the same characters of euphoria and depression may exist as permanent states differentiating individuals, these well-defined associates of euphoria are listed here.

Test associates of reported Euphoric Mood (opposites for Depressed Mood).

1. More (frequency and length) of spontaneous and "unnecessary" conversation
2. Less "regression" to childhood events and ideas in thought and memories
3. Greater speed of decision (on sensory material) (nearly 50 per cent increase)
4. Larger, more expansive movements in gesture, handwriting (larger and less cramped), and drawing

Less definitely:

5. Sizes and distances, marked off by hand, judged less than they are
6. Reversible perspective fluctuation rate slower
7. Less profound and long sleep

For linking Q factors with T factors, Johnson's findings on subjectively reported associates are included here.

1. Feeling of augmented physical energy
2. Gain of confidence in oneself and one's powers
3. More sense of outgoing friendliness to others
4. Diminution of a "generalized feeling of indecision"
5. Greater inclination to talk and less inclination toward shy withdrawal
Possibly also: feeling other people are more friendly to oneself, change from emotional apathy (though some depressed cases report anxiety and "jitters" rather than apathy).

Cluster T. (*XXXVIII*). *Laughter.* Evidenced by (110). Not a true cluster but only correlates of greater tendency to laughter (in children).

	r with
Frequency (time spent) of laughing	(.75 consistency)
Weight divided by normal weight for that age	.89
Talkativeness (No. words spoken)	.60
Actual age (C.A.)	.44
Frequency (time spent) crying	− .11
IQ	.07
Height-weight ratio	.00

Cluster T. (*XXXIX*). *Crying.* Evidenced by (111). Not a true cluster but correlates with crying, as follows:

	r with
Frequency of crying	
Chronological age	— .47
Weight divided by weight normal for age	— .36
Height-weight ratio	.00

Functional unities in ego dynamism tests. In recent years a variety of indirect tests of personality have grown up which, deliberately or otherwise, converge on the use of the ego defense mechanisms (or dynamisms) to measure those aspects of personality of which the individual is not conscious or is unwilling to accept. For these the writer has suggested the inclusive title of *ego dynamism tests*. The defense mechanisms which hold promise of being used in this way are projection, rationalization, identification, repression, and reaction formation.

Projection was first employed in tests by Murray, Sears, and the present writer, independently, in 1937, and most experiment has been on this one dynamism. Many tests using so-called projective technique — e.g., the Rorschach — do not, however, clearly employ the mechanism of projection, and there is at present some confusion in this field both as to the principles of test design and the question of whether one expects to get correlations with overt personality or with hidden and unconscious dynamic trends. The writer has suggested that there are really three distinct kinds of projection at work in the usual projection situation (56) and that the assessment of temperament and cognitive traits might result from one of these, though the others are more truly dynamic, but unequally concerned with drives in the unconscious and the self-regarding sentiment.

The tests so far used (with inventive answers in the Murray's Thematic Apperception test and selective answers in the present writer's Dynamism tests) have aimed at measuring dynamic traits (needs, ergs, dispositions) and have employed unfinished stories, ink blots, cloud phantasies, free play and dramatization, free associations on pictures, picture interpretation, similes, and completion of sentences.

Despite the attraction which the Rorschach test seems to have exercised — especially on psychiatrists — and the resulting great expenditures of time upon it, its validity and reliability seem to be little improved since its defective psychometric construction and poor level of prediction were reviewed (*46*) in 1936. It remains a mixture of ill-defined intentions, analogous to a patent medicine, devoid of clear-cut theoretical bases which would permit refinement through research.[1]　No factor or cluster has been established among its separate measurements, which are defined in terms of highly subjective and *a priori* notions.　One of the most recent studies (Sanford) shows its predictions to be "slightly but reliably above chance."　But this average is achieved because "intellectual power, special abilities, work habits were more reliably predicted than temperament (introversion-extraversion) or motivation."　In short, it succeeds in measuring abilities for which there are already more valid tests, rather than dynamic and temperamental traits in which research should now be interested.　Thurstone's recent study (*262a*), factor analyzing the Rorschach with other perceptual measures, found the factor to be specific to the test, not carrying over to other situations.

True projection procedures and studies of wit reaction undoubtedly have immense importance for the objective measurement of personality, but the beginning is too recent and the workers too few for much to have emerged.　Sanford (*225*), who has presented one of the few substantial studies yet published, obtained, as did Cattell (*56*), negligible correlations between projection measures of needs and rated needs

---

[1] Judging by the material, the Rorschach measures the Fluency of Association Factor (T. XXVII), Oscillation (T. XX), "g" (T. I), and possibly a persistence factor, but none clearly or with sufficient items to be reliable.

(on overt behavior). Cattell, however, obtained significant correlations at the same time between projection scores and appreciation of wit employing the dynamic tendency in question. Sears (*230*) got positive correlations among subjects lacking self-insight and significant negative correlations among those ranked high for insight. Sanford has shown that the measurements have high reliability, that they vary in an ordered way with age, sex, etc., and that they related, in clinical study, to *covert* needs studied by free association and other techniques. Similar relation of projection measures to the clinical picture have been demonstrated by Vernon (*269*) and by Balken and Masserman. The clusters of covert needs as found by Sanford are as follows: Their mean intercorrelation (uncorrected for attenuation) seems to be about .27, which is decidedly lower than is necessary for obtaining clusters among ratings and other test measurements. It has been suggested that the findings can be better understood by admitting *three* varieties of projection mechanism (*56*).

Cluster (XL). "*Strong Character.*" Evidenced by (114).

> Need Blamavoidance
> Need Inviolacy
> Need Abasement

Cluster T. (XLI). "*Ego Defense.*" Evidenced by (115).

> Need Infavoidance
> Need Counteraction
> Need Defendence
> Need Seclusion
> Need Understanding

Cluster T. (XLII). "*Anti-social.*" Evidenced by (116).

> Need Acquisition-antisocial
> Need Aggression
> Need Dominance
> Need Recognition
> Need Autonomy
> Need Harmavoidance
> Need Blamescape

Cluster T. (XLIII). *"Self-assertion."* Evidenced by (117).

> Need Exhibition
> Need Play
> Need Recognition

Cluster T. (XLIV). *"Social."* Evidenced by (118).

> Need Affiliation
> Need Nurturance
> Need Sex
> Need Deference
> Need Cognizance
> Need Acquisition-personal
> Need Exposition

Humor as a personality indication. Wit and humor may be considered among ego dynamism tests, if the Freudian theory is correct that the keenest pleasure derives from expression of repressed drives. The correlation of wit appreciation with personality requires first, however, that the factors in wit appreciation as such be explored and a sufficient battery of jokes having known factor complexity be accumulated. Two studies, (10), (58j), have so opened up this field, yielding six and seven factors respectively.

The definition of a factor presents difficulty, for inspection may sometimes suggest common matter, sometimes common form, and sometimes common dynamic satisfaction in the jokes with high loadings. The present writer sees suggestive evidence, however, that these factors are essentially personality factors. If this is so, the difficulties encountered in attempting to define them in narrow categories of wit *per se* are explained and the better course, followed below, would seem to be to attempt at present a less concise, more tentative and broader description of each group of jokes, in whatever terms suggest themselves, but principally in dynamic terms. It is at least known that the *form* of the joke *per se* (limerick, cartoon, joke) has no relevance.

Factor T. XLV (156, not in (10)). Coarse aggression against authority and all conventions of decency, order, morality, idealism *vs.* whimsy.

Factor T. XLVI (157, possible "reaction to debauchery" in (10)). Gallic wit, quick, light humor with sexual emphasis. Pleasure in the ridiculous and farcical. "Laughing at life."

Factor T. XLVII (158: 5 in (10)). Sex themes of a pretty direct nature.

Factor T. XLVIII (159: 7 in (10)). Derision, superiority, masculine assurance. "The horse laugh."

Factor T. XLIX (160; possibly 3 in (10)). Subtle, light humor — hard of definition.

Factor T. L (161: 4 in (10)). Play on words; pleasure in intellectual play.

Factor T. LI (161*a*). Pleasure in poised, unpunctured egotism, in ignoring the politeness and the foibles and pretensions of society.

Factor T. LII (6 in (10)). Ridiculous wisecracks. Interpersonal aggression?

Cursive miniature situation test correlations. A "miniature situation" test measurement differs from experimental measurements in general in that the miniature situation is designed actually to measure a trait, occurring widely in major real-life situations, within a definite miniature experimental situation. It presumes a stylistic similarity of behavior and attempts to find the laboratory test situation which will give the maximum measurement of the true trait. Most of the above factors are in terms of objective measures that are experimental — e.g., rate of reading, perseveration, pressure on a dynamometer. But a few, notably those of Hartshorne and May, are in miniature situations. The present data arise from cursive miniature situations — i.e., those in which the experimental situation is made to move and change, requiring adaptations from the subject to an unfolding situation.

Factor T. LIII. Impulsivity-Inhibition. Evidenced by (109). A general factor in the twelve June Downey tests — e.g., speed of movement, flexibility, speed of decision, motor impulsion, coördination of impulse — which correlates 0.3 with scholastic success when intelligence is held constant.

The cursive miniature situation test designed by the present writer (50) (55) and consisting of a moving strip with lines of various kinds which have to be crossed with a pencil as they pass a small window presents situations demanding the following traits: (1) Honesty, in not marking after the items pass a certain line. (2) Honesty in not attempting to score on "slanting" lines. (3) Ability to make good judgments of a total situation rapidly. (4) Persistence in face of difficulties. (5) Emotional stability in face of unexpected frustrations and conflicting instructions. (6) Foresight and the postponement of immediate for better later opportunities of scoring. (7) Resource and initiation in scoring whole blocks and patterns in new ways. (8) Ability to profit by past errors. (9) Flexibility in responding to pressure and emergency output demands. There are also measures of change of performance with different kinds of motivation.

At present it seems desirable only to list the following "total goodness of response" cluster and a "leadership" cluster, though differentiations between delinquents and psychotics and between obsessional, manic depressives and schizophrenics are already adumbrated in other clusters.

Cluster T. (LIV). *Integration of Character Responses.* Evidenced by cluster (112) in C.M.S. data.

Score on decision situations
Score on caution and foresight items (saving up "Circle Mass" scores)
Score on honesty (refusal to cross slanting lines)
Score on honesty (refusal to pass over forbidden boundary to improve score)

This cluster has negligible correlation with age or "g" and is decidedly higher for delinquents than normals (C.R. about 3.0) and for psychotics than delinquents (C.R. about 7.0). It correlates positively significantly with ratings on will-character and foresight.

Cluster T. (LV). *Forceful Leadership.* Evidenced by cluster (113) in C.M.S. data.

Score on resourcefulness (patterns wholistically handled)
Score on slanting lines crossed
Score on freedom from emotional upset as recorded by small change after frustrations and surprises
Score on foresight in use of circle mass items

This cluster correlates .80 to .95 with ratings of leadership in face-to-face situations.

That the ratio of finally "confirmed" and accepted factors (Roman numerals) to experimentally demonstrated factors is so small in this chapter (155 to 82), compared with those from rating and questionnaire data, is of course due to (1) the greater difficulty of merging phenomenal factors as a consequence of test items having a less wide reference (and therefore being less likely to have much in common) than verbally defined general traits. Special researches to test the relations of these factors may prove later that we have been too cautious, and that certain reductions in the total number can be made by matchings of which we are not now aware. (2) To the fact that test factors can be catalogued as "established" on the basis of fewer researches than would be demanded for the more tenuous questionnaire or rating researches.

Chapter Twelve

THE ESTABLISHED PRIMARY TRAITS: THEIR MEAS-
UREMENT AND USE IN PERSONALITY PREDICTIONS

1. THE PROBLEMS OF INTEGRATING RESULTS FROM DIVERSE FOUNDATIONS

Purpose of the final chapter. The present study in personality, having proceeded through an ordered exposition of the
known facts in various fields, can now culminate in an attempt
to define the primary personality traits which are of major
importance for theory and practice. Rating, questionnaire,
test, and clinical factors are to be put side by side, so that we
can recognize the same source trait in its diverse clothing.
At the same time we shall seek perspective on the relative
importance of these essential factors, range the first dozen in
order, concentrate on their interpretation, and try to understand their interaction in the total personality. The concentrated study of these traits which may be considered established, and the survey of their practical and theoretical importance, will include both surface and source traits.

At the same time we shall illustrate and repeat briefly for
emphasis the basic theoretical positions attained earlier in
the study and proceed to certain refinements and extensions
which could not be appropriately undertaken in the initial
exposition.

Finally, we can now attend to the practical problems of
efficient prediction in applied psychology and begin also to
indicate the fertile vistas immediately opened up to research.

469

The matching of source traits. The cross-matching of BR, Q, T, and C source traits faces difficulties additional to those of (1) sample, (2) choice of variable, and (3) system of rotation, encountered in matching within any one field.

Since *no* variables are exactly the same in different fields of data, no mechanical, objectively scientific method of matching is possible. A rated "shyness" or "emotionality" *may* be different from a questionnaire response "Yes, I am shy" or "Yes, I become easily emotional." Indeed, we shall find in actual matchings of such factors clear indications that self-ratings are distorted, that certain forms of behavior cannot be assessed in questionnaires, that some forms of behavior are misinterpreted or underemphasized by the external rater — e.g., anxiety — and that, in general, behavior does not always "look" as it "feels." Imagination, psychological experience, and intuition based on intensive study are necessary in getting the best possible matches between patterns drawn from different source material.

An extensive research is now in progress at the writer's laboratory to get intercorrelations of the actual factors in these diverse fields, to fix finally their relationships. Meanwhile, for lack of such a "straddling" study, we have proceeded with cross-identifications (1) by matching factors having approximately synonymous variables in their patterns, having about the same order of saturation in these variables, and having the same "feel" of the whole pattern, as sensed in the manner indicated above. (2) By checking, in appropriately similar studies, to see that major factors, high in mean contribution to the variance, are matched with major factors and minor factors with minor ones.[1] (3) By being alert to see that no factor in one research is matched with more than one factor in any other research. (2) and (3) provide quite considerable assistance. In the end the

---

[1] It is significant that, with one possible exception, the ten or twelve most important factors in each realm were those that found matches in cross-identifications — i.e., they *are* of the same order of importance.

goodness of the individual match is partly attested by the goodness of the whole matched series. Any one change in the present matching would in general precipitate a whole series of re-identifications, most of which would be somewhat less likely than those now made.

Occasionally, as in Reyburn and Taylor's studies, and in a small *ad hoc* comparison of our own factors with Guilford's questionnaire factors, good windlasses have aided our approach across the chasms which separate various data. But it is not claimed that the matching attempted here is objective and of an accuracy which can be quantitatively expressed. The matching has been an art of psychological judgment, improved by practice and immersion in the data, and resulting in matches the varying degrees of confidence in which have been indicated at the appropriate places.[1]

List of confirmed factors in each field. The final exposition of agreed factors in C, BR, Q, and T fields, as set out respectively in Chapters 3, 9, 10, and 11, began in each case with the most clearly established, overdetermined factors and petered out eventually in tentative factors found only in one research or in researches with inadequate technique. Before attempting cross-matching among the diverse fields, it seems desirable to restrict the lists for these fields by considering only those factors in each which can be considered, with a reasonable degree of confidence, to be established.

A conspectus of the factors considered as established is presented in the lists of Table 25 below. For admission to these lists a factor must have been found in at least three independent researches, each meeting reasonable standards of technical soundness regarding population or mode of trait assessment. In a few special instances (some 10 per cent) this regulation is modified, in view of the unusual clearness of a factor contributed by fewer researches or smaller populations.

---

[1] The writer wishes to express his thanks to the six psychologists and psychiatrists who gave time to this matching. They came to unanimous verdicts except where indicated.

It is noticeable that the highest proportion (90 per cent) of "phenomenal" factors which fail to achieve mutual confirmation and extension occur in the test-measurement realm. This doubtless arises partly from the greater difficulty of recognizing the nature of trait elements here. Unless test procedures are the same in detail, they cannot be recognized as identical, nor does one risk considering them as such, though in fact they may be, whereas in verbally defined traits the universal coin of language indicates at once if the trait elements are in the same area. Again, the failure may result from the test factor's covering relatively small and sometimes unimportant facets of personality. In later cross-identifications it is also noticeable that the test-measurement factors are less frequently matched and identified.

TABLE 25

LIST OF CONFIRMED FACTORS IN RATING, QUESTIONNAIRE, AND TEST FIELDS

The factors are referred to by their standard numbers in Roman figures. The number after each indicates the number of researches in which it has appeared. A question mark, which occurs before three or four of the variables, indicates that their confirmation is not quite of the same order of reliability as the rest.

CLINICAL SYNDROMES
(19 syndromes)

C. I. Simple Schizophrenia
C. II. Catatonic Schizophrenia
C. II. Hebephrenic Schizophrenia
C. IV. Paranoid Schizophrenia
C. V. Manic Depressive Personality
C. VI. Manic Syndrome
C. VII. Depressive Syndrome
C. VIII. Involutional, agitated Melancholia
C. X. Psychopathic Personality
C. XV. Conversion Hysteria
C. XVI. Anxiety Neurosis
C. XVII. Anxiety Hysteria
C. XVIII. Obsessional or Compulsive Neurosis

BEHAVIOR RATING FACTORS
(12 factors from 83 delineated in research)

BR. I. (A) Cyclothymia and Schizothymia (7)
BR. II. (B) General Ability — v. — Mental Defect (A very large number)
BR. III. (C) Emotional Stable Character — v. — Demoralized General Emotionality (10)
BR. IV. (E) Dominance (Hypomania) — v. — Submissiveness (12)
BR. V. (F) Surgency — v. — Agitated Melancholy (11)
BR. VI. (I) Sensitive, Anxious Emotionality — v. — Rigid,

TABLE 25 — *Continued*

CLINICAL SYNDROMES

C. XIX. Neurasthenia
(?) C. XXV. Migraine and Allergy
(?) C. XXVI. Enuresis
C. XXVII. Neuropathic Constitution
C. XXXIa. Anal Character
C. XXXII. Mental Defect

BEHAVIOR RATING FACTORS[1]

Tough, Poise (6)
BR. VII. (G) Positive, Character Integration — *v.* — Immature Dependent Character (5)
BR. VIII. (J) Neurasthenia — *v.* — Vigorous, Obsessional-determined Character (7)
BR. IX. (D) Hypersensitive, Sthenic Emotionality — *v.* — Phlegmatic Frustration Tolerance (4)
BR. X. (H) Kindly Rhathymia — *v.* — Obstructive, Withdrawn Schizothymia (4)
BR. XI. (K) Trained, Cultured Mind — *v.* — Boorishness (2)
BR. XII. (L) Paranoia (2)

QUESTIONNAIRE, SELF-INVENTORY FACTORS

73 personality factors (P), 56 interest factors (I), 10 attitude factors (A), 21 factors out of 139 delineated in research.

Q(P) I. Shyness-Withdrawal — 7 sensitivity — 4
Q(P) II. General Emotional Hypersensitivity — 4
Q(P) III. Melancholy Agitation — 3
Q(P) IV. General Neurotic Maladjustment — 3
(?) Q(P) V. Schizoid Asthenia — 2
Q(P) VI. Confident Self-Assertion — 5
Q(P) VIII. Self-Sufficiency — 4
Q(P) IX. Will-Character — 3
Q(P) X. Obsessional, Inflexible Will-Character — 3
Q(P) XI. Relaxed Independence — 3

TEST MEASUREMENT FACTORS

13 factors out of 182 delineated in research.

T. I. General Ability — 50(?)
T. XII (?). Honesty-Integrity — 2
T. XIII. Active, Reliable Will-Character (Conscientious Thoroughness) — 3
T. XIV. Determined Will-Character — 5
T. XVI. Smooth, unwilled dynamic momentum and absorption — 7
T. XX. Oscillation — 7
T. XXIa. Speed of Ideomotor Skills — 7
T. XXVII. Fluency of Association — 6
T. XXXII. Disposition "Inertia-Rigidity" or Motor Perseveration — 15

[1] The order of final numbering is that of mean variance contribution as we judge it most likely to be modified when research is more complete. Naturally, since constitutional and environmental mold traits will to some extent be complementary in variance, and since their variance ratio will depend on cultural circumstances, there is no such thing as an *absolute* order of factors in variance magnitude. Moreover, mean variance is meaningless apart from an agreed personality sphere.

TABLE 25 — *Continued*

Questionnaire, Self-Inventory Factors	Test Measurement Factors
Q(P) XIII. Nervous Anxiety and Instability — 3	T. (SF) I. Metabolic or General Autonomic
Q(P) XV. Paranoid Schizothyme — 3	T. (SF) II. Sympathetic (Adrenergic) Activity — 3
Q(P) XVII. Liking Thinking — 3	T. (SF) III. Thyroid — v. — High P.G.R.
Q(I) Ia. Sociable Activity — v. — Detached Independent, Creative Work — 8	Also six humor factors (T. XLVIII–LIII), several factors of somatic structure, eleven ability factors, and many significant clusters.
Q(I) Ib. Guiding People for their Presumed Good — v. — Being Coldly Objective — 4	
Q(I) IIa. Thoughtful Interest in Understanding Nature — 9	
Q(I) IIIa. Verbal Persuasion — v. — Practical Control of Material — 8	
Q(I) IVa. Philistine Go-getting — v. — Aesthetic Interests — 5	
Q(A) Ia. Radicalism — v. — Conservatism — 6	
Q(A) II. Hard-headed, Rational — v. — Sentimental	
Q(A) III. Personal Liberty — v. — Coercion	

On general psychological grounds it seems unlikely that the factors operative in personality are as few as the dozen or so which might result from matching the factors manifested in these four fields. We should expect fewest, in initial researches, in the BR data, both because the mode of estimation is such as to permit slender factors to be missed and because the personality sphere on which it is based would result in only *truly general factors* being found. Many of the factors found in test and questionnaire data are almost certainly highly local group factors. Later research may well reveal a hundred or two of such factors over very limited fields of behavior.

The BR data are probably right in indicating that only

about half of the variance of traits is accounted for by truly general factors, but we suspect that finer methods of measurement, permitting more exact rotations, and by improved methods, will reveal these factors to be nearer to 20 in number than 6, and this general argument has been an additional reason for our preferring the 12 factors of our α rotation to the 6 factors of the β rotation.

2. THE TWELVE PRIMARY SOURCE TRAITS MANIFESTED IN ALL DATA

System of description. At the beginning of each trait description a set of reference numbers will be given indicating the BR, Q, T, and C items which have been matched. (The reference numbers are those in Table 25 above, and in the appropriate special chapters.)

To avoid the necessity of too much retrospective reference, the chief "phenomenal" source traits incorporated will be further indicated by the names of their discoverers. The main factor descriptions in rating terms will not be set out again, since they can be obtained by reference to a single page in Chapter 9; but a brief sample of the questionnaire factor items will be given. A final short résumé at the end of each source-trait section will attempt to give an overall picture of the source trait as it emerges from the combination of overlapping factor findings in all fields.

The following accounts are intended to combine discussion of the reasons for matchings — since no space is given elsewhere to the pros and cons, doubts and certainties, of individual matchings — with the actual descriptions.

Factor I. A. Cyclothymia — *v.* — Schizothymia

From matching BR I, QP I, QI. I, C I. See main list of BR traits, page 313.

The questionnaire data offer two factors — QP I and QP XV — which compete almost equally for identification. The first is the *shyness* factor, appearing variously as Self-confidence (Flanagan (*88*)), Social initiative (McCloy Layman (*159*)), Social introversion (Mosier (*187*)), Social inactivity (Darrow and Heath (*71*) [1]), Social introversion or S (Guilford and Guilford (*105*)), Shyness (Guilford (*102*)), Sociability (Reyburn and Taylor (*215*)), and Approach-withdrawn (Pallister (*200*)). This is highest in the responses

1. Troubled with shyness
2. Keeps in background on social occasions
3. Does not make new friends easily
4. Has feelings of being watched on street

However, if it is not safe to assume that the hostile, obstructive characteristics are hidden by the questionnaire responses, a better identification is with a paranoid factor instanced by Layman's (*159*) Sensitive, excitable emotionality, Darrow and Heath's (*71*) Paranoid excitability, and Reyburn and Taylor's (*215*) Perseveration. (See description under factor L.) The weighty objections to this alternative, however, are that it is a relatively obscure factor, whereas shyness is one of the largest and best established, like the A factor. Moreover, the paranoid factor already identifies very well with our L factor. We conclude, therefore, that the questionnaire has omitted, or failed to get true answers to, items dealing with the irritability, rigidity, hostility, and coldness which agree so well in this factor and in the clinical picture.

Throughout, confirmed T factors — which are, in any case, rare — cannot be matched with the same confidence as BR, C, or even Q factors; for they do not deal at all with verbal terms, in which the others are couched, or with everyday behavior. Fortunately, in about half of the few researches yielding factors in specific test performances, a rating, or one or two questionnaire items, have been correlated in with the test

---

[1] Darrow and Heath's findings are not those of a true factor analysis, but because of their valuable physiological correlations have been roughly reinterpreted in factor form.

material, thereby giving some orientation. With regard to about half the factors, however, the T matching remains at the low level of guesswork, aided by some mathematical facts and psychological intuitions. There is no trace of a T factor to match factor A: only the cluster T. (SS) VII of Kretschmer.

Among C factors, or, rather, clinical syndromes, the psychiatrists agreed at once in picking out the cyclothyme-schizothyme distinction to match the present factor. It is interesting that the distinction which has dominated clinical observation for fifty years should be confirmed as that with the greatest mathematical role in the variance of normal personality traits.

If one attempts to anticipate relations between factors and the four main varieties of schizophrenia — simple, hebephrenic, catatonic, and paranoid — he has to bear in mind that these four surface-trait patterns (syndromes) could be accounted for either by a smaller number of factors, producing four clusters by overlap, or alternatively by one factor to each cluster. In the former situation there might be one main cyclothyme-schizothyme factor and two factors producing four modifications of it. In the latter situation these two factors at right angles to the main factor need not in themselves involve any general schizoid traits: they would merely be modifiers of the primary schizoid factor, A. There is also the possibility to be considered that the factors in psychosis will not be found *at all* in a normal range population sample, but will manifest themselves as emergent factors only in a sample from some extreme slice of the population distribution.

The fact that we find in our results four factors which, at one end, very definitely depict forms of schizoid behavior suggests that the second of the above two possible explanations is likely. We shall deal with the alignment of these four factors with the clinical syndromes as we encounter the later schizoid factors.

Résumé concerning A. The behavior ratings in A (BR I) center on easygoing, genial adaptability, trustfulness, warm-hearted emotional expressiveness, and generosity. The negative aspect stresses inflexibility, coldness, suspicion, secretiveness, timidity, cynical hostility, and pessimism. The questionnaire findings emphasize the shyness and excessive sensitivity in the schizoid pole. A common misapprehension on schizothymia consists in tying up shyness with submissiveness. The ratings show self-assertiveness decidedly high among the schizothyme traits, and some of the self-conscious egotism of the schizothyme may be due to the inherent conflict between shyness and self-assertion. The high rating of the cyclothyme in idealism must be considered a rating in practical idealism, adventurous coöperativeness, and charity; for the refined "religious" idealism of the schizothyme is an equally certain characteristic when one penetrates deeper. Indeed, the schizothyme is slightly higher in the traits which sometimes add up to "character" in life situations; for the tenacity, obstinacy, and freedom from overt emotionality which are part of the temperament connote greater steadfastness in some — e.g., academic study — situations. All the factorizations yielding an A factor support squarely the more detailed elaborations of cyclothyme-schizothyme differences as made in the insightful clinical type studies of Kretschmer (*154*). The cluster produced by A and H together is undoubtedly one describable as "temperamental." But the discussion below (page 491) suggests that H rather than A is truly a temperament factor, correlating with pyknic-leptosomatic body build.

Factor II or B. Intelligence, General Mental Capacity — *v*. — Mental defect.

Matching BR II, QP XXI, T. I. and C. XXXII. See main lists of rated traits, page 315.

Résumé concerning B. This is the well-known general mental capacity factor, g, as it affects personality. One must stress strongly that it contains more moral character traits than are normally thought of as associated with intelligence. Their presence in the syndrome is confirmed by excellent agreement of the α, the β, and the actual intelligence-test correlations. They are: wise, emotionally mature, reliable, independent, thoughtful, deliberate, not frivolous, persevering, painstaking, mentally alert and vigorous, conscientious, having intellectual and wide interests, etc. Presumably, if educational influences in home and school favor good character development, the more intelligent individual, over the course of years, learns more completely and effectively to acquire the habits of good self-discipline, the self-regard, and the consistency in the approved social mold. The correlations with general energy and with emotional stability may be indirect products of the good hygienic and general environment likely to surround the child of intelligent parents.

Factor III or C. Emotionally Mature Stable Character — *v.* — Demoralized General Emotionality

Matching BR III, QP IV (but some resemblance also to II and III), T. XII, and C. X. See main description of BR traits on page 317.

The equivalent in Q data is well defined. It appears as Vernon's (*269*) Self-depreciation and Neuroticism, Mosier's (*187*) Depression, and Darrow and Heath's (*71*) General Neuroticism (though their "Melancholy Agitation" is also similar). Bridges, Garrison, and Slawson found it highly differentiating delinquents and nondelinquents, which helps tie it up with Burt's General Emotionality. Vernon (*269*) found it the largest single factor in character disintegration (or neuroticism), which agrees with its rank in variance here. On qualitative grounds it could also be identified with the Q factors associated with D and F. The most loaded questionnaire items are:

1. Frequently in low spirits
2. Lonesome, even with others

4.* Frequently feels grouchy
6. Gets discouraged easily
7. Feels not adjusted to life

In T data this factor seems well matched by Brogden's (*20*) Honesty factor (which has a slightly lesser resemblance to G, already matched by his Will-Character) and by the factor implicit in Hartshorne and May's (*111*) Integration cluster (Coöperativeness, Persistence, Inhibition). The former has loadings as follows:

Not cheating on coördination test	.63
False book list statements	.55
Questionable character preferences	.34

In clinical data its most obvious match is the psychopathic personality, though there is a faint resemblance to a manic-depressive onset. The objections to the former are that it might match G almost equally and that it is in fact a clinically poorly defined syndrome. G seems to be more a matter of character training and C of constitutional or earlier and deeper integration or disintegration. The G match therefore seems better, but perhaps psychopathic personality should be split into a major and a minor syndrome corresponding respectively to our C and G.

Résumé of C. The essence of positive C seems to be emotional stability, realism in facing life's problems, trustworthiness, steadfastness, freedom from inner emotional upsets, and outer susceptibility to temptations, and therefore power to show loyalty, perseverance, thoroughness, honesty, self-respect, and self-control. Its obverse is emotional changeability, high general emotionality, evasion of responsibilities, and tendency to general neurotic manifestations. Subjectively this appears as emotional dissatisfaction, a feeling of discouragement, loneliness, and maladjustment, chronically above that of the average person in an average situation.

* Throughout, these numbers are the order in the *complete* Q-factor list, from which these items are sampled.

There is yet no proof — apart from (1) Burt's observations on delinquents and (2) the resistance of psychopathic personality to psychotherapy — that this is a temperamental rather than an acquired character integration; but its appearance is at any rate that of some deep-seated lack of personality integration and not of a mere absence of good character training. Everything points to this *general emotionality* factor as being of central importance in the prediction of delinquency.

Factor IV or E Dominance-Ascendance (Non-euphoric Hypomania) — *v.* — Submissiveness

Matching BR IV, QP VI, and C.VI. See description of BR traits on page 321.

In Q data, this appears as Flanagan's *(88)* Dominance, Layman's *(159)* Inferiority of (alternatively but less probably) social aggressiveness, Mosier's *(187)* Inferiority, and the Guilfords' *(102)* Dominance-Masculinity.

A sample of the highest items is:

1. Does not lack self-confidence
2. Does not keep in background on social occasions
4. Is not easily discouraged — e.g., when opinions of others differ from his own
6. Is not troubled by feelings of inferiority
7. Likes to sell things or solicit funds for a cause in which he is interested

Among T factors one might be tempted to identify this factor with Thornton's *(258)* Masculinity and Rethlingshafer's *(212)* Controlling desire to escape discomfort, which weight: dynamometer grip, physical size, endurance in pain and holding breath, and length of time sticking at a problem. Also there is resemblance to the T factors matched with J. But the former match is ruled out by Thornton's *(258)* finding a dominance factor, as follows:

Score on Wang questionnaire on persistence	.67
Score on Allport Vernon A–S Test	.56
Self-rating on self-confidence	.51

which involved no tests significantly in its loading (though all types of tests were present). Dominance seems to be more a social than a will quality.

The clinical diagnosis was hypomanic or manic with its obverse of "simple" depression. No other in the range of abnormal syndromes seems to have any relevance here. Note, however, the evidence of two forms of mania, and the relation to factor D.

Résumé on E. There is a slight difference of the α and β factorizations, the latter stressing more the ascendant, adventurous, expressive, elated, widely interested, vigorous-active side of self-assertion and the former the egotistic, willful, extrapunitive, embittered, and conceited aspects. The supporting factorizations overlap both of these modifications. They stress antisocial sociability, anger and destructiveness, extrapunitiveness, curiosity, sex, self-confidence, forcefulness, and lack of tact, of kindness, and sometimes conscientiousness. The Q data stress the core of self-confidence, the insensitiveness to social disapproval, and the pleasure in manipulating people.

Probably the pattern of this factor alters more than others with age and the reaction of the cultural patterns to dominance — e.g., the comparative social disapproval of dominance behavior in Britain as compared with America and Germany. As Williams's study of three-year-olds shows (*278*), in infancy it seems to fuse with the obverse of the character factor. Possibly later social disapproval of the antisocial aspects clears it increasingly of the disapproved overt predatoriness, but adds embittered and extrapunitive aspects. Since Maslow's (*165*) (*166*) extensive investigations were of a surface trait, clinically defined, rather than of a precise factor, it is uncertain just how many of the associates which his thorough search turned up can yet be confidently attached here.

One of the more absurd misunderstandings of this factor is that which assumes it is identical with leadership. Leadership in different situations needs to be very differently predicted, and the role of dominance-ascendance will almost certainly never be more than a fraction of the variance of the leadership criterion.

The modality and origin of dominance can at present be only sheer speculation, but its role in the surface trait of somatotomia suggests that it may have dispositional and bodily (mesomorphic) associations. This factor has a noteworthy negative correlation with factor I.

Factor V or F. Surgency — *v.* — Agitated Melancholic Desurgency

Matching BR V, QP III, T. XXVII, and C. VIII (also C. VII). See description of BR traits on page 324.

(NOTE. In the β rotation this factor has slightly less mean variance than factor VI or I, but is listed as V because in the α rotation it is decidedly larger than I.)

The title Surgency-Desurgency was given to the surface trait constituted by the outcrop of this factor by the present writer in 1933. But since the clinical syndrome of agitated melancholy is now seen to be the extreme obverse of surgency, the factor is given this combined description.

In Q data there is some resemblance to the factor put under C above. There is also, naturally, a close resemblance to the Q factor which expresses that BR factor — H — which closely resembles F. There was, however, a very definite consensus of diagnoses that surgency corresponds to a Q factor which happens to be as well established, as important in terms of variance, and as clear cut as the BR factor itself. This is Layman's (*159*) Emotionality-Moodiness, Mosier's (*187*) Cycloid tendency, and Guilford's (*102*) Depressive tendency or D factor, the total picture of which the present writer has called Melancholy Agitation. It is defined by the responses:

1. Is often just miserable (for no reason)
2. Worries over possible misfortunes
3. Has frequent ups and downs of mood
5. Is meditative and introspective
6. Is not carefree and cannot relax

A test factor — fluency of association (T.XXVII), as established by Hargreaves (*108*), the present writer (*41*), Thornton (*258*), Rethlingshafer (*212*), Notcutt (*194*), and Thurstone (*262*) — has been in use for some time as a measure ($r = .65$) of the cluster surgency (*46*). Now that the cluster has been resolved into two and possibly three factors, it remains to be seen if the present factor, as one might suspect, will carry off the main correlation with Fluency. Fluency loads:

Verbal ability (very easy opposites)	0.71
Speed of reading	0.5–0.6
Associations to ink blots	0.5–0.6
Finishing sentences, pictures, and stories	0.5–0.6

A confident clinical identification of F can be made with melancholia (agitated, "constitutional," involutional). Simple depression resembles the pattern in many respects but is probably better classified under E. Certain dissimilar items — e.g., absence of fatigue in the above — rule out the otherwise related patterns of neurasthenia or anxiety neurosis.

Résumé on F. The essence of high F is a placid, unemotional, realistic cheerfulness, with talkativeness, geniality, enthusiasm, sociability, and a witty originality. All factorizations stress cheerful joyousness, gregariousness, friendly assertiveness and talkativeness, adaptability, quick resourcefulness, humor that tends to wit, and (less definite) sympathy, curiosity, and trustfulness.

The obverse is sorrowful, pessimistic depression, with fear and worrying. There is marked emotionality, brooding, some suspicion, anger, disgust, and aloofness; general neuroticism, nervous habits, whining (children), sensitive introspectiveness, and a tendency toward habit-bound precision, thrift, and conventionality. Subjectively the individual feels miserable, troubled by worry, depression, and instability of mood, and inability to relax.

This factor may be the level of nervous energy or a predisposition to an over-powerful super ego. Some results suggest that F factor varies, more than any other, in the same person from time to time, especially in those already highly endowed with A factor.   Incidentally, since this variability obscures the present ratings, it is possible that accurate immediate measurement would assign this factor greater variance than it now shows.

Factor VI or I.   Sensitive, Anxious Emotionality — *v.* — Rigid Tough Poise

Matching BR VI, QP XIII, T. III or IV, and C. XVI or C. XIX.   For description of BR traits see page 330.

Two Q factors have some claims to be matched here: Reyburn and Taylor's Flexibility-speed and their Tension-high-strungness; but as these were established in a single factorization, both cannot be right.   Good matchings can be seen also in Darrow and Heath's (*71*) Sleep difficulties, Guilford's (*104*) Nervousness, and Reyburn and Taylor's Nervousness (*215*).   The items in these latter are:

1. Is easily startled
2. Suffers from insomnia
3. Is easily distracted
8. Is inclined to express emotions easily
10. Feels that he uses more energy than most in getting things done

If this identification is correct (see clinical discussion below), it illuminates the nature of the factor a good deal; for it brings in all kinds of somatic associations (indigestion, anemia, heart trouble) now being focussed in researches in psychosomatic medicine.

Alternatively, among Q matchings, the first Reyburn factor stresses impulsiveness and inability to relax, while the second emphasizes speed.   Of these, the first seems definitely more likely, if the above identification has to be superseded.   The choice between these two Q matchings must be considered to be still open.   The present match is a little unsatisfactory because it drags in neurasthenia-like traits when a Q factor has already been well matched with the J factor (neurasthenia).

However, one must bear in mind that anxiety neurosis and neurasthenia are notoriously difficult of separation.

The T. III Hyperthyroid and T. IV Hypersensitive factors have both a decided resemblance to the picture given by the Q factor, while cluster T(XXXV) Masc.-Fem. is a third alternative.

Clinically, I and J factors are easily seen to comprise the symptomatology of anxiety neurosis and neurasthenia, but because of their close resemblance further research will be necessary to decide with certainty which factor is which. At present, judges agree by a great majority in considering I to be, in its extreme form, a description of anxiety neurosis. The only difficulty here is the absence of outstanding emphasis on anxiety itself in the ratings. (It is present as "Nervousness" in I, which has higher saturation here than in J.) But this lack of outstanding emphasis on anxiety in the I pattern may be due to the fact that the anxiety of anxiety neurosis is more an introspected than an obvious, overt, behavioral component. Both anxiety neurosis and neurasthenia clinically have psychosomatic associations, and with this picture our I and J factors also agree. The BR description fills out the pre-anxiety neurosis personality with some interesting, and usually insufficiently noticed, associated behavior traits, and sets a tough, mature, assured, and rigid poise as its opposite.

Résumé on I. The essential character is more elusive than with most source traits. There is every indication in the duality of the above matchings that the I factor is really two highly "coöperative" factors requiring to be "split" by more exact research techniques. The positive loadings show primarily a tenderhearted, sensitive, sympathetic emotionality and imaginativeness, with some emotional dependence, gregariousness, neuroticism, and timidity.

The obverse is represented by a hard-boiled, mature, independent, unemotional, poised individual with some smugness, overprecision, and blinkered logic. Ancillary factors throw in at this pole also sexual sensuality, curiosity, popularity, noncoöperativeness, frankness, and courage.

Burt has suggested autoerotic sensuality as the essence; others have pointed out its connection (evidenced in 74) with masculinity and femininity. The connection with sex differences is striking, but the factor also exists in a population of one sex only. It may, however, arise from the ratio of testosterone to female sex hormone. The present writer considers the connection with anxiety central. Also, the questionnaire match stresses anxiety, tension, jumpiness, and signs of subliminal anxiety generally; but the greater timidity of women and their greater liability to anxiety neurosis would fit in with this. The factor could also be one of sex repression — i.e., libido into anxiety.

Factor VII or K. Trained, Socialized, Cultured Mind — *v.* — Boorishness

Matching BR VII, QP VIII. Description on page 334.

From factor VII and onward the source traits are considered less clearly established and are arranged in diminishing order of certainty rather than of variance. The justification of the α factorization which creates these factors rests partly, as indicated, on such a factor having been found in other BR or in Q, T, and C investigations. The degree of certainty, therefore, is based on the number of such rediscoveries.

Two similar Q factors have a claim here. The best match, which might be called Intellectual Leadership, appears in the Guilfords' research most clearly, as Thinking Introversion. In their second research they identify this with their sixth factor (Thinking), but the writer would judge it closer to the third (Liking Thought). It seems the same also as Whisler's (276) Interest in Controversies. In this case its chief items are:

1. Is not more interested in athletics than in intellectual matters
3. Generally prefers to lead in group activities
4. Inclined to study motives of others
6. Thinks the problem of "whether the industrial age dulls most people's appreciation of beauty" is vital (Etc.)

As a T factor K might seem so broad — comprising all educational habits, knowledge, and achievement — as to escape detection in past, detailed, analytical, scholastic testing researches. Almost certainly any good test of general, scholastic, and aesthetic education would tap this factor pretty directly. However, one does not have to fall back on mere supposition, for a research by Brogden (*20*) actually shows a clear-cut factor, distinct from intelligence and the character factors, as follows:

Vocabulary	.55 to .60
Willingness to face discomfort for sake of duty	.47
Good ethical choices in story test	.44

(This, being for twelve-year-olds, may be regarded as the foundation of the developed personality qualities in the above BR factor among adults.)

Résumé on K. This may be either a factor of education generally — i.e., as the title indicates, a trained, cultured mind such as is likely to be produced by an "intellectual" background, or it may be actually a more restricted tendency within the above area to think more than most, to be more conscious of and forceful about social and moral duties, and to have refined aesthetic satisfactions.

Factor VIII or G. Positive Character Integration — *v.* — Immature, Dependent Character

Matching BR VIII, QP IX, T. XIII, and C. V. Description on page 326.

This factor apparently appears in Q data in Layman's (*159*) Changeability, Reyburn and Taylor's (*213*) Will-Character, and their confirmation of it in a second research (*214*) and probably in Whisler's (*276*) Conventional Ethical Principles. On purely qualitative grounds, Guilford's (*102*) Rhathymia might be the obverse; but we believe closer inspection and general considerations veto this identification.

1. Does not desire constant change of work
4. Does not worry about possible misfortunes

5. Is not suspicious of others' motives
7. Is not impulsive
8. Is slow and deliberate in manner

Of the three T factors in the realm of character as such, that best fits the present G factor which is distinguished by high loadings in persistence (not of a brute, physical kind), conscientiousness, and independence (resistance to suggestion). This is the factor found by O'Neil (198) (Will-Character), Brogden (20) (Will-Character), and perhaps embedded in the Hartshorne and May (111) "integration" cluster. In the former it loads

Resists suggestion in picture interpretation, etc.	53
Conscientious over details of instructions	37
Perseveration	− 46

(Also: Accuracy in sorting cards, tendency to stick to a choice, persistence on dynamometer or insoluble maze.)

Clinically the lower (right) pole of this factor most directly resembles that psychopathic personality which has strong hysterical components. It is distinguished from low C (general emotionality) by emphasis on emotional dependence, irresponsibility, and immaturity. It is possible that it is essentially the conversion hysteria personality — i.e., one of the "character neuroses" of psychoanalytic theory.

Résumé on G. This seems to be the self-conscious "willed" aspect of character, as distinct from that steadfastness due to deeper emotional stability — i.e., an environmental mold source trait in character, supplementing the probably constitutional C factor with which, in past researches, it has constantly been confused and combined. It is presumably the result of good integrative training, and is likely to correlate with age and maturity. However, one can point with confidence only to the traits of responsibility, reliability, painstaking, hard-working perseverance and conscientiousness, systematicness, and ability to control impulsiveness, worry, suggestibility, and the effects of distractions.

**Factor IX or H.   Charitable, Adventurous Cyclothymia — *v*.
— Obstructive, Withdrawn Schizothymia**
Matching BR IX, QP XI, C. II.   List of BR traits on page
328.

The most ready agreement in the Q factors is found with
that factor instanced by Guilford's (*102*) Rhathymia, Reyburn
and Taylor's (*215*) fourth factor, and Vernon's (*269*) Carefreeness.   These agree well mutually, but do not indicate the
kindness, still less the conscientiousness, seen in the outside
observer's rating.   If it be true that this factor involves true
charitableness, and "charity vaunteth not itself," this discrepancy is precisely what would be expected.   But there is
doubt here, for a minority of judges identified with other Q
factors, though with factors already well matched elsewhere
(A and, less often, F)
The Q items are:

1. Is carefree
2. Is happy-go-lucky
3. Does not worry
4. Is impulsive
6. Craves excitement
8. Is unconcerned what others think

No T factor is known definitely to tie up with this BR
factor, though some correlation with fluency measures is
almost certain.   (See F, page 483.)
That A and H are the best examples we have of coöperative
factors (page 528) has already been mentioned.   Why two
independent influences should be capable of affecting very
much the same pattern of traits is not easy to understand, but
in this, even more than in our other instance (C and G), general clinical knowledge points definitely to the same phenomenon and suggests a clear hypothesis.   We know that schizophrenia can appear (*a*) with little hereditary indication, with
comparative suddenness, with strong environmental stress,
or (*b*) with strong hereditary and pre-psychotic constitutional
indications, with slow insidious onset and with no discernible

excess of infantile trauma. Review of the newly available data on shock therapy likewise indicates two extremes, (*a*) being responsive and (*b*) unresponsive to shock. There seems also to be some greater association of the hereditary pattern with catatonic and hebephrenic than with simple and paranoid forms (*139a*).

Our hypothesis is, therefore, that our two factors correspond to the two chief sources instrumental in producing the schizophrenic pattern. Only faint indications exist as to which is which. But the fact that A has the larger variance, just as environment seems to have the larger clinical role, and that paranoid trends, suggestive of a "frustration and aggression" situation, are more marked in A factor, inclines one to theorize that A is the environmental mold trait and H the constitutional source trait in the genesis of the schizoid cluster syndrome. Anthropometric correlations should therefore be sought with H, not A.

Résumé on H. This factor is clearly very similar to Cyclothymia-schizothymia. It stresses more, however, carefree adventurousness, frankness, kindness, some seeking of the limelight, impulsiveness, and spirited love of excitement. Conversely, the obverse brings out more sharply the inhibited, fearful, withdrawn, and obstructive aspects of schizothymia, rather than the emphasis on hostile, hard, frustrated, and vindictive in A minus.

Factor X or J. Neurasthenia — *v.* — Vigorous, "Obsessional Determined" Character

Matching BR X, QP X, T. XIV, and C. XIX. Description of Br traits on page 332.

A well-established Q-data factor which has been called "Obsessional Inflexible Will-Character" was repeatedly matched by the judges with this description. It recurs as Layman's (*159*) Impulsive action, Reyburn and Taylor's (*215*) Inhibition, and Vernon's (*267*) Scrupulousness. On qualitative grounds there is good reason also to include here a factor of "schizoid asthenia," though there is no adequate ground for identifying this (as a polar opposite) with the above Obsessional Will-Character. It is represented by Layman's (159) inability to meet reality, Mosier's (187) autistic tendency, and Stagner and Krout's (238) (239) forgetfulness with the items: daydreaming, loneliness, self-consciousness, troubled by useless ideas running through head, and poorness of memory. The objection to identifying this second Q factor with the neurasthenic pole of the present factor is that Layman's two factors are not opposites, while the generally neurasthenic picture of the Q factor also has some distinct compulsive items. Moreover, it is possible that J should be identified with whichever of the Speed and the Nervousness Q factors is not identified with I, which would preclude the simultaneous identification with the "Schizoid asthenia" Q factor. We shall, therefore, list only the identification with the "Vigorous Obsessional" pole of the rating factor, with the above Q factor of Reyburn and Taylor, Vernon, and others, as follows:

1. Is not impulsive
3. Is persevering and stable
5. Is very particular about dress and personal property
7. Is able to concentrate well
10. Does not relax easily

T data yield a factor which almost certainly belongs either here or with E. A possible argument for matching with E (apart from its general character) is the existence of a specific r of .44 with the A–S test. Against this, however, are the lowness of the correlation; the presence of ascendance (Variable 21) in the present factor at about the expected low level of correlation, and, most cogently, Thornton's finding of a true dominance factor additional to this factor from the same correlation data.

Accordingly, the T factor, which we finally match here, is that which has variously been called determined, self-sufficient, endurant Will-Character and reappears recognizably in the researches of Howells (*28*) (Endurance), Thornton (*52*) (Withstanding Discomfort), Rethlingshafer (*44*) (Discomfort), Brogden (*3*) (Self-control), and Brintnall (*2*) (Confidence-Persistence), with the following outstanding items:

Strength and time of dynamometer grip	.55–.79
Time S will endure painful pressure or electric shock	.62–.69
S's self-rating on persistence	.42
Score on Allport A–S Test	.44
Translates slang terms into precise English rather than slang terms (also prefers better to questionable reading)	.55
Indicates preference for duty at cost of discomfort	.50

Clinically the left polar extreme of this factor is pretty clearly Neurasthenia (with the emphasis on fatigue and inability to concentrate, but little on irritability). However, neither pole can be considered extreme good adjustment; for at the right pole one cannot mistake the continual indications of what has sometimes been called the "obsessional character" (not the obsessional *neurosis* with asthenic symptoms).

Résumé on J. This seems to be a factor of nervous vigor, energy, perseverance, speed, smartness, initiative, industry, independence, capability, and conscientiousness with inability to relax. The obverse brings in languidness, daydreaming, poor health, lack of confidence, slackness about dress, etc., ignoring environment, and emotional dependence. It may be a source trait of deep, chronic nervous fatigue, or spring from some physiological disorder — e.g., lack of vitamin B.

Factor XI or D. Hypersensitive, Infantile Sthenic Emotionality — *v.* — Phlegmatic Frustration Tolerance

Matching BR XI, QP II, T. (SF) II or T. (SF) IV*a*, C. VI (Special Form). Description of BR traits on page 319.

Despite the veiling of aggressive aspects in the Q data, the factor was pretty confidently identified by most judges. This factor, which the present writer contingently called "general emotional hypersensitivity," occurs as Layman's Inability to meet reality, Mosier's Hypersensitivity, Darrow and Heath's Neurasthenia with excitability, and perhaps as Reyburn and Taylor's second factor.

From the items with highest loadings we sample:

1. Feelings are easily hurt
2. Often gets excited, is easily rattled
6. Expresses his emotions readily
7. Cannot stand criticism
8. Indulges in self-pity

No T factor can be pointed out with confidence in this case. One suspects that this pattern may correlate with Fluency (as does F more definitely) or, again, with the oscillation factor (page 418). Hyperactivity and hypersensitivity of emotion, however, have loadings in two rather similar T. (SF) factors, namely, T. (SF) II and T. (SF) IV*a*. The former, which is more likely, has

High pulse rate	No average available
High respiration and B.M.R.	No average available
High Psychogalvanic Reflex Magnitude Minus Systolic Blood Pressure	.80
Low Actual Skin Resistance	.70
High Systolic Blood Pressure	.54

Clinically, again, no match is obvious and unquestionable. There is some resemblance to Moore's "Non-euphoric Manic," but this was established from clinical material statistically and is not a commonly recognized clinical entity. There is also a very decided resemblance to conversion hysteria and a lesser one to the "neuropathic constitution." We believe this is a core of traits in common to hysteria and non-euphoric mania, not previously clearly recognized and which could be called the "hysteric-manic" diathesis.

Résumé on D. This factor probably has only small variance and needs to be better defined. It expresses a form of unrestrained emotionality and changeability in which sympathy-seeking and quarrelsomeness are combined. Excitability is stressed, rather than emotionality, and there are many neurotic concomitants. It may be the character neurosis of the late Oedipus phase, which psychoanalysts connect with the hysterical personality. Like factor B (Mental capacity), it has in a peculiar degree the character of leaving extremely few aspects of personality unaffected — a possible indication of being a temperamental trait.

Factor XII or L.   Surgent Cyclothymia — v. — Paranoia

Matching BR XII, QP XV, and C. IV*a*. Description on page 335.

The only Q factor which comes up for consideration here is one which has already been discussed for A and rejected there, because its small general magnitude and infrequent appearance in factorizations suggest that it belongs to a lesser factor in our series than the first.   Qualitatively and quantitatively, therefore, this Q factor fits excellently here.   It appears as Darrow and Heath's (*17*) complex consisting of a paranoid tendency, excitability, and depressive tendency; perhaps as Reyburn and Taylor's (*46*) Perseveration; and has some overlap with Layman's (*31*) Emotionality factor identified with F. The Q factor, therefore, is a good match but is itself not sufficiently confirmed.

1. Thinks most people are self-seeking or malicious
2. Dislikes many people
3. Does not usually trust people; or prefers to work alone
4. Believes found fault with more than he deserves; or feels easily hurt
6. Often gets in a state of excitement
8. Has high perseveration score on a "p" test

Clinically the factor is readily identifiable as paranoia or paranoid schizophrenia.   The only unsatisfactory aspect of this match is that paranoia is an important and fairly widespread condition, whereas this is the least of our factors. The apparent contradiction may be reconciled, however, when one reflects that this small factor stands on the shoulders of the major factors of schizophrenia — A and H — giving the schizoid make-up this final twist.   It fits in also with the fact that pure paranoia — as distinct from paranoid schizophrenia — has always been an elusive, debated syndrome. This one would expect from a factor which is of such small variance that it would be a submerged factor syndrome unless aided by combination with some other factor in forming a single cluster.

Résumé on L.   The trait elements in L are so highly correlated with those in A (and to a lesser extent H) that unless we believe in allowing a substantial role to coöperative factors we may doubt its existence.   Its contribution to the variance is in any case very small.   The Q and C evidence, slight as it is, does, however, support the notion of a small factor here.

Its description is that of an unhappy, frustrated, hostile, rigid, brooding, and suspicious, withdrawn personality — i.e., of what is commonly called paranoia — though within the "normal" range of the factor there is no evidence of delusions as such.

The interpretation of source traits.   As pointed out elsewhere, "interpretation" is, in a sense, only continued description — the accumulation of associations and knowledge which increase the field within which prediction can be made. The above descriptions contain already, therefore, our essential interpretation of the main source traits.   Research will carry the pattern farther and perhaps in some cases confirm our hypotheses about some one physiological or cultural influence which *is* the factor.   It will also decide whether the given source trait is a temperamental, dynamic, ability, or wholistic factor.   Our present position is that, by reason of being based on the whole personality sphere, these factors, in contrast to those obtained from most artificially "conditional" tests, are almost certain to be wholistic factors.   However, judged by their apparent psychological nature, a surprisingly high proportion of them are predominantly temperamental or constitutional in nature.   Indeed, the indication seems to be that *environmental mold traits will prove only rarely to be general factors*.   These important traits perhaps need to be looked for among group and specific factors.

Some psychologists may be interested in a direction of "interpretation" with which we have concerned ourselves very little — namely, allowing these source traits to inherit the name and meaning of historically eminent concepts. This could readily be done.   Historical type dichotomies and syndromes have been so numerous that at least *one* could doubtless be found to resemble each and every one of our source and surface (pages 246 and 507) traits.   On the other hand, some of the historical patterns seem to have been complete impostors, either because they posed as source traits — i.e., as springing from a single cause or principle — when in fact they are revealed as only composite surface traits, or because they do not actually exist with the characters described, even as surface traits.   Extraversion, for example (as used by later writers if not as used by Jung), is definitely not a source trait, but a rough approximation to a large surface trait.

Our view is that the less the present factors and clusters are encumbered with vague associations and false meanings from doubtful ancestors the better.   We have accordingly made historical identifications only where the match is very clear. Interpretation seems best confined to physiological and social correlates, to genetic origins, transformations, and modes of interaction and especially to predictive importance in all sorts of real-life situations.

3. THE NATURE OF THE PRINCIPAL SURFACE TRAITS AND THEIR RELATION TO SOURCE TRAITS

Relative utility of surface traits. For most purposes the psychometrist will do well to deal with source traits rather than surface traits.   This practice is justified because (1) measurement has more precise meaning for factors than for wide clusters of uncertain extent, (2) factors are, as true functional unities, presumably more stable, permanent, and less circumstantially determined than clusters formed by factor overlap, and, most cogently, (3) factors, as true functional influences, can be used predictively and analytically in far more situations than can clusters.

Nevertheless, for sheer descriptive purposes the surface trait is frequently superior. It corresponds directly to what the observer sees in behavior. For this reason surface traits or syndromes are generally more convincing entities to the experienced naturalistic observer than are factors, and, as a glance at the list below will show, the outstandingly successful historical attempts at systems of describing and "typing" people have converged on the chief *surface* traits as we now know them. Probably it will be found that, in terms of ratings, surface traits can be estimated with greater reliability. Source traits always have to be assessed indirectly, from a weighted mean of several separate trait-element estimates, but the surface trait elements are usually so similar, obvious, and closely knit that they can be rated with high reliability as a single trait. The novelist, the dramatist, and the psychiatrist define the subjects of their study in terms of surface traits; the refined and potent technique of psychometric analysis and predictions, at the hands of the psychologist, in terms of measured, understood source traits, is only now dawning.[1]

The theory regarding the creation of clusters either through a "heaping up" of several factors or through the emphatic expression of a single factor has been amply described in preceding chapters. Here it remains to illustrate such relations by reference to actual examples among our surface traits, and particularly with respect to psychiatric syndromes.

Illustrations of relations of surface to source traits. As the variables of our main factor analysis were themselves clusters,

---

[1] The distinction we make may be viewed historically as anticipated by (1) the very use of the term "personality," from *persona* or mask. This led to talk of "inner" and "outer" personality, but inner and outer meant all things to all men and frequently implied moral evaluation; (2) the use of the terms "phenotype" and "genotype"; (3) the "geisteswissenschaftlich" Gestalt approaches as opposed to reflexology. None of these was clear or precise enough to provide a method.

any clustering of these produced by factors or factor overlaps will actually be clusters among clusters. Are these to be found among our catalogue of surface traits (Chapter 8), or, if not, where else?

Such clusters or surface traits will be larger and shallower (lower mean intercorrelation) than those we have called individual surface traits in Chapter 8. They will correspond to the "sectors" in which those clusters are there bunched. They may be detected also as the clusters — very obvious ones — in the original *correlation matrix between clusters*, on which our large-scale factor analysis was based. These latter clusters actually correspond fairly well with the "sectors" of Chapter 8. Finally, since some of the surface-trait clusters of Chapter 8, especially those established in earlier research by Sheldon, Maslow, and the present writer, are very wide and shallow, the overlap of the present narrow cluster variables may be expected to result in clusters from that list.

If the reader will look at the factor loading table (*58a*), he will see that there are six variables which have appreciable loadings, and in the same sense, in both factors B and C, as follows:

Variable	B	C
3	− .44	− .26
4	.45	.30
10	.32	.40
17	.34	.38
27	.30	.39
28	37	.36

A brief multiplication of the factor loadings will show that the mean intercorrelation of these six variables, due to common possession of the two factors, is 0.32 — e.g., $r_{34} = - 44 \times 45 + (-) 26 \times 30 = - 0.28$; again, $r_{27} = 0.53$. Since every possible "linkage" is appropriately made among these variables, they constitute a low cluster. This cluster (with three reflected to the opposite quadrant) can be readily seen in Diagram 17 below. The trait-element variables involved are: reliable, mature, independent, thoughtful, deliberate, austere, balanced, loyal, honest, emotionally stable, unemotional, content, phlegmatic, self-controlled, self-respecting.

This wide shallow cluster will be found essentially to constitute the A sector (especially within the AB province) of the main cluster catalogue of Chapter 8. As no other factors are systematically effective, even to a slight degree, in all five of these variables we can conclude that the surface trait — the wide AB sector surface trait described above — which we have called *"Realism; emotional integration"* is a product of two source traits — intelligence (B) and (negative) general emotionality (C).

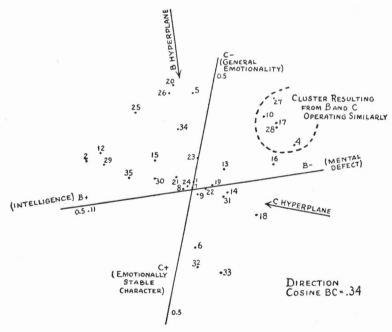

DIAGRAM 17. EXAMPLE OF POSITIVELY OBLIQUE FACTORS

Psychiatrically it is interesting to note that the more highly correlating items in this cluster, namely 3, 4, and 27 (mean r about 0.5), constitute the narrow surface trait AB 4, which seems to be essentially the personality commonly described for the conversion hysteric.   This implies that both emotional dissociation *and* low intelligence are involved in hysteria, which agrees with the usual findings of lower than average intelligence for hysterics.[1]

As an example of a surface trait which our analysis shows to be the product of overlap of as many as three or four factors we may take sector CB, particularly as it outcrops in the two narrower clusters CB 1 and CB 4.   This is essentially the surface trait which Sheldon has written about at length under the name of "cerebrotonia," while CB 1 may be taken as an extreme manifestation in neurasthenia.   The trait elements in the broad, shallow CB 1–4 sector are: sensitive, hurried, absent-minded, timid, awkward, introspective, shy, high-strung, excitable, poor self-control, melancholy, unsociable, and shiftless.   If we examine the variables in this area — principally 5, 13, 18, 20, 29, 30, 32, 33 — we find that most of them do indeed have a very similar and quite complicated common factor weighting, consisting of very high negative F, moderate negative A and C, and a loading on E, which is negative and slight in 5, 13, 18, and 20 and positive in 32 and 33.   Cerebrotonia and neurasthenia seem to consist of the first factor pattern: extreme desurgency, slight schizothymic tendency, appreciable general emotionality (lack of integration), and a tendency to dominance rather than submissiveness. This results in the shallow cluster hypochondriacal, high-strung, hurried, vivacious, neurotic, sensitive, insecure, emotional.   This seems to be the "ground plan" out of which surface trait E 1 or cerebrotonia, CB 1–2, might develop.

[1] A more detailed analysis of the conversion hysteric syndrome and other clusters in actual neurotic symptoms into factors has been carried out elsewhere (58g), with results well in accord with these.

If, now, dominance is reversed in its influence (as in 32, 33), adding submissiveness to the same A, C, F pattern, we get the cluster AC 1, which has been labeled agitated melancholy.[1] (In short, though the melancholia syndrome is largely F, it may not be an entirely pure factor syndrome.) The mean correlation produced by the heaping up of these four factors is, in fact, not high (about .30), in spite of the agreement of all traits in their general factorial composition. Consequently the true surface traits both of cerebrotonia and of E 1 may require, as further research could show, some added limited group factor to "bring them out" with the high intercorrelations usually assigned to them.

It is interesting to note that if positive and negative endowments in the main source traits are about equally frequent, high endowments in such a surface trait as cerebrotonia, which requires simultaneous *positiveness* in *five* factors, will be relatively rare. This difference in distribution between source trait endowments and compound surface trait endowments is worthy of further inquiry, and may explain the rarity of pathological syndromes which are nevertheless nothing more than the products of source trait endowments possessed in such degrees very widely.

The pattern of the surgent temperament, explored some years ago by the present writer, as a surface trait (40), is now revealed as due primarily to the surgency-melancholy factor, F, but aided also by the cyclothyme-schizothyme factor, A — i.e., the most marked surface cluster of surgency develops only on the bases of cyclothyme temperament, while the fullest expression of the desurgent cluster occurs only when low F supervenes on schizothyme temperament. Since extremes of F are presumably less frequent in the schizothyme than the cyclothyme, the surgent cluster is presumably more frequent than its opposite — i.e., we should expect the distribution to be skewed.

[1] This suggests that circumstances producing a change merely in dominance may precipitate a CB 1 personality into agitated melancholia.

Instances of surface traits which are the direct and pure expression of a single source trait are relatively easily found with the "big" factors of high variance, and examples are given in section 2, above, of pathological syndromes which appear to be of this type; but they are naturally not easily to be found among factors which do not load any variables very highly and which have the character only of "submerged factor syndromes" (page 140). An instance occurs with variables 9, 14, and 19, which are intercorrelated about .38 as the result of factor A alone, and have no other factor whatsoever with a common influence. A surface trait having these trait elements is recorded as the F sector in Chapter 8, and outcrops especially in F 2 and F 5. Similarly factor B appears as the whole shallow cluster of the B group; while factor E (Dominance) outcrops as CB 1 and CB 2, called by Sheldon somatotonia and related as such to body build. These examples suffice to illustrate the heterogeneity of surface traits — i.e., their varying degrees of compositeness and the consequent limitations in using them in research and applied problems in lieu of pure source traits. Furthermore, one must bear in mind that two individuals equally endowed with a certain surface trait may represent quite different proportions of the source traits which enter into it — i.e., apparently the same trait can be differently produced, a high influence of one source trait compensating for the lack of another. Obviously this variety of causation of what is roughly the same surface trait can occur only in the middle ranges of endowment; the upper limits require both source traits to go "all out."

Factor combinations yielding paradoxical surface traits. A serious defect of the earlier, clinical and observational approach to surface traits is that it tends to recognize only the salient patterns formed when factor is piled upon factor and not the fainter patterns, equally numerically represented in a population, wherein factors somewhat alike in nature act in opposite directions. For example, extraversion is probably a combination of four factors, all operating in the same direction as regards the trait-element of sociability and a number of related traits — e.g., quickness, expressiveness. Let us consider the two principal factors only — A, cyclothymia, and F, surgency — for simplicity's sake. It is obvious that the number of individuals in whom these both manifest high positive loadings is no greater than those in whom one is positive and the other negative; yet surface traits notice only the first combination.

The seeming "paradoxical" combinations — i.e., those in which qualitatively like factors operate in opposite directions — are likely to produce subtle trait element patterns worthy of special remark and study. For example, the individual whose sociability one would expect to find high because of positive A endowment and low because of negative F endowment manifests, in the writer's rather sporadic observation, a kind of passive, clinging sociability. He does not appear very sociable, actively seek society, or participate by talking, etc., but he feels sociable, desires company, and is highly accessible (in the psychiatric sense).

Many instances of complex behavior which are cited as criticisms of the notion of a trait are in fact those which most beautifully illustrate the prediction of behavior through the use of source traits. By redefining the nature of the trait element which is taken into our correlations — in this case redefining "sociability" in the direction of the complex behavior considered above — we could, as discussed on page 124, get a trait element more purely saturated in one factor. In this case, by redefining as a passive, clinging type of sociability, we should get something which enters more into A, cyclothymia, and less into F, surgency. Experiments in such redefinition aid in defining the source trait A. They also help to remind us that behavior in the middle range of "sociability" is, by virtue of its mixed factorial composition, very sociable in one sense and very unsociable in another. In short, properly to understand and use the loadings of a composite "logical" trait element we must stick to the precise definition of the element used in the original factor analysis. Next we can get fuller prediction from a single source trait by using "organic" trait elements which we have invented and defined in the light of our increasing knowledge of the factors operating.

Among other common instances of "paradoxicalness" the following may be briefly indicated. Negative A (Schizothymia) and positive E (Dominance) lead to a combination of self-confident self-will with shyness and withdrawal producing behavior that turns on a knife edge. Such an individual rapidly becomes dominant with individuals he knows while remaining very shy with strangers. Again, the individual with positive G (Character integration) and negative C (General emotionality) is likely to show qualitative complexity in such trait elements as self-control and realism of thinking. On the one hand he is persistent, consciously moral, and idealistic; on the other he suffers from an emotionality which renders him unexpectedly unfairminded, prejudiced, and unreliable in that he shifts his attitudes without conscious warning. It may be that the high loading of "feels remorseful" in the Q factor for C springs from the (chance) association with G which calls the individual's attention sharply to the C behavior. Again, it would be worth while to make a special study of the person Cyclothyme on H (presumably constitution) and Schizothyme on A, in whom such trait elements as secretive, obstructive, withdrawn, might well be very different from those in the opposite combination. Marked opposite loading of certain traits could also occur from B (intelligence) and K (education?) being in opposition and from E (dominance) and J (neurasthenia).

The more complete interpretation of surface traits. The notion of "interpreting" surface traits may seem to involve a contradiction in terms. Surface traits are purely descriptive devices. A surface trait can be interpreted only by revealing the source traits which go to produce it and which are themselves of known nature and origin, as we have just done.

As stressed before, however, description readily extends into "interpretation," since fuller understanding is always a contribution to interpretation. Therefore we can interpret surface traits more completely, as such and without reference to source traits, by the same measures as we adopted with source traits, viz.:

(*a*) Relating them to historical and popular concepts and labels and to standard psychiatric syndromes — i.e., increasing their associations — and

(*b*) Proceeding to more detailed operational descriptions of the behavior connoted by the trait-element terms in which they have so far been couched. This involves also a deliberate widening of the base of behavioral, introspective (self-inventory and other), test performance, clinical and physiological referents which are the main manifestations of the trait in question.

Historical connections. Relating established clusters to historical types and traditional syndromes in the literature could be an endless task. Any experimental psychologist who gazes at the literary productions even of the last two hundred years only (as viewed, for example, in such a complete compendium as that of Roback (*217*)) must feel the words of a famous disconsolate coming aptly to his lips, "Fie on 't! oh fie! 'tis an unweeded garden, that grows to seed; things rank and gross in nature possess it merely." Much of the exuberant self-deception of the typologists has to be set aside, finding no counterpart, except by further deception, among confirmed surface traits; but the following identifications perhaps do not strain the concept of identity unduly. At least their listing (already foreshadowed in Section 8 of

Chapter 7) may facilitate the relating of past discussions to the present variables, though one does not claim that the matchings are carried out with the thoroughness applied above among the existing patterns of modern research. Some of the syndromes are not "historical" but existing clinical syndromes, already discussed in connection with source traits and here roughly equated with surface traits.

TABLE 26

CROSS-IDENTIFICATIONS OF SURFACE TRAITS AND CLINICAL SYNDROMES

PRESENT DESCRIPTION TITLE OF SURFACE TRAIT	CLUSTER INDEX NUMBER	HISTORICAL TYPE OR CLINICAL SYNDROME
Integrity-Altruism *vs.* Dishonesty-Undependableness	AA 1	Psychopathic Personality
Conscientious Effort *vs.* Incoherence	AA 2	Anal Character. Vagotonic Type
Practicalness, Determination *vs.* Daydreaming, Evasiveness	AB 2	Simple Schizophrenia or Subjective-Objective (Stern)
Neuroticism, Self-deception, Emotional Intemperance	AB 3	General Neuroticism
Infantile, Demanding, Self-centeredness *vs.* Emotional Maturity, Frustration, Tolerance	AB 4	Conversion Hysteria
Agitation, Melancholy *vs.* Placidity, Social Interests	AC 1	Agitated Melancholia
Balance, Frankness *vs.* Secretiveness, Immoderateness	AC 2	Catatonic Schizophrenia (Obverse of Labile. Pavlov)
Emotional Maturity *vs.* Infantilism, Dependence	B 1	Emotional Maturity (Willoughby)
Disciplined Thoughtfulness	B 2	Classical Type (Ostwald)
Creativity, Self-determination	B 3	Romantic Type (Ostwald)
Intelligence, Penetration, Talent	B 4	"g" General Intelligence
Crude Social Assertion, Exhibitionism	CA 1	Inferiority Overcompensation (Adler)
Energy, Boldness *vs.* Timidity, Languor	CB 1	Somatotonia (Sheldon)
Lack of Restraint, Adventure *vs.* General Inhibition	CB 3	General Inhibition. Unrestrained-Restrained (Guthrie)

TABLE 26 — *Continued*

Present Description Title of Surface Trait	Cluster Index Number	Historical Type or Clinical Syndrome
Poised Sociability, Toughness *vs.* Sensitivity, Haste	CB 1–2 and CB 4	Hyperthyroid Sensitivity, or Cerebrotonia (Sheldon)
Sociability, Heartiness *vs.* Shyness, Reserve	D 1	Extraversion (Jung)
Sociability, Warmth *vs.* Independence, Aloofness	D 2	Cyclothyme-Schizothyme (Kretschmer). Viscerotonia (Sheldon)
Pleasure-Seeking, Frivolous *vs.* Earnest	D 4	Active *vs.* Reflective (Jordan)
Cheerful, Enthusiastic *vs.* Sour, Mirthless	D 5	Sanguine *vs.* Melancholic (Classical)
High-Strung, Impulsive *vs.* Relaxed, Deliberate	E 1	Explosive Type (James)
Sthenic Emotionality *vs.* Self-control, Patience	E 2	Hypomanic
Intrusive, Frivolous, Unstable	E 3	Hebephrenic Schizophrenia
General Emotionality, Dissatisfied	E 4	General Emotionality
Friendly *vs.* Hostile, Mean, Obstructive	F 3	Obsessional-Compulsive Personality
Cynical, Suspicious, Dishonest	F 4	Paranoid Schizothyme.　(1) Sadistic Type (Apfelbach)
Sadistic, Vindictive *vs.* Good-tempered, Complaisant	F 7	Paranoid Schizothyme.　(2) Choleric (Classical)
Austerity, Thoughtfulness, Stability	G 1	Jaensch's T-type.　Disintegrate.
Verbal Skill, Interesting Ideas	G 2	Theoretical Type (Spranger)?
Creativity, Emotional Color	G 4	Jaensch's B-type.　Integrate.
Thrift, Tidiness, Obstinacy	H 1	Anal-Obsessional-Character. Hysteroid Obsessoid
General Aesthetic Interests	J 1	Spranger's Aesthetic Type
Hypochondriacal, Taciturn, Retroversion	O 1	Antevert-Retrovert
Asceticism, Eccentricity	P 1	Eccentric Schizothyme Character (Bleuler)
Inflexibility, Wandering	Q 1	"Ambulatory Schizothyme"

Expanded operational "Interpretation" of surface traits AA 1, CA 1, and CB 1

Chapter 8 revealed 50 nuclear clusters subtending 20 sectors of personality. Clusters appearing incidentally in other chapters, notably that on test measurements, added a few more, bringing the total to some 65 reasonably well-confirmed surface traits.

Space does not permit any general attempt to expand the meaning of all these traits; so we shall take three only — AA 1, CA 1, and CB 1 — to illustrate the direction of development which a complete personality scheme could take.

CA 1 and CB 1 are deliberately selected to illustrate the situation of a pair of closely similar traits often confused in amateur discussion. The operational "interpretation" of surface traits should be a simple process of behavioral exemplification of trait terms, themselves only slightly less concrete than the behavior; for the surface trait, by origin and definition, is descriptive of *behavior*, not of any underlying *cause* of behavior.

AA 1, labeled *Integrity-Altruism vs. Dishonesty-Undependableness*, is represented at the core by the traits Honest, Self-controlled, Self-denying, Loyal, Fair-minded, Reliable *vs.* Dishonest, Selfish, Fickle, Partial, Undependable, in that order of diminishing centrality. Around the core are found, on the positive side, Having good judgment, Idealistic, Intelligent, Being a good follower, Understanding, Stable in emotion, Thoughtful, Self-respecting, and Emotionally mature; and on the negative side, Changeability, Unreflectiveness, Lack of Self-respect, and Emotional infantilism. If one examines the expansion of these terms into their synonym groups, as originally set out in Section 4, Chapter 7, one finds, on the positive side, upright, principled, truthful, incorruptible, self-disciplined, self-mastering, stoic, faithful, stanch, single-hearted, fair, just, trustworthy; and on the negative side, cheating, thievish, lying, egotistic, self-interested, uses people, inconstant, prejudiced, biased, not steadfast.

The label terms for the cluster and still more those for each trait element tend to be more abstract than the synonyms which they represent from each individual study, so that the truly operational situations are best reached through studying the more particular terms merely "represented" by the label. Thus the individual high in the present surface trait will not cheat, thieve, or lie to gain advantage, will resist bribes or temptations, will show control of his emotions and little liability to moods. He will direct his behavior by principles of an idealistic nature, be unselfish and considerate, prove capable of judging situations without prejudice, be loyal to friends and institutions. He will also tend to be reflective and to be capable of bearing pain and discomfort stoically. It is noteworthy that this cluster contains little of the perseverance, conscientiousness, industry, and other esteemed character qualities which belong to the cluster AA 2. It deals with the capacity to renounce, forego, inhibit, accept delayed satisfactions and long-circuited expression, to take frustration without regression, and to see life's situations in perspective.[1]

CB 1 and CB 2–4 correspond to what Sheldon has called, respectively, Somatotonia and Cerebrotonia. In our more noncommittal, purely descriptive labels CB 1 is called *Energy, Boldness, Spiritedness vs. Apathy, Timidity, Languor.* It has at the core, positively: Energetic-spirited, Enthusiastic, Alert, Debonair, Strong Personality, Quick, Bold, Independent; and negatively, in descending importance: Languid, Apathetic, Absent-minded, Slow, Timid, Dependent. Less central trait elements are, positively: Vivacious, Assertive, Hearty, Daring, Being a Leader, Active in Games, Proud, Adventurous, Competitive, Not sensitive, Unrestrained, Noisy, Friendly but fighting, and Humorous; and negatively: Submissive, Quiet, Not Given to Domination.

[1] One writer has called the cluster "Passive but Constructive Virtues."

The expansion into the synonym groups of other studies produces the more particular terms: forceful, chipper, high-spirited, zestful, zealous, ardent, observant, jaunty, dapper, dominating, impressive, well knit, quick of apprehension; and, negatively: listless, languorous, world-weary, resigned, dreamy, indefinite, depersonalized, desireless, sluggish, retarded, clinging, and passive. Since this cluster seems to be the essence of that for which Sheldon invented the term "Somatotonia," his description of a typical somatotonic would be an operational exemplification. Thus he describes (*231*, page 121) Boris ———: "pugnacious, aggressive, loud . . . an excellent football player . . . popular. There appears to be no relaxation at all."

The CB 1 endowed individual will not be easily discouraged or repressed by failure, inhibited by authority, or reduced by fatigue. He will take up all kinds of activities, especially physical activities, with enthusiasm. In social situations he will be dominating and insensitive to danger signals. He will be quick in decision and independent in thought.

CA 1, labeled *Crude Social Assertion and Exhibitionism vs. Modesty and Obedience to Authority,* is in some ways very close to the above, yet different. Its core trait elements prove to be, positively: Exhibitionist, Argumentative, Talkative, Boastful, Arrogant; and, negatively: Self-Effacing, Peaceable, Taciturn, Modest, and Humble. Less central elements are, positively: Conceited, Headstrong, Restless, Autocratic, Bossy, Restless, Careless of appearance (in boys, unkempt), Extrapunitive, Treacherous, High-strung, Forward, Active, Persistent, Obstinate, Independent, Plucky; and, negatively: Deferring, Avoiding blame, Gentle-tempered, Relaxed.

The expansion into synonym groups brings: Contentious, factious, self-displaying, seeking admiration, voluble, vociferous, blustering, vauntful; and, negatively: not limelighting, not demanding recognition, meek, silent, incommunicative, and unassuming. The individual with high CA 1 endowment will seek the limelight in most situations, will talk too much, will blame others when things go wrong, will let people down or betray them behind their backs, will be high-strung and restless, will bluster and attempt to be autocratic. These "insecure" characteristics should alone suffice, for the psychologist having insight, to distinguish it from the energetic, zealous dominance of CB 1. However, the goal of immediate research must be to express these grouped trait-element terms in precise operational tests which will distinguish one surface trait from another without leaning upon individual insight into the essential character below the overt behavior.

4. THE MEANING OF OBLIQUE AND HIGHER–ORDER FACTORS IN RELATION TO THE PERSONALITY SPHERE

Available covariational entities. Initially the attempt to express covariation entities in mathematical form lead to two mutually assisting concepts: (*a*) Clusters, which are of vague boundary, and correlated, (*b*) Factors, which are initially treated as uncorrelated (orthogonal).

Further study may suggest more subtle concepts, some being hybrids or modifications of the above. Principally — indeed solely — we have to consider (*a*) a "hybrid" entity, consisting of a "factor" put through a cluster, when the factor is supernumerary to the factor space and hence dependent on other factors. This concept, due to Tryon, we called a *qualitative cluster*. (*b*) Second- and higher-order factors obtained from factor analyzing oblique, intercorrelating factors. The former, we concluded, has only a limited utility as a representational device,[1] but the use of oblique

---

[1] Three qualitative clusters in two-space might, it is true, give better "simple structure" in the sense of accounting for three clusters of variables more simply — except for the complication of an extra axis. Also one must consider, speculatively, the possibility that distinct, real psychological influences might operate to produce such mathematical relationships. For example, the skills of swimming and those of diving

factors and the second-order factors which may appear among
them is a highly naturalistic representational device and one
which needs to be clearly understood by those concerned with
the further progress of personality trait systems.

Oblique factors. Cogent reasons have already been set out
(page 279) for considering that true psychological source
traits will normally be represented by oblique factors, while
orthogonal factors represent an artificial, mathematically
dictated attempt at oversimplification very rarely corresponding to anything in nature. The associated characteristics
and consequences of oblique factors must now be considered
more fully.

That oblique factors are commonly very clearly required by
the nature of the correlation data themselves can be illustrated
by the two specimens (see Diagrams 17 and 18) taken at
random from the factor diagrams made while seeking for
simple structure in our main research on the twelve primary
source traits. In Diagram 17 the hyperplane for C is so clear
as to admit of nothing but obliqueness. The B hyperplane is
not too clear in this drawing (intelligence is one of two or
three factors which consistently show poor hyperplanes of
unloaded variables, being too general in their effects).

Here it can be clearly seen that a good simple structure is
obtained by shifting the C factor slightly away from orthogonality; for a hyperplane, well defined by a collection of
variables almost in a straight line, lies slightly athwart the
axis of the A factor. If we believe that a hyperplane is
properly defined by this simple structure criterion — and it
is hard to believe that in any highly varied collection of

could be independent in training origin yet so alike in quality that they appear as two
clusters in one plane. Experiment, especially with sociological and genetic factors of
known mode of operation, can only decide if this occurs; but if so it is almost certainly
a rare mental structure. If and when this exists, it presents a set of trait elements
having the origin and meaning of a source trait, yet appearing mathematically as a
cluster. Such clusters could, of course, be defined and measured, like any other
clusters not lying in one plane, by the centroid line of the cluster.

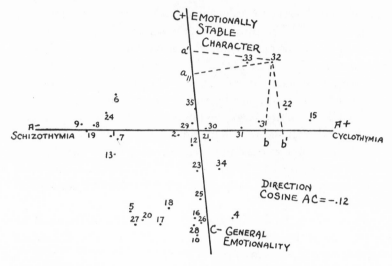

DIAGRAM 18.   An Instance of Negative Oblique Factors

variables more than about half of them will be involved in any particular factor — we must accept that in the majority of instances somewhat oblique factors are indicated by the data themselves.

Some confusion has arisen in oblique factor representation by reason of the fact that the standard mathematical textbook representation of oblique coördinates is different from that required in the field of factor analysis. The coördinates of the variable 32 above are, by the conventional method, a^1 and b^1 as shown, whereas by the factorial method they are a and b. (Otherwise the variables in the hyperplane would not have zero loadings.)

Oblique factors, as those familiar with the usual mathematical procedures know (see (120) (254)), require for their complete description both a *factor structure* and a *factor pattern*. These become identical in the special orthogonal case. An unavoidable complication in handling personality predictions in terms of oblique factors is that the calculation of performance in one particular trait element from the correlations of the trait element with the factors is a decidedly longer mathematical process than with orthogonal factors (see Equations, page 560). The estimation of a factor endowment from trait element, knowing the correlations, is, however, straightforward (page 562). Nevertheless, if the natural structure of personality consists of correlated (oblique) source traits, the greatest economy in prediction in all fields will in the end be achieved by dealing with oblique rather than artificial orthogonal entities.

The most marked correlations (obliquities) between our primary factors arise positively between (1) General Emotionality (C $-$) and Low Intelligence (B $-$); (2) Dominance (E $+$) and Emotional Stability (C $+$); and (3) Independent Character (G) and Emotional Stability (C $+$). There is also evidence of some slighter positive correlation among the three schizothyme factors, A, H, and L; between I and F and between B, intelligence, and I, cultured mind.

These examples call attention to the fact that it is necessary to distinguish clearly between correlated factors and what have been called, below, coöperative factors. Factors influencing similar variables in a similar way, and therefore having similar profiles — e.g., intelligence (B) and education (K) — are called coöperative factors. But apparently coöperative factors may be themselves uncorrelated, or even negatively correlated. Though, as influences, they work the same way, the operation of one of these influences may or may not tend to be associated with more than expected strength and frequency of operation of the other.

Probably, coöperative factors will appear most often positively correlated, because, through family and social linkages, the presence of one will tend to favor the presence of another. Thus, in the well-substantiated correlation of the intelligence factor (B) with the emotional stability factor (C), above, the following causal connections can readily be envisaged. (1) *Through the Family.* Because of heredity, more intelligent children will tend to have their emotional stability built up by intelligent parents. Because of wiser handling of their emotional problems their general character integration will be better. (2) *Through Society.* By reason of what has been called *socially conditioned genetic adhesion (57a)*, genetic endowment favorable to social promotion — e.g., ability and emotional stability — will tend to become linked in classes and, through class-assortative mating, in individuals.

Similarly, the positive connection ($r = .43$) between the presumed constitutional trait of emotional stability (C) and the presumed environmental mold trait of character integration (G) may be due to more stable parents exercising better character-training influences. It may also be aided by emotional stability, "sensitizing" in the individual the traits potentially acted upon by character training (or, seen inversely, by general temperamental emotionality putting obstacles in the path of operation of the character-molding influences).

Second- and higher-order factors. It is obvious that, from a mathematical point of view, factors — "second-order" factors — can be extracted from a matrix of correlations among oblique factors. Higher-order factors could be extracted from the correlations among second-order factors, and so on in indefinite regression. Whether actual psychological correlation matrices will yield such factors and whether they can be given psychological meaning is another question.

For the first attempt to put this to the test of practice we are indebted to Thurstone (*263a*). He isolated some seven primary abilities, as correlated (oblique) simple-structure factors. Their correlations were found to be susceptible to analysis into one general factor — a factor of general ability, apparently Spearman's "g."

Thurstone next illustrated the matter on a simpler physical

system by factor-analyzing the correlations among a population of rectangular boxes measured in many different ways. A factor analysis, rotated for simple structure, revealed three factors corresponding to length, breadth, and height. But the simplest structure required correlated factors, and a factor analysis of their correlations yielded a general, second-order factor of "total size." Consequently the loading in each of these could be predicted from so much of the second-order general factor plus so much of a specific.

Our primary personality factors (α rotation, see matrix page 89 in $(58a)$) subjected to a further factorization and rotated for simple structure yielded three factors, as follows:

TABLE 27

FACTORS IN PERSONALITY

FIRST-ORDER FACTORS	SECOND-ORDER FACTORS				
	F_1 (SS)	F_2 (TT)	F_3 (ER)	F_4 (SH)	F_5
A. Cyclothymia-Schizothymia	.1	.4	− .2	.3	.3
B. General Ability	.3	.2	− .1	.3	.6
C. Stable Character — General Emotionality	.6	.1	0	.6	0
D. Sthenic Emotionality — Frustration Tolerance	.2	0	− .1	0	.3
E. Dominance — Submissiveness	.6	0	0	− .3	0
F. Surgency — Melancholy	.4	.4	.5	0	0
G. Character Integration — Dependent Character	.4	− .2	0	0	0
H. Adventurous Rhathymia — Withdrawn Schizothymia	− .2	0	0	.5	.3
I. Anxious Emotionality — Rigid Poise	0	0	.8	0	0
J. Neurasthenia — Vigorous Character	0	.7	.1	0	.1
K. Cultured Mind — Boorishness	− .2	− .5	− .2	− .2	0
L. Surgent Cyclothymia — Paranoia	0	.4	− .1	− .2	.5

TABLE 27 — *Continued*

APPROXIMATE INTERCORRELATIONS OF SECOND-ORDER FACTORS

	F_1	F_2	F_3	F_4	F_5
$(SS)F_1$					
$(TT)F_2$	.35				
$(ER)F_3$	− .10	0			
$(SH)F_4$	.05	10	0		
F_5	0	.50	− .30	.20	

TENTATIVE INTERPRETATIONS

SS = Social Status (or Forceful, Positive Qualities)
TT = Tenacity Tension — *v.* — Adjustment, Coöperation
ER = Excessive or Easy Reactivity — *v.* — General Inhibition
SH = Security — Good Heredity — *v.* — Anti-Social Qualities

No instance of higher-order factors has yet been presented in psychological data, and one may well doubt whether so complex a structure will ever be found. The problem, therefore, is primarily to give psychological meaning to second-order factors in general and to those in the present inquiry in particular.

A second-order factor is clearly a cause of covariation which is in some, but not all, senses more fundamental than a first-order factor and which, in any case, is more pervasive and extensive. If, for example, higher social status favors the individual's being subjected more strongly to (*a*) an environmental mold of better academic education, (*b*) a pattern of vigor arising from better nutrition, and (*c*) certain neurosis-producing inhibitions, it might happen that three distinct factors would be found corresponding to these influences, but that all three would have low positive intercorrelations due to a factor of social-status influence on personality.

Obviously, in the great plexus of socio-psycho-physio-economic influences constituted by the social organism we find tangled chains of causes, instances of circular causation, and many possibilities of explaining phenomena by alternative concepts which are equally true because they are equivalent ways of conceptualizing the same events. The alternative factorizations correspond to these alternative conceptualizations. You may say that more intelligent people tend to get a better education because they come from smaller families which can afford to educate their children; or you may say that more intelligent people tend to restrict their families because they get a better education which teaches them to plan their families (57a).

In opposition to Thurstone's second-order factor of general ability Spearman has argued for a resolution into factors which require no second-order factor, all the variance being taken by a dominant first-order factor and less variance being left in the special abilities (51). For prediction the explanations amount to the same in the end; but if simple structure is better obtained by the correlated factors, then they may prove more convenient practical predictors in most situations. Since the individual is so entangled in the social organism, we should expect the psychologist's second-order factors often to be the same as the sociologist's first-order factors; indeed, there should be a very busy common market in psychology, physiology, and sociology for factors which are primary in one and second order in another.

An apparent difficulty in extracting second-order factors and giving meaning to them lies in the fact demonstrated by Thurstone (236a), that selection operating within a group with respect to one or more variables alters the angles between factors (though not the nature of the factors). To get an undistorted view of second-order factors, therefore, a normal population, free of selection according to specific variables, is necessary, and since this is rarely fully attained, second-order factors from a single study need to be interpreted cautiously. Our own second-order factors are five in number, three of which are tolerably well supported by the alternative β factorization. However, since the accurate determination of the angles between our factors was not a primary and thoroughly pursued aim of the study, we do not consider the present second-order factors to be more than a sketchy outline of what is likely to be found in that realm by the more thorough study now proceeding.

We shall adopt the convention of indicating second-order factors by two-letter symbols. The first factor, *SS or Social Status*, is so designated because it loads very definitely the factors which an independent study (57*a*) indicates to be the chief psychological variables associated with social status — namely B, intelligence; E, dominance; C, emotional stability, and G, character integration. (It also loads surgency, F.) The second, *TT or Tenacity-Tension*, is best viewed reversed. There it loads vigorous obsessional character (J), the two "acquired" schizoid factors (A) and (L), and the agitated melancholy factor (F). This indicates some general character of frustration-tenacity-tension which we have merely labeled descriptively, for lack of sufficient grounds for interpretation. The third, *ER or Easy Reactivity*, loads anxious emotionality (I) quite heavily and surgency (F) moderately. These are the factors of expressiveness and have indications of being temperamental in nature. ER might be a hyperthyroid or autonomic factor, gaining alternative expressions in cheerful or anxious overactivity. The fourth and fifth factors are *PI, Pyknic Inconative*, covering carefree rhathymia and lack of assertiveness, and *CI or Cyclothyme-Intelligence*, a factor underlying all three cyclothyme-schizothyme factors and intelligence. The latter may be connected with the common clinical observation of relatively high intelligence in manic-depressives and may represent a unitary genetic endowment. The only appreciable correlation of second-order factors exists between SS and TT (positive), though lesser correlations are indicated with others.

Second-order factors, as causes of organization among personality factors, might be expected to fall generally into either socio-historical or bio-physiological entities. We are still too near the threshold to pursue their significance, for theory or practice, further.

The personality sphere and higher-order factors. A little reflection will show that the question of second- and higher-order factors is tied up with our earlier problem of defining the surface of the personality sphere. If a researcher took for the initial correlation a small but widely separated set of variables, he could get directly, as a first-order factor, the factor which, if he had taken a more dense and numerous set of variables, he would have obtained only as a second-order factor. This would happen if each of the actual behavior variables happened to measure fairly purely one distinct general factor, a specific factor and very little else.

This is rather unlikely to happen by chance, but it becomes a probability when more relatively pure tests of factors — e.g., intelligence tests, fluency tests, character tests — come into general use and form common constituents of test batteries. Even without this aid from circumstances it is likely to happen in partial fashion, and the danger has to be faced that any given analysis may result in a mixture of first-order and second-order factors, confusing our concepts and our attempts at matching from one research to another.

It must be remembered that a particular factor may appear as specific, group, or general, in proportion to the density of representation of variables, in a particular area, in our correlation matrix. The factor identification problem that arises through uneven sampling can be illustrated by a historical example. When a set of ability measures, representative save for a certain concentration in the verbal field, was factorized, it yielded a general factor "g" and a verbal (group or general) factor "V." Thurstone's later analysis of a larger trait population, with dense representation from other than verbal fields, yielded a set of seven or more group or general factors, marked off by simple structure, and such that "g" only appeared as a second-order factor, though "V" remained first-order.

As trait density increases, therefore, first-order pass to higher-order factors. Consequently the agreed definition of orders awaits an agreed definition of density — in fact, of the "area" of the personality sphere. One basis for defining the personality sphere — language — has been set out above: it yields twelve major first-order factors. Probably these will appear as second- or higher-order factors in increasing microscopic studies. Another possible "sphere" basis is to sample performances according to time expended in them — e.g., a variable from every fifteen minutes of the average citizen's day. Other possibilities should be examined; for until the demarcation and division of the "personality sphere" is faced and solved as a theoretical problem, the objectives of factor analysis — and an anastigmatic view of the total personality structure — cannot be scientifically assured.

5. SOME STATISTICALLY MORE REFINED CONCEPTIONS
   ON PERSONALITY STRUCTURE

The need for flexibility of concepts. In this section we propose to look at some more refined and more speculative possibilities of detecting patterns and of statistically analyzing personality than would have been apt earlier, where the initial presentation would have been made unduly complicated and confused.

At the advancing frontiers two types of ignoramus rush in where statisticians fear to tread. First the weaver of fine verbal, philosophical, and frequently entirely mystical concepts of personality who doubts that the mathematical treatment is subtle enough to follow his intuitions and who, if he could grasp the statistical concepts, would probably object to such simplicities as normal distribution, linear correlation, and direct additive interreaction of factors. Secondly, the businesslike applied psychologist, who is struck by certain empirical relations and who, in blind trial and error unhampered by theory or over-nice statistics, sometimes hits upon unusual covariation patterns and uses crude, incongruous modes of representation which a "classical" statistician would have missed, by reason of his too rigid frame of thought. Both of these blind critics nevertheless deal with possibilities which the keen, flexible researcher needs always to keep in mind. Though these extreme observations are hurled at him destructively, he must use them as guides to refinements which need ultimately to be made in adapting analytical representations to the more minute contours of reality.

"Fission" and multiplication of factors with more intensive research. Before dealing with further theoretical analysis, however, it is necessary to refine and clarify our thought on a rather neglected issue within the existing practice of factor representation. Consternation sometimes greets the remark that later research has "split" into two a factor which was once considered unitary, or that several factors are now recognized as operative in a field — e.g., musical ability,[1] neuroticism — where one or two were deemed to explain the variance.

Such a view of the matter is in one sense true, in another entirely misleading. The reader should refer back to the introductory discussions on this topic with respect to factor matching on page 310. The matter becomes clear only if we distinguish two situations: (1) where the earlier factor or factors have been truly located, with a sufficient number of variables, a very good estimate of the communalities, and a sound rotation for simple structure; (2) where the earlier factors are based on incomplete research or rotation.

In the first situation a once discovered factor is never "split" by later research. Research with new variables confirms loadings in the old field and merely extends the mapping

---

[1] Here four factors have actually been increased by recent research (*142*) to eight.

of its profile into other fields. If a factor is defined by loadings in the three variables *a*, *b*, *c* (example, page 309), the introduction of variables *d* and *e* into the matrix will not alter the loadings in *a*, *b*, and *c*. The latter may bring into existence a new factor shared by *d* and *e* and *one* of the variables *a*, *b*, and *c*, or introduce such substantial variance as to give meaning and true dimensionality to a factor in *a*, *b*, and *c* previously jettisoned as a mere residual (see diagram below).

Probably the chief root, however, of this disturbingly paradoxical "splitting of the atom" of factor analysis is our inability accurately to estimate communalities. Consideration of the basic formula on page 558 will show that if the loadings S_1 and S_2 of two factors are the same we can substitute $S_1(T_1 + T_2)$ for the usual two terms, with respect to all variables. T_1 and T_2 can then be considered a single factor, T_{1+2}, and the correlation matrix yielded by multiplying the equations appropriately is indistinguishable from that based on two factors T_1 and T_2. Only the communalities in the two matrices are different, being $2 S_1^2$ in the first case and $(2 S_1)^2$ in the second.

In other words, where an insufficient variety of variables has been taken, so that the ultimate dissimilarity of loading profile of two factors is not betrayed, and where communalities have been systematically rather overguessed, one factor may appear where in fact there are two. It is not surprising, therefore, that our research of Chapter 9, in which the communalities proved to be closely estimated and in which a larger number of variables were employed (also aiding correct estimation), the single general character factor "w" of earlier, briefer researches was split into C and G and the schizothyme factor into A and H.

Failures to recognize the compound nature of a factor as a result of poor communality estimates are likely to become more rare as researches become carried out on larger matrices and with time for iterative techniques. The second cause of belated splitting, however, due to omission of particular

variables which give meaning to what would otherwise be
mere residuals, is likely to persist and needs to be studied more
closely, in geometrical as well as algebraic representation.
The problem includes that discussed in the preceding section,
wherein an originally first-order factor is either modified in
profile or becomes a second-order factor through more dense

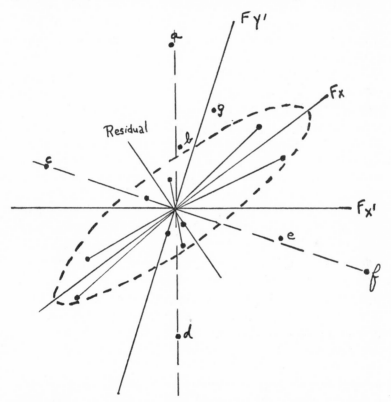

DIAGRAM 19.   Fission of a Factor by More Representative Research
Variables

representation — i.e., through narrower and more numerous
and peculiar forms of behavior being included.

When additional variables add variance and give status to a
residual, causing a new dimension to be recognized, it will

readily be seen, by considering the process of rotation, that the integral nature of other factors than the residual may also be affected. For consider the plot of two last factors when the variables fall into an elongated ellipse as covered by the broken line of Diagram 19. Normally one puts one axis, Fx, down the length of the ellipse and considers the short axis a mere residual. If in a later research, however, new variables a, b, c, d, e, f are added, all loaded in Fx but all happening to introduce the hitherto unrepresented dimensions, one is compelled to recognize two factors here instead of one. And it may well happen that the disposition of the new points clearly requires a rotation of the original Fx to Fx′, at the same time defining a hyperplane for a new factor Fy′.

Of course, the new variables *may* confirm the position of the original Fx; but there are several historical instances where they have not. The new factors, Fx′ and Fy′, as the diagram shows, will generally tend to split the loadings of the old variables in Fx in about the same proportion for all variables, though their loadings in new variables will be quite different.

To guard against such initial false views of a factor, it is desirable for any research to take a wide range of variables, preferably a pair (for a specific factor would not help) from each of every suspected factor field. Having to "split" a factor thus means that it was not originally defined adequately as an invariant factor on a hyperplane of adequate dimensions as a result of wrong communalities, insufficient variety of variables, or even of a mathematically insufficient number of variables to determine a factor.

Probably the worst example in applied psychology of confusion through inadequate factoring occurs with respect to the alleged "neuroticism factor." Later studies show half a dozen such factors and the first has no more claim than the others to be *the* neuroticism factor. The discovery of a second factor should, of course, be a signal for rejecting from the test originally chosen for routine measures of the first factor those which also have a heavy loading in the second. For example, if good tests of "g" (intelligence) are later found also to share verbal factor, they have to be rejected in favor of equally saturated ones which do not.[1]

The need to keep second and later factors in view can be illustrated in verbal as well as mathematical terms, for it is not at all an uncommon source of confusion in verbal discussions. A researcher may, for instance, set down the trait *excitable* and try to define it more precisely by listing also the polar opposite *reserved* or *suppressed*. Later it may occur to him or to someone else that *phlegmatic* is the proper opposite of *excitable*. Or, worse still, both may use only the label *excitable* but may implicitly use different opposites in rating. Actually a new dimension has thus become involved — that separating natural lack of excitability from suppression of excitement according to a cultural pattern,[2] and a new factor similar in many variables and loadings to the first, yet distinct, may then appear.

Consideration of such pitfalls again makes it clear that the cross-identification of factors, between diverse researches, as in the present study, can be no casual process, decided merely by agreement of lists of variables in which the factors

[1] The extent to which a set of traits can enter into the definition of further and further factors depends, of course, upon the amount of the variance of those traits already accounted for by known factors. The progress of personality research can be gauged by, among other things, the diminishing amount of variance unaccounted for in the traits that are of major importance in life. (Important perhaps in guidance psychiatry, occupational, social, and other competencies.) For when all the variance is accounted for, we shall know all the factors, hereditary, social, physical, environmental, and physiological, which determine personality traits in any way. Such perfection of understanding of every act of behavior can doubtless never be attained, but we can aim to get as close to it as possible. In this connection it is significant that the present factor-analytic research, taking into account a more complete sampling of all personality aspects than any previous factorization, has decidedly higher communalities than are usually found and accounts for a yet greater fraction of the total variance of major personality traits.

[2] An instance very much to the point is one which occurred to the present writer when discussing with vocational guidance workers the use of Strong's Interest Test. A first factor sets "interest in people" over against "interest in things." A possible second factor sets "interest in nature" over against "interest in mechanical things"; but this factor can show itself to any extent only in the responses that fall in the "interest in things" of the first factor. This is found confusing by some. Burt's use of bipolar factors is particularly enlightening in settings of this kind.

are high, but must be based on awareness of *what has happened to the total variance of trait elements* and of what other factors could be matched in the same field.

Coöperative and permissive factors. Recently the present writer has observed some peculiar relations between factors which suggest that though factors may be independent or only slightly correlated as regards their axes they may have very definite interrelations regarding their field of operation in personality. This points to more complex "integration" of factors than has previously been suspected and, if substantiated, opens up a new field of facts to help in understanding the nature of source traits.

If factors are independent in both possible senses — i.e., uncorrelated and uncoöperative — there would be no reason to expect any relation between the loadings of a series of variables on each. When one plots the distribution of variables with respect to any two factors, it should appear homogeneous, except for (*a*) a concentration at each of the hyperplanes and (*b*) presumably a normal distribution positively and negatively of loadings on each factor giving greatest density at the means.

Logically the possible departures from such homogeneity seem to be three in number. First, factor 1 could have all its high positive and negative loadings only in the high positive region of the second factor (and therefore its negligible loadings all in the negative region of the second factor). We may then call the first factor a *unilaterally operating*, and the second a *permissive* factor, because only when variables have a positive loading on this second are they permitted to have any (appreciable) loadings on the first. We have found no sufficiently clear or intelligible instance of this to justify illustration or discussion, but A is to some extent permissive to F, and K and D to E. Secondly, the high positive loadings in one factor might occur only where there are high positive loadings also in the second, and vice versa. Since negatives would then go also with negatives, the variables will tend to fall largely in two opposite quadrants; but by simply reflecting the variables we can, if we wish, throw them all in *one* quadrant. (The third theoretical possibility is positive factor 1, with negative factor 2, and vice versa, but this again is a picture of concentration of variables in diagonally opposite quadrants and could be made into our second case by reflecting one factor.)

This second theoretical possibility we shall call the phenomenon of *coöperative* factors, because it is as if the presence of the first factor in any amount permits and encourages the action of the second in the same direction in the same variables. This justifies discussion, because we have found several instances of it. A surprising proportion of them arise from among three factors, A, C, and E, which seem especially "coöperative." Curiously enough, one of the few published personality factor diagrams, that of Reyburn and Taylor (*213*), shows this same phenomenon and with respect to a factor which can definitely be identified with our C.

A fairly extreme instance is illustrated in Diagram 20. Here the variables which are most loaded in A tend also to be most loaded in H, to such an extent that it is rather difficult to distinguish the psychological nature of A from that of H. Our tentative interpretation is that A is a cyclothyme *environmental* and H is a cyclothyme *constitutional* mold trait. A "cyclothyme environment" acts most powerfully on those traits which are in the cyclothyme constitutional pattern. We may say that one factor *sensitizes* certain traits to the action of another factor.

Of course, in extreme instances of this kind, as in our A and L factors, it is always questionable whether simple structure does not demand that a hyperplane be run right through the length of the ellipse (the diagonal of the opposing quadrants). Our β rotation was a concession to this alternative, and, in the above instance, it abolished H and L by combining them with A. But in fact a majority of the diagrams thus

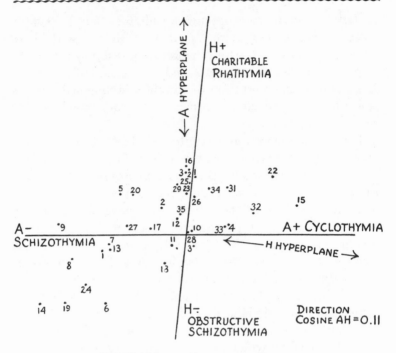

DIAGRAM 20. Coöperative Factors

"simplified" contained, like Diagram 20, quite definite and satisfactory hyperplanes for the coöperative factors. (Thus one can increase the number of variables in the H hyperplane from 10 to, say, 12 by the "gross" simplifications, but this gain of 2 is more than offset by losses from the A hyperplane when A is rotated to its natural position at about 90° to the new H. The use of the major axis of the ellipse as the invariable position of the factor axis is argued against by the cases discussed in connection with Diagram 19 on page 525. Finally, the writer has shown by examples elsewhere (58d) that the falseness of the "simple structure" obtained by using the main axis of an ellipsoidal nebula of points can be revealed by a simple test of "goodness of fit" of a hyperplane.

Admittedly, until the proportional profiles method of directing rotation can be brought to the aid of the simple structure method, the question of whether the rotation should put a hyperplane along the ellipse cannot be definitely answered in all instances, for the indicators we have discussed above are sometimes too faint or ambiguous. Meanwhile we may ask ourselves whether the apparent phenomenon of coöperative factors seems psychologically likely, or conceivable in instances in this or some more tangible field. One can, indeed, readily find examples of such action.' Hunger and fatigue affect many variables of behavior similarly, some very differently; altitude and distance from the equator operate similarly on a host of flora characters; the engine horsepower and the plane weight (reciprocal) or quality of gasoline used act similarly on a variety of plane performance measurements. These examples suggest, incidentally, that in some instances of coöperative factors we shall find the distinct factors operating through some single intermediary to their expression. In the case of flora we might be tempted to rotate to bring out a single factor, along the ellipse, of "mean annual temperature," a permissible but perhaps less satisfactory means of prediction of all characteristics.

Further possible complications in mathematical treatment likely to be required by the nature of personality. Though most students are likely to complain of the complication of present-day personality study, there are some more critical minds who object rather that the mathematical treatment is not complicated enough and argue that the real subtlety of personality is depicted too clumsily by the coarse mosaics of present mathematical approximations. Let us take stock of the simplifying assumptions by which, in the pioneer stages, we save ourselves from despair, and see how venial they turn out to be.

The chief mathematical conveniences that have been employed in the past in addition to orthogonal axes are (1) simple additive relations between factor endowments, (2) linear regression underlying the correlation coefficients, and (3) normal distribution of measurements. The first has not yet been questioned by any known data, but it is conceivable that when two influences come to bear on a trait element, one *multiplies* the effect of the other. Thus in an extreme instance one factor might act as a catalyst to the influence of the other. The issue is at present too speculative to justify launching out here on a survey of parabolic regressions and the very considerable mathematical modification which would be required.[1]

Regarding non-linear regression it is to be noted first that examples *do* exist in psychological data, though rarely. Well-known instances are the perseveration and will-character factor relationship, fluency and age in young children, and in certain projection-test responses when related to overt personality. Three major situations arise, as indicated by the following diagram. In the first situation any factor analysis

DIAGRAM 21. THREE POSSIBILITIES OF UNUSUAL REGRESSION

carried out with product moment r's would be only a very rough approximation. This situation, in which deviants in both directions from the average of one variable deviate in the same direction from the central values of the other, is perhaps the most likely, on psychological grounds, of the exceptions to linearity. It can only be handled, somewhat clumsily, by splitting the population and establishing factors in those above

[1] Burt (*27*, pages 239 ff.) offers an excellent discussion of the broader aspects of this question of refined mathematical representation.

average different from those existing in the below average. The second, monatonic situation can be handled very satisfactorily by making a simple transformation of one variable, compressing its units at one level and expanding them at another, so that a linear relation exists among the derived units. A situation of this kind might exist with tact and intelligence. Near the mental-defective level slight increases of intelligence bring marked increases of tact, but in the upper ranges of intelligence it is rarely that differences of tact spring to any extent from differences of intelligence. This might be handled also by having curved factor coördinates, representing different degrees of obliqueness at different levels of endowment.

The third situation (non-homoscedasticity) is one in which variable A predicts B relatively well in the lower ranges of A but not in the upper ranges. This happens in some data when A is age. It can occasionally be handled by a simple transformation, but it may be necessary here also to split the distribution and admit the existence of a factor in the lower ranges not present in the conditions of the upper ranges.

6. THE UTILITY OF ESTABLISHED PERSONALITY TRAITS IN APPLIED PSYCHOLOGY

Is practical psychology practical? Despite the inability of scientific psychology to supply sound measuring devices — except in the realm of abilities — psychologists in clinical, industrial, and educational practice have had to use some sort of personality assessment. They have been too closely at grips with practical necessities, and with the obstinate fact that personality variables are of paramount importance, to neglect, even temporarily, the dynamic and temperamental aspects of human nature. Unfortunately, in default of nourishment from pure research, they have filled their emptiness from extremely doubtful sources.

They have, for example, used "rating scales" in personnel work the merest glance at which is enough to show that the variables are chosen without any scientific plan or any definite concept of personality structure. Usually they contain a hodgepodge of unevenly overlapping variables, with the highly uneconomic result that some major factors are estimated several times over, others are completely missing, and all are thrown together in a weighted total having no relation to any explored weighting of the needs of the job.[1] Alternatively the practitioners fall for some mysterious "patent medicine" type of test, as has happened to some extent in psychiatry with the Rorschach, dealing with no well-established variables and having lower validity than many less-complicated devices. But most branches of applied psychology depend on a generous use of the questionnaire, with arbitrary divisions and based on no knowledge, beyond intuition, of the relevance of each of these categories to success in the occupations concerned or to prognosis under psychotherapy.

Probably the most fundamental criticism of the direction — or lack of direction — in existing personality-assessment schemes in applied psychology is one to which reference has already been made in the introductory chapter. This refers to the tendency, shown sometimes even by capable research workers, to believe that a given adjustment problem — a vocational selection scheme, a military psychiatric screening test, a prediction of scholastic success — can be considered solved by obtaining a blind empirical correlation between the criterion and some specific test or test item made up *ad hoc*. The spectacle of the rank growth of pretentious specific tests claiming to measure any marketable aspect of personality — tests of unknown factorial complexity, and unrelated to

---

[1] A graduate student working with the present writer recently made a detailed study of the rating scales used by a very large New England business concern. Twelve supposedly independent aspects of personality were rated and combined in different profiles for different purposes. Actually all fell into a single surface trait with a mean intercorrelation of .70! Many major independent aspects of personality were thus completely neglected.

basic research — in the psychometry of the past twenty years makes a sad page of psychological history. These have been expensive vanities, for if the time and energy spent in standardization, etc., had been devoted to psychological research, we should now be in possession of knowledge of personality structure permitting insightful designing of tests. The tendency of the psychiatrist, the educator, and the industrial and the military psychologists to attempt to solve their problems in mutual isolation shows complete failure to recognize that the human personality, with the same structure and aspects, operates in all these situations. Still worse, it implies a failure to envisage the complexity of the problems the psychologists are facing, the flexibility of personality and the great variety of recombinations of factors that may be required to predict success even with slight changes in the conditions and population samples. Yet no one seems so surprised as the psychometrist when the correlation he obtains with the criterion for selecting foremen at the A plant fails to sustain itself at all in the B plant!

Even if the test-to-criterion correlation method without any understanding of personality structure or of the factors involved in the given situation were successful in giving a good validity, it would still be highly uneconomical. For it would be an *ad hoc* research finding, permitting no generalization to other situations and requiring to be re-proved in each of a thousand situations.[1]

The cardinal importance of source-trait measurements. The neglected problem of scientific personality assessment in applied psychology now stands, however, on the threshold of a radical solution. That solution will come through an exact delineation of the profiles of the dozen or so general

---

[1] The government has recently published a fat volume recording the correlations found in some thousands of wartime experiments correlating specific tests with specific criteria. This expensive monument to short-sighted psychometric industry and expediency unfortunately contributes practically no guidance to personality structure theory and to predictive problems in psychometry generally.

factors, and the more numerous group factors operative in every field of personality expression. It will require the validation of objective tests of these factors and their standardization in norms of performance, adjustment, and success with respect to a host of occupations, life situations, psychiatric clinical impressions, and educational situations. This information will in turn lead to understanding of the life course, the origins and destinies, of the various source traits. This program, the first stage of which is now partly attained, obviously requires much industry and wide organization for the fulfillment of the last stage. Yet the work involved is not a tenth of that which will be wasted if psychiatry, industry, and education continue to flounder on their own, seeing each, through a glass darkly, some dim corner or purely local aspect of what is a general personality problem. Fortunately, even without overall organization, we may confidently expect that, once sound measures of the factors *per se* are set up, the usefulness of the source-trait measures will grow in snowball fashion, increasing their usefulness in one realm by each increment of knowledge about their functioning in another.

Psychiatrists have in the main proceeded qualitatively in their observation of syndromes. Even in ordinary practice, however, the majority of patients raise not only the question of *what* syndrome, but also the question of *how much* of a given syndrome. Is the patient *really* manic enough to require hospitalization? From what degree of neurasthenia can this patient be said to be suffering? If the practitioner has instruments and scales to answer such questions, the scientific basis of his art is raised to a finer level. Undoubtedly we may expect, in the long run, to see psychiatry recapitulate in the field of personality syndromes its course of development in regard to the syndrome of mental defect. There a "qualitative" syndrome became enriched and, indeed, far more fully understood, through the development of precise concepts about the "g" factor (our B factor) and about special abilities, together with the growth of instruments for their exact measurement.

The need for gaining power to measure slight changes in the intensity of neurotic or psychotic syndromes is even more imperative in research, for in general the influences examined in research are likely to produce effects too slight for estimation by gross observations.

Diagnosis and prognosis promise to be improved by source-trait measurements in two major senses. First, it would lead to a proper regard for the role of those temperamental, constitutional powers which, quite as much as the ability measures which the psychometrist now records, affect the outcome of any mental conflict in which the individual becomes involved. One would wish to know, for instance, the individual's constitution on the H axis — of cyclothyme-schizothyme temperament. In the first place, these measurements would aid interpretation of observed behavior. For example, some forms of behavior might occur in an individual high in general emotionality (C factor) which would need to be regarded much more seriously if they appeared in an individual low in constitutional emotionality. Again, marked withdrawal behavior could be viewed with less alarm if the associated questionnaire responses were those of factor QP VIII than if they were found to be those of the schizoid factor, QP I.

Secondly, the use of the established factors, accurately measured, could provide a "temperature chart" for prognosis and checking on the efficiency of routine psychotherapeutic treatment. The writer has already encountered clear instances in which fluency test measures, of the F factor of Surgency-depression, have strongly indicated, before any clinical signs appeared, the onset of a depression or manic phase which later materialized overtly and clinically. Similarly, Stephenson (240) has described instances where perseveration measurements have indicated changes in the course of schizophrenic psychosis. It is not asserted that *objective* tests are yet at a stage where they can be successfully used by other than research workers; but the *factor* patterns which are of importance as continuations of psychopathic syndromes within the normal range are now themselves clear, so that they can already be estimated by whatever contingent devices the situation may suggest, while time may provide better and objective devices.

Educational psychology has barely begun to take accurate personality measurement into its practice, despite the axiom that personality development is the better part of education. Even in the attempts to predict purely scholastic achievement there could be no more sorry contrast than that between the refined meticulousness of educational-measurement scales, recording special abilities, aptitudes, and achievements, and, on the opposite side, the utter failure to organize, or to grasp the importance of, those temperamental and dynamic traits which must account for quite as much of the variance in educational achievement as do abilities.[1]

A few researches, such as those of Line (*162*) or Oates (*196*), have already indicated how predictive these personality factors, even with the poor validity of our present objective tests, can be in respect to school performance. The present writer has shown that certain temperament measures (*44*) apparently decide the fundamental direction of interests more consistently than superficial *ad hoc* interest inventory measures. Indeed, there is a growing support for the assertion that an altogether higher level of educational prediction will be obtained when "wholistic" factors, taking into account the

---

[1] An error very prevalent in the present decade of educational psychometric research is to assume that whatever is not specific — i.e., whatever is common to all educational achievement — is general intelligence. Fuller analysis shows (*58e*, *58f*) that a good deal of the common element is due to general personality factors, not general intelligence. Similarly, Woodrow's studies of actual year-to-year progress in school subjects show general intelligence to be one of the least of the general factors responsible for increments (*281b*); indeed, the prediction of annual school progress from intelligence alone is almost negligible.

personality traits linked with abilities, are regularly employed. For example, it seems that high verbal ability (with intelligence constant, of course) is associated with low sociability, seclusiveness, and introspectiveness. In the prediction of verbal ability, therefore, it may well be that we should take into account any influences likely to shift the individual toward greater or lesser sociability in the period in question.

Provision of educational opportunity through "scholarship selection" has reached vast proportions in Britain and is likely to become more extensive in America. Criticisms of the methods of selection, to the effect that they favor unduly the academic type of mind, will consequently become more relevant and frequent. Shifting the emphasis from existing scholastic accomplishment to measures of intelligence and special abilities has increased the soundness of selection, as judged by the better predictions now obtained of future success. But this is only a beginning. The testing program needs to include personality measurements of those factors, often not obviously important as seen by the school-teacher observer at the time, which are so important for the successful use of intelligence beyond the school period.

The utility of measuring well-defined unities among personality traits could be equally strongly urged in industrial psychology and personnel work. In guidance and personnel work the practical, non-academic psychologist has, it is true, been sufficiently insistent on considering the total personality; but he has built on the shifting sands of scientifically uninformed guesswork. Even so, it may well be that he has succeeded better than those highly technically trained psychometrists who seem to think that personality testing can be achieved by a pedantic repetition or extension of the ideas and methods used with scholastic measurement. These questionnaires following so tritely in the well-worn track of intelligence and scholastic tests connote a very poverty-stricken conception of personality! The self-inventories, interest check lists, etc., along these lines, directed to narrowly occupational or scholastic purposes, can be regarded, in the light of clinical and other approaches, as a mere nibbling at the edge of the problem.

Both the makeshift devices of the practical man and the academic psychometrist's displays of technical virtuosity in an inadequately conceived medium fail to handle the problem of personality prediction. As we have stressed earlier, they suffer, above all, from lack of integration. The applied psychologists have worked too much like psychological clerks, each in a small department of his own, each seeking an oversimplified system of accounting which will work in his own field, regardless of the others. Only by research embodying the total clinical viewpoint, directed to finding the structure of the whole personality and to introducing the calculus of dynamic psychology, can these problems be sincerely handled.

At present the batteries of, for example, interest tests, devised by guidance and personnel psychometrists, are quite useless for clinical work and are practically unknown to psychotherapists. They deal with small, arbitrary, occupational categories of interest, unrelated to primary dynamic make-up or to temperament. On the other hand, the categories of the clinical psychologist float in a void as far as occupational and educational prediction are concerned. Despite the fact that the majority of intelligent but educationally retarded children turn out to be primarily maladjustment problems, when insightfully examined, the special ability and disability categories — e.g., reading, number — of the educational psychologist remain unilluminated by relation to the temperamental and dynamic trends of the total personality. This is the situation which proper attention to the description and measurement of personality could radically remedy.

Description of traits as an aid to psychiatry. There is one further utility of statistically exact trait definition which might be overlooked, because it reaches over into what is usually thought of as qualitative psychiatric diagnosis. If one considers, for example, the notion of "schizoid," he will realize that diagnoses often differ or remain uncertain because, although all are agreed as to the collection of trait elements which constitute the schizoid personality, there is doubt as to which are comparatively central and primary and which relatively inessential. Now the factor-analysis loadings, or the mean correlations in a surface-trait cluster, indicate at once which trait elements constitute the core of the pattern. Clinical description alone has been equally powerless to settle, to the satisfaction of all psychiatrists, the most constant and essential elements in many other patterns — e.g., psychopathic personality, hypomania, or neurasthenia. In actual diagnoses discussed by psychiatrists familiar with the present findings, these findings have been found to give greater certainty to practical decisions.

7. PRACTICAL MEASUREMENT OF COMMON AND UNIQUE TRAITS

Dimensions before scales. It might be objected to this book that despite its title, "The Measurement of Personality," eleven out of twelve chapters are exhausted before beginning to take up the actual measurement techniques which the applied psychologist is most eager to possess. One may lead a horse to the water without presuming to show it how to drink, however, and to the qualified psychologist a detailed demonstration of the translation of one of these well-defined factors into an actual scoring system and a scale might be somewhat of a reflection on his resourcefulness and his training. However, in an age of specialization, the practicing psychometrist may not have time to construct and validate his own tests. We have recently undertaken sufficiently large-scale experiments, therefore, to validate objective tests

— both for individual testing and for group, pencil-and-paper situations — of the twelve primary personality factors. These tests will soon be released for publication, with appropriate training arrangements and precautions against indiscriminate lay use, so that they may be used in conjunction with the theoretical preparation gained from the present volume. Meanwhile we can set out provisional rating scales for the chief source traits and discuss the more detailed problems of validation and scaling as they concern the design of the further testing devices.

Ratings of the chief source traits. In Chapter 9 it has been pointed out that behavior rating has been too uncritically criticized by many psychologists, and that those who have paused to investigate its validity and reliability, with intent to "debunk" it, have frequently ended by admiring it. Rating means all things to all psychologists. The requirements of good rating as understood in these discussions have been set out in Section 5 of Chapter 9, and it will be assumed that ratings of the traits described below will be taken only when these conditions prevail.

If the true and essential nature of each source trait were known, it would be possible to describe precisely the quintessential behavior and to rate on that. Since research has not progressed to this point, it is safer to rate the behavior of some half-dozen traits (trait elements) high in the source trait, and to average them. A weighted average, weighting those traits with greater loadings in the factor concerned, might seem an improvement on this; but in practice it has generally been found that the resulting improvement in assessment is slight and far from justifying the trouble taken.

The half-dozen or so trait elements chosen to estimate a personality factor, like the subtests chosen to measure the factor of general ability in an intelligence test, must meet the following requirements: (1) They must be loaded as highly as possible with the personality factor and as little as possible with specifics. (2) They must not share any specifics (if it is *truly* a specific they cannot) or group factors — i.e., they must be diverse apart from *the* general factor concerned. (3) They will, of course, share other general factors, but the trait elements chosen for one factor should (*a*) be as low as possible in all other general factors and (*b*) disperse its higher loadings among several other general factors, rather than repeat them in *one* extraneous factor (when such higher loadings in extraneous factors cannot be avoided); (*c*) if possible balance the positive loadings of one element in an extraneous factor by negative loadings of another element in that extraneous factor. Such balanced elements are called *suppressors*.

These conditions cannot be ideally met when 12 factors have to be estimated from 35 trait elements, as at the present stage of personality study. Until a greater gamut of elements is available, we cannot find enough of them highly loaded in one factor which also satisfy condition (3) above. Consequently, as commonly happens in practice — e.g., in estimating questionnaire factors from actual items — the items chosen to measure one factor are inevitably weighted more with some one or two of the remaining factors than with all the others. The choice of variables is too restricted to permit selection of good suppressors. The result is that factors estimated from averaging a bunch of traits are not pure, and so correlate among themselves more than would the factors correctly and laboriously estimated according to the full-dress procedures of mathematical theory (*120*).

Below, a set of traits (indicated by index numbers as recorded on page 295) is suggested for use in estimating each of the 12 factors of the α analysis or the 6 factors of the β analysis. The principal "spurious" correlations between factors introduced by this optimum, but still not ideal, collection of "estimating traits" are indicated after each factor. For most practical purposes — i.e., for other than refined research — it is suggested that each factor be estimated by those traits (the great majority) common to the α and β factorizations, whereby the issue of α and β systems no longer arises.

TABLE 28

SETS OF TRAITS FOR ESTIMATING FACTORS

	TRAITS THE RATINGS OF WHICH ARE TO BE POOLED	FACTORS WITH WHICH SOME CORRELATION IS PRODUCED
Factor A α	1, 7, 8, 9, 15, 19, 24, 32	Moderately H, F, E
β	1, 7, 8, 14, 15, 19, 22, 24	Very slightly E
Factor B α	2, 3, 11, 12, 28, 29	Slight: J, K; Slighter G
β	2, 3, 11, 12, 29	None
Factor C α	5, 10, 16, 18, 20, 25, 33	Very slight: A, E, G
β	4, 5, 10, 16, 20, 26, 32, 33	None
Factor D α	7, 13, 26, 27	Moderate: A, C, E
Factor E α	1, 7, 21, 25, 30, 33, 35	Very slight: C, D, A
β	1, 21, 30, 31, 35	Very slight: B, A
Factor F α	15, 21, 31, 32, 33, 34	Moderate: A, H
β	5, 15, 32, 33	Slight A, C
Factor G α	1, 3, 10, 11, 20, 27, 35	Moderate: B, C, J
Factor H α	6, 16, 19, 23, 25, 26, 30	Moderate: A Slight: F, L
Factor I α	3, 5, 6, 20, 34	Slight: C Very slight: D, G
β	3, 5, 6, 20, 27, 30, 34	Very slight: A, C
Factor J α	11, 12, 21, 30, 32, 35	Moderate: B, G, E Slight: C, K
Factor K α	11, 12, 14, 15, 29, 33, 35	Moderate: B, G, E Slight: J, H
Factor L α	8, 9, 14, 15, 20, 22, 24	Moderate: A Slight: F, H, E

It will be noticed that the β descriptions of the factors give easier and clearer (less correlated) estimation, especially of the earlier factors; but this is no proof of their greater "truth," only of their greater convenience when sheer description is involved.

Validation and standardization: essential or internal *vs*. peripheral or external.   Any test device directed to measuring personality along the major dimensions here indicated, whether by a battery of behavior-rating scales or a set of objective tests, has to be subjected to the dual validation process which faces all psychological tests claiming a role in applied psychology.   It has to be validated first as a true psychological functional entity, and secondly it has to be validated and standardized as a predictor of performance in various current real-life situations.

This duality of validation has never been clearly envisaged and stated in psychometric theory.   The essential or internal validation takes a set of laboratory or other measures in a field of responses which is suspected, on common-sense or intuitive grounds, to have a psychological unity and which, usually, has also some claim to be of importance for practical, everyday-life predictions.   It validates each test by proving that it belongs to the single functional unity concerned. This may be done either by factor or cluster analysis, or by some less basic procedure such as "item validation."   The latter, of course, is extremely approximate, proving neither that the item has loadings in a factor nor even that it belongs to a cluster (for the inter-item correlations are not computed). But it indicates at least the probability of a cluster and prepares the ground for study by better techniques.

Internal validation means proving that a unitary trait exists to be measured and that the test in question partakes of this trait.   It means, further, deciding whether what is common to the elements of the unitary trait is what the experimenter wants to measure.   One might set out to measure mechanical aptitude by throwing together a dozen tests that look like mechanical aptitude, yet discover that the largest factor among them saturates most highly the tests showing more manual dexterity than mechanical sense.   One has then obtained internal validation of certain manual dexterity tests, but the validation of mechanical aptitude tests must be begun with a fresh pool of better-chosen tests.

It will be obvious that in a strict, logical sense there is only one kind of validation — namely, the internal validation through obtaining the correlation of the test with the cluster or factor among test variables or life situations constituting the unitary trait in question. The duality of approach suggested here arises from the fact that the purposes of the investigator involve preconceptions as to what is "the trait in question" and from the chasm that lies between test situations and life situations. The peripheral validation seeks proof that the test, already internally validated as a measure of a unitary trait, predicts in practically important real-life situations and in the situations in which the psychologist's preconceptions said it should be predictive. It is sometimes possible to get a unitary trait among laboratory measures or tests which has no discernible role in any situation of importance in everyday life. The peripheral validation is strictly, however, not a validation but an exploration of the correlations of the test (and the unitary trait it represents) with real-life successes.

Of course, a factor can be established among real-life situation measurements and the test then correlated with it; but the practical difficulty of getting measured data on a sufficiency of real-life situations has so far prevented such carrying out of internal and external validation in a single process. Behavior rating studies come nearest to this, and our personality factors may be said to be established in the world before they are established in the laboratory. In the great majority of traits it is more practicable to validate a test against a unitary trait in the controlled conditions of the laboratory or schoolroom and then to seek the peripheral validation or illumination of what the test measures, by organizing the field data — e.g., regression coefficients on occupational success — as they slowly accumulate.

One of the worst misunderstandings of validation is that which begins peripherally by saying, for example, "What I mean by intelligence is that which brings success in life" and proceeds to obtain test correlations with various criteria. Here a test of unknown factorial composition is correlated with an equally mixed, non-unitary undefinable criterion. But absurdity in validating procedures reaches its climax when science sets up an apostolic succession by validating each new intelligence test against its predecessor, going back to the Binet!

As research penetrates to less obvious and familiar traits, however, it would seem desirable and probable that essential validation will be completed *before* meaning is extended by peripheral validation. Thus perseveration at first was established as a unity only within restricted, controlled test performances; it was a theoretical "laboratory toy." Later it was found to have meaning, value, or validity with respect to some important manifestations in delinquency and psychopathology. A final difference in the two validation goals and procedures is that in internal validation one correlates tests against estimates of a unitary trait; in peripheral validation one seeks correlations of the unitary trait with real-life situations with respect to which it is expected to give valid predictions.

Internal and *peripheral* validations can be best illustrated by some matured, well-understood field of measurement, such as that of general mental capacity. Spearman's or Thurstone's approach provided the internal validation, showing that many diverse tests in the field of general ability correlated together highly as by a single general factor and that these measures all manifested in common a demand on "ability to perceive complex relations." An intelligence test could henceforward be validated against this factor and the clearer definition of ability which had emerged from it.

Simultaneously many psychologists were validating intelligence tests peripherally, saying that to know the structure of the psychological ability, and to see its essential nature analyzed from test material, is not enough. One wants to know what it does outside the laboratory. Thus in the case of intelligence the peripheral or external validation will consist in finding out how important this general ability is for success in this and that kind of occupation, and to what extent it may be taken as the quality lacking among mental defectives, whether it has much or little connection with lunacy, whether people very highly endowed with it are what have been called geniuses, and whether it predicts success in a wide variety of real-life performances or only some very special fields. In short, one asks, as Terman did, what does the trait *mean* in terms of existing real-life situations of our present culture.

With gross, obvious traits like intelligence, the role of which in everyday life can be foreseen, peripheral validation can begin early, but in other cases it has brought confusion.

Corresponding to *essential vs. peripheral validation*, one finds the contrasting notions of essential and peripheral *standardization*. Essential standardization consists simply in expressing the test-measurement standards in relation to some basic frequencies of population distribution (perhaps also in relation to age). One obtains thereby a table of normative units such as IQ or percentile scores, in terms, for example, of items per second in the given test. *Peripheral standardization*, on the other hand, gives meaning to scores in terms of levels found in everyday life. For when the essential validation and standardization are completed, the meaning of the measurement and the magnitude of any given individual's score may still be said to remain relatively bare of meaning. They require to be enriched by further associations and implications. When a thermometer is validated and standardized (calibrated) to the satisfaction of a theoretical physicist, he has reached the point when he knows relatively precisely what he means by temperature and that his standard degree is one hundredth of the range between the freezing and the boiling of water. But until he discovers a good deal about the *effects* various temperature changes have upon many chemical and biological processes, his concept of temperature is a relatively empty one; and until he knows that the normal body temperature is 98.6° F., that the earth's coldest regions go down to − 90° C., that iron melts at 1535° C., and so on, the units of his "standardization" also do not convey any immediate notion of "how much."

In the instance of intelligence, the peripheral standardization has increasingly revealed the actual levels of average intelligence in various occupations, the meaning of various clinical divisions of mental defect, the range of scores in various kinds of selective and unselective schools and colleges, the mental age of army draft recruits, and so on. In the perspective of these landmarks any given score in the original essential (percentile and mental age) standardization has taken on a richer significance.

Some applied psychologists — e.g., Strong (*245*) — apparently do not give recognition to the principle of dual validation, and some theorists — notably Thomson (*254*) — seem actually to have wished to avoid it. The latter would cut out the concept of intelligence as an unnecessary "intermediate variable" and proceed straight from a measure on a particular test to a prediction about a particular occupation. The alternative procedures may be schematized as follows:

1. TEST (Internal Validation) TRAIT (Peripheral Validation) REAL-LIFE PREDICTION
2. TEST (Particularized Validation) REAL-LIFE PREDICTION

In the writer's view particularized validation is not only devoid of proper scientific interest but deceptive in its promise of practical economy. It is scientifically weak for reasons maintained throughout this book.[1] One needs to measure

[1] The plainly indicated necessity of the present day, though one may be optimistic to expect to see it realized in the next decade, is that every industry interested in personality prediction, every clinic and educational institution, should support a central institution for research into personality. There are only one science and one person-

known functional unities. But its absurdity is most cogently argued by the demands of practical economy and efficiency alone; for a specific test for every occupation and life situation is its logical and impossible conclusion.

General principles in prediction. The peripheral *validation* of a source-trait measurement — i.e., its correlation with, or

ality to be studied. The "practical" man who thinks he can get efficient prediction by looking only at that small surface area of personality which seems to have contact with his problem, and who tries to go from an unanalyzed test direct to an occupational or educational prediction, confining his thought only to the needs of the institution he serves, is guilty of *lèse majesté* against the dignity of nature! He is doomed to get hopelessly entangled in the protean varieties of the situations, which change and multiply about him; attracted by the false glitter of immediate test-to-job barter, he can never hope to see the real meaning of his measurements and extract their latent possibilities.

The rank and file of industrial and guidance psychologists seem to be pathetically hypnotized by this mirage of some sort of one-to-one correspondence between a mental test and success in an occupation. This is, in one sense, a variant of the "perfect niche" illusion, or the belief that there is for each person an occupation which he fits as a key the wards of a lock. It springs also from the loose thinking which presupposes the existence of a special ability corresponding to each occupation. As indicated, one has to look rather for certain combinations of personality traits, which have little or no relation to the occupations produced by any culture at any particular moment of its life.

The parochialism of viewpoint among applied psychologists mentioned also in the opening chapter may be illustrated by a recent debate in which a number of guidance and personnel workers concerned with "occupational interest tests" denied that any such "clinical" concept as, for instance, the cyclothyme-schizothyme temperament pattern could have any relevance to their problems. But on regarding the operational interest tests in which they place their robust faith one finds that their predictive power, as individual tests, is very fleeting. Though one may predict the occupational interests of a man of 25 from his recorded interests at 20, it is not practical to do so from his interests in early adolescence. The interest-measure responses, however, are found to group themselves in certain factor patterns, in a way which suggests (in consonance, for example, with the greater resemblance found between identical twins than between fraternal twins, in interests) that the interest measurements are really indicators of temperament, and that the ultimate prediction of congeniality of an occupation is, in fact, being made from temperament. Our factor analysis proves, and the interest analyses of Strong suggest, that the cyclothyme-schizothyme pattern is in fact responsible for more of the variance of interests as a whole than could be taken into account by any specific interest test. Moreover, such broad underlying factors maintain themselves with a certain continuity through adolescence, so that we may suppose that the same temperamental tendency is showing itself in turn in the interests appropriate to each age. If this is a correct analysis of the situation, it would be more economical as a testing technique and more realistic scientifically to admit temperament as the real predictor or intermediate variable, and to measure it directly as such, not as a passing collection of interests.

regression upon, performance in many real-life situations — as well as its peripheral *standardization* — i.e., the score levels existing in various real-life performances — need to be achieved before source traits can be efficiently used in applied psychology.

However, in dealing with personality traits, far more than when dealing with strict abilities, there are certain complexities needing to be observed in the art of prediction. First and most obvious is the fact that whereas abilities generally have one "good" direction, personality traits frequently do not. For some occupations — e.g., art and music — high endowment in C factor (emotionality) may be essential; for others — e.g., aircraft pilots — the same endowment will appear on the debit side.

Secondly, it is hardly necessary to emphasize that until more is known about the nature-nurture ratio of each of these factors, the fact that a person has a given percentile score at a certain age is no basis for predictions about his behavior some years hence. The available evidence points to a marked constitutional and hereditary determination of factors A or H, B, and C. On the other hand, Dominance, E, character integration, G, and I, are almost certainly very responsive to personal history. It has been shown in regard to Fluency measures, which correlate with F, that F or Surgency is rather more determined by environmental influences than by heredity (*48*). Until more is known, therefore, it seems necessary to have norms for every age and condition; to be careful not to assume that these norms can be carried on to other ages, and to assume the probabilities of environmental change in individuals in the factors indicated by this discussion.

Although psychologists may not fall into the above common error of assuming that some traits are desirable and others undesirable *per se* (as may be done with abilities), they sometimes uncritically assume that an optimum level for a given trait in a given situation is indicated by the actual average level found in that trait among those who are success-ful in the situation. But if, for example, those who adjust themselves successfully to the occupation of telephone operator have an average IQ of 115, it by no means follows that higher intelligence would not lead to still more successful performance.

The observed endowments of "successful" people in various occupations are equilibrium levels in a social adjustment of supply and demand, and by no means psychologically op-timum levels. Society might prosper better with more intelligent surgeons and teachers, and less intelligent stock-brokers, lawyers, or criminals. Again, with the help of unusually skilled psychologists a firm could pirate the labor market and capture many talented individuals, unaware of their latent talents, so that the levels in that firm might be made well above those regarded in similar firms as optimal, to the benefit of that firm and possibly to the impoverishment of other occupations. We know practically nothing about *true* optimal levels (*a*) psychologically and (*b*) in relation to the good of the whole community. Our ignorance of true optimal scores is especially glaring with respect to neuroticism factors — e.g., factor J — the usefulness of which to a voca-tion or to the whole community is bound to be systematically misunderstood by any psychologist suggestible to popular stereotypes and valuations, and who does not await the empirical evidence as to what neuroticism means, in the long run, in terms of creativity and success in various occupations.

Admittedly, however, until experiment gives the psychol-ogist more understanding of the real needs of the community, he has to accept the existing occupational and educational standards as those governing his guidance practice. This procedure is at least far in advance of the practice of deciding by mere inspection of an occupation what traits are required therein, or elaborating from one's inner consciousness the effect of various temperament factors upon the course of a neurosis, or accepting popular stereotype valuations as indicated above.

Among those oversimplified practices in applied psychology which provoke the failures exposed by some recent surveys — failures which indeed cry to heaven — is that which assumes the same test or even the same factor will have the same correlation with success in an occupation (or the same prognosis in therapy) in different contexts. Some pyschometrists protest indignantly against the test when they find their expected correlations defaulting in a particular industrial concern or guidance group. When factors are used, by those who clearly understand factors, this too simple mechanical treatment by the psychometrist is unlikely to arise. For the psychometrist sensitive to statistical intricacies realizes the effect of such influences as range of sample, or systematic preselection, and the influence which the change in correlation between one factor and a criterion will have upon all variables. For example, the correlation of intelligence with "success in a teaching situation" is high in any representative sample of the general population. In a group of teachers, however, already selected for intelligence and other qualities by success in academic performance, the correlation of teaching success with intelligence may be very low or even systematically negative.[1]

Finally, the psychologist of personality, to a greater extent than the psychometrist restricted to abilities, has to consider the likelihood that success in an occupation, or prognosis in a situation of mental conflict, will be predicted from a pattern of factors rather than from scores in individual factors. In such situations it may well be that one factor can to some extent and over certain ranges "do duty" for another —

[1] This has actually been found in some training colleges. If we suppose passing academic standards is a product of intelligence and personality traits together, the individual who has just got through and has low intelligence will have high character qualities. If, now, in passing the practical teaching test more emphasis is placed on personality qualities, the less intelligent become more successful, for they have more of the personality qualities.

e.g., cyclothymia for surgency, or character factor G for emotional stability C. This makes the fixing of a profile pattern a more difficult task and raises some very interesting theoretical and mathematical questions, the study of which here and now, however, would be gratuitous pedantry, until the progress of research has revealed the nature of the actual interactions. Commensurate with this problem is the theoretical possibility of what Stout called creative synthesis and others creative emergence — i.e., the rise of certain powers through a particular combination of factors. This possibility, however, is already taken into account in factor analysis itself, though admittedly our present practical techniques, notably in rotation, are not subtle enough infallibly to catch these more ghostly derived factors. (Some of the factors in the α rotation, but not the β rotation, may be of this kind. In another sense "second-order factors" may be emergents rather than deeper sources of covariation.)

The practical role of specific and unique traits. As indicated in Chapter 5, we regard specific, group, and general traits as purely relative, not absolute divisions. Furthermore, these are divisions which come to have meaning only when the concept of trait sphere is employed and when its area can in practice be delimited by psychologists who have agreed upon an objective method of sampling trait populations. As indicated in the theoretical discussion (Chapter 5), a specific trait often remains such merely because the experimenter has not been sufficiently ingenious or alert to perceive that the variable can be included, by the use of a more insightfully selected trait population, in some group or general trait.

Our experience with the present personality analysis suggests rather strongly the novel possibility that specific and group factor traits will, more frequently than general factors, be environmental mold source traits. At least, the most obviously temperamental, constitutional source traits come out strongly and without apparent omissions as general factors. Moreover, on *a priori* arguments, we should expect environmental mold influences to be able simultaneously to affect only limited and restricted regions of the personality sphere. Our single variables, it must be remembered, are themselves clusters, and perhaps these clusters are definite products of environmental mold influences. Genetic and developmental research can alone answer this. However, in the meantime the measurement of these "specific clusters" certainly cannot be omitted, for they are needed to account for fully half the total variance in general behavior. Moreover, as pointed out earlier, it may be more important to know to what particular objects a man more strongly directs his aggression (unique trait or loading in a "specific" common factor) than to know how strong his over-all aggressiveness is in an average of all fields (common general trait of "aggressiveness of disposition"). It is suggested, therefore, that the psychometrist should look over the surface traits in Chapter 8, which are largely "specifics" in relation to our main general factors, to select those which, over and above the general factor source traits relevant to every research or applied problem, seem likely to be relevant to his particular problem.

Regarding unique traits one may guess that the dispute as to the relative importance of common and unique traits is likely to swing in the near future, as psychologists get time to attend more closely to unique traits, in the direction of overestimating the latter, which will at least be better than totally neglecting them, in the manner of psychologists in the last decade. However, the psychologist in his first rapture over the unique trait is nevertheless bound to admit that time and circumstances make delimitation of true unique traits an impractical ideal in most mass guidance and educational programs. It is, then, sometimes more practical and always quite simple to measure unique traits in an arbitrarily bounded, "logical" trait unity, using interactive units. In psychotherapy, on the other hand, we may surely expect a rapid growth of objective, metric P-techniques, suitably abbreviated, for discovering and watching the boundaries, growth, and decline of unique dynamic and cognitive traits constituted by various symptom manifestations. The measurement of such traits is bound to be interactive or ipsative, and except for research purposes, necessarily rough.

Probable peripheral validities of primary source traits of personality. Naturally there are practically no experimental findings of the occupational and other correlations of factors so recently discovered as these — with the exception of B, general ability, and E, dominance. But we may suggest those directions in which the intrinsic nature of the trait, and circumstantial evidence too scattered to describe, indicate that research should look for the most substantial correlations.

H factor, as Kretschmer has shown, has outstanding validity for predicting success in occupations involving mixing with many people. A positive H endowment is found in realistic, practical, compromising business organizers and foremen. A negative H endowment favors academic and research inclinations, and dealing with things rather than people. Persons thus endowed adjust better to order and system and avoid the occupations with undefined professional and moral boundaries, with ups and downs of fortune and risk.

In its extreme endowments H factor has importance for the psychiatrist, as a measure of liability to manic-depressive or schizophrenic outcome in situations of mental conflict.

B factor has already almost adequate peripheral validation and standardization in terms of occupational norms of intelligence, correlation with success in school subjects, etc. One must not overlook, however, its value as a predictor of character qualities and in particular its regression on delinquency.

C almost certainly has high predictive significance with respect to delinquency and also neurosis. On its positive side it should be a selector for persons required in positions of responsibility, where mature, sound judgment, fair-mindedness, and freedom from bias are required — e.g., in administration.

D may be diagnostic in psychiatric work, of liability to hysteric and manic outcome of mental conflict.

E already has established correlations, through the work of Allport and Maslow, with leadership (foremen are significantly higher than clerks), with readiness to break conventions, with tendency to reject the renunciatory attitudes of religion. It may be an ingredient in face-to-face leaders, explorers, soldiers, and scientists.

F in its positive measurements is strongly indicative of success in social contact occupations, especially salesmanship. In negative endowments it indicates depressive and agitated melancholic trends which should render it an indispensable diagnostic measure for the psychiatrist.

G is valuable whenever character integration needs to be assessed — e.g., as a measure of educational progress in noncognitive fields, as a psychiatric measurement of the extent of disintegrative mental conflict, as a prognosis of delinquency in unfavorable surroundings. On the positive side it is probably high where success in positions of responsibility, best use of given abilities, and leadership through example are concerned.

A is presumably a measure of acquired schizoid-cycloid trends and accordingly valid in psychiatric prognosis.

I may prove to be prognostic of liability to anxiety neurosis. It seems likely also to have predictive validity (in negative loadings) of fitness for executive positions requiring poise and a cool head, and probably also for air pilots and other occupations requiring ability to deal with emergencies.

J may be principally of psychiatric importance, as an indicator of neurasthenia and exhaustion conditions, though the obverse has importance for success in most tasks requiring concentration and energy.

K probably has correlations with intellectual leadership and leadership through persuasion generally.

L, as a measure of paranoid trends, is a contra-indication, for example, for admission to the armed forces, or wherever getting on with a large group of people under trying circumstances is involved.

8. SYSTEMATIC PRESENTATION OF THEOREMS ON THE NATURE OF PERSONALITY

Basic theorem. Our theory of source traits must now be briefly reviewed and clearly stated in its final form. The first theorem is that every behavior manifestation of personality, PR (Personality Response), for an individual i, can be predicted by the following type of equation:

$$(1) \quad PR_{j \cdot i} = S_{1 \cdot j} T_{1 \cdot i} + S_{2 \cdot j} T_{2 \cdot i} + S_{3 \cdot j} T_{3 \cdot i} \cdots + S_{n \cdot j} T_{n \cdot i} \cdots$$
$$T_{j \cdot i} + e_j$$

where T_1, T_2, etc., are source traits — i.e., mathematical factors obtained through certain unique, psychological meaningful conditions of rotation, etc. Some of these are general to many performances; but at least one, T_j, is peculiar to the situation in which PR_j is measured. e is some experimental error of measurement (*not* function fluctuation[1]).

$T_{1 \cdot i}, T_{2 \cdot i}$, etc., are the personal endowments of the individual i in the source traits concerned and $S_{1 \cdot j}$, $S_{2 \cdot j}$, etc., are factor loadings peculiar to the situation of PR_j. All measurements — the performance, PR_j and the factor endowments $T_{1 \cdot i}$ and $T_{2 \cdot i}$ — are in standard scores.[2]

---

[1] e_j and function fluctuation, f_j, are together proportional to $\sqrt{1 - r_c{}^2}$, where r_c is the repeat or *consistency coefficient*. e_j alone is proportional to $\sqrt{1 - r_r{}^2}$, where r_r is the split-half *reliability coefficient*. From there e_j and f_j can thus be separately estimated. f is not introduced into the above equation because strictly it should go with each T measurement, which would complicate and obscure the basic form of the equation.

[2] Since most readers of this book will not be, primarily, statisticians, I have adopted a notation which is reasonably in line with that commonly used in statistics — PR_j, any variable; i, any individual; T_p, any factor; a total of r variables and n factors — but have used other symbols more directly suggestive of the verbal symbol — e.g., PR for performance or response.

Prediction of individual performance in one variable.
Actually, since personality source traits seem to be themselves not independent, but correlated, formula (1) has
finally to assume a somewhat more complicated form. In
technical terms formula (1) represents the *factor structure* of a
performance variable — i.e., the correlations of the variable
with each of the factors. When factors are orthogonal, the
individual's score in the variable is obtained by adding his
score in the factors, in the *factor pattern* equation — i.e.,
structure and pattern are the same. But when factors are
oblique, at least three important derivatives of the *factor
structure* have to be derived in more complex ways. These
are (*a*) the original correlations between variables, (*b*) the
total communality of a variable, and (*c*) the individual's endowment in a variable. The individual's endowment in a
variable PR_j now becomes a function both of the factor endowments and of the angles between the factors. It is
debatable to what measures we should apply the term
"loadings" in this situation. If we draw Cartesian coördinates and follow the usual mathematical convention, the
projections on the factor coördinates are different from the
correlations with the factors. When we reduce "loadings"
to zero in a hyperplane in a simple structure, it is these correlations rather than the conventional type projections which
we reduce to zero, so that the term "loading" is perhaps more
appropriately used for the structure than the pattern. Again,
one might measure projections on the factors by dropping
perpendiculars on the factors concerned, in which case structure and pattern remain the same, as in orthogonal factors.
(See page 514.) In this case the contributions of the factor
endowments to endowment in a variable are different from
the loadings, but it might be less confusing to make the
distinction between loading (correlation) and contribution,
than that between structure and pattern. The "contributions" of the factors are obtained from the pattern of correlations with the factor from the following equation.

	(A)	(B)	(C)
(1a)	Structure Matrix (Correlation of *r* variables with *n* factors)	= Pattern Matrix (Contributions of *n* factors to *r* variables)	× Matrix of factor intercorrelations (*n* × *n*)

whence

	(B)	(A)	(C⁻¹)
(1b)	Matrix of contributions to factor (*r* × *n*)	= Oblique factor matrix (*r* × *n*)	× Inverse of matrix of factor intercorrelations (*n* × *n*)

If one deals with twelve factors, the above equation means that each of the twelve loadings or contributions of factors to the variable is itself the sum of twelve products — a not inconsiderable increase in computational labor, yet small compared with that involved in factor-analytic procedures as a whole. Where the true interrelationships of personality performances are such that the greatest overall economy in many psychological situations and problems is obtained by dealing with second-order factors, equation (1) becomes[1]

$$(2) \quad PR_{j.i} = S_{I.j}T_{I.i} + S_{II.j}T_{II.i} + \cdots S_{1.j}T_{1.i}^{1}$$
$$+ S_{2.j}T_{2.i}^{1} \cdots + T_{j.i} + e_{j}$$

where T_I and T_{II} are second-order factors, T_1^1, and T_2^1 are the "group specifics" left in the first-order factors T_1 and T_2 when the variance of the second-order factors is removed, and $T_{j.i}$ and e_j are the test specifics and the error measurement as before. At present this theoretical proposition belongs to the future, save for one practical instance — the prediction of performance in abilities from "g" and Thurstone's primary abilities.

Misconceptions about traits. A very frequent objection to the notion of unitary trait, which on examination has no foundation, deserves comment here. It is said that the concept of unitary trait is impossible because common observation shows inconsistency, in that a man who is, say, aggres-

---

[1] A novelist expresses our equation when he says (Antoine de St.-Exupéry, *Night Flight*), "Courage is . . . a touch of anger, a spice of vanity, a lot of obstinacy, and a tawdry 'sporting' thrill."

sive in one situation is not necessarily so in another. Two contentions are confused here, neither of which is really an objection. (1) Naturally aggression is a function of the situation as well as of the trait. A man is aggressive if someone knocks his hat off, not if someone shakes his hand. Clearly this "inconsistency" is not what the critic means. (2) If Smith shows more aggression than Jones in provoking situation A, it is observed that he does not always show greater aggression than Jones in provoking situation B; i.e., *perfect* correlation does not exist between aggressive behavior in different situations.

If we deal with surface traits, the answer is simple: correlation clusters form recognizable unities without the correlations needing to be perfect. If the criticism is directed against source traits, it can be answered by considering the simplest possible illustration, as follows: Let us take two persons, x and y, and two situations, a and b. Now we know that no behavior is ever determined by one trait only. Thus aggressive behavior may be determined by an ergic trait of dominance F^1 and a metanergic trait of inhibition by society F^{11}, the latter having, of course, negative loadings in positive aggression situations such as a and b.

For the sake of simple arithmetical illustration we shall suppose certain actual endowments of the two individuals in these traits — namely, .4 and .2 for x, and .5 and .6 for y. Then we shall also suppose that a is a social situation where most people would hesitate to show aggression, so that the loading of F^{11} is high, say $-.7$, whereas b is a home situation in which the tired businessman drops his inhibitions, so that F^{11} is loaded only $-.2$. The actual provocation to aggression in a and b is represented by .4 and .8, respectively. Then the prediction of the four performances is as follows:

First Situation

$$PR_{ax} = .4\ F_x^1 - .7\ F_x^{11} = .4 \times .3 - .7 \times .2 = -.02$$
$$PR_{ay} = .4\ F_y^1 - .7\ F_y^{11} = .4 \times .5 - .7 \times .6 = -.22$$

Second Situation

$$PR_{bx} = .8 \, F_x{}^1 - .2 \, F_x{}^{11} = .8 \times .3 - .2 \times .2 = .20$$
$$PR_{by} = .8 \, F_y{}^1 - .2 \, F_y{}^{11} = .8 \times .5 - .2 \times .6 = .28$$

In the first situation i is about averagely aggressive and j is decidedly below average. In the second both are above average but j is more so; i.e., the two aggressive situations do not correlate positively. Thus the seeming inconsistency of overt behavior is compatible with an underlying constancy of endowment in the source traits.

Estimation of the individual's factor endowment. The precise calculation of an individual's endowment in any one factor has so far not been described. It is obtained from his endowments in each of the performances, PR, by the following equation:

$$(3) \quad T_{pi} = \beta_{pa}.PR_{a\cdot i} + \beta_{pb}.PR_{b\cdot i} + \cdots \beta_{pn}.PR_{n\cdot i}$$

Here the β symbols represent, as in the commonest statistical convention, the *regression coefficients* of the performances on the factor. These are very roughly proportional to the correlations of the factor with the performances and are calculated from these correlations in conjunction with the correlations among the performances, as follows:

$$(4) \quad \beta_{pj} = -\frac{D_{pn}}{D_{n\cdot n}} \text{ where } D_{n\cdot n} \text{ is the minor of the elements}$$

containing the correlations of factor p with the n variables and D_{pn} is the co-factor of the element containing all the correlations of the performance PRj, in the matrix of performance intercorrelations bordered by the correlations of the performances with factor Tp.

This may be expressed, alternatively, to cover all regression coefficients:

$$(4a) \quad \beta_{pj} = R_{jj}{}^{-1} \cdot R_{jp}, \text{ where } R_{jp} \text{ is the transpose of the}$$
factor matrix and R_{jj} is the correlation matrix.

Various modifications of the above basis of calculation — e.g., Aitken's pivotal condensation, Harman's method using factor instead of variable intercorrelations — offering shortened devices for practical computation, should be consulted by the reader in the standard textbooks — e.g., (27), (120), (261), (254).

Multiplying the regression coefficient of each performance by its correlation with the factor, adding for all performances involved and taking the square root, we obtain the multiple correlation indicating with what accuracy we can estimate the factor in question from the variables employed.

In applied psychology, however, such estimation by weighted scores is usually considered to involve more trouble than is justified by the slight gain in accuracy. It is sufficient to find half a dozen or more variables heavily loaded in the factor concerned, and little in any other (or with mutual suppressors in others). These are weighted unity and all others zero; i.e., one averages this group.

Through understanding the essential nature of the source trait and ingeniously designing tests highly saturated with it and of low complexity (of factor structure) — as has been done in measuring intelligence — one avoids any calculation (other than adding) in estimating the factor.

This analysis should be considered in connection with the earlier general, clinical discussion in which it was pointed out that a trait endowment is thus an averaging of many situation responses and an abstracting — e.g., of a simple ergic drive — from many fields in which it normally manifests itself. The mathematical analysis reminds us that the choice of situations is not arbitrary, but directed by factor analytic findings to those in which the erg in question is most frequently involved for most people. The areas of involvement of a trait are thus part of its definition and, since cultural changes may sometimes shift them, they need to be resurveyed at not too lengthy intervals.

Systematic position relative to more general psychological viewpoints. The reflexological standpoint in psychology committed itself to the paradigm

$$S \rightarrow R \quad \text{or} \quad R = f(S)$$

seeking to explain behavior through considering responses as functions of stimuli. By contrast, dynamic psychology adopted the common-sense view that organisms strive for goals, having "minds of their own" and not waiting to respond mechanically to stimuli. Conditioned response psychology studied all variables determining the response except the dynamic state of the animal. The present writer has always maintained, in opposition to this view, that the basic formula should be

$$R = f(O,S)$$

i.e., that an expression O, for the organism, its purposes and states, should be introduced, instead of leaving the organism a mere hyphen between S and R.

Now it will be at once obvious that formula (1) is really the required more complete and adequate statement of the $R = f(O,S)$ theorem. Therein the T's are statements about the abilities, temperament qualities, and drive strengths of the organism; while the S's are what we might call *situational indices* (for the term "situation" is preferable to "stimulus"). They describe how much each unitary reactivity capacity of the organism is brought into action by appropriate aspects of the total situation. The T's, of course, describe the organism's constitutional endowment, its modification through previous experience, and its present dynamic state.

Clarity of theory is aided, and more apt research may be stimulated, if we recognize three varieties of situational indices: (*a*) Complexities, loading ability factors, (*b*) Incentives, loading dynamic unitary traits, and (*c*) Constancies, loading temperament traits. This approach gives us one more character of the situation (*c*) than we found it necessary to recognize when attempting to define modality. The inconsistency must be left to the verdict of research; but some reconciliation may be effected by supposing that "constancies" represent the media, as it were, through which the complexity and incentive characters of the situation are presented. Incidentally we might expect these to vary less than (*a*) or (*b*) from one situation to another — an additional argument for temperament factors being characterized by a lower and smoother loading pattern than abilities or dynamic traits.

Incentives can in turn be divided into those which affect constitutional dynamic traits or ergs and those which affect acquired dynamic patterns or metanergs. These we shall call respectively *pro-ergs* and *pro-metanergs*. The study of situational indices is likely to be of great importance for many distinct reasons. In dynamic psychology, for example, the understanding of the nature of the primary unlearned situation for the provocation of each erg or propensity can be approached by locating the situations in which the pro-ergs concerned have a high loading value. In applied psychology the number of situations for which situational indices need to be experimentally determined and listed is very great. But by studying the field[1] characters associated with various indices it will almost certainly be possible to some extent to estimate the magnitude of the index to be associated with a trait of some particular character, without the necessity of making an actual experiment in every such case. For example, study of the loadings of the general ability factor in various situations indicates that the situational complexity character is one of complexity or abstractedness of general "relation eduction" and that, with average adults, analogies or classifications tests of a certain difficulty have loadings around 0.7. From this it is not difficult to deduce that a series test will also have loadings about 0.7 but that a speed of reading test will be far lower.

---

[1] I employ this in the sense of the usual topographical metaphor. So-called topological psychology does not seem to contribute anything — unless it be elaborate confusion — and the present approach carries the prediction of behavior to a higher degree of precision than has been attained with any topological mathematics.

Job analysis, which is concerned precisely with estimating these situational indices for various source traits, and advertising, which is much concerned with the magnitude of pro-ergs, would both be carried to a new level of scientific dependability by the systematic exploring, collation, and comparison of situational indices in a great number of occupations, life situations, etc. Similarly, psychiatry would gain in technical control by the working out of situational indices, especially pro-metanergs, for those important emotional landmarks in the typical environment which Murray (*190*) has called "presses" and of which he has prepared preliminary inventories.

The definition of personality. The concept of personality to which the above methodological approach leads may be defined as follows:

(1) Personality is concerned with and deduced from all the behavior relations between the organism and its environment. It is that which predicts behavior, given the situation.

(2) The attributes by which it is described and measured are traits (structures or dispositions defining potential behavior) which may be considered properties of the organism, but which can only be defined in terms both of the organism and its environment — i.e., as relationships between the physiological organism and its environment.

(3) Traits are functional unities manifested in the case of common traits by covariation with respect to individual differences and also, in the case of individual traits, with respect to occasions. It is not yet known whether the unities found in different covariational circumstances always match, but there is evidence that they frequently do. However, covariational unities have different degrees of persistence with change of circumstance, so that a hierarchy of potency must be admitted.

(4) Common traits are defined not only by the organism and the environment, but also through the group or species to which the organism belongs.

(5) Complete description of personality may also require truly unique traits, measurable in attributes (dimensions) of behavior not found in any other individual.

(6) The functional unities within the organism are themselves interrelated in broader unities springing both from biological sources and sources in the social structure. Consequently the truly self-contained whole is not the organism but the cosmos, and completely efficient prediction can be attained, theoretically, only by consideration of this greater whole. However, the organism is a center of organization of functional unities only one rank removed from the whole, so that personality is one of the most convenient points of reference for the approximate prediction of events, especially of the events largely determined by individual human decisions and strivings.

9. RESEARCH VISTAS

The fields of research opened up by the present advances, and the more urgent problems a solution of which is required for the proper and full use of the present findings, may be summarized as follows:

(1) An inquiry in which BR, Q, T, and C data are thrown into a single analysis, to confirm the interrelations stated in hypothesis in this chapter and to provide thereby the objective tests required for true measurement. As stated elsewhere, a study to match these "interior" and "exterior" factors, and to invent and validate objective tests of them, is in progress at the University of Illinois, on 400 subjects; but in order to clarify all issues and yield a thoroughly firm foundation such studies need to be done with different age groups and different populations of variables.

(2) A more precise determination of the hyperplanes of and angles between factors, if possible by application of the method of proportional profiles, to determine more reliably, for an unselected population, the second or higher order

personality factors, in order that their nature and meaning may throw further light on personality structure.

(2) A renewed exploration of the best rotation of the personality sphere data — i.e., of the basis of factors D, G, H, J, K, and L present in the α and not in the β rotation. This can be done only with objective tests, set among sound ratings, as in (1), in order that (*a*) the existence of the fainter hyperplanes employed in the simple structure of α may be verified or disproved and (*b*) the more basic principle of proportional profiles may also be applied.

(3) A systematic exploration of the wider associations — i.e., a "peripheral validation" — of these factors, especially physiological, sociological, and psychiatric; together with a recording of associations and norms in applied fields — e.g., occupational guidance, educational prediction, and psychotherapy.

(4) An investigation, as early as possible, of nature-nurture ratios, to decide which factors are environmental mold traits and which constitutional. With regard to the latter, investigations on mode of inheritance can then be profitably undertaken and correlations with body build, physical diatheses, etc., more profitably undertaken. Once the source traits due to environmental molding are picked out with certainty, it will become worth while to make a thorough search for their causes — e.g., of the role of super ego pressure in determining the degree of F; of social, parental, and sibling rivalry in fixing E; the relation of I to mental conflict and anxiety; of J to exhaustion; of G to moral training; of L to frustration; and so on.

A great variety of animal experiments, when and where comparable factors have been established in animal populations, could be used most advantageously to throw light on the genesis of these patterns.

(5) A systematic elucidation of the relations of well-known surface traits to well-established source traits. This would

involve revising many inconclusive research findings of the past which started to find causes and consequences of ill-defined and poorly established surface traits such as introversion, extraversion, suggestibility, inferiority, viscerotonia, etc. Such existing suggestive findings need restating and clarifying in terms of (*a*) established surface traits and (*b*) the pure source traits of which the surface traits are sometimes composite resultants. In particular, studies are needed of clinical populations to discover the factorial genesis of the surface traits which we call pathological syndromes.

(6) The personality sphere might next be explored in more detail, by studying more restricted areas with more numerous, specific, restricted trait elements, especially narrow dynamic and cognitive traits, notably specific interests, attitudes, skills, and limited specific aspects of shyness, dishonesty, self-assertion, etc. Formally, this means a proper exploration of the nature of *group* and specific factors. A vital methodological point, disastrously neglected in many intensive, special area researches, is the necessity for keeping *at least two landmark variables from each of the primary personality factors among the more numerous variables concentrating on the factor intensively studied*, to give cardinal orientation. If our assumption is correct that the environmental mold traits are most frequently group and specific factors, this extension of the survey would net a haul of common traits of great practical importance. Theoretical curiosity would also be met by explaining the very substantial amount of trait variance still unaccounted for by the big general factors.

(7) Of paramount importance to ultimate advance is research on more theoretical and methodological matters. In particular: (*a*) Investigation of the relations of functional unities obtained through different varieties of covariational data — e.g., cross-sectional, incremental, longitudinal, and of the variations in "potency" of functional unities. (*b*) Testing of the theory of conditional modality factors and their

relation to wholistic factors propounded here. (*c*) Examination of the concept of the personality sphere, of various means of objectively determining its "area," and of the effects of various past accidental limitations of variable population in distorting factor interpretation, especially in confusing first- and second-order factors.

(8) Exploration of the incidence and range of specific factors and their importance relative to common factors in determining what are usually considered important aspects of personality.

(9) Exploration of the change in the loading pattern of each factor as it emerges from populations and individuals studied at a number of distinct, significant age levels. These studies of change with age, etc., would reveal also changes in the relative importance of factors (variance contribution) and their intercorrelations (organization about second-order factors).

⌞ (10) The end of the study of the individual differences is the understanding of general laws about mind. The writer would argue on theoretical grounds — though the history of psychology offers empirical support — that the statistical analysis of individual differences, because it deals with a richer and more natural interplay of processes than can be involved in an experimental situation, offers a better road to the understanding of these processes than does the laboratory. It is probable that some of the most important general laws of mind are only to be revealed by study of the personality-as-a-whole, or even of personality-society-cosmos as a whole. The psychologists who wish to preëmpt the title of "experimental psychologists," because they have unreflectively and even slavishly followed the piecemeal procedures of respectable sciences such as physics, are likely to find that the statistical-experimental psychologist has yet unlocked the door they howled without. For the most important dynamic, adjustive, and learning phenomena of man cannot be brought into the laboratory, and the investigator becomes an experimentalist only by ceasing to be a psychologist.

Yet this is not the only, or even the chief, reason for advocating the more complex and arduous path of experimental-statistical investigation *in situ;* nor is it more than a preliminary step to the achievement of methodological perspective. Perhaps the major reason for considering factor analysis, and the still more sensitive analytical techniques about to grow out of it, to be preferable to simple experiment at the present stage of psychology is that it offers hope of asking rightly the questions which experimental psychology is asking wrongly. Experimental psychology begins by taking for its dependent and independent variables quite arbitrary aspects of behavior. It starts by naïvely assuming a unity where it has used a name and has practically never stopped to investigate, first, the existence of a unitary trait — e.g., in "reaction time," various perceptual processes, variables in learning curves. Consequently the whole approach to the analysis of the learning process, for example, has been in terms of artificialities lying athwart the natural functional entities and factors operative in the organism.

Beginning with the analysis of personality structure by statistical methods, however, we aim to converge upon certain clear concepts and pure manifestations of process which can then appropriately be attacked by experimental methods. In the ultimate aim of understanding laws of mental operation ingenious statistical treatment of uncontrolled, observed data and resourceful experimental design for controlled observation are, at the right times, essential mates. But in the last twenty years of psychology it seems to have been insufficiently recognized that the study of psychological processes does better to begin, rather than attempt to end, with the investigation of personality — i.e., with the reactions of the organism-as-a-whole.

Bibliography

1. ABERNETHY, E. M. Dimensions of "introversion-extroversion." *J. Psychol.*, 1938, 6, 217–223.
2. ALLEN, E. A. Temperament tests. *Brit. J. Med. Psychol.*, 1927, 7, 392–446.
3. ABRAHAMS, A. Effort syndrome. *Lancet*, 1941, 240, 437–438.
4. ACKERSON, L. *Children's Behavior Problems: 2. Relative Importance and Interrelations among Traits.* Chicago: University of Chicago Press, 1942.
5. ALEXANDER, W. P. Intelligence, concrete and abstract. *Brit. J. Psychol.*, Monogr. Suppl., 1934, 6, No. 19.
6. ALLPORT, G. W., and ODBERT, H. S. Trait-names, a psycho-lexical study. *Psychol. Monogr.*, 1936, 47, 1, pp. 171.
7. ——, and VERNON, P. E. *Studies in Expressive Movement.* New York: The Macmillan Company, 1933.
8. ALLPORT, G. W. *Personality: A Psychological Interpretation.* New York: Henry Holt & Co., Inc., 1937.
9. ANASTASI, A. A group factor in immediate memory. *Arch. Psychol.*, 1930, No. 120.
10. ANDREWS, T. G. A factor analysis of responses to the comic as a study in personality. *J. Gen. Psychol.*, 1943, 28, 209–224.
10a. ARLUCK, E. W. A study of some personality characteristics of epileptics. *Arch. Psychol.*, 1941, No. 263, 77.
11. ASCH, S. E. An experimental study of variability in learning. *Arch. Psychol.*, 1933, 22, No. 143, 1–54.
12. AVERBUKH, E. S. (A separate form of obsession.) *Neuropat. Psikhiat. Psikhogig.*, 1936, No. 10, 1730–1738. (From note in *Psychol. Abstr.* only.)
13. BALKEN, E. R., and MASSERMAN, J. H. The language of phantasy: 3. The languages of the phantasies of patients with conversion hysteria, anxiety state and obsessive-compulsive neuroses. In TOMKINS, S., *Contemporary Psychopathology.* Cambridge: Harvard University Press, 1943.
14. BEAR, R. M., and ODBERT, H. S. Experimental studies of the relation between rate of reading and speed of association. *J. Psychol.*, 1940, 10, 141–147.

15. BENON, R. *La Mélancolie.* Paris: Librairie Médicale Vigné, 1937.

16. BERNSTEIN, E. Quickness and intelligence. *Brit. J. Psychol.*, Monogr. Suppl., 1924, 3, No. 7.

16a. BLACKER, C. P. *The Chances of Morbid Inheritance.* London, 1934.

17. BRACKETT, C. W. Laughing and crying of pre-school children. *Child Devel.*, Monogr., 1934, No. 14, pp. *15* and 91.

18. BIESHEUVEL, S. The measurement of the threshold for flicker and its value as a perseveration test. *Brit. J. Psychol.*, 1938, 29, 27–38.

19. BRINTNALL, A. K. A preliminary study of persistence and ability. *Psychol. Bull.*, 1940, 37, 585.

20. BROGDEN, H. E. A factor analysis of forty character tests. *Psychol. Monogr.*, 1940, 52, No. 3, 39–56.

20a. ——. A factorial analysis of the interest values test. (Publication to be announced.)

20b. ——. A multiple factor analysis of the character trait intercorrelations published by Sister Mary McDonough. *J. Educ. Psychol.*, 1944, 397–410.

20c. ——, and THOMAS, W. F. The primary traits in personality items purporting to measure sociability. *J. Psychol.*, 1943, 16, 85–97.

21. BROWN, C. H. The relation of magnitude of galvanic skin responses and resistance levels to the rate of learning. *J. Exp. Psychol.*, 1937, 20, 262–278.

22. BROWN, W. S. A note on the psychogalvanic reflex considered in conjunction with estimates of character qualities. *Brit. J. Psychol.*, 1925, 16, 130–141.

23. ——, and STEPHENSON, W. A test of the theory of two factors. *Brit. J. Psychol.*, 1933, 23, 352–370.

24. BURRI, C. The present status of the problem of individual differences in alternating activities. *Psychol. Bull.*, 1935, 32, 113–139.

25. BURT, C. L. The analysis of temperament. *Brit. J. Med. Psychol.*, 1938, 17, 158–188.

26. ——. The relations of educational abilities. *Brit. J. Educ. Psychol.*, 1939, 9, 55–71.

27. ——. *The Factors of the Mind.* London: University of London Press, 1940.

28. CALDWELL, J. M. The constitutional psychopathic state: 1. Studies of soldiers in the U. S. Army. *J. Crim. Psychopathol.*, 1941, 3, 171–179.

29. CAMERON, K. Chronic mania. *J. Ment. Sci.*, 1936, 82, 592–593.

30. CAREY, N. Factors in the mental processes of school children 1, 2, and 3. *Brit. J. Psychol.*, 1915, 7, 453–490; 1916, 8, 70–93 and 170–182.

31. CARLSON, H. B. Attitudes of undergraduate students. *J. Soc. Psychol.*, 1934, 5, 202–213.

32. ——. Factor analysis of memory ability. *J. Exp. Psychol.*, 1937, 2, 477–492.

33. CARPENTER, A. The differential measurement of speed in primary school children. *Child Devel.*, 1941, 12, 1–7.

34. CARROLL, J. B. A factor analysis of verbal abilities. *Psychometrika*, 1941, 6, 279–308.

35. CARTER, H. D.; CONRAD, H. S.; and JONES, M. C. A multiple factor analysis of children's annoyances. *J. Genet. Psychol.*, 1935, 47, 282–298.

36. ——; PYLES, M. K.; and BRETNALL, E. P. A comparative study of factors in vocational interest scores of high school boys. *J. Educ. Psychol.*, 1935, 26, 81.

37. CASON, H. An annoyance test and some research problems. *J. Abnorm. Soc. Psychol.*, 1930, 25, 224.

38. CATTELL, R. B. The significance of the actual resistances in psychogalvanic experiments. *Brit. J. Psychol.*, 1928, 19, 1, 34–44.

39. ——. Experiments on the psychical correlates of the psychogalvanic reflex. *Brit. J. Psychol.*, 1929, 19, 357–386.

40. ——. Temperament tests: 1. Temperament. *Brit. J. Psychol.*, 1933, 23, 308–329.

41. ——. Temperament tests: 2. Tests. *Brit. J. Psychol.*, 1934, 24, 20–49.

42. ——. Friends and enemies: A psychological study of characters and temperament. *Charact. and Person.*, 1935, 3, 54–63.

43. ——. On the measurement of perseveration. *Brit. J. Educ. Psychol.*, 1935, 5, 76–92.

44. ——. Perseveration and personality: Some experiments and a hypothesis. *J. Ment. Sci.*, 1935, 81, 151–167.

45. ——. The measurement of interest. *Charact. and Person.*, 1935, 4, 147–169.

46. ——. *A Guide to Mental Testing.* London: University of London Press, 1936.

47. ——. Temperament tests in clinical practice. *Brit. J. Med. Psychol.*, 1936, 16, 43–61.

48. ——, and MOLTENO, E. V. Contributions concerning mental inheritance. 2. Temperament. *J. Genet. Psychol.*, 1940, 57, 31–47.

49. ——. Sentiment or attitude? The core of a terminological problem in personality research. *Charact. and Person.*, 1940, 9, 6–17.

50. ——. An objective test of character-temperament. *J. Gen. Psychol.*, 1941, 25, 59–73.

50a. ——. *General Psychology.* Cambridge: Sci-Art Publishers, 1941.

51. ——. The measurement of adult intelligence. *Psychol. Bull.*, 1943, 40, 3, 153–193.

52. ——. The description of personality: 1. Foundations of trait measurement. *Psychol. Rev.*, 1943, 50, 6, 559–592.

53. ——. Fluctuation of sentiments and attitudes as a measure of character integration and temperament. *Amer. J. Psychol.*, 1943, 41, 195–216.

54. CATTELL, R. B. The description of personality: 2. Basic traits resolved into clusters. *J. Abnorm. Soc. Psychol.*, 1943, 38, 476–507.

55. ——. An objective test of character-temperament. *J. Gen. Psychol.*, 1944, 28.

56. ——. Projection and the design of projective tests of personality. *Charact. and Person.*, 1944, 12, 177–194.

57. ——. A note on correlation clusters and cluster search methods. *Psychometrika*, 1944.

57a. ——. The cultural functions of social stratification. *J. Soc. Psychol.*, 1945, 21, 3–23.

58. ——. Psychological measurement: ipsative, normative, and interactive. *Psychol. Rev.*, 1944, 51.

58a. ——. The description of personality: 3. Principles and findings in a factor analysis. *Amer. J. Psychol.*, 1945, 58, 69–90.

58b. ——. Factor analysis for proportional profiles: The formulae and an example. (Publication to be announced.)

58c. ——. Parallel proportional profiles and other principles for determining factor rotation. *Psychometrika*, 1944, 9, 267–283.

58d. ——. Simple structure in relation to some alternative factorizations of the personality sphere. *J. Gen. Psychol.*, 1946.

58e. ——. Personality traits associated with abilities: 1. With intelligence and drawing ability. *Educ. and Psychol. Meas.*, 1945, 5, 131–146.

58f. ——. Personality traits associated with abilities: 2. With verbal and mathematical aptitudes. *J. Educ. Psychol.*, 1946.

58g. ——. The diagnosis of neurotic conditions: A reinterpretation of Eysenck's factors. *J. Nerv. Ment. Dis.*, 1946.

58h. ——. Oblique, second-order and coöperative factors in personality. *J. Gen. Psychol.*, 1946.

58i. ——. Simple structure in relation to some alternative factorizations of the personality sphere. *J. Gen. Psychol.*, 1946.

58j. ——, and LUBORSKY, L. B. Response to humor as a test of personality structure. (Place of publication to be announced.)

58k. ——. A hypothesis in answer to the riddle of perseveration and disposition rigidity. *Charact. and Person.*, 1946, 15.

59. CHI, P. L. Statistical analysis of personality ratings. *J. Exp. Educ.*, 1937, 5, 239.

60. CHORNYAK, J. Some remarks on the diagnosis of the psychopathic delinquent. *Amer. J. Psychiat.*, 1941, 97, 1326–1340.

61. CLARKE, G. Some character traits of delinquent and normal children in terms of perseveration. Aust. Counc. *Educ. Res. Publ.* No. 29, 1934.

62. CLECKLEY, H. *The Mask of Sanity*. St. Louis: The C. V. Mosby Company, 1941.

63. COX, J. W. *Mechanical Aptitude: Its Existence, Nature, and Measurement*. London: Cambridge University Press, 1929.

64. Cox, J. W. *Manual Skill, Its Organization and Development.* London: Cambridge University Press, 1934.
65. Crutcher, R. An experimental study of persistence. *J. Appl. Psychol.*, 1934, 18, 409–417.
66. Cummings, J. D. Variability of judgment and steadiness of character. *Brit. J. Psychol.*, 1939, 29, 4, 345–370.
66a. Cureton, T. K., and Others. *Endurance of Young Men.* Monograph No. 40 of Soc. for Res. in Child Development. Washington, D. C.: National Research Council, 1945.
67. Darley, J. G., and McNamara, W. J. Factor analysis in the establishment of new personality tests. *J. Educ. Psychol.*, 1940, 31, 5.
68. Darling, R. P. Autonomic action in relation to personality traits of children. *J. Abnorm. Soc. Psychol.*, 1940, 35, 246–260.
69. Darroch, J. B. A further note on the degree of variation in the score of a motor test of perseveration. *Brit. J. Psychol.*, 1939, 29, 427–428.
70. ——. Variation in the score of a motor perseveration test. *Brit. J. Psychol.*, 1938, 28, 262.
71. Darrow, C. W., and Heath, L. L. Reaction tendencies relating to personality. In Lashley, R. S., *Studies in the Dynamics of Behavior.* Chicago: University of Chicago Press, 1932.
72. Dessoir, M. Psychological types. *Charact. and Person.*, 1934, 5.
73. Deutsch, H. Ueber einen Typus der Pseudo-affektivität ("als ob"). *Int. Z. Psychoanal.*, 1934, 20, 223–235.
74. Dexter, E. S. Personality traits related to conservatism and radicalism. *Charact. and Person.*, 1939, 7, 230–237.
75. Drake, R. M. Factorial analysis of music tests by the Spearman tetrad-difference technique. *J. Musicol.*, 1939, 1, 6–10.
75a. Draper, G.; Dupertuis, C.; and Caughey, J. *Human Constitution in Clinical Medicine.* New York: Harper & Brothers, 1944.
76. Dubois, P. H. A speed factor in mental tests. *Arch. Psychol.*, 1932, 22, 141, pp. 38.
77. Dudycha, G. J. An objective study of personality. *Arch. Psychol.*, 1936, No. 204, pp. 53.
77a. Dunbar, F. *Psychosomatic Diagnosis.* New York: Paul B. Hoeber, Inc., 1943.
78. Eisenson, J. A note on the perseverating tendency in stutterers. *J. Genet. Psychol.*, 1937, 50, 195–198.
79. El Koussy, A. A. H. The visual perception of space. *Brit. J. Psychol.*, Monogr. Suppl., 1935, 7, No. 20.
80. Entwhistle, W. H. Oscillation. *Brit. J. Psychol.*, 1937, 27, 313–328.
81. Estes, S. G. A study of five tests of spatial ability. *J. Psychol.*, 1942, 13, 365–371.
82. Eysenck, H. J. Personality factors and preference judgments. *Nature*, 1941, 148, 346.

82a. EYSENCK, H. J. An experimental analysis of five tests of "appreciation of humor." *Educ. and Psychol. Meas.*, 1943, 3, 191–214.

83. ——. The appreciation of humour: an experimental and theoretical study. *Brit. J. Psychol.*, 1942, 32, 295–309.

83a. ——. Types of personality: a factorial study of seven hundred neurotics. *J. Ment. Sci.*, 1944, 90, 851–861.

83b. ——. General social attitudes. *J. Soc. Psychol.*, 1944, 19, 207–227.

84. FERGUSON, L. W. Primary social attitudes. *J. Psychol.*, 1939, 8, 217–223.

85. ——. The stability of the primary social attitudes: 1. Religionism and humanitarianism. *J. Psychol.*, 1941, 12, 283–288.

86. ——; HUMPHREY, G.; and STRONG, E. K. A factorial analysis of interests and values. *J. Educ. Psychol.*, 1941, 32, 197–204.

87. FINCH, F. H., and ODOROFF, M. E. Sex differences in vocational interests. *J. Educ. Psychol.*, 1939, 30, 151–156.

88. FLANAGAN, J. C. *Factor Analysis in the Study of Personality.* Stanford University, California: Stanford University Press, 1935.

89. FLEMMING, E. G. A factor analysis of the personality of high school leaders. *J. Appl. Psychol.*, 1935, 19, 596–605.

90. FLUGEL, J. C. Practice, fatigue, and oscillation. *Brit. J. Psychol.*, Monogr. Suppl., 1929, 4, No. 13.

91. FOLEY, J. P. Factors conditioning motor speed and tempo. *Psychol. Bull.*, 1937, 34, 351–394.

92. FRANK, J. D. Recent studies of the level of aspiration. *Psychol. Bull.*, 1941, 38, 218–226.

92a. FREEMAN, G. L., and KATZOFF, E. T. Individual differences in physiological reactions to stimulation and their relation to other measures of emotionality. *J. Exp. Psychol.*, 1942, 31, 527–537.

93. FRISCHEISEN-KOHLER, I. The personal tempo and its inheritance. *Charact. and Person.*, 1933, 1, 301–313.

94. GARDNER, J. W. The relation of certain personality variables to level of aspiration. *J. Psychol.*, 1940, 9, 191–206.

95. GARNETT, M. J. C. General ability, cleverness and purpose. *Brit. J. Psychol.*, 1919, 9, 345–360.

96. GARRISON, R. C. An investigation of some simple speed activities. *J. Appl. Psychol.*, 1929, 13, 167–172.

96a. GIBB, C. A. Personality traits by factorial analysis. I. *Australasian J. Psychol. and Philos.*, 1942, 20, 1–15.

96b. ——. Personality traits by factorial analysis. II. *Australasian J. Psychol. and Philos.*, 1942, 20, 1–27.

96c. ——. Personality traits by factorial analysis. III. *Australasian J. Psychol. and Philos.*, 1942, 22, 1–27.

97. GOODMAN, C. H. A factorial analysis of Thurstone's sixteen primary mental abilities tests. *Psychometrika*, 1943, 8, 3, 141–151.

98. GOULD, R. An experimental analysis of "level of aspiration." *Genet. Psychol.*, Monogr., 1939, 21, 3–115.

99. GOULD, R., and KAPLAN, N. The relationship of "level of aspiration" to academic and personality factors. *J. Soc. Psychol.*, 1940, 11, 31–40.

100. GUILFORD, J. P. Unitary traits of personality and factor theory. *Amer. J. Psychol.*, 1936, 48, 673–680.

101. ——, and BRALY, R. W. Extroversion and introversion. *Psychol. Bull.*, 1930, 27, 96–107.

102. ——, and GUILFORD, R. B. Personality factors D, R, T, and A. *J. Abnorm. Soc. Psychol.*, 1939, 34, 1.

103. ——. An analysis of the factors in a typical test of introversion-extroversion. *J. Abnorm. Soc. Psychol.*, 1934, 28, 377–399.

104. ——. Personality factors N and GD. *J. Abnorm. Soc. Psychol.*, 1939, 34, 2, 239–249.

105. ——. Personality factors S, E, and M, and their measurement. *J. Psychol.*, 1936, 2, 109–128.

106. GUNDLACH, R. H., and GERUM, E. Vocational interests and types of ability. *J. Educ. Psychol.*, 1931, 22, 505.

106a. HALVERSON, H. M. Infant sucking and tensional behavior. *J. Genet. Psychol.*, 1938, 53, 365–430.

107. HAMILTON, N. Perseveration and stability in school children. Thesis, Dept. Psychol., University of Sydney. Recorded by WALKER, G. V., 1944.

108. HARGREAVES, H. L. The "faculty" of imagination. *Brit. J. Psychol.*, Monogr. Suppl., 1927, 3, No. 10.

109. HARRISON, R. Personal tempo and the interrelationships of voluntary and maximal rates of movement. *J. Gen. Psychol.*, 1941, 24, 343–379.

110. ——, and DORCUS, R. M. Is rate of voluntary bodily movement unitary? *J. Gen. Psychol.*, 1938, 18, 31–39.

110a. HARSCH, C. M. A factor analysis of the responses to an annoyance inventory. *Psychol. Bull.*, 1935, 32, 535.

110b. HART, H. H.; JENKINS, R. L.; AXELRAD, S.; and SPERLING, P. I. Multiple factor analysis of traits of delinquent boys. *J. Soc. Psychol.*, 1943, 17, 191–201.

111. HARTSHORNE, H.; MAY, M. A.; and SHUTTLEWORTH, F. K. *Studies in the Organization of Character.* New York: The Macmillan Company, 1930.

112 HEALY, W., and M. F. *Pathological Lying, Accusation, and Swindling.* Boston: Little, Brown & Co., 1915.

113. ——, BRONNER, A. F., and BOWERS, A. M. *The Structure and Meaning of Psychoanalysis.* New York: Alfred A. Knopf, 1931.

114. HEATHERS, L. B. Factors producing generality in the level of aspiration. *J. Exp. Psychol.*, 1942, 30, 392–406.

115. HERMAN, M.; HAPHAM, D.; and ROSENBLUM, M. Non-schizophrenic catatonic states. *N. Y. S. J. Med.*, 1942, 42, 624–627.

116. HERRINGTON, L. P. The relation of Physiological and Social Indices of Activity Level. In MCNEMAR, Q., and MERRILL, M. A., *Studies*

in Personality: In Honor of Lewis M. Terman. Stanford University, California: Stanford University Press, 1942.

117. HERTZMAN, M. The influence of the individual's variability on the organization of performance. *J. Gen. Psychol.*, 1939, 20, 3–24.

118. HIRSCH, N. D. M. *Dynamic Causes of Juvenile Crime.* Cambridge: Sci-Art Publishers, 1937.

119. HOCH, P., and RACHLIN, H. L. An evaluation of manic-depressive psychosis in the light of follow-up studies. *Amer. J. Psychiat.*, 1941, 97, 831–843.

120. HOLZINGER, K. G., and HARMAN, H. H. *Factor Analysis: A Synthesis of Factorial Methods.* Chicago: University of Chicago Press, 1941.

121. ——, and SWINEFORD, F. A study in factor analysis: the stability of a bi-factor solution. Suppl. Educ. Monogr. No. 48. Chicago: University of Chicago Press, 1939.

122. HORN, D. Some clusters in personality traits. *Charact. and Person.*, 1944.

123. HORST, P. *The Prediction of Personal Adjustment.* Social Science Research Council, Bulletin 48, 1941.

124. HOTELLING, H. Analysis of a complex of statistical variables into principal components. *J. Educ. Psychol.*, 1933, 29, 417–441, 498–520.

125. HOWARD, C. Perseveration. Unpubl. Thesis. University of London. Referred to by WALKER, G. V., 1944.

126. HOWELLS, F. H. An experimental study of persistence. *J. Abnorm. Soc. Psychol.*, 1933, 28, 14–29.

126a. HOWIE, D. Aspects of personality in the classroom: a study of rating. *Brit. J. Psychol.*, 1945, 36, 15–29.

126b. HUNTLEY, W. Judgments of self based on records of expressive behavior. Thesis. Cambridge: Harvard University, 1938.

127. HUMM, D. G., and WADSWORTH, G. W. The Humm-Wadsworth temperament scale. *Person. J.*, 1933, 12, 314–323.

128. HUMPHREYS, L. G.; BUXTON, C. E.; and TAYLOR, H. R. Steadiness and rifle marksmanship. *J. Appl. Psychol.*, 1936, 20, 680–688.

129. JAENSCH, E. R. *Eidetic Imagery.* New York: Harcourt, Brace & Co., Inc., 1930.

130. JAENSCH, W. *Grundzüge einer Physiologie und Klinik der Psychophysischen Persönlichkeit.* Berlin: Springer, 1926.

131. JASPER, H. H. The measurement of depression-elation and its relation to a measure of extroversion-introversion. *J. Abnorm. Soc. Psychol.*, 1930, 25, 307–318.

132. ——. Is perseveration a functional unity participating in all behavior processes? *J. Soc. Psychol.*, 1931, 2, 28–51.

133. ——; FITZPATRICK, C. P ; and SOLOMON, P. Analogies and opposites in schizophrenia and epilepsie. E. E. G. and Clinical Studies. *Amer. J. Psychiat.*, 1939, 95, 835–851.

133a. JENKINS, R. L., and GLICKMAN, S. Common syndromes in child psychiatry. *Amer. J. Orthopsychiat.*, 1946. (In press.)

134. JENSEN, M. B. Some psychological aspects of migraine. *Psychol. Rec.*, 1938, 2, 403–430.

135. JOHNSON, D. M., and REYNOLDS, F. A factor analysis of verbal ability. *Psychol. Rec.*, 1941, 4, 183–195.

136. JOHNSON, W. B. Euphoric and depressed moods in normal subjects. 1 and 2. *Charact. and Person.*, 1937–1938, 6, 79–98, 188–202.

137. JONES, E. Traits of the superior personality (in business executives and salesmen). *Person. J.*, 1932, 11, 86–96.

138. JONES, L. W. Individual differences in mental inertia. *J. Nat. Instit. Indust. Psychol.*, 1929, 4, 282–290.

139. ——. Temperament and the threshold for flicker. *Brit. J. Psychol.*, 1939, 29, 422–426.

139a. KALLMANN, F., *The Genetics of Schizophrenia*. New York: J. J. Augustin, Inc., 1938.

140. KANTOR, J. R. Character and personality: their nature and interrelations. *Charact. and Person.*, 1938, 6, 306–320.

141. KATZENELBOGEN, S. Hypochondriacal complaints with special reference to personality and environment. *Amer. J. Psychiat.*, 1942, 98, 815–822.

142. KARLIN, J. E. A factorial study of auditory function. *Psychometrika*, 1942, 7, 251–279.

143. KELLEY, T. L. *Interpretation of Educational Measurements*. Yonkers-on-Hudson, New York: World Book Company, 1927.

144. ——, and KREY, A. C. *Tests and Measurements in the Social Sciences*. New York: Charles Scribner's Sons, 1934.

145. KELLEY, T. L. *Essential Traits of Mental Life*. Cambridge: Harvard University Press, 1935.

146. ——. An experimental study of three character traits needed in a democratic social order. *Harvard Educ. Rev.*, 1942, 12, 294–322. Also in KELLEY and KREY, *Educational Measurement*.

147. KENDIG, I. Studies in perseveration: 5. Theoretical significance of the perseveration and repetition of conative activity. *J. Psychol.*, 1937, 3, 253–259.

148. KENNEDY, M. Speed as a personality trait. *J. Soc. Psychol.*, 1930, 1, 286–299.

149 KISKER, G. W. Constancy in the manic-depressive syndrome. *J. Nerv. Ment. Dis.*, 1941, 93, 163–168.

150. KLINEBERG, O. *Race Differences*. New York: Harper & Brothers, 1935.

151. KLING, CARLOS. A statistical study of the relations of neurasthenic, dyspeptic, and allergic symptoms. *J. Gen. Psychol.*, 1934, 10, 328–343.

152. KNIGHT, F. B. The effect of the "acquaintance factor" upon personal judgments. *J. Educ. Psychol.*, 1923, 14, 129.

153. KOCH, H. L. A multi-factor analysis of certain measures of activeness in nursery school children. *J. Gen. Psychol.*, 1934, 45, 3, 482–487.

153a. ——. A factor analysis of some measures of the behavior of pre-school children. *J. Gen. Psychol.*, 1942, 27, 257–287.

153b. KREMER, A. H. The nature of persistence. *Stud. in Psychol. Psychiat.*, 1942, 5, No. 8.

154. KRETSCHMER, E. *Körperbau und Charakter* (seventh edition). Berlin: Springer, 1929.

154a. KREYENBORG, G. *Körperbau Epilepsie und Charakter. z. f. d. ges. Neur. u. Psychiat.*, 1928, 112, 506–548.

155. KRUGER, B. L. A statistical analysis of the Humm-Wadsworth temperament scale. *J. Appl. Psychol.*, 1938, 22, 641–652.

156. KUJATH, G. Generativer Mechanismus und Persönlichkeit bei den Schizophrenen. *Allg. Z. Psychiat.*, 1941, 117, 181–221.

157. LANDIS, C. The justification of judgments. *J. Person. Res.*, 1925, 4, 7.

158. LARSON, L. A. A factor analysis of motor ability variables and tests, with tests for college men. *Res. Quart. Amer. Assn. Hlth. Phys. Educ.*, 1941, 12, 499–517.

158a. ——. A factor analysis of cardiovascular variables and tests. 1940. See page 457. Physical Fitness Supplement to *Res. Quart. Amer. Assn. Hlth. Phys. Educ.*, 1941, 12, No. 2.

159. LAYMAN, E. M. An item analysis of the adjustment questionnaire. *J. Psychol.*, 1940, 10, 87–106.

160. LENTZ, F. F. Generality and specificity of conservatism-radicalism. *J. Educ. Psychol.*, 1938, 29, 540–546.

161. ——. Personage admiration and other correlates of conservatism-radicalism. *J. Soc. Psychol.*, 1939, 10, 81–93.

162. LINE, W., and KAPLAN, E. The existence, measurement, and significance of a speed factor in the abilities of public school children. *J. Exp. Educ.*, 1932, 1, 1–8.

162a. ——; GRIFFEN, J.; and ANDERSON, G. The objective measurement of mental stability. *J. Ment. Sci.*, 1935, 81, 61–106.

163. LURIE, W. A. A study of Spranger's value types by the method of factor analysis. *J. Soc. Psychol.*, 1937, 8, 17–37.

164. MADIGAN, M. E. A study of oscillation as a unitary trait. *J. Exp. Educ.*, 1938, 6, 332–339.

164a. MARTIN, A. H. An experimental investigation of the factors and types in voluntary choice. *Arch. Psychol.*, 1922, 12.

165. MASLOW, A. H. A test for dominance feeling in college women. *J. Soc. Psychol.*, 1940, 12, 255–270.

166. ——. Dominance feeling, behavior and status. *Psychol. Rev.*, 1937.

167. Maslow, A. H., and Flanyb, M. S. The role of dominance in the social and sexual behavior of infra-human primates. *J. Genet. Psychol.*, 1936, 48, 310–338.

168. Masserman, J., and Carmichael, H. Diagnosis and prognosis in psychiatry. *J. Ment. Sci.*, 1938, 84, 893–946.

169. Maurer, K. M. Patterns of behavior of young children as revealed by a factor analysis of trait "clusters." *J. Genet. Psychol.*, 1941, 59, 177–188.

170. McCloy, C. H. A factor analysis of personality traits to underlie character education. *J. Educ. Psychol.*, 27, 375.

171. ——. The measurement of speed in motor performance. *Psychometrika*, 1940, 5, 173–182.

171a. ——. A study of cardiovascular variables by the method of factor analysis. Pages 107–113. Second Biennial Meeting of the Soc. for Res. in Child Development. Washington, D. C.: National Research Council, 1936.

172. McDonough, M. R. The empirical study of character. *Cath. Univ. Amer. Stud. Psychol. Psychiat.*, Washington, D. C. 2. Nos. 3 and 4, 1929.

173. McDougall, W. *An Outline of Psychology.* London: Methuen & Co., Ltd., 1923.

174. ——. *The Energies of Man.* London: Methuen & Co., Ltd., 1935.

175. ——. On the nature of Spearman's general factor. *Charact. and Person.*, 1934, 3, 127–143.

175a. ——. *National Welfare and National Decay.* London: Methuen & Co., Ltd., 1921.

176. McGehee, W. Judgment and the level of aspiration. *J. Gen. Psychol.*, 1940, 22, 3–15.

177. McNemar, Q. On the number of factors. *Psychometrika*, 1942, 7, 9–19.

178. ——. Practice and "general" motor ability. *J. Gen. Psychol.*, 1930, 3, 67–97.

179. Menninger, K. A. Recognizing and renaming "psychopathic personalities." *Bull. Menning. Clin.*, 1941, 5, 150–156.

180. Miles, D. W. Preferred rates in rhythmic response. *J. Gen. Psychol.*, 1937, 16, 427–469.

181. Miller, C. W. The paranoid syndrome. *Archiv. Neurol. Psychiat.*, 1941, 45, 953–963.

182. Miller, E. B. Physical and physiological studies, pp. 25–87, in Sanford, R. N., and Others. *Physique, Personality, and Scholarship.* q. v. 1943.

183. Mirk, M. The difference of emotional stability in girls of different ages. *Australasian J. Psychol.*, 1930, 8, 229–232.

184. Moore, H. A comparison of linguistic and non-linguistic ability. *J. Soc. Psychol.*, 1931, 2, 245–252.

185. MOORE, F. W. The empirical determination of certain syndromes underlying praecox and manic-depressive psychoses. *Amer. J. Psychiat.*, 1930, 9.

186. MORGAN, J. J. B., and HULL, C. L. The measurement of persistence. *J. Appl. Psychol.*, 1926, 10, 180–187.

187. MOSIEV, C. I. A factor analysis of certain neurotic symptoms. *Psychometrika*, 1937, 2, 263–286.

188. ——. On the validity of neurotic questionnaires. *J. Soc. Psychol.*, 1938, 9, 1, 3–16.

188a. MURPHY, M. A. A study of primary components of cardiovascular tests. *Res. Quart. Amer. Assn. Hlth. Phys. Educ.*, 1940, 11, 57–71.

189. MURPHY, G., and JENSEN, J. *Approaches to Personality.* New York: Coward-McCann, Inc., 1932.

190. MURRAY, H. A., et al. *Explorations in Personality.* New York: Oxford University Press, 1938.

191. NESTELE, A. Schwererziebarkeit und Psychopathie. *Zbl. Jugendr. Jugendwohlf.*, 1937, 28, 450–460.

192. NEWCOMB, F. M. The consistency of certain extrovert-introvert behavior patterns in fifty-one problem boys. F. C. Contrib. Educ. No. 382. New York: Columbia University Press, 1929.

193. ——. An experiment designed to test the validity of a rating technique. *J. Educ. Psychol.*, 1931, 22, 279.

194. NOTCUTT, B. Perseveration and fluency. *Brit. J. Psychol.*, 1943, 32, 4, 200–209.

195. NOYES, A. L. *Modern Clinical Psychiatry.* Philadelphia: W. B. Saunders Company, 1940.

196. OATES, D. W. Group factors in temperament qualities. *Brit. J. Psychol.*, 1929, 20, 118–136.

197. OLINICK, S. L. Studies in trait-names. Honor Thesis. Cambridge: Harvard University Library, 1936.

198. O'NEIL, W. M. Department of Labor and Industry, Vocational Guidance and Juvenile Employment Section, Sydney, Australia. Personal communication to the present writer, 1936.

198a. ONSLOW, H. Fair and dark: Is there a predominant type? *Eugenic Reform.*, 1920, 12, 212–220.

199. PACE, C. R. The relationship between liberal-conservative attitudes and knowledge of current affairs. Ph.D. Thesis. University of Minnesota Library, 1937.

200. PALLISTER, H. The negative or withdrawal attitude: a study in personality organization. *Arch. Psychol.*, 1933, No. 151.

201. PERRY, R. C. A group factor analysis of the adjustment questionnaire. Los Angeles: Southern California Educ. Monogr., 1934, No. 5.

202. PERSCH, R. Epileptoide Persönlichkeiten und Pyromanie. *Mschr. Psychiat. Neurol.*, 1937, 95, 173–212.

203. Philip, B. R.   Studies in high speed continuous work: 1. Periodicity. *J. Exp. Psychol.*, 1939, 24, 499–509.

204. Philpott, S. J. F.   Fluctuations in human output.   *Brit. J. Psychol.*, Monogr. Suppl., 1933, 6, No. 17.

205. Pinard, J. W.   Tests of perseveration: 1. Their relation to character. *Brit. J. Psychol.*, 1932, 23, 5–19.

206. ——.   Tests of perseveration: 2. Their relation to certain psychopathic conditions and to introversion.   *Brit. J. Psychol.*, 1932, 23, 114–128.

207. Porter, J. P.   A comparative study of some measurements of persistence.   *Psychol. Bull.*, 1933, 30, 664.

207a. Porteus, S. D., and Babcock, M. E.   *Temperament and Race.*   Boston: Richard C. Badger, 1926.

208. Rabinowitz, A. J.   Aspects of psychopathic personality.   *U. S. Veterans' Bureau Med. Bull.*, 1941, 18, 179–181.

209. Rangachar, C.   Differences in perseveration among Jewish and English boys.   *Brit. J. Educ. Psychol.*, 1934, 4, 186–208.

210. Reik, F.   *From Thirty Years with Freud.*   New York: Farrar & Rinehart, Inc., 1940.

211. Repond, A.   Le lattah; une psychonévrose éxotique.   *Ann. Med. Psychol.*, 1940, 98, 311–324.

212. Rethlingshafer, D.   The relation of tests of persistence to other measures of continuance of action.   *J. Abnorm. Soc. Psychol.*, 1942, 37, 71–82.

213. Reyburn, H. A., and Taylor, J. G.   Some factors of personality: a further analysis of some of Webb's data.   *Brit. J. Psychol.*, 1939, 30, 1, 151–211.

214. ——.   Factors in introversion and extraversion.   *Brit. J. Psychol.*, 1940, 31, 335–340.

215. ——.   Some factors of temperament: a re-examination.   *Psychometrika*, 1943, 8, 91–104.

216 Reymert, M. L.   The personal equation in motor capacities.   *Scand. Sci. Rev.*, 1923, 2, 117–222.

216a. Richards, T. W.   Factors in the personality of nursery school children.   *J. Exp. Educ.*, 1940, 9, 152–153.

217. Roback, A. A.   *Bibliography of Character and Personality.*   Cambridge: Sci-Art Publishers, 1927.

218. Rogers, C. R.   Measuring personality adjustment in children 9–13 years of age.   F. C. Contrib. Educ. No. 458.   New York: Columbia University Press, 1931.

219. Rogers, M.   Research on arithmetical abilities.   F. C. Contrib. Educ. No. 130.   New York: Columbia University Press, 1923.

220. Rogerson, C. H.   The differentiation of neuroses and psychoses, with special reference to states of depression and anxiety.   *J. Ment. Sci.*, 1940, 86, 632–644.

221. Ross, V. R. Relations between intelligence, scholastic achievement, and musical talent. Sacramento, California: *Calif. Bar. Juv. Res.*, 1937.

221*a*. Rostan, L. *Cours Elementaire d'Hygiène.* Paris, 1828.

222. Ryans, D. G. An experimental attempt to analyze persistent behavior. *J. Gen. Psychol.*, 1938, 19, 333–353.

223. ——. The meaning of persistence. *J. Gen. Psychol.*, 1938, 19, 79–96.

224. Sahai, M. Circular mentality and the pyknic body build. Thesis. London: University of London Library, 1931.

225. Sanford, R. N., and Others. Physique, personality, and scholarship. Vol. 8, No. 34 of the monographs of the Soc. for Res. in Child Development. Washington, D. C.: National Research Council, 1943.

226. Sarbin, F. R., and Bordin. E. S. The relation of measured interests to the Allport-Vernon study of values. *J. Appl. Psychol.*, 1940, 24, 287–290.

227. Schiller, B. Verbal, numerical, and spatial abilities of young children. *Arch. Psychol.*, 1934, No. 161.

228. Schwantz, L. A. Social situation pictures in the psychiatric interview. *Amer. J. Orthopsychiat.*, 1932, 2, 3, 124–133.

229. Sears, P. S. Level of aspiration in relation to some variables of personality: clinical studies. *J. Soc. Psychol.*, 1941, 14, 311–336.

230. Sears, R. R. Experimental studies of projection: 1. Attribution of traits. *J. Soc. Psychol.*, 1936, 7.

231. Sheldon, W., and Stevens, S. S. *The Varieties of Temperament.* New York: Harper & Brothers, 1942.

231*a*. ——; Stevens, S. S.; and Tucker, W. B. *The Varieties of Human Physique.* New York: Harper & Brothers, 1940.

232. Shen, E. The influence of friendship upon personal ratings. *J. Appl. Psychol.*, 1925, 9, 66.

233. Shevach, B. J. Studies in perseveration: 8. Experimental results of tests for sensory perseveration. *J. Psychol.*, 1936, 3, 403–427.

234. Slater, P. Speed of work in intelligence tests. *Brit. J. Psychol.*, 1938, 29, 1, 55–69.

234*a*. Snyder, L. H. *Medical Genetics.* Durham, North Carolina: Duke University, 1941.

235. Spearman, C. *The Abilities of Man: Their Nature and Measurement.* London: The Macmillan Company, 1927.

236. Spencer, D. *Fulcra of Conflict.* Yonkers-on-Hudson, New York: World Book Company, 1939.

237. Sprague, G. S. The psychopathology of psychopathic personalities. *Bull. N. Y. Acad. Med.*, 1941, 17, 911–921.

238. Stagner, R. Intercorrelation of some standardized personality tests. *J. Appl. Psychol.*, 1932, 16, 453–465.

239. STAGNER, R. *The Psychology of Personality*. New York: McGraw-Hill Book Company, Inc., 1937.

240. STEPHENSON, W. P score and inhibition for high p praecox cases. *J. Ment. Sci.*, 1932, 78, 908–928.

241. ——. An introduction to so-called motor perseveration tests. *Brit. J. Educ. Psychol.*, 1934, 4, 186–208.

242. ——. The inverted factor technique. *Brit. J. Psychol.*, 1936, 26, 344–361.

243. ——. The foundations of psychometry. *Psychometrika*, 1936, 1, 195–210.

244. STERN, A. Borderline group of neuroses. *Psychoanal. Quart.*, 1938, 7, 467–489.

244a. STEVENS, S. S., and DAVIS, H. *Hearing, Its Psychology and Its Physiology*. New York: John Wiley & Sons, Inc., 1938.

244b. STOCKARD, C. R. *The Physical Basis of Personality*. New York: W. W. Norton & Co., Inc., 1931.

245. STRONG, E. K. *Vocational Interests of Men and Women*. Stanford University, California: Stanford University Press, 1943.

246. STUDMAN, L. G. Studies in experimental psychiatry: 5. "w" and "f" factors in relation to traits of personality. *J. Ment. Sci.*, 1935, 81, 107–137.

247. SUTHERLAND, J. D. The speed factor in intelligent reactions. *Brit. J. Psychol.*, 1934, 24, 3, 276–294.

248. SUPER, D. E., and ROPER, S. An objective technique for testing vocational interests. *J. Appl. Psychol.*, 1941, 25, 487–498.

249. SWEET, L. *The Measurement of Personality Attitudes in Younger Boys*. New York: Association Press, 1929.

250. SYMONDS, P. M. *Diagnosing Personality and Conduct*. New York: D. Appleton-Century Company, Inc., 1931.

250a. TCHERNORUK, V. G. The question of structure of traumatic neuroses. *Psychol. Abstr.*, 1937, 11, 142.

251. TERMAN, L. M. The measurement of personality. *Science*, 1934, 80, 605–608.

252. ——, and Others. *Sex and Personality*. New York: McGraw-Hill Book Company, Inc., 1936.

253. THOMAS, D. S.; LOOMIS, A. M.; and ARRINGTON, R. E. Observational studies of social behavior patterns. Vol. I. Social behavior patterns. New Haven: Instit. Human Relat., Yale University, 1933.

254. THOMSON, G. H. *The Factorial Analysis of Human Ability*. London: University of London Press, 1939.

255. THOMPSON, R. The depressive phase of manic-depressive insanity. *Ulster Med. J.*, 1941, 10, 29–39.

256. THORNDIKE, E. L. The interests of adults: 2. The interrelations of adult interests. *J. Educ. Psychol.*, 1935, 26, 497–507.

257. THORNDIKE, R. L. *Children's Reading Interests*. New York: Teachers College Bureau of Publications, Columbia University Press, 1941.

258. THORNTON, G. R. A factor analysis of tests designed to measure persistence. *Psychol. Monogr.*, 1939, 51, 3, pp. 42.

259. THURSTONE, L. L. A multiple factor study of vocational interests. *Person. J.*, 1931, 10, 198.

260. ——. The vectors of mind. *Psychol. Rev.*, 1934, 41, 1–35.

261. ——. *The Vectors of the Mind*. Chicago: University of Chicago Press, 1935. Revised Edition, 1944.

262. ——. *Primary Mental Abilities*. Chicago: University of Chicago Press, 1938.

262a. ——. *A Factorial Study of Perception*. Chicago: University of Chicago Press, 1944.

263. ——. Second-order factors. *Psychometrika*, 1944, 9, 71–100.

263a. ——. The effects of selection in factor analysis. *Psychometrika*, 1945, 10, 165–198.

263b. THURSTONE, L. L., and THURSTONE, F. G. *Factorial Studies of Intelligence*. Chicago: University of Chicago Press, 1941.

264. TINKER, M. A. The significance of speed in test response. *Psychol. Rev.*, 1931, 38, 450–454.

265. TRAXLER, A. E. The relation between rate of reading and speed of association. *J. Educ. Psychol.*, 1934, 25, 357–365.

266. TRYON, C. M. Evaluations of adolescent personality by adolescents. In BARKER, R. G.; KOUNIN, J. S.; and WRIGHT, H. F., *The Development of Personality*, pp. 545–566. New York: McGraw-Hill Book Company, Inc., 1943.

267. TRYON, R. C. *Cluster Analysis*. Chicago: University of Chicago Press, 1939.

268. VERNON, D. The "dream technique" in projection tests. Unpublished data. Cambridge: Harvard Psychological Clinic, 1943.

269. VERNON, P. E. The Assessment of Psychological Qualities by Verbal Methods. Indust. Health Res. Council. Rep. No. 83. London: H. M. S. O., 1938.

270. WALKER, K. F.; STAINES, R G.; and KENNA, J. C. P-tests and the concept of mental inertia. *Charact. and Person.*, 1943, 12, 1, 32–46.

271. WALTON, R. D. The relation between the amplitude of oscillations in short-period efficiency and steadiness of character. *Brit. J. Psychol.*, 1936, 27, 181–188.

272. ——. Individual differences in amplitude of oscillation and their connection with steadiness of character. *Brit. J. Psychol.*, 1939, 30, 36–46.

273. WASHBURNE, M. F., and Others. Reaction time, flicker and affective sensitiveness as tests of extroversion and introversion. *Amer. J. Psychol.*, 1930, 42, 412–414.

274. Webb, F. Character and intelligence. *Brit. J. Psychol.*, Monogr. Suppl., 1915, 1, No. 3.

275. Weber, C. O. Function fluctuations and personality trends of normal subjects. *Amer. J. Psychol.*, 1938, 51, 702–708.

275a. Wenger, M. Some relations between muscular processes and personality and their factorial analysis. *Child Devel.*, 1938, 9, 261–275.

275b. ———. Interrelations among some physiological variables. *Psychol. Bull.*, 1940, 37, 466.

276. Whisler, L. D. A multiple-factor analysis of generalized attitudes. *J. Soc. Psychol.*, 1934, 5, 283–297.

277. Whitehead, F. N. *The Industrial Worker: A Statistical Study of Human Relations.* Cambridge: Harvard University Press, 1938.

278. Williams, H. M. A factor analysis of Berne's "Social Behavior Patterns in Young Children." *J. Exp. Educ.*, 1935, 4, 2.

279. Willoughby, R. R. The relationship to emotionality of age, sex, and conjugal condition. *Amer. J. Sociol.*, 1938, 6, 920–931.

280. Winiarz, W., and Wielanski, J. Imu — a psychoneurosis occurring among Ainu. *Psychoanal. Rev.*, 1936, 23, 181–186.

280a. Wittels, F. Der hysterische Charakter. *Psychoanal. Beweg.*, 1931, 3, 138–165.

280b. Wolff, W. *The Expression of Personality, Experimental Depth Psychology.* New York: Harper & Brothers, 1943.

281. Woodrow, H. Two quantitative laws relating to goodness of performance. *J. Psychol.*, 1937, 4, 139–159. See also data on retentivity in *J. Educ. Psychol.*, 1917, 8.

281a. ———. Interrelationships of measures of learning. *J. Psychol.*, 1940, 10, 49–73.

281b. ———. Intelligence and improvement in school subjects. *J. Educ. Psychol.*, 1945, 36, 155–166.

282. ———. The relation between abilities and improvement with practice. *J. Educ. Psychol.*, 1938, 29, 215–230.

283. Yde, A.; Lohse, E.; and Faurbye, A. On the relation between schizophrenia, epilepsy, and induced convulsions. *Acta Psychiat.*, Kbh., 1941, 16, 325–388.

283a. Young, P. T. *Emotion in Man and Animal.* New York: John Wiley & Sons, Inc., 1943.

284. Yule, E. P. The resemblance of twins with regard to perseveration. *J. Ment. Sci.*, 1935, 81, 489–501.

285. Zilboorg, G. Ambulatory schizophrenia. *Psychiatry*, 1941, 4, 149–155.

286. Zillig, M. Experimentelle Untersuchungen über Umstellborkeit. *Zt. f. Psychologie*, 1925, 97, 30.

Subject Index

Index of Names